INSIDERS' GUIDE® TO

KANSAS CITY

THIRD EDITION

KATIE VAN LUCHENE

INSIDERS' GUIDE®

GUILFORD, CONNECTICUT
AN IMPRINT OF THE GLOBE PEQUOT PRESS

The prices and rates in this guidebook were confirmed at press time. We recommend, however, that you call establishments before traveling to obtain current information.

INSIDERS' GUIDE®

Text design by LeAnna Weller Smith
Maps by XNR Productions, Inc. © Morris Book Publishing, LLC

ISSN: 1542-7404
ISBN: 978-0-7627-4554-8

Manufactured in the United States of America
10 9 8 7 6 5 4 3 2 1

CONTENTS

Greater Kansas City

North of the River

River Market, Downtown,
and Crown Center

Country Club Plaza and Westport

East Metro
and South Kansas City

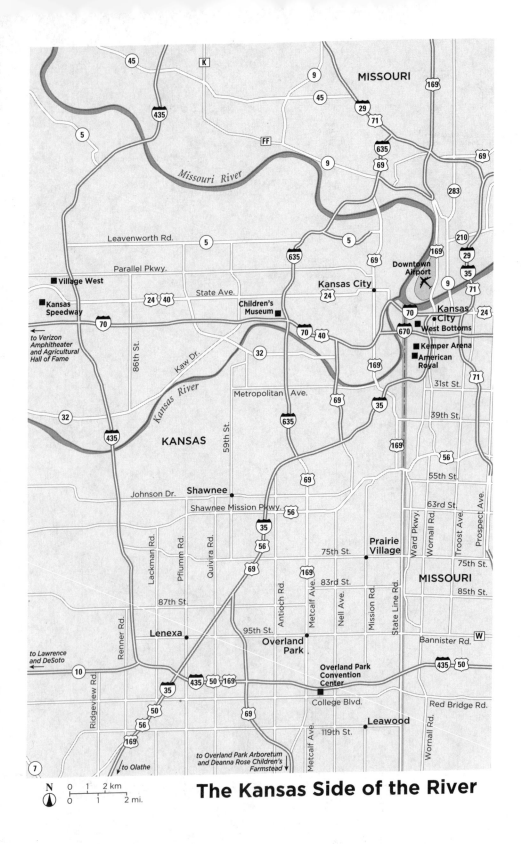

The Kansas Side of the River

PREFACE

Ah, there you are! We couldn't start the party without you.

What are we celebrating? Just the most dramatic transformation in our city's 150-plus-year history, that's what. The conga line forms at the Power & Light District, a nine-block entertainment hot spot that's the star of our $4.9 billion downtown revival. The glowing glass spaceship that landed a few blocks away? That's our new Sprint Center, ready to host sporting events and music's biggest names. Nearby, the Kansas City Convention Center just got a gorgeous makeover to the tune of $135 million.

But our jazzed-up downtown is home to more than just bistros, nightclubs, and shops; for many urbanites, it literally *is* their home. We've added thousands of residences—fresh new condos and brick-lined lofts carved from century-old warehouses—sprinkled amid the commercial spaces to create a compelling 24/7 lifestyle.

If you're staying just for the weekend, your lodging options have expanded as well. Here's where the "new" becomes "old," in such beautifully renovated hotels as the Aladdin and the Hilton President, where Frank Sinatra once crooned in the Drum Room's nightclub. History buffs will also salute our recently opened museum at the Liberty Memorial, the nation's only dedicated WWI memorial.

You're also invited to join the street party in our vibrant Crossroads Arts District—what the national press has dubbed the SoHo of the Midwest. Stroll or catch a trolley to peruse eight blocks of artists' galleries and studios along with unique boutiques filled with antiques, giftware, and home decor—even a gourmet chocolate factory!

Areas north of the river are also turning on the spotlights to show off their new entertainment districts, Zona Rosa and Briarcliff Village, where upscale shops mingle with top dining choices.

In fact, confetti is flying in every direction. NASCAR fans will discover an ever-expanding stay-and-play shopping and entertainment district surrounding the Kansas Speedway in Wyandotte County, Kansas, offering everything from live concerts and salsa dancing to the nation's first T-Rex Café.

Overland Park, a suburb in Kansas, has plenty of reasons to celebrate as well, with its stunning new Nerman Museum of Contemporary Art. Its neighbor, Leawood, continues to grow as a shopping mecca with the opening of the region's first Crate & Barrel store as well as dozens of other discoveries popping up every day.

Toss in what *Time Magazine* calls "the world's most anticipated building in 2007"—the Nelson-Atkins Museum of Art's Bloch addition—and you'll understand why we've set off the Roman candles.

It's definitely Kansas City's time to shine. The whole world is watching, and we're so glad you're here to share in all the hoopla.

ACKNOWLEDGMENTS

In the history books, 2007 will be remembered as the year Kansas City turned from a great city to one of the country's most exciting destinations. More than ever we are *the* place to be for visitors seeking a vacation wonderland, the individual or family searching for the ideal place to call home, or the resident who wants to discover what all the national buzz is about.

A heartfelt thank-you is in order for those who contributed to our remarkable rebirth, starting with Stanley Durwood. After watching his beloved downtown languish for decades, Stan poured his heart (and considerable cash) into plans for a Power & Light District, named for the art deco building that housed his company, AMC Entertainment. His dream would have died with him in 1999 if newly elected Mayor Kay Barnes hadn't picked up the torch. By her second term she made good on her promise to create a vibrant urban core filled with residences and commerce, a stadium, and, yes, her friend's Power & Light District.

Thanks as well to Carol Marinovich, Kay Barnes's counterpart in Kansas City, Kansas, who brought the Kansas Speedway to sleepy Wyandotte County. Today the entertainment district surrounding the racetrack is the state's most popular tourist destination. Best of all, it gave new pride to a city that has taken a backseat to its more glamorous sister for decades.

While these women were making money for the region, others were spending it: Henry Bloch and his wife, Marian, contributed millions for the Steven Holl–designed building that bears their name at the Nelson-Atkins Museum of Art. Across the state line, Jerry and Margaret Nerman can see their moniker on the side of a stunning new contemporary art gallery at the Johnson County Community College campus. They follow in Crosby Kemper's rather enormous shoes; he brought us the Kemper Museum of Contemporary Art in 1990.

Others contribute to our culture in more modest—but just as important—ways. Artists carved galleries and studios out of warehouses in what is now the Crossroads Arts District, and shopkeepers and restaurateurs soon followed. This bohemian neighborhood is home to a lively gallery crawl the first Friday of every month.

Hats off to these visionaries, along with all the musicians and chefs, historians and innkeepers whose passions and talents make this city positive vibrate with excitement. And for the thousands of mentors, teachers, caregivers, philanthropists, and volunteers: You're the reason we're known as the Heartland.

I'm saving my most personal thank-you note for my husband, the handsome guy by my side as I explore this marvelous city. Jerry Foulds, you continue to be my best friend and my hero.

HOW TO USE THIS BOOK ❓

Naturally, as a travel guide, this book is ideal for anyone planning a visit to Kansas City, whether it's a vacation, as home base for a series of day trips, or a few days before or after a business meeting. Pass right by the velvet ropes; this is your official VIP pass to the best Kansas City has to offer in attractions, dining, nightlife and shopping. As a mover and a shaker, you won't want to miss a thing.

We've also put together a helpful guide just for the *movers*. If you're thinking of making Kansas City your new home, you'll find information about the local real estate market; a tour of wonderful neighborhoods; and an overview of area health care, child care, and education options in the Relocation chapter. This section also includes a listing of service providers, such as gas companies and new-neighbor groups, to help you quickly feel at home in your new town. This chapter makes the *Insiders' Guide* an ideal resource for real estate companies to send to potential out-of-town buyers and for companies to give to employees who are being transferred to the City of Fountains.

Traveler or transplant: Welcome! But perhaps the optimum use for this book is the reader who lives in Kansas City but hasn't really lived it up yet. You'll tour neighborhoods otherwise unknown, tap your foot at jam sessions, talk to natives and newcomers, meet historians and artists and gardeners and zookeepers. And, oh, the food! Consider it research.

Using this book as a guide, start your own romance with your hometown. Along the way you're guaranteed to discover more about the city and its surrounding small towns . . . and you might just learn more about yourself by taking part in the poetry readings, pottery painting, tango lessons, and cooking classes listed throughout these pages.

If you have children, this guide will help quiet that "There's nothing to doooo" whine. There's *plenty* to do in Kansas City for kids of all ages. Parents will be happy to note the number of attractions, many of which are free. This guide might also encourage a student to learn more about the history of the Midwest.

For pioneers headed to Santa Fe, Oregon, and California, Kansas City was the gateway to the future. But for you it might be the gateway to your past. Independence, Missouri, is home to not one but two vast genealogical libraries. Family-history seekers come by the busloads to the Mid-Continent Public Library's Genealogy and Local History branch and the Jackson County Historical Society Archives and Research Library in the Independence Square Courthouse.

So whatever the reason for purchasing this book, we sincerely thank you and hope you'll enjoy it—and Kansas City—to its fullest. *NOTE:* Unless otherwise indicated all listings in this book are located in Kansas City, Missouri; other cities and towns will be designated MO (Missouri) or KS (Kansas).

HOW THIS BOOK IS ORGANIZED

Travelers familiar with the *Insiders' Guide* series will recognize the easy-to-use format used throughout this book. Those friendly

ℹ️ No wonder one of our nicknames is The City Beautiful. Kansas City maintains 36 public fountains, in addition to those on private property, as well as 55 monuments and sculptures. And you'll find 201 public parks within our borders, 19 with swimming pools, 36 with tennis courts.

features you appreciate are all here, including Insiders' Tips—designated with an ℹ—that let you in on (shhh!) local secrets and Close-ups that provide an in-depth look at some of our top attributes.

Like all *Insiders' Guides*, this one has been organized to help make the most of your trip to the City of Surprises, from how to navigate our streets to where to find the culinary dish you crave. If that happens to be barbecue, we shudder to picture you hunched over the hotel room's yellow pages trying to choose a winner from the 100 or so barbecue restaurants listed. We'll tell you where to find a smoked brisket that will bring tears to your eyes. Want fries with that? Skip the Idahos: You won't want to miss the sweet potato fries at one popular joint.

If you're new to the *Insiders' Guide* series, here's a quick overview of what you'll find in several of the chapters and a suggestion about where to start, depending on why you're here.

You might want to spend a few minutes with Getting Here, Getting Around. It explains how to divide Greater Kansas City (which actually encompasses 18 counties in two states) into five manageable areas. The rest of the book refers to these districts to make finding a particular place easy.

Because many of you will be looking for a particular type of food (is that Kansas City strip calling your name yet?), restaurants are indexed by fare. Lucky for you, no matter what food you fancy—whether it's a luscious eggplant casserole (even this carnivorous city has a strong vegetarian contingency!) or the garlicky chicken spiedini at Garozzo's Ristorante—it's never more than 20 or so minutes away.

If, however, your passion is dashing for a dressing room at a chichi boutique, you're in luck. In Shopping you'll discover the inside scoop on where to find fashions, antiques, decor, and discount shoes.

In The Arts you'll discover our world-class museums, symphony, ballet, live theater, and opera. You'll also see why Kansas City is gaining national recognition as an art town, thanks to our three major art museums, the Nelson-Atkins, Kemper, and Nerman.

Next we suggest you head to Annual Events and Festivals. Chances are there's a music festival, street fair, tour of a historical area, or neighborhood block party going on right now. You wouldn't want to miss the revelry while you're reviewing this book.

Looking for more outdoor fun? Spend an afternoon at the Kansas City Zoo or one of our beautiful arboretums or lakes and you won't miss the mountains or beach; pack a picnic basket (find out where in the Food and Gifts section in Shopping), then open the book to Parks, Lakes, and Recreation.

Perhaps your culinary choices run more to hot dogs and roasted peanuts—fare that's best savored at the ballpark. You won't go wanting here: With Royals and T-Bones baseball, Chiefs football, and professional hockey and soccer teams, there's a game in town nearly every week. And our Kansas Speedway offers NASCAR fans an exciting day at the races. Start your engines in Sports.

Whew! That should get you started. Pace yourself, go easy on the incendiary salsa at Southwest Boulevard's Mexican restaurants, and you should do just fine.

Finally, the small print. We made every attempt to provide the most accurate and up-to-date information to help make your visit to Kansas City a success. But if you disagree with anything or discover a hot spot we missed, please let us know. Send your comments or suggestions to editorial@Globe Pequot.com, or write to:

The Globe Pequot Press
Reader Response/Editorial Department
P.O. Box 480
Guilford, CT 06437

ℹ You may have such a good time visiting Kansas City you won't want to leave. Our many charms have earned us a spot in Expansion Management's "America's 50 Hottest Cities for Expansions and Relocations." We rank way up there at No. 4.

AREA OVERVIEW

Kansas City has always been known as a vibrant mix of urban sophistication and small-town friendliness. But now there are five billion more reasons to love us. That's the price tag for our downtown makover alone. There's also more of us to love. We've recently grown from eleven counties to eighteen in both Kansas and Missouri, representing more than 9,100 square miles filled with two million happy, friendly folks.

So now more than ever, when you say "Kansas City," you're really talking about one diverse, exciting region that encompasses two states and fifty unique communities. Our unified advantage—along with our central location, well-educated and productive workforce, and low cost of running a business or buying a home—makes us a magnet for corporations to build headquarters here. And our enviable quality of life means individuals and families are thrilled to make their homes here. In fact, we have a slogan that shows off our city's strength in numbers: "OneKC."

Just witness the entertainment area in Wyandotte County, Kansas, that quickly became the number-one attraction in the state. Village West zoomed into being with the NASCAR Kansas Speedway, Cabela's outdoor gear emporium, Nebraska Furniture Mart, and Great Wolf Lodge. Restaurants and attractions followed, and now—just a few years after opening—the area draws more than seven million visitors a year.

Our urban core renaissance includes a new library—one of the most beautiful in the nation—plus a thriving art and shopping scene in the Crossroads Arts District. Our skyline, already a beauty, is stunning with the H&R Block Headquarters, the Power & Light District, the Sprint Center, and other draws planned for the next few years.

But for right now, there's plenty to love about our town. So let's get started with a whirlwind tour.

Although the metroplex known as Kansas City encompasses just over 9,000 square miles, locals think of home as separate neighborhoods (such as Brookside), destinations (Country Club Plaza), or geographical areas (the Northland). Before your eyes glaze over, we've divided the region into five handy little areas, described below. Maps of each are found in the front of this book. We'll refer to these areas throughout the book. And remember, just about any destination in the metro is twenty minutes away or less.

METROPOLITAN AREAS
North of the River

In 1972 when the city planners approved the new Kansas City International Airport a whopping 21 miles north of downtown, they expected an immediate surge in housing and services in the Northland. It took twenty-five years before new homes and golf courses began to dot the hillsides facing the Mighty Mo. But the real reason to head north isn't for new delights but old: the charming city of Parkville with its storefronts filled with art

i Want to save money during your visit? Go to the Kansas City Convention and Visitors Bureau Web site, www.visitkc.com, for ready-to-print coupons for some of Kansas City's most popular attractions. Recent values included discounted admissions to the zoo, Truman Library, Powell Gardens, and Vaile Mansion, plus coupons to redeem at Crown Center. Check often, because selections change.

Resources for More Information

Hungry for more? Although this book provides a portable entree into the City of Surprises, following are sources to enhance your visit.

Media
Our daily newspaper, the *Kansas City Star*, publishes several photo-rich books on a variety of subjects from history to barbecue to the Flood of '51. Write to Kansas City Star Books, Attn. StarInfo, P.O. Box 410457, Kansas City, MO 64141-0457, or call (816) 234-4636.

KC Magazine provides a well-rounded, well-written look at the town's most interesting people, places, and sometimes-quirky habits. Each monthly issue also includes a calendar of events, restaurant reviews, and a dining guide. It's a must-read for locals and welcome lifeline for expatriates. Call (913) 894-6923 for subscription information, or check out www.kcmag.com for a taste.

Every city needs an "alternate" paper and ours is *The Pitch*. Read it for irreverent takes on culture, music, film, and politics; if nothing else read it for Charles Ferruzza's restaurant reviews. It's available free at kiosks all over town, or at www.pitch.com.

An online source, www.presentmagazine.com, gives an interesting view of the food, music, and art scene in town.

Tourism Sites
Well before your trip, access these chamber of commerce and visitor center Web sites for up-to-the-minute information about festivals and events. Or call to receive brochures, maps, and special offers by mail.

Convention and Visitors Bureau of Greater Kansas City
If you only have the time—or patience—to contact one visitor center, this should be it. Its quarterly magazine, *Goin' to Kansas City*, lists a calendar of events, information about dining and nightlife, kid-friendly activities, and even area day trips. The staff is adept at helping out-of-towners plan successful conventions and even family reunions. Write to the bureau at 1100 Main, Suite 2550, Kansas City, MO 64105-2195; call (816) 221-5242 or (800) 767-7700; or log on to www.gointokansascity.com or www.visitkc.com. Satellite locations at Union Station and 4709 Central on the Country Club Plaza offer a wide variety of brochures and maps.

galleries and festive eateries. And if gambling floats your boat, you'll want to cross the bridge to reach our four riverboat casinos.

River Market, Downtown, Crown Center

Here's where it all began 150 years ago. And despite the mass exodus to the suburbs during the 1950s and 1960s, the central core remains the heart of our city. Fortunately it's coming back into its own thanks to entertainment venues such as the River Market, newly refurbished urban lofts that draw upscale professionals, and late-night attractions such as the 18th and Vine Historic Jazz District.

Popular galleries throughout the Crossroads Arts District have attracted some of the

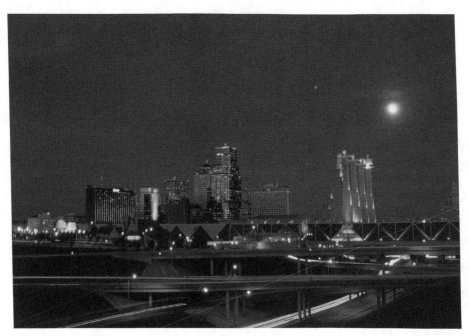

Full moon over downtown skyline. CVB OF GREATER KANSAS CITY

area's most dynamic restaurants to the area, while just south, Crown Center offers a stay-and-play mecca for travelers with its hotels, restaurants, and shopping. This city-within-the-city is linked via skywalks to the newly refurbished Union Station, which houses Science City, an interactive museum for kids; a three-story Extreme Screen, the region's only 3-D theater; and dining options that range from lobster to burgers.

Coming up are a new sports arena, an exciting entertainment district, and a performing arts center.

Country Club Plaza and Westport

Any trip to Kansas City must include a day of shopping on the Country Club Plaza, a 14-city-block potpourri of over 180 stores, boutiques, and dining establishments set among forty fountains and fifty sculpted works of art. If the "Rodeo Drive" of the Midwest is a little too upscale for you, Historic Westport offers a more laid-back social scene.

Nearby is the popular 39th Street corridor, which boasts more top-notch restaurants than any other real estate in town, and the 45th and State Line Art and Antiques district will thrill the collectibles hunter. The Plaza and Westport area is also home to the nationally respected Nelson-Atkins Museum of Art and the Kemper Contemporary Museum of Art. Take a short drive south past neighborhoods filled with million-dollar homes to find Brookside, an old-fashioned Main Street USA enclave with a collection of cafes, a toy store, an ice-cream parlor, and even a five-and-dime store complete with creaking wooden floors.

East Metro and South Kansas City

Independence, Missouri, is still Harry's town, with the Truman Presidential Museum and Library all spiffed up and ready to tour along with his home. Our famed double-header sports complex also bears the thirty-third president's name; tickets to a Chiefs football or Royals baseball game draw sports enthusiasts

Contact Information for Other Area Towns

Atchison, KS
(913) 367-2427
www.atchisonkansas.net

Blue Springs, MO
(816) 228-0209
www.bluespringsgov.com

Bonner Springs, KS
(913) 422-1020
www.bonnersprings.org

Cameron, MO
(816) 632-2177
www.cameron-mo.com

Chillicothe, MO
(660) 646-4281
www.chillicothemo.com

Clay County, MO
(816) 468-4989
www.clayedc.com

De Soto, KS
(913) 583-1585
www.desotoks.org

Excelsior Springs, MO
(816) 792-7733
www.ci.excelsior-springs.mo.us

Gladstone, MO
(816) 436-2200
www.gladstone.mo.us

Grandview, MO
(816) 761-6505
www.grandview.org

Independence, MO
(816) 325-7111
www.visitindependence.com

Jackson County, MO
(816) 881-4440
www.co.jackson.mo.us

Johnson County, KS
(913) 715-0748
www.jocoks.com

Kearney, MO
(816) 628-3343
www.kearneyareadevelopment.com

Lansing, KS
(913) 727-6111
www.lvarea.com

Lawrence, KS
(785) 865-4411
www.lawrencechamber.com

Leavenworth, KS
(913) 727-6111
www.lvarea.com

Leawood, KS
(913) 498-1514
www.leawood.org

from all over. South Kansas City is also home to the Kansas City Zoo, where hundreds of animals from exotic lands gambol and roam in their natural habitats.

The Kansas Side of the River

Just a few years ago this guide would have discounted the "other" Kansas City across the state line completely. But thanks to forward-thinking former mayor Carol Marinovich, Wyandotte County in Kansas has zoomed into

the picture with its new Kansas Speedway, which brings droves of NASCAR fans from a four-state region. Bring your earplugs. And bring your credit cards to the shopping havens sprinkled throughout Prairie Village, Overland Park, and Leawood.

OUTLYING AREAS

Earlier we mentioned that Kansas City recently added seven counties to our region.

Lee's Summit, MO
(816) 525-6617
www.leessummit.org

Lenexa, KS
(913) 888-1414
www.Lenexa.org

Liberty, MO
(816) 792-6033
www.ci.liberty.mo.us

Miami County, KS
(913) 294-4045
www.miamicountyks.org

North Kansas City, MO
(816) 274-6040
www.nkc.org

Olathe, KS
(913) 764-1050
www.edc.olathe.org

Ottawa, KS
(785) 242-1000
www.ottawakansas.org

Overland Park, KS
(800) 262-PARK (7275)
www.opcvb.org

Parkville, MO
(816) 505-2227
www.parkvillemo.com

Platte County, MO
(816) 270-2119
www.plattecountyedc.com

Shawnee, KS
(913) 631-6545
www.shawnee-edc.com

Southwest Johnson County, KS
(913) 764-6566
www.swjocoks-edc.com

St. Joseph, MO
(816) 764-6566
www.saintjoseph.com

Topeka, KS
(785) 234-2644
www.topekachamber.org

Warrensburg, MO
(660) 747-0244
www.warrensburgecodev.com

Weston, MO
(816) 640-2909
www.ci.weston.mo.us

Wyandotte County, KS
(913) 371-3070
www.kckcvb.org

Welcome, we say: The more the merrier! You can learn more about each county's many charms by logging onto their Web sites listed in "Community Profiles," found elsewhere in this chapter. But for now, here are snapshots of some of our favorite new neighbors.

Atchison, Atchison County, KS

Located 50 miles northwest of downtown Kansas City and only 35 miles from Kansas City International Airport, the town of Atchi-

son is a historic town known for its picturesque setting on the Missouri River and Victorian mansions on brick-lined streets. But its real claim to fame is Nell Hill's, a home decor emporium that draws busloads of shoppers from surrounding states. Discover details about this proud little community in Day Trips and Weekend Getaways.

Topeka, Shawnee County, KS

Topeka, Kansas's capital city, offers a quality

7

of life that includes a terrific zoo, parks, festivals, and Washburn University. A remodeled Topeka and Shawnee County Public Library designed by noted architect Michael Graves is considered one of the most modern libraries in the country.

St. Joseph, Buchanan County, MO

A hop, skip, and a jump from downtown Kansas City, St. Joseph provides a wealth of attractions that celebrate both our Wild West roots (you can visit the Jesse James home and the Pony Express Museum, for example) and our cosmopolitan upbringing, evidenced by drop-dead-gorgeous Victorian homes such as the Shakespeare Chateau, which is now a bed-and-breakfast. Walking tours of the Museum Hill and Cathedral Hill neighborhoods will introduce you to glorious residences from long ago.

Excelsior Springs, Clay County, MO

You might say this town is all wet. But that's a good thing: Once dubbed "the Health Center of the Nation" thanks to its therapeutic waters, today the town's two spas have undergone extensive renovations. Once a favorite of President Harry S. Truman and Al Capone (but never on the same weekend!), the Elms Resort offers a graceful style with new amenities; see details in Accommodations. And the Hall of Waters boasts the longest mineral water bar in the world, along with pampering spa services.

Lawrence, Douglas County, KS

To University of Kansas alumni, Lawrence has always seemed like part of Kansas City as Kansas Highway 10 becomes bumper-to-bumper Jayhawkers going back and forth on game day.

With an exciting arts community and thriving downtown, it's no wonder Lawrence is one of the fastest growing areas in the region. Get the scoop on what we affectionately call Larry Town in Day Trips and Weekend Getaways.

THE CENTER OF IT ALL

Although it's true that Kansas City is just 250 miles from the geographical center of the United States, we like to think that the term "heartland" refers more to our lovable people than the logistics. After all, we're home to Hallmark Cards, Helzberg Diamonds, and Russell Stover Candies—so you might say Cupid is a permanent resident.

We're all heart, too, when it comes to helping people in need and supporting the arts. Perhaps our generosity of spirit is a holdover from the days when homesteaders showed up with hammers and hampers of food to help a neighbor raise a barn.

Today, it's *money* we're raising to make Kansas City a better community. In fact, if you have the cash, conscience, or closet space you can attend a different black-tie fund-raiser every weekend, all year long. If you'd rather provide a little sweat equity instead, you can participate in a charity road race, bike ride, or golf tournament most weekends from spring through fall.

When we're not giving, we're taking—taking in the sights and smells of our town, that is. Some of the best aromas come from hickory smoke swirling around the barbecue restaurants that dot our city. We'll admit we didn't invent this method of slow cooking—we just perfected it.

Just ask the members of the Kansas City Barbecue Society, the largest organization devoted to the artform in the world. The group, whose motto is "Barbecue: not just for breakfast anymore," sanctions more than 120 national barbecue contests each year,

i If you're coming to Kansas City in the summer, do you pack a sweater or suntan lotion? Maybe both. A recent July day topped out at 99 degrees, but the recorded high was a bit warmer at 103. The lowest temperature on record for that date was 55 degrees. To get current temperatures plus a five-day forecast, log on to www.kansascity.com.

Vital Statistics

Mayors: Mark Funkhouser (Kansas City, MO) and Joe Reardon (Kansas City, KS)

Governors: Matt Blunt (Missouri) and Kathleen Sebelius (Kansas)

United States senators: Christopher Bond and Claire McCaskill (Missouri); Sam Brownback and Pat Roberts (Kansas)

Average maximum temperatures (degrees Fahrenheit): 38 (January); 65 (April); 89 (July); 69 (October)

Average minimum temperatures (degrees Fahrenheit): 21 (January); 45 (April); 70 (July); 48 (October)

Average precipitation (in inches): 1.30 (January); 3.37 (April); 4.02 (July); 2.98 (October)

Average annual snowfall (in inches): 21

Total population (as of March 2004): 1,967,405 (27th largest U.S. city)

Kansas counties: Atchison, Leavenworth, Wyandotte, Johnson, Franklin, Miami, and Linn

Missouri counties: Caldwell, Clinton, Clay, Ray, Jackson, Lafayette, Cass, Johnson, and Bates

Total combined region: More than 9,100 square miles; 132 miles from the northwest tip of Atchison County to the southeast corner of Bates County

Median age: 35.4

Average household income: $66,700

Median price for house: $155,800 (vs. $185,200 nationally)

Major airports: Charles B. Wheeler Downtown Airport, Kansas City International Airport

Major interstates: I-435, I-35, I-70, I-29, I-635, I-670

Total consumer spending: $35.9 billion

Hotel and motel rooms in the area: More than 30,000

Nicknames: City of Fountains, City of Surprises, The City Beautiful, Number 1 "Kid-Friendly City" (Overland Park, KS)

Major colleges and universities: Avila University, Johnson County Community College, MidAmerica Nazarene University, Park University, Rockhurst University, University of Missouri–Kansas City, William Jewell College

Famous Kansas Citians: Harry S. Truman, Jean Harlow, Casey Stengel, Ginger Rogers, writer Calvin Trillin, Walter Cronkite, golfer Tom Watson, handbag designer Kate Spade, actor Chris Cooper, jazz musician Pat Metheny, and Maurice Greene, once the fastest man on Earth

Just passing through (important people who lived in Kansas City): Count Basie, Ernest Hemingway (journalist at the *Kansas City Star* for six months), and Walt Disney

Homegrown companies: Hallmark Cards, Sprint, H&R Block, Helzberg Diamonds, Garmin International, AMC Theatres, Lee Jeans, Russell Stover Candies, American Century Investments, Applebee's, Black & Veatch, YRC Worldwide, and Three Dog Bakery

Products invented here: McDonald's Happy Meal, K.C. Masterpiece Barbecue Sauce, Teflon coating, Valomilk, Eskimo Pies, Hostess Twinkies, Rival Crock-Pot, the multiscreen movie theater, the outdoor shopping center, and the swing style of jazz

Notable events in Kansas City's history:

June 26, 1804: Lewis and Clark camp here during their first expedition to the Louisiana Territory.

1821: Francois Chouteau, a Frenchman from St. Louis, establishes a fur company at the Kaw River.

1821: Missouri is admitted to the Union.

1833: John Calvin McCoy opens a supply store 4 miles south of the river on the Santa Fe Trail. .

June 1, 1850: Town of Kansas (in Missouri) is incorporated.

1854: Kansas-Nebraska Act; many historians consider this the beginning of the Civil War.

1859: Thriving town welcomes 1,500 steamboats.

July 3, 1869: Hannibal Bridge opens, first rail bridge to span the Missouri River and provide a direct rail link to Chicago.

1871: Stockyards expand, giving us the start as prime meatpacking center. That means steaks, folks.

1889: Town officially becomes Kansas City, Missouri.

1899: City's first convention hall is built.

1900: Convention hall burns to the ground.

1900: Three months after its destruction, convention hall is rebuilt, just in time to host Democratic Convention.

1903: Missouri River floods the West Bottoms, leaving 22,000 people homeless.

1905: William Strang Jr. builds an interurban railway to encourage residential area in what is now Overland Park, Kansas.

1910: Joyce Clyde Hall sells postcards out of his suitcase at the YMCA—the start of Hallmark Cards.

1914: Union Station is built; during its heyday, 271 trains passed through daily.

1915: Parks and boulevard system is built, earning us the title "City Beautiful."

1921: The Liberty Memorial site is dedicated; completion is on November 11, 1926.

1923: The Country Club Plaza opens for business.

1931: While the rest of the country sagged under the Depression, Kansas City thrived, thanks to the Ten-Year Plan, which created jobs and saw the construction of the City Hall, new courthouse, and miles of new roads.

1933: Nelson Gallery of Art opens.

1943: Kansas City Monarchs, the all-black baseball team, celebrates forty-three straight wins.

October 15, 1949: WDAF, Kansas City's first television station, begins regular programming.

Friday the 13th, 1951: The Kansas River floods the West Bottoms again, leaving more than 20,000 homeless.

1960: The Chiefs football team plays its first season in Kansas City.

April 8, 1969: The Kansas City Royals play their first game.

January 12, 1970: Chiefs win Super Bowl IV, beating the Minnesota Vikings 23–7.

1972: River Quay, entertainment area near the River Market, takes off.

1972: Kansas City International Airport opens.

1973: Worlds of Fun opens, as does Crown Center's hotel and entertainment complex.

1974: Westport, a restaurant and entertainment district in midtown, becomes shopping and dining magnet.

1976: Kansas City hosts the Republican National Convention.

1985: Royals win the World Series.

1988: City hosts the NCAA Final Four basketball tournament.

1991: Emanuel Cleaver II becomes the first African American mayor of Kansas City. He serves until 1999, when Kay Barnes is elected the city's first female mayor.

1996: Voters across five counties pass the Bistate Cultural Tax, the first two-state effort of its kind in the country. Work begins to restore Union Station.

1997: 18th & Vine comes back to life with jazz venues, the Kansas City Jazz Museum, and the Negro Leagues Baseball Museum.

2000 and beyond: Kansas City, Missouri's urban areas begin a revitalization period, thanks to warehouses being converted to lofts. Neighborhoods such as the Crossroads Arts District attract artists, unique shops, and restaurants.

2001: Kansas Speedway opens in Kansas City, Kansas, home to NASCAR races. It's soon joined by a 400-acre tourism district called Village West.

2004: Bill passes to build a downtown arena; also on the drawing board is a new downtown entertainment district and a Performing Arts Center.

2004: Groundbreaking takes place for the South Loop redevelopment area including the H&R Block Headquarters, the Power & Light District, the Sprint Center, and the renovated President Hotel. Filming starts on *Mending the Heart of an American City,* the documentary that will capture it all. Kansas City International Airport completes a three-year, $258 million renovation project.

2005: The downtown Kansas City residential development continues to boom, with nearly 700 lofts and condo units completed. MAX, a rapid transit system, offers faster commutes for the areas between the Country Club Plaza and the River Market.

2006: The *Kansas City Star* unveils its $200 million Press Pavilion at 17th and McGee Streets. H&R Block's world headquarters opens downtown. The Kauffman Performing Arts Center breaks ground at 16th and Wyandotte. The Legends at Village West continue to add new shops and entertainment venues, as does Zona Rosa up north. Briarcliff Village opens north of the River with shops, restaurants, and lofts.

2007: Kansas City welcomes the new Power & Light District, Sprint Center, and Bartle Hall ballroom expansion. The city's cultural world expands with the Bloch Building at the Nelson-Atkins Museum of Art and the Nerman Gallery of Contemporary Art at Johnson County Community College.

including the granddaddy of 'em all, the American Royal, held next door to our celebrated stockyards each fall. See the Restaurant chapter for more information about Kansas City barbecue as well as a listing of some of our most celebrated joints.

But don't box us in as just a place to get barbecue—or world-famous steaks, for that matter. We offer the hungry visitor a variety of dining experiences that rival any other cosmopolitan city.

Have a hankering for Argentine chimichurri sauce or crawfish étouffée? How about authentic pollo mole, osso buco Milanese, sauerbraten, or spanikopita? Do you savor sushi or designer pizza? Brittany-style mussels or Moroccan lamb kabobs on your mind? Dim sum sound good? Or would an ice-cold beer and chili dog hit the spot?

Answer yes to any of these culinary cues and you've come to the right place.

Jazz and Blues

Our music came to us from cities such as New Orleans by way of the Mississippi and Missouri Rivers. And, like our barbecue that incorporates tomatoes for texture and molasses for sweetness, we created our own distinct recipe for jazz.

Musicians such as Count Basie took aspects of gospel, ragtime, and blues and turned them into swing, an infectious rhythm that got people out of their chairs to dance at the Reno Club in 1936. Charlie "Bird" Parker's alto sax propelled the art form even further with a new manic yet compelling sound called bebop.

The 12th Street nightspots where these geniuses jammed are long gone, but you can still hear live music in clubs, restaurants, and festivals all over town. A jazz museum and nightclub at 18th and Vine celebrates their influence and provides a forum for today's talented newcomers.

Our Climate, Both Weather-wise and Culturally

You'll find Kansas City to be a casual, friendly place where shirtsleeves—even nice shorts and sandals in summer—are appropriate for most restaurants. When in doubt call to ask, but long gone are the days when diners were handed ill-fitting jackets in order to be seated.

As for the temperature, the old saw "if you don't like the weather, just wait a few minutes and it will change" is certainly true here. Situated in the temperate zone, Kansas City experiences an annual average temperature of a pleasant 55 degrees, with a few days in winter that drop below 20 and a few in summer that go above 90.

It's hard to pick a favorite time to visit: Nature has blessed us with a paintbox of pleasing hues throughout the year. Spring comes early in the heartland, wearing a little girl's wardrobe of pink dogwood and yellow daffodils. Summer means cornflower blue skies, emerald lawns, ripe red tomatoes at the farmers' markets, and enough outdoor festivals to keep you from noticing the humidity.

In fall the landscape becomes a jewelry store window of crimson and gold as elms, maples, and giant oaks take on autumn's hues. In fact, many first-time visitors are amazed at the forestlike vistas throughout our city. Our forested bluffs, parks, gardens, and tree-lined boulevards are never more inspiring than when the weather turns brisk. During winter the colors—although man-made—are no less brilliant as 250,000 holiday lights outline the towers and spires of the Country Club Plaza, our spectacular Spanish-style outdoor shopping and entertainment district.

You'll be glad you brought a just-in-case umbrella any time of year. Here in the home of corn-fed beef, we rarely complain about the rain that grows that golden crop. You won't either the first time you taste a char-grilled Kansas City strip at Plaza III The Steakhouse.

GETTING HERE, GETTING AROUND

You might take a train, you might take a plane
. . . but no matter how you get here, you'll
enjoy it just the same!

GETTING TO KANSAS CITY

As you're driving in from the airport or on an
interstate you might wonder, "Where's the
city?" We assure you, it's here—and worth the
trip. But before you see our skyline rising like
the Emerald City out of limestone bluffs, you'll
pass fields of corn and pastures of bovine.
And just to prove the Midwest isn't all flat
plains, on the way you'll be treated to gently
rolling hills lush with trees: pink redbud in
spring, garnet-hued sycamore in autumn.
Relax and enjoy the view as your vehicle
becomes a decompression chamber: You're in
Kansas City now, where the pace is carefree
and the natives are so nice that you'll want to
stay longer than you'd planned.

Getting to the City
from the Airport

Chances are if you're flying the friendly skies
to our friendly city, you'll be coming into
Kansas City International Airport, or KCI.
(Read more about this award-winning airport
in the Close-up.)

The KCI Shuttle provides transportation
between the airport and more than ninety
metro-area hotels and runs from 4:00 a.m. to

i When buying tickets online, enter
KCI (for Kansas City International
Airport) and you might wind up in Kono,
Indonesia. (How's the weather?) You'll
find us instead at MCI, a holdover from
our Mid Continent International days.
And because all the airport codes starting
with "K" were taken, we'll remain MCI.

11:55 p.m. daily. If your flight arrives after 9:00
p.m., call to make reservations. Ticket counters
are located near each airline baggage claim
area at Terminal A—gates 1, 15, 30; Terminal
B—gates 31, 50, 60; or dial "5000" on a white
airport courtesy phone. Expect to pay around
$17 per person from the airport to the Plaza.
Call (816) 243-5000 or (800) 243-6383 for more
information, or log on to www.kctg.com. Nonstop travel to and from Johnson County is available for $45 for up to three passengers.

A private car service is a convenient way to
go—and besides, isn't it an ego-booster to be
greeted at the airport with your name printed
on a sign? Carey Limos has courteous drivers
and plush Lincoln Town Cars at your disposal.
Call (816) 471-1234 or (800) 808-1131. Another
quality service is Leader Limo, which offers luxury sedans, vans, minicoaches, and stretch
limos. Call (866) 770-5323 or (816) 753-5323, or
visit www.leaderlimo.com.

Other Area Airports

Although Kansas City International handles all
scheduled commercial flights, several smaller
fields support private pilots flying into town.
Kansas City's old Municipal Airport, located just
north of downtown, is now called Charles B.
Wheeler Downtown Airport and serves arriving
and departing corporate jets and charter
flights. For more information call (816) 243-5248
or check www.flymkc.com. Other airports
include the New Century AirCenter in Johnson
County, (913) 782-5335; Independence Memorial Airport, (816) 795-8774; and Lee's Summit
Municipal Airport, (816) 251-2492.

Private air charter companies serving the
metropolitan area are Air Charter Team, (816)
283-3280 or (800) 205-6610, and Executive
Beechcraft Inc., (816) 842-8484 or its KCI location at (816) 243-6440.

GROUND TRANSPORTATION

Bus Services

We'll admit our city bus system isn't as convenient or all-encompassing as those of other cities our size. But until—make that if—Kansas City voters ever agree on a light rail system, it's the best we've got. Voters approved funding for a system in 2006.

The Kansas City Area Transportation Authority maintains the city bus system we call the Metro, which serves primarily the central corridor of Kansas City, Missouri. The Metro Area Express (MAX to his friends) is a new rapid-transit service that runs from the River Market to the Plaza and all points in between including downtown and Crown Center, the trendy Crossroads Arts District, and Westport. Stylish MAX buses use dedicated lanes during rush hour and (get this) can prolong green lights to stay on schedule. We'd like to have that toy. That means the average travel time from the Plaza to downtown is less than seventeen minutes, with no fumbling for quarters to feed the meter once you get there.

MAX is rolling seven days a week, from 5:00 a.m. to 1:00 a.m., and transit times range from every nine minutes during rush hour to every thirty minutes after 7:00 p.m. Even the price is right at $1.25, which includes free transfers to all other buses. MAX has an easily identified logo. If you like it, it can be yours; you can purchase a MAX T-shirt for $12 to ride in style. Visit www.kcata.org for details and routes. For a cheap, two-hour tour of the city, catch the 51 Ward Parkway line, which passes through some pretty neighborhoods. Call (816) 221-0660 for schedules or log on to www.kcata.org.

Not that many SUV-wielding suburbanites take the bus, but those who do have access to the Johnson County Transit, affectionately called "The Jo." The buses stop at park-and-ride locations throughout the county and cover the county before heading across the state line. The blue buses take on a scarlet hue when hundreds of Kansas City Chiefs football fans don red jackets and caps to party all the way to the stadium. For schedules and fare information call (913) 362-3500 or go to www.thejo.com.

Taxis

You'll find taxis in Kansas City; just don't expect to find them queued up on every street corner as in Chicago. Most taxi companies have direct-connection phones at the airport, but a cab ride to the Plaza will cost around $40; better to choose the shuttle or limo service listed above. Most large hotels have taxi stands, or call Yellow Cab at (816) 471-5000 for round-the-clock service. The entire fleet is air-conditioned and drivers accept credit cards. Wheelchair-accessible vehicles are available.

Trains and Interstate Buses

On December 17, 2002, after a seventeen-year absence, Amtrak returned to Union Station with a new $4.6 million ticketing and boarding facility. The waiting room in the renovated train station features five of the original wooden benches and a large, historic wall clock.

Passengers enter at the northeast corner of Union Station's Grand Hall (with a capital G), adjacent to Pierpont's Restaurant. Short-term parking is available in front of the station; long-term parking is provided in the West Yards parking lot.

Three trains with four departures daily serve Kansas City: the Southwest Chief, between Chicago and Los Angeles; the Ann Rutledge, between Kansas City and Chicago; and the Kansas City Mule and St. Louis Mule, which travel daily between Kansas City and St. Louis. For station information only call (816) 421-3622. For reservations and schedules call (800) 872-7245 or (800) USA-RAIL or visit www.amtrak.com.

i   Wearing your seatbelts isn't just a good idea; it's the law on both sides of the state line. In both Missouri and Kansas, children ages four and younger must be in car seats.

Greyhound and Jefferson Bus Lines share terminals at 1101 Troost Avenue in downtown Kansas City, Missouri. Call (800) 231-2222 or (816) 221-2835 for fare and schedule information. A word of caution here: This location is not the safest in town, especially at night.

Car Travel

Depending on where you're staying during your visit, you can certainly enjoy areas of Kansas City without a car. On the Country Club Plaza, for example, some of the city's best dining, shopping, and nightspots are just a lovely stroll away from several fine hotels. Westport, too, offers the car-less crowd plenty to see and do. Stay at Crown Center and you won't even need an umbrella: overhead skywalks link the two hotels with entertainment, shopping, and the renovated Union Station, which houses Science City Museum.

However, if your lodging is in a suburb like Overland Park, you'll need a car to get around. There's nothing scarier than watching a group of conventioneers with name tags sprint across six busy lanes of Metcalf Avenue in search of burgers and beers.

Auto Rental Companies

Avis, (816) 243-5763, (800) 331-1212
Budget, (816) 243-5757, (800) 677-3681
Dollar, (816) 243-5600, (800) 800-4000
Enterprise, (816) 966-8188 or (913) 383-1515 in Kansas, (800) 736-8222
Thrifty Car Rental, (816) 842-8550

Freewheelin' Freeways and Roundabout Roads

Wherever you want to go in the metropolitan area, you can get there if you have directions and about twenty minutes. Since opening our first expressway, Southwest Trafficway, in 1950, we've developed a network of roadways that circle and circumvent the city. Today the Kansas City area has far more freeway miles per person than any other major U.S. city.

As you'll learn in the History chapter,

Traveling through Kansas City is far more luxurious today than for the 360,000 or so pioneers setting out on the Santa Fe and Oregon Trails in the early to mid-1800s. Back then 1 in 10 died. Learn their stories at the National Frontier Trails Center in Independence by viewing films, maps, and artifacts and reading diaries kept on the trip.

Kansas City began its life at the banks of the Missouri River. Numbered streets—those running east and west—follow a grid that starts at the river and are numbered sequentially both north and south. Main Street divides the town between east and west. Kansas City, Missouri, and most of Johnson County, Kansas, follow this pattern, but there are exceptions to the rule. Some streets meander along the land's natural contours, creating ribbonlike roads around lakes and ponds. Some of the prettiest such avenues pass through Mission Hills and Sunset Hills, where Tara-like mansions stand on acres of manicured lawns and back up to golf courses. No trip to Kansas City is complete without an eye-popping drive through these neighborhoods. Go ahead and gawk; we still do.

As in many other cities, it can be confusing to follow driving directions when streets change names at a whim. For instance, head to the airport from the Inter-Continental Hotel on the Plaza and you'll change streets five times within 4 miles as Ward Parkway becomes Baltimore, then J.C. Nichols Parkway. Cross Westport Road and the street sign says Broadway, then Pennway Park before becoming West Pennway—then (urrgh!)—Broadway again. Our advice? Take a limo, or the KCI Shuttle, or call a friend.

In both Missouri and Kansas you may turn right on a red light after stopping unless otherwise posted. Failing to do so—and pronto, buster—is a sure way to get a beep from the car horn behind you. We're a friendly bunch, but behind the wheel some drivers go from nice to nasty. Tailgating, changing lanes without signaling, and driving through red lights are some

Close-up

Welcome to the World's Friendliest Airport

If Kansas City International is your starting point you may not care for the airport's location—about 20 miles northwest of downtown or about a half hour drive—but you're certain to appreciate the user-friendly design. Opened in 1972, it features an innovative layout that connects three C-shaped terminals to a central loop. From the air it looks like Mickey Mouse's head sporting an extra set of ears. This configuration provides the shortest distance from curb to gate—75 feet—of any major U.S. airport. Check-in counters, baggage retrieval, and parking are also just steps away. One trip here and you'll see why *Travel Digest* in 2000 named KCI the world's "Most People-Friendly Airport."

How friendly, you might ask? Well, we recently spent $62 million for 15,000 economy parking spaces. While we're wondering where's the economy in that figure, you might like to know that the spaces are just part of a ten-year, $1.2 billion renovation project that includes some pretty spiffy artwork, including designs imbedded into the floors.

Facelifts are fine, but what you'll really enjoy are the expanded dining options throughout our three terminals. Now you can savor our famous Arthur Bryant's BBQ while waiting for a flight, or enjoy a cold brewsky from one of the Midwest's best microbreweries at Boulevard Brew Pub. And that reminds us: We've also added roomier lounges and more restrooms, including those that are more convenient for passengers with disabilities and people traveling with children.

Parking
Now, about that parking. The nearest parking lots to the terminals (A, B, and C) provide free parking for the first half hour. After that it's $2 for one-half

of the bad habits you may encounter, although some districts are putting up stoplight-mounted cameras to catch these last lawbreakers. Simply give an "I'm new here" shrug and forgive our manners. Please. Thank you.

As in all cities, you'll want to lock your car doors and place valuables such as cameras and suitcases in a locked trunk. And avoid walking alone at night. Unfortunately, that isn't just on deserted downtown streets; there have been incidents of crime, albeit rare, in nearly every area of greater Kansas City.

If you're planning to drive here in the middle of winter, check out the road conditions posted by the departments of transportation. For Kansas it's (800) 585-7623 or www.kanroad.org, and in Missouri (800) 222-6400 or www.modot.state.mo.us/roadcond/. But by the time you finish typing this last one, the flurries may have ended.

Tours

Discover Kansas City while you leave the driving to. . . well, somebody else. For the grooviest ride, catch the Magic Bus, decked out with to one hour, then $2 per hour up to a maximum of $18 per day. Circle parking is the same price, except the maximum is $12 per day. Economy parking is available at satellite lots for $5.50 per day. To reach these lots, take Paris Street off Cookingham Drive before you reach the terminal. Park in the lot (again, A, B, or C) that matches the terminal for your flight. For instance, if you're flying on Southwest Airlines, park in Lot B. The free shuttle will take you to your terminal.

Airlines Serving KCI

	Phone	Terminal	Gate
Air Canada	(888) 247-2262	A	10–12
AirTran	(800) 247-8726	A	15
American	(800) 433-7300	C	76–79
Continental	(800) 523-3273	C	67–69
Delta Connection Comair	(800) 354-9822	B	56–60
Delta	(800) 221-1212	B	56–60
Frontier	(800) 432-1359	C	84–85
Midwest Airlines	(800) 452-2022	A	23–30
Northwest	(800) 225-2525	C	61–64
Skybus	(website only) www.skybus.com	C	87–88
Southwest	(800) 435-9792	B	31–39
United	(800) 241-6522	A	10–12
USAirways	(800) 428-4322	A	1–9

love beads, lava lamp, and classic TV shows from the '70s. The Gangster Tour provides a look at mob houses and infamous crime scenes, from May through September. Visit www.kctg.com or call (816) 243-5000.

You won't need a get out of jail free pass, but we do recommend comfortable shoes to view our town's diverse architecture on a Historic Kansas City Foundation walking tour. These popular excursions include downtown's art deco buildings; our first exclusive neighborhood, Quality Hill, featuring homes dating from 1865; Union Cemetery, the final resting place for many of Kansas City's founders and Civil War casualties; 18th and Vine, with museums devoted to Kansas City jazz and the Negro Baseball Leagues; the Country Club Plaza; and more. Tours, which are led by enthusiastic volunteers, last from forty-five minutes to ninety minutes and cost—what a bargain!—around $6 per person, with a six-person minimum. Call (816) 931-8448 or visit www.historic kansascity.org to reserve a tour at least two to three weeks in advance. Some of the tours are adaptable for van or buses.

Downtown at twilight. CVB OF GREATER KANSAS CITY

Some of the best views of Kansas City can be found at the Liberty Memorial tower at Penn Valley Park, the glass-enclosed elevator at the InterContinental Hotel at the Plaza, and the City Hall Observation Deck at 414 East 12th Street.

Agenda Kansas City can plan sightseeing tours of your choice, including historic sites, a day of shopping, or a night on the town via vans, minicoaches, or limos. Call (913) 268-4466 or (888) AGENDAKC, or check out www.agendakansascity.com.

HISTORY

There's real drama in our town's 180-plus-year history, a story filled with fascinating heroes and colorful rascals. Yet, unlike an old-fashioned Western it's not always easy to tell if the central characters are wearing white hats or black.

In our struggle to change from mudville to metropolis, we've endured heartbreak such as cholera, fires, and a Civil War that left emerging towns on both sides of the state line bloodied and raw. And like every city that dared to stake its future on a river—in our case, two rivers, the Missouri and Kansas—there have been devastating floods.

Yet our history is also filled with stories of pluck and perseverance. Our up-from-our-bootstraps triumphs over natural and man-made tragedies earned us the slogan "Kansas City Spirit." We've always been a town that drew people of grit and tenacity. Our early trailblazers—men such as McCoy, Swope, Nelson, Van Horn, Vanderslice, and Volker—often came here looking to make a buck or build a reputation, fell in love with the town, and became our most staunch boosters. Their names are carved into cornerstones, printed on street signs, and embellished on entry markers throughout the city they loved.

Today, a century and a half later, we honor the new pioneers who are taking us forward with vision and vitality. The last part of this chapter is devoted to the men and women whose names adorn new buildings, art centers, and organizations that were created to assist families, find cures for diseases, and train tomorrow's leaders.

Our story starts where it all began: at the river.

WHERE THE RIVERS MEET

Our landscape—fertile valleys and tallgrass prairies, limestone bluffs and wide rivers—was formed when glaciers inched across the shallow seas covering the areas now known as Kansas and Missouri. Ages later other emigrants traveled here by way of the Missouri River. Indians came—the Hopewell, Shawnee, Delaware, and the Kanza who gave us our name—in wooden canoes. French traders arrived in pirogues and keelboats. These were followed by steamboats, often magnificently appointed, before railways and roads crisscrossed our lands.

On June 26, 1804, explorers Meriwether Lewis and William Clark camped on the confluence of the Kansas and Missouri Rivers during their first expedition to the Louisiana Territory. The view they saw from the bluff that would become Quality Hill is still a commanding one today. A handsome statue commemorating the expedition stands at Case Point near downtown. (See details in Attractions.)

It would be nearly two decades before the town really came into being. In 1821—the year Missouri was admitted to the Union—a Frenchman from St. Louis, Francois Chouteau, established the American Fur Company at

> **i** Trek to Clark's Point at Eighth and Jefferson to take in the view of the river below and imagine what it was like for the area's first visitors, such as Lewis and Clark. The overlook didn't get its name for half the famous expedition party, however. It was named to honor former city councilman Charles H. Clark in 1933.

Kawsmouth to feed Europe's craving for beaver-felt hats. Five years later Chouteau's post was destroyed by flood. Would he leave this spot? *Mon dieu!* At the time his enterprise brought in what would now amount to $5 million a year. He moved to higher ground upriver near what is now Troost Avenue. It wouldn't be the last time the river (America's second longest after the Mississippi) would turn on the people who tried to tame her.

By 1833 the area just east of Indian Territory had captured the attention of another early entrepreneur. John Calvin McCoy, a college-educated surveyor and son of a Baptist minister, opened a supply store 4 miles south of the river on the Santa Fe Trail. He called the place West Port. Today Westport is still a thriving center of commerce, filled with restaurants, shops, and bars. One of its most popular, Kelly's, started life as a tavern in 1836.

McCoy also founded Westport Landing on a rock ledge across the river from Chouteau's settlement. In 1838 McCoy and thirteen other men formed a company and bought a 271-acre tract surrounding the river landing for $4,220. The growing town needed a name and, perhaps inspired by the passing of a jug, the group rejected Possum Trot and Rabbitville for Town of Kansas. The name stuck, and the town was incorporated on June 1, 1850. We wouldn't become Kansas City until 1889.

The township thrived, thanks in part to the romanticized depictions of the frontier by writers such as Washington Irving. How many Easterners packed up possessions to travel halfway across a continent after reading *A Tour on the Prairies* in 1832? How much wanderlust was inspired by the description in *The Oregon Trail* of a land "at the height of its freshness"?

Yet travelers seeking the land of the quixotic passages in books and newspapers were disappointed by their first glimpse of our corrugated landscape. By 1840 the settlement was a square mile of land carved out of 130-foot limestone canyons so rugged its 500 residents called it Gully Town. Thick vines and dense forests of oak, hickory, elm, hackberry, and walnut awaited workers. The land was slashed with deep ravines plowed out by rushing streams. After a rain, Gully Town became Mudville.

Yet still they came.

CHOLERA STRIKES

In 1849 the burgeoning settlement met with its first serious setback when cholera killed nearly 30 percent of its residents and drove out hundreds more. There were scarcely enough people left to bury the dead.

Yet by March 1853, fewer than three years after the plague, the port was thriving once more, driven in part by the Mexican trade over the Santa Fe Trail and the discovery of gold in California. In a frontier version of "Last gas for 50 miles," the wagon trains fueled up on provisions at the westernmost point reachable by Missouri River boats. In 1850, 600 wagons got their start at Kansas City. Just ten years later the trade amounted to 16 million pounds of merchandise each year. In 1859, 1,500 steamboats landed at the site.

Tens of thousands arrived here before heading west. Many decided to stay, and today our diverse personality comes from the immigrants who moved here and brought their colorful cultures. Over the decades Scandinavians went to work in the packinghouses. Italians grew the produce sold at the City Market. Five thousand Greeks arrived in Kansas City within a fourteen-year span and called their community around Fifth Street "Athens." The Irish, Germans, and Jews came, each bringing rich traditions along with suitcases and knapsacks. African Americans were brought to the area by white slaveholders. A

i Get a glimpse—actually an eyeful—of what our river town must have looked like around 1840. A mural that depicts riverboats and a tiny settlement on the bluffs has been painted on a brick building just east of the Broadway Bridge in the River Market area.

Serbo-Croatian community sprang up on Strawberry Hill, overlooking the Kaw River in Kansas City, Kansas.

The city's first hotel—a two-story frame structure at Main Street and the levee—was established in 1846 by Thompson McDaniel to handle the travelers.

At the same time the Wyandot tribe owned and operated a ferry across the Kansas River, then known as the Kaw, which today's Lewis and Clark Viaduct spans. The name of the tribe has presented some debate: Wyandot is the correct Indian spelling. The English added another *T*, and the French tacked on an *E*. But that's nothing compared to the confusion created when the township was incorporated as Kansas City, a duplicate of the larger city across the water.

THE CIVIL WAR

But soon the division between Kansas and Missouri was deeper than the river that cut through the land. By 1850 one in five Jackson County residents was African American. Of these, nearly 3,000 were slaves. Communities, even families, were divided on the issue of slavery.

Many historians trace the beginning of the Civil War to May 1854, when the Kansas-Nebraska Act opened the former Indian Territory to settlement. The conflict between abolitionists and pro-slavery groups plunged the land, known as "Bleeding Kansas," into political and military strife. The fighting gained intensity when William Clarke Quantrill

i Civil War history buffs will want to pick up two brochures produced by the Civil War Round Table—a twenty-five-stop driving tour that includes important battle sites throughout the Kansas City region and a walking tour that details important locations, including Loose Park and the John Wornall House. Call (888) 397–1236, or write to the Monnett Battle of Westport Fund, P.O. Box 22528, Kansas City, MO 64113-0528.

and 450 guerrillas swooped into nearby Lawrence, Kansas, before dawn and slaughtered more than 200 men and boys. A year later a battle known as the "Gettysburg of the West" was waged across Westport and west into what is now Mission Hills.

The Civil War decimated both sides of the state line. In Kansas City, Missouri, the population dropped 25 percent to 3,000 or so. The city treasurer's statement showed municipal assets were $16,120.20 and its liabilities, $13,090.84. Cash on hand was $87 and change.

A RETURN TO PEACE AND PROSPERITY

In 1863 the government sent troops to protect the Santa Fe traders and business began to boom once more. The chamber of commerce was organized and real estate became salable again. A vacant lot on Sixth near Main brought $500; another on Walnut near Fifth sold for $305.

Yet the city, after four years of neglect, was in deplorable shape. The streets were quagmires, hub-deep with mud even weeks after a rain, and washouts and gullies made traffic almost impossible. In the spring of 1865 the city negotiated a loan of $60,000 to improve road conditions and open thoroughfares. Once again things began to hum, and soon the hotel on Main Street was registering 27,000 arrivals a year.

In the meantime the settlement across the Kansas River was also growing, although more slowly. In 1855 a group of Kansas City, Missouri, businessmen purchased the core of the town from the Huron Indians. Growth escalated when the settlement's first packing plant was built in the Central Industrial District in 1868, and it soon developed a solid base of railroads, stockyards, and industries. Later that year the Town of Wyandotte and the adjacent towns Kansas City, Kansas, and Armourdale were incorporated into a single city.

During this time Kansas Citians began riding to work, school, and the movies on a "bunch of bananas": yellow streetcars that numbered 700 at the height of their eight-decade run beginning in 1869. For a 2-cent fare travelers could get quite a thrill traversing the city's hilly streets; the Ninth Street line from Quality Hill to the West Bottoms was as steep as anything San Francisco had to offer. The influx of rubber-tired buses and personal vehicles retired the last of the streetcar bells in June 1957.

BRIDGE TO THE FUTURE

In those days, despite our growth, the towns of Leavenworth, Kansas, and St. Joseph, Missouri, were leaving Kansas City, Missouri, in their dust. They had populations of 15,400 and 15,000, respectively, to our 4,000. But what these lusty rivals didn't have were city boosters such as Robert Van Horn and Kersey Coates, who helped secure the first rail bridge to span the Mighty Mo and provide a direct rail link to Chicago. On July 3, 1869, the opening of the Hannibal Bridge was celebrated by a parade, barbecue, and fireworks. More than 20,000 people watched as the *Hannibal,* the pride of the Hannibal & St. Joseph Railroad, steamed across the bridge with ten railcars in tow.

Other railroads followed from every direction until the present great aggregation of systems was built up and Kansas City's future was assured. Within five years our population had soared to 32,000, while the other cities had grown by only a few thousand each. A Main Street lot worth $400 in 1856 brought $11,000 in 1871.

SIN CITY AND ITS SAVIORS

Yet not all of our newfound prominence was positive. According to writer Charles Gleed, by 1878 the town was filled with "renegades, Indians, demoralized soldiers, unreformed bushwhackers, and border ruffians, thieves, and thugs imported from anywhere, professional train-robbers of home growth, and all

i World leader and bank robber: We celebrate both our famous native sons, Harry S. Truman and Jesse James. The lives of both men are celebrated in museums and homes dedicated to their importance in the Midwest and the world.

kinds of wrecks from the Civil War."

Those homegrown train robbers were, of course, Frank and Jesse James. In 1866 the James Gang began its crime spree by robbing a bank on Liberty, Missouri's town square. Along with ten compatriots they made off with $62,500; one bystander was killed. The James farm near Kearney, Missouri, was one of several safe havens for the boys, but in truth they had plenty of willing help. Many Southern sympathizers saw the outlaws as romantic Robin Hoods who were avenging the loss of the Civil War. During the 1870s the gang was linked to nearly two dozen heists.

There was plenty of money to go around. In those days we had more gambling houses than any other city in the nation. One of these, Marble Hall, was a favorite of Wyatt Earp, Bat Masterson, Buffalo Bill Cody, and Wild Bill Hickok.

This era also marked the start of our meatpacking industry. Two plants for slaughtering cattle and hogs were opened, and in 1871 the stockyards were expanded in the West Bottoms. Cowboys who moved the herds spread news about the "Queen of the Cowtowns," where saloons had French glass, gleaming mahogany bars, and no last call.

By 1878 the freewheeling town had a growth rate of 70 percent and was labeled a Modern Sodom by the local newspaper. There were eighty saloons, actually a lifesaver because the murky water supply made drinking whiskey a virtue. Annie Chambers's posh brothel at Third and Wyandotte Streets was doing brisk business as well, and if customers tired of her establishment, they had forty other bordellos to sample.

Our prosperity also brought conveniences.

In 1879 the Missouri and Kansas Telephone Company printed its first directory, listing forty-six subscribers in Kansas City, Missouri, and twelve in Kansas City, Kansas. We had an opera house, Exposition Hall, a public waterworks system with 15 miles of water mains, and a two-man fire department.

Yet when William Rockhill Nelson moved to Kansas City from Indiana in 1880, he was appalled to find unpaved roads and haphazard walking boards instead of sidewalks. Soon he was using his newspaper, the *Kansas City Evening Star,* to instigate change. After he won his crusade for better fire protection and street lamps, he focused on public recreation and parks. Read more about this benevolent bear of a man in the Media chapter.

Nelson also convinced others of the importance of green spaces and planned roadways. Colonel Thomas H. Swope donated the largest gift of land in the city's history, before or since: a 1,334-acre tract of land 4 miles from downtown. It became the park that bears his name: the second largest public green space in the United States after New York's Central Park.

In 1891 landscape designer George Kessler was hired to create boulevards and parks using classical architecture while celebrating our eccentric topography. He carved roadways out of gorges and around hills to create wonderful scenic drives. By 1915 we had a feature that would forever rival cities blessed with mountains and ocean views: a parks and boulevard system that earned us the title "City Beautiful."

Buildings were springing up as fast as the roses in one of the city's loveliest green spaces, Loose Park. By the late 1880s a building spree had given the town the nickname "Athens of the West," based on architecture with high ornamentation and neo-Gothic styling. We built the third largest train station in the world, Union Depot, in the West Bottoms and constructed the luxurious Coates House Hotel and Coates Opera House . . . never mind that the latter was next to a cow pasture.

Real estate developers were following Kessler's boulevards to the south. J. C. Nichols built Crestwood, a small shopping area, at 55th and Oak to serve his residences. He sited homes on generous lots that kept the existing terrain as natural as possible, often creating curving streets to save large trees and preserve brooks and streams. His Mission Hills area, with its rolling meadows, ponds, and walkways, set examples that were repeated by developers all over the country.

By 1890 we had twenty-five schoolhouses, 35 miles of cable car track, and nearly 6,000 new houses. Scottish immigrants laid out the city's first golf course in the Hyde Park neighborhood in 1894. The game was a hit: These days 240,000 Kansas Citians—or 15 percent of our population—are golfers.

KANSAS CITY SPIRIT

In 1899 the city's first convention hall, designed by Frederick E. Hull, opened to the rousing music of John Philip Sousa's band. The cost was high—double the original estimates—but the structure was debt-free thanks to the donations of generous Kansas Citians. It's a legacy of philanthropic pride we follow today.

A year later, fire destroyed the building just three months before the Democratic Convention was to be held, an event boosters hoped would bring us national acclaim. But even as the fire blazed people circulated through the crowd soliciting donations for the building's reconstruction. A frenzied ninety days later, the convention nominated William Jennings Bryan in one of the world's largest indoor arenas—certainly its newest. The phrase "Kansas City Spirit" was coined that day. Locals strutted around town wearing badges boasting, "I Live in Kansas City—Ask Me."

Six hundred visiting journalists picked up the story and soon newcomers were jamming the streets. One person drawn to the vivacious city was eighteen-year-old Joyce Clyde Hall, who in 1910 sold postcards from a suitcase under his bed at the YMCA—the

Close-up

Kansas City's Colorful History

- Artist Frederic Remington sold his first painting in Kansas City. The twenty-three-year-old arrived here in 1884 and his commercial endeavors—a hardware store and a saloon—failed miserably. His paintings, however, were popular and he sold them through an art supply dealer before moving to New York.

- In 1904 Lyda Burton Conley studied law and became the first Native American female lawyer in the country. She used her new degree to petition Congress to pass a bill prohibiting the removal of the Huron Indian Cemetery in downtown Kansas City, Kansas. The resting place remains there today, a small plot of land surrounded by businesses between Sixth and Seventh Streets on Minnesota Avenue.

- The City Union Mission received a much-needed boost from a most unlikely patron when, in 1934, ninety-two-year-old bordello owner Annie Chambers was moved to tears during a funeral sermon by Reverend David Bulkley. She deeded her opulent brothel to his cause, and her residence at Third and Wyandotte Streets was converted into a women's shelter.

- One of the world's most successful companies started at the YMCA. In 1910, eighteen-year-old Joyce Hall arrived in Kansas City from Norfolk, Nebraska, with a shoebox of postcards, which he kept under his bed at the Y. His room became the company's first address, and today the "Shoebox" line of cards honors that humble beginning.

- A mural in the Missouri Capitol in Jefferson City by Kansas City artist Thomas Hart Benton depicts our rambunctious town in the 1930s. The

start of Hallmark Cards.

The city's resolve would be tested again in 1903 when spring rains turned the Missouri River into an inland sea, flooding the West Bottoms. It destroyed bridges, swept away the stockyards, filled the Union Depot, and left 22,000 people homeless. Public relief money came pouring in, and the area began to rebuild within days.

The trauma of the flooding drove William B. Strang Jr. to develop a flood-free residential area in Johnson County, Kansas. To encourage development he built an interurban railway in 1905 to take residents from downtown to home and back. It extended to the small town of Olathe farther west. The Strang Line building is still standing, now home to Traditions Furniture Store in Old Overland Park.

Another peril—this time man-made—soon took over the West Bottoms and eventually spread over the entire city. An infamous political machine started when Jim Pendergast opened a saloon in the area. Soon his younger brother, Tom (profiled in this chap-central character in the colorful painting was Boss Tom Pendergast—for which Pendergast himself posed—dealing with real estate developer J. C. Nichols and banker William T. Kemper.

- When John Calvin McCoy married Virginia Chick in 1838, he was late for the wedding. His future father-in-law sent out a search party and found him—in his wedding attire—feverishly finishing a neighbor's barn roof just minutes ahead of a thunderstorm. Six years later a tornado hit the McCoy house, blowing three-month-old Spencer—crib and all—out of the house. He was found some distance from the destroyed home, uninjured and still in bed.

- Mayor Milton McGee laid out Grand Avenue—the first road from the Missouri River to the town of Westport—just wide enough to get his horse and buggy turned around without having to back it up.

- *The Muse of the Missouri* fountain between Eighth and Ninth on Main celebrates the river's importance in Kansas City's history. Sculptor Wheeler Williams had planned to model the fish fountainheads after native Missouri River fish. But when he deemed our catfish too ugly he fashioned his own hybrid with a carp body and bluefish head.

- At one time Alexander Majors's Pony Express freight and stagecoach company employed 4,000 circuit riders, including fifteen-year-old wagonmaster Billy Cody. But by 1860 the telegraph and railroad spelled doom for the operation, and "The Great Bullwhacker" lost his fortune. In 1895 the entertainer, now known as Buffalo Bill Cody, made his former employer part of his Wild West show. Majors's home at 81st Street and State Line is now a museum. Read more about it in Attractions.

ter's Close-up), was named superintendent of streets.

Those same streets continued to carry Kansas City's population southward and away from its river origins as urban sprawl settled in. J. C. Nichols began selling houses for $1,000 in Kansas City, Kansas.

By 1912 the city had 55,000 telephones, 221 churches, 72 public schools, 2,100 acres of parks, 70 miles of boulevards, and 260 miles of street railway. It also had 81 movie theaters with an average weekly attendance of nearly 450,000, almost twice the population of the city. General Hospital, an institution built to serve the city's 24,000 black residents, became the first hospital in the nation to be run and staffed completely by African Americans.

We had other reasons to be proud. Workers hung a 6-foot clock in the archway at Union Station in the fall of 1914. The Beaux Arts–style station replaced the Union Depot in the flood-worried West Bottoms. The new $60 million station at Pershing Road and Grand featured a 95-foot ceiling in the Grand Hall, three 3,500-pound chandeliers, and a North Waiting Room that held 10,000 people. During its heyday, 271 trains passed through the depot daily. Read more about Union Station's sad decline and remarkable restoration in Attractions.

By 1914 the city had another important industry, this time in the service sector. The Federal Reserve Bank opened that year and by 1921 ranked fifth in bank-clearing volume nationwide. This attracted other federal agencies to the area, and by 1939 more than 100 federal offices were located in the metropolitan area.

Money was indeed flowing during the Gilded Age. Millionaires built mansions to rival any in the country. To give his Corinthian Hall the northeast bluff view he desired, lumberman Robert A. Long moved three smaller mansions down the street. His 72-room townhome cost $1 million to build and furnish— shocking in that day. Today the majestic building houses the Kansas City Museum and Planetarium. Read more about this fascinating display in Attractions.

Ladies were decorating more than just their parlors. Charles Tivol opened his jewelry store on Petticoat Lane, where a suitor could purchase a one-carat diamond for $175. The diamonds are a bit pricier these days, but the service is still unmatched at the family-owned business now located on the Country Club Plaza. Petticoat Lane—so named for the lacy lingerie ladies would show on windy days— was also home to the Emery, Bird, Thayer general store.

THE JAZZ AGE: GOOD TIMES AND BAD

On January 16, 1920, prohibition of liquor became part of the U.S. Constitution, yet here the Pendergast political machine kept the city wide open. It was the start of the Roaring Twenties, and no town bellowed louder. Nightclubs flourished thanks to police who were paid to ignore gambling, prostitution, and liquor. Tom Pendergast's own gambling

hall had two windows, marked DONATIONS and REFUNDS.

Jazz musicians knew they could always get a gig in Kansas City. Duke Ellington, Cab Calloway, and other bandleaders stopped here on tours, and our local groups kept the beat with the best of them. Pianist William "Count" Basie got his start with Bennie Moten's Kansas City Orchestra. Music poured out of nightclubs along 12th Street and 18th and Vine. The Reno Club, Harlem Nite Club, and big dance halls such as the El Torreon kept swinging all night. One young player frequented the Reno Club to listen to his idol, saxophonist Lester Young. Eventually this young man, Charlie Parker, would create a musical style all his own.

Kansas Citians had plenty of other amusements. Fairyland Park opened on 80 acres of farmland at 75th and Prospect Avenue in 1923. That same year the first retail building on the Country Club Plaza made its first sale and the Pla-Mor Ballroom, billed as America's largest indoor amusement center, opened in 1927. It was soon attracting 4,000 dancers nightly. When they weren't shopping, dancing, or riding the Ferris wheel, residents could listen to four local radio stations.

We stopped moving long enough to salute when five prominent Allied commanders, including General John J. Pershing and French Marshal Ferdinand Foch, joined Vice President Calvin Coolidge to dedicate the site of the Liberty Memorial in 1921. It was the country's only monument to World War I. Coolidge, by now president, returned on November 11, 1926, to formally dedicate the completed memorial, with its majestic 200-foot shaft rising from a hill overlooking Union Station.

We had other heroes to celebrate as well. Formed in 1919, the all-black Kansas City Monarchs baseball team traveled the Midwest in the 1920s and 1930s, when baseball was segregated. The players thrilled fans with forty-three straight wins in 1943. A team member, Jackie Robinson, was the first black player to sign with a major league team, the

Brooklyn Dodgers, in 1947. Pitcher Satchel Paige eventually played for the Cleveland Indians and the St. Louis Browns before returning to Kansas City to star for the A's.

Another Kansas Citian got his start during this decade. Harry S. Truman, unsuccessful as a haberdasher, was handpicked by Tom Pendergast to run for a post on the administrative court that governed Jackson County. He won, but Pendergast soon learned that Truman would not become one of his lackeys. Independence is still Harry's Town; you can visit his museum and farmhouse. Find out more in Attractions.

HIGH TIMES

Kansas City said "What Depression?" and continued to thrive during the nation's darkest days, thanks in part to Pendergast. In 1931 the Ten-Year Plan created jobs and spawned a new City Hall, a courthouse, and miles of new roads. The art deco–style Kansas City Power & Light building was completed at 14th and Baltimore. For years it was the tallest building in Missouri; it remains the most stunning, especially at night when its prismatic glass and automated lighting system change the tower's colors. Two years later the Nelson Gallery of Art and Atkins Museum opened on the property formerly occupied by newspaper publisher William Rockhill Nelson.

It was the end of a decade—and the end of an era—when in 1939 Pendergast pleaded guilty to income tax evasion and

i Some of our city's liveliest history happened in nightspots along 18th and Vine during the Jazz Age. You can relive those days—to a more refined degree—at the district's American Jazz Museum; the Blue Room, which doubles as a museum and nightclub; and during jazz jams on Saturday night at the Mutual Musicians Foundation. Get event information on the twenty-four-hour Kansas City Jazz Ambassadors' Hotline, (816) 753-5277.

was sentenced to fifteen months in Leavenworth Prison.

WAR AND RESURGENCE

When the United States went to war, Kansas Citians went to work. Before the 1940s our economy seemed forever grounded in livestock, grain, and freight. But our central location—and farmlands full of willing workers—made the Midwest ideal for wartime industry. Remington Arms Company built an ammunitions plant on 3,200 acres east of Independence, and within three years the Lake City Ordnance Plant was churning out 200 million rounds of ammunition a month. When the Army Air Corps picked Kansas City for a bomber plant, it predicted it would employ 8,000 to 10,000 workers. But when the announcement was made—one year to the day before the bombing of Pearl Harbor—no one could have guessed the factory would soon have a workforce of 26,000.

Defense jobs drew 40,000 workers to Kansas City between 1940 and 1943. Most of them clocked in at the Pratt & Whitney aircraft engine plant at Bannister Road and Troost Avenue, where former homemakers and farmhands built the 2,000-horsepower engine used in Navy fighter planes. The facility was the first major employer on the suburban south side and required new four-lane roads and trolley tracks. There were six cafeterias to feed the riveters and workers, 40 percent of whom were women and 6 percent black. And they did the city proud: Kansas City companies consistently won prestigious "Army-Navy E" awards for production performance. The garment district, in the meantime, outfitted America's fighting forces.

On August 14, 1945, Missouri's favorite son, President Harry S. Truman, declared that the war was over. The troops came home, minus some 1,250 soldiers from Jackson County who died in action.

The jubilant country was dancing to Charlie Parker's bebop music. And here in the Midwest, we stared at our Philcos as the town's first television station, WDAF, began regular programming on October 16, 1949. By the fall of 1950 kids were watching Whizzo the Clown on KMBC–TV. His audience was growing fast; during the next decade 100,000 babies were born in Kansas City.

As we celebrated the centennial of the city's incorporation, things looked rosy. We had a new outdoor venue, Starlight Theatre. Mickey Mantle played outfield for the Kansas City Blues, a team in the American Association. And the Katz Drug store was selling Davy Crockett coonskin caps for 98 cents.

Then, on Friday the 13th, 1951, after forty days of rain the Kansas River poured over its dikes to flood the Argentine district and the West Bottoms . . . again. By Saturday the Kaw had engulfed the stockyards and factories in the area and forced the evacuation of 15,000 people. City crews dumped junked cars onto the embattled levees to fight the surging water and try to keep the Municipal Air Terminal dry. Five people died and 20,000 were made homeless.

Once again the city rallied. In memory of the city's mettle when it rebuilt the Convention Hall in three months in 1900, workers rebuilt the destroyed American Royal facilities in time for the livestock show weeks later. The country marveled at the collective Kansas City character. Illustrator Norman Rockwell painted *The American Spirit* showing a worker rolling up his sleeves while holding a blueprint.

In 1956 the Hannibal Bridge was replaced by the Broadway Bridge. Kansas City streetcars made their final run in 1959, and only twenty trains a day pulled into Union Station. In the following decade, news about transportation would continue to fill the front pages of the *Star*.

THE TIMES THEY ARE A-CHANGIN'

By 1962, when Interstate 70 was replacing U.S. Highway 40 as the primary entry from the east and west, city commuters were already touting the new 55-mile Interstate 35.

Soon it would link folks who lived in Johnson County with their downtown jobs. Within a few years office parks and shopping malls would pop up in every direction to take workers and shoppers out of the inner city.

The exodus from downtown began in earnest in 1947 when Sears Roebuck and Co. opened its first suburban store on the Country Club Plaza. The movement gained momentum in 1958 when Blue Ridge Mall opened in east Kansas City and Ward Parkway Center opened to the south. They were followed by Metcalf South Shopping Center and a parade of other malls in the suburbs, whose expanding populations packed the parking lots. Downtown stores became increasingly irrelevant. Emery, Bird, Thayer closed in 1968. Dillard's, which replaced the venerable Macy's store, moved to the suburbs in 1989. Only the Jones Store Co. was left, and it turned off the lights in 1998.

The city's central core also lost its airport. The Municipal Airport just north of downtown was too confining for growth; pilots and passengers complained that landings seemed to miss nearby skyscrapers by inches. Its replacement, Kansas City International, opened in fall 1972 on a 5,000-acre tract of land northwest of the city.

Some teenagers, in the meantime, were getting high on their own. The Midwest had its share of hippies during the 1960s. Most hung out at Volker Fountain (now called Thies Park) and neighborhood coffeehouses, where they heard local musicians such as Brewer and Shipley. Some participated in protest marches.

Some historians were protesting, too—

i Where will you find the only monument and museum in the world dedicated solely to World War I? It's not Washington, D.C., or Normandy—it's the 217-foot-tall Liberty Memorial right here in Kansas City. Major renovations, started in 2002, have returned the site to its former glory and added a fascinating museum.

not for change but for conservation. It was a time when landmarks were destroyed to make room for expressways and parking lots. More than 125 buildings came tumbling down, including the former Lyric Theater at 622 Main Street, Kansas City's first public school at Independence Avenue and Cherry Street, and Bob Potee's glittering gambling house at No. 3 Missouri Avenue in the area now known as the River Market.

But the '60s also brought plenty to cheer about. The Chiefs professional football team played its first season in Kansas City after owner Lamar Hunt transplanted the team from Dallas. Kansas City voters approved an ordinance that required taverns, amusement parks, and public pools to admit minorities. And on September 17, 1964, the Beatles played a half-hour concert to screaming fans at Municipal Stadium. The Fab Four eventually would record their own version of "Kansas City," the city's anthem.

Another crowd filled the stadium when the Kansas City Royals pitched the first ball on April 8, 1969. It was Ewing Marion Kauffman, the man who started Marion Labs, who brought the team to Kansas City after the A's moved to Oakland.

We crowded the streets on January 12, 1970, to welcome home the Chiefs, who had just won Super Bowl IV in New Orleans, beating the Minnesota Vikings 23–7. We continued our move to official sports town with the construction of a twin stadium. Arrowhead Stadium opened for the Chiefs in fall 1972; Royals Stadium housed the Royals a year later. Today the baseball facility is called Kauffman Stadium—or simply "The K"—to honor the baseball team owner.

We were going after crowds of tourists as well with two shining new attractions that opened in 1973. Worlds of Fun created a loopy new skyline of roller coasters and rides on 175 acres in North Kansas City. And the Crown Center complex replaced an eyesore called Signboard Hill across the street from Union Station, offering a city-within-a-city of shopping, restaurants, and hotels linked by glass-enclosed skywalks.

When we hosted the Republican National Convention in 1976, Crown Center impressed delegates and media representatives, as did the elegant new Alameda Plaza Hotel, the first large luxury hotel to grace the Country Club Plaza. Its popular Rooftop Lounge and restaurant offered unparalleled views, food, and libations. Those looking for a more casual atmosphere could find it at the Gilbert-Robinson Plaza restaurant, Houlihan's Old Place.

If anyone visited River Quay (pronounced key), an entertainment district near the City Market, it would be their last chance. The area opened in spring 1972 with thirteen antiques shops, restaurants, and art studios taking over refurbished buildings, some dating back to the Civil War. Within a year the streets along Delaware and Wyandotte were jammed every weekend. This was, after all, where it had all started for Kansas City, and preservationists and partygoers were pleased. Then organized crime took over and sleazy bars began to proliferate. Several buildings were leveled by suspicious explosions, and before the end of the decade River Quay was kaput.

But good things often come from disasters, and the demise of River Quay also helped signal the end of organized crime in Kansas City. Thankfully for visitors today, the area, now called River Market, is stronger than ever with dining spots and shops set around the outdoor farmers' market. On weekends festivals and music fill the streets. And it has become one of the trendiest places to live, thanks to dozens of lofts that have transformed warehouses into sleek condos.

While River Quay was folding, Westport was growing. By fall 1974 extensive sections of the old town were being revitalized for restaurants and shops. With restaurants from casual to fancy, and bars that cater to sports crowds to cigar-smoking highbrows, Westport is our city's most happening place, especially for the younger crowd. Along these brick-lined streets, last call doesn't come until the wee hours of the morning.

Early on one of those mornings our city

Thomas J. Pendergast

The powerful Pendergast political machine began, fittingly enough, with a horse race. Jim Pendergast used his winnings to launch a saloon below the bluffs in the West Bottoms, an area filled with warehouses, rail lines, and livestock pens. His watering hole also served as a bank for the working class. He was elected alderman in 1892 and soon extended his influence to the north end of the city. Eighteen years later his younger brother, Tom, replaced him as alderman. The Pendergast tradition of finding jobs for the unemployed and feeding the poor during holidays continued, even after Tom moved out of the West Bottoms into a mansion at 5650 Ward Parkway.

Boss Tom parlayed five years on the city council into a thirty-year reign over graft, prostitution, gambling, and rigged elections. And he determined that real power and wealth was tied to business. His Riverside Racetrack pulled in plenty of dough, his Jefferson Hotel was the place to buy liquor and a little action, and his Ready-Mix Concrete Company paved Brush Creek, which fronts the Country Club Plaza.

The Pendergast power reached its zenith (many would say its nadir) between 1925 and 1939. Hundreds of nightclubs operated around the clock. Operators, gamblers, and prostitutes didn't fear police raids; they knew they'd soon go free.

The rest of the nation was noticing. NBC Radio tagged Kansas City a "hot spot" for hoodlums. In 1938 the *Christian Science Monitor* called Kansas City "wider open than any place outside Reno" and blasted residents for being "astonishingly complacent about it all." Not everyone was. Missouri Governor Lloyd C. Stark—who had once sought Pendergast's support and was denied—called for a federal probe of Boss Tom. The crime? An insurance fix he set up through the statehouse, a place referred to as "Uncle Tom's Cabin."

Crime may have been high during this period, but so, too, was the city's growth. Some say Kansas City avoided the worst of the Depression because the Pendergast connections attracted federal funds to the area. Pendergast supported a $40 million public works project, a ten-year plan that changed the city's skyline. By 1930 the city had impressive new buildings, including the Federal Reserve Bank Building, Board of Trade, Kansas City Power & Light building, the twenty-nine-story City Hall, Jackson County Courthouse, and the Municipal Auditorium, these last two constructed with concrete from Pendergast's concrete company. The 200-acre Lee's Summit Lake kept work crews busy as well. Pendergast's company also provided the materials for the Nelson Art Gallery and the runways at the new Municipal Airport.

Pendergast handpicked politicians, including a Jackson County judge, Harry S. Truman, who became a candidate for the U.S. Senate in 1934. Truman, a celebrated straight shooter himself, admired Pendergast's ability to get things done but stood up to Boss Tom when it came to shady dealings. According to Truman, he received only one request from Pendergast, to support a political ally. Truman refused, saying he was already backing another man, and that was the end of that.

Was Pendergast a friend or foe? Most historians admit he was both. To workers, particularly immigrants who came to a new city without connections, he was a godsend. The city paid 400 Pendergast captains to stop by houses during the 1930s and 1940s to make sure there was enough coal for the winter, enough food for hard times, a job if you needed one. At Christmas the captain—who would mention his allegiance to the Jackson Democratic Club—would show up with food, heating fuel, even toys for the children. The gift tags simply said "A friend," but people knew Pendergast was behind it. The grateful masses kept electing Pendergast's picks.

"Boss Tom" Pendergast ran Kansas City for thirty years. SPECIAL COLLECTIONS DEPARTMENT, KANSAS CITY PUBLIC LIBRARY, KANSAS CITY, MISSOURI

Ballots, in fact, would be Boss Tom's downfall. Over 60,000 of those votes were found to be cast by "ghosts" who were falsely registered. A funeral parlor listed seventeen voters. Vagrants were paid 25 cents for every vote. Eventually 259 Pendergast supporters were convicted by federal juries for conspiracy involving voting fraud.

Pendergast's own betting addiction ended his glory days. He was arraigned in 1939 for failure to pay taxes on a bribe he took to pay off gambling debts. After serving fifteen months in prison, he lived quietly at his home at 5650 Ward Parkway until his death in 1945. His stronghold on city government was over, but he left another legacy: When the books were audited the city was $22 million in debt.

With a new reform group in control, what we lost in revenue and vibrancy—slot machines were trucked away and jazz clubs lost their crowds—we made up for with a renewed civic pride.

was once again ravaged by floodwaters. In mid-September 1977, residents in northwest Wyandotte County and Bonner Springs were driven out of their homes and a wall of water hit the Country Club Plaza. The death toll eventually reached twenty-five and property damage (mostly on the Plaza) was over $100 million. Within days the U.S. Army Corps of Engineers and the city began to work out plans to deepen and widen Brush Creek's channel, which fronted the famed shopping district.

The 1970s was also the decade when Kansas City started to take a long look at its public persona. We were proud of our city's natural beauty and growing sophistication. Now we wanted the rest of the world to discover our many charms. We began to shirk our cowtown image while holding tight to our Midwestern values. The phrase "It's a great place to raise children," after all, had long been a selling point for real estate agents.

We began to embrace and encourage public art. We had a head start thanks to the fountains and sculptures throughout the Country Club Plaza. And thanks to the pull of students to the Kansas City Art Institute and artists to Hallmark Cards, art appreciation had a strong base in Kansas City. So the world may have been surprised—but we weren't— when world-famous artist Christo chose our Loose Park for one of his high-profile displays. For two weeks in October 1978, bright orange fabric ribboned and swirled around 3 miles of the park's walkways. It was fascinating, it was frivolous, it was fun.

HIGH INFLATION, HIGH EXPECTATIONS

Like every other American city, we were hit hard in the 1980s with skyrocketing inflation rates and high unemployment. But we momentarily forgot 17 percent mortgage rates when the Royals won the 1985 World Series. A champagne-soaked Ewing Kauffman celebrated with third baseman George Brett, pitcher Dan Quisenberry, the other players,

and 41,628 screaming fans. Within days Grand Avenue was wall-to-wall with revelers as we gave the team a rousing victory parade.

At the ballpark, more and more license plates were from Johnson County as that county grew by 85,000 residents during the decade. Money continued to shift from Missouri to the Kansas side as mini-mansions sprang up in Johnson County subdivisions such as Hallbrook, which opened in 1989. Houses in this enclave cost on average $550,000.

Kansans had other things to celebrate: In 1986 voters did away with the past century's temperance law and approved liquor by the drink, a state lottery, and racetrack betting. The Woodlands dog- and horse-racing track opened in Wyandotte County a few years later.

Local business was racing ahead as well when a local company, US Telecom, merged with the long-distance arm of GTE in 1986. The world headquarters of the resulting company, Sprint, became one of the area's largest employers.

Kansas City continued its reputation as a sports town when we hosted 15,000 visitors for the NCAA Final Four basketball tournament in April 1988. We celebrated other sports heroes, for reasons that often went deeper than skills with a club or a bat. Golfer Tom Watson resigned from the Kansas City Country Club (where he learned to play golf) in 1990 because the club would not allow a Jewish businessman, Henry Bloch, to join. In 1992 George Brett made the 3,000th hit of his career at Royals Stadium. Two years later he retired, perhaps because his biggest fan, Ewing Kauffman, was no longer in the stands to watch him play. The philanthropist had died the year before.

WORKING TOGETHER

As we started looking toward our 150-year anniversary, city leaders began to push for a renewed interest in our central core. At the top of the list was the dilapidated Union Station. It was clear that revitalizing the once-beautiful landmark would take cooperation—and money—from both sides of the state line. In 1996 voters across five counties passed the Bi-state Cultural Tax, the first two-state effort of its kind in the country. Work began to convert the grand old depot into a science museum and entertainment venue, a project that would cost more than $200 million. Soon voters were also saying "yes" to restoring the Liberty Memorial.

Sprawl continued to move the city in all directions. By the mid-1990s the Northland was a boomtown with new, luxurious subdivisions popping up in Clay and Platte Counties. More than 100,000 residents were drawn to the area's rolling hills and lush-treed landscapes dotted with lakes and golf courses.

Everyone, it seemed, headed north of the river to try his or her luck at the new gambling casinos. Today we're home to four casinos where guests can play games of chance before sitting down to a bounteous buffet, elegant dinner, or stage show featuring national headliners. We bet you'll want to see the Attractions chapter for more information about these exciting venues.

We maintained our interest in public art. Bartle Hall got its *Sky Stations*—some call them "hair curlers"—in 1994. Giant *Shuttlecocks* dotted the lawn at Nelson-Atkins Museum of Art. We continued our love affair with fountains: Water displays define the entrances to business parks, government buildings, and neighborhoods.

We stopped razing and started restoring historic buildings from the River Market area to the downtown Garment District, Hyde Park and the Northeast area, Quality Hill and West Bottoms to the east side of town. Meanwhile places such as Parkville and Weston added to their "Main Street USA" charm with new cafes, galleries, and shops.

We also began to honor our history by paying tribute to the people, places, and events that formed our city. In 1997 we opened the Negro Leagues Baseball Museum and the Kansas City Jazz Museum at 18th and Vine Streets, once the heart of the African-American neighborhood. The driving force behind these redevelopments was Emanuel Cleaver II a Methodist minister who was mayor of Kansas City from 1991 to 1999. Cleaver made history as the first African-American mayor of the city. His replacement, Kay Waldo Barnes, was the first woman to hold the office.

Other cities within the metropolis began to thrive under fresh leadership. Even the sister city across the river awoke from more than a century of slumber. Carol Marinovich, the new mayor/chief executive of the Unified Government of Wyandotte County/Kansas City, Kansas, thrilled residents and surprised some neighboring cities when she announced plans for the new Kansas Speedway. The track, which opened in 2001, sponsors three NASCAR-sponsored races each year to bring an estimated $170 million boost to the city's economy, the equivalent of a Super Bowl every year. Surrounding it is Village West, a 400-acre entertainment and shopping district anchored by Cabela's outdoor emporium, which—along with camouflage on every conceivable piece of apparel—includes a 55,000-gallon walk-through aquarium and a museum-quality African diorama with trophy elephants, rhinos, lions, and water buffalo. No wonder the average visitor stays three and a half hours. Village West is also home to Nebraska Furniture Mart, billed as the largest home furnishings store in the world, and the Great Wolf Lodge, a combination hotel and indoor water park (see more in the Shopping, Attractions, and Accommodations chapters).

Meanwhile, Ed Eilert, mayor of Overland Park, Kansas, for 20 of the city's 40 years, has transformed the bedroom community into the state's fastest-growing city. This suburb is continuing to go after a tourism market with a handsome new convention-and-hotel center (See Accommodations).

LOOKING FORWARD

Visitors and newcomers have always been surprised to find in Kansas City a town that's vibrant and varied, friendly yet sophisticated.

The best is yet to be. There's a palpable new energy here, especially in the urban core that's been neglected for so long. Like many positive changes it started on two fronts. Corporate leaders stopped waiting for a master plan and slowly began to put their money and influence into opening offices, living spaces, and cultural venues downtown. Meanwhile young artists began to create lofts and studios out of abandoned buildings between downtown and Crown Center, creating an exciting avenue of arts that brought in patrons and encouraged restaurants and retail shops. Even the storied West Bottoms are coming back with new art galleries, cafes, and businesses.

It has paid off in one of the country's most spectacular downtown transformations, including an entertainment district, a new arena, and two new art galleries. Adding to the mix will be more hotel rooms, condos and lofts, restaurants, and shopping venues. And thanks to a "Let's share" attitude among the eighteen counties that make up the region, we're busy attracting even more business to our area. It's a great time to work and live in Kansas City—and an exciting time to visit.

KANSAS CITY'S PROMINENT CITIZENS

Kansas City's leaders are continuing a tradition that began almost as soon as the town took hold: that of giving back to the community through endowments, expertise, and plenty of cash. There is, however, an important distinction between our early-day givers and those of today: The patriarchs of a century ago have been replaced, in many cases, by pairs as husbands and wives jointly decide how best to use their time and funds. In many cases the matriarch controls a separate foundation with its own unique mission.

There are, of course, thousands of do-gooders whose names will never appear on a bronze plaque; these are the folks who build homes for Habitat for Humanity, spending weekends each fall to paint, clean, and fix up inner-city houses through an organization called Christmas in October. They send a $5 or $50 check when they read about a family in trouble, donate coats in winter, fans in summer, and toys for holidays. They volunteer to visit the elderly and read stories to children, line up for blood drives, and sign up for their turn in food kitchens. And their cash contributions have made Kansas City one of the top philanthropic cities in the country: The Greater Kansas City Community Foundation (www.gkccf.org) has provided more than $800 million in grants, making it the seventh-largest in grants made among 582 community foundations nationwide.

So cheer these modern-day heroes—named and unnamed—who continue to make this city a great place to live and work. As you'll see in the profiles below, their reach often extends beyond our borders to help millions through education and medical research.

Henry Bloch

The cofounder, with brother Richard, of H&R Block Inc., the national tax preparation firm, has enhanced the lives of many residents. Since 1985 the Henry W. and Marion H. Bloch Foundation has provided money to expand facilities at the University of Missouri–Kansas City business school, now called the Henry W. Bloch School of Business and Public Administration. The Blochs have also financed scholarships at Avila College and capital improvements at the Kansas City Art Institute. And when Mr. Bloch retired in 2001, his company's parting gift didn't arrive in a watch box: His name is on one of the city's newest and most exciting fountains in front of Union Station.

But this couple's most lasting legacy will always be the remarkable Bloch Building expansion to the Nelson-Atkins Museum of Art. The late Richard Bloch founded the R. A. Bloch Cancer Foundation with his wife, Annette. The foundation's cancer hotline offers support to those newly diagnosed and has established cancer survivor parks in dozens of cities across the United States, including a lovely sculpture garden on the west side of the Country Club Plaza.

Donald and Adele Hall

"When you care enough to give the very best" could be the slogan for this couple's generosity as well as that of Hallmark Cards, the company founded by Donald's father.

For more than four decades Donald Hall has changed the landscape of the city for the better, with his Crown Center complex, the Henry Moore sculpture garden at the Nelson-Atkins Museum of Art, and funds for Union Hill housing and Union Station's renovation. Adele Hall has donated time and money for the Nelson-Atkins Art Museum expansion, the United Negro College Fund, Wayside Waifs, and countless other organizations. She's had the rare honor of being named both Kansas Citian of the Year and Johnson Countian of the Year.

The couple recently sent the city "its very best"—a $60 million check to the Nelson-Atkins Museum of Art. That brings to a total of $100 million the amount the Hall Family Foundation has contributed to the museum over the years.

Barnett and Shirley Helzberg

Open any Sunday's *Star* society page and there's Shirley Helzberg at a gala fund-raiser for Starlight Theatre, the Kansas City Symphony, the Shakespeare Festival, and the new Arts Council of Metropolitan Kansas City. Yet she doesn't just show up on Saturday night—she's deeply involved in these organizations and dozens more.

As for cold cash, the couple gave one of the largest personal gifts to save Union Station, $1 million for a garden at Starlight, and seed money for a new Kansas City charter school.

Barnett, who was mentored by Ewing Kauffman, has made helping young entrepreneurs his second career after selling his jewelry business to Warren Buffett of Berkshire-Hathaway. He established the Helzberg Entrepreneurial Mentoring Program in 1995. And

Rockhurst University, where he has been an adjunct professor for more than ten years, recently renamed its business school the Helzberg School of Management to honor the couple.

Shirley also spent untold millions renovating an old schoolhouse south of downtown into a marvelous antiques store called Webster House. See Shopping for more on this classy venue.

R. Crosby Kemper Jr.

Kemper's banking empire, UMB Financial Corporation, spans several states, yet his generosity remains chiefly in his hometown. In 1973 he donated $3.2 million to construct Kemper Arena in the West Bottoms, and a $6 million gift in 1990 resulted in the Kemper Museum of Contemporary Art. Kemper has always been one to come through for a worthy cause, such as his $1 million gift to rebuild the city's bankrupt orchestra, now the Kansas City Symphony, and a $2 million donation to the Liberty Memorial restoration fund.

James and Virginia Stowers

A decade ago few people around town had heard the name Stowers. Although his fortune from the mutual fund empire he founded, American Century Investments, put them at the top of Kansas City's elite, the reserved twosome shunned the limelight.

Yet today this couple is turning the city into a center for biomedical research. As cancer survivors, they've poured millions into the Stowers Institute for Medical Research, a handsome center built along the thriving Brush Creek Corridor. And they're proving wrong the experts who advised them to develop the institute on one of the coasts. After all, what respected international scientist would want to move to the Midwest? Since opening its doors in 2000, the Stowers Institute has attracted the world's top research talents, who, incidentally, have fallen in love with their adopted hometown.

Ewing and Muriel Kauffman

Everyone in Kansas City knows the story about how Mr. K saved the Royals baseball team, and most have heard of his Project Choice program, which helped students succeed on both sides of the state line (we cover Project Choice in the Higher Education section of the Relocation chapter).

But Kauffman is also credited with encouraging entrepreneurs through mentoring programs. Today the Ewing Marion Kauffman Foundation has about $2 billion in assets and includes the Kauffman Center for Entrepreneurial Leadership. His vivacious wife helped get a 911 system in the Kansas City area, and the Muriel McBrien Kauffman Foundation has assets of about $300 million.

Muriel's daughter, Julia Irene Kauffman, now oversees the foundation's works. Its most generous gift to date is more than $100 million for the new Kauffman Center for the Performing Arts, which will turn a hilltop just south of Bartle Hall into a $330 million civic landmark when it opens in the next few years. (Read more about this exciting project in the Arts chapter.)

OTHER RESOURCES

We celebrate our rich history at dozens of museums and visitor centers throughout Kansas City. You'll find listings for interesting places such as the Grinter House, the first home built in Kansas City, Kansas; Missouri Town 1855; the Jesse James Farm and Museum; President Harry S. Truman's farm and museum; and the Gem Theater, which showcases our jazz heritage, in the Attractions chapter under History.

TRACE YOUR OWN FAMILY HISTORY

The Kansas City area—in particular Independence, Missouri—offers genealogists and

family historians a wellspring of information. A good place to start your search is the Jackson County Historical Society Archives and Research Library (www.jchs.org), located in the Jackson County Courthouse at 112 West Lexington Avenue, Room 103. It contains 20,000 photographic images and a 2,000-volume library of reference books, periodicals, letters, and more. The society's bookshop sells more than 600 titles, including maps and books relating to Jackson County, the westward expansion, and the Civil War. The society also operates two historical sites, the 1859 Jail Museum and Clinton's Old Fashioned Soda Fountain, where a young Harry Truman once worked. Call (816) 461-1897 for information.

The Mid-Continent Public Library (www.mcpl.lib.mo.us) and its adjacent 12,000-foot Genealogy and Local History Department are wonderful resources for tracing ancestors. The collection includes the U.S. population censuses for 1790 to 1920 as well as family and county histories. The branch is located at 317 West 24 Highway, Independence; call (816) 252-7228 for hours. A new genealogy center will open in spring 2008.

The Black Archives of Mid-America Inc., at 2033 Vine, Kansas City, Missouri, is one of the largest collections of African-American memorabilia, artifacts, and research materials in the Midwest. There is an admission fee. Call (816) 483-1300 or visit www.black archives.org for information.

At the Johnson County Archives (www.archives.jocogov.org) you'll find documents relating to the history of Kansas and the county, including marriage licenses, wills, and naturalization records from the late 1880s. The center is located in the County Administration Building, 111 South Cherry, Suite 500, Olathe, Kansas; call (913) 715-0400.

ACCOMMODATIONS

When staying in Kansas City for a night, a weekend, or a month, you can expect to be treated to the friendly service that defines our town. That means the person behind the front desk will actually look up and smile as you approach. Innkeepers—sometimes accompanied by a tail-wagging dog—may greet your arrival with a plate of fresh-baked cookies. Then there's the owner of an Overland Park motor hotel who paid a guest's bail one Saturday night. We trust you won't test our hospitality quite that far.

Good manners abound, yes, but you'll also find great accommodations. Your footsteps will echo across lobbies lined with enough marble to rebuild ancient Rome, and when one hotel boasts of running water, it's referring to the five-story waterfall to your left. Plenty of famous folks have registered at our front desks over the years, including movie stars and rock stars, glamour queens and gangsters—Al Capone used one area resort as his hideout—and more than our share of presidents. Harry S. Truman, in fact, showed the world he was still commander-in-chief, despite the headlines, at one of our downtown hotels.

There are rooms to fit every taste and pocketbook, from ultraposh retreats and bed-and-breakfast inns to budget-pleasing motels and even campsites. Naturally for a city our size, every hotel, motel, and extended-stay chain is represented—just right for ratcheting up your frequent-travel points. In addition to these national names, we offer some one-of-a-kind lodging choices. To see a complete roster of available accommodations, check out the Hotel and Motel Association of Greater Kansas City's Web site at www.kansascitylodging.org.

Guests with special needs will find that most hotels offer nonsmoking or allergen-free rooms—sometimes even entire floors—and unless specified, every hotel listed is partially or wholly wheelchair-accessible. To be on the safe side, we recommend that you call ahead to check. Travelers with small children or pets should also check on services available.

As for where to stay, it depends on what you desire during your visit. The downtown area is home to our financial, business, and convention services. It's also where you can see our city in stages—or "on" stages, as it were. Our grandest theaters—many of them turn-of-the-twentieth-century gems—are downtown. We have a treasure chest of other gems for you in the urban core: Our grand old hotels have been renovated into spectacular boutique accommodations. Here you can roam the hallways, ballrooms, and nightclubs, such as the Hilton President Hotel's Drum Room, which once hosted Frank Sinatra, the Marx Brothers, and Patsy Cline. You can help make it famous again after its recent $45 million renovation. The Aladdin Hotel is the "newest" old lodging choice, which originally opened in 1936 and after a considerable makeover offers up its vintage-hip guest rooms and a Martini Loft. And between downtown and Crown Center are dozens of art galleries and artists' studios in the Crossroads Arts District. During nice weather the neighborhood becomes a street party as art lovers go from gallery to gallery. And where the crowds go, great restaurants are sure to follow. The Crossroads and nearby Freighthouse District seem to sprout a fabulous new restaurant every month.

Speaking of Crown Center, we call this complex a city-within-a-city because it combines two luxury hotels and dining, shopping, and attractions all in one neat package, along with an old-fashioned town square that sports an outdoor ice-skating rink, fountains, and live entertainment. Union Station and Science City are connected to the center via an elevated, climate-controlled walkway called The Link. And it's all in the shadow of our magnificent Liberty Memorial, the country's only museum and memorial dedicated solely to World War I.

Locations in and around Westport and our famous Country Club Plaza offer so many dining, shopping, and nighttime entertainment options you could book a room for a month and not see it all. This area also boasts two world-class art museums, lovely parks, and the reason we're called the City of Fountains. If gambling is your game, it's a sure bet you'll enjoy our riverboat casino-hotel resorts. History buffs who are wild about Harry will find hotels and bed-and-breakfasts close to his museum and home in Independence.

But don't discount accommodations in outlying areas. For instance, Overland Park offers some of the best shopping west of Fifth Avenue. And when we say take it outside, we're not being rude: Johnson County has miles of walking trails linking public parks and waterways. Dozens of private and public courses make this a golfer's paradise. Wyandotte County, Kansas, will tempt you with brand-new hotels in Village West, the 400-acre entertainment area surrounding the NASCAR race track. And you won't have to gamble on getting a good night's sleep, along with grand entertainment, at the spectacular new $66 million Argosy Casino Hotel and Spa with a view of downtown. Not to be outdone, Kansas City's Harrah's Casino hit the jackpot with updates to its hotel. But the action at the tables and top-notch acts in the VooDoo Lounge may mean you'll never touch the king-size bed.

As for *when* to come, spring and fall are our most glorious times of year, when gardens and trees look particularly pretty, and during summer there's a festival or event every weekend. Every winter our entire city dresses for the holidays. We open our decorated homes for tours, offer cookies and hot cider in shops, and invite the world to watch as 250,000 colored lights illuminate the Country Club Plaza on Thanksgiving night. Hotel rooms overlooking the magical ceremony —our version of Mardi Gras—often are booked a year in advance. Come anyway; the dazzling view continues through mid-January.

Reservations are always recommended. Especially with new hotels and amenities in downtown, Overland Park, and elsewhere, Kansas City is a popular convention town, drawing groups of 40,000 or more. It seems folks can't get enough of our blues and barbecue. And during racing season at Kansas Speedway, rooms go as fast as the NASCAR cars. So it won't hurt to call well in advance for reservations; you'll have that much longer to dog-ear pages in this book.

So let's get you checked in. We've divided this chapter into four categories: Hotels and Motels, Extended Stays, Bed-and-Breakfasts and Inns, and RV Parks and Camping. The first two categories are listed by location. The others are listed alphabetically. All places to stay are located in Kansas City, Missouri, unless otherwise noted.

Price Code

Prices reflect the average rate for high season, double-occupancy accommodations. Keep in mind that most hotels offer a price range based on size of room, amenities, and desirability. Prices listed do not include special services such as babysitting, valet laundry, parking (if charges apply), telephone calls, room service, or hotel-motel taxes. Many hotels and most bed-and-breakfasts offer packages; several places provide Internet-only discounts.

$	Less than $60
$$	$60 to $110
$$$	$111 to $160
$$$$	$161 and up

HOTELS AND MOTELS

Country Club Plaza and Westport

Embassy Suites Hotel $$
220 West 43rd Street
(816) 756-1720
www.embassysuites.com

The waterfall and mini-rainforest in this all-suite hotel's twelve-story atrium is so gorgeous you might want to pitch a tent. But check out your room instead; the bedroom and separate living room make it ideal for families and business travelers. Each suite offers home-away-from-home amenities such as two TVs, refrigerator and microwave, coffeemaker, and more.

More pluses include a made-to-order complimentary breakfast and an afternoon manager's reception where you'll be treated to your favorite beverage. And the location, halfway between the Plaza and Westport, means you have sixty or so restaurants to choose from within minutes. Now aren't you glad you booked another day?

Hampton Inn & Suites $$
4600 Summit
(816) 448-4600, (877) 410-4600
www.hamptoninnkc.com

Here's how to have the Country Club Plaza practically at your front door and still have enough cash left for a big-shot dinner out. This nine-story hotel has 203 oversized guest rooms, including two-room suites with fully equipped kitchens bigger than many apartments. A continental breakfast and evening reception with appetizers and beverages are complimentary. There's also a fitness room and indoor pool to help you keep in shape for those days of nonstop shopping. The Hampton is a top pick for family reunions and other group get-togethers.

Holiday Inn Express-Westport $$
801 Westport Road
(816) 931-1000, (800) HOLIDAY
www.ichotelsgroup.com

A Holiday Inn is a Holiday Inn—right? Well, that's true until you toss in a little history. A plaque above the door shows that this site was once part of the original Santa Fe Trail, while a trail map in the lobby shows the westward route.

The hotel continues the Western theme with Southwest fabrics and a Frederic Remington sculpture. Rooms—109 in all—offer workstations, dataport phones, and coffeemakers. The executive kings have separate sitting areas, and welcome baskets greet guests. A complimentary continental breakfast is included, and of course there's that terrific location next door to Kansas City's favorite entertainment center, Westport.

The Quarterage Hotel-Westport $$
560 Westport Road
(816) 931-0001, (800) 942-4233
www.quarteragehotel.com

Don't let the modern brick exterior fool you; inside, the Quarterage is a nineteenth-century beauty with warm oak, tin ceilings, and marble appointments. A cozy wood-burning fireplace beckons you to hunker down with a good book, and even the complimentary full breakfast and evening cocktail hour seem like an innkeeper's thoughtful touches from days gone by.

You'll also appreciate the twenty-first-century features such as passes to a nearby health club with aerobics classes, soothing hot tub and sauna, and two-line phones with high-speed data connections. It may be hard to leave, particularly if you have a prime spot near the fire, but the excitement of Westport beckons. Just steps away are some of the city's best nightspots, restaurants, and shops.

> **i** You didn't hear it from the hotel's staff—they would never impinge on a guest's privacy—but when performers such as Sting end their gigs in town, they often end the evening with an impromptu concert at the piano in the InterContinental Hotel's lounge.

Close-up

The InterContinental Kansas City

Step into this marble-lined lobby and you could be at an InterContinental in any great city: San Francisco, Tokyo, Shenzhen. All stellar to be sure, but none of the others have what the InterContinental Kansas City has—the world-famous Country Club Plaza just a heartbeat away.

Kansas City's four-diamond hotel began its life in 1969 as the Alameda Plaza with a Spanish theme to coordinate with the Country Club Plaza's architecture and art. It changed briefly to the Ritz-Carlton before becoming The Fairmont in 2000. A $10 million renovation returned it to its role as the city's premier hotel soon after.

Now, in the hotel's latest transformation, the InterContinental logo appears on the signage and the in-room note cards. The company has wisely kept what's best about the hotel and added its own flourishes. Indeed, the hotel is undergoing another impressive multimillion-dollar makeover as we speak. But have no fear; the renovations will be seamless. A hotel that prides itself on guest services would never disrupt anyone's slumber with construction racket next door. It's only right that a grand hotel in the City of Fountains would have a liquid landmark. The waterfall that fronts the InterContinental is a backdrop for a statue of Diana, goddess of the hunt—quite possibly in honor of the 180 shops awaiting guests across the street.

The hotel's entrance is located at the end of a short drive around back, a configuration that saves all the best views for guest rooms and public areas. It's an especially pretty picture from the lobby-floor lounge where fresh sushi (available on Friday and Saturday nights) is served along with more than 300 types of martinis. Local jazz musicians perform every Tuesday through Saturday night, one of the reasons the Oak Bar was named one of the top hotel bars in the world by Continental Airline's *Inflight Magazine*. Hotel guests have been surprised to see renowned musicians, such as Billy Joel, show up here after an in-town gig for an impromptu turn at the piano.

The Raphael Hotel $$$
325 Ward Parkway
(816) 756-3800, (800) 821-5343
www.raphaelkc.com

Villa Serena, a name that sounds like a Spanish lullaby, was the 1927 apartment hotel that would become the Raphael. In 1975 legendary hotelier Phil Pistilli created a treasure out of the nine-story structure by expanding rooms while keeping the Andalusian architecture borrowed from the Country Club Plaza across Brush Creek.

The Raphael more than lives up to its reputation as the city's most romantic hotel. Sometimes the staff plays Cupid to set the stage for proposals. One suitor requested rose petals leading from the lobby, into the elevator, and through hallways, ending with a dozen roses and an engagement ring in the suite. She said yes.

The Oak Room is tucked just beyond the lounge and is open for breakfast, lunch, and dinner as well as Sunday brunch. You may choose from the spa cuisine, but we usually opt for the luscious corn chowder or the rib eye steak with a Jack Daniel's peppercorn cream sauce. Anyone would be charmed with the high-style afternoon tea from 2:00 to 4:00, complete with a selection of sweets and tiny sandwiches. Call for reservations.

The twelve-story InterContinental has 346 guest rooms, including 20 suites, 3 wheelchair-accessible rooms, and 220 nonsmoking rooms. Rooms are luxurious retreats with marble bathrooms, three telephones (including one in the bathroom), and an in-room safe. All the suites and the rooms on the Executive Level have access to a private lounge with complimentary food presentations throughout the day and the personal services of a concierge.

Self-parking in the covered parking lot is free; valet parking is also available. The outdoor heated pools overlook the Plaza from one story above street level, and on-call massage services are available seven days a week at the fitness center. A variety of meeting rooms, banquet space, and a 12,000-square-foot ballroom makes this one of Kansas City's preferred addresses for weddings and other celebrations. Another plus is the services of Larry Wheeler, the on-site florist, whose designs are legendary.

The winter holidays are an enchanting time to be here. Wait until you see the spectacular display on Thanksgiving night, just moments after the Plaza's famous lighting ceremony ends. Fireworks timed to hundreds of musical cues appear over the rooftop to leave spectators breathless, especially those with the best vantage points throughout the hotel. It's a thrilling addition to the lighting extravaganza that has defined the Plaza for more than seventy-two years.

No wonder Plaza-view rooms are often booked a year or more in advance. Just remember, kids, the holiday lights stay on through mid-January. And with indulgences like these, there truly isn't a bad room in the house. The InterContinental Kansas City is at 401 Ward Parkway; for more information call (816) 756-1500 or (888) 424-6835, or visit www.kansascityic.com.

The Raphael Restaurant has also served up amorous scenes such as diamonds frozen in ice cubes or tucked into bouquets delivered to the table. But even without a solitaire in sight, this dining room is special. Chef Peter Hahn develops a new menu weekly by giving continental twists to classic American fare. Dark smoky mirrors, deep recessed booths, piano music filtering in from the bar lounge—it all makes for a wonderful dinner out where—get this—you can actually hear your dinner partner. You can read more about this Kansas City favorite in the Restaurants chapter.

The Raphael has thirty-five rooms and eighty-eight spacious suites filled with amenities as plush as the robes. Business travelers will enjoy extra touches such as computer dataports, a state-of-the-art voice mail system, and even ergonomic work chairs in every room. If you ever want to leave your room, an entire fourteen-block wonderland of shopping, entertainment, and dining awaits you on the Country Club Plaza. Loose Park, with its famed rose garden, duck pond, and walking paths, is just a stroll up the hill. The Nelson-Atkins Museum and Kemper Museum are close by as well. And of course the hotel staff will be happy to arrange trips to other attractions around the city.

The Raphael will also woo you with special packages such as the Girlfriends Getaway, a grown-ups' pajama party complete with margaritas, popcorn, chick flicks, and a disposable camera to document the fun. We suppose what happens at the Plaza stays at the Plaza. The Romance Package takes a cue from that suitor from years past—or is it the other way around?—with Plaza-view accommodations, two keepsake monogrammed robes, and rose petals scattered across the pillows. Hold our calls.

Crown Center

Hyatt Regency Crown Center $$–$$$
2345 McGee Street
(816) 421-1234, (800) 233-1234
www.crowncenterhyatt.com
The Hyatt's lobby lounge makes quite a first impression with a dazzling sculpture that drops from the two-story ceiling like golden raindrops. It's an elegant place to listen to piano music or the restful sounds of a fountain while you enjoy a cocktail. With Hyatt's renowned attention to detail and Kansas City's friendly charm, you may never want to leave.

You won't have to. The hotel is connected to the eighty-five-acre Crown Center complex via an elevated walkway, so you can stroll in climate-controlled comfort to shops, restaurants, live theater, and movie houses. Crown Center Square, called Kansas City's "Rockefeller Center" by *National Geographic Traveler*, is host to year-round entertainment and the city's only outdoor ice-skating rink. Another skywalk takes you to Union Station, the city's historic train station that includes an

i How many balls are suspended in the sculpture hanging in the lobby of the Hyatt Regency Crown Center? Give up? We've counted them for you: The striking artwork designed by Vermont artist Irv Harper contains 1,965 small silver globes.

interactive science museum, great restaurants, and unique entertainment choices.

The Hyatt's 731 rooms and suites feature twenty-four-hour room service, minibars, and movie channels. Other amenities include a complimentary health club, an all-weather pool, tennis courts, and a downtown view.

And within the Hyatt are two dining choices so superb they'll forever change your concept of "hotel restaurants." You'll find detailed descriptions in the Restaurant chapter, but for now think about the Peppercorn Duck's rotisserie-roasted duck and buffet filled with every chocolate dessert imaginable. Or combine a little sightseeing with your grilled steak at Skies, the hotel's revolving rooftop restaurant. The lounge provides a breathtaking view as well.

The Westin Crown Center $$$$
1 Pershing Road
(816) 474-4400, (800) 228-3000
www.westin.com/kansascity
Thank goodness for the Hall family, owners of Hallmark Cards, who converted an eyesore called Signboard Hill into one of the city's most exciting tourist areas. At its heart is the Westin, whose five-story lobby waterfall makes dramatic use of the original hill's natural limestone.

The 729-room hotel's location just keeps getting better and better. Its neighbor is the renovated Union Station, with several excellent restaurants, entertainment, and Science City, all accessible via an elevated walkway that looks like something out of Disneyland's Tomorrowland. And hotel guests are just a brisk walk from our beautifully restored Liberty Memorial and a taxi ride from the vibrant Crossroads Arts District neighborhood.

But you can enjoy plenty of action without

leaving Crown Center. Enjoy a burger in a streetcar, take in a movie, or shop dozens of unique boutiques. Kids can learn new artistic skills at Kaleidoscope or simply color a placemat at Crayola Cafe. (See Restaurants, Attractions, Shopping, and Kidstuff for details.)

As a guest of the Westin, you'll have a ringside seat for the activities at Crown Center Square, including summertime concerts, hunting for the Great Pumpkin, and lighting the mayor's Christmas tree. Even when there's nothing happening outside, the downtown skyline view from Benton's rooftop steakhouse is stunning.

Downtown

The Aladdin Holiday Inn
Downtown $$–$$$
1215 Wyandotte Street
(816) 421-8888
www.hialaddin.com

One of Kansas City's newest boutique hotels is also one of its oldest. After an extensive renovation, this historic building, originally built in 1926, offers the kind of retro-chic that would make it popular in any major city. But the slender, brick sixteen-floor beauty is situated right in the heart of our downtown's convention and entertainment district with an architectural styling that echoes the more than sixty art deco buildings in the area.

Today's Aladdin offers 193 guest rooms, including two suites, with exquisite bedding (including a menu of pillow choices) and such amenities as a fitness center and iPod loaded with music. But what we enjoy most are the revamped restaurant, the Zebra Room, and the Martini Loft.

i The Link—the 880-foot-long, enclosed elevated walkway between the Hyatt Regency Hotel and Crown Center's shops—contains 2,000 panes of glass, which are cleaned three times a year. A second, 810-foot link was added in 2000 to connect the Westin Crown Center to Union Station.

The dinner menu makes the most of our Midwestern cravings for meat with a carpaccio of beef, Kansas City strip, and grilled ostrich. One popular dessert is an upscale look at a childhood favorite with a trio of S'mores Shooters with toasted marshmallow and milk chocolate in shot glasses with amaretto. The Zebra Room is open for breakfast and lunch as well. The Martini Loft gives guests history with a twist, shaking up such classic cocktails as the old-fashioned and French 75 Martini. The Mojito Martini could be the most refreshing way to spend ten bucks.

Hilton President Kansas City $$–$$$
1329 Baltimore
(816) 221-9490
www.hilton.com

The word "spectacular" comes to mind as you enter this lovingly renovated historic gem. Located in the heart of downtown's renaissance, including the Power & Light District and the business district, the President offers luxury and style.

If you like to say "They don't build 'em like they used to," you'll enjoy all the lush trappings from the 1920s when the President first arrived on the scene: gorgeous marble and intricate plasterwork decorate every inch of public space. The rooms may be cozy, but you'll appreciate modern touches such as the wireless high-speed Internet access and two-line phones. If you're in the market for an impressive corporate shindig or special event, such as a wedding, the President's grand ballroom will wow your guests with an elegant space and unmatched views of downtown. All in all, we'd say the $45 million for the makeover was well spent.

Kansas Citians rejoiced when the President reopened and brought back its famous Drum Room from the 1940s. Luminaries such as Frank Sinatra, Tommy Dorsey, and Duke Ellington all performed here. Today guests can sit in the Rat Pack booth and enjoy live entertainment on Friday and Saturday nights along with the Drum Room's tasty nine-ounce martinis. Alas, the Marx Brothers won't be on the stage, but some of Kansas City's best jazz talent will be.

The restaurant side is also getting noticed with its laid-back atmosphere and unique menu choices that favor a Caribbean Fusion flair—a wink and a nod to the Cuban influence that was all the rage in the 1940s. Here's where a Cuban blackened snapper or guava grilled yellowfin tuna might come to the table along with the more classic (but just as tasty) KC strip. Just look for the huge red drum and DRUM ROOM in neon on the corner.

Kansas City Marriott
Downtown $$$–$$$$
200 West 12th Street
(816) 421-6800, (800) 228-9290
www.marriotthotels.com

With an ideal downtown location, underground link to the convention center, and superb meeting facilities, the Marriott is convention central. It's also the place where Kansas Citians stop in for cocktails before heading across the street for a night at the Folly, Midland Theatre, Music Hall, Lyric Opera, or Kansas City Symphony. Riverboat gambling is nearby, and Crown Center, Westport, and the Country Club Plaza are just a trolley or short cab ride away.

In 1997 the 573-room Marriott nearly doubled in size by merging with the historic Muehlebach Hotel at 1213 Wyandotte. During its prime the Muehlebach was Kansas City's favored host for celebrities, presidents, and four musicians from Liverpool who held a news conference in the ballroom on September 17, 1964. Other news was made here as well: In the wee hours of November 3, 1948, Harry S. Truman hurried back to the hotel to join his campaign staff to announce that he had won reelection.

A recent renovation has reclaimed the Muehlebach's gracious past: Sparkling crystal chandeliers once again cast a warm glow on the lobby's mosaic tile floors, and deeply carved mahogany gleams. Along with a tantalizing feeling of "If these walls could talk," the

i The 60-foot waterfall in the Westin Crown Center hotel's lobby often contributes to more waterworks—by way of happy tears. The beautiful spot has been the site of more than a hundred weddings since it opened in the late 1960s.

Muehlebach offers guests 410 rooms and 37 suites.

The two hotel towers are now linked via a covered walkway. Together the properties offer 10,000 square feet of meeting space, including two ballrooms, thirty-two breakout rooms, and a 12,000-square-foot exhibit hall. The complex features a fully equipped health club and indoor pool, full-service business center including secretarial services if requested, and gift shop. Attached, covered parking is available for a fee; valet service is available.

There are also plenty of places to dine, enjoy a cocktail, or simply relax. For breakfast, lunch, or dinner head to Lilly's or the Pam Pam Room, a Kansas City tradition for generations. The Muehlebach Lobby Lounge offers a refined cocktail hour, and the 12th Street Bar on the lobby level of the Marriott adds jazz to the mix on Friday and Saturday nights.

Radisson Hotel & Suites $$–$$$
1301 Wyandotte Street
(816) 474-6664, (888) 201-1718
www.radisson.com/kansascitymo

This twenty-eight-story high-rise has had several names and personalities, beginning as the Americana in the 1970s. It closed its doors in 1994 and reopened to great fanfare as the Omni three years later when it helped usher in a renaissance of the downtown area. Today, as the Radisson, it's more handsome than ever, graced with rich woods, mission-style furnishings, and a hint of the art deco architecture found in many of its surrounding buildings. The location puts Kansas City's cultural attractions and business services at its door.

A $26 million renovation made sure the 388 guest rooms and 99 king suites have

Hotel Phillips $$

106 West 12th Street
(816) 221-7000, (800) 433-1426
www.hotelphillips.com

Even before this address was transformed into an exquisite boutique hotel, it had a place in Kansas City's heart. When completed in 1931, the twenty-story, 450-room hotel was the tallest in town. It was also the most high-tech: Every room had a radio receiver—the first commercial structure in the Midwest so equipped—which gave the crews a syncopated beat during construction. Even the site's first occupant, the Glennon Hotel, which was razed to make room for the Phillips, had a story to tell. Among its first-floor shops was a haberdashery operated by Harry S. Truman.

In 1979 Hotel Phillips was placed on the National Registry of Historic Places as a stunning example of art deco architecture. The lobby is particularly handsome, with twin staircases, intricate metalwork, and black glass on the ceiling to create the illusion of endless space. The centerpiece is a gilded 11-foot likeness of the goddess of Dawn created by Norwegian-born sculptor Jorgen Dreyer. In classical mythology Dawn was the mother of the stars. At this hotel she's the patron saint of travelers passing through Kansas City.

The new owner, Marcus Hotel group, spent $20 million to restore Phillips Hotel to its magnificence while adding to its comfort. There are now 215 spacious guest rooms and two suites, each smartly decorated with exquisite fabrics and furnishings.

Even the restaurant is something special, which, as any frequent flyer will agree, is rare. With hot new executive chef Marshall Roth (easily identified by his spiky white rock-star hair), the ChopHouse has the culinary, er, *chops* to match its beautiful surroundings. See a full description in Restaurants. The 12 Baltimore lounge is a trendy place to entertain guests and enjoy a cocktail and appetizers while listening to live music.

The hotel encourages art lovers to visit during the monthly gallery walk in the nearby Crossroads Arts District by offering its First Fridays Package from March through December. The special includes a one-night stay plus a $25 gift card to the hotel's 12 Baltimore Bar & Café. At printing the price starts at $129. Check out other specials including one for fans of the Royals—as in our baseball team, not the queen.

Diana Fountain in front of the Fairmont Hotel. CVB OF GREATER KANSAS CITY comfort and luxury to match the company's reputation.

The Radisson is also a fashionable choice for grand events. Its crown jewel, a circular rooftop ballroom, offers a breathtaking view of the city's skyline. Bistro 1301 offers guests American cuisine and wood-fired pizzas, complemented by a 2,000–bottle wine cellar.

East Metro

Adam's Mark $$–$$$
9103 East 39th Street
(816) 737-0200, (800) 444-ADAM
www.adamsmark.com

At this handsome high-rise you can almost hear "Play ball!" coming from Kauffman Stadium. Its convenient location across from the ballpark makes it a top choice for sports fans. The fact that it's also close to Worlds of Fun and Oceans of Fun, the Kansas City Zoo, and the IMAX Theatre makes it particularly family-friendly.

Amenities at this 374-unit hotel include indoor and outdoor pools and a health club with saunas. And when a hot dog at the stadium just won't do, Adam's Mark serves up American fare at Remington's Steak and Seafood Grill and casual dining at the Pantry. At Players Sports Bar a big-screen TV and a cold beer are waiting for you. Better yet, take advantage of one of the hotel's packages that include Chiefs or Royals tickets plus shuttle passes.

North of the River

Ameristar Casino Hotel $$–$$$
3200 North Ameristar Drive
(816) 414-7000, (800) 499-4961
www.ameristar.com

If your interpretation of "a little R & R" is "I'm ready to roll the dice," the Ameristar is for you. The 184 guest rooms and suites are quite nice, but it's the entertainment outside that keeps the reservations phone ringing.

The casino's decor—with an arched, blue-sky ceiling and dancing water fountains—makes it one of the most beautiful in the Midwest. Guests can partake of more than

160 table games, Kansas City's largest collection of slot and video poker games, eighteen state-of-the-art movie theaters, or a stroll along the Victorian-era streetscape. And everyone gets lucky at the hotel's restaurants. Choose from Orlean's, a white-tablecloth seafood restaurant; Arthur Bryant's, an offshoot of the famous barbecue joint downtown; an international buffet; and an ice-cream parlor. And Ameristar makes sure children have fun while parents play; Kids Quest provides activities in a safe, supervised environment.

Ameristar's three live music venues pay off big as well. The Grand Pavilion hosts top touring talent such as Chris LeDoux, Chuck Mangione, Diane Schurr, and Glen Campbell, while the Hofbrauhaus brings down the house with rock 'n' roll and blues. At the Phoenix, a twin of the popular downtown nightclub, you can enjoy jazz and blues with steaks, barbecue, or pasta.

Argosy Casino & Spa $$–$$$
777 Northwest Argosy Parkway
Riverside, MO
(816) 746-3100
www.argosycasinos.com/kansascity

You can bank on having a great time at the new Argosy now that a luxurious, state-of-the-art hotel and spa has been added to the newly renovated casino. The feeling is pure top-rate, from the minute you enter the Tuscan-style lobby to the moment you sink into the plush bedding in your suite. And do book a suite if you're feeling in the chips. They're not just nicely appointed, they are *extravagant*. Request one that provides a view of the twinkling downtown skyline off in the distance.

Opened in 2007, the Argosy offers 250 regular rooms and 8 suites with upscale fabrics and details that make anyone feel like a high roller here, especially the enormous bathrooms with double-sized showers, rain showerheads (trust us, you'll want one for your home), and jetted tubs, all set in beautiful mosaic tiling. Two 42-inch HD plasma-screen televisions and an in-room refrigerator add to your comfort. Although it's hard to pull yourself away from lounging in that plush robe, you have too much to do, such as treat yourself to a massage or facial in the elegant day spa, or try one of five dining venues— from fancy wood-fired steakhouse and Kobe beef burgers to a casual deli. Don't worry: You can work off those calories in the fitness center where each treadmill has its own TV.

And of course Argosy offers all the gaming action you could want, including a plush new poker room with seven tables dealing out Seven-Card Stud and Omaha and Texas Hold 'Em. Any open seats are announced throughout the casino, so you can enjoy the slots until it's time to get your game face on. A recent jackpot was up to $96,000 and change.

You'll learn more about the 62,000-square-foot casino's many attributes in Attractions, but when it's time to head back upstairs to the hotel, you'll appreciate the small details, such an electronic doorbell/do not disturb feature, which means you won't have to hang a tag on your doorknob. That, and the thought of Kansas City's own Roasterie coffee waiting for you in the morning, is enough to send you to dreamland.

The Elms Resort & Spa $$
401 Regent
Excelsior Springs, MO
(816) 630-5500, (800) THE-ELMS (843-3567)
www.elmsresort.com

You never know whom you might meet at this retreat just thirty minutes from Kansas City; Presidents Harry S. Truman and FDR slept here. So did Al Capone. In fact, plenty of national celebrities and much of Kansas City society have stayed here. The Elms's history actually precedes its grand opening date of 1912: The property was originally built in 1888 as a luxury resort to take advantage of the purported healing properties of the area's mineral waters. When the building's wide wooden verandas and pine interiors twice were destroyed by fire, they was replaced by native Missouri limestone.

The hotel is still a haven of serenity and style, with 152 guest rooms and suites. A world-class spa and wellness center includes Swiss and Vichy showers and services such as mud, seaweed, and aloe wraps; massage treatments; facials; manicures and pedicures. With its sixteen acres of gently rolling hills, the Elms also provides plenty of opportunities for an afternoon stroll or jog.

When you're ready for cocktails you can unwind in the lobby lounge or the second-level library lounge, where a scenic view accompanies your favorite libation. The Elms's upscale dining room, Adega, serves innovative American cuisine with style (on weekends only). A more casual option is the Dining Room, where guests can enjoy breakfast, lunch, and dinner or sumptuous Sunday brunch in a graceful setting with high ceilings, a wood-burning fireplace, and a wall of windows overlooking the landscaped grounds.

If you can pull yourself away from that late-morning massage, there's plenty to do in Excelsior Springs. Along with golf courses and antiques shops, there's the fascinating Hall of Waters Spa and Mineral Baths, where you can choose your favorite bottled water from around the world or indulge in other spa treatments. And the Jesse James Farm and Museum in nearby Kearney, Missouri, provides a fascinating look at the area's favorite bandit hero. You can find more information about these in Attractions, or through links on the resort's Web site.

Harrah's North Kansas City
Casino & Hotel $$–$$$
One Riverboat Drive
North Kansas City, MO
(816) 472-7777, (800) HARRAHS
www.harrahs.com

Harrah's hotel and convention center is so attractive that you might come here without so much as peeking in the gaming area. The 392 rooms and suites are luxurious and amenities abound, including twenty-four-hour room service, an indoor swimming pool, and an exercise room. There's even an arcade to keep kids and teens happy for hours.

But you'll be tempted to play once you

see Harrah's 30,000-square-foot addition to its Mardi Gras Casino, highlighted by marble floors, sparkling chandeliers, and a spectacular fountain. With over 2,000 slot machines and plenty of tables, we're betting you'll find lots to keep you entertained.

When you're hungry head to one of four themed restaurants, including casual choices such as Toby Keith's I Love This Bar & Grill, and Moby's Fish Tales. The Range rustles up sizzling steaks, seafood, and prime rib in an upscale Southwestern setting. Every meal includes a loaf of warm honey-wheat bread, a choice of Caesar salad or trip to the incredible salad bar, and scrumptious poblano-spiked salsa with blue corn chips. And the smoking-hot nightclub, VooDoo Lounge has put Harrah's on the map. See details in Nightlife.

Overland Park, Kansas

The Doubletree $$–$$$
10100 College Boulevard
Overland Park, KS
(913) 451-6100, (800) 222-TREE
www.doubletree.com

This hotel's name is certainly appropriate: It's surrounded by a densely forested park that includes a 4-mile hiking and biking trail, wildflower meadows, and park benches. In fact, guests have watched deer graze, herons glide silently by, and families of ducks paddle along the streams that meander through the woods.

Expect to find some creature comforts inside as well, starting with Doubletree's signature chocolate chip cookies. Each of the 356 rooms and 17 suites on eighteen floors is tastefully decorated and well appointed for both business and pleasure travelers. The hotel's entertainment options include a lounge where you can relax over cocktails while watching the sun set over that magical parklike vista.

And the newly renovated and named Trofi Restaurant, with its beautiful fountain and multitiered design, is a favorite with the Johnson County set. The dining room serves regional cuisine for breakfast, lunch, and din-

ner accompanied by piano music. Each Sunday an eye-popping champagne buffet brunch gives you a reason to head downstairs, where chefs will prepare omelets to your liking, carve juicy roast beef, or place a piping-hot Belgian waffle on your plate. Other tables are filled with cold shrimp, fresh salads and fruits, grilled vegetables, baked goods, hot egg dishes, sausage and bacon, and desserts.

The Doubletree is also tops when it comes to location. Guests soon realize there's plenty to do in the southern part of our metropolis. If you like to shop, you're just minutes away from Oak Park Mall, one of the largest shopping centers in Kansas. Anchors include Nordstrom, Macy's, and JCPenney along with 185 specialty shops such as Coach, Aveda, Ann Taylor, and Gap. Back at the hotel, take a stroll along the adjacent hiking trail or head to the bowling alley across the street. Dozens of great dining options are close by as well.

And NASCAR fans will be glad to know the Doubletree is just two minutes from the new Kansas Speedway . . . if you drive like Jeff Gordon. For the rest of us it's about a fifteen-minute journey.

The Marriott $$–$$$
10800 Metcalf
Overland Park, KS
(913) 451-8000, (800) 228-9290
www.overlandparkmarriott.com

This 398-room hotel is an island of style in the heart of bustling Overland Park. The public areas are plush and inviting, and three distinct dining choices give you plenty of reasons to make this your home-away-from-home. At Pitcher's the bartender can toss you a highball or beer to enjoy with appetizers, burgers, or salads from midafternoon until late at night. Allie's is a popular lunch spot, serving such all-American cuisine as fried catfish, burgers, and soups and salads along with a breakfast menu.

The Marriott is also home to Nikko Japanese Steakhouse, which combines an evening's entertainment with fabulous food. Skilled chefs chop and prepare tappan-style dinners in front of you on large stainless-steel grills. And if you smile just right you might get a shrimp tossed into your open mouth! Nikko is open for dinner only.

To work off your meal, do some laps in the indoor pool, head to the fitness center, or take advantage of nearby outdoor activities. Swing by a golf course or check out one of the area's beautiful public parks. Or slip on comfortable shoes and head to the shopper's paradise known as 119th Street, where a shopping center, mall, or major store is on every street corner. Big names include Ann Taylor, Talbots, Restoration Hardware, and Coldwater Canyon, and there are boutiques, spas, and more. When it's time for lunch or dinner, tuck into one of the area's great restaurant choices, from barbecue and burgers to upscale cuisine. And isn't it nice to know that your 300-thread-count sheets and fluffy down comforter are waiting for you back at the Marriott?

Sheraton Overland Park Hotel at the Convention Center $$–$$$
6100 College Boulevard
Overland Park, KS
(913) 234-2100, (888) 625-5144
www.sheraton.com

It's really the second half of this lodging's title—the Convention Center—that's its claim to fame. Opened in November 2002, this 240,000-square-foot facility is helping put sleepy suburban Overland Park on the tourism map. The space boasts the largest ballroom in Kansas and a 60,000-square-foot exhibit hall that's often filled with conventions and meetings . . . and always filled with regional art. More than sixty pieces of fine art enliven the space, including massive metal sculptures and landscapes that capture in oil our glowing sunsets.

The Sheraton Hotel, which is connected to the convention center via landscaped courtyards and an all-weather walkway, offers 412 rooms, a fitness center, and high-speed Internet access.

Its restaurant, 1906 Bar and Grille, takes its name from the year in which William Strang Jr. developed the railroad that led to the development of Overland Park. The 148-seat restaurant has the feel of a masculine chophouse, done in rich shades of hunter green, cream, and khaki. And because this is beef country, expect thick, juicy steaks to dominate the menu, along with double-cut pork chops.

White Haven Motor Lodge $
8039 Metcalf
Overland Park, KS
(913) 649-8200, (800) 752-2892

Since 1957 the White family has been turning guests into friends at their pretty little motor lodge. And even though Metcalf has become cluttered with car dealerships and retail shops, White Haven continues to be a nifty place to stay. Its charm, after all, comes from a blast-from-the-past design with a swimming pool out front, retro sign that once was considered modern art, and furniture that leans toward French provincial. It provides the kind of comfort, value, and friendliness that make you expect to see Ward and June Cleaver and the boys pull up in a station wagon.

Brothers Bob and Eugene, along with their wives, children, and grandchildren, maintain one hundred neat-as-a-pin rooms here, from singles to spacious suites. Stay as long as you like; lots of folks rent the rooms for weeks. To encourage the extended-stay trade, every room has a refrigerator, and a continental breakfast is served each morning in the coffee lounge. Expecting a fax? They'll take it at the front desk and deliver it personally. Lock your keys in the car? They'll get it open. One of the sons is a mechanic who has helped many a stranded traveler get back on the road.

It's this kind of special service that keeps the flowers and candy coming from satisfied customers; one guest even sent fresh eggs from her farm. And it must have been some thank-you gift after Bob paid bail to get a guest out of jail one night.

Repeat business and word of mouth keep the NO VACANCY sign lit, particularly during summer, so reservations are in order. And say, isn't that Wally and the Beav in the swimming pool?

Wyandotte County, Kansas

Chateau Avalon $$$–$$$$
701 Village West Parkway
(Interstate 435 and State Avenue)
Kansas City, KS
(913) 596-6000, (877) KC-AVALON
(52-282566)
www.chateauavalon.net

What's Cleopatra doing on the plains of Kansas? Looking pretty pleased with herself, relaxing in a two-person jetted spa with Chroma therapy lighting, that's what.

This latest entry into the wildly successful Village West entertainment district is a cross between a bed-and-breakfast and a high-end resort. The plush amenities include custom-made mattresses and posh linens, 60-inch flat-screen TVs with DVD players and surround sound, a rose-petal turndown, and made-to-order in-room breakfast. Cleo, baby, you never had it so good.

Chateau Avalon offers sixty-two luxurious themed suites, including six two-story accommodations, such as the Castaway Isle, where being shipwrecked may not be a bad idea. The hurricane left your ship in a tree on this tropical island paradise. Coconut oil, anyone? Or perhaps the Casablanca is more to your tune; here you'll slumber in a replica of 1940 Morocco, complete with piles of plush pillows and a DVD of the famous movie.

The hotel is also destined to be a popular site for weddings and events, thanks to its opulent French country design and lavish landscaping, including fountains and courtyards.

Great Wolf Lodge $$$–$$$$
10401 Cabela Drive
Kansas City, KS
(913) 299-7001, (800) 608-WOLF (9653)
www.greatwolflodge.com

Dorothy, I don't think we're in Kansas anymore. That overused line suddenly had new meaning

when this massive northwoods lodge opened in the Village West entertainment district in 2003. From its hand-carved totem poles to the rustic furniture throughout the lodge, it could be situated on a snowcapped mountain peak.

But the main draw is pure tropics: an indoor water park where an eye-popping assortment of fountains, pools, slides, and jets stay a pleasant eighty-four degrees year-round. Every few minutes a giant bucket atop the twelve-story tree house tips and drenches the crowd below. Hold on to your swim trunks!

It's a vacation for the entire family, with eight waterslides, hot tubs, and Treehouse Island, where kids of all ages can explore twelve levels of interactive water fun with more than sixty amazing water features, cargo nets, and web crawls. At any moment, a fountain or water jet might soak you. During warm weather, take it outside at Thunder Bay Outdoor Park. Certified lifeguards are always on duty.

After dinner in the Bear Claw Cafe, a chance to win prizes in the Northern Lights Arcade, and an ice-cream treat, it's story time in the lobby as children cuddle with parents by a massive stone fireplace. Sleepy eyes snap open when a menagerie of animated woodland creatures brings a giant clock tower to life. One of the most compelling attractions of Great Wolf, however, is its six different themed suites, including the Wolf Den with a decorated enclosure for tired little cubs.

Great Wolf Lodge came just in time for those sports enthusiasts who want one more day to shop at nearby Cabela's outdoor-goods emporium or families in town to attend a NASCAR race at the Kansas Speedway. But with its year-round watery wonderland, it's become a favorite of locals looking for a fun birthday venue or an overnight getaway. Moms can get their own version of water therapy with a trip to the Aveda Spa on the premises.

EXTENDED STAYS

With Kansas City's growing base of national and international corporations, extended-stay facilities are popping up all over to give newly hired executives a homey place to board. Individuals and families relocating to our city will find temporary residences that truly feel like home. Following are a few choices, ranging from rooms with efficiency kitchens to luxe townhomes with fireplaces. For more options, Extended Stay (www.extendedstaydeluxe .com) matches fully furnished apartments, duplexes, and homes to specific needs.

Crown Center

Residence Inn by Marriott–
Union Hill $$–$$$
2975 Main Street
(816) 561-3000, (800) 331-3131
www.residenceinn.com/mciuh

When Hallmark hires a new manager from out of town, they'll often treat the trainee to these deluxe townhomes overlooking the company's headquarters at Crown Center. The services are amazing, including complimentary grocery shopping, van transportation up to 5 miles, breakfast, and an evening hospitality hour with beverages and a light meal. During nice weather the social hour moves to the pool area, where burgers and hot dogs are on the menu.

Accommodations include studios, doubles, and a two-level penthouse that includes a queen-size bed on each floor, plus a pullout sofa bed. Some rooms have fireplaces. And of course, the location is superb, with the entertainment, restaurants, and shopping at nearby Crown Center, plus downtown, Westport, and the Plaza just a van drive away. No wonder guests stay thirty, sixty, even ninety days or more; why would you ever want to leave?

South Kansas City

Windsong Corporate Apartments $
114 West 103rd Street
(816) 942-5997, (800) 692-2468

A convenient location, attractive units, good value—prices equate to about $40 a day— and friendly service? No wonder so many corporations book their transplanted employees and managers here. Windsong has eighty-

nine apartments ranging from one to three bedrooms, all completely furnished including all household supplies. There's also weekly maid service, a laundry room in each building, and carports. Windsong is located just south of I-435, so it's convenient to every part of the city, and the Sprint campus is just minutes away.

BED-AND-BREAKFASTS AND INNS

Rocking chairs on wide verandas, breakfast sausages grilled on a tree-shaded patio, a grand piano in the parlor, and fresh flowers on your nightstand . . . for those who treasure the personal touches found only at a bed-and-breakfast, we have just the cozy spot for you. Several, in fact. This list includes urban settings, Plaza addresses, and a horse ranch in the tallgrass prairies of Kansas. And what, pray tell, could be more fun than sleeping in a renovated church?

Circle S Ranch Guest Ranch &
Country Inn $$
3325 Circle S Lane
Lawrence, KS
(785) 843-4124, (800) 625-2839
www.circlesranch.com

If the welcoming committee seems particularly happy to see you, you've just met Lucy. The friendly pooch is one reason guests of the Circle S feel at home immediately. Another is Mary Cronemeyer's smiling face welcoming you to her inn, nestled amid rolling hills 40 miles west of Kansas City.

It may as well be a million miles away. The inn is set in 1,200 acres of sprawling prairie and wooded glens that have been in Mary's family since the mid-1800s. Since opening in May 1998, Circle S has won enough awards to turn a cowgirl's head. It has become a popular place for everything from business meetings to marriage proposals, but rarely in the same weekend.

In fact, Mary has coordinated dozens of weddings, from sweet ceremonies in the wildflower meadow to blowout bashes at the

Party Barn. This 5,000-square-foot barn, when not hosting a hoedown, is a mini-agricultural museum with farm implements, tack, and tools hanging on walls and from ceilings. Little cowpokes can even ride a 1950s-era grocery store mechanical horse for a dime.

Back at the inn, twelve spacious guest rooms feature decor ranging from pioneer quaintness to cowboy whimsy—witness the showerhead in a bucket—plus private bath and breathtaking view. An eight-person hot tub in the silo will give you something to talk about for months. It was built by Mary's husband, Jack Cronemeyer, a fifth-generation carpenter who also crafted most of the inn's beautiful woodwork.

If you're looking for peace and quiet, you'll find it in these endless blue skies and pastures. The only sounds are soft mooing of the cattle, an occasional scream from a peacock, and—early in the morning—the timpani of tree frogs. Late at night you might hear the unmistakable arr-arr-arrooooo of a far-off coyote.

Unless you want to rise at 5:00 a.m. to bottle-feed a motherless calf like one guest did, mornings start at 8:30 with a ranch hand's breakfast of scrambled eggs, biscuits and gravy, crispy hash browns, and—if you're lucky—some golden preserves from Mary's grandmother's apricot tree. Spend the rest of the day browsing boutiques in nearby Lawrence, or stay home. Call dibs on a rocking chair on the wraparound porch, explore the tallgrass prairie on mountain bikes, or stroll the trails until a hammock calls your name. Chances are you won't be alone: White-tailed deer, quail, and wild turkey share the ranch with 200 head of cattle and quite a few bison.

If you take along a picnic basket, ask for extra apples for Pepper, Cricket, and Crazy Alice. When these horses aren't working the land, they're hoping a guest shows up with a Red Delicious and a soft spot for big brown eyes. And if you have horses of your own, bring 'em; you can ride the trails with the ranch hands and help out with daily activities during summer months. For the safety of the other animals, however, Circle S cannot accept pets.

Along with personal retreats and special occasions, Circle S has found a niche with old-fashioned slumber parties—adult style. Mary greets guests with whirling blenders of margaritas while manicures, pedicures, and massages await. All-night videos and popcorn complete the theme.

The Inn on Crescent Lake $$–$$$
1261 St. Louis Avenue
Excelsior Springs, MO
(816) 630-6745
www.crescentlake.com

Motor up the long curving drive to this majestic 1915 Georgian-Colonial with stately white columns and you might expect Scarlett O'Hara to sashay down the steps. Instead a contemporary—yet just as gracious—couple welcome you into their majestic inn. The setting is spectacular as well: twenty-two wooded acres including two crescent-shaped ponds that inspired the inn's name.

If the inn looks familiar, that's because it has been featured on Bob Vila's *Restore America* on HGTV and in *Travel Holiday*, *Midwest Living*, the *Columbus Dispatch*, *KC Magazine*, and half a dozen other publications. Soon you'll discover what the buzz is about. When Anne and Bruce Libowitz turned the home into an inn in 1997 they kept its architectural charm—such as the sun-filled solarium and sweeping staircase—while providing modern conveniences. Scarlett wouldn't have been nearly as petulant after soaking in a 6-foot whirlpool tub. In 2004 Ed and Irene Heege became the new innkeepers, maintaining the charm and adding new amenities.

Each of the ten rooms and suites has a private bath and unique personality. The black-and-white Art Deco room features a red claw-footed tub, the third-floor Treehouse Suite offers a cozy bower feeling, and the Train Room appeals to the inner child with a model train circling an overhead track. The ballroom, also known as the Honeymoon Suite, is the most requested room. Painted a buttery yellow, the airy room has a king-size iron bed draped in lace, separate sitting room, and daybed-filled dormers that create lots of places for curling up together.

Two suites are particularly appealing. The Garden Room's private deck comes complete with a hot tub for wishing on a star. It also affords a private entrance and is wheelchair-accessible. The two-story Cottage, separate from the main house, is a little love nest that would be perfect for a weekend of bliss or a week of reconnecting with each other. It offers a living room, half bath, and kitchen on the lower level and king-size bed, sitting area, whirlpool tub for two, and walk-in shower above. A TV and stereo system are on each floor, but the real entertainment is a few steps away at the lunar lakes . . . or perhaps back in the bubbly tub.

The water does, indeed, beckon guests during nice weather. Share a paddleboat; take a dip in the pool; or aim a fishing pole at the bass, sunnies, or catfish. Or take a walk around the estate's paths. Off-site activities include golf, antiques shopping in Olde Town, or a thirty-minute drive to Kansas City's attractions. During winter, retreat to the warmth of the solarium to watch snow fall gently on the expansive lawn.

Or simply while away the hours anticipating the hearty breakfast the next mornig, which may feature sour cream waffles with banana syrup or biscuits and sausage gravy.

The inn is also available for corporate events and the most glorious wedding imaginable. Packages include a girl's getaway and a romance weekend that combines a suite for two nights with champagne. Draw our bath, please; we'll be there in thirty.

The James Inn $$
342 North Water
Liberty, MO
(816) 792-4335
www.thejamesinn.com
This bit of heaven-on-earth was originally the St. James Catholic Church, built in 1913. By the 1980s the parishioners had outgrown the

place, and a decade later David and Mary Anne Kimbrell began turning the belfry, vestibule, and bell tower into a lovely bed-and-breakfast. As an infant Mary Anne was baptized in the very space that is now the dining room.

The architecture lends itself beautifully to its new purpose. Exposed bricks and aged beams make wonderful backdrops to the couple's antiques and Oriental rugs. Sunlight floods the rooms through tall arched gothic windows, and fireplaces that once warmed churchgoers now add a glow to guests. The guest rooms are special as well, with queen-size four-poster beds, fireplaces, goose-down mattresses, comforters, and pillows. Jetted tubs overlook the bedrooms from lofts above.

A licensed massage therapist/aesthetician is available for a massage, body wrap, or spa treatment, and the inn's gift shop sells lotions, bath salts, and aromatherapy candles so you can scent your room as well. The pampering continues in the hot tub located on a two-tiered deck.

Guests also delight in meals here: David's Belgian waffles and quiche are sinfully good, and on Friday night there's prime rib to enjoy by candlelight. These dinners sell out quickly, so it's best to book well in advance. David and Mary Anne also host wine-tasting events and murder mystery weekends, and non-guests can reserve room at the table for Saturday and Sunday brunches.

The inn is also popular during parents' weekends at nearby William Jewell College. And it is just 2 blocks from Liberty Square, a place to shop for antiques or visit the bank Jesse James robbed. And if you missed David's prime rib, there's the Hardware Cafe on the square, a place that once sold hammers instead of ham steaks.

Ophelia's $$
201 North Main
Independence, MO
(816) 461-4525
www.opheliasind.net
Cocktails, dinner, a little light jazz, and you're

off to dreamland. It's all part of the package at Ken and Cindy McClain's stylish inn just upstairs from the restaurant of the same name. The couple have even tossed in a little history: Ophelia's is across the street from Clinton's Soda Shop, where a young Harry Truman used to dish up ice cream.

At the inn, as well as at the restaurant below, Cindy's artistic talent is on view with beautifully decorated rooms, special touches, and a few paintings displayed here and there. The seven rooms and one spacious suite each have a private bath. The amenities rival those of a fine hotel, with down comforters and pillows, voice messaging, cable TV, and wireless Internet. A continental breakfast is brought to your door in a basket.

Ophelia's is on historic Independence Square with its centerpiece, the Jackson County Courthouse. Part of the original 1836 building remains today, and the office Truman occupied as county administrative judge is largely unchanged. It's a fascinating look back in time, or you could get your nostalgia fix at one of the many antiques shops within the square. There are five restaurants as well, but if you've experienced lunch or dinner at Ophelia's, you won't want to stray far from the inn.

For more information about other nearby attractions, including the Truman Museum and home, the buck stops at the Attractions chapter.

Southmoreland on the Plaza $$–$$$$
116 East 46th Street
(816) 531-7979
www.southmoreland.com

Perhaps the Midwest's most celebrated inn, the Southmoreland is a magnificent 1913 colonial revival on a quiet residential street just 2 blocks from the Country Club Plaza. Inside you'll understand its long list of kudos, including being six-time winner of the Mobil Four-Star award, one of America's Top 25 Favorite Inns, and Inn of the Month from *Travel and Leisure*.

In 1999 owners Mark Reichle and Nancy Miller Reichle didn't so much buy the inn as inherit it from its founders. The couple treat it like the precious gem it is, continuing the tradition of ambience and adding a few amenities of their own. The best of these is the new carriage house suite named for George Kessler, the landscape architect who designed the inn's namesake park. The suite is separated from the main building by a lovely brick courtyard and offers unmatched privacy and comfort. Guests can relax in front of the wood-burning stove—bright red to match the room's cheery wallpaper and bed linens—or in a jetted tub for two. There's a king-size antique iron bed and small balcony, and on the antique walnut dresser, a book describing local flora and fauna from Kessler's day.

Similar charming details appear in the inn's other twelve rooms, which are named for Kansas City celebrities. Guests in the pastel Clara and Russell Stover Room, for example, find a tiny box of chocolates on their pillows, and the Satchel Paige knotty pine sleeping porch re-creates the baseball legend's favorite fishing cabin. Pictures of the Kansas City Monarchs line the wall.

Each room has a private bath and such special treats as a fireplace or jetted tub. And in one, shafts of upward-beaming light from Frank Lloyd Wright's 1940 Community Christian Church make a delightful nightlight. Other thoughtful in-room touches include cut-crystal decanters of sherry, fresh flowers, and a copy of the book *Here Lies Kansas City* opened to the section about the room's namesake.

You'll also appreciate what's happening in the kitchen. Guests are treated to wine and hot hors d'oeuvres upon arrival. For dinner you'll have your choice of dozens of restaurants on the Plaza. After an afternoon of museums and shops, a fresh batch of Monster Cookies—a combination of chocolate chips, oatmeal, and peanut butter—await your arrival.

In the morning awake to an incredible breakfast that may include the inn's famous French toast stuffed with Swiss cheese and brown-sugar ham, fresh fruit, and chocolate-zucchini bread. In warmer weather Mark often treats guests to grilled sausage or ham steaks on the patio shaded by sugar maples. It's just one highlight of what makes staying in a bed-and-breakfast so special—you're treated like family.

If you're lucky (or quick) enough to book a room over Thanksgiving, you'll arrive home from the famous lighting ceremony on the Country Club Plaza to find about thirty types of homemade pies waiting in the dining room. Dibs on Mark's Key lime!

Woodstock Inn   **$$–$$$**
1212 West Lexington
Independence, MO
(816) 833-2233, (800) 276-5202
www.thewoodstockinn.com

Sweet dreams are nearly guaranteed at this lovingly restored inn in the historic district of Independence. The original 1900 building was Ruby Short-McKim's studio, where the artist designed quilts and created her famous Kimport porcelain dolls until the 1980s. Charles Woodstock turned it into an eleven-room bed-and-breakfast in 1987, and today it's owned and managed by Todd and Patricia Justice. The couple, who met in Korea, where they taught English, brought back several things from their world travels, including a sensitivity to guests' needs and some beautiful furnishings. The Oriental Suite, for example, features a museum-quality antique wedding bed and black lacquer and mother-of-pearl armoire from the country where the innkeepers fell in love.

Love, in fact, is the overriding emotion at Woodstock Inn. Details such as fresh flowers, fireplaces, silky bed linens, and lace-draped canopies help set the mood, and honeymooners will find a page of love quotes in their rooms.

All eleven guest rooms and suites have private baths, many have jetted tubs, and some have fireplaces. In the morning, a delightful breakfast will stir you from beneath cozy bedcovers. Todd's specialty is malted Belgian waffles topped with fresh fruit sauce; other creations include apple and peach

crepes, ham-and-cheese-stuffed French toast, and garden-fresh frittatas.

A short walk to the sights of Independence will help work off the calories. Historians often choose Woodstock while exploring the world of Harry S. Truman, and Kansas City's other attractions are a short drive away.

The inn offers several special packages, including the Romantic Rendezvous, which includes chilled champagne or sparkling grape juice, a twenty-seven-exposure one-use camera to capture those special moments, and a dinner voucher for one of the area's premier restaurants. Husbands may want to book the "Honey, I'm Sorry!" package to get out of the doghouse.

RV CAMPSITES AND RESORTS

Basswood Country Inn and
RV Resort   **$$–$$$**
15880 Interurban Road
Platte City, MO
(816) 858-5556, (800) 242-2775
(reservations only)
www.basswoodresort.com

Here's a campsite and fishing resort that hits all the right notes. At least that's what Bing Crosby and Rudy Vallee thought when they were guests of millionaire A. G. Stephens's Basswood Sportsmen's Club in the 1940s. Hedy Lamarr often stopped by, and Bess Truman hosted her bridge club here for many years. At one time it was on the railway line that linked Kansas City with St. Joseph between 1913 and 1933.

But like so many grand places of that era, the sporting lodge lost favor and was neglected. Don and Betty Soper saved it in 1979 and spent eight years returning it to its former charm. Today the bed-and-breakfast inn, country store, and modern RV resort, according to *Peak Magazine,* is "perhaps the most beautiful wooded lakefront setting in the Kansas City area." It's without a doubt the fishiest: Four freshwater lakes, fed by the original spring that Stephens once bottled and sold worldwide, are stocked with catfish, bass, crappies, and carp. Check the resort's Web site for a photo of one happy angler hoisting a 19½-pound catch.

Basswood packs a summer's worth of activities into the site, including a swimming pool, volleyball, shuffleboard, children's playground, and walking trails. There's a large selection of videos to rent at the store, where you'll also find basic groceries, RV and camping supplies, packaged liquor, and gifts. And mmmmm—is that pizza you smell? Yep, they bake up fresh pies every day from 5:30 to 8:00 p.m.

Accommodations include the private Mother-in-Law Cottage with two bedrooms and full kitchen; the Celebrity House Suites where Bing Crosby, Rudy Vallee, and the Trumans often stayed; and Country French Suites. There are 139 full hook-up RV sites (thirty and fifty amp) plus 24 water/electric-only sites for tents and pop-ups, including 35 deluxe sites with patios. Guests can use the two picnic shelters, playground, spacious laundry facilities, and superclean bathhouses with shower stalls and vanities. A meeting hall is available for parties and family reunions.

Basswood Resort, open year-round, is just 5 miles from Kansas City International Airport and near the attraction-packed towns of Independence, Parkville, Weston, and St. Joseph.

Jackson County Parks and Recreation Campgrounds
(877) 528-4748
www.co.jackson.mo.us
(click on "Parks and Recreation")
Discover the reason we don't miss beaches and mountains here in the landlocked Midwest. Our breathtaking lakes, timberlands, and parks provide plenty of recreation and relaxation. Our well-maintained campsites give outdoor enthusiasts a chance to rough it just enough. Just be sure to practice your "Kum ba yah" before it's your turn to lead the campfire sing-along.

Jackson County, Missouri, offers three public campgrounds with a total of 236 camping sites, all about fifteen minutes from Kansas City proper. They are available by reservation for stays up to fourteen days, and at least one camper must be twenty-one or over. The camping facilities include showers, restrooms, attendants, picnic tables, and ice.

Longview Lake Campground is within nearly 5,000 acres of parkland and includes a 930-acre lake with full-service marina including disabled fishing docks. Attractions include a 4-mile nature trail, horse park, launching ground where colorful hot air balloons take off and land, swimming beach, and twenty-seven-hole public golf course. The campground is open April 27 through September 30. Its 119 sites include 59 with electricity at $14 to $17 per day and 60 tent-ready at $10 to $13 per day.

Lake Jacomo Campground is within beautiful Fleming Park, at 7,800 acres, the largest parkland in Jackson County. At its heart is 970-acre Lake Jacomo, and there's a smaller Blue Springs Lake as well. More than 1.3 million visitors a year make the best of its many pleasures, including a nature preserve, an Audubon center, a marina that hosts a sailboat regatta nearly every weekend, a swimming beach, nature trails, and more. Watch for things flying overhead, such as Frisbees—this is a popular dog hangout—and model airplanes. The campground has sixty large, tree-lined sites: ten full hookup, thirty-eight electric, and twelve tent, for $10 to $23 per day. The site is open year-round; call for specific availabilities.

Blue Springs Lake Campground, also within Fleming Park, is open from April 13 to October 31, with fifty-seven sites (twenty full hookup, seventeen electric and water, twenty electric) that range in price from $14 to $23 per day. This site is five minutes from the beach.

RESTAURANTS

Of all the things that surprise first-time visitors to Kansas City—from our cosmopolitan ambience to our far-from-flat topography—nothing seems to floor them more than our food. Not just how good it is, mind you, but how diverse it is.

Tourists already know about the superiority of our beef thanks to Calvin Trillin's 1974 book, *American Fried,* which begins, "The best restaurants in the world are, of course, in Kansas City. Not all of them; only the top four or five." Other writers picked up the scent and have been gushing about our steaks, barbecue, and burgers ever since.

But here's the amazing thing: You don't have to be a card-carrying carnivore to eat well here. Foodies can have a world tour of authentic cuisine from Mexico to Mongolia and cooking styles from Cajun to Catalan. Vegetarians can get their five-a-day at a number of excellent eateries in town. And even the staunchest of steakhouses offers at least one meatless dish.

Enjoy fresh fish? We'll get along swimmingly. We may be landlocked, but we can still serve you a piping-hot sea bass thirty-six hours after it met its last fisherman. And wine aficionados will want to raise a toast to this city. *Wine Spectator* hands out awards around here like party favors. Two of our restaurants have received the magazine's Grand Award, a distinction only one hundred in the world can claim. But sometimes it's what's not on the menu that makes it worth your trip. Lots of dining rooms serve a side of blues or jazz with their burgers or beefsteaks. For a complete list, see Nightlife.

Hungry yet? Following are a few tips to keep you from being disappointed in your quest for a fabulous meal. We've done our best to provide current information about the restaurants listed, but we suggest you call first before heading out the door. As for payment, major credit cards are accepted unless noted. And a word about reservations. Actually two: Make them. On weekends there's often a wave of people trying to get into the flavor of the month—which can create up to a two-hour wait at places that don't take names. Houston's comes to mind, although their roasted chicken is so divine you'll gladly accept a pager at the door.

Speaking of Houston's, you'll find this and just about every other national chain here, including Ruth's Chris Steakhouse, P.F. Chang's China Bistro, Cheesecake Factory, and Morton's Steak House. We have (at last count) twenty-one Applebee's, which makes perfect sense because it was born and raised here. These are all fine dining experiences, to be sure, but this book focuses on independent restaurants to introduce you to our regional cooking and original recipes.

Although we cover a lot of dishes in this chapter, you can find additional restaurants listed in the *Kansas City Star* Friday Preview, monthly issues of *KC Magazine,* and *The Pitch,* where Charles Ferruzza's tart-as-Key-lime-pie wit makes for entertaining restaurant reviews. We'd give him the last curl of calamari on our plate any day. Another handy resource is the *Restaurant Guide of Kansas City,* a free quarterly magazine available at hundreds of restaurants, hotels, and outdoor boxes. It's published by Kathy and Laurent Denis, a couple who met in his hometown of Bordeaux, France, moved back to her home state, and now share their love of fine food with the rest of us. The guide's Web site (www.kcrestaurantguide.com) also provides restaurant links that include up-to-date menus, recipes, and maps. You can even purchase gift certificates online.

Finally, in this chapter we've listed restaurants by cuisine rather than location because in KC we'll drive across town for the ribs and onion rings at Fiorella's Jack Stack barbecue or the pasta special—no questions asked—at YiaYia's in Overland Park. A forty-minute trek to Parkville for mussels in white wine sauce at Cafe des Amis? We're on our way.

To help you find your way, we've added a geographic key in parentheses beside the restaurant's name. Or you can simply follow your nose. All restaurants are in Kansas City, Missouri, unless otherwise noted.

Price Code

Our price code is based on dinner for two, without appetizers, dessert, alcoholic beverages, tax, or tip. Your own bill may be higher or lower depending on what you order and normal fluctuating prices. Lunch prices are generally less. Bon appétit.

$. . . . . **Less than $20**
$$ . . . . **$21 to $40**
$$$ . . . . **$41 and up**

AMERICAN/CONTINENTAL

**The American Restaurant
(Crown Center)**   **$$$**
25th and Grand Avenue
(816) 545-8000
www.theamericankc.com

With a glamorous movie-star entrance and sparkling view of downtown, this American beauty is the place to woo a lover or wow a client. The soaring space was designed by Walter Platner two years before he did Manhattan's late, great Windows on the World, and it's stunning. Curving wooden louvers adorn the 20-foot-tall ceilings—a lacy valentine to the city from the American's owner, Hallmark Cards. Shutters on the floor-to-ceiling windows are opened just at sunset, often to applause from a room of delighted diners. During the winter holidays the view includes a twinkling 100-foot mayor's Christmas tree in the Crown Center Square below.

i Save 40 percent on dinner? We'll drink to that. Sign up on www.kansascitymenus.com for discounted gift certificates to some of KC's top restaurants. The offer arrives via e-mail once every quarter, and the best ones are gone within minutes, so be quick or go hungry. The site also has handy links to dozens of dining choices.

The food easily matches the theatrics. The legendary James Beard was brought in as a consultant in 1974 to create refined yet soul-warming interpretations of classic American cooking.

Kansas City's only Mobil Four-Star hired executive chef Celina Tio in 2001 when celebrated couple Michael Smith and Debbie Gold left after six years to open 40 Sardines in Overland Park.

Celina's menu continues to pay homage to the Midwest's bounty of meats, game, and produce. But before you think "meat, potatoes, and plenty of gravy," take a look at a recent midwinter menu: duck breast and thyme-roasted spaghetti squash with orange-juniper oil and antelope and braised chestnuts with a syrah grape reduction. And grandma never made a shepherd's pie like this; here it's studded with lobster, wild mushrooms, and roasted cipollini onions and served with truffled mashed potatoes. Celina won the coveted James Beard Award for the Midwest in 2007.

Thanks to maitre d' Victor Hugo Berndt Jr., the service is stellar as well. And although the American has been trying to lighten its formal reputation—jackets at dinner are merely *suggested* now—it's still a refined restaurant where you might see black tie and ball gowns before opening night at the Lyric Opera.

The American is open for lunch Monday through Friday and dinner Monday through Saturday. Call to ask about cooking lessons. Maybe Celina will teach you how to make that lobster sheperd's pie.

Bluestem (Midtown) $$$
900 Westport Road
(816) 561-1101
www.kansascitymenus.com/bluestem

When husband-and-wife chefs open a restaurant, it can't help but be high on the romance meter. That's the mantra at this forty-three-seat bistro that Colby and Megan Garrelts opened in spring 2004—and it has been rocking the local foodie contingent ever since. What makes it romantic is the pacing—don't expect to eat and run to catch an eight o'clock movie. Dinners start with *amuse-bouche,* a complimentary sampling of tastes. This is your first glimpse of the chefs' attention to detail: Each miniature canapé is presented like a gem at a jewelry counter.

Appetizers include fois gras glazed in sauterne jelly and served with fig jam and brioche, just as luscious as it sounds. Entrees might have you reaching for your camera before tucking into such masterpieces as wild salmon with crispy sweetbreads or a beautifully grilled strip steak next to mahogany-colored roasted onions. The chefs also offer a six-course fixed-priced dinner menu accompanied by paired wine from their impressive list. Megan's skill with pastries is evident in the dessert selection, which includes a citrus crème brûlée and silky malted-chocolate sponge pudding.

Bluestem also offers a brunch where eggs are served Benedict-style, topped with smoked salmon and asparagus. Health nuts may opt for the crunchy house-made granola.

Brunch, dinner, or a late-night sweets spree—Bluestem is the perfect date spot. Recently Bluestem made it even more delicious to spend the evening here by opening a swanky wine bar right next door. The cocktail menu is as inventive as Colby's food menu, and light bites are available as you converse with friends on the velvet sofas.

Cafe Sebastienne
(Country Club Plaza) $–$$
4420 Warwick Boulevard
(816) 561-7740
www.kemperart.org/cafe

No one would blame executive chef Jennifer Maloney if she skimped on food presentation; her restaurant's location within the Kemper Museum of Contemporary Art should be visual stimulus enough. But her menu and its plating are more than up to the challenge. And now that a covered courtyard is open for year-round dining, there's more room for the hungry masses.

Her salads—such as the ode to autumn, with seasonal greens, smoked Gouda, turkey, pears, honey-baked pecans, and curry-mustard dressing—are works of art. The foie gras–stuffed quail and risotto are simply dreamy, the roasted beef tenderloin with turnip-and-fig gratin divine. And for some fans, the meal isn't over until they've polished off a wedge of chocolate budino, a decadent flourless torte served with fresh fruit and whipped cream. Lunch is served Tuesday through Saturday, and dinner is available Friday and Saturday with a Sunday brunch.

You may read more about the Kemper Museum in The Arts. But for now you'll be thrilled to learn that admission is free seven days a week. Spend the savings on a serving of budino.

Cafe Trio $–$$
3535 Broadway
(816) 756-3227
www.cafetriokc.com

This bustling bistro is so friendly and hip, the food doesn't have to be good. But lucky for you, Chef Karl Martens oversees one of the most innovative menus in town. This is the kind of spot where regulars show up, sit

---

i Although lots of restaurants and bars offer early-evening happy hour drink and appetizer specials, KC's young and beautiful crowd are more apt to venture out late at night. Voila! The reverse happy hour, usually from 9-ish to close. Grand Street Cafe, re:Verse, and Kona Grill are just three. We feel an afternoon nap coming on.

We can't imagine you can get through this chapter and still be hungry. But if so, you'll find more menus listed in our Nightlife chapter. It's not all chicken fingers, either. Several of our lounges offer fine cuisine, but their claim to fame is a mean martini or wine selection.

down and—while their favorite cocktail is being shaken—simply announce to the server, "I'll have the usual." Popular choices include the Mac Daddy (a gooey macaroni masterpiece with three gourmet cheeses, bacon, and red peppers—we often ask for it made with chicken), seafood-stuffed tilapia, and a sixteen-ounce KC strip rubbed with fresh cracked pepper, then flaméed in brandy sauce.

Live music plays nearly every night of the week in the Starlet Lounge, a tiny space between the dining room and bar area that's been known to become an ad hoc dance floor. Many Trio fans choose to sup on their small-plate favorites, such as the Blue Cheese Bistro (slices of grilled filet topped with melted cheese) or one of the popular pizzas, at a booth or table in the bar. For intimate parties, there's a private room in back; with artwork, deep-red walls, and drapes that can further separate you from the crowds, it seems like your very own Shangri-la.

Trio attracts a wide variety of patrons, and they're all welcome: the city's most stylish gay men, straight couples from the suburbs on their way to an arts performance downtown, young singles meeting friends right after work. Perhaps it's the roster of attractive servers that makes this look like the next version of *Friends*.

Owners Chris and Tai (Al, the third member of the trio, must be invisible) are almost always on hand to make sure your time here is memorable—right down to a selection of Christopher Elbow chocolates (see page 142) presented with the check. Be sure to get on the e-mail list for updates on art shows, discounts, and events. Women wearing out-

landish hats, for instance, have been rewarded with free dinners, and dads have dined on $15 steaks during Father's Day week. There's indoor parking just to the north of the entrance, but don't overindulge in martinis; it's a tight fit.

Classic Cup Cafe
(Country Club Plaza) $$
301 West 47th Street
(816) 753-1840
www.classiccup.com

This longtime Plaza favorite offers a running fashion show as bags tagged with Sak's Fifth Avenue, Gucci, and Halls pass by its row of tables on the sidewalk. Didn't get a front-row seat? Don't worry. There's a huge deck out back, and the inside tables have wall-to-wall windows plus a fireplace for coolish weather.

The food is good from any vantage point. Half the lunch crowd seems to be sighing over the spicy Thai pizza. Other top picks are the salads and pastas. If you're ravenous after all that power shopping, go for heartier fare such as the grilled tenderloin medallions with a creamy blue cheese sauce.

Dinners might start with gnocchi, Italian potato dumplings served in a tomato-basil or Gorgonzola-walnut sauce. Entrees continue the world tour with such specialties as grilled rack of lamb and roasted chicken. To accompany your meal there are forty wines by the glass as well as an 800-bottle wine cellar. You'll be glad you saved room for dessert once you taste the Classic Cup's legendary bread pudding with hot caramel sauce. If chocolate is more to your liking, the pot de crème is made with dark Belgian chocolate and espresso from Kansas City's own Roasterie coffee.

The Classic Cup is also one of those rare restaurants that offer gourmet breakfasts. Many a business meeting has taken place over its buttermilk griddlecakes, eggs Benedict, or biscuits and gravy. The breakfast menu is available weekdays and Saturday, and on Sunday the options increase during brunch with selections such as a Florentine ham frittata with layers of spinach, ham, and Jack cheese baked in a savory egg custard. The grits and grillades—grilled Italian sausage atop garlic cheese grits with red sauce—will make any Southerner feel at home. The Classic Cup is open seven days a week, and reservations are a good idea.

One more note: If you're in town when the Classic Cup offers a wine or beer tasting dinner in the wine cellar, we suggest you sign up. Along with good spirits and excellent food, experts from celebrated wineries or breweries will explain their craft. It's a wonderful evening, usually at a remarkably good price. The restaurant's Web site lists upcoming events.

EBT Restaurant $$–$$$$
1310 Carondelet
(I-435 and State Line, in the atrium of UMB Bank)
(816) 942-8870
www.ebtrestaurant.com

It's always fun to introduce someone new to EBT. First there's the location. The restaurant is on the ground floor of what may be the least-attractive bank in the region. But step inside its big cement edifice and you'll see why it's one of our picks for a romantic anniversary or first date.

The name comes from Emery, Bird, Thayer, our town's first department store, founded in 1863 at 11th and Grand. The grand store closed in the '60s, and decades later its gorgeous mezzanine tearoom was reborn as EBT Restaurant using such artifacts as the massive sandstone column capitals, exquisite chandeliers, and stained glass. But what really sets the room apart are the private dining booths in the ornate brass elevator cages.

A major makeover in 2006 created an environment to appeal to a younger crowd

I'll have the KC strip . . . and a hog, please. That's hog as in Harley-Davidson. It's just one of the perks of working at Grand Street Cafe, YiaYia's, or any other PB&J Restaurant—your very own motorcycle after fifteen years of employment.

without saying goodbye to its longtime fans. Rich colors and textures, along with enormous lighting fixtures that look as if they've been borrowed from a Moroccan palace, retain the right to call this the place for a special occasion.

Executive Chef Russ Muehlberger's menu is masterfully done during lunch and dinner. Dinners there have wowed us with coriander grilled lamb chops served with shallot marmalade glacé and sweet potato puree, and parmesan-breaded Chilean sea bass with pasta and an Alfredo sauce. The chef takes chicken on an Asian tour with a sweet chili glaze, jasmine rice, and grilled baby bok choy. Lunch is popular as well when executives conduct business over peppered beef tenderloin, Caesar salad, or blackened pork tenderloin sandwich. Owner Ed Holland (who also grows the roses you see throughout the room) has been known to flambé a mean Cherries Jubilee. General Manager Thomas Goerdel does double-duty as well; he's also the sommelier, so choosing from the vast wine menu is easy as punch.

EBT also caters to music lovers. The lounge offers live jazz Monday through Saturday and a delightful new small-plate menu that includes an artisan cheese plate, grilled shrimp with avocado salsa, and luscious smoked salmon and spinach dip—all for under $10. More hidden delights await in that big bank box: wine dinners and vodka tastings. Now *that's* rich!

40 Sardines $$–$$$
11942 Roe Avenue
Overland Park, KS
(913) 451-1040
www.40sardines.com

A world-class restaurant in back of a shopping center in Overland Park? Absolutely! That's because 40 Sardines has Debbie Gold as its chef and owner. She's half of the celebrated couple (with ex-husband Michael Smith) that rose to stardom as executive co-chefs of the American Restaurant, winning accolades and awards since 1994. Debbie trained with

Michelin-starred chefs in France, and she and Michael met in the kitchen of Charlie Trotter's in Chicago. They've hosted the Friends of James Beard Benefit at least five times—that's like taking home a quintet of Oscar statuettes—and helped put Kansas City on the culinary map. When Debbie and Michael left the American in 2001, fans prayed the team would remain in the city, and they did—shining the spotlight on a Johnson County suburb. In kitchens, as in life, things change, and the duo split in 2006. Thankfully, Debbie has remained at 40 Sardines, serving what she calls "contemporary American bistro" fare, influenced by the cuisine of countless countries where she has traveled or lived, including France, Italy, and Spain. Her desserts, especially the lemon meringue pie with candied kumquats, are not to be missed.

Sign up for special wine dinners and those that are love-fests to certain foods, such as heirloom tomatoes, along with cooking classes in the expanded back room. The small but stylish room includes a private dining room and communal table in front of the open kitchen. This premium spot is the hottest ticket in town—and we don't mean from the gas flames. We recommend calling well in advance for reservations. It will be a memorable meal, guaranteed. Lunch served weekdays; dinner, seven days a week.

Grand Street Cafe (Country Club Plaza) $$
4740 Grand
(816) 561-8000
www.eatpbj.com.com

This is the PB&J restaurant group's flagship place, designed with an exuberant floral-pattern wallpaper, handsome rattan chairs, and food that lives up to its slogan, "Dining so amazing, so refined, so memorable, they named a thousand-dollar bill after us." You'll agree with your first slurp of the potato, leek, and smoky bacon soup, a rib-sticking chowder so popular they sell a staggering ten gallons a day. But it's the double-cut pork chop that will cinch the deal. With executive chef Marc Valiani at the helm, it's always juicy and

> **i** Some of our top restaurants make happy hour positively giddy by offering hors d'oeuvres and cocktails for pocket change. Pierpont's serves around ten appetizers; Morton's, steak sandwiches; and McCormick & Schmick's, shrimp cocktails and burgers with fries for $1.95.

flavorful, and the stewed apples on the side are the perfect touch. We like to introduce guests to the dish and watch them try to finish the entire thing.

Like most other great Kansas City restaurants, the Grand does a fine filet of beef. But don't overlook the succulent seafood. The signature dessert is a chocolate ganache in phyllo pastry served with vanilla crème anglaise and raspberry puree.

During nice weather there's romantic alfresco dining on the deck overlooking the Plaza's meandering Brush Creek. The main dining room can get a bit crowded and noisy, but it's grand fun to dine at the bar and watch pasta getting saucy in the open kitchen. And the normally packed entrance and bar area overflow during happy hour when people queue up for flavored martinis and discounted appetizers. Things are more serene during Sunday brunch, a fine start to an afternoon at the Nelson-Atkins Museum of Art a few blocks away. Grand Street provides the whole package—food, service, and atmosphere—seven days a week.

Grand Street Cafe is open for lunch Monday through Saturday, dinner daily, and brunch on Sunday.

Jardine's Restaurant and Jazz Club
(Country Club Plaza) $–$$
4536 Main Street
(816) 561-6480
www.jardines4jazz.com

Live jazz seven nights a week and on Saturday afternoon may be the biggest pull for this cozy nightclub near the Country Club Plaza, but it serves some mighty fine food along with the tunes (see Nightlife for details). Chef

Antonio Gaytan's menu is a symphony of steaks, chops, and seafood, including a luscious peppercorn-crusted filet of beef with brandy cream sauce, fried catfish, and some inventive pasta dishes. Everything, including the salad dressings, is made in-house.

Lunch items are priced extremely well, with a nice selection of salads and sandwiches for around $7. But the best bargain is that there's no cover charge for evening performances. Dinner reservations are always a good idea and a must on weekends when popular stylist Angela Hagenbach or Ida McBeth is on stage.

JJ's (Country Club Plaza) $$
910 West 48th Street
(816) 561-7136
www.jjs-restaurant.com

In 1996 JJ's was one of only six restaurants worldwide to receive the Grand Award by *Wine Spectator* magazine. Although the list has grown to eighty-five, some say that Jimmy Frantze's intimate bistro still has no equal when it comes to ambience. Part of its charm is the location—a quiet tree-lined side street just west of the Plaza, hidden among apartment buildings and defined by its tile roof and deep-red awnings. By late afternoon the tables in the sunny bar start to fill with neighbors reading the paper over a glass of wine, catching up on gossip, or waiting until their favorite table is open.

Dinner is served through the arched doorway where white linen–topped tables and tall plants divide the open space. Exuberant paintings by local artist Mike Savage add color to the walls. There's colorful food as well, starting with Paco's Shrimp, a savory appetizer of jumbo shrimp stuffed with a horseradish sauce, deep fried, and served with a mustard sauce and red-pepper coulis.

The menu focuses on steaks, including a pan-seared filet medallion with a peppercorn and red wine cream sauce. Fish, pasta, chops, and chicken are available as well, all expertly done. The wait staff is friendly without hovering and well trained on which wines will per-

fectly complement your meal. JJ's is open for lunch on weekdays and for dinner seven days a week.

Joe D's Wine Bar-Cafe (Brookside) $$
6227 Brookside Plaza
(816) 333-6116
www.joeds.com

Lots of us discovered that not all wine comes in screw-top bottles at this cafe's previous incarnation, called the Monastery. The brown-robed, sandaled servers are long gone, but you might say the building stayed in the family: Good local Catholic boy and Notre Dame alumnus Joe DiGiovanni bought the place in 1986 and it has been packed ever since. Although Joe sold his namesake in 2006, it's still a winner.

The kitchen is in the talented hands of chef Devin Wilson, who prepares an amazingly diverse list of soups and salads, pastas, and entrees defined by fresh seafood, steaks, and chops. By all means peruse the menu, but don't miss the long list of daily specials printed on a chalkboard. Recent entries included shrimp and artichoke hearts in a lemon basil cream sauce over pasta, duck enchiladas, and mixed grill of Denver elk and veal tenderloin served with a gin and raspberry demi-glace. Devin, you are a genius.

The place to be from mid-May until late fall is the patio, where Brookside neighbors congregate and others stop by with cones of Foo's frozen treats from down the street. Get there early for a ringside seat, as these tables are first-come, first-served. Reservations, however, are taken for the inside rooms. And instead of coveting that ice-cream cone, order the famous bread pudding with chocolate and caramel sauces and see who's jealous now.

Joe D's is open for lunch Monday through Friday and dinner Monday through Saturday, with brunch on Sunday.

M&S Grill $-$$
4646 JC Nichols Parkway
(816) 531-7799
www.mandsgrill.com

Kansas City Originals

As in all *Insiders' Guides*, we try to focus on local flavor, whether in shopping destinations, coffee shops, bookstores, or restaurants. It's not that there aren't some fine national chains in town; it's just that we like to celebrate the independent owners and chefs who are driven by a desire to offer something unique and homegrown.

In Kansas City we're lucky to have Kansas City Originals, an organization that supports the cause of restaurants with one or two locations. At this writing, thirty-one individual dining spots make up the roster, with more coming on board every year.

You'll find a terrific online directory on the organization's Web site (www.kcoriginals.com) with links to individual restaurant sites that include menus, directions, and hours. And be sure to sign up for a KC Originals PowerCard. This free frequent-diner card accumulates points every time you dine at one of the member establishments; 150 points gets you a $10 gift certificate for your next meal. Join at any of the members' locations or online.

So here you go: a different restaurant for every day of the month. And then, of course, you'll have to start over because menus will have changed. You'll find many of these restaurants elsewhere in this chapter, but the entire Kansas City Originals roster is worth repeating. All addresses are in Kansas City, Missouri, unless otherwise stated.

Aixois
2501 East 55th Street
(816) 333-3305
www.aixois.com

The American Restaurant
2450 Grand Boulevard
(816) 545-8001
www.theamericanrestaurant.com

Bar Natasha
1919 Main Street
(816) 472-5300
www.barnatasha.com

Cafe des Amis
112½ Main Street
Parkville, MO
(816) 587-6767
www.cafedesamiskc.com

Cafe Maison
408 East 63rd Street
(816) 523-3400
www.cafemaisonkc.com

Cafe Sebastienne
Kemper Museum of Contemporary Art
4420 Warwick Boulevard
(816) 561-7740
www.kemperart.org/cafe

Cafe Trio
3535 Broadway
(816) 756-3227
www.cafetriokc.com

Cafe Verona
206 West Lexington
Independence, MO
(816) 833-0044

City Tavern
101 West 22nd Street
(816) 421-3696
www.citytavern.net

Coach's Bar and Grill (two locations)
414 West 103rd Street
(816) 941-2286

14893 Metcalf Avenue
Overland Park, Kansas
(913) 897-7070

40 Sardines
11942 Roe Avenue
Overland Park, KS
(913) 451-1040
www.40sardines.com

Garozzo's (four locations)
www.garozzos.com
528 Harrison
(816) 221-2455

9950 College Boulevard
Overland Park, KS
(913) 491-8300

1547 NE Rice Road
Lee's Summit, MO
(816) 554-2800

13505 South Mur-Len Road
Olathe, KS
(913) 764-6969

Harry's Country Club
112 Missouri Avenue
(816) 421-3505
www.harryscountryclub.com

Hereford House (four locations)
www.herefordhouse.com
2 East 20th Street
(816) 842-1080

5001 Town Center Drive
Leawood, KS
(913) 327-0800

19721 East Jackson Drive
Independence, MO
(816) 795-9200

8661 North Stoddard Avenue
Zona Rosa Shopping Center
(816) 584-9000

Jardine's Restaurant and Jazz Club
4536 Main Street
(816) 561-6480
www.jardines4jazz.com

JJ's
910 West 48th Street
(816) 561-7136
www.jjs-restaurant.com

Joe D's Wine Bar–Cafe
6227 Brookside Plaza
(816) 333-6116
www.joeds.com

Kokopelli Mexican Cantina
5200 West 95th Street
Prairie Village, KS
(913) 385-0300
www.kokopellimexicancantina.com

Le Fou Frog French Bistro
400 East 5th Street
(816) 474-6060
www.lefoufrog.com

The Majestic Steak House
931 Broadway
(816) 471-8484
www.majesticsteakhouse.com

The Mango Room
1111 Main Street
(816) 268-4600
www.kcmangoroom.com

Marina Grog & Galley
22 A Street, Gate 1 at Water's Edge
Lake Lotawana, MO
(816) 578-5511
www.marinagrogandgalley.com

MelBee's
6120 Johnson Drive
Mission, KS
(913) 262-6121
www.melbees.com

continued

Close-up

Ophelia's Restaurant
201 North Main Street
Independence, MO
(816) 461-4525
www.opheliasind.com

Pierpont's
Union Station
30 West Pershing Road
(816) 221-5111
www.pierponts.com

Piropos at Briarcliff Village
4141 North Mulberry Drive
(816) 741-3600
www.piroposkc.com

The Raphael
325 Ward Parkway
Raphael Hotel
(816) 756-3800
www.raphaelkc.com

The Shields Manor Bistro
121 Main Street
Platte City, MO
(816) 858-5557
www.shieldsmanorbistro.com

Starker's Restaurant
201 West 47th Street
(816) 753-3565
www.starkersreserve.com

Tatsu's French Restaurant
4603 West 90th Street
Prairie Village, KS
(913) 383-9801
www.tatsus.com

Webster House
1644 Wyandotte
Webster House Antiques
(816) 221-4713
www.websterhouse.com

Think about your favorite dinner at home—real comfort food, such as meatloaf and pot roast with rich brown gravy. If Mom's no longer interested in turning on the oven for you, head to M&S Grill for these classics along with dishes that are way out of your mama's league.

Of course the food and ambience are terrific; they're by the team that brought you McCormick & Schmick's (see separate listing), one of the city's premier seafood emporiums. M&S is a bit more laid-back but the bar area is just as bustling come happy hour when the barkeeps are slinging cocktails featuring fresh-squeezed juices, and a juicy cheeseburger or crisp calamari will set you back only $1.95. The din is high-decibel to match the energy of the mostly young, single crowd.

If you're here to dine, you're also in luck. The dry-aged steaks are from L&C Meat Com-

pany, locally owned and operated since 1948. The menu proclaims the T-bone the "greatest steak in the world," and with it in weighing a hefty twenty-four-ounces, we'll have to take their word for it. We'll go for the pecan-crusted catfish or that pot roast, complete with mashed potatoes and green beans. Regulars opt for the crab "tater tots," little morsels of heaven, complete with jalapeño tartar sauce. But save room for a generous slice of that Southern specialty, red velvet cake with cream cheese frosting.

MelBee's Bar & Restaurant $$–$$$
6120 Johnson Drive
Mission, KS
(913) 262-6121
This little gem looks like it was plucked from a trendy Chicago neighborhood and plopped into a block of retail shops on busy (and

frankly, boring) Johnson Drive. Inside is one of Kansas City's sexiest spaces, with low lights, a curvy bar where the martinis are top drawer, live piano music nightly, white linen–draped tables, and an ever-changing art display. The food presentation is just as sexy: Instead of huge portions, entrees are served like jewelry on small plates with glistening sauces done in dots and swirls. It's an elegant, quality versus quantity way to dine.

We suggest each diner choose one or two entrees from the list of thirty or so cold and warm selections and then share. Favorite entrees include the sumptuous wild mushroom potpie (just the cognac-kissed aroma under that puffed pastry will make you swoon) and the sautéed halibut with mango Thai chilies, a lovely composition in red and gold. Or opt for the prix fixe dinner and choose from four or five selections to enjoy with a cocktail or glass of wine. Service is poised and friendly at MelBee's, and the clientele is a sophisticated mix of straight couples and gays.

Lunch is also special here, with a variety of soups, salads, and sandwiches. The Mel-Bee Club, made with chicken breast, prosciutto, Havarti, and smoked tomato aioli, is terrific, especially when crisp, bronze sweet potato fries share the plate.

Michael Smith $$–$$$
1900 Main Street
(816) 842-2202
www.michaelsmithkc.com

Frankly, we'd follow Michael anywhere. He first came on the Kansas City scene in 1994 as half of a talented team with then-wife Debbie Gold that wowed guests at the American Restaurant. This attractive couple—she's a pretty blonde, he's sexy in that pulled-back-ponytail kind of way—were our very own celebrity chefs for all the years they ruled at the city's most elegant digs. The duo launched the annual James Beard Foundation dinners right here, coaxing some of the country's top chefs to participate, and in 1999 he shared the James Beard Best Chef

in the Midwest award with Debbie, a first for Kansas City.

Then, bam! In 2002 they left the cozy confines of the American to open their own place and stunned the entire town when they chose a Johnson County address for 40 Sardines. They made history again by actually drawing a crowd to this urban vibe in the suburbs with their signature comfort food. Cooking lessons and wine dinners followed when they opened an event space in the back.

But it seems these two can't keep out of the news. Their breakup rocked the foodie world again in 2006. Relief came when we learned Debbie would continue at 40 Sardines (see separate write-up) and Michael would open his own self-named place in the Crossroads where the late, great Zin used to reside. Not only that, but he'd take over the popular art space next door, Blue Gallery, to open a more casual tapas joint called Extra Virgin.

Michael has warmed up Zin's rather austere environment and replaced the low-slung banquettes in the bar with cafe tables. Even the color scheme, created by local designer Eric Negrete, sounds good enough to eat: chocolate brown, olive green, and cream. Sheer draperies on the wall-to-wall windows will add a cozier feel but take away a bit of the "I have a table and you don't" status on First Fridays (see page 221) when reservations are as hard to come by as truffles in July.

Michael continues his focus on Mediterranean fare: a little Spanish, a soupçon of French, a dash of Italian. His sides are never an afterthought; they are perfectly suited to the main dish. Tender braised rabbit is served with gnocchi, morels, and persillade; a Spanish serrano ham salad comes with avocado, frisee, and aged sherry vinegar and olive oil dressing; slow roasted pork is joined by a scallion risotto, blistered tomatoes, and marinated goat cheese.

The restaurant will open for lunch as well; good news for a neighborhood that continues to grow as a daytime shopping destination.

Next door, Michael's Extra Virgin is a more casual venue with small plates and decor that reflects the happy colors, aromas, and tastes from Spain and Italy—burnt sienna, saffron, and red—with braised meats and fresh pastas. An open kitchen, wood-fired oven, good-sized bar, and patio out front will be a decided pull.

Ophelia's $$
201 North Main
Independence, MO
(816) 461-4525
www.ophelias.net

When Ken and Cindy McClain turned this boarded-up space into a hip, urban restaurant and inn, they gave after-hours life to historic Independence Square. The American regional cooking with European flair is as artfully done as Cindy's paintings on the walls. Favorites include his brandy-laced crab soup and roasted rack of lamb. And at just under $18 the salmon and jumbo sea scallops in a saffron white wine beurre blanc isn't just a culinary standout, it's a bargain.

Lunch is casual with a kick, such as chicken salad with port wine apples and candied walnuts and a smoked pork sandwich with pickled red cabbage. A low-fat spa menu is also available for lunch and dinner, a thoughtful touch for guests staying at the inn upstairs. Lunch and dinner are served every day but Monday, and brunch is available on Sunday. On Friday and Saturday evenings there's live jazz in the bar; the large open space makes it easy to listen and still enjoy a conversation.

To turn a delightful evening into a good night, reserve a room at the inn, where Cindy has worked her creative magic with seven rooms and one luxurious suite. See Accommodations for more information.

Pachamama's $$–$$$
800 New Hampshire
Lawrence, KS
(785) 841-0990
www.pachamamas.com

When this handsome restaurant opened a few years ago, it gave us a reason *besides* University of Kansas basketball to drive thirty minutes to this college town. Pachamama's food is distinctive and the atmosphere is romantic. Lush greenery creates a rainforest effect, a visual reference to the restaurant's Incan name, which means Mother Earth.

That's where the maternal theme ends: Mom never cooked like this. Chef/owner Ken Baker's menu takes us around the world with stops in Asia, India, Mexico, and Italy. A roasted portobello and carrot tower, for example, is enhanced with a ginger-soy-mirin essence; spaghetti verde brings together roasted poblano chiles, tomatillo, and cilantro crema; and a rolled pork loin is cured in a maple-red chile rub and served with wild rice pilaf and balsamic wild cherry sauce. If the Tahitian vanilla bean crème brûlée is on the dessert list, order two. It's too good to share.

Dinner here is always exciting but even more so during a wine-tasting dinner or cooking class events. Call or check the Web site for details and dates. Pachamama's is open for lunch Tuesday through Saturday and dinner Tuesday through Sunday.

Peppercorn Duck Club
(Crown Center) $$–$$$
2345 McGee
(816) 435-4199
www.hyattkc.com/pcdc

The folks at Hyatt Regency somehow missed the memo that said hotel restaurants must be mediocre. Even after two decades the Peppercorn is *still* one of the best places to seal a business deal or pop the question. Any celebration is more special with a trip to the over-the-top Ultra Chocolatta dessert bar. Before you say "no thanks," just remember this chocolate-lover's paradise is complimentary. And didn't your mother tell you it's impolite to refuse a gift?

As befitting its name, duck in all its crisp and succulent glory reigns supreme on the menu, fresh from one of the rotisseries on view. The duck strudel—prepared with portobello mushrooms, Boursin cheese, and a truffle demi-glace—is particularly delicious. Other popular choices include barbecued shrimp in a spicy sauce that calls for extra napkins, and game including pheasant, venison, and bison. You can indulge for lunch on Thursday and Friday and dinner Monday through Saturday. Service is as smooth as you would expect in a venue this plush. There's more royal treatment: a matchbox printed with your name and a rose presented to each lady. And be sure to leave something on your plate: Leftovers arrive in duck-shaped aluminum foil packages.

Phillips ChopHouse
Hotel Phillips $$$–$$$$
106 West 12th Street
(816) 221-9292
www.hotelphillips.com

A gorgeous space with rich carved oak and marble appointments, impeccable service including tableside flambéed desserts, and a sophisticated menu . . . what more could you want? Perhaps a luxurious hotel room upstairs? You've got it! In fact, the ChopHouse is one of those rare finds—a hotel restaurant you'll want to visit even if you're not staying the night.

Especially since rock star–looking chef Marshall Roth is in the house, true foodies will appreciate the presentation as much as the well-executed food. His culinary surprises will keep you talking for days. Balsamic-marinated cipollini risotto accompanies the cedar-planked salmon, and seafood cassoulet—starring house-made seafood sausage— complements a meltingly tender pan-roasted monkfish. The steak choices are always top notch, too.

If the gourmets are satisfied, wine aficionados will be beside themselves here; the glasses are Riedel, a fitting tribute to a fine wine selection and a wait staff, led by award-winning sommelier Kathi Rohlfing, knowledgeable enough to suggest stellar vintages. Wine dinners here are remarkable. Just save room for the bananas Foster, flamed at your table. You could also ignite your own flame upstairs

(see Accommodations).

Lunch service is smooth as well, if you can get past the fact that the attractive lady at the next table is the ex-mayor. Here's where Kansas City's movers and shakers seal deals, pitch ideas, and celebrate new business. Or sometimes they just come to enjoy good food, such as the duck spring rolls or BLT with seared diver scallops nestled among the smoked bacon and tarragon aioli on sourdough.

Pierpont's (Crown Center) $$
Union Station, Pershing and Grand
(816) 221-5111
www.herefordhouse.com

When Union Station opened in 1914, even the women's and children's lounges were grand affairs, with marble stonework and ornate oak leaf plaster. In 1999 Rod Anderson, owner of the Hereford House, turned these rooms into one of the city's most glamorous restaurants. The bar is particularly stunning with its dark woods, richly detailed high plaster ceilings, and mirrored liquor shelves that bartenders reach by climbing a fourteen-step rolling ladder. It gives a whole new meaning to "I'll take that straight up."

Named "best place to entertain out-of-town guests" by the local press, Pierpont's is also a top choice for small groups thanks to its swanky private Wine Cellar dining rooms. Close the French doors and you'll have the space to yourselves. Larger banquet rooms overlook the grand dining space below. Although the restaurant has a sophisticated feeling, it also attracts casually dressed clientele during happy hour when a variety of appetizers—including hamburgers, calamari, and skewered chicken—are available for less than two bucks. It's a terrific light meal before heading to one of the theater venues within Union Station.

But we suggest you reserve a dark, cozy booth and stay for dinner. This is part of the Hereford House group, remember, so the steaks are superb. Pierpont's is also known for its fresh seafood, and the duck is fabulous, spit roasted and served with a raspberry-hoisin sauce that suits the rich duck meat. But for rich, you can't get more decadent than the macaroni and lobster casserole made with shiitake mushrooms, fresh asparagus, and smoked Gouda cheese sauce.

Rod has made a commitment to his wine cellar, with more than 300 labels on the menu and 3,000 more stored below. It makes for a terrific wine tasting dinner. Reservations are necessary for these monthly events and highly recommended for lunch and dinner, served seven days a week.

Raphael Restaurant
(Country Club Plaza) $$
325 Ward Parkway
(816) 756-3800
www.raphaelkc.com

For decades, patrons have referred to the Raphael as the most romantic restaurant in town. It could be the piano music coming from the lounge, the dark paneling with smoked glass and mirrors, the private booths, or the food that can make even the toughest customer starry-eyed. Or it could be that, unlike so many other bistros in town, you can actually hear your partner's sweet nothings whispered from across the table.

Adding to its lovey-dovey ambience is the fact that the Raphael Hotel's lobby is just a few steps away. In fact the restaurant has served as preamble to many an amorous evening, and the staff has contributed to marriage proposals by hiding ring boxes under dinner domes or inside bouquets of roses.

Although the restaurant's atmosphere and service say Old World, chef Peter Hahn keeps the menu fresh with items borrowed from Asian, French, Italian, and even Southwest cuisines. Appetizers, for example, include grilled sea scallops with papaya and an orange-cilantro sauce and prosciutto-grilled pears with a Gorgonzola-walnut relish and port wine glaze. Even the spinach salad is special here, enlivened with smoked salmon bacon and a lemon-horseradish dressing.

The entrees change weekly to take advantage of the season's bounty. Past menus have included bison rib-eye steak rubbed with chili oil then grilled to medium rare and served with roasted corn-poblano mashed potatoes. A delightful veal scaloppini is stacked with pancetta, fried tomatoes, and Stilton cheese; and vegetarians can be very happy with the eggplant Parmesan. Entree descriptions include wine suggestions from the Raphael's extensive list. Desserts include a macaroon nut tart that would be lovely with a cream sherry . . . or there's always that chocolate waiting on your pillow upstairs.

Lunch and dinner are served Monday through Saturday. Breakfast is served daily.

Room 39 $–$$
1719 West 39th Street
(816) 753-3933
Room 39 Mission Farms
10561 Mission Road
(913) 648-7639
www.rm39.com

With walls painted mustard-yellow and tomato-soup red and a scattering of cute chairs, this tiny eatery looks like your mother's kitchen, but trust us—Mama doesn't cook like this. The owners, Ted Habiger and Andy Sloan, are pretty darn cute, too. And smart. They quietly opened their space for breakfast and lunch, then waited for fans of their comfort-food-with-a-kick to beg them to serve dinner as well.

The beauty of Room 39's food is its take on simple fare: lunch could be a pork loin sandwich, but it's jazzed up with caramelized onions; chicken livers (maybe Mom *is* in the kitchen after all) are served on toasted focaccia with brandy butter, oyster mushrooms, and an arugula salad. Fresh-squeezed lemonade, coming up.

Dinner is more upscale, but don't worry; there are still no white linen tablecloths or prices to match. Any given night might offer only six entrees, but the wide variety will make everyone happy. Braised pork belly so tender you could cry, softshell crabs, paella, and a beef tenderloin with toasted brioche, foie gras, and truffled demi-glace.

Good luck getting a table in the morning, when there's often a wait to lay claim to the best brioche French toast around. The Spanish-style omelet served with hash browns and toast will set you back a mere eight bucks, and steak and eggs (served only on Saturdays) just north of $10. Room 39's coffee is legendary as well; it serves Danesi espresso, Italy's beloved brew. Have your caffeine in your dessert instead, perhaps, with an affogato (espresso poured over vanilla ice cream) or indulge in a tender lavender panna cotta.

Fans of Room 39 who live out south were thrilled when the owners opened a second location at the very ritzy Mission Farms in summer 2007. But this time they know they have a winner, so the dining room is open for lunch and dinner seven days a week, with brunch on Saturday and Sunday. The decor may be a little more refined, but don't worry; the food retains the same quality.

Rozzelle Court (Country Club Plaza) $
4525 Oak Street
(816) 751-1279
www.nelson-atkins.org

Perhaps it's the setting that compels us to place this cafeteria-style eatery in the same category as the most lauded, and often luxurious, restaurants in town. The space is a trip to Tuscany with carved stone, a ring of arched openings in the balcony above, a gurgling fountain, and the golden glow from skylights three stories above. And where else can you fold your napkin, stand up, and say, "Now where do you suppose they keep the Rembrandt?"

Frankly, once you've tasted the food you won't mind pushing a brown plastic tray through the line. You might think artists have arranged the salads here, especially the grilled salmon on spring greens dressed with balsamic vinaigrette. The soup of the day never fails to impress, whether it's curried chicken or rich seafood bisque. Desserts are always delectable as well, ranging from Key lime pie to almond cheesecake.

An On the Town Passport Unlimited card (888-273-6392; www.passport unlimited.com) gets you a free entree when you pay for one of equal or higher value. The roster includes around 36 places ranging from brewpubs to fine dining, and you could easily recoup the $87 annual membership fee over a long weekend in town.

Lunch is served Tuesday through Sunday (the museum is closed Monday), and the live music that accompanies Friday dinners turns this enchanting room into one of the most popular in town. Admission to the museum is free, and the food is reasonably priced. Now *that's* art. Read more about the Nelson-Atkins Museum of Art in the Close-up in the Arts chapter.

Savoy Grill (Downtown) $$$
219 West Ninth Street
(816) 842-3890
www.savoygrill.net

As the city's oldest restaurant, there simply isn't another place in town so imbued with history, romance, and gentility. If those accolades sound dated, so be it. The deeply carved wood paneling, stained glass, and cushy dark booths certainly worked for Harry S. Truman, who was such a regular customer they named Booth No. 4 in his honor.

While you're contemplating your order, take note of the surroundings, which haven't changed much since 1903. The lanterns were once gaslights, and the twelve murals were painted by Edward Holslag to depict the pioneers' arduous trek on the Santa Fe Trail. The first mural near the entrance shows steamboats arriving at the Missouri River levee with limestone bluffs in the background—what would become downtown Kansas City.

But the Savoy didn't make or keep its reputation with artwork alone. Perfectly grilled steaks and steamed lobsters are the mainstays here, and dinner might start brilliantly with steamed mussels brought to the table in a big tin bucket. Owner Don Lee and white-jacketed waiters providing impeccable service will make sure your meal is perfection. Take your time; after all, it took a scene in *Mr. and Mrs. Bridge* fourteen hours to film here.

Reservations are a must for both lunch and dinner. Lunch is available Monday through Saturday, dinner seven days a week. And here's good news for theatergoers and night owls: Dinner is available until midnight on Friday and Saturday.

Skies (Crown Center) $$-$$$
2345 McGee
(816) 435-4199
www.crowncenterhyatt.com

Breathtaking panoramic views of the skyline are on the menu at this revolving restaurant on the forty-second floor of the Hyatt Regency. In fact, with seventy-two windows and twenty-three color murals gracing the walls, you're surrounded by the sights of Kansas City wherever you look. There's no chance of getting dizzy, however; the rotation is so smooth you may not notice it until the red neon Western Auto sign is out of sight.

Although the menu offers nothing revolutionary (sorry, we couldn't resist) the mesquite-grilled steaks are expertly prepared. Other choices include tender steamed crab legs and a mixed grill of fish, chicken, and beef. For dessert, bid farewell to your diet and go for the Sky High Pie, three layers of homemade ice cream on a graham cracker crust. Or head to the lounge for an after-dinner drink and tell the bartender, "One more trip around the city, please." Skies is open for lunch on weekdays, cocktails and dinner seven days a week, and brunch on Sunday.

Starker's Reserve
(Country Club Plaza) $$$
201 West 47th Street
(816) 753-3565
www.starkersreserve.com

This Kansas City gem provides everything fine dining should be: beautifully prepared food served with Old World style in a gorgeous setting. Cliff Bath also founded Harry Starker's around the corner, a much-loved restaurant named for a gregarious fifteenth-century British gourmand. Harry, it was said, often indulged in whiskey and wine before engaging in naked public jaunts, hence the phrase "stark naked." Starker's, alas, served its last meal in 1996. But by then the elegant Mr. Bath had opened the current space as a private restaurant.

Today Starker's Reserve is open to public dining as well, making it one of the most coveted reservations in town. Now that chef John McClure is also the owner, it's better than ever. The surroundings are exquisite, with country French furnishings, lovely second-story views of the Plaza, and chandeliers crafted of wine bottles that reflect color and light around the room. Dinners here are long, leisurely affairs featuring contemporary cuisine and the freshest ingredients. A winter menu could start with butternut squash–leek soup with bacon and chives or pan-seared shrimp dumplings with lobster broth and crème fraîche. Maroon-colored roasted baby beets enliven a watercress and goat cheese salad with spiced pecans and Pommerey mustard vinaigrette.

Entree specialties include rack of lamb served with sundried tomato and porcini risotto sauced with a mint demi-glace, and a potato-wrapped salmon so moist its dill-flavored buerre blanc sauce might go untouched. Are you sighing yet? Perhaps the chocolate truffle mousse will send you over the edge. And it gets better: Starker's wine cellar is stunning. It was the first Missouri restaurant to earn a Grand Award from *Wine Spectator*. It remains on the esteemed list today. Reservations are a must here, and although casual attire is welcome, Starker's is worth dressing for. Hear that, Harry?

Starker's Reserve serves dinner Monday through Saturday, and John, bless his heart, now serves lunch from 11:30 a.m. to 2:00 p.m. Monday through Friday.

Yahooz $$
4701 Town Center Drive
Leawood, KS
(913) 451-8888
www.eatpbj.com

We wouldn't steer you wrong; don't let the cowboy-like decor (think spurs, lots of tooled leather, and rawhide 'round the lamps) keep you away from this place. It is, after all, part of the PB&J group, which owns Grand Street Cafe and YiaYia's, so you couldn't get a bad meal here if you tried.

Hefty steaks, naturally, are on the menu, but other items might tempt you as well. Yahooz makes the most of locally raised products, including pork from Alma Farms and free-range chickens from regional farms. The dishes are always expertly prepared and served with great sides, such as cheddar scalloped potatoes. You'll want to eat every bite, so make sure you don't fill up on the cast-iron skillet of warm corn bread with honey butter before dinner.

Kids will love the place thanks to its giddyap look, comic books, and special menu with corn dogs, cheeseburgers, and peanut butter and jelly sandwiches. And the wait staff seem to be selected for their aptitude in making children feel special. One server offered to whip up some applesauce from scratch when a young diner requested the nonmenu item.

Yahooz is open for lunch Monday through Saturday and dinner every night and rustles up a Sunday brunch fit for a hardworking cowboy. Along with carved ham and roast beef, the buffet offers made-to-order omelets, smoked salmon, an egg-cheese-and-sausage casserole, fresh fruits, breakfast pastries, and desserts. Reservations are recommended, especially on weekends. Watch for their famous wine dinners.

YiaYia's Eurobistro $$
4701 West 119th Street
Overland Park, KS
(913) 345-1111
www.eatpbj.com

The PB&J group went all out in designing this striking decor with limestone walls, slate floors, and a lodgelike ambience. The menu is heartwarming too, with appetizers such as wild mushroom ragout over creamy polenta. We've noticed people trying hard not to pick up the shallow bowl to slurp every last bit; thank goodness the servers provide crusty sourdough bread for that task.

The menu offers flavorful choices for lunch and dinner including a grilled salmon salad and tasty oak-fired gourmet pizzas. The linguini with shrimp, spinach, and oven-dried tomatoes in a rich brown butter sage broth is one of the best pasta dishes in the city, and the sautéed sea bass with rock shrimp and fennel risotto is a work of art. No wonder the servers seem proud to bring the custom-designed charcoal-and-white plates to your table.

The nightly specials—typically grilled fish, pasta, and pizza—are always winners. As a nice touch they offer the pasta servings in two sizes; order a half portion and you'll still be amazed at the number of noodles placed in front of you. Half of Johnson County must have Styrofoam boxes in their fridges marked with "YY" and the date. But the double-cut pork chop is so savory you'll want to eat every morsel in one sitting. Ditto for the grilled beef tenderloin with a black pepper and Gorgonzola-Chianti sauce served with marinated vegetable kabobs and mashed potatoes.

The desserts are fine as well. Order the crème brûlée and you'll get a trio of tiny pots: chocolate, raspberry, and a classic version. It's the perfect way to share a dessert with the rest of the table. You'll see plenty of families and large groups dining here, but you can still find a romantic booth in a corner. On a balmy evening, a table on the plant-lined patio is worth requesting. Lunch is served Monday through Saturday, and dinner is available every night. A brunch menu is offered on Sundays.

Webster House Restaurant
(Downtown/Crossroads) $–$$$
1644 Wyandotte
(816) 221-4713
www.websterhousekc.com

In this beautifully renovated schoolhouse-turned-antiques shop, it's the dining rooms that go to the head of the class. Whether you're seated in the red room, sunny market, or New York–style library, this is a popular place for the ladies who lunch, folks who work downtown, and shoppers who have discovered the nearby stores in the Crossroads Arts District.

Chef Charles D'Ablaing keeps the mix fresh with a menu that changes daily, but with any luck the list will offer the goat cheese soufflé—a tender mound of baked cheese served with greens and sliced fruits of the season. Add one of the desserts, such as the just-tart-enough lemon bar, and it's a lovely way to spend an afternoon before searching the rooms for stunning eighteenth- and nineteenth-century European and American antiques and unique giftware (see write-up in Shopping).

This is also one of high society's favorite spots for special events such as wedding receptions and parties. The galleries filled with antiques make a stunning background for brunch, luncheons, and after-hours soirees. The culinary team can create an elegant repast specifically for your needs, or you may choose from one of Webster House's private-dining menus. For special occasions the antique school bell may be rung in honor of the celebration. For us, the Webster's roast rack of lamb with walnut crust and pear-bourbon sauce is a bell-ringer!

ASIAN

Saigon 39 (Midtown) $
1806 ½ West 39th Street
(816) 531-4447

This family-owned Vietnamese cafe is often voted the best in Kansas City thanks to its award-winning dishes. Stir-fried dishes are very popular, and the spicy pineapple soup is a unique taste sensation you could easily learn to love. Think you can take the heat of the kitchen? Better watch how you order your dishes—mild, medium, or hot—because the cooks will comply. An extra-spicy version of the crabmeat-and-squid soup has become an ad hoc prescription during cold and flu season; it's guaranteed to knock the germs right out of you.

Other soups, as well as stir-fries, can be customized with combinations of meat and fish or served vegetarian style. Order a side of their ethereal spring rolls and you have a fine meal. Bring cash—nothing else is accepted—and call ahead because Saigon 39 is open on a limited and ever-changing schedule. But their curry dishes alone are definitely worth a phone call.

Thai Place $-$$
9359 West 87th Street
Overland Park, KS
(913) 649-5420

11838 Quivira
Overland Park, KS
(913) 451-THAI (8424)

Interstate 29 and Northwest 64th Street
(816) 584-THAI (8424)

4130 Pennsylvania (Westport)
(816) 753-THAI (8424)

100 East Seventh Street
(Arun Thai Place Grill)
(816) 472-THAI (8424)
www.kcthaiplace.com

There may be no other cuisine as marvelously diverse and intricate as Thai, and Ann Liberda does it to a "T." Since opening her first Thai Place in Overland Park, she and her son, Ted, have introduced Kansas Citians to unusual sauces that include everything from slightly sweet coconut milk and refreshing basil and lemongrass, to a head-exploding concoction flecked with slivers of bright red peppers we've nicknamed "hurt me." It's all delicious, as long as you understand that hot and spicy means just that.

Although it's fun to experiment with new dishes (huge servings make it easy to share), you can't go wrong with the popular seafood *phad Thai*, a delightful marriage of sweet, salty, and spicy flavors made with rice noo-dles, shrimp, mussels, squid, and crabmeat in a fermented fish sauce called *nam pla*. We've decided that most of the menu sounds like a teenager who just came home with a pierced tongue. Just point and smile, and let your friendly server do the rest.

Large groups might want to try a variety of appetizers, such as the fried mussels, four huge garlic tempura-battered fritters served over stir-fried bean sprouts; cordovan-colored pork ribs; and delicate, translucent spring rolls fat with grilled chicken, cilantro, and carrot shreds. Entrees include Chilean sea bass, and a ginger-laced Duck Paradise in a rich brown sauce alongside fried rice studded with roasted cashews and pineapple instead of peas and carrots. The curry dishes are particu-larly lush blends of sweet and savory flavors.

The location at Seventh and Walnut is a boon to city workers hungry for more than a burger at lunch. Service is quick, the food superb, and free parking across the street a real bonus.

BAKERIES, DELIS, AND DESSERTS

Andre's Confiserie Suisse (Midtown) $
5018 Main Street
(816) 561-3440
www.andreschocolates.com

This combination European-style tea shop, bakery, and candy store is wildly popular with ladies who lunch, midtown office workers, and even men who do eat quiche. In fact, the only way to sample the elegant food is to get here before 11:15 a.m. or after 1:30 p.m. because Andre's doesn't take reservations and there's always a crowd. No matter. People will gladly wait in line for the prix fixe lunch, which includes a choice of two specials such as goulash or vol-au-vent, plus a fresh-baked roll, choice of confection from the dessert tray, and beverage for less than $11. A quiche or two always appears on the menu as well. All the desserts are incredible, but the Linzer torte is simply to die for.

Marcel Bollier, son of the late founder, Andre Bollier, runs the tiny place, and his mother, Elsbeth, oversees the ever-changing menu. Together they make sure Andre's famous quality continues. Before you leave the shop—and you can bet someone in line hopes you will—stop by the cases of exqui-site handmade chocolates and desserts. The artistry of the truffles and chocolate boxes filled with confections is superb. Out of town fans can order from the Web site.

Andre's is open for lunch Tuesday through Saturday.

d'Bronx Deli $
3904 Bell
(816) 531-0550

2450 Grand Avenue (Crown Center)
(816) 842-2211
www.dbronx.com

This cheerful, bustling New York–style deli serves massive sandwiches but perhaps is most beloved for its thin-crust pizza piled nearly 2 inches high with toppings. Its 30-inch version is a party in a box whether you're tak-ing it home for a night in front of the tube, back to the office for lunch, or sneaking it past the hotel's front desk. But the best part is eating in because of the never-ending stream of people. You'll see suited business execs, construction crews, moms with hungry kids, and starving artists. This place is the great equalizer because no matter what your background, everyone faces the same dilemma: What sand-wich should I order today? There are fifty on the menu, but here's a hint: The Italian meat-ball is hard to beat. Or try a house specialty, such as the Wild Bill, which is salami, pro-volone, coleslaw, and spicy mustard and horse-radish on rye. Let's rodeo!

And while you're waiting for your food, don't be surprised if a television crew shows up. d'Bronx has been featured on Food TV's *The Best Of,* a program that spans the nation looking for top eateries. And just in case you doubt the name's authenticity, d'Bronx own-ers Janet and Robert Bloom are originally from that famous neighborhood. More important, they beat out plenty of famous New York addresses to be named one of the six top delis in the country.

The deli is open seven days a week. Now that they opened a second location, in Crown Center, there's even more to love.

Foo's Fabulous Frozen Custard (Brookside) $
6235 Brookside Plaza
(816) 523-2520

3832 West 95th Street
Leawood, KS
(913) 383-3667
www.foosfabulousfrozencustard.com
What could be better on a sultry night than sharing a Sticky Hickey? Especially when the treat is actually a concrete—a richer, denser version of ice cream mixed with marshmallow, caramel, and chocolate chips. Foo's is fun anytime of year but especially when you slurp your cup, cone, or sundae as you window-shop the beautiful Brookside neighborhood. You can choose from dozens of ingredients to mix with your frozen custard, including fruits, nuts, chunks of Snickers and Heath Bar, and flavorings such as maple, rum, and coffee. Make your own recipe or go for a Foo's favorite, such as Mint Oreo Twist or a Blue Devil, which incorporates raspberries, crème de menthe, and chocolate chips. Divine. And JoCo rejoiced when Foo's came south with a second location.

Murray's Ice Creams & Cookies (Westport) $
4120 Pennsylvania Avenue
(816) 931-5646
Murray's may be the reason we don't mind the heat and humidity in mid-July—it gives us one more reason to head to Murray's. This tiny spot at the end of a horseshoe-shaped loop in Westport lists sixteen or so flavors on the wall with around 200 other recipes waiting their turn. With any luck Chocolate Flake Fromage will be on the list when you visit. This cream cheese–flavored ice cream with semisweet chocolate flakes has its own fan club. Other specialties are smooshies, which

merge ice cream with such toppings as chunks of candy bars, and lumpies, which are malts made chunkier than normal. Try to control yourself.

Murray's has a few tables indoors and out, but most people prefer to walk around Westport to window-shop and people-watch. During December and January, when Murray's is closed, you'll just have to dream about Fudge Raspberry Rhapsody or One Drunk Monk. But they do a very nice send-off: On the last Sunday in November all ice-cream tubs are half price. See? Now you have plenty of time to buy a bigger freezer.

Plan to visit? Here's the scoop: Murray's opens at noon Tuesday through Sunday and closes between 9:00 and 10:30 p.m. depending on the day. Closed Monday.

A word of advice? Bring some extra cash. The ice cream is rich, and so are the prices.

Natasha's Mulberry & Mott $
1621 West 39th Street
(816) 531-5999
www.natashagoellner.com
The shop's name is a mouthful, but so is the pain au chocolate when you try to consume an entire warm, flaky roll of heaven all at once. We have a general rule about never partaking of pastries baked by anyone this tiny, but rules are meant to be broken. The darling Natasha received her diploma from the French Culinary Institute in New York before returning to Kansas City to open a wedding cake business with her mother, Vicki, in 2004. A year later, the duo created a cute bakery shop on 39th Street's Restaurant Row where they sell impossibly tender croissants, delightful cupcakes and cookies, the impossibly good pain au chocolate, and other lovelies, all from scratch.

Tasha's weddings cakes, however, are what put her on the map; she crafts exquisite flowers out of sugar and fondant that, truth be told, can take some of the spotlight away from the bride's gown. And get this—the cakes and fillings are utterly delicious. It's enough to make us cry at weddings.

BARBECUE

Arthur Bryant's Barbeque (East Side) $
1727 Brooklyn
(816) 231-1123
www.arthurbryantsbbq.com

Celebrities and presidents have made the pilgrimage to this landmark since 1930, and today, despite the spot's location in a neglected neighborhood, the lunch line still forms by 11:30. Even then you'll wait as much as half an hour to yell "Beef and fries" to the man standing in front of that smoking pit, but it's worth it to get your hands around 4 inches of brisket.

In fact, it's worth the wait just to witness the decades-old ritual as the counterman slaps two pieces of Wonder bread on a plate and—using his catcher's mitt–size hand—grabs a fistful of just-sliced beef brisket to completely cover the bread. No tongs, no gloves, and no complaints from us. He then slathers on a thick layer of sauce using a paintbrush. The sauce is an alarmingly orange mixture that's a bit more vinegary—and a lot grainier—than anything else in town. You'll no doubt notice big vats of the stuff curing in the front windows. Although they introduced a sweeter, tomato-based version a few years back, go for the original; after all, it's one reason *New Yorker* columnist Calvin Trillin named Bryant's "the single best restaurant in the world." The sandwich is accompanied by an enormous portion of unpeeled fries hot from a lard bath. Don't forget to fish a good number of pickle slices from the jar on your way to the cash register.

The beer is served in a frozen mug that turns the brew into a slushee for adults. You can eat in the restaurant or have your meal

i Burnt ends might sound like a restaurant reject, but around here it's a delicacy. The dish is cut from the ends of a barbecued brisket and served alone with sauce or as a sandwich. The high-flavor, slightly chewy treat is on the menu at just about every barbecue joint in town.

to go, whereupon it will be wrapped in two layers of butcher paper that will only partially protect your car's upholstery. Eat in or take out, take the time to savor every morsel. After all, it's been cooking for thirteen hours or so.

Bryant's serves lunch and dinner seven days a week, and because it's just a block from the historic 18th and Vine district, it's a tasty way to make a day of killer 'cue, cold beer, and hot jazz.

BB's Lawnside Bar-B-Q
(South Kansas City) $
1205 East 85th Street
(816) 822-7427
www.bbslawnsidebbq.com

For a full shot of what Kansas City does best—blues and barbecue—you can't beat Lindsay Shannon's roadhouse. The Louisiana-style gumbo is mighty good, but BB's excels at hickory-smoked ribs. The aroma alone will practically pull you from the front seat of your car and into the front door. Grab your barbecue and a locally brewed Boulevard Beer and pull up a chair at one of the long tables filled with temporary strangers. Once the ragtime, boogie-woogie, or blues starts up you'll be sitting next to your new best friends. A seat at the bar will give you a vantage point to plenty of people-watching. BB's is open for lunch and dinner Wednesday through Sunday, and there's live music every night. Check out the listing in Nightlife for more information about this popular joint.

Danny Edwards Famous
Kansas City Barbecue
(Downtown) $
2900 Southwest Boulevard
(816) 283-0880

Dan's not kidding; this is the kind of 'cue that made Kansas City famous. Owner Danny Edwards learned well from his pop, legendary smokemaster Jake Edwards. He dry-rubs his ribs in a secret spice mixture before smoking them out back for about eight hours. The result is a deep-down flavored slab that's tender but with just enough chewy texture to make you work at falling in love.

The brisket sandwich—arguably the most tender in town—is the top seller, with ribs and burnt ends running close behind. Danny also does a mean barbecued chicken. Now that Danny has moved from his tiny eighteen-seat spot downtown to this more spacious sixty-seat digs, he may have to come up with a new motto to replace the "Eat it and beat it" painted on the forty-five-pound pink pig. Another change is that now there's a parking lot to the side for twenty-five cars. Expect it to be full most of the time. With his new location, he's expanded the hours. Someone alert Zagat voters, will you?

Fiorella's Jack Stack Barbecue　　$–$$
13441 Holmes (Martin City)
(816) 942-9141

9520 Metcalf
Overland Park, KS
(913) 385-7427

4747 Wyandotte Street (Country Club Plaza)
(816) 531-7427

22nd and Wyandotte
(Freight House District)
(816) 472-7427
www.jackstackkc.com

Around here, we tend to steer clear of barbecue chains. A famous rib place tried to infiltrate our town a few years ago and soon went back to North Miami wondering, "What happened? They loved us in Dallas!" But Jack Stack's growing empire is just fine with us, because they started right here in the 1950s.

The location next to Lidia's in the bustling Freight House area near Union Station is a fancy-pants version with a gorgeous bar, soaring ceilings, and cushy booths. One diner walked in, whistled, and said, "This is where gluttony gets an etiquette lesson." If purists refuse to eat 'cue at any restaurant with a wine rack it's their loss; Zagat reviewers say this is the best barbecue in the nation. And it's casual enough to show up in jeans. They

finally opened a restauraunt on the Plaza to introduce tourists to this treasure.

The original restaurant in Martin City is definitely laid-back. It looks like a house that's been expanded a few times to make room for relatives. The second location, on Metcalf, is an attractive space with a huge parking lot that is still overflowing on weekends. The menus at all four locations are big enough to blanket the table, filled with a mind-boggling selection of barbecued meats, hickory-grilled poultry and fish, and certified Angus steaks. Kiss your low-fat diet goodbye and start with a rack of thick-cut, battered onion rings big enough to wear as bracelets. They come to the table stacked like a kid's toy on a copper skewer. Other side dishes include a rich cheesy corn casserole, slightly sweet coleslaw, and fabulous hickory pit beans thickened with chunks of burnt ends, ham, and meat drippings.

Jack Stack serves five types of ribs, including pork and beef spare ribs, baby back, and lamb ribs that got rave reviews in the London Times and New York Times. Along with steaks, sausage, pork chops, and crown prime rib, there are fire-grilled chicken, fish, and shrimp. Sandwiches include the Martin City Mayor—named for the restaurant's original home—made with chopped burnt ends topped with coleslaw on a French bun.

All four locations are open for lunch and dinner seven days a week. And here's good news for you unfortunate souls who can't get to Kansas City often enough: Jack Stack's ships their award-winning ribs and other smoked meats anywhere. Check www.jackstackbbq.com or call for information.

Gates Bar-B-Q　　$
1325 East Emanuel Cleaver II Boulevard
(816) 531-7522

2001 West 103rd Street
Leawood, KS
(913) 383-1752

3205 Main Street (Downtown)
(816) 753-0828

1221 Brooklyn (East Side)
(816) 483-3880

10440 East 40 Highway
Independence, MO
(816) 353-5880

1026 State Avenue
Kansas City, KS
(913) 621-1134
www.gatesbbq.com

It's always fun to watch a tenderfoot walk through the door and take a step backward when assailed by a loud "May I help you?" from behind the counter. Answer quickly because with these crowds, they don't ask twice. The menu is printed on the wall above the open kitchen, but if you get flustered just remember you can't go wrong with the ribs and fries.

Or go for the mixed plate to try the ribs, beef brisket, and beef sausage. Once you're handed your plate of smoky 'cue, head to the side table to load up on one or all four flavors of sauce. The mild version makes a fine ketchup substitute for dipping fries. And don't be surprised if you find yourself heading back to the line, this time yelling back at the order taker, "Yeah, you can help me. Give me a slab to go."

Lunch and dinner hours vary by location. Call ahead.

Hayward's Pit Bar-B-Que $
11051 Antioch Road
Overland Park, KS
(913) 451-8080
www.haywardsbbq.com

Hayward Spears and his family have been adding a smoky haze to Johnson County since the mid-1970s. Far too classy to be considered a barbecue joint, Hayward's offers a chance to relax and enjoy succulent ribs and sandwiches piled high with beef, pork, ham, or combinations. For lots of flavor condensed into a bite-size package, try the burnt ends as a sandwich or part of a combo meal. The onion rings are big, fat crunchy affairs, and the beans have plenty of meaty chunks.

This place does a huge take-out business, and Hayward was smart enough to build a separate order-taking alcove so things don't get quite so crowded on Friday and Saturday nights. If you're eating in, check out the collection of Angus and Hereford horns on the walls, 3-foot testaments to our cowtown heritage. Hayward's is open for lunch and dinner seven days a week and does a brisk catering business.

L.C.'s Bar-B-Q (East Side) $
5800 Blue Parkway
(816) 923-4484

This is the place to find true Kansas City lip-smacking barbecue: smoky ribs, brisket that will make you weep, and perhaps the best fries in the world. Although not as famous as Arthur Bryant's, it's usually on the top-five list of people who really know their smoked meat. The sauce is sweet and tangy. You'll want to eat until you hurt.

Table space is generally gone by a quarter to noon, and when there's a Saturday game at Kauffman Stadium, cars line up early. Be forewarned, though: This is far from a fancy location. Perhaps there's a good reason for the bars on the windows, and even the smoker in the parking lot is chained to a utility pole. Lunch and dinner are served Monday through Saturday.

Oklahoma Joe's BBQ $
47th and Mission Road
Kansas City, KS
(913) 722-3366

11950 South Strang Line Road
Olathe, KS
(913) 782-6858
www.oklahomajoesbbq.com

No doubt Jeff and Joy Stehney heard every imaginable joke using "gas" and "restaurant" in the same sentence when they started serving barbecue in a space shared by a filling station, convenience store, and liquor store. Now they're laughing all the way to the bank as people line up noon and night for award-winning fare. The walls are lined with just a

Kansas City Barbecue

Welcome to the barbecue capital of the world. Oh, we know: The Carolinas claim to be the cradle of American barbecue, and Texas has the brisket circuit sewn up. But here in the Midwest we've perfected the technique so well it's often referred to by the generic term "Kansas City barbecue," as if the city and the food are forever intertwined.

To really appreciate barbecue you've got to talk the talk. First off, true aficionados consider "barbecue" a noun, not a verb, although the rest of us tend to use it both ways. It refers to beef or pork that's been slow-cooked over wood—often hickory, cherry, or apple to add a subtle flavor—for hours. And we do mean hours. It's a commitment of time and constant attention, turning it into a recreational sport that calls for cold beer and good friends. A brisket or slab of ribs can take eight hours or more of monitoring the fire to make sure the temperature doesn't vary more than a dozen degrees. This patient technique makes barbecue distinctly different from Kansas City's preferred method of cooking steak, grilling quickly over a flame stoked as high as 1,400 degrees F.

The result is a succulent morsel of meat. But saying ribs are so tender they fall off the bone is not necessarily a compliment; it may mean they've been parboiled—a real no-no that local experts call *faux 'cue*. Say it fast and you'll get the message.

And don't expect your barbecue to show up slathered with sauce. Although meat is often dry-rubbed with a spice mixture before going into the smoker, the sauce—if applied at all—is mopped on right before serving or during the final minutes of cooking so the sugars in the sauce don't burn. That's another thing: Although there are exceptions such as the vinegary version at Arthur Bryant's, for the most part Kansas City sauce is on the sweet side thanks to its molasses-spiked tomato base. If you want more sauce with your brisket sandwich, you'll usually find a bottle or two of the thick, mahogany-colored liquid on the table, often sporting the restaurant's label. Don't even think about asking for the recipe. Around here ingredients are guarded as carefully as Zsa Zsa Gabor's birthdate.

If you're getting the idea that barbecue isn't merely a food group but our city's true identity, you're halfway there. Or as members of the Kansas City Barbecue Society like to say, "Barbecue. It's not just for breakfast anymore." Membership in the KCBS—the world's largest, with more than 6,000 members worldwide—is $35 a year. Contact them at 11514 Hickman Mills Drive, Kansas City, MO 64121. Or call (816) 765-5891 or (800) 963-KCBS, or visit www.kcbs.us.

KCBS members—and the rest of us—are eternally grateful to Henry Perry. He introduced the food group to Kansas City in the late 1920s when he started selling ribs out of a trolley barn at 19th and Highland. A slab back then—wrapped in pages of newsprint—cost 25 cents. Henry's barn became 'Cue University for such local legends as George Gates and Charlie Bryant. Charlie eventually bought the place and expanded it with help from his brother Arthur. After Charlie died Arthur tinkered with the sauce—the original was so hot it nearly caused blisters—and moved the business to 1727 Brooklyn. The lunch lines have never stopped.

As for its preparation, though the main ingredients and basic techniques passed down from Henry are universal, the sauce recipe and even the hardwoods used for smoking often are closely guarded secrets. In Kansas City, saying one barbecue restaurant is the best in town can start a heated debate. Heck, we can't even agree on one single spelling of the name: barbecue, barbeque, BBQ, or bar-b-que. When it comes time for locals to pick their favorites, the criteria are usually split into categories like best fries, best ribs, best brisket, or best sauce.

We'll let you decide. But pace yourself; there are eighty or so barbecue outlets in town. We've listed some of the top achievers in this chapter. But before you go, here's a quick primer, courtesy of the Kansas City Barbecue Society, to help you place your order.

- **Baby back ribs:** Also known as loin back ribs, these are cut from the pork loin and usually weigh about two pounds per slab.

- **Barbecue:** To slow cook meats over hardwood (some folks use charcoal or a mix of the two) at a temperature of 200 to 375 degrees F.

- **Burnt Ends:** Blackened, somewhat charred pieces of brisket that are too charred to slice. These are served with plenty of sauce and highly prized at restaurants. Sometimes they're called "brownies."

- **Glaze:** A finishing sauce applied to meat—what's called mopping—during the final minutes of barbecuing.

- **Long end spare ribs:** The first six ribs from the breastbone on back.

- **Pit:** The cooking unit used to barbecue. You'll see everything around here, from black barrels on legs to cement or brick open structures. A good smokemaster can produce great barbecue from a hole in the ground.

- **Rib tips:** The breastbone at the top of a slab of spare ribs.

- **Rub:** A dry marinade—usually a closely guarded mixture of dry spices and herbs—that's liberally massaged into meats to impart flavor.

- **Short end spare ribs:** The last seven or eight ribs in a slab of spare ribs. We're calling dibs right now.

- **Wood chips:** Small chips of wood used to impart smoky flavor to barbecued meats. Hickory is perhaps the most popular, but plenty of experts use fruitwood like apple or cherry because it's slightly sweeter. Some people cut the bitterness of hickory by mixing in fruitwood.

If preparing barbecue sounds like a huge commitment in time and trouble, we have a solution: Skip the wood, get on the road, and let a master smoker prepare it for you. You'll find some of the city's most popular barbecue restaurants elsewhere in this chapter. Happy eating.

few of the 300 or so trophies Joe and his team have won at contests around the country, including a coveted Grand Champion statue the size of a three-year old.

This is simply outrageously good barbecue. And while competitors often excel at one or two items, at Oklahoma Joe's everything is superb. Favorites include lip-smacking ribs, burnt ends, and Carolina-style sandwiches, that Southern treat of pulled pork topped with spicy slaw. The gumbo, a rather unusual menu entry, is thick with chunks of smoked chicken, ham, and okra. It's as good as anything served in New Orleans. By 11:30 the lunch line to Joe's snakes around the corner, with folks sharing stories of their first time here or eager to get their mitts on a Hog Heaven (pulled pork and sliced sausage on a bun) or a Lean-n-Mean (smoked turkey on Texas toast topped with spicy slaw).

They'll slap smoked meats on anything here, including salads. You can have your greens topped with shredded pork, cold sliced brisket, or hot boneless chicken. Have a salad if you must, but don't skip the fries. In super-size-me portions, they're some of the best in the city. So are the rest of the sides, which are—along with that mighty fine gumbo—available in pint and quart containers to go. The sauce is also for sale, a garnet-colored, slightly sweet concoction called Cowtown Bar-B-Q that ranked first at the 2001 American Royal Barbecue Contest. Jeff also sells four seasonings to rub into meats before smoking or grilling. And of course you'll want an "I got smoked to the bone" T-shirt designed by local cartoonist Charlie Podrebarac.

The line starts to form again for the dinner specials. Prices can't be beat: on Monday and Tuesday half a smoked chicken with two sides and Texas toast is just $5.95. Thursday is rib night, when a full slab goes for just shy of 13 bucks. The menu suggests a slab will serve two to three people; they obviously haven't watched some of us eat.

Oklahoma Joe's has a great atmosphere where families, couples, and singles pack into three booths, sixteen tables, and a long counter facing a view of regular and premium pumps. The beer is flowing, the barbecue is smoking, and the stereo is blaring "Got My Mojo Workin'." Can it get any better than this? Well, yes. They could be open on Sunday. And if they would just do something about that name.

Though we still favor the original location, we're happy to have an Oklahoma Joe's in Olathe now. But it's still not open on Sunday!

Rosedale Barbecue $
600 Southwest Boulevard
Kansas City, KS
(913) 262-0343

Naturally this joint knows how to smoke meaty ribs and flavorful brisket. They've been doing it since 1934, longer than anyone else in Kansas City. For years this no-frills place was called a "bucket shop" because it sold beer in metal cans. Although a little more sterile since remodeling a few years back, it still retains a slightly funky atmosphere. And Rosedale certainly passes the litmus test for good 'cue: Lines extend out both side doors by noon. It can be a madhouse, but you can always show up when the crowds are gone; it's open until 10:00 p.m. Monday through Saturday and until 8:00 p.m. on Sunday.

Fans go for the hearty beef, pork, and ham sandwiches, or "half bird and fries," tasty barbecued chicken and crispy zigzag-cut fries served hot in a waxed paper bag. The baby back ribs are tender and lean but are available only on Sunday. And Wednesday brings another rare treat: all-you-can-eat riblet dinners. If you don't care for barbecue—say it isn't so!—there's also homemade chili and a kielbasa sandwich.

CAJUN/CREOLE

Jazz—A Louisiana Kitchen $–$$
1823 West 39th Street
(816) 531-5556

1859 Village West Parkway
Kansas City, KS
(913) 328–0003
www.jazzkitchens.com

Kick the fun up another notch at this rowdy Kansas City mainstay where the walls are covered with Mardi Gras posters and graffiti from past visitors. You'll want to add your own comment or signature after digging into such traditional Cajun dishes as blackened seafood, gumbo, oysters on the half shell, and po'boy sandwiches. Or just order the all-you-can-eat hushpuppies for $139; the order includes a free bottle of Dom Perignon.

At night this becomes party central as live jazz, Dixieland, and blues play five nights a week. During the day it's often a hangout for interns from the KU Medical Center up the street looking for a little relaxation and roux between rounds. They can replace their stethoscopes with Mardi Gras beads. Make sure to get your own colorful necklace before you leave.

Jazz is open from 11:00 a.m. to midnight daily. At the new Jazz, in Kansas City, Kansas, "roules" out the fun seven days a week.

CASUAL DINING

Harry's Country Club $–$$
112 Missouri Avenue
(816) 421-3505
www.harryscountryclub.com
You bet we're wild about Harry, and we have been ever since Mr. Murphy ruled Westport from his spot behind the bar of the New Stanley (which became the Old Stanley, then the New . . . oh, never mind). When he opened his own place in the River Market, he gave his thirsty patrons a glimpse of what their dads or granddads may have enjoyed decades ago in a relaxed neighborhood honky-tonk. Ice-cold yard beers. Two-fisted turkey sandwiches. Pan-fried catfish. The prices haven't even changed much since then: A fried bologna sandwich and bottle of Pabst Blue Ribbon will set you back just $3.75. A devoted downtown lunch crowd bellies up to the bar for salads, homemade soups, and daily specials including meatloaf, and lasagna. You might be surprised to see some upscale items on the menu, including a

seductive penne with spicy vodka, tomato, and cream sauce.

Those who are too refined for brewskies can indulge in flights of premium tequila, which simply means three one-ounce pours of different brands for $12, or choose to fly first class with samples of the premium aged fire water for $17. Whiskey flights also are departing from Harry's Country Club, with three different one-ounce pours for just $10—including top-notch bourbons and single malts. Another reason to love Harry? While other bars charge $8 and up for a mixed drink, at the Country Club a well drink is a mere $3, a martini just $4. The unmatched view of a glittering downtown skyline is free.

And what's good grub and booze without live music? Wednesday through Saturday during good weather, the friendly deck's the place to hear bands with such names as Tater and the Gravy Train and the Good Old Boys (usually with a $5 cover charge). At other times the jukebox takes over. Save us a seat on the deck and order up a round of ice-cold Schlitz, will ya?

The Mixx $
4855 Main Street
(816) 756-2300
www.mixxingitup.com
The proprietor of The Mixx, Jo Marie Scaglia and her sister, Kathy Green, who owns Twenty/20 in the Freighthouse District, are the queens of casual dining. They come by it naturally; papa Maria introduced Kansas City to grinders, those two-fisted sandwiches made from meatballs, sauce, and cheese stuffed into a hollowed-out Italian roll.

i Dining out with little ones? Lots of our restaurants cater to kids, with special menus, coloring books, or toys to keep them happy and occupied. Some of the best are Yahooz! in Leawood, the Crayola Cafe in Crown Center, and Winstead's, where children can share a Skyscraper ice-cream soda and listen to the jukebox.

The Mixx is Jo Marie's concept and it's a doozy. Diners walk up to the counter at this small restaurant and order a salad, then watch as the chefs mix in your choice of extras from a list of forty. And we're not talking carrot sticks—gourmet goodies such as candied pecans, caramelized onions, and balsamic mushrooms. Pick your greens and house-made dressing, such as the nonfat pear ginger vinaigrette, and ta-daaa—an enormous bowl of freshness for about what you'd pay at a drive-through. Huge portions of grilled chicken, steak, or salmon—even tofu—are available for a few dollars more.

Not feeling creative? Jo Marie also offers specialty salads, such as the incredibly good Knife & Fork, a medley of wild field greens with grilled steak, roasted potatoes, caramelized onions, and blue cheese with a balsamic vinaigrette with just enough bite. At less than 10 bucks, it's big enough to share (just get another roll). Another must-try is the Thai salmon salad tossed with edamame (tender soybeans) and an Asian sesame dressing.

Nine signature sandwiches, all for around $8, are also terrific here: The Thanksgiving Favorite pairs roasted turkey with cranberry-apple chutney for a holiday in your mouth. Or create your own masterpiece from a list of ingredients. Soup and salad combos are available as well, and the daily pasta is definitely worth trying. Kids get grilled cheese sandwiches and Mom's Buttered Noodles, and everybody needs to grab one of Jo Marie's famous cupcakes.

No wonder this small, bright spot off the Plaza is popular with the lunch crowd, families, young singles, groups of giggling teens, and couples heading off to see a movie or touring the nearby Nelson-Atkins Museum of Art or just the Kansas City Library across the parking lot.

Here's swell news for Johnson Countians: Jo Marie is opening a second location out south. Check her Web site for time and location.

Stroud's (North Kansas City) $
5410 Northeast Oak Ridge Drive
(816) 454-9600
www.stroudsrestaurant.com

Mention the name Stroud's to anyone in Kansas City and watch a moon-eyed look come across their face. This is the home of legendary pan-fried chicken, where folks are willing to wait for hours for a table. The rickety 1920 roadhouse under a bridge was part of the charm, as was singing along to the piano player. That's why our hearts were broken (if not somewhat healed from all that cholesterol) when we learned Stroud's would be torn down as part of a construction project.

The owners have vowed to find a new location, and we're hoping for floors that lean a little to the south like the old place. But in the meantime, we still enjoy the same food at Stroud's Oak Ridge Manor, a homestead that dates back to a log cabin built in 1829. Through three families the site has served as a place of great hospitality, which always includes good food. Mike Donegan, the last of the three guys who started Stroud's, continues the legacy here.

There's still a long line; Stroud's takes reservations only for parties of ten or more Sunday through Thursday, never on Friday or Saturday.

But most people don't mind the wait—except perhaps parents with small children—because the crowd is festive, there's a full bar, and the aroma of fried chicken serves as a constant reminder of the final reward. Once seated, remember that everything is served family style, so whatever chicken dinner you order will arrive at the table on large platters and in bowls to pass around. Don't worry, we've never seen a table run out of fluffy mashed potatoes, slow-cooked green beans, peppery cream gravy, cottage fries, or french fries. Skip the ketchup and dunk the fries in gravy like most guests do.

To start you'll have your choice of chicken noodle soup or salad, and every dinner ends with a basket of warm cinnamon rolls. Like magic your server will show up with doggie bags and packets of hand wipes. But back to that chicken. Stroud's serves it steaming hot from the 14-inch cast-iron skillets. The crispy golden brown crust falls away to reveal tender, juicy chicken that was deemed "the best chicken on the planet" by the *New York Times*.

If chicken isn't your thing, there are tasty pork chops served pan-fried or broiled in garlic butter sauce, chicken-fried steaks, pan-fried catfish, and deep-fried shrimp. The waitresses are friendly, efficient, and polite enough to laugh at whatever chicken joke you care to share. And if you're looking for a reminder of your visit beyond that doggie bag, buy a "We Choke Our Own Chickens" T-shirt.

Stroud's is open 5:00 to 9:30 p.m. Monday through Thursday, 11:00 a.m. to 10:30 p.m. Friday, 2 to 10:30 p.m. Saturday, and 11:00 a.m. to 9:30 p.m. Sunday.

Twenty/20 $
2020 Baltimore
(816) 471-2020

This sliver of a bistro on one of the busiest corners in the Freighthouse District gets positively crammed on the first Friday of every month, thanks to its proximity to the Crossroads Arts District. Well, that and the fact that owner Kathy Green hires a DJ to pump out the tunes for patrons sitting outside with cocktails and wine.

What's on the menu board is pretty heart-thumping, too, such as Kathy's salmon salad and big, fat sandwiches. Her pastas, such as a rigatoni with sausage and spicy red sauce, and pizzas are favored neighborhood noshes. There's a brisk lunch business, with people dining in the upstairs loft, dotting the outdoor cafe tables, or grabbing a to-go box. And when you see that Twenty/20 is the caterer for an event, you know it's going to be good.

Kathy's little corner of the world is also a quiet spot (when the gallery crawl isn't going on) for an early dinner, huddled upstairs holding hands, admiring the groovy architecture and art, and savoring one of the Scaglia sisters' culinary treats.

Westport Flea Market $
817 Westport Road
(816) 931-1986

Usually when someone buys a restaurant, he acquires long hours, a few headaches, and long-lost buddies mooching free meals. Joe Zwillenberg got a bit more when he plunked down cash to buy the Westport Flea Market: hero status. The Flea is a local phenom—a hamburger joint in the center of a ragtag collection of flea market booths. When the owner decided to sell the establishment to Hooter's, a national chain of bar and grills featuring waitresses in hot pants, the neighborhood went ballistic. Local boy Joe Z. came to the rescue and saved this treasure.

"Treasure" may be a bit strong: The place is a dive where seekers of all things beefy have to wind through a chockablock entrance, find a table amid all the pinball machines, order at the counter, then wait for the cheeky announcer to call their name. Sally, your order's up. Raymond, come and get it. While you're waiting, notice the wall of awards announcing Best Burger in KC. It is that, indeed. It's all in the meat, and this is fresh from McGonigle's, one of the true great butcher shops left in Kansas City. The Mini-Market Burger, at 5½ ounces, is plenty of protein, especially when you doll it up at the condiment table filled with lettuce, sliced tomatoes and onions, real mayo, and pickles. The Flea Market Burger is a 10-ounce bad boy. The curly fries are good and greasy. The menu also lists BLTs, hot dogs, and paninis, but who cares? It's all about the burger.

So now you know what to order; all you need to know is when. Mondays, margaritas are just $3.50 to go with live music. After 5:00 p.m. every Tuesday you'll get two burgers for the price of one. Wednesday night is a trivia party where the joint is packed with teams who know all the battles of the Crimean War and every TV theme song ever written. It's great fun just to watch.

The Flea is open seven days a week for lunch and dinner starting at 11:00 a.m., then until 11:00 p.m. Sunday through Thursday and 11:30 p.m. Friday and Saturday.

Winstead's (Country Club Plaza and other locations) $
101 Brush Creek Boulevard
(816) 753-2244

Since 1940 this has been the place to come for burgers and shakes, and other than a few menu updates not much has changed since then. The waitresses still wear jaunty uniforms, the jukebox still plays great tunes—no quarters required, just punch in your favorite rock 'n' roll tunes—and most important, they continue to live up to their sixty-year motto, "We grind U.S. choice steak daily for the sandwich."

For newcomers, it's only fair to describe the famous Winstead's steakburger—available as singles, doubles, or triples. But don't expect quarter-pound patties. These are flat, thin circles of beef that are broiled on a greaseless grill. In fact the onion slice is thicker than the burger, so you won't be remiss if you order a double. But it's the combination of flavors—the grilled beef with slightly crispy edges, fat slice of sweet onion, tangy mustard-and-ketchup sauce, pickle sliced the long way, and unadorned bun—that beats all other burgers hands down. It's even wrapped in paper and presented on your plate like a gift.

To complete your experience get the Special Chocolate Frosty, "the exclusive Winstead drink you eat with a spoon." They mean it; try to suck this creamy concoction through a straw and we know for a fact your head will cave in. Only after the drink has partially melted, on the off chance there's any left, should you even consider unwrapping the straw. During hot summer days the limeade is a refreshing substitute, made with plenty of shaved ice and a perky hat of lime sherbet. For families or a table of teens it's great fun to order a Skyscraper Soda; this monster of an ice-cream treat is served in a glass about a foot tall and is meant to be shared by two to four people.

Winstead's is open daily for breakfast, lunch, and dinner.

CHINESE

Blue Koi (Midtown) $–$$
1803 West 39th Street
(816) 561-5003

107th and Mission Road (Mission Farms)
Leawood, KS
(913) 383-3330
www.bluekoikc.com

The sponged aqua walls Blue Koi aren't the only cool thing about this dumpling and noodle shop. The menu lists unexpected dishes that appeal to vegetarians and carnivores alike. And for the kid in all of us there are eleven flavors of bubble tea, which is all the rage in San Francisco's Chinatown. This iced milk and tea drink is made with tapioca balls that float to the bottom of the glass, waiting for you to slurp them up through a straw. Like your tea straight? You'll find an extensive list of aromatic brews, including a slightly floral scented jasmine, to go with your meal. If you have the time or interest, invest in the Gong Fu tea ceremony, available from 2:00 to 5:00 p.m., which includes an array of small cups and fragrant tea that's been scented seven times.

But it's the Chang family's comfort food that has people filling the long, narrow space for lunch and dinner. The Chinese pot roast, a slab of slow-roasted, fork-tender beef ladled over wide strips of noodles, is addictive. Or follow the menu's lead and order Ants on a Tree, a Taiwanese dish of sautéed minced pork and shredded cabbage served with amber-colored cellophane noodles.

Seven types of dumplings are available to order either boiled or pan-fried as a meal or an appetizer to share. The duck wrap is another excellent starter; shredded roasted duck is mixed with cucumber, cilantro, and a tangy and slightly sweet hoisin sauce and served in a soft breaded wrap.

Vegans will be happy to find several tempting dishes, including a vegetarian dumpling, lettuce wrap, and braised tofu with shiitake mushroom entree.

The savory fare is now also available in

fancier digs, where JoCo's kids can discover bubble tea.

Bo Lings $
9055 Metcalf Avenue
Overland Park, KS
(913) 341-1718

4800 Main Street (Country Club Plaza)
(816) 753-1718

9574 Quivira Road
Lenexa, KS
(913) 888-6618

7105 West 135th Street
Overland Park, KS
(913) 239-8188

8870 Northwest Prairie View Road
(Zona Rosa)
(816) 587-7880

20 East 5th Street
(River Market)
(816) 841-5465
www.bolings.com

When Kansas Citians are hungry for Chinese food, those in the know head for one of Richard and Theresa Ng's restaurants. Their original place, a beautiful showroom in pale teal and dark wood in the Plaza's Board of Trade Building, gained them a loyal following. Johnson County fans were thrilled when they opened more locations closer to home.

Richard's food is fresh, flavorful, and authentic; in fact he often visits Hong Kong's best restaurants for ideas to bring back home. The extensive menu includes Cantonese lettuce wraps, General Tso's Chicken, shrimp and scallops in garlic sauce, sizzling black pepper beef, and fried noodles. Even the rice is special: a blend of aromatic jasmine and fluffy American long grain. A house specialty is succulent Beijing roasted duck. These plump, rice-fed ducks are cooked in custom-designed hanging ovens that let the fat drip away as the skin becomes crisp and russet colored. The duck is then carved and tucked into soft steamed buns along with slivers of cucumber, green onion, and sweet plum sauce. It may become your new favorite dish.

On Saturday and Sunday a dim sum brunch is served at the Plaza and Metcalf locations. This wildly popular event offers over fifty appetizers, including steamed barbecue pork buns, shrimp dumplings, and stuffed eggplant. All six locations are open seven days a week.

Genghis Khan Mongolian Grill
(Midtown) $
3901 Bell
(816) 753-3600

8634 North Boardwalk (Northland)
(816) 587-8883
www.genghiskhankc.com

This large corner restaurant with exposed brick walls and wooden floors is always packed thanks to the variety of food, a fun atmosphere, and incredible value. Although the menu offers tempting dishes, most regulars ignore the printed list and head for the all-you-can-eat buffet.

For lunch grab a plate and start piling on your choice of twenty fresh vegetables and sliced beef, chicken, pork, crab, catfish, and squid. At night the selections expand to include shrimp, scallops, lamb, Chinese sausage, and mahimahi. Then add a splash of sauce. You can create your own flavor from twenty ingredients such as soy sauce, ginger, and garlic, or use the handy recipes provided. Finally, hand your overflowing plate to the barbecue cook, who will grill it before your eyes. Prices include appetizers, such as crab rangoon and spicy chicken wings, and dessert.

Expect a crowd by noon, when this becomes a hangout for interns and staffers from nearby KU Hospital, vegetarians, and anyone else looking for fresh flavorful food at a bargain price. Lunch starts at just $7.50, and dinner is around $13.00 depending on whether your creation includes meat. Unique cocktails add to the fun.

The original location is open Monday through Saturday for lunch and dinner; Northlanders get an extra day of Khan cuisine.

FRENCH

Even though our first official settler was French, it would be some 150 years before we acquired more than one restaurant serving Gallic food. Today we have some of the finest French bistros this side of the Atlantic, attended to by chefs who, more often than not, came here for love and ended up falling in love with the city as well.

Aixois (Midtown) $$
251 East 55th
(816) 333-3305
www.aixois.com

Pronounced *Ex-WAH*, this chic bistro came to be when Megan and Emmanuel Langlade met at another French restaurant in Parkville, fell madly in love, married, and left to open their own place. And what a charming rendezvous it is, snuggled in the back corner of a block of antiques and design shops in the genteel Crestwood neighborhood. In fact, to reach the restaurant you can enter through the outdoor patio or the coffee bar that's kid- and dog-friendly. The coffee service alone hints of what's ahead; stirrers are mismatched silver spoons rather than white plastic sticks.

Inside the bistro, mustard-yellow walls and exposed bricks and ceiling beams set the mood. And though the menu is small, there are enough daily specials to warrant a weekly reservation. Many devotees would be quite happy to order Emmanuel's truite saumon meunière every single day; this ruby trout sautéed in lemon butter and topped with slivered almonds is so popular it's served for both lunch and dinner. For sheer presentation, it doesn't get much better than coppery salmon peeking out from beneath a golden brown parchment paper package.

But if a restaurant can make its name simply for potatoes, this one can. We hate to use the term french fries when describing pommes frites, because no fast-food joint ever offered such crisp-tender slivers of spuds. They're served with a number of items, including the peppered flank steak, Kansas City strip, and Prince Edward Island mussels in a luscious cream sauce. Starters are also delicious, especially a classic salade niçoise, a lovely composed salad of tuna, tomatoes, tiny black olives, and hard-boiled egg on a bed of greens with a tangy vinaigrette, and the peppery arugula and strawberries with warm goat cheese. The luxurious pâtés are all made in-house.

If you can't decide which dessert to have, enjoy them all with the assiettes Aixoise, a decadent display that includes crème brûlée, chocolate mousse, fresh fruit with puree, and profiterole's with chocolate. Aixois serves lunch and dinner Monday through Saturday. The coffee bar is open seven days a week.

Cafe des Amis $$
112½ Main Street
Parkville, MO
(816) 587-6767
www.cafedesamiskc.com

It's easy to pretend you're in a village in France while sitting on this sun-dappled deck with the fragrance of roast duck swirling around you. The clincher is handsome owner Didier Combe's accent as he asks if the escargot is to your liking.

Didier's recipes, from his mother's kitchen in Aix-en-Provence, are brought brilliantly to life by his chef. The menu includes classics such as coquilles Saint Jacques and new masterpieces such as a casserole of organic vegetables, aromatic herbs, and tangy goat cheese. For lunch there are lovely crepes, and at night the filet in a sauce of cognac, peppercorns, and Roquefort will have you swooning.

Desserts include crepes filled with a dark chocolate sauce and a shimmering tart served with caramel sauce. Although the deck seating is divine, the bistro also has small—and we do mean small—rooms inside. But no one's complaining; the close quarters give you one more reason to sit knee-to-knee with your sweetheart.

Cafe des Amis serves lunch Tuesday through Saturday, dinner Tuesday through Sunday, and Sunday brunch from noon to 3:00 p.m.

Cafe Provence $$
3936 West 69th Terrace
Prairie Village, KS
(913) 384-5998
www.cafeprovence.net

When famed French Chef Patrick Quillec opened this charming cafe, he collected new fans. And if the windows look out over a parking lot rather than the Seine, who cares? It's the food that counts, and the chef does not disappoint. As for atmosphere, the television at the bar is always tuned to a French station, where even a traffic report sounds romantic.

And the food—especially the sunny, saffrony bouillabaisse—looks like you've traveled to Provence. But if you really want to savor your seafood, opt for the mussels in a white wine, garlic, and shallot sauce so decadent you'll beg for more bread. Other classic French dishes include steak tartare and pan-seared frog legs served with a rosy tomato coulis. And, ah, for dessert, there's crème caramel, lemon tart, and profiteroles, which are pastry puffs topped with ribbons of chocolate ganache and served with home-made ice cream. Lunch and dinner are served Monday through Saturday.

Cassis $$$
Town Center Plaza
4821 West 117th Street
Overland Park, KS
(913) 383-1000
www.cassiskc.com

In the land of plenty known as Overland Park, where bowls of pasta feed a family of six and pork chops come double-cut, there's a tiny bistro that focuses on quality, not quantity. Frankly, we'd follow the French chef/owner, Patrick Quillec, anywhere, and not just for his charming accent. The courses sing of his mastery of flavored oils and subtle emulsions and reductions. The Tomato Farci is a modern take on the classic Caprese salad, with three small peeled tomatoes stuffed with Boursin cheese, warmed slightly, served on organic basil pesto, and drizzled with hazelnut vinaigrette.

Patrick may change your mind about trying anything out of the ordinary, such as rabbit, frog's legs, or chicken livers. With his sauces, a wedge of the phone book could be a hit. His cream of asparagus soup is the culinary equivalent of Kate Hudson—frothy but with substance. We rarely order chicken out, but the Raised Right Organic Chicken, with its mahogany-hued crisp skin, is superb.

More than twenty-five wines are served by the glass, with the rest divided by bottle prices ($27, $37, $47—how brilliant is that?), along with a category called Paragon, composed of "if you have to ask" varietals such as Dom Perignon and Mount Veeder Reserve Red. A full bar is available as well.

Not surprisingly, the desserts are standouts, including a warm plum clafouti for those who favor a not-too-sweet ending, and a trio of chocolate mousses for those, like us, who do. Service is just as rewarding, with well-trained servers who never rush you during lunch or dinner. The leisurely pace will give you time to appreciate the sexy interior with textured walls painted a glossy currant-red (appropriate for the restaurant's name, which means *currant*), while a private dining room next to the bar is the color of mascara. No wonder the ladies-who-lunch favor this place!

The rich colors and large, original paintings—interspersed with enormous gold-framed mirrors—make the 65-seating space feel so sumptuous you don't mind sharing secrets with the couple at the next table. Perhaps you should learn to whisper in French. More good news: Cassis is open for dinner seven days a week, lunch is Monday through Saturday.

Le Fou Frog (River Market) $$–$$$
400 East Fifth Street
(816) 474-6060
www.lefoufrog.com

It only makes sense that this cozy French bistro would land in the historic River Market district not far from where our famous first Frenchman made his home. The rest of us are just glad chef Mano Rafael followed his heart—and his bride, Barbara, a Kansas City native—to our river town as well. The move was easier for him than you might think, because the area reminds him of the port city of Marseille.

Since opening the restaurant in 1997, Mano has thrilled guests with classic French dishes such as escargot with garlic butter and seared rack of lamb coated with Dijon mustard and herbs. Order the steak au poivre with pommes frites, those thin and crispy fried potatoes, and pretend you're sitting in a small cafe on the rue de la whatever.

After more than a decade, there's still a steady buzz about Mano's moules marinieres, which are Prince Edward Island mussels steamed in a broth of white wine, shallots, mustard, and heavy cream. But don't overlook the osso buco Corsican, slow-braised veal shanks in a red wine–veal broth topped with thin slices of prosciutto and shaved mozzarella. His cassoulet of duck breast is a savory mixture of sausages from Toulouse, lamb, flageolet beans, rosemary, and garlic. If there's room left for dessert, the warm apple tart is a fitting ending to the evening.

Le Fou Frog, which means "the crazy Frenchman," is open for dinner Tuesday through Sunday. It also hosts such events as a Bastille Day celebration, wine tastings, and a Valentine's Day feast that features food declared to be aphrodisiacs. To turn even a winter's evening into a party, a heated tent is available year-round. One bit of warning: This place is very noisy and boisterous, and that's just how the owner and most of the patrons like it. But if you're looking for a quiet, intimate evening, this may not be your best choice.

Tatsu's $$
4603 West 90th Street
Prairie Village, KS
(913) 383-9801
www.tatsus.com

Don't let the location in an unassuming strip mall dissuade you from coming here. Just pop in a French CD and pretend you're driving your Renault past the Eiffel Tower rather than a firehouse in Johnson County. Inside, the space is lovely with candlelight, fresh flowers, and even fresher food. Japanese-born owner and chef Tatsu Arai has been adding a delicate touch to classic French cuisine, to the delight of his longtime fans, since 1980. Specialties include braised oxtails cooked in a red wine sauce and Jacques a la Moutarde, which is poached shrimp, scallops, and mushrooms in mustard sauce served in a puff pastry shell. Entrees come with salad, fresh vegetables, and home-baked bread. And after you've fallen in love with the house-made salad dressing, you'll be glad to know it's available by the bottle.

By now we hope you've ordered the Grand Marnier soufflé. It's a lovely sight on a pool of crème anglaise and stripes of dark chocolate sauce. And notice, please, the two dollar signs in Tatsu's heading. It is truly amazing to find food and service this splendid for so few francs.

Lunch is served Monday through Friday; dinner is served seven days a week.

INTERNATIONAL

La Bodega (Midtown) $$
703 Southwest Boulevard
(816) 472-8272
www.labodegakc.com

This boisterous cafe is where you'll find out which of your friends learned to share in kindergarten. For at La Bodega, most of the menu is composed of hot and cold tapas— little savory appetizers—that are meant to be passed around the table. We've come to love the Basque way of socializing so much we often graze this way for hours, with a different dish arriving every few minutes to a round of applause. Complete the Spanish tradition with a glass of sherry. La Bodega also serves lovely old ports, wines, and a fabulous sangria.

Top-selling cold tapas include marinated olives, roasted red peppers stuffed with tuna and rice, and asparagus spears wrapped in smoked salmon. Hot versions to try are skewered chicken and chorizo with garliccumin mayo, squid sautéed in olive oil and garlic, and Pimento Del Piquillo Relleno, meatballs in a spicy garlic cream sauce. This last dish is so savory you'll want to make a boat with your bread—*hacer una barco* in Spanish—and sail it around the plate to pick up every bit of sauce.

If you still have room for entrees, two of the most popular are grilled steak with blue cheese and the Spanish paellas. The seafood version is loaded with shrimp, chunks of whitefish, scallops, mussels, and littleneck clams and served with lots of saffron-yellow rice. Skip the dessert and spend your last pesos on the special coffee made with several types of liqueurs. As you're sipping you'll have time to study the colorful decor, especially the mosaic bar and fabulous mural by local artist Peregrine Honig.

Lunch is available Monday through Saturday. Dinner is served daily.

Piropos $$–$$$
4140 North Mulberry Drive
(Briarcliff Village)
(816) 741-3600

1 West First Street (Private dining)
Parkville, MO
(816) 741-3600
www.piroposkc.com
In Buenos Aires the women are so beautiful that admirers have created an art form—loosely translated into *piropos*—for paying them compliments. The lovely Cristina Worden received a particularly fine piropo from husband Gary; he built a restaurant to showcase her country's cuisine.

The view alone will have you whistling in admiration. The restaurant makes the most of a hilltop setting overlooking the lights of Kansas City's skyline in the distance. In winter, the fireplace is another enchanting view.

At Piropos the food is the star, especially since it's based on ingredients we appreciate in the Midwest: excellent steaks and fresh salads. It's the trio of sauces that sets this cuisine apart: creamy garlic aioli; criolla made with peppers, tomato, celery, and vinegar; and chimichurri, that Argentinean staple made with parsley, garlic, vinegar, and olive oil. The sauces are served in tiny pots along with empanadas—the spiced beef version is especially flavorful—so you can pick your favorite.

There are some surprises on the menu. The fact that nearly half of Argentina is made up of Italians is evident in pasta dishes, such as ricotta and spinach–stuffed ravioli with a walnut-studded butter sauce. A pan-seared halibut brushed with a roasted red pepper puree leads the fish choices. But it's the grilled meats that stand out at Piropos, including succulent steaks, lamb, and pork chops. You'll find yourself asking for more sauces for dipping.

The desserts provide another nod to the Argentinian way of life. Dulce de leche—a caramel known in South America as milk candy—is drizzled over creamy flan, chocolate cake, and apple-filled crepes. Piropos serves lunch Monday through Friday and dinner daily. The original Parkville location is open for special (and we mean special) events only.

re:Verse (Country Club Plaza) $$
618 Ward Parkway
(816) 931-7811
www.reversekc.com
La Bodega owner James Taylor had an instant hit when he opened this hip place on one of the Plaza's most visible corners. The Beat Generation theme doesn't matter to the mostly twentysomethings at the bar, but the retro cocktails certainly do. The list includes grasshoppers, stingers, and martinis and a refreshing mojito made by adding white rum to a muddled mix of mint, sugar, and lime. The cocktails keep coming until 1:30 a.m., making it one of the late-night lounges of choice.

The decor is just as stylish as the crowd, with lipstick-red walls and ceiling, stainless steel panels, and viewing screens that let you peek into the kitchen. It can be quite a show on busy nights. The menu stars tapas, like its sister restaurant on the Boulevard: spicy tidbits to share with dining partners. The trio of ahi tuna slices is a nice choice; they're seared, tied with scallions like little packages, and served with a peanut-chili sauce. The sautéed calamari and spicy chorizo is a sensual delight on a stark white plate.

Pasta dishes are just as artfully dressed, and the grape leaf–wrapped sea bass is roasted, then placed on a bed of sautéed chard and creamy Israeli couscous. It's a dish that's big enough to share, especially if you've spent the first half of the evening trying several tapas. Re:Verse is open for lunch Monday through Saturday and dinner seven nights a week. A DJ or live music is on tap seven nights a week. For early birds, re:Verse serves espresso starting at 6:45 a.m. and breakfast from 7:00 to 10:30 a.m. Monday through Friday.

The sexy Red Room is our choice for private parties.

Shiraz (Crossroads Arts District) $$
320 Southwest Boulevard
(816) 472-0015

Stephanie and Ali Shirazi's first eatery was the West Side Cafe, a phone booth–sized place in a reconditioned gas station. When they moved to a bigger and prettier space a few blocks down the street, loyal fans followed, hungry for Ali's black beans and rice, tandoori chicken, and anything he decided to curry that day.

With its exposed brick walls, artwork from local artists, and metal cutouts at the windows casting intricate shadows at noon and night, Shiraz has a welcoming bohemian atmosphere. Low lights, flickering candles, and the heady fragrance of exotic spices make for a very sexy evening. If you notice that half the patrons have ordered the roasted red pepper appetizer, there's a reason. This terra cotta–colored dip of peppers, walnuts, pomegranate syrup, and tahini is addictive. It's served with warm toasted pita bread, and for another dollar a tasty black olive hummus will share the plate. Split the appetizer with a friend, add two fresh Greek-style salads, and you have a marvelous lunch.

Standouts on the dinner menu include pork chops served with a piquant pomegran-

ate glaze, and Ali's signature dish, gormeh sabzi: lamb shank braised with aromatic Persian herbs and sun-dried lemons until tender and flavorful. His eggplant Marrakesh stuffed with rice, tomatoes, and feta cheese is one of the most coveted vegetarian meals in town. Listen carefully to the dinner specials as well; if the server mentions sea bass, raise your hand immediately. It's always meltingly tender, a dish you'll dream about for weeks. With food this flavorful and plates filled to brimming, it's hard to save room for dessert. But it would be a shame to miss the flourless chocolate cake, hazelnut praline crunch, and chocolate mousse served with hazelnut ice cream. It's divine.

During nice weather ask for a table in the courtyard where, especially on balmy Saturday nights when a guitarist is playing lush flamenco music, there simply isn't a more romantic urban setting. Shiraz is open Monday through Friday for lunch and Tuesday through Saturday for dinner.

ITALIAN

The Copa Room $-$$
3421 Broadway
(816) 931-5200

Well, ring-a-ding-ding—if it isn't Frank, Dino, and Sammy! Well, the Rat Pack certainly would feel right at home at this small family-run Italian eatery. Handsome Carlo Fiorello turned to the best cook he knew to open his restaurant—his mom, Kathy (also known as Nani, Italian for "grandmother"). There must be something in those meatballs, because she's got to be the youngest-looking grandma in Kansas City.

It really is a family affair: Along with Nani, Carlo's cousins serve diners and even wife Lenae fills in when needed.

You'll find all the classics here, many served with Nani's famous sugo, a rich tomato sauce: ravioli, lasagna, stuffed artichoke, fried meatballs. Looking for something lighter? Basa, a delicate whitefish, is sautéed and served with a lemon wine sauce. Or order the

i We love to eat. On average, every man, woman, and child in Kansas City spends $938 dining out each year, according to the National Restaurant Association. That puts us third in U.S. metropolitan areas; just $30 less than first-ranking New York City and $17 less than Washington, D.C. We spent $29 more per person than San Francisco!

Frank, Dean, and Sammy Combo with chicken spiedini, lasagna, and penne Alfredo for less than 20 clams, and kiss your diet goodbye. Then go all out and order Nani's cheesecake.

Wednesday through Saturday night, the place is as lively as an Italian wedding, with music by Rudy Amato or Frank Vig, who perform your Rat Pack favorites from 9:00 p.m. until 1:00 a.m. There's no cover charge.

Parking for this pretty storefront restaurant is on the street, in a small lot in back, or across the street at the Missouri Gas and Energy building. How appropriate —The Copa Room *is* a gas.

Garozzo's Ristorante $–$$
526 Harrison (East Side)
(816) 221-2455

1547 Northeast Rice Road
Lee's Summit, MO
(816) 554-2800

13505 South Mur-Len
Olathe, KS
(913) 764-6969

Cafe Garozzo
9950 College Boulevard
Overland Park, KS
(913) 491-8300
www.garozzos.com

Some people have a standing reservation at the original Garozzo's on Harrison every Friday night, rebuilt after a fire destroyed it in 2003. Is it the 5-inch-high lasagna, Frank Sinatra tunes in the background, or owner Mike Garozzo singing along in his gravelly voice? Sorry, Mike. It's the food.

This multiroom restaurant is where many of us tasted our first chicken spiedini, that flavorful rolled breast of chicken smothered in a piquant garlic-lemon sauce. It's a recipe Mike brought from the Italian section of St. Louis known as the Hill in 1989, and every year more of us fall in love with the tangy taste, especially since he seems to add another restaurant every five years or so and all locations are open for lunch and dinner seven days a week.

Spiedini fans may find it hard to branch out, but the menu offers other wonderful items, particularly specialties named for Garozzo family and friends, such as the Gambretti Angelina, charbroiled, jumbo shrimp in a white wine butter sauce with mushrooms and fresh broccoli. The Bistecca Salvatore Alla Siciliano is a sixteen-ounce porterhouse that's breaded, charbroiled, and basted in amogio sauce, that garlicky lemon concoction that defines so many dishes here. Thanks, Sal, wherever you are.

All entrees are served with a house salad, pasta or vegetable on the side, and bread and butter. Skip the yellow spread and dip your bread in what's known as Italian butter, a small plate of olive oil, freshly ground black pepper, grated Parmesan cheese, and a sprinkling of red pepper flakes. The appetizers are hard to pass up. Pray that cream of artichoke is the soup of the day; it's worth every bit of butter and cream. The Heaven and Hell is pesto-stuffed ravioli and lawn prawn charbroiled in fiery diablo sauce.

Pastas are, naturally, excellent here, and a variety of tubular and ribbon noodles are available with tomato sauce, Alfredo, or simple crushed tomatoes and garlic. If you're lucky somebody will order the Three Way Pasta, a platter overflowing with ravioli, spaghetti, and mostaccioli and topped with a softball-sized meatball. We've been waiting to see it polished off in one sitting. And on Thursday the lunch specials often include short ribs that are so delicious they often sell out early.

You'll be happy to know Garozzo's also

sells house-made sauces, salad dressings, and its own line of pasta at each restaurant and several grocery stores throughout the Kansas City area.

Jasper's (South Kansas City) $$–$$$
1201 West 103rd Street
(816) 941-6600
www.jasperskc.com

For nearly five decades the Mirabile (pronounced *Mir-AH-bill-ee*) family, led by Jasper Sr., collected culinary rating stars, diamonds, and a multistate fan club for serving classic Italian food at its formal dining room on Wornall Road. When it moved south patrons followed the aroma of grilled sausages, roasted lamb shanks, and garlic to its new home. And now thanks to a more casual atmosphere—it's not unusual to see shorts in summer—a younger crowd has discovered this Kansas City treasure. Loyal customers were happy to see such favorites as baked lasagna and veal scaloppini on the menu even after the patriarch passed away.

Jasper Mirabile Jr.—friends call him JJ—has been running the kitchen for many years. His respect for traditional Italian cuisine and genius for creating new dishes have earned him accolades around the world. He's been a guest chef at the James Beard House—the first Kansas City chef so honored—and featured in the *New York Times*, *Midwest Living*, and *Italy's Cucina*. And he's always improvising: A tour of Venice inspired entrees such as grilled sea bass with truffle sauce and fire-roasted duck with blood orange and dried cherry balsamic demi-glace. Did we mention his lobster and ricotta ravioli? Bellisimo!

JJ also finds time to share his passion with others. He teaches cooking classes at the Culinary Center of Kansas City (see www.kcculinary.com for schedules) and at the organic farmers' market at Barstow School each summer.

Finding the door to the restaurant can be a bit confusing. You enter through the family-owned Marco Polo's Italian Market, a tiny shop filled with cheeses, meats, condiments, and homemade take-out dishes such as savory Italian meatloaf. Make a mental note to stop by during lunch for a grilled sausage and pepper sandwich.

On pleasant evenings ask for a table on Jasper's patio, where the quiet gurgle of Indian Creek and canopy of trees can make you forget you're near a busy intersection. The restaurant is open for lunch and dinner seven days a week, and reservations are accepted for parties of six or more. For smaller groups, you may call an hour or so before you plan to arrive and ask to be placed on a wait list.

Always improvising and improving on ways to treat his customers like family, JJ recently added a lovely wine bar to his restaurant. The first Italian *enoteca* in Kansas City, it's a wonderful way to relax with friends over a flight of reds and whites from Piedmonte, Tuscany, Umbria, Sicily, and more. Colorful blown-glass lighting fixtures add a warm glow to the cozy room. Ask to see the tasting chamber, a charming choice for a private party.

Lidia's (Freighthouse District) $$
101 East 22nd Street
(816) 221-3722
www.lidiasitaly.com

It was quite a coup when famed restaurateur and public TV cooking show host Lidia Bastianich chose Kansas City for her first restaurant outside New York. Locals who'd been dazzled by her northern Italian cuisine at Becco and Felidia helped create a buzz that hasn't abated even after several years.

Lidia and her team decided to open in the Freighthouse District near Union Station, an area that had been neglected for decades. It's now the hottest area in town thanks to the nearby art galleries and shops in the Crossroads Arts District. The three-story room is dominated by spectacular blown-glass balloons fashioned into chandeliers, which are reminiscent of Dale Chihuly's famous work. Oversized wine bottles in silhouette create another dramatic decoration.

For those who thought Lidia's would raise the bar on restaurant prices, the opposite is true. Servings are generous and prices are surprisingly low. It may be hard to select just one entree from the expansive, evocative menu, so no one will blame you for simply ordering the pasta trio. It takes "all you can eat" to an entirely new level as servers circle the rooms to refill plates with pastas fresh from the kitchen. The selection changes daily but usually includes a ravioli, sauced ribbon shape, and aromatic risotto. For around $13 it is without a doubt the most delicious bargain in town.

The regular menu includes roasted veal shank with saffron-scented barley risotto and grilled salmon over braised lentils with a zesty chive-mustard sauce. Even the rib-eye steak gets an Italian lesson with a rosemary, sea salt, and anchovy rub before it's grilled.

Lidia has left her namesake restaurant in the capable hands of executive chef Dan Sweeny and pastry chef Cody Hogan, whose contributions include bonet al caffe, a molded custard flavored with chocolate, amaretto, and espresso, and a tiramisu some consider the best in town. No room for dessert after your fifth helping of pasta? Then end the evening as the Italians do, with a caffe corretto, "corrected coffee," that's braced with shots of grappa and liqueur.

Lidia's is open for lunch Monday through Saturday, dinner daily, and brunch on Sunday. The deck is one of the most romantic places in town.

Seven   **$$–$$$**
100 East 7th Street
Kansas City, MO
(816) 777-1107
www.seven-kc.com
At last! Kansas City has an upscale venue that's worthy of our downtown's renaissance. The look is sexy and lush, with a long agate table lit from underneath, white curtains that change colors with the beat of the music, a bar area that magically turns into a DJ-run dance floor at night, and an intimate loft area where you can watch all the action from cushy sofas while imbibing with your own VIP drink service. For around $250 you can host your own private party with a bottle of Grey Goose and all the accoutrements. The stunning view of downtown is free.

But for our money, we'll take a hand-shaken cocktail any day. Fans of Susan Avery, an alchemist who won *KC Magazine*'s Bartender of the Year twice while at the late, great Zin, will recognize her hand in creating the Seven Deadly Sins cocktail menu featuring her flower- and fruit-infused vodkas. Envy, anyone?

Meanwhile, longtime devotees of co-owner Victor Fontana will recognize several northern Italian dishes from the time he ran the trendy Fanny's, Veco's, or Frankie's on the Plaza. Steak Modiga, short ribs, calamari, and a terrific pistachio-crusted salmon top the dinner menu, which also repeats the list of pastas and pizzas (including a heavenly sweet fig and Gorgonzola number) from lunch. The Ragu of Wild Mushrooms over Creamy Polenta is the classiest comfort food you'll ever have.

Parking is on the streets or free in the spacious lot across the street. This is the place for the city's most attractive singles to be seen late at night. Our advice? Dress to the nines to show up at Seven at 10.

MEXICAN/SOUTHWESTERN

La Fonda El Taquito (Midtown)   **$**
800 Southwest Boulevard
(816) 471-1675
Drive up and down Southwest Boulevard and you'll find the real deal: Mexican restaurants where the owner's grandmother stirs the pork chili while a younger sister presses tortillas one at a time. El Taquito is just such a place. It got its start in 1978 when Augustin Medina opened a tortilla factory in a tiny storefront. When he began serving lunch to help with the cash flow, the food was so tantalizing it became his chief business.

Twelve years ago La Fonda moved to its current location at the corner of Summit and Southwest Boulevard, where those fresh tortillas scoop up succulent pork chili. Like true family-style Mexican food, the flavors are not hot, but you can crank up the heat by adding freshly made salsas in temperatures ranging from mild to wild.

Flavorful pork is also used for the taquito carnitas, soft-shell tacos that satisfy right down to your soul. The taquitos can also be ordered with chicken or chorizo. Burritos are popular as well, but leave room for the sopapillas, fried bread dusted with cinnamon sugar, or the smooth flan.

On Friday and Saturday nights live Latino music turns the front area into a salsa and merengue dance floor. Things cool down a bit a few hours later, just in time for a Sunday brunch when huevos rancheros and other classic dishes liven up the menu. La Fonda is open seven days a week.

Tarahumara Mexican Restaurant $$–$$$
10001 West 87th Street
Overland Park, KS
(913) 403-9211
www.tarahumaramexicanfood.com

Your mouth may stumble over the name of this rustic restaurant, but local foodies are raving about this place—despite the fact that it's in the suburbs instead of midtown's Southwest Boulevard. Seeing the words "mozzarella cheese" on a Mexican menu is usually the tip-off that the food isn't the real deal, but the flavors are authentic.

Although you'll find all the usual suspects, from enchiladas to tamales and burritos, Tara is known for its specialties. Chuletas Adobadas are pork steaks in adobo sauce; Puerco en Salsa Verde, chunks of pork that have been cooking for hours served in a tomatillo sauce; and Bistek con Papas, grilled steak served with potatoes, jalapeños, and onions. Regulars simply go for the addictive soft tacos filled with barbacoa and cilantro for $1.50 each. Just add a bowl of chunky guacamole and an icy margarita, and who needs a strolling mariachi band?

Along with classic margaritas, Tarahumara serves Mexican and domestic beers. And mole? Olé!

SEAFOOD

Fresh seafood lovers, your ship has come in. Thanks to overnight shipping, several restaurants receive fresh fish and shellfish shipments six days a week. Then they fry, grill, roast, blacken, or pan sauté them with finesse. Following are some of the seafood restaurants that really float our boat.

Bristol Bar and Grill $$–$$$
5400 West 119th Street
Overland Park, KS
(913) 663-5777
www.bristolseafoodgrill.com

Fans of this Kansas City classic were crushed when it left its longtime spot on the Country Club Plaza (where Capital Grill now resides), but they didn't have long to pine. It reopened, gorgeous stained-glass dome and all, near one of our *other* open-air shopping centers, Town Center Plaza. The Bristol also kept its slightly sweet drop biscuits that servers bring around throughout your meal, as well as the beloved Sunday brunch. This button-popping buffet features dozens of dishes including seafood pasta, cheese grits, crab soufflé, peel-and-eat spiced shrimp, carved prime rib, scrambled eggs and egg casseroles, fresh fruit, a Belgian waffle bar, and decadent desserts such as Key lime tarts, bread pudding, and chocolate-dipped strawberries.

At lunch and dinner, however, it's the seafood that rules. Several types of fish are available seared, grilled, baked, or blackened, including yellowfin tuna, salmon, and mahimahi. The Bristol is open seven days a week for lunch or brunch and dinner, and the huge parking lot is always filled on weekends, when reservations are a must.

McCormick & Schmick's
(Country Club Plaza) $$–$$$
448 West 47th Street
(816) 531-6800
www.mccormickandschmicks.com

Is it our imagination, or does this place look like a casting call for *Friends?* Perhaps it's the cosmopolitan martini that casts a rosy glow. Whatever the reason, here's where the beautiful people show up to see and be seen and partake of happy hour appetizers. The rest of us get happy by heading to a dinner table. And if you want to get positively silly, reserve one of the booths (called a "snug") with curtains that can be drawn discreetly shut.

Good luck choosing from this eye-popping menu of no less than thirty fresh seafood entrees. And they do mean fresh: Fish is shipped in six days a week. You might start with oysters on the half shell from Washington, Long Island, Prince Edward Island, and British Columbia; a sampler plate will get you a few from each location. During cold weather the traditional oyster stew is the perfect comfort food.

The menu changes daily based on the latest coastal catch but usually includes specialties such as salmon roasted on a cedar plank and served with a pinot noir sauce or stuffed with crab, shrimp, and Brie; and cashew-crusted tilapia with a Jamaican rum butter sauce. Grilled steaks and imaginative pasta dishes are also available.

For dessert, there's a delightful white chocolate mousse encased in a dark chocolate bag served with fresh berries and whipped cream. Now don't you wish you'd requested one of those secluded snugs?

Lunch and dinner are served Monday through Sunday. Reservations are highly recommended for the main dining rooms and the outdoor patio overlooking the Plaza.

Trezo Mare Ristorante $$–$$$
4105 North Mulberry Drive
(Briarcliff Village)
(816) 505-3200
www.trezomare.com
The story behind this glamorous restaurant includes a local boy, an Italian beauty, a playboy, and an ex-*Vogue* model. With all that brewing, how could a night here be anything but romantic? Even the name, a marriage of Spanish and Italian meaning "treasures of the sea," has panache.

Los Angeles interior designer Hal Swanson (who hails from Kansas City), carved out a handsome wine room, bar and lounge, and open dining room, all in the golden colors of Italy. Unfortunately, the only room that makes use of that glorious view of downtown is the bar, where you can enjoy happy hour on the patio or indoors. The fireplace is a nice touch on cool evenings. Also pretty cool is the cocktail menu, featuring house-infused spirits that change with the seasons. The Russian 80 is a refreshing summertime cooler that serves a cucumber-infused gin in a lemon-sugar-rimmed martini glass.

Befitting the name, seafood is the star here. Appetizers include fresh Manila clams, seared crab cakes, and a cruda "duet" that pairs bigeye and king salmon prepared two ways. Treat your tablemates to a Trezo feast, (for around $45), which comes chilly, with an assortment of lobster, shrimp, and more, or crispy, with tempura versions of shellfish.

The menu changes daily—as it should with a menu made of fresh seafood—but a few recent temptations included grilled cold-water lobster on rigatoni tossed in a lobster cream sauce, seared day-boat scallops, and wood-fired ahi tuna with red chili fried rice and jalapeño-wasabi slaw.

Order wine from the extensive menu, or keep a stash in your personal wine locker. This VIP treatment comes with membership in the Wine Cru, which includes invitations to special events and discounts on wine purchases during the year.

SOUL FOOD

The Mango Room $–$$
1111 Main Street
(816) 268-4600
www.kcmangoroom.com
Take a Caribbean vacation at this lively downtown spot where the walls are a sunny yellow and the food is a happy fusion of island cuisine and soul food. It's the love child of Grand Street Cafe veterans Thelma Oliver and Chef Ian Hockenberg, who got his cooking chops at

Spago and Chez Panisse. This is the only place in town to find such a savory mixture of Jamaican meat patties, braised oxtails with a jerk dry rub, fried chicken and catfish, and brown sugar–brined pork chops.

Daily lunch specials such as green pork chili, along with fresh salads topped with salmon or grilled chicken, bring in the crowds. Every meal includes a breadbasket filled with sweet-potato muffins and other home-baked goodies. The macaroni and cheese is also special; done in a casserole style, it comes sliced into a wedge and drizzled with Mornay sauce.

Dinners here might start with a pineapple-infused Bob Marleytini served in a chilled stainless-steel vessel. Once you're in the mood, go for the plantain-crusted halibut or jambalaya. Braised greens may be your cup of tea, but we'll order the cheddar grits anytime. But do save room for the hot mango cobbler with homemade ice cream.

A happy hour, friendly service, and validated parking in the Town Pavilion garage at 12th and Walnut make this a perfect spot for before or after an arts performance downtown. Or make it your prime destination and relax for the evening. A jazz trio plays on Friday and Saturday nights, and the Mango also hosts wine dinners. It's our favorite form of island-hopping.

Peachtree   **$–$$**
1512 East 18th Street
(18th and Vine District)
(816) 472-8733

The Peachtree Buffet
6800 Eastwood Trafficway
(816) 923-0099
www.peachtreerestaurant.com
Real lard. Real butter. Real home cooking made with soul. That's Peachtree's way at both the original all-you-can-eat buffet on Eastwood and the pretty new place in the heart of the historic 18th and Vine District. The buffet tables practically groan under the weight of all the fried chicken and catfish, smothered pork chops, macaroni and cheese,

candied yams, and salad fixings—more than twenty selections prepared fresh daily. Save room for the famous peach cobbler and bread pudding, but you might want to order a dozen sweet potato corn bread muffins to go.

In the jazz district, the Peachtree is a fine start or finish to your trip to the American Jazz Museum or Negro Leagues Hall of Fame (see Attractions) or before heading to one of Kansas City's top performers at the Blue Room. But the restaurant entices you to stay in your seat for the evening when it serves up great music on Friday and Saturday nights. That's just as well; after partaking in all the Southern dishes, you may not want to move a muscle except to clap or snap your fingers to the beat.

Prized choices include zesty "Sister Baby" baby back ribs, "Ole Time" salmon croquettes, Ragtime rib eye, and plenty of Southern fried chicken and spiced shrimp. Of course there's okra, corn bread and greens. Is the sweet potato pie calling your name yet?

STEAKHOUSES

As the city that gave the world the Kansas City strip—please don't ask for a New York strip around here—we're known for our steaks. This particular cut came to be in 1946 when Eddie Williams bid $35.05 per pound—ten times the going rate—for a champion Hereford at the American Royal livestock auction. It made T. O. Pride's sixteen-year-old owner $44,375 richer and created national attention for Kansas City steaks. Following is a cowtown primer on cuts of beef, along with a few suggestions about where they do them up royally.

- **Filet:** Selected from the finest beef tenderloin, this cut is the tenderest, most melt-in-your-mouth of all red meats. Usually available in six–, eight–, and ten-ounce cuts.
- **Kansas City strip:** A beautifully marbled, boneless cut loaded with flavor. Typically available in ten- and twelve-ounce sizes.

- **T-bone:** A very thick, very juicy cut that's fit for a king or queen. Better save room for this one; it's often served in twenty-two-ounce cuts.
- **Rib-eye:** Very juicy and flavorful, this steak is hand-cut from the naturally aged prime rib.

Benton's Steak and Chop House $$–$$$
1 Pershing Road in the
Westin Crown Center Hotel
(816) 391-4460
www.bentonskc.com

Ah, decisions, decisions. Shall we have the Western Auto sign, the Marriott Hotel light display, or the Liberty Memorial flame? Those aren't menu items, they're just three of the spectacular views from Benton's floor-to-ceiling windows twenty floors above the Westin Hotel. One early July visit brought a 360-degree panorama of fireworks from all over the city, and a midwinter dinner gave us a scene of ice skaters and the mayor's Christmas tree in the Crown Center square below.

The interior is nearly as spectacular, especially the sixteen original works by namesake and beloved Kansas City artist Thomas Hart Benton. A recent renovation brought on soothing tones of pale wood, stacked-stone fireplaces (with elegant fireballs instead of logs), and crisp white tablecloths offset by cobalt-blue glassware. It's chic but not intimidating; you'll see travelers in khakis and cropped pants, couples dressed up for date night, and families enjoying Sunday brunch. More about that extravaganza later.

Chef Martin Hueser deftly supervises a panorama of dishes, from double-cut pork chops to tasty holdovers, such as steamed dumplings, from the days of the popular Asian eatery downstairs, Trader Vic's. And if you think a steak is a steak is a steak, you'll be pleasantly surprised. Benton's starts with twenty-one-day-aged certified Angus beef flavored with a signature seasoning that adds a unique, tangy hickory flavor. The chargrilled top sirloin is as tender as a filet and flavorful as a KC strip; it could change a vegan's mind.

Fish lovers will also find plenty to love with such succulent entrees as wild striped bass, lobster tails, and swordfish steaks served with a pineapple relish. The wine list is well rounded as well. Pastry chef Damian Fraase delivers with such treats as his Chocolate Gateau, made of sinfully rich chocolate mousse with a center of cheesecake, all topped with soft chocolate ganache. View? What view?

The Sunday brunch is a popular choice for holidays such as Mother's Day or Easter, but it's a celebration any weekend. Service is from 10:00 a.m. to 2:00 p.m. Between the eggs Benedict, Thai chicken salad, and lobster bisque, you may not notice the ice sculptures, fantastic dessert display, and mounds of caviar. After all, what's champagne without it? Pace yourself; there are over a hundred items to choose from, including healthy fresh fruit, an omelet station, and carving stations with prime rib.

Another "prime" time to come is Thursday through Saturday evenings, when the pretty lounge offers live jazz to go with the view. Check the Web site for wine flights and appetizer specials. In fact, that's where we snagged a coupon for a free flambéed dessert prepared tableside one evening. Or you could simply watch the flame over the Liberty Memorial to your left.

The Capital Grille (Country Club Plaza) $$$
4740 Jefferson Street
(816) 531-8345
www.thecapitalgrille.com

When readers of *KC Magazine* named this the best steakhouse in town, they raised a few eyebrows. Frankly, it's rare that a transplant—and a thirty-two–location national chain at that—can win the hearts of such a loyal crowd. But this ultraplush restaurant earns its accolades. It provides just the right clubby atmosphere, starting at the handsome granite-and-mahogany entrance. There's even a signature martini, the Stoli Doli, made with slices of pineapple marinating in glass crocks of Stolichnaya vodka on the bar.

The seating is sumptuous whether you're in a plush booth, at a white linen–draped table, or in one of the private dining rooms that are usually taken by the bigwigs from our football organization. As you're escorted to your table, you'll pass the glass case where beef is dry aging for fourteen to twenty-one days. When they're at the peak of flavor, steaks are hand-cut, well seasoned, and seared at 1,100 degrees Fahrenheit to seal in the juices and provide that distinctive caramelized crust. And that, according to the executive chef, is the key to the Capital's extraordinarily good steaks.

Purists will simply order a fourteen- or twenty-ounce Kansas City strip or filet sans topping, but the steak au poivre with Courvoisier cognac cream sauce is pretty remarkable, too. So are the signature veal chops with Roquefort butter sauce.

But first things first. Dinners can start with cold baby lobster with confetti mayonnaise, a sinfully rich lobster bisque, or the "Wedge," an enormous portion of iceberg lettuce with blue cheese and crumbled bacon. As for lunch, the steak salad is large enough for two, or one diner with dreams of a second meal.

Service is refined yet friendly, with servers who say "My pleasure" to any request—and mean it. Don't be surprised if you receive a handwritten note a day or two after your visit. An impressive wine list includes more than 300 bottles ranging from $27 to well over $500. A few large and half bottles are available as well. And true wine connoisseurs will appreciate the fine crystal glassware without a rolled rim. At about $12 a stem, it's an investment in quality that sets the right tone. Wine lockers are available to store your personal collection; the brass plaques lining the wall read like a "Who's Who" of Kansas City elite.

If you need one more reason to make a reservation, consider the deep-dish Key lime pie with toasted pistachio crust. The restaurant is open for lunch on weekdays and dinner seven days a week, including a 9:00 p.m. last call on Sunday.

Hereford House $$–$$$
20th and Main Street (Downtown)
(816) 842-1080

5001 Town Center Drive
Leawood, KS
(913) 327-0800

19721 East Jackson Street
Independence, MO
(816) 795-9200

8661 North Stoddard Avenue
(Zona Rosa)
(816) 584-9000
www.herefordhouse.com

Since 1957 the Hereford House's downtown restaurant has been serving perfectly aged, trimmed, and grilled steaks seven days a week to willing carnivores. It's even rumored that the phrase "juicy and tender" was coined in this very spot.

So naturally longtime fans were relieved when new owner Rod Anderson kept the restaurant's ambience and most of its tenured staff when he remodeled the downtown landmark in 1987. A year later he opened a location in Leawood, then Independence, and now he's planted his brand in Zona Rosa.

For real beef lovers, the thrill begins with a charred carpaccio sliced paper thin and served chilled with a peppy chipotle mayonnaise. Or try plump mushroom caps stuffed with shrimp and crab in a creamy cheese sauce. The steaks, of course, are delicious, either simply grilled or topped with a cracked pepper and blue cheese sauce or Dijon mustard and brown sugar glaze. Fish is done right here as well, particularly the cedar-plank salmon that's oven roasted and served with a garlic herb butter. Side dishes include the signature cowboy baked beans and twice-baked potato. As for the creamy Italian and cheddar cheese salad dressings, regulars refer to them as "pink" and "yellow" and usually order a little of both.

Hereford House is also a business-lunch mecca, usually packed with nearby office staff and conventioneers who've heard about the daily specials, such as twin beef medallions,

French dip, or meat loaf with mashed potatoes and gravy. Leave room somehow for the heavenly white chocolate bread pudding or peach cobbler served with vanilla ice cream.

All four restaurants are open seven days a week. The Leawood location offers kosher dinners with advance notice. The dress is casual, and reservations are recommended. For a beef-eater's bargain, try the Sunset Dinner special.

J. Gilbert's $$–$$$
8901 Metcalf
Overland Park, KS
(913) 632-8070
www.jgilberts.com

This restaurant has the high honor of being named for Joe Gilbert, the beloved restaurateur who helped build the Gilbert-Robinson empire. It's a fitting tribute. The interior is a handsome mix of stone and dark woods with an enormous bar area and some of the friendliest bartenders in town. While you're enjoying a cocktail you'll have time to sample the addictive house-made potato chips with blue cheese sauce.

The dining areas are beautiful as well, with a cozy fireplace, big cushy booths, and a golden glow from the low lighting. Take your time with the menu; although J. Gilbert's fashions itself a steakhouse, it offers some excellent seafood, chicken, and pasta dishes, such as a five-spice chicken penne with a smoked Gouda sauce.

But this place definitely knows how to put the sizzle into a steak. They select only cornfed Black Angus beef, then sear the steaks on a wood-fire grill hot enough to seal in the flavorful juices within seconds. Purists will go for the tender filet mignon, and those who hanker for something fancy might like the bourbon-based sauce. The side dishes really shine here as well, especially the poblano potatoes au gratin.

J. Gilbert's provides the right atmosphere for a romantic anniversary dinner, yet is casual enough for families. It's open for dinner only, Monday through Sunday.

Jess & Jim's Steak House
(South Kansas City) $$
517 East 135th Street
(816) 941-9499
www.jessandjims.com

A tornado took this place off the map in the 1950s, but it landed forever on the culinary map in 1972 when Calvin Trillin announced in *Playboy* that it served the best steak in the universe. The notoriety resulted in expansion—twice—and a new menu that included a twenty-five-ounce Playboy Strip.

The restaurant's namesakes are gone; Jim for good in 1981 and Jess on the West Coast, where he no doubt misses Midwest beef. But the tradition lives on with Jim's kin, the Van-Noy family. And just to prove that lightning *can* strike twice, Jess & Jim's was recently mentioned again in *Playboy,* when the magazine called it "the quintessential Midwestern steakhouse." The article got it right; the place is next to railroad tracks, meat hangs in the window, and the waitresses are stunned if someone asks to see a dessert menu.

There are ten cuts of steaks available, including filets ranging in size from five to fourteen ounces, and an eye-popping, button-flying thirty-ounce porterhouse. Steaks are served sizzling on big hot silver platters. You can order them any way you like, but please note that steaks cooked beyond medium well are not guaranteed.

Other entrees include lobster—available either steamed or battered and fried—frog legs, chicken gizzards, and shrimp. And most come with your choice of a football-sized baked potato, fabulous cottage fries, plus soup or salad and homemade garlic toast. There's even a surprisingly varied wine list that includes twenty-three cabernets.

Jess & Jim's steaks are also available for carryout, as are gallon jars of their famous pickled beets. And here's a secret: Sometimes you'll find a money-saving coupon on their Web site. The promotion changes based on the time of year, but you can bet it has nothing to do with dessert.

The restaurant is open for lunch and dinner Monday through Saturday.

The Majestic Steakhouse (Downtown) $$$
931 Broadway
(816) 471-8484
www.majesticgroup.com

This slim three-story building once housed Fitzpatrick's saloon and a bordello, making it a popular place for gangsters and political bigshots during the 1930s. Pressed tin ceilings, tile floors, and stained-glass lights reveal its turn-of-the-twentieth-century age and helped put it on the National Register of Historic Places.

Since 1993 the landmark has gone from making history to serving historically good steaks. The Majestic is justly proud of its twenty-one-day dry-aged prime beef. True carnivores will simply point to the twelve-ounce Kansas City strip, a marbled steak so flavorful you may not notice the flaky baked potato and sautéed vegetables on the side.

And that brings up a good point regarding prices. Unlike a lot of steakhouses that offer salads and side dishes a la carte, the Majestic's entrees come fully loaded, including a salad with a tasty house-made basil-walnut dressing. Owner Doug Barnard—a wine buff himself—has peppered the 800-label wine list with bottles starting at just $12. All in all it makes for a rather reasonable evening out, especially when you add in the free entertainment. You can hear some of Kansas City's finest jazz musicians seven nights a week in the lower level, and there's never a cover charge. Lunch is served weekdays and dinner every night.

And don't hesitate to order a before- or after-dinner drink here; Prohibition has been over for years. Not that it mattered when Tom Pendergast ran the city from this address. You'll find out more about him in the History chapter, but in the meantime you can visit his cigar club on the third floor, complete with walk-in humidor, stained glass, and leather chairs. Although it's a private club you can be a temporary guest of the restaurant as long as there's no special event going on.

Plaza III The Steakhouse (Country Club Plaza) $$$
4749 Pennsylvania
(816) 753-0000

5020 West 137th Street
Leawood, KS
(913) 239-8499
www.plazaiiisteakhouse.com

The fact that this place still packs them in, even after big-name national steakhouses moved into the neighborhood, is affirmation of its excellent food and great service. The Spanish-style decor hasn't changed much since duo Joe Gilbert and Paul Robinson, along with Joe's son Bill, opened it in 1963.

Dinners start with complimentary chilled vegetables and ranch-style dip, but our advice is to save yourself for what's on the menu. Standout appetizers include the famous Plaza III Steak Soup, a thick broth of ground beef and vegetables, and a spinach salad with spiced roasted walnuts and hot bacon dressing. Side dishes include a one-pound baked Idaho potato and delectable creamed spinach, and crispy latkelike hash browns with onions.

But let's get down to why Plaza III is consistently rated one of the country's top steakhouses. It's the beef. They hand-select only cornfed, center-cut USDA-graded prime beef and then age it from three to four weeks in their own beef locker. Optional diable, béarnaise, and pan-gravy sauces are available but totally unnecessary with steaks of this caliber. If you're not in the mood for steak, lobster and salmon are also on the menu.

The extensive wine list has won acclaim from *Wine Spectator*. And before or after

Beyond barbecue and steaks, we have a few other hometown recipes to sample. The Plaza III steak soup is a perennial favorite, as is the baked potato soup at the Grand Cafe. You'll also want to try a brew from Boulevard Beer, and finish your meal with java from the Roasterie Coffee. Several top restaurants also serve their own blends.

dinner you can head to the cozy bar through the side door or downstairs to the jazz lounge for live music.

Plaza III recently brought its legacy—along with Sunday brunch—to Leawood. The buffet, served from 10:00 a.m. to 3:00 p.m., has over sixty selections.

Lunch and dinner are served Monday through Saturday. Dinner only is available Sunday.

VEGETARIAN

Vegans and the diet conscious can usually find at least one or two meatless meals on the menus of most of the restaurants listed above. But the following places cater to those who love veggies and grains.

Blue Bird Bistro (West Side) $
1700 Summit
(816) 221-7559
www.kansascitymenus.com/bluebirdbistro
At this storefront cafe located above the downtown bluffs, you'll see a diverse crowd enjoying inventive dishes and a cozy atmosphere. Although dishes with free-range chicken and chemical-free beef and pork have been added, many still consider this their favorite vegetarian menu.

Salads include a quinoa with peppers, red onion, dried apricots, and currants with a lemon and olive oil dressing. Add a cup of curried red-lentil and tomato soup and it's a dandy lunch. The whole-wheat thin-crust pizzas topped with an assortment of vegetables and homemade tomato sauce are popular anytime, as is the veggie lasagna.

There's also a full bar, where you can try a chilled Japanese sake. Lunch and dinner are served Monday through Saturday, with a Sunday brunch.

Eden Alley Cafe (Country Club Plaza) $
707 West 47th Street
(816) 561-5415
Hidden in the basement of the Unity Temple on the Plaza, this fun and funky place evokes the feeling of a hippie hangout from the 1960s. The patrons, however, are a mixed bag. At any given table you can see business types from surrounding offices, book club participants, and, yes, vegetarians looking for delicious dishes starring whole grains, beans, and greens.

The day's menu appears on a blackboard above the tiny kitchen, and always includes tasty salads and a veggie burger that could change your mind about meatless fare. Other frequent offerings include pizza and cheesy quesadillas. With what you've saved in animal fat, you can splurge on a yummy cake or brownie. But be sure to bring cash, because Eden Alley doesn't take credit cards or checks. It's open for lunch only on Monday and Tuesday, and lunch and dinner Wednesday through Saturday. Saturday brunch, from 11:00 a.m. to 4:00 p.m., is a la carte, and the new patio is beautiful.

SUNDAY BRUNCH

Some folks save all their calories for Sunday, when several restaurants offer items from an a la carte menu or a brunch buffet. Show up and you'll be rewarded with made-to-order omelets, boiled spiced shrimp, carved prime rib of beef, fresh pastries, and everything in between. And on special occasions such Easter, Mother's Day, and Thanksgiving, lots of other places fire up the chafing dishes, so call ahead and ask. If a restaurant listed below does not appear elsewhere in this chapter, we include the address in its description.

Many rate the brunch at **Tofi Restaurant** in Overland Park, Kansas's Doubletree Hotel the "Best in Kansas City." One look at the six-station feast and you'll understand why. Chefs will prepare omelets to your liking, carve prime rib as thick as you'd like, and pop out hot, crispy Belgian waffles. There are also peel-and-eat shrimp, fresh fruits and salads, grilled asparagus and red peppers, a medley of fresh breakfast pastries, fluffy scrambled eggs, ham, crisp bacon, and desserts including brownies, chocolate cake, lemon tarts, and the chocolate chip cookies this hotel is known for.

Ophelia's on Independence Square serves brunch items from its inventive menu and is a great place to begin a trip to nearby the Truman Library and Museum. The big-daddy brunch is part of Benton's charm, along with the stunning view of midtown.

At **YiaYia's Eurobistro**, where the service is like a big comfortable hug, a diverse brunch menu greets you every Sunday. Two standouts are Corey's crab omelet and the Big Guy, an eye-popper that includes eggs Benedict, lox and bagel, a blueberry pancake, strawberry French toast, oven-roasted potatoes, and bacon or sausage. Add a cup of YiaYia's private coffee blend and you're set for the day. At **Yahooz!**, its cousin across the street, you can enjoy a brunch buffet that includes egg-based casseroles, roasted meats, fruit parfaits, and more.

Brunch may be the best—certainly the quietest—time to try **Tomfooleries Restaurant & Bar** (612 West 47th Street, 816-753- 0555) because all the twentysomethings are still in bed. You'll be treated to an amazing number of pastries, hot dishes, cold shrimp, made-to-order omelets with fifty choices of ingredients, and unusual buffet items such as cold pizza and hot corned-beef hash.

ALFRESCO DINING

During nice weather it's grand to dine outdoors on a deck or patio where you can hold hands with your date or hold court with a group of friends. Following are some suggestions, many of which you'll find detailed elsewhere in this chapter.

At **Lidia's** umbrella-dotted patio you can enjoy dinner or simply dessert and Italian coffee while listening to the gurgle of a water fountain or the roar of a freight train rushing by. The scent from the restaurant's herb garden adds more appeal. The skinny brick-lined patio at **Shiraz** is popular on pleasant evenings. With soul-stirring guitar music and Ali's fabulous menu, this is an urban paradise. The **Classic Cup** on the Plaza is the place to see and be seen, particularly if you get a coveted spot on the front sidewalk, where the people-watching is as lively as the food. There's also a large deck in back. During a sunset or on a starry night, there's perhaps no better place to be than the tiny European-style balcony at **Figlio** on the Plaza overlooking beautiful Mill Creek Park and the J. C. Nichols fountain. **McCormick & Schmick's** is even more popular when the calypso music plays starting in May. A steel-drum duo and bar specials will make you feel like you're in the tropics. On Thursdays, jazz provides a sultry beat as you meet and mingle. If that's not enough to put you in the mood, cocktails are discounted and the peel-and-eat shrimp are a steal.

Baja 600 (600 Ward Parkway, 816-931-6600) offers an enormous deck area right on the Country Club Plaza's most visible street where margaritas are as fresh as the cute guy at the next table.

The Cheesecake Factory (4701 Wyandotte, 816-960-1919) has a flower-decked patio where patrons indulge in the town's biggest salads and sandwiches, then share a slice of heaven for dessert.

Trezo Mare's patio has a stunning view of downtown. It's almost as tempting as the fruit-infused cocktails and the seared ahi tuna waiting for you inside.

For a lovely waterfall view and fabulous Italian food, head to **Jasper's** patio. Here, surrounded by shady trees and the quiet splashing of Indian Creek, you'd swear you were at a private retreat instead of in the suburbs. And at **Joe D's** in Brookside, any table will guarantee you a wonderful meal, but during nice weather patrons fight over the last seat on the patio. The sidewalk fronting **re:Verse** on the Plaza is where the young and beautiful hang out.

NIGHTLIFE

To taste the true essence of our town, you simply must spend an evening listening to jazz. It was that syncopated, soulful, savory stew of many different musical styles, after all, that put Kansas City on the musical map.

That, and the atmosphere that surrounded it. During the Jazz Age, Kansas City earned the name "Paris of the Plains," not so much for our wide boulevards but for the variety of vice available twenty-four hours a day. At one time this wide-open town was home to hundreds of nightclubs, speakeasies, cabarets, dance halls, and honky-tonks, chiefly clustered around 12th Street and Vine on the east side of town.

Along with jazz, Kansas City had another thriving entertainment option in the 1920s and 1930s: female impersonators. The city's most popular drag club was Dante's Inferno on Independence Avenue. The club is long gone, but its sign lives on in the front window of Retro Inferno, an ultracool vintage furniture store downtown (see more details in Shopping).

Those honky-tonk days are long gone, but on any given night and even some afternoons you can still hear jazz pouring out of clubs and restaurants, on street corners on the Country Club Plaza, and at annual festivals such as the Juneteenth Celebration, Parkville's River Jam, and the Jazz Lover's Pub Crawl (see Annual Events and Festivals for information). But today "Satin Doll" shares air space with other musical styles, including rock, R&B, zydeco, Irish folk songs, country, and reggae.

When you get enough people together to listen to music, it's a sure bet many of them will want to get up and dance. Whether you want to scoot your boots, learn the tango, or practice your West Coast Swing, you'll find an open dance floor somewhere in town.

Night owls can also find plenty of other entertainment around here. We have our share of comedy clubs and bars and taverns, including some that serve up their own microbrewed beer. Before you head out, however, a bit of housekeeping: In both Kansas and Missouri, the legal drinking age is twenty-one. Most of our nightlife is clustered in the downtown, Westport/ midtown, and Plaza districts, and a few are within walking distance of one another; club-hoppers most likely will need a car.

Enough of the rules, already—let's go! To make it easier to locate your personal predilection, we've divided this chapter into entertainment categories.

COCKTAIL LOUNGES, WINE BARS, AND TAVERNS

When it's cocktail time, you can order a cold one at bars found within some of the city's finest restaurants, such as Plaza III–The Steakhouse and McCormick & Schmick's on the Plaza and Pierpont's in Union Station, where the bartenders will climb a ladder to fetch the mixings. But if you *really* want to get high, head to Skies, the revolving restaurant and lounge atop the Westin Regency Crown Center Hotel. When you've seen the red neon Western Auto sign go by for the fourth time, it's your cue to call it a night.

Here's a list of other places ready to serve up your drink order. For a real taste of Kansas City, order a pint of our hometown brew, Boulevard Beer.

Blonde
100 Ward Parkway
(816) 931-2525
www.blondekc.com

i If you've had too much nightlife around the holidays, get a ride or call a cab when it's time to hit the road. Each year Holiday Cab offers free rides home (the first $25 worth of fare, or about 20 miles) between Christmas and New Year's from 7:00 p.m. to 3:00 a.m. Call (816) 276-7899, or ask the bartender for the free cab.

Forget all the blonde jokes; this nightspot is one smart cookie. The word posh comes to mind, with brown suede walls, pale woods, and the sexiest bathrooms in town. Shut the stall door and the glass magically becomes opaque—at least you hope. The bar area is crowded with pretty people, the dining area subs as a tiny dance floor with DJs spinning hip-hop to techno sounds, and the mezzanine area offers plush chairs and even a bed for lounging.

Blonde introduced Kansas City to bottle service, a swanky way to entertain your group of up to ten with premium liquor (Absolut will set you back around $200), Red Bull, mixers, a fruit and cheese plate, and chocolate-covered strawberries. Blondes may not be able to do the math, but we can: It's a great deal. Taste Wednesdays are also a sure bet; for just $12 you get a cocktail, appetizer, entree, and dessert. The eye candy, as always, is free. More good news: The food is quite good. We enjoy the flats (grilled steak or chicken with tomatoes, rosemary, and cheese), the satays, and Devil Chips, which are potato chips drizzled with blue cheese. Did we mention martinis? Those aren't crickets you hear—it's the constant *click, click, click* of ice hitting aluminum shakers.

Blonde raised some eyebrows when it rolled out Body Sushi, where you can play with your food . . . to some degree. Selections of sushi rolls and sashimi are placed on a seminude female model and patrons are allowed to remove their appetizers. It's all tastefully done.

With all its many pluses, we have to warn you that Blonde has a reputation for being a bit snobby. A doorman is selective about whom he allows into the pale confines, there's often a line to get in, and only the sophisticated will feel at home here. But if you've played the game at any fancy nightclub in Chicago or New York, it's nothing new. Required are $600 shades. Failing that, reservations are a must by phone or the Web site.

Blonde is open Sunday from 8:00 p.m. to 2:30 a.m. (when it's about the *only* thing open); Monday through Saturday lunch is served from 11:00 a.m. until 2:00 p.m., then happy hour kicks in at 4:00. The Blonde whispers "nighty-night" at 1:00 a.m. Monday and Tuesday; 2:30 a.m. other nights.

The Cashew
2000 Grand
(816) 221-5858
www.thecashew.com
What do you call a more upscale version of a string of bars called The Peanut? The Cashew, of course. And while the Peanut (5000 Main Street, 816-753-9499 plus five other locations) is known for hot wings, the world's best BLTs, and peanut shells on the wooden floor, this more refined legume serves cashews in a bowl.

On balmy nights you'll see urban professionals and a few artists from nearby studios hanging out over beers and martinis when the garage doors are up and the view of downtown is spectacular. So's the red sangria and the Cashew "3" Martini, made with soy vodka. It's a cool place to start the gallery stroll through the Crossroads Arts District on First Fridays. Or come for the live music Monday through Wednesday. The Cashew also rents out its second floor for private parties. Or have a really small private party in the photo booth tucked in a corner.

Cigar Bar
1519 Grand Boulevard
(816) 421-7222
There are always a few hidden gems in town that the locals would prefer we not mention. This smoky lounge is one of those. On the

seedy side, the long, slender room has every-thing you want in a bar—a cheesy lounge singer, Al Latta, who performs at 8:30 p.m. Tuesday through Saturday; pretty cocktail waitresses with plenty of cleavage; and a print of a naked woman smoking a cigar behind the bar.

Did we mention the lasagna? It's fabulous, as are the rest of the mostly Italian dishes served here. That's one of the reasons the person sitting next to you at lunch could be a titan of industry or a stripper from the club down the street. A walk-in humidor contributes to the endless cigar smoke. But when you're singing "Volare" along with Al, slurping a cold martini, and waiting for your plate of spaghetti and sausages, you won't mind a bit. The Cigar Bar is open from 11:00 a.m. to 3:00 a.m. Monday through Saturday and 6:00 p.m. to 3:00 a.m. Sunday.

JP Wine Bar
1526 Walnut Street
(816) 842-2660
www.jpwinebar.com

In trendy shades of chocolate and chartreuse, this wine bar and coffeehouse came on the scene in an ideal location halfway between the hip Crossroads Arts District and the hot-as-a-pistol downtown loop. Here's where the urban sophisticate drops by after work or couples end the night over a pinot and a cheese plat-ter that's as pretty as the room. There's a comfy nook by the door, overstuffed chairs by the fireplace, and during nice weather cafe tables and chairs on the sidewalk.

JP's features wine flights, refreshing moji-tos, and concoctions that marry wine with

i Around here, Sunday is made for S.I.N. That's nothing naughty; it's the acronym for Service Industry Night, when restaurants and bars offer steals and deals on food and liquor to other chefs, waitstaff, and managers. No secret handshake necessary; they'll recognize you from your comfortable shoes and it's-been-a-long-week attitude.

alcohol. Recently, owner Ryan Maybee expanded his space to handle all the traffic. Check into special events such as wine tast-ings. But don't worry about wine snobs; here they call sweet red wine Stickies, and smooth whites are Like Butta. You're invited to join the wine club if you're rich or, lacking wealth, simply because you're pompous and want to show off. Ryan is kidding, of course. Club membership means you can store your wine (or liquor bottles, for that matter) and get invited to exclusive events. JP's opens at 6:00 a.m. with coffee drinks, then lunch is served from 11:00 a.m. to 4:00 p.m. with sal-ads, sandwiches, and soups, like a luscious acorn butternut squash number. Small plates and cheese platters (along with terrific desserts) are available from 4 to 11:00 p.m. Hang up your cup or glass at 1:30 a.m. Not open on Sunday.

Kelly's Westport Inn
500 Westport Road
(816) 561-0635
www.kellyswestportinn.com

History buffs might like to know that Kelly's is the oldest building in Kansas City. Well, at least they have a bronze plaque saying it is. Even the owners aren't sure. What they do know is that this corner establishment was once a grocery store run by Daniel Boone's grandson and became a saloon by 1933. Since then it's been where a cross section of the city—lawyers, salespeople, real estate agents, and artists—meets for lunch on Fri-day and never seems to make it back to the office. Perhaps it's the bright-red Jell-O shots that get to them: at $1 a pop, they do seem to slide down easy. By evening the crowd is younger and rowdier and, in summer, barely dressed. Kelly's is such a tradition on St. Paddy's Day that in 1989 they closed the doors for fear that the floors would cave in. Get a glimpse of the mob scene on the Web site. On weekends those wooden floors are wall-to-wall with returning college kids and boomers who make regular pilgrimages to their favorite hangout.

Martini Corner
31st and Main
www.martinicorner.com
When hipsters in Kansas City mention "the corner," this is what they mean: an entire neighborhood of bars a few blocks from Crown Center (the KCTV5 Tower is an excellent landmark). There's a variety of vibes to match any mood, but you can show up only if you fit the following description: punk rocker, investment banker, nursing student, or soccer mom. That means just about everyone. And we're pretty sure the corner served as a magnet for all the singles moving into the new condos and refurbished homes sprinkled around Union Hill (www.unionhill.com). Either that or it's the stunning view of downtown.

It all started with the Velvet Dog (400 East 31st Street, 816-753-9999), Kansas City's original martini lounge. The retro decor, terrific jukebox, and bocce ball court out back make it one of those great neighborhood bars your dad may have visited long ago. Play pool indoors or out while you chow down on such typical bar fare as ravioli and pita pizzas. It's girl power every first Thursday of the month, when a local fashion group takes over with a trunk show, $7 manicures, and $3 appletinis and cosmos from 5 to 9-ish.

Across the street, the Empire Room (334 East 31st Street, 816-561-2640) is more upscale but still friendly. The front lounge is open Monday through Thursday, and the dance floor pulses with energy on weekends. It's a good thing you like to dance; the couches are reserved for patrons paying $150 and up for bottle service. Reserve this VIP treatment online. You've got to love a lounge that celebrates the start of the workweek with a "Blo" party, "because Mondays don't have to suck."

On breezy summer nights, the young business crowd spills out of the patios and tiki bar at Sol Cantina (408 East 31st Street, 816-931-8080), where happy hour starts just after siesta time—3:00 to 7:00 p.m., with reverse happy hour from 10:00 p.m. to midnight. Keep the margaritas coming, *por favor*. For sustenance, there are the famous fish tacos, bruschetta, paninis, and other tasty grub.

A pool table, a dozen TVs, pizza, stromboli, and friendly owners. What more could you want? That's the setup at Tower Tavern (401 East 31st Street), which stays open until 1:30 every night. Here's where you'll see locals chatting at the bar after work or on weekends when flip-flops are the footwear of choice. The menu runs the regular bar food gamut but is actually quite good. For our money (and not a lot), the Tower Slides are tops. The two-ounce burgers come three to an order, topped with caramelized onions and cheddar cheese. The meat-filled stromboli and, dare we say, *gourmet* pizzas are terrific as well, especially the Philly-steak version.

New kid on the block The Drop (409 East 31st Street, 816-756-DROP) came on strong with great, cheap food—from 4:00 to 7:00 p.m., when starters are half off, a plate of marinated olives will set you back two bucks and change—and a kitchen that stays open until midnight. That's good news, because we guarantee you've never tasted a grilled cheese sandwich like this. The paninis and bruschettas are also excellent, and the sweets menu includes cookies and milk.

Mike's Tavern
5424 Troost Avenue
(816) 444-3399
www.mikestavernonline.com
Mike's is just what a neighborhood bar should be, with friendly bartenders, a casual atmosphere, and cheap drinks. Students and alumni from nearby University of Kansas City–Missouri and Rockhurst University congregate in the afternoons to play pool, hang out at the bar, and watch sporting events on one of fifteen or so screens. The jukebox plays mostly fifties rock, there's karaoke every Wednesday night, and local bands often show up on weekends. If that's not enough, there's always a game of darts, Golden Tee, or the half-pound burgers and crispy Tater Tots to keep you happy.

The Wine Bar
13657 Washington Street
(in Lukas Liquor Super Store)
(816) 942-8707
www.kcwinebar.com
Hidden inside this enormous liquor supermarket really is something super: a wine bar that invites you to experience more than ninety wines plus premium ports and single-malt scotches. The technology alone is enough to make you woozy: This is the first place in town to use Enomatic, an Italian-designed wine-serving system. Essentially, you simply decide on the wine you want to try from the long line of winners, press a button, and the perfect pour is siphoned into your waiting wineglass. The wine is always fresh because there's no oxidation.

The entire space is attractive and smoke free, but what we really appreciate is the big teddy bear in the apron, executive chef Terry Barkley. When he's not hosting a cooking demonstration, he's in the kitchen whipping up innovative and delicious fare to go with your wine. Appetizers, small plates, and other savories are always on tap. One night it could be a rustic orzo with grilled vegetables, another night spinach salad with Pinky's vodka-and–rose petal sorbet vinaigrette. Check the Web site or get on the e-mail list to find out when the next salsa party will be. While Chef Terry concocts a Spanish-theme dinner and sangria, you'll be taught the steps to the romantic dance. Prices for special events range from zip to $40.

COMEDY CLUBS

Since the days of burlesque, Kansas City has always been a circuit for top-name comedians, a tradition that continues today thanks to more than our share of comedy clubs. Over the past decades we've welcomed such up-and-comers as Rosie O'Donnell, Ellen Degeneres, and a guy named Jerry Seinfeld. At one time our first official comedy club, Stanford & Sons, located above the Westport restaurant by the same name, was ranked first in the Midwest and third in the nation by *Rolling Stone* and *Variety*.

ComedyCity
300 Charlotte
(816) 842-2744
www.comedycity.cc
Home of Kansas City's original Comedy Sports, where tag teams improvise to suggestions from the audience. You won't hear the "blue" language used in other clubs; this is good, clean family fun that's appropriate for groups of all types and sizes. And when the audience participates and the players are on, this can be a hilarious night out, Wednesday through Sunday.

The Improv
7480 Northwest 87th Street (Zona Rosa)
(816) 587-4500
www.themajestictheatres.com
This world-famous name has been the career launching pad for dozens of familiar faces of TV and film. David Spade in Tempe, Arizona, Bette Midler in New York, plus Lily Tomlin, Robin Williams, and Drew Carey. Now Kansas City has its own franchise with a top-notch setting. The comedy lounge is part of the Majestic Theatre complex, a beautiful venue that also includes three luxurious movie theaters and a cafe with a complete bar and tableside dining.

And if you wish you could have another drink while the show is going on, you can. Simply beckon your server and that dirty martini can appear as fast as the next racy punch line. Like fries with that? No problem: At the Improv it can be dinner and a show with appetizers, sandwiches and salads, and entrees all available before, during, or after the performance. And it's nice to see that the

i If you're taking a cab, be aware that—unlike some other major cities—taxis here don't cruise, so allow time for the doorman to call one, and make sure you keep the cab phone number handy.

management doesn't gouge guests on food and drink prices. A Southwest panini is just $8, grilled salmon complete with fresh veggies and potato is a mere $16. Wine is by the bottle or glass and your favorite martinis are available as well for fair prices.

The talent and the venue are first-rate, as is the seating system for this 350-seat, blissfully smoke-free club. It's strictly first come, first seated, so our suggestion is to get there early. Check the Web site for details on reserving your place and opening times. The laughter starts at 7:30 p.m. Wednesday through Saturday with a second, 9:45 p.m. show Friday and Saturday and a 7:00 p.m. show on Sunday. And if you think you're the next Robin Williams, check out the next open-mic night.

Stanford & Sons
1867 Village West Parkway
(In the Legends at Village West,
Kansas City, KS)
(913) 480-7500
When Craig and Jeff Glazer—along with comic David Naster—opened a comedy shop above dad Stanford Glazer's restaurant in 1979, it catapulted the Westport neighborhood into the city's nightspot scene. When Craig convinced Robin Williams to try out new material here in 1981, *Variety* picked up the story and the rest is history. A few decades later, the sons picked up their microphone and moved to a space behind Hooter's in a strip mall in Overland Park, Kansas, and did brisk business.

After some contentious lawsuits with their dad regarding the name, the boys have the last laugh with their new 6,000-square-foot, half-million-dollar club in Wyandotte County's mega-successful Village West near the Kansas Speedway. With 300 fixed seats, three levels of plush seating, and a full-service bar and appetizers (don't miss Mario's meat grinders), the club has attracted celebrity and up-and-coming comics. You'll recognize names from TV shows such as *Last Comic Standing* and movie roles. If you think you have a shot at stardom, bring three minutes

of material to open-mic night every other Thursday.

DANCE

Nearly every night in our fair metropolis, couples are putting on their dancing shoes and twirling, dipping, or boogying to music somewhere in town. Perhaps surprisingly, the fastest-growing age group at dancing events is twentysomethings, who are taking to the Lindy Hop and West Coast Swing with wild abandon. For a complete list of venues, classes, and dance organizations to join, complete with pictures, check out Mike Strong's well-organized Web site (www.kcdance.com). Following are a few of the most popular locations.

Barumba in Mi Cocina
620 West 48th Street
(816) 960-6426
Getting an invitation to this Latin lounge in the downstairs of a popular Mexican restaurant on the Country Club Plaza hearkens back to the "are you cool enough?" days of Studio 54 in New York. If you're not a regular, you have to have dinner upstairs first and then meet the approval of the manager. Once in, though, the music is hot, the dancing is hotter, and the patrons are friendly. It's the cocktails that will get you: Specialty drinks like the Mambo Limousine will run you over fast. You'll have plenty of time to nurse that highball, though. The nightclub, which opens at 10:00 p.m., stays open until 2:30 a.m. No food is served.

El Caribe Cafe & Lounge
12112 West 87th Street Parkway
Lenexa, KS
(913) 599-2270
At this restaurant located 1 block west of Quivira, it's time to put down your Caribbean Jerk Chicken when the Latin dance lessons start at 8:30 p.m. or you might be wearing the spicy brown sauce. By the time the DJ arrives at 10:00, the place is generally packed, and the sensuous salsa and tango moves continue until 2:00 a.m.

GAY AND LESBIAN CLUBS

Balanca's
1809 Grand
(816) 474-MEOW (6369)
www.balancaskc.com

Gay, straight, singles, couples, biker chick, or accountant—well, maybe not an accountant—but everyone else will feel welcome here. In fact, owner Lori Burroughs won't tolerate closed-minded jerks. It can get pretty rowdy here, and that's just the way Lori likes it. The upstairs lounge is a teensy bit more chill, and here's where you come for a game of darts or pool before heading back down to the Pyro Room, where DJs and sometimes live music gets the floor crowded. The 3:00 a.m. closing time makes it the place plenty of folks head for a nightcap. The action starts at 9:00 p.m. Tuesday through Thursday, 6:00 p.m. Friday and Saturday. And if you were here Saturday night you'd understand why it's closed Sunday and Monday. That's when all the kitties sleep.

Bar Natasha
1911 Main Street
(816) 472-5300
www.barnatasha.com

Since opening on New Year's Eve 2003, this bon vivant of a bar and nightclub has attracted the city's most sophisticated gays along with mostly urbane straight couples. When it first opened there was a sense of secrecy to the place—almost as though you needed a special knock for admittance. There was no sign over the door as there is now, and from the sidewalk the cabaret seemed like another office building on the block.

i Kansas City is home to a vibrant, growing gay and lesbian population that includes high-society sophisticates and the bohemian set made up of actors and artists. We list several nightspots that cater to them, but the truth is that straights are just as welcome. It's all about tolerance, except when it comes to dressing with style. No slobs allowed.

The secret-club atmosphere may be gone, but the cavernous space still has several things going for it: a piano smack dab in the center of the room where a variety of artists perform (if you know the lyrics to popular show tunes, you're in) and lead sing-alongs; a tasty menu that raises the bar for typical bar food; and a statuesque co-owner, Missy Koonce, who can be seen mixing a cocktail, greeting her immense network of friends, or belting out a tune on stage. This popular Kansas City actress named her club for Natasha Fatale, the cartoon character she played in a production of *Rocky & Bullwinkle* at the Coterie Theatre.

The menu is short—about twelve savory items and six sweets—with prices that range from 5 bucks for a chutney cream cheese spread with crackers to $70 for blini with caviar. The most popular dish is the sliced steak with blue-cheese butter; at $10 it's a terrific meal paired with the cheese platter and a chocolate flourless cake chaser. The singing may drown out your party's conversation, but no matter. Sing right along and enjoy the fun.

Bar Natasha is open from 4:00 p.m. to 1:00 a.m. Wednesday through Saturday and is a popular venue for events such as private birthday parties and fund-raisers, particularly those that benefit AIDS research.

Bistro 303
303 Westport Road
(816) 753-2303

Talk about night and day! At noon a mix of ladies-who-lunch and workers from nearby offices enjoy a menu that leans toward fine French food. Must-tries include a marvelous croque-monsieur and crème brûlée, pizza with feta, or a delectable 303 Club piled high with turkey and brie. The space is bright with windows and floor-to-ceiling mirrors.

Come evening, twinkling votive candles and the city's most sophisticated gay men are reflected in the mirrors. And we do mean crowded. Although you can order from the small blackboard listing a handful of appetizers at night, the kitchen closes at 9:00 p.m. because it's all about cocktails and flirting. In fact, 303 doesn't even offer food service on Friday or Saturday nights; the servers just couldn't make it through the throng. In fact, the wall-to-wall bodies make it hard to see the room's other charms, such as exposed brick walls, high tin ceiling, and copper-encased bar—or even the Louis VIII plaque gracing one of the niches. After all, one of the owners is a respected antiques dealer in town. Hours are 11:30 a.m. to 1:30 p.m. Monday through Saturday.

Missie B's
805 West 39th Street
(816) 561-0625
www.missiebskc.com
This good-time place opened its doors in April 1994 as a piano lounge, and when Belle Starr began doing Monday-night drag shows, that became its claim to fame. The region's best female impersonators perform here five nights a week; add twice-weekly karaoke and you've got plenty of reasons to buy those new silver heels you've been eyeing. The outrageous Flo Show is every Saturday from 10:00 p.m. until 3:00 a.m. Closing on week-nights is 2:00 a.m.

You have to love a bar that advertises the most affordable drinks in town *starting at noon.* Bootlegger's Club is located upstairs and is the home of Kansas City Leather University and Mr. Dixie Belle 2007. A DJ keeps the light-drenched dance floor busy seven nights a week; twin stripper poles are at the ready (two poles! No waiting!) for those inclined to exhibit special dance skills. Sunday afternoons you'll find a tea dance followed by a beer bust that is often a private party or fund-raiser for a social cause. Bootlegger's also has a leather shop, which is open Thursday through Sunday.

Outabounds Sports Bar
3601 Broadway
(816) 756-2577

People thought Doug Knetzer and Alan Rogers were crazy to open a gay sports bar, but look who's crazy now—as in happy crazy. It's wall-to-wall on Chiefs Sundays and just about any other time a game is on one of the multiple plasma-screen TVs. The bar food and decor are pretty standard, except the poster of local legend George Brett has longer hair. And just like any sports bar, when the favored players come on the screen, the entire place cheers—but here it might be more for how cute he looks in his uniform. But it's all in good fun. Although it's mainly a gay hangout, the friendly staff welcome straight folks as well.

Sidekicks Saloon
3707 Main
(816) 931-1430
www.sidekicks-saloon.com
Who says gay men can't wear cowboy hats and line dance? At this saloon and dance hall, everyone's welcome, but it mainly caters to the gay crowd of cowboys and leathermen. Friday night features drag shows, and Saturday night brings on dancing to country and pop music. Tuesday is a retro-music affair, and on Wednesday get ready to vote for your favorite contestants in their boxers. Drag queens and singers are on the stage most Thursdays. Hours are 2:00 p.m. to 3:00 a.m.

LIVE MUSIC

Some of the venues below offer a true night-club atmosphere with cocktail tables surrounding a stage and an appreciative audience that's there to actually *listen* rather than gab with tablemates. Answer a cell phone here and you might find yourself stared down or even out on the street.

There are also dozens of places—restaurants and hotel lobbies all over town—where trios or piano players provide background music to clinking glasses and conversation. But whether you take your jazz with a side of sirloin or like it a la carte, you'll discover talent that can soar above the din.

Some locations charge covers ranging from $3 to $5 depending on the night and the talent; many invite you to sit and enjoy the music gratis as long as you order an occasional cocktail or two.

Blues and Rock 'n' Roll

Rhythm and blues was the father of jazz, and Papa never really left the Kansas City music scene. These days there are as many blues venues in town—and at least as many fans—as there are jazz emporiums. You can catch a case of the blues nearly anywhere, any night in Kansas City. For times and locations, check out the schedule on the Kansas City Blues Society's site at www.kcbluessociety.com.

A word about tickets: For the venues that bring in major bands (such as Grand Emporium and the Uptown), advance tickets, which are highly encouraged, are available at the nightclub's box office or on its Web site. Tickets can also be purchased through Ticketmaster (816-931-3330, www.ticketmaster.com), or at ticket centers including Hen House grocery stores and other outlets detailed on the Web site. Be aware that Ticketmaster charges a substantial additional fee.

BB's Lawnside Bar-B-Q
1205 East 85th Terrace
(816) 822-7427
www.bbslawnsidebbq.com
Owner Lindsay Shannon combines his passions for blues, beer, and barbecue in this homey roadhouse, which plays live music Thursday through Sunday. The food's pretty hot, too; try the spicy jambalaya, Smoky Jo's Gumbo, or ribs and burnt ends. And to wash it all down order a "Bucket of Blues," which will get you five

> **i** If smoking bothers you, call ahead to inquire about a nightspot's smoking policy. Some confine cigarettes and cigars to the bar, some—like the Blue Room—forbid smoking entirely. Nearby Lawrence, Kansas, bars are now smoke free, and the rest of Kansas may be next.

Pabst Blue Ribbons in a galvanized tin. Nothing fancy here, but when the joint is jumping with blues, jazz, or Terence O'Malley's ragtime piano, it's a guaranteed good time. See if you can identify the lineup of blues greats on the mural behind the stage.

Blayney's
415 Westport Road
(816) 561-3747
www.blayneys.com
Now that this quintessential blues spot has a presence on the street in the form of Blayney's Irish Tavern, you don't have to hunt for the underground bar. The tavern hosts live acoustic music Monday through Saturday, so we advise you to take the stairs, pay at the door, and get ready for good rockin' tonight. Blayney's is the sort of hangout where bartenders have your usual draft ready before you sit down, where the entire space—and many of the patrons—are in desperate need of daylight, and the dance floor is so crowded you may find yourself dancing with several people at once. In short, it's a blast. Folks from all age groups and walks of life show up to hear longtime favorites, such as the smoky-voiced leader of the Bob Harvey Band, the Nace Brothers, and Four Fried Chickens and a Coke (that's a band, not a menu special), six nights a week. It's easy to figure out the owner's given name: bartenders wear T-shirts saying, "I work for Dick . . . but I prefer cash." It's our pick for best Kansas City souvenir.

During warm weather the deck out back is the place to be.

Grand Emporium
3832 Main
(816) 531-1504
www.kcclubs.com
It's obvious the moment you enter—once your eyes adjust to the inky interior, that is—that this place has soul. Built in 1912, the building once served bathtub gin in the speakeasy downstairs and other vices in the bordello above. But starting in 1985 owner Roger Naber made it famous for the blues,

reggae, rock and rockabilly, jazz, and swing it serves up seven nights a week; in fact it's the only establishment to be twice voted "Best Blues Club in America" by the Blues Foundation.

As of spring 2004 it has a new owner, proving that old rockers never die—they just get married and have children. Naber may be gone, but the music continues in a slightly tidier space.

Some longtime fans were peeved when decades' worth of rock posters came down and the bathrooms lost their somehow endearing divelike quality when the G.E. changed ownership. We say ignore the environment and just enjoy the national-headliner music and other events.

Between the live music, Salsa Fridays, and Saturday night DJs who cater to the young, single gay crowd, there's something for everyone here. Well, perhaps except those allergic to smoke. But if you can see yourself through the blue haze, you are guaranteed a good time. You can always burn that shirt when you get home.

The place seats 175, but often it's too crowded to even see the chairs, let alone find one, as 300 folks move en masse to the music. Even during the day time there's music, thanks to the jukebox that's loaded with a hundred rare 45s, from Howlin' Wolf to James Brown.

John's Upper Deck
928 Wyandotte Street
(816) 474-5668
There's no better view of the city than from this three-story rooftop known to regulars as simply "the deck," where downtown workers head after clocking out to hear rock 'n' roll and rendezvous with friends. But don't miss out on the other two floors. DJ John packs the second-level dance floor every weeknight while nondancers head straight for the pool tables.

The second floor is also where you can find one of the best bargains downtown: a lunch buffet for under $6. The first floor's diner has served lunch and dinner to downtown workers for more than twenty years. The huge menu features mostly sandwiches (the fajita steak version is especially tasty), pastas, salads, and burgers. On Friday, two pounds of crab legs will cost you just under $12, ready to be washed down with discounted shots of liquor. What a way to start the weekend. John's is also one of the only downtown joints that's open seven days a week and until 3:00 a.m. on weekends.

The Levee
16 West 43rd Street
(816) 561-2821
www.thelevee.net
Truth be told, about half of Kansas City tipped back their first tequila shooter right here in this neighborhood bar just north of the Plaza. Long popular with folks from twenty-one to the well-over-fifty crowd, the Levee is the place for dancing on the tables (go ahead, we've all done it at least once) and listening to flat-out blues and rock 'n' roll Wednesday through Saturday. The fun continues until 3:00 a.m. and often spills out onto the deck or patio.

There's plenty of parking in a lot across the street, but on warm summer weekend nights, there's often a line to get in. Expect a cover charge.

Raoul's Velvet Room
119th and Metcalf (Rosana Square
Shopping Center)
Overland Park, KS
(913) 469-0466
www.raoulsvelvetroom.com
Who says there's no place to party in sleepy suburban Overland Park? You'd never know it from the outside of this club smack dab in the center of a shopping mall off busy 119th Street, but inside it's a throwback to the ritzy supper clubs of the 1930s, with a smoke-filled bar and a separate, dark and moody dining area. Cocktail tables and a dance floor surround the stage area, where you can hear a variety of music from acoustic guitar to jazz to

A few years ago Kansas City caught martini mania in a big way. Several of our bars and restaurants have entire martini menus, with everything from the classic to a chocolate version. Some of the longest lists are found at the Inter-Continental Lobby Bar, Raoul's Velvet Room, and the Velvet Dog.

Disco Dick and the Mirror Balls. Raoul's is open seven days a week from 4:44 p.m. (and not a minute too soon) until 2:00 a.m. But don't worry, it's easy to find your car in that big parking lot.

The Uptown
3700 Broadway
(816) 753-8665
www.uptowntheater.com

God bless Larry Sells, the man behind the restoration of this magnificent movie palace. When it opened in 1928, the Uptown thrilled patrons with its elaborate Mediterranean courtyard design complete with balconies, twinkling stars, and mechanical flying birds. Ten years later the theater copyrighted the "Fragratone" system, which piped fragrances through the ventilation ducts.

Through the years all the greats played here, from Bob Hope to Bob Dylan, and it continued to serve as a live concert venue until it closed in 1989. After a $15 million restoration, it has reopened in all its glory. And although the opulent decor and red velvet curtain might contrast with the occasional heavy metal acts that appear on stage, it provides the appropriately upscale atmosphere for performers such as Ben Vereen or Nancy Wilson. Even when there's nothing happening on stage, the new Nowhere Club is a fun place to enjoy a cocktail and happy hour buffet four nights a week.

Along with an event calendar, the Web site offers photos and 3-D views of this breathtaking place with the curved marquee. And if you're looking for a delightful preconcert dinner, there's the Grille on Broadway (816-531-0700). Tickets may be purchased at the Uptown or through Ticketmaster.

Casino Entertainment

Although Kansas City's four casinos provide plenty of gaming action, you can exchange the blackjack tables for a cocktail table to hear live music in a variety of pavilions and piano bars. In Attractions we provide additional details about each casino.

Ameristar Casino
8201 Northeast Birmingham
(816) 414-7000, (800) 499-4961
www.ameristarcasinos.com/kc

Consistently voted "Best Casino" by readers of *KC Magazine,* Ameristar could also win prizes for the entertainment lineup in its Star Pavilion. Since 1997 it has brought in such acts as Keith Urban, Tony Bennett, and even the Smothers Brothers to its elegantly appointed stage. Tickets range from $12 to $65. Or head to the more intimate Casino Cabaret.

Argosy Casino
777 Northwest Argosy Parkway
Riverside, MO
(800) 270-7711
www.argosycasinos.com/kansascity

With a $105 million makeover, this stunning casino has plenty of action outside the blackjack tables. The local jazz and rock stars in the Casino Stage Bar and Crazy Olives Bar and Restaurant are as cool as the margaritas and martinis. One of our favorites, Lonnie McFadden, brings soulful R&B, a right-on impression of Louis Armstrong, and even some old soft-shoe to the stage. And if a steak is calling your name, the Journey is the place for wood-fired beef. As for us, we think we'll journey upstairs to one of the stunning new suites. See more details in Accommodations.

Harrah's
One Riverboat Drive
(816) 472-7777
www.harrahs.com

Although Harrah's bills itself as the place for serious slots, when it comes to music the emphasis is on fun. Your first hint is the sound of jazz horns or head-thumping rock coming from the VooDoo Lounge, one of the city's best nightclubs. The lineup continues to thrill, with such headliners as Violent Femmes to jazz stylist Dave Koz. Even when there's no live music, it's still the place to hang with friends or flirt with new ones as attractive bartenders mesmerize you by tossing the shakers overhead. Got enough liquid courage yet? Then head to the dance floor with great lights and a fantastic sound system as the DJ plays the hits. VooDoo is definitely the place to wear your trendiest club gear. And the mezzanine-level VIP section gives you the best shot of the entire venue—your own private sanctum to do that voodoo thing you do.

For a more laid-back (way, way back) vibe, there's Toby Keith's I Love This Bar and Grill. Yes, *that* Toby Keith, and you can bet the big guy showed up to kick off its first weekend. The Whiskey Girls will pour you a cold one as you listen to live country music.

The entire casino recently had a major renovation, helping to earn its "Best of KC" from readers of *KC Magazine*. Along with the gaming choices, diners are well served at the Range Steakhouse, Moby's Fish Tales, and more casual venues. See Accommodations for more.

Located on the northern bank of the Missouri River 3 miles from downtown, Harrah's offers a classy play-and-stay option with an attached hotel, as well as four dining options to keep you happy for an evening or a weekend. There's even a car wash so you can get your automobile cleaned and detailed while you enjoy yourself.

Isle of Capri Casino
1800 East Front Street
(816) 855-7777, (800) THE ISLE
www.islandcapricasino.com
You can't miss this casino, with lights outlining the paddleboat so bright it rivals the nearby downtown skyline. Inside, the music is lively as well, with steel drums beating out a Caribbean beat to continue the island theme, or jazz trios on weekends that link Kansas City's heritage with calypso.

Country

Although we sometimes try to ignore our cowtown heritage like it's a pesky younger brother who follows us around, there's no disputing our Western roots. Throughout much of 1980, in fact, the most popular radio station and most of the jukeboxes in town played nothing but country hits. Most of us have hung up our spurs these days, but you can still join in a line dance at these two nightspots when the mood strikes.

The Beaumont
4050 Pennsylvania
(816) 561-BOOT (2668)
www.kcclubs.com
The first thing you notice upon entering this popular club in Westport is the mechanical bull. How convenient that it's right in front of one of three bars in the joint, all the better to wrestle up some nerve. If that action is a little too much for you, perhaps taking a free line-dance lesson is more your style.

Thanks to its size and open design, the Beaumont can bring in some top-name acts that are too big for other clubs. Don't be surprised, however, to hear decidedly noncountry bands here; there wasn't a single Stetson in sight when rock band They Might Be Giants appeared. And then there are the Friday salsa nights when professional dancers practice sensuous moves on the giant dance floor while crowds gather to watch.

But the Beaumont's "urban cowboy" appeal is its best draw. You've just gotta love a band called Insane Clown Posse. It's closed Sunday, which is why, we suppose, even cowboys get the blues.

You'll get the blues if you show up with anything except cash or a debit card. No credit cards, please.

Denim and Diamonds
1725 Swift
North Kansas City, MO
(816) 221-7300
www.denimdiamonds.com

Although there's no live music here, the place is plenty lively without it thanks to a great staff and an enthusiastic crowd. Loosen up those new Levi's with free dance lessons Wednesday through Sunday from 7:30 to 8:30 p.m., then be ready to two-step all night. The crowd often breaks into a line dance, and even if you don't know the steps you'll have fun. Double D is known for some of the prettiest cowgirls in the Midwest, especially on Thursday, which is Ladies' Night.

Irish Pubs

The success of our stockyard industry in the West Bottoms was built, for the most part, on the broad backs of Irish workers who moved here in the late 1800s. They brought their music, dance, and a passion for a pint to their new home, and the rest of us become at least a little Irish when we partake of it. No wonder ours is the third largest St. Patrick's Day parade in the country. But you won't have to wait until March: There's an Irish festival or sing-along nearly every weekend somewhere in Kansas City.

We even lay claim to one of the finest Irish soloists, Connie Dover, who resides in Weston (a charming town just north of Kansas City; see Day Trips and Weekend Getaways) and appears at local festivals when she's not touring the world or appearing on National Public Radio's *Prairie Home Companion*. With the voice and face of an angel, she can bring a crowd to tears—or its feet—with a simple ballad. See her schedule at www.conniedover.com. Other local talent includes Eddie Delahunt, Bob Reeder, and groups like the Shenanigans. Hear them at the following locations, or purchase their CDs at Browne's Market (3300 Pennsylvania; 816-561-0030; www.brownesmarket.com), Kansas City's oldest retail establishment and the oldest Irish business in the country.

Harling's Upstairs
3941-A Main Street
(816) 531-0303
Harling's is just outside the craziness of Westport, but you won't miss it once the music

starts. In fact, you might not even find it unless you're looking; its largely unmarked entrance is a single door that leads to a staircase that opens to huge rooms with an eagle's-eye view of the busy street below. Its Irish heritage comes out when crooners get the crowd going with Gaelic songs Wednesday and Thursday. Mama Ray and Rich Van Sant serve up the blues on Sunday from 2:00 to 6:00 p.m. to help bid a soulful farewell to the weekend.

O'Dowd's Little Dublin
4742 Pennsylvania Street
(816) 561-2700
www.odowds.com
On summer nights the upstairs deck of this Plaza establishment is packed with young, attractive people whose motto seems to be "the more the merrier." Many a date has been made on the slender staircase that joins the two floors. You can enjoy live Irish music, often erupting into sing-alongs, with your ale and traditional Irish fare. With its busy Plaza corner location, it's a fine place to meet up with friends or make new ones.

O'Malley's Pub
500 Welt Street
Weston, MO
(816) 640-5235
www.westonirish.com
When a German immigrant named John Georgeans started a brewery (the oldest brewery west of the Hudson River) in the early 1840s, he dug three rooms 55 feet underground and lined them with limestone blocks to create an even temperature for the fermenting process. At one time the brewery produced up to 20,000 barrels of beer a year before it was closed during Prohibition. Today the trilevel space is home to Sean O'Malley's Pub, which is the perfect escape on a hot summer evening. Just upstairs, Sean's parents operate the American Bowman Restaurant, so you can literally dine and drink without leaving the premises.

Gem Theater. CVB OF GREATER KANSAS CITY

When entertainers take the stage, the atmosphere is unlike anything else in town. Every October, Sean hosts an Irish Festival with three additional stages outside (see more in Annual Events and Festivals). There's authentic Irish food, imported libations, and great entertainment, including bawdy limericks. Watch for appearances by Connie Dover.

Jazz

The Blue Room
1600 East 18th Street
(816) 474-2929
www.americanjazzmuseum.com

Back in the 1930s and 1940s, the Blue Room, located in the swank Street Hotel, was one of the hottest nightspots in the country. Six decades later it serves as a museum by day, with a wall of images of local musicians who made Kansas City swing. The glass-topped cock-tail tables are display cases filled with such rare artifacts as Count Basie's 1936 Musician's Union card, while the jukebox serves up tunes and videos from performers such as Louis Armstrong, Charlie Parker, Billie Holiday, Fats Waller, and John Coltrane. Don't miss seeing Charlie Parker's saxophone or Ella Fitzgerald's rhinestone eyeglasses among the displays.

At night the Blue Room comes to life as a jazz club where four nights a week it welcomes local and national jazz greats. Since opening in September 1997, the club has built a loyal and ever-growing following. Although food and smoking are prohibited to preserve the artifacts, alcoholic beverages are available at the bar. The crowd tends to be older and well dressed. The Blue Room is part of the American Jazz Museum but has its own entrance. There is a small cover charge.

The Kansas City Jazz Ambassadors can provide a pub crawl for you any time of year. The all-night party includes visits to at least three hot jazz spots, plenty of local music history, and authentic barbecue. They'll even provide live music on the bus. Tariffs start at $40 per person for groups of forty or more. Call (913) 967-6767 or (816) 478-8378.

The Gem Theater
1615 East 18th Street
(816) 474-6262
www.americanjazzmuseum.com

Opened as a movie theater in 1912, the Gem has a facade that's still beautiful, with its stained-glass and distinctive neon marquee. But inside it's been updated to a 500-seat theater with the latest in lighting, sound, and acoustical design. The theater has hosted concerts, workshops and symposiums, and an annual Jammin' at the Gem Concert Series featuring outstanding national performers such as Lionel Hampton and James Moody. Call for event information, or check the Web site.

Jardine's Restaurant & Jazz Club
4536 Main Street
(816) 561-6480
www.jardines4jazz.com

This cozy club has become one of Kansas City's hottest night spots to hear some of the city's top performers, including Angela Hagenbach and Lisa Henry, every Tuesday through Saturday. And when blues stylist Ida McBeth has a birthday, she celebrates in this hideaway with several dozen of her closest friends and fans. The late-night jam session is also popular every Saturday after midnight when musicians show up after ending gigs elsewhere; anyone with a voice or a horn is encouraged to get up on stage.

The restaurant serves better food than you might expect, too (see listing in Restaurants). Everything—from the skillet-fried chicken and crunchy-crusted fried catfish—is made from scratch. Want to really live?

Reserve a cozy, dark booth and order the peppercorn-crusted filet mignon in brandy cream sauce. And here's good news for night owls: Jardine's is one of the rare places that serves dinner until midnight on weekends. Just a stroll from the Country Club Plaza with plenty of well-lighted parking in back. No cover.

The Majestic Steakhouse
931 Broadway
(816) 471-8484
www.majesticgroup.com

If walls could talk they'd drown out the music played seven days a week at this historic nightspot. Originally built in 1911 as the Fitzgerald Saloon, the handsome brick building served as a bordello, speakeasy, and office where politicians met with lobbyists and thugs, businessmen, and favor seekers. The downstairs space now provides a cozy nightclub featuring some of the city's favorite vocalists, such as Julie Turner. No cover charge.

This is another example of great food nearly upstaging the entertainment; the dry-aged steaks here are renowned (see more details in Restaurants). In fact, locals remember the Majestic from its forty-year span at East 31st Street and Holmes. Although you won't be able to hear the jazz in the dining room, a solo acoustic guitarist provides music to dine by.

The night isn't complete without at least a peek at the members-only, third-floor Pendergast Cigar Club with its brick walls, leather chairs, and walk-in humidor. Memberships cost from $500 to $3,000 a year, but here's a real Insiders' tip: For the cost of dinner—no sacrifice there—you can be escorted up the stairs as a guest of the restaurant as long as there isn't a private party in session.

The Mutual Musicians Foundation
1823 Highland Avenue
(816) 471-5212
www.thefoundationjamson.org

This living shrine to jazz is where Charlie Parker, Jay McShann, Bennie Moten, Lester

Kansas City—and All That Jazz

During the 1920s and 1930s, Kansas City was at the heart of the music scene. Because the city was a railroad hub, some of America's best musicians would stop here on their way to or from New Orleans, Chicago, or New York, and many, such as Bill "Count" Basie, liked what they saw and heard and soon made the city their home.

Kansas City was a prosperous place during these decades and patrons had their pick of grand palaces, such as the Pla-Mor, which opened Thanksgiving Day 1927 at the northwest corner of Linwood and Main. The "million-dollar ballroom" featured an enormous dance hall along with a bowling alley, swimming pool, and ice-skating rink that doubled as the home ice for the town's minor league hockey team. Local stars shared marquee space with top-name touring acts such as Louis Armstrong. And Hoagy Carmichael premiered a new tune called "Stardust" on the Pla-Mor's stage.

The city's seedier side was represented by such joints as the Chesterfield Club, where waitresses were clad in nothing more than cellophane.

But no matter whether the nightclub was ritzy or raunchy, it was packed with talent. Local musicians such as Count Basie, Charlie Parker, and Joe Turner eventually influenced jazz across the nation. Basie practically invented the infectious, syncopated style called swing at his piano at the Reno Club, bringing in soaring solos to drive the crowds wild.

Parker is generally considered most responsible for the creation of bebop, taking the music known as jazz into its modern incarnation. Certainly, others like Dizzy Gillespie and Thelonious Monk contributed mightily. But even among his peers, Parker was recognized as a leader, one of the rare musicians who actually earned the tag "genius." Had he not died in his thirties he might have gained even more of a mainstream following.

The legendary "cutting session" between tenor sax greats Lester "Pres" Young and Coleman "Bean" Hawkins depicted in Robert Altman's film *Kansas City* really happened. It went down on December 18, 1933, and continued until the wee hours at a joint called the Cherry Blossom. Pianist and bandleader Count Basie kept time.

Some say famed saxophonist Charlie Parker came by his nickname "Yardbird," later shortened to just "Bird," because of his fondness for fried chicken. But others say his handle came from his "free as a bird" lifestyle that would cause his untimely death.

As musicians such as Basie and Parker became better known, they often left for the East Coast and bigger gigs. But it was the fall of political boss Tom Pendergast (read more about his reign in the History chapter) that marked the end of the Jazz Age in Kansas City. Once reformers closed the nightspots, the remaining bands took the A Train to places like New York and Chicago.

So the term "Kansas City jazz" is a handy handle for a musical mix that owes its life to gospel, ragtime, blues, swing, and bebop. No wonder it's so

The sound that put Kansas City on the musical map—jazz—still can be heard at nightclubs, restaurants, and courtyards all over town. RICK McKIBBEN

hard to define. Our advice? Don't overanalyze it. Just listen.

You'll have plenty of chances. Kansas City has given birth to some remarkable jazz talents over the decades, and it continues today. A few, such as singer Kevin Mahogany and Grammy-winning guitarist Pat Metheny, have moved away. But others are happy to call the heartland home between tours to Chicago, New York, and Europe. While they're touring there are others to keep your fingers snapping: A two-page list of local musicians printed in *JAM,* the Kansas City Jazz Ambassadors' bimonthly magazine, includes eighty-five bands, fifty-five vocalists, and one tuba player. You'll find them performing almost every night at some nightclub or restaurant or headlining at music festivals all over town. Look for listings in the *Kansas City Star*'s Friday Preview or *The Pitch,* or call the twenty-four-hour Kansas City Jazz Ambassadors' Hotline at (816) 753-5277.

By the way, when Charlie Parker's plastic horn came up for auction at Christie's in New York, forward-thinking Kansas Citians, led by then-mayor Emanuel Cleaver II, outbid a Japanese investor to bring it back home for $145,000. The instrument is now displayed at the American Jazz Museum at 18th and Vine.

Jazz at the Phoenix. CVB OF GREATER KANSAS CITY

Young, Mary Lou Williams, and other greats got their start and where today, musicians jam from around midnight until dawn—or as long as the audience is there. There's no cover charge, but donations are gladly accepted at the door, and you'll want to pony up a few bucks after a particularly soulful solo. The city has gone back and forth on this, but as of now liquor is served here.

Located in the 18th and Vine District, the building was designated a National Historic

Landmark in 1982 after undergoing major reconstruction. The district is also home to the Negro Leagues Baseball Museum and the American Jazz Museum, both well worth a visit (information is available in Attractions), along with the Gem Theater and the Blue Room, described earlier. If you hurry you might still see some of the movie sets from Robert Altman's 1995 film, *Kansas City.*

On weekends musicians and music students get in free; other guests pay $8.

Phoenix Piano Bar & Grill
302 West Eighth Street
(816) 472-0001
www.phoenixjazz.com
You can't miss this cozy neighborhood club; just drive around downtown until you hear music or spot the giant smiling face mural painted on its brick wall. Folks inside are grin-

i Although you'll see plenty of jeans and even shorts during summer, lots of jazz club patrons tend to dress up a bit on Saturday night. So pull out that cocktail dress and black suit when you paint the town red. Didn't pack the fancy duds? Don't worry: You'll be welcome no matter what you're wearing.

ning as well, thanks to the friendly atmosphere. Expect visits from top performers such as internationally respected jazz stylist Karrin Allyson (who lived in town for a while), Max Groove, and the Dave Stephens Swing Band. The menu features steaks, pasta, and fresh seafood for lunch and dinner, but the main pull is the live music and casual vibe. Originally the Phoenix Hotel built in the 1880s, today it's where to get your weekend started right. No cover.

SPORTS BARS

Kansas City is officially a sports town, so nearly every bar in town—even the more sophisticated versions with highly polished wood and real ferns—has a big screen or two tuned to a game, tournament, or race. And when a professional sports team or college game is on the tube, one of these bars is the place to go to commiserate or celebrate with friends.

810 Zone
4800 West 119th Street
Leawood, KS
(913) 469-9663
www.the810zone.com
The name of this bar and grill isn't the code name for a football play (810 . . . hike!); it refers to the hyper-popular Sports Radio 810 station. That means it's the ultimate spot for sports fans where live broadcasts, buckets of Corona, and eighty TVs (including four HD

big-screens) are always on tap. Naturally the walls are lined with sports memorabilia, and the crowd gets noisy when the game is on. But what we really dig are the ballpark franks and frosty malts just like you can get at the stadium. Funnel cakes? You bet. Save us a seat at the bar.

Harpo's
4109 Pennsylvania
(816) 753-3434
www.harposkc.com
With nightly happy hour specials from 4:00 to 7:00, a menu loaded with appetizers and burgers, and plenty of strategically placed TVs, it's no wonder Harpo's was named best sports bar by USA Today. There's even a nifty courtyard when you want to escape the non-stop cheering or grousing during a Chiefs game. The fun continues until 3:00 a.m.

River Market Brewing Company
500 Walnut Street
(816) 471-6300
www.rivermarketbrews.com
During the day and most evenings this attractive brewpub does a brisk lunch business serving beer, salads, burgers, and pretty good barbecue. But woe is the couple expecting a quiet evening out when a KU or MU football game is being televised on what seems like an endless number of screens. That's when noisy alumni take over the wooden booths and barstools to cheer on the teams.

SHOPPING

In the mid-1800s, as the last civilized stop on the way out West, Kansas City welcomed wagon trains and riverboats with provisions, pickaxes, and camaraderie. Shoppers still come here in droves, although today they show up for style rather than mere sustenance.

In fact, several times a year entire busloads of ladies disembark at the shopper's paradise known as Kansas City. Shoppers from hundreds of miles away make annual, sometimes quarterly, pilgrimages to our city-sized antiques centers, enormous outlet malls, and one-of-a-kind emporiums such as Nell Hill's in nearby Atchison, Kansas.

Of course, the high-winter holidays wouldn't be the same without a visit to the Country Club Plaza, our 14-block extravaganza of retail stores and entertainment with 250,000 glowing Christmas lights outlining every building, spire, and arch. And for those who enjoy one-of-a-kind shops rather than big-name stores that could be in any city in North America, there's the Crossroads Arts District, a vibrant neighborhood with more than seventy art galleries, boutiques, and showrooms, all within a mile walking radius. We'll give you the full tour in this chapter's Shopping Districts section, but we've also singled out a few shops in cross-referenced categories, such as antiques.

Our shopping opportunities are so stupendous that when people call us a sports town, they're often referring to the action in the *aisles*, not the stadiums. Our renowned buying power and sophisticated lifestyle have naturally attracted giant retailers, often for their first forays into the Midwest. Examples include Nordstrom, Ralph Lauren, and Crate and Barrel. And where these giants go, smaller exclusive boutiques and stores such as Armani, St. John Knits, Dean & Deluca, MAC Cosmetics, and Burberry follow, giving

us enough cachet to be considered the heartland's Rodeo Drive.

Other retail adventures await you just outside our city limits. Drive just forty miles or so to Weston, Missouri, or Lawrence, Kansas, and you'll find charming, old-fashioned downtowns filled with antiques shops and flea markets, art galleries, unique fashion emporiums, and more. We take you there in the Day Trips and Weekend Getaways chapter.

And don't overlook the dozens of one-of-a-kind shops you'll find only in Kansas City. Asiatica fashions exquisite garments from antique kimonos, and Retro Inferno sells designer furniture from the 1930s to 1970s in prime condition, just right for that so-in loft look. Both shops were "discovered" by collectors in New York and Los Angeles before their own hometown. Ditto for local artists Markus Pierson, whose famous Coyote series is owned by the rich and famous, and his wife, Sheryl Pierson, whose collages grace the homes of Whoopi Goldberg and Sir Elton John. The Piersons' work can be acquired through Blue Gallery (see separate listing under Art). Metal sculptor Tom Corbin (see separate listing) counts Jack Nicholson, Tom Hanks, and Alec Baldwin as fans, and Joscelyn Himes (www.jhtextiles.com), whose studio and shop is in the Crossroads Arts District, creates ethereal fabrics for the design collections of Bill Blass, Donna Karan, and Vera Wang.

Don't be shy about calling or dropping by any of the places mentioned. One thing you'll learn about shopping in Kansas City is that, unlike some other cities, you'll be greeted by a friendly hello whether you're in a major department store or a tiny shop with a tinkling bell above the door. Go ahead and touch the goods, sit down to test the cushions, and ask where to get a good meal nearby. And don't be surprised if they place your purchase in a gift bag complete with tufts of tissue paper and a jaunty bow.

Expect most of the shops to be open Monday through Saturday, unless listed otherwise. But because many of the stores are owner- or artist-operated, it's always best to call ahead.

The shops in this chapter are grouped by category of goods and then listed alphabetically. All the shops are in Kansas City, Missouri, unless otherwise noted.

Many of these special places are unadvertised, and several are off the beaten path. When the shopkeepers ask how in the world you discovered them, just say an Insider gave you the scoop. So put on those comfortable shoes, grab that credit card, and let's go shopping!

ANTIQUES AND COLLECTIBLES

It's true: We're one of the country's best-kept secrets when it comes to the quality and value of the antiques available here. And often, just to make the hunting even more delightful, we've grouped dozens of shops together in a huge antiques mall or neighborhood. You can literally shop all day at one location, returning to your vehicle just long enough to store another treasure in the trunk. When it's time for a break, a cafe or coffee shop is usually just a shopping bag's throw away.

Antiquities & Oddities
Architectural Salvage
2045 Broadway
(816) 283-3740
www.aoarchitecturalsalvage.com
If the name doesn't get you, just driving by the beautiful two-story Broadway Bank–turned–antiques shop with intriguing treasures peeking through the windows will. For decades, long before slightly chipped architectural remnants, bronze urns blackened with age, and enormous marble sculptures became the look

for upscale gardens and homes, Architectural Salvage has been collecting interesting and priceless pieces from razed buildings, churches, and movie palaces and selling them to interior decorators, set designers, and savvy shoppers.

Here's where to find massive carved wooden doors, rusted gates, salvaged church pews, stained-glass windows, Tara-sized porch columns, discarded fireplace mantels, and red velvet fold-down seats. You can spend hours just digging through boxes of doorknobs and cases of rescued hardware. Pace yourself, and leave the nice clothes at home; it can get pretty grungy here. But to find that perfect gargoyle for your garden, what's a little eighty-year-old dust? The store is open 10:00 a.m. to 5:00 p.m. Thursday through Saturday or by appointment. Owner Rick Bettinger may have just the baluster or newel post you need.

Cheep Antiques
500 West Fifth Street
(816) 471-0092
www.kansascityrivermarket.com/cheep antiques
The name sounds like "bargain," but the quality and variety of antiques found inside this three-story shop in the River Market are about as rich as it gets. There are so many hall stands, armoires, buffets, bedroom sets, dining tables, and washstands in this 30,000-square-foot space that you'll have to squeeze between them sideways to get to the next room.

The bounty also includes rugs, clocks, upholstered furniture, and an odd assortment of baskets, boxes, and even humidors. The Porter family (one is always in residence,

i You'll find a number of charming, old-fashioned "Main Street" shopping districts throughout Kansas City, each filled with unique stores and antiques shops. Some of the best are in Parkville, Brookside, Independence Square, 45th and State Line, Crestwood, and the eclectic Crossroads Arts District.

ready to share the history of each piece) can convert nearly any armoire into an entertainment or computer center. Layaway and delivery are available. Look for the big sign on the building 1 block west of the Broadway Bridge. Open Tuesday through Friday 9:00 a.m. to 3:00 p.m.; 9:00 a.m. to 5:00 p.m. Saturday and Sunday. Closed Monday.

The Curious Sofa
3925 West 69th Terrace
Prairie Village, KS
(913) 432-8969
www.curioussofa.com
Stopping by Debbie Dusenberry's antiques and home furnishings shop is like a minivacation as your senses are assailed by scented candles, offbeat treasures longing to be touched, and a danceable French tune on the stereo. On any given day you might find a peeling-paint medicine cabinet, funky mirror covered in shells, or beaded Barbie-size chandelier. Her selection of new and antique jewelry is divine.

Here, vintage is cleverly mixed with made-to-look-old new items, such as the sofas tufted to within an inch of their lives. Her devoted followers were nervous when she closed up her original shop in the Crossroads Arts District a few years ago and moved to (gasp!) Prairie Village. But Deb transformed a standard space into a vintage wonderland with tin ceilings, cubbyholes, and her legendary more-is-more sensibilities. The voluminous interior also gave her room to blossom with even more delicious displays. We adore her, as do editors of such magazines as *Country Living, Cottage Living,* and *Romantic Home* (notice a pattern here?) who have all featured her store or her home in their pages. We dare you to visit Curious Sofa and not fall hopelessly in love. For just a taste, visit her flirty, evocative, totally sexy Web site, or, as we like to call it, foreplay.

45th & State Line Antique,
Art & Design Center
45th and State Line Road
(816) 531-4414

If you have a penchant for the old, the unique, or the collectible, then snoop to your heart's content in this quaint historic district that features over twenty antiques shops and galleries, all within charming row houses. Despite the number of shops in one place, they rarely repeat each other, so it's a sure bet you'll be here for hours. The prices bring back buyers again and again.

One not to miss is Christopher Filley (816-561-1124), where unique antiques and decorative arts are stacked to the rafters. Although it specializes in garden art including architectural remnants, statues, bird fountains, and pitted stone balls, you'll also spy hand-carved santos, a nice selection of mercury glass, mirrors set inside enormous industrial gears, and other delightfully quirky finds. Prices are not marked, but don't be afraid to ask Christopher or his associate, Rich Hoffman. You'll get a price and perhaps a fascinating story about the item's history.

European Express (816-753-0443) may sound like a fast-food cafe, but it's actually three floors filled with antiques, including enormous armoires and marble washstands. And make sure to stop by Morning Glory Antiques (816-531-5554), and . . . oh, what the heck. Visit them all; each is totally different, all are wonderful. And the proprietors are truly happy to greet you and answer questions. During the holiday open house they'll even set out cookies and hot spiced cider.

Locust Grove Antiques & Interiors
25180 Missouri Highway JJ
Weston, MO
(816) 640-3203
www.locustgroveweston.com
Locust Grove isn't an antiques *mall*, but with its barnlike size it may as well be. It's amazing that two partners own the entire inventory, which is part antique, part new, all sensational. Kate Parsons, a talented interior designer, teamed up with daughter Christy Shafer to create small vignettes of themed treasures to make browsing fun and collecting a breeze.

A recent walk-through spied a dining room area with pierced silver servers, topiaries, and a tapestry throw; a bar service with silver cocktail picks in a vintage shot glass and an old seltzer bottle; and a glorious bedchamber with antique bedroom set, vintage linens, and needlepoint pillows. They also have some of the most incredible faux florals and botanicals available, including dried wreaths. Locust Grove is definitely worth the 40-mile drive out of town, especially if you're heading to Weston (see Day Trips and Weekend Getaways) for the afternoon or weekend. The shop is open every day but Monday.

Mission Road Antiques
4101 West 83rd Street
Prairie Village, KS
(913) 341-7577
www.missionroadantiquemall.com
Better get plenty of rest the night before you plan to attack this 50,000-square-foot mall, considered to be one of the finest in the Midwest. The building is as historical as some of its contents; sixty years ago it was a stable for Thoroughbred horses, including the 1938 Kentucky Derby winner, Lawrin. Today the "stalls" have been taken over by 350 dealers displaying their wares, which include European antiques, primitives, stained glass, vintage housewares, Oriental porcelain, estate jewelry, military collectibles, and more. The mall is open Monday through Saturday 10:00 a.m. to 7:00 p.m. and Sunday 11:00 a.m. to 6:00 p.m.

Some vendors specialize in one category, such as original oil paintings or Christmas decorations, but most offer an engaging array of goods. Expect to spend at least half a day to see it all. And just as you've reached sensory overload, there's a cozy cafe in the mall to offer a place to sit down to some tasty food. The Bloomsbury Bistro's menu changes every Friday, but expect to find items such as veggie lasagna and chicken salad along with soups and wraps. The chef knows her way around a cake pan, too. Homemade desserts include pies and German chocolate cake. The bistro is open 11:00 a.m. to 3:00 p.m. Monday through Saturday and is closed Sunday.

River Market Antique Mall
115 West Fifth Street
(816) 221-0220
www.kansascityrivermarket.com/river marketantiques
No wonder this mall has been voted "Best Antique Shop in Kansas City" by readers of *The Pitch*. First, there's the size. With more than 30,000 square feet of booths and showcases spread out over four floors, it's enough to make you just plain giddy with anticipation of what you'll find. Here's just a teaser: American, European, and primitive furniture including mission and Wakefield; pottery and glassware featuring plenty of Roseville; vintage clothing and jewelry; quilts and lamps; antique toys; and old advertising art. The vendors are friendly enough to answer questions and point you to another booth if you're seeking something specific. And the location creates the perfect environment for finding treasures as old as our city: The mall is a few blocks from the very spot where our town began. Open 10:00 a.m. to 6:00 p.m. seven days a week.

Webster House Antiques and Restaurant
1644 Wyandotte
(816) 221-4713
www.websterhousekc.com
If you're from the old school of thought, you'll love shopping for antiques in what's considered to be Kansas City's oldest surviving school. While renovating the Romanesque Revival building, built in the late nineteenth century, workers removed plasterboard to find blackboards with homework assignments written in chalk.

Now the rooms hold the marvelous antique and decorative accessories that used to grace Crestwood Galleries Antiques & Cafe, which spent thirty years at the Crestwood Shops at 55th and Oak. Thanks to owner Shirley Bush Helzberg's vision, the new location has more than double the retail space, plus room for a charming restaurant and additional galleries on the second floor. Loyal fans of Crestwood Galleries will be thrilled to see the same friendly faces at Webster House, including general manager Keitha Kaminski and talented designer Joe Haas. As for the aroma wafting around the Chinoiserie and Chippendales, it's probably executive chef Charles d'Ablaing's latest creation. We tempt you further in our Restaurants chapter.

Woodson Place Antiques & Interiors
318 West Walnut
Raymore, MO
(816) 331-2701

Sleepy little Raymore's population nearly doubles when Roy and Jane Park announce they're back from Europe with the latest container of antiques. Caravans of buses, cars, and vans show up at this turn-of-the-twentieth-century home turned shop set back from a busy commercial street. Thank goodness there's plenty of parking—and a separate warehouse to hold the overflow.

It's Jane's unerring eye for quality that draws customers from twelve states—she has an instinct for what people want—but it's the jaw-dropping prices that keep them coming back. Recently a magnificent tiger mahogany armoire, circa 1860, sold for a mere $1,789. Bring measurements and be ready to buy as soon as you fall in love; at these prices nothing lasts long enough to tarry. Raymore, Missouri, is located about 40 miles south of Kansas City. Be sure to call for dates of the next open house.

BED AND BATH GIFTS

Indigo Wild
3189 Mercier
(816) 221-3480, (800) 361-5686
www.indigowild.com

This tiny company produces delightfully scented bath and beauty products made of good-for-you ingredients. The Zum bars, for example, include goat's milk, pure essential oils, and herbal extracts and come in lots of yummy scents, such as lavender-mint and sandalwood-citrus. The bars, which look like tie-died artwork, with swirls and chunks of colors, come in fun, corrugated shapes. The company also makes paraffin-free candles, baby care products, body lotions, and all-natural lip balms in flavors such as tangerine. That's Zum kiss! Products are available by phone, online, or through a clever catalog.

Perfect Scents
5037 West 119th Street
Overland Park, KS
(913) 469-1737
www.perfectscentsinc.com

"Come inside and play," Nancy McAnany beckons to those who enter her shop of earthly and ethereal delights. Since 1989 she's been turning customers into alchemists as they create unique body lotions, massage oils, and home products using dozens of aromatic essential oils. Nancy figures there are at least 3,424 different custom-scented products you can conjure up. Or choose one of her designer oils that smell like expensive versions without the hefty price tags.

The shelves and counters reveal other treats, such as spearmint-flavored lip balm, gentle baby care products, lamp rings that send a subtle fragrance throughout the room, and car diffusers that do the same for that long drive home. And who could resist the red mineral facial treatment she calls the "Hoover vacuum cleaner" of masks?

Scandia Down—Kansas City
501 Nichols Road (Country Club Plaza)
(816) 753-4144
www.scandiadownkc.com

Welcome to Ursula Terrasi's little corner of the world. Literally. This merchant—with the grace of Italian royalty and the warmth of a Midwesterner—searches the globe for luxurious bedding (can you count to 800 threads per inch?), hand-finished furniture, heavenly scented bath potions, and beautiful tableware for her shop on the Country Club Plaza. But it's the meringue-high, down-filled comforters that have shoppers wanting to jump in bed. Each cozy store vignette has been dressed to the nines in sumptuous fabrics and masses of pillows.

No wonder Scandia Down is favored for its bridal registry service: Climb into one of these sumptuous confections every night and the honeymoon may never end. And following Mother Nature's course, the shop has a new line of beds and accessories for babies. No one leaves empty-handed, now that Ursula has added lovely jewelry and personal accessories.

The shop is located on the corner of Pennsylvania and Nichols Road, at the delightful Penguin Courtyard, where live musical concerts are held from spring through fall. If Ursula has her way, they'll play a medley of Dean Martin hits.

BOOKSTORES

Naturally we have our share of national book dealers, such as Waldenbooks, Borders, and Barnes & Noble. But we also have an amazing number of independent booksellers who succeed because of their special services. Rainy Day Books, for instance, consistently brings well-known writers to town for speaking engagements. At Bloomsday Books and Reading Reptile, the owners have found a market and nurture it so well, customers wouldn't think of being disloyal. So here, dear readers, are some of our best and brightest booksellers.

Bloomsday Books
313 East 55th Street
(816) 523-6712
www.bloomsdaybooks.com
Lawyer-turned-bookseller Tom Shawver is thrilled to take your gently used books in for trade; it's his confirmation that one more person has the reading bug. The bookstore's location is ideal: a large sunny space in the quaint Crestwood Shops, where his neighbors include antiques stores and bustling bistros. The shelves are well organized with varied categories, and the staff is made up of avid readers who can talk about nearly any book or author.

Relax with an espresso and croissant, scone, or a slab of peanut butter fudge from the Aixois Coffee Bar a few doors down. Then take your beverage back to Bloomsday, choose a chair in the sun-filled window, and relax while you make your literary selection. Tom certainly won't rush you: There's no doubt this guy holds literature—especially the works of Irish author James Joyce—in high esteem. He named his shop for Leopold Bloom, the central character in Joyce's *Ulysses,* and every June 16 holds a nonstop reading of the novel. Hold the latte; could you make that an Irish coffee, please?

The Complete Traveler
7321 West 80th Street
Overland Park, KS
(913) 648-1560
www.completetrav.com
Gerry and Mary Buckley wholeheartedly recommend traveling—they met on Mary's trip to Ireland and you might say he was her favorite souvenir. They married in 2001 and purchased this shop two years later. Beyond providing a staggering amount of travel guides, globes, and personal accessories, such as money belts, they dispense valuable advice. Though they are experts in Ireland (golf, anyone?), South Africa, and Australia, the Buckleys can arrange travel to any destination and can issue Rail Europe tickets with no additional fees. If you're sending a student off on a trip, this couple can help make you and your young scholar more at ease.

The Complete Traveler is an authorized representative for Eurail and BritRail passes and is one of a few retailers to carry the Thomas Cook European Rail Timetable, which some call the bible of European rail travel. And because you have to put your new travel guide in something, the store stocks a nice supply of luggage.

I Love a Mystery
6114 Johnson Drive

Mission, KS
(913) 432-2583
www.iloveamystery.com

It's no mystery why this place is so popular with book lovers: It's stocked with more than 24,000 new and used mystery books, including a large selection of signed first editions and all things Sherlockian. But it's the decor that sets it apart. Visitors are greeted at the door by a gargoyle, while a life-sized skeleton guards the coffee bar. Daggers, skulls, and poison bottles are tucked into nooks and crannies, but never fear. You're welcome to sit down in an overstuffed chair and settle in for a read or a nap. And signing up for a book club wouldn't kill you, would it?

Prospero's Books
1800 West 39th Street
(816) 531-WORD (9673)
www.prosperosbookstore.com

Since November 19, 1997, owners Will Leathem and Tom Wayne have created more than a bookstore, they've built a place to celebrate the written and spoken word. In 2002 they moved book, stock, and barrel to a historic hardware building across the street, restoring pressed tin ceilings and rolling library ladders. A dramatic staircase links the main floor and basement, marrying the late 1800s with today's urban chic. The casual reader or antiquarian collector can find a gem here, while listening to the city's longest-running and largest open-mic poetry readings. Songwriters perform here as well, and in 2002 Prospero's launched the 39th Street Artwalk the third Friday of each month. The team also publishes books.

Rainy Day Books
2706 West 53rd Street
Fairway, KS
(913) 384-3126
www.rainydaybooks.com

Vivien Jennings and Roger Doeren somehow manage to convince top authors that they can't sell a single book unless they appear in Kansas City. Since 1975 Rainy Day has hosted thousands of book signings—several a month—for authors including Ray Bradbury, Anne Rice, John Grisham, Martha Stewart, Garrison Keillor, and Nigella Lawson.

This corner store in Fairway near the Country Club Plaza is all that a bookseller can hope to be: a friendly place where there's someone on the staff who can recommend a book whether the subject is murder, cooking, home repair, romance, or coping with a baby sister. Rainy Day also sponsors writers' seminars throughout the year to encourage local authors to keep those bookshelves filled. And Vivien writes a regular column, "Book Ends," in a weekly society magazine, the *Independent*. Heavens, if *she* can find time to read, anyone can.

Reading Reptile
328 West 63rd Street
(816) 753-0441
www.readingreptile.com

Is this someone's living room or a bookstore? Actually, it's both. Since 1988 owners Pete and Debbie have made this cheery shop their home-away-from-home, where they've brought up their four adorable kids, made lasting friendships, and introduced hundreds of children to the joys of the written and spoken word. They hold free story hours for preschoolers and school-aged children every week and host book clubs for young readers.

Once a year Reading Reptile sponsors a two-day event (a literary love-in, they call it) so that children, adults, teachers, and librarians can meet some of the top authors and illustrators. The store is fun, the Web site is a hoot, and the T-shirts, in which a fellow implores his dog to "Read, dammit!" would make a fine gift for the serious booklover.

STEALS AND DEALS

Act II
1417 West 47th Street
(816) 531-7572
www.actiiinc.com

Yes, it's true that Act II is a consignment shop,

ℹ️ Local folklore credits Olathe boot-maker Charles H. Hyer with the innovation of making boots shaped differently for right and left feet in the late 1800s. Before that, shoes were identical, and—one would imagine—a little tough to break in.

but owner Gloria Everhart is so picky about quality that the goods might as well be right off the retail rack. Savvy women and men shop here first for eveningwear with labels from Bill Blass, Calvin Klein, St. John, and other designers. The after-five and ball gown selection is amazing thanks to the number of black tie affairs held each year in Kansas City; some social denizens attend four or more a season and wouldn't dare wear the same sequined number twice.

Gloria also sells tailored suits, casual clothes, outerwear—yes, even furs—and like-new handbags and shoes. The store is just up the hill from the Plaza.

Bob Jones Shoes
1914 Grand
(816) 474-4212
www.bobjonesshoes.com
You're bound to find your sole-mate at Bob Jones. At any given time more than 100,000 pairs of designer shoes line the racks at up to 70 percent off retail. Sure, a few in the back room are a little dated, unless you want bright blue pumps with six-inch heels, but 98 percent of the inventory consists of top names found at the finest department stores. For women that includes Enrico Gori, Via Spiga, Stuart Weitzman, Joan & David, and Calvin Klein. Men can choose from Johnston Murphy, Kenneth Cole, Bostonian, Rockport, and more. Bob Jones also carries a limited number of athletic shoes and unique women's handbags. Just look for the wooden Indian in front.

Bushnell Factory Outlet
8500 Marshall Drive
Lenexa, KS
(913) 752-6166

445 Northwest Murray Road
Lee's Summit, MO
(816) 525-2220
www.bushnell.com
Take a look at the pair of binoculars in your hall closet or backpack; if they're good, chances are "Bushnell" is printed on the case. This Kansas City–based company has been manufacturing high-performance optics for more than fifty years, but until these outlets opened, you'd have to pay retail prices at sporting goods stores. You'll still pay retail for some merchandise, including first-run binoculars, telescopes, night-vision scopes, and laser rangefinders. But you'll find significant discounts, from 25 percent to 50 percent off retail, on discontinued items, and up to 75 percent off retail on factory demonstration goods that are still in great shape.

The outlets hold plenty of attraction for any birder, astronomer, or sports enthusiast, even if that means someone who pulls a beer tab at a football game instead of a trigger in the woods. Plus Bushnell carries Bolle and Serengeti, some of the most stylish sunglasses in the world.

Cargo Largo
(formerly Recovery Sales Outlet)
13900 East 35th Street South
Independence, MO
(816) 350-6101
www.cargolargo.com
This may be the only place on Earth to find a limited-edition Italian fountain pen worth $3,000, an antique Japanese tansu chest, a ten-pound bag of kitty litter, and a Big Bird costume all in the same place. But don't bother rushing over for the yellow feathered suit: it's long gone by now. In its place is something else just as bizarre. Cargo Largo handles about 15,000 shipments of lost, unwanted, or otherwise undeliverable cargo every week, all discounted up to 80 percent off the retail price.

In fact, its parent company, Kansas City–based Recovery Management Corp., is the biggest single buyer of all misdirected freight in the country. And although it does a

The Country Club Plaza

What do you get when you combine an art and sculpture gallery, shopping center, flower garden, and jazz club? You get the Country Club Plaza, and admission to this outdoor extravaganza is free of charge.

Nestled against the banks of Brush Creek, this architecturally stunning, 14-block plaza offers everything you could want—shopping, dining, hotels, services, and entertainment—all within walking distance. Or if you're so inclined, you may view the elegant surroundings from a horse-drawn carriage.

The Plaza was the brainchild of Jesse Clyde (J. C.) Nichols, a real estate developer who changed a swampy tract of land into the country's first shopping center in 1922. He envisioned a shopping area that was automobile-friendly at a time when many thought the auto was a passing fad. And he wanted his little village filled with the romantic courtyards, ornate towers, red-tiled roofs, ornate ironwork, art, and sparkling fountains he had admired in Spain. Today the artwork alone is worth far more than the $1 million he originally paid for the fifty-five-acre site.

In the early 1920s new shops opened and thrived on the Plaza, and soon long-standing downtown stores opened second locations here. It became the center of style and fashion. The permanent wave was introduced in a Plaza beauty salon, and top Hollywood movies debuted at the ornate Plaza Theater. J. C. continually looked for ways to attract shoppers.

In 1925 a single strand of lights heralded the start of the holiday shopping season. It's a celebration that has grown into a world-famous event as 250,000 jewel-colored bulbs outline every spire, swag, and tower beginning Thanksgiving evening. And it doesn't matter if the weather is frigid; with thousands of people packing the streets it's always warm. The lights continue to shine until mid-January.

During the Depression the Plaza Art Fair began in 1932 as a promotional tool to encourage visitors. More than seventy years later, the event is the Midwest's premiere art fair, drawing an annual crowd of more than 275,000 during the three-day event. This celebration of the arts transforms 9 blocks into a giant art gallery representing more than 250 artists from nearly every state. Entertainment includes a free children's workshop, culinary specialties from twenty-five Plaza restaurants, and live music on three stages. The event is held each fall near the end of September.

Before J. C. Nichols died in 1950 he had seen his idea influence other developers around the country. Miller Nichols built on his father's dream, adding hotels and apartments to the Plaza's landscape and buying outstanding artwork and fountains from around the world to adorn his museum without walls. Some of the most spectacular pieces include the J. C. Nichols Memorial Fountain by Henri Gerbert, the Pool of the Four Fauns, the 130-foot-tall reproduction of the famous Giralda Tower of Seville, and the endearing *Sleeping Child* sculpture that slumbers in the median of a busy

The holiday shopping season officially begins Thanksgiving night when the Plaza lights are turned on.
CVB OF GREATER KANSAS CITY

street. An illustrated Walking Art Tour is available from the Plaza Customer Service center (816-753-0100) at 4745 Central, or find photos and maps at www.countryclubplaza.com.

For some, shopping is an art form, and the Plaza provides plenty of opportunity to practice it. Among more than 150 unique stores you'll recognize such retailers as Brooks Brothers, Coach, Eddie Bauer, Z Gallerie, Betsey Johnson, Gap and Gap Kids, J. Jill, St. John, Tiffany and Co., AIX Armani Exchange, Banana Republic, MAC Cosmetics, Anthropologie, The Sharper Image, Barnes & Noble Booksellers, and Tommy Bahama.

But we're perhaps even more proud of the hometown retailers presented here. They include Halls (see separate listing under Fashion and Accessories), an elegant emporium with fashions for men and women, fine jewelry, giftware, and accessories for the home; jewelry stores including Tivol, Swirk, Vinca, and Helzberg Diamonds; Diebels Sportsman Gallery; Three Dog Bakery with treats for pets; Superlatives, a world-class antiques and home decorating shop; and Scandia Down, where the service matches the exquisite display of European linens and gifts.

The culinary arts are well represented as well. Nearly forty restaurants, bistros, and pubs will tempt you. Frequent travelers will be happy to know

continued

their favorites are here, including Ruth's Chris Steakhouse, McCormick & Schmick's Seafood Restaurant, The Capital Grille, Houston's Restaurant, P. F. Chang's China Bistro, Uno Chicago Grill, and the Cheesecake Factory. But don't miss some of our hometown dining experiences; one taste of Bo Lings Chinese Restaurant, Baja 600, re:Verse, Starker's Reserve, The Raphael Restaurant, or Plaza III The Steakhouse and you may find a new favorite. Look for details about some of the best in the Restaurants chapter.

The Plaza is also home to fourteen or so specialty food options, including the Better Cheddar, a purveyor of gourmet food and wine; Panache Chocolatier, where you'll find decadent fudge, truffles, and addictive chocolate-dipped popcorn; and Topsy's Popcorn Shop, the place to get freshly popped treats and perhaps the world's best limeade. And because you shouldn't have to go too far without an espresso, LatteLand has two separate locations on opposite ends of the Plaza.

Just as J. C. Nichols intended, the Plaza is a self-contained city with personal services galore. Get your shoes shined or repaired, suits tailored, and boxes shipped, handy for all those purchases you plan to take home. Looking for a new hairdo or personal pampering? The Plaza boasts five salons or spas, including Mario Tricoci Salon & Day Spa, Beauty Brands, and the elegant new House of Elan Med Spa (www.houseofelan.com) just up the street. To pay for it all, you'll find four ATMs within the area.

Kansas City's musical heritage is well represented on the Plaza. Beginning each May, free "Plaza Live" concerts bring some of the area's best jazz, blues, and folk musicians to the outdoor courtyards. The entertainment goes from 5:00 to 8:00 p.m. every Thursday, then again each Saturday and Sunday from noon to 5:00 p.m. It's the perfect way to enjoy a latte or lap some ice cream, sit on the side of a fountain or find a bench, and listen to stylists such as Ida McBeth confessing the blues. Music lovers can also hear tunes at several venues throughout the Plaza, including the InterContinental and Raphael hotels.

It's true, there is a lot to see and do on the Plaza. May we give you a lift? One of the most exciting ways to experience the magic is in a carriage. Two companies, Pride of Kansas City and Surreys Ltd., will escort you around the open-air marketplace in a festive old-fashioned carriage pulled by horses. For a truly enchanting evening choose Cinderella's Coach, a pumpkin-shaped carriage outlined in sparkling white lights.

If all this shopping, dining, and sailing has you exhausted, sweet dreams are just a stroll away at four hotels—the InterContinental (formerly the Fairmont), Raphael, Four Points by Sheraton, and Hampton Inn & Suites—and the Southmoreland Inn, an award-winning bed-and-breakfast. In the Accommodations chapter, you'll get officially tucked in.

The Country Club Plaza was a gift to Kansas City from J. C. and Miller Nichols. And this visually stunning, wildly exciting fantasyland of shopping, dining, music, and entertainment is our gift to the rest of the world.

big Internet business, most of the goods end up on shelves in this airplane hangar–size warehouse. Here's a recent haul for one shopper: a Winston fly-fishing rod at half its $700 price, an Oriental rug for $60, a fax machine, a floor lamp, Doc Marten boots, and massive quantities of caulking supplies. He passed on the framed Red Sox shirt signed by Ted Williams and Budweiser neon sign in the shape of a football helmet. Hours are 9:00 a.m. to 8:00 p.m. Monday through Saturday; 11:00 a.m. to 6:00 p.m. Sunday.

Cargo Largo also holds a Thursday-afternoon bid sale, which is more fun than a barrel of monkeys; a container of live simians is perhaps the only thing you won't see. Items include retail, commercial, industrial, and hard-to-classify categories. The sale is held in Unit 800 of Carefree Industrial Park (call Cargo Largo for directions) the second Tuesday of each month from 6:00 to 8:00 p.m.

FARMERS' MARKETS

We're blessed to be surrounded by dozens of small farms and orchards, many of them certified organic. Farmers drive to town in the wee hours every Saturday and Sunday to bring us fresh sweet corn, snap beans, juicy peaches, and tomatoes so good you can eat 'em like apples. Following are some of the most popular markets where the rows of nature's best are laid end-to-end like colorful quilts.

Brookside Market
63rd Street and Wornall Road
(Border Star Montessori School parking lot)
www.farmerscommunitymarket.com
This lively mix of local and certified organic famers provide freshly picked vegetables and fruits, fragrant herbs, edible cut flowers, and free-range egg and honey products. Many of the regulars show up for the hot coffee and breakfast burritos and perhaps a chance to see Chef Jasper Mirabile teach a new dish for those heirloom tomatoes. These colorful, craggy specimens are so popular here there's

i Stores on the Country Club Plaza stay open until 9:00 p.m on Thursday nights year-round to give you an opportunity to hit your favorites while in town. And beginning Thanksgiving night, the stores stay open every night except Sunday during the holidays to help make the season bright.

a festival in their honor in late July. Opening day at Brookside is mid-April and goes until mid-October. You'll want to schedule the entire day here; after you pick up a dozen ears of sweet-as-sugar corn and get a bag of brownies to go, visit the Brookside shops just across the street.

City Market
Fifth and Walnut
(816) 842-1271
www.kc-citymarket.com
This is the big kahuna, the biggest open-air market in six states, where nearly 200 vendors hawk fresh produce on Wednesday, Saturday, and Sunday year-round. For the pick of the crop, it's best to get here early, around 7:00 a.m. on Saturday, 9:00 a.m. otherwise. That's when all the chefs arrive to sniff cantaloupe, inspect zucchini, and plan for that evening's special. That pale yellow ear of corn might end up in a chipotle-laced chowder tonight.

Restaurants aren't the only ones buying in bulk; you'll see couples lugging flats of strawberries to cars parked down the street. And beyond ripe produce, expect to see a hodge-podge of arts and crafts such as twig furniture, jewelry, and paintings from local artists. It's always a party atmosphere, especially on weekends, when crowds can swell to 30,000 or more a day. If the fruits and vegetables make you hungry, your table is waiting at Winslow's Barbecue, Bo Lings, or Minsky's Pizza. If you have time, tour the steamboat *Arabia,* a riverboat that sank during the early days of our town. It's a fascinating museum that we cover in Attractions.

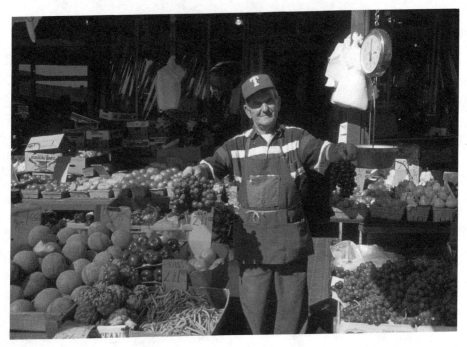

Produce at City Market. CVB OF GREATER KANSAS CITY

KC Organics
Minor Park (Just east of Holmes on Red Bridge Road)
(816) 444-FOOD (3663)
www.kcorganics.com

This market doesn't draw nearly the crowds of others in town. But that's just fine with the picky consumers who show up every Saturday from May through mid-October. Shorter lines mean you can actually talk to the farmers about their green beans, fingerling potatoes, apples, peaches, and exotic-looking Japanese eggplant. But don't expect picture-perfect specimens. A few bug-ravaged tomatoes prove that everything is certified pesticide- and chemical-free.

Many of the growers also bring prepared foods such as jellies, jams, salsas, and even hand-milled soap. You may also be treated to live music and cooking demonstrations.

Marche du Jour
3848 West 75th Street

Prairie Village, KS
(573) 584-3385
www.delawareinteriors.com/marche
Every Saturday from May through October, Mother Nature shows up in the guise of Sally at Widgeonwood Farms (even the name sounds like something organic) with just-picked heirloom tomatoes, wild plums, slender asparagus stalks, and other organic delights. And for Sally, a dusty pickup truck wouldn't do: She displays her colorful fare in the courtyard of Delaware Interiors (913-384-0330), a delightful home furnishings shop whose goods are almost as glorious as the glossy eggplant on display outside.

But some regulars come to Marche du Jour to stock pantries rather than vegetable bins. Each week brings new jars of treats, such as dilled green beans, Italian parsley pesto, port wine cranberry relish, tomato-basil-Vidalia dressing, and wild plum butter. There is rarely enough to go around; get there by 9:00 a.m. or you may be disappointed.

Sally also makes decadent sweets, including biscotti dipped in white chocolate, chocolate English toffee, and chocolate raspberry truffle sauce. Here's our recipe for heaven: a couple of truffles and a warm bath fragranced with her rosemary-and-lavender French bath salts.

Thank goodness you needn't go the entire year without a jar of Sally's gazpacho. She hosts a holiday market in early December at Delaware Interiors. Call for details; they also ship.

Overland Park Farmers' Market
Marty Street between 79th
and 80th Streets
(913) 642-2222
www.downtownop.org
It can get pretty crowded on a summer Wednesday or Saturday morning as people stand in line for just-picked watermelons, fat blueberries, Big Boy tomatoes, and peaches-and-cream corn, a variety so sweet and tender you can practically eat it raw. There's always a display or two of cutting flowers in bouquets, locally produced honey, and more. To keep things lively, several times a month a live band will entertain the crowds at the Clock Tower, an old-fashioned public square a few stairs up from the market area. Get there early for a seat outside, or duck into Farm to Market Cafe or Homer's Coffeehouse for a cappuccino and a muffin and grab a chair on the patio.

FASHION AND ACCESSORIES

Asiatica Ltd.
4824 Rainbow Boulevard
Westwood, KS
(913) 831–0831
www.asiaticakc.com
Fans of this shop report Asiatica sightings all over the world—in a posh hotel lobby in New York City, in the shadow of the Sistine Chapel—because its fashions, made from old Japanese kimonos, are so distinctive. Each year Elizabeth Wilson and Fifi White travel to the Far East to hand select vintage fabrics or exquisite new textiles, then bring them back home to get glorious new lives as vests, flow-ing jackets, blouses, and wraps.

These gorgeous garments are available only through Asiatica's showroom near the Country Club Plaza and a handful of trunk shows in major markets around the country. Each piece of clothing is a work of art, a one-of-a-kind artifact created from a nonrenewable resource.

The shop also offers an ever-changing selection of antiques, unique tableware, ceramics, scarves, and jewelry picked up from around the world. And you never know when you'll be tapped on the shoulder somewhere in Rome with the question, "Say, aren't you wearing Asiatica?"

Churchill
5240 Belinder
Fairway, KS
(913) 262-5240
www.churchillinfairway.com
This gem of a find is in the delightful, block-long shopping-and-dining destination known as the Fairway Shops. And while Churchill is known for its incredible selection of antique furniture, it's also the place to spy accessories and jewelry favored by Hollywood's young A-list stars, such as Kate Hudson and Gwyneth Paltrow. Chances are the booty in the coveted Oscar swag bag is on Churchill's shelves before the telecast is over. Just how does a tiny shop in the heart of Kansas City get such a scoop? Leave it to Churchill's vivacious owner, Sally Hilkene.

Frankly, we'd follow this trendsetter any-where. Sally's unerring eye for taste (she has been a much-sought-after interior designer for more than twenty years) serves her well, as she fills her shop with an eclectic collection of treasures for the home and personal adorn-ments. Fancy the handbag on Sharon Stone's arm in a celebrity magazine? Check with Sally first. Those fabulous scented stones Elton John likes to give as gifts? Churchill's, again. And this warm and energetic merchant is known for her exquisite one-of-a-kind jewelry, culled from estates all over the world—such as the glorious pair of chandelier earrings one famous actress wore on the cover of *Vogue*.

Though Sally follows the trends, her inventory consists of pieces that will stand the test of time. And speaking of that, did you see her selection of divine watches?

feng
5029 West 119th Street
(Hawthorne Plaza)
Leawood, KS
(913) 498-0530
www.fenglookeast.com

Just look at the handcrafted door handles and you know you're entering a shop of a woman who digs the details. In feng (as in feng shui, the Asian art of design and placement that brings harmony) Beth Zollars has created an oasis of style and refinement in the middle of suburbia. The deep-red walls and furnishings are nearly as compelling as the inventory. Just for an hour you'll be transported to a chic neighborhood in SoHo or L.A. or Hong Kong, filled with precious antiques, designer fashions, and one-of-a-kind accessories that you simply must have.

Beth's own famous taste is reflected in the designer goods displayed out in the open: Chan Luu, Anna Sui, Alice Roi. And the shoes! The selection is tiny—just a handful—but they are exquisite little creatures that Beth often helps design. Follow your nose to the Tea Market in the back of the store; a wall of shelves holds tins of loose tea in aromatic blends meant to heal, nurture, and pamper you. Everything is gift-worthy here, with exquisite packaging and labels. Beth, who is as warm and friendly as she is fashion-savvy (she may have the best laugh in Kansas City), calls feng a lifestyle store. This is just the sort of life you'll want to experience.

Halls
211 Nichols Road (Country Club Plaza)
(816) 274-3222

200 East 25th Street (Crown Center Shops)
(816) 274-8111
www.halls.com

Kansas City's only true, homegrown department store was created in 1913 by Hallmark Cards founder Joyce C. Hall. It continues to be the town's crown jewel. Here's where Kansas City's women and men of style find clothes—from ball gowns and tuxedos to tees and jeans—acquire fine stationery and home decor, register for weddings, and purchase corporate gifts. The shoe department is divine and Jennifer in couture can zip you into an Oscar de la Renta or Badgley Mischka (and never, ever let you attend the Symphony Ball wearing someone else's dress). Room after room is filled with the most delectable giftware and table accessories and everything for the gourmet. Naturally, Halls has an extensive Hallmark card department. Halls Plaza also houses the Midwest's only Steuben Gallery, and the beyond-fabulous Jewel Room shows off several exclusive lines including Van Cleef & Arpels. Personal shopper Krystal Pina-McGill makes life simple.

Halls is also the anchor of the Crown Center shopping complex, offering business and dressy attire to the urban set. An extensive housewares department, gourmet food section, and paper-goods selection make up the three-story mix.

Nolte's Bridal
5057 West 119th Street
Overland Park, KS
(913) 345-1122

4149 North Mulberry Drive
(816) 587-5575
www.noltesbridal.com

Weddings are all about the dress; once that's conquered, everything else falls into place. Mike Nolte has been fitting Kansas City's most knowing brides for more than twenty-five years. Beyond the tulle, Mike and his team offer all the wedding services you need to stay calm and enjoy the most important day in your life. Naturally, Nolte's carries the best designers, including Vera Wang, Badgley Mischka, Monique Lhuillier, and Priscilla of Boston. But the responsive team can also coordinate the invitations to the mints on the tables. At the new Briarcliff Village location (possibly the most glamorous wedding salon in the land), the ever-charming owner introduced an exciting collection of cocktail dresses and formal gowns for weddings and beyond. A monthly "Sass at Six" fashion show serves as a benefit for a local cause; pink was the theme for the Susan G. Komen fund-raiser. The show is limited to the first fifty women who RSVP.

Serendipity
2710 West 53rd Street
Fairway, Kansas
(913) 722-2101
On any given Saturday, you may run into three friends (two with dogs, one with a teenage daughter) seeing what's new at this hipper-than-hip store in the Fairway Shops. What's the draw? Clearly it's the runway-hot collection of clothes Miriam Garvey displays throughout the tiny shop. You'll pick her out right away—she's a ravishing redhead. Oh, wait, that's her equally beautiful daughter, Leslie. There's usually a fashion show running on the flat screen overhead, and it's incredible how many of the latest pieces are hanging right at your fingertips. All the names you read about in *W* and *Bazaar* are found here: Michael Stars, Tracy Reese, True Religion, Seven for all Mankind. With Miriam's or Leslie's just-us-girlfriends guidance, you can put together an outfit for daytime or cocktail that looks smashing on you, but never contrived. Add a bracelet or earrings from their fun displays and poof! You will turn heads at the soiree. When Miriam says she dresses the most beautiful women in Kansas City, she means beautiful both inside and out. Just like her.

Standard Style Boutique
5076 West 119th Street
Leawood, KS
(Town Center Plaza)

447 West 47th Street
(Country Club Plaza)
(913) 685-4464 (for both stores)
www.standardstyle.com
It was a good day when Matt and Emily Baldwin followed their hearts (and Matt's family)

and moved back to the Midwest from California. They brought with them a passion for fashion that created the shop that is the exact opposite of its name. There is nothing standard about a boutique that showcases the most sought-after designers in the world. With nearly 150 lines in all, women will lust after casual to glam clothes from Jean Paul Gaultier, Marc Jacobs, Trina Turk, and DVF. Guys will locate just the right screen printed T-shirt, jacket, and jeans for the nightclub that night. Rumor has it that Matt and Emily made an emergency visit to Oprah's show to dress George Clooney. We do know this for a fact: Standard Style has a loyal following with trendsetters all over the country who shop on the Web and make a beeline for one of their two stores when in Kansas City. We happen to love the fact that this movie-star gorgeous couple is one of us: friendly, helpful, and fun.

FINE ART

We have more than our share of talented artists in Kansas City, thanks in part to the influence of the Kansas City Art Institute and Hallmark Cards. We cover the galleries that show their work in the Arts chapter. But in the meantime, here's your chance to visit the studios, showrooms, and even classrooms where they create their craft.

Blue Gallery
118 Southwest Boulevard
(816) 527-0823
www.bluegalleryonline.com

ℹ️ You can buy one of Rhett Johnson's found-art sculptures at his studio in Dearborn, Missouri, or simply admire them at a Hen House grocery store. The store commissioned Rhett to create 6-foot-long chickens out of tractor seats, painted steel, gelatin molds, and various gizmos. The Hen House at Quivira and College Boulevard in Overland Park, Kansas, has the fanciful fowl hanging above the produce display.

This gallery in the Crossroads Arts District caters to both novice buyer and serious collector with a thoughtful mix of styles and prices. Blue just moved around the block to a glorious new larger space, providing even more opportunities to find something you can't live without. Owners David and Kelly Kuhn (she's beautiful enough to be an artist's model and wise enough to be a muse) have a knack for attracting artists with a salable look. Nothing here is so out-there that you instantly feel like the only person in the world without a tattoo or pierced appendage. Not that that's a bad thing, mind you.

Like many gallery owners, David and Kelly will bend over backward to help you own the art you fall in love with. They'll let you take it home to live with for a few days or even come out to take a picture of your intended wall, then digitally drop in the artwork to see how it would look. Out-of-town buyers can peruse art on the Web site and have it shipped. But trust us; you'll want to visit this space yourself, if for no other reason than to meet Stella, the lovable gallery mascot. With any luck, you'll be here for First Friday when Blue is the epicenter for the gallery walk. Sign up for such upcoming events as artist receptions and parties.

Other must-see galleries in the Crossroads Arts District include Sherry Leedy Gallery (2004 Baltimore, 816-842-2626, www.sherryleedy.com) in a two-level converted warehouse that's art in and of itself. Sherry displays outstanding pieces from international as well as emerging regional artists. You can't miss the amazing Dale Chihuly glass piece hanging from the ceiling. Leedy-Voulkos Art Center (2012 Baltimore, 816-474-1919, www.leedy-voulkos.com) is owned by Jim Leedy, whom many consider the father of the Crossroads district. Along with regional and national artists, Jim's diverse talents are showcased here. Known for his expressionist ceramics, he has had a major exhibition nearly every year somewhere in America since 1962. A new addition to the space is the Cross Gallery (816-651-3480, www.thecrossgallery.com), owned by Michael and Rane Cross.

Corbin Bronze Ltd.
201 Wyandotte Street
(816) 842-0496
www.corbinbronze.com

You can see Kansas City sculptor Tom Corbin's work at the Firefighter's Memorial Fountain at Penn Valley Park, the Kauffman Memorial Garden near the Plaza, and in galleries and designers' showrooms across the country. Or simply rent the movies *Ransom* and *A Perfect Murder,* where his stunning furniture and statuettes set the tone for the characters' privileged lifestyles.

Better yet, view the work in person at his showroom in the River Market area. Tom has sold more than $1 million worth of sculptures, furniture, and lighting, forever knocking him out of the starving-artist category. His trademark is slim, ethereal female figures that seem light enough to float despite their bronze heft. Prices range from $200 to more than $100,000 each.

The Kansas City Art Institute
Annual Ceramics Sale
4415 Warwick
(816) 474-5224, (800) 522-5224
www.kcai.edu

Discover emerging artists and incredible bargains during this student sale at one of the country's most respected art institutes. The event is always held a few weeks before the Christmas buying season, usually the first weekend in December. Doors open promptly at 10:00 a.m. on Saturday and noon on Sunday, but shoppers start showing up hours before to secure a place in line. Insider hot tip: Show up for the Friday-night preview to stake your claim. Once the doors open it's every art lover for himself or herself. During years when the snow is higher than a lined rubber boot, students bring out hot cider to keep things lively. Here's the drill to keep from being trampled by the crowds behind you: As soon as the doors open, grab one of the empty cardboard boxes off to the left and start moving around the stations. When you see something you like, grab it or it will be gone.

The proceeds help keep the artists in clay and supplies, so that's a good thing.

Rhett and Kelly Johnson
Dearborn, MO
(816) 450-3616
www.rhettjohnson.com
Rhett is a monumentally talented sculptor who works with such found objects as old cobalt-blue bottles, engine parts, and iron he shapes and leaves outside to rust. His garden art features graceful birds landing on arches and stakes. Kelly creates exquisite beaded art and witty painted papier-mâché masks, which she also sells at Missouri Bluffs, a women's clothing store in Weston, Missouri (see Day Trips and Weekend Getaways). Their studios in Dearborn, Missouri, just north of Kansas City, are open by appointment only and definitely worth the 35-mile trip.

River's Bend Gallery
201 Main Street
Parkville, MO
(816) 587-8070
www.riversbendgallery.com
This sunny shop on Parkville's quaint Main Street has a diverse grouping of art, including oils and pastels, photography, jewelry, and even whimsical martini glasses. The focus, however, is on art glass—gorgeous vases in a kaleidoscope of colors, iridescent jellyfish caught in elongated globes—that makes you wonder how the pieces ever could have been in a molten state.

Robyn Nichols, The Pearl Gallery
1818 McGee
(816) 474-1731
www.robynnichols.com
This raven-haired enchantress turns calla lilies, nasturtium blossoms, and gingko leaves into gleaming sterling silver jewelry so their delicate beauty lasts forever. Robyn's exquisite work is admired at high-end stores and

i When Barnett Helzberg brought the Hope diamond to town to promote his new store on the Country Club Plaza, security was tight as the public took turns viewing the priceless gem. But when it came time to transport the legendary rock to the store's Topeka location, Barnett simply dropped it in his coat pocket and drove away.

galleries around the country. And she always draws a crowd at the Plaza Art Fair each fall as people cluster around the booth to see her jewelry and elegant serving pieces: spoons shaped like seedpods, ladles like lily pads.

The artist also creates commissioned work for individuals and companies. Her work can be viewed at her gallery, The Pearl, which also exhibits other artists' three-dimensional work throughout the year. Call for specific dates and times. And if you live in or near Kansas City, get on Robyn's mailing list; her annual holiday parties are renowned.

FOOD AND GIFTS

Andre's Confiserie Suisse
5018 Main Street
(816) 561-3440

4929 West 119th Street
Overland Park, KS
(913) 498-3440
www.andreschocolates.com
When Master Confiseur Andre Bollier and his wife, Elsbeth, came here from Switzerland in 1955 to set up a candy shop, few residents had ever tasted premium chocolates; it would be decades before "Godiva" meant anything but a lady with a horse. So the Bolliers served lunches at their tearoom while they began educating the Midwest palate. We tell you about the lunch specials in Restaurants, but for now let's rhapsodize about the confections within the glass cases. Son Marcel and his wife, Connie, joined the company in 1974, and in 2001 their son René and his wife, Nancy, came on board.

All the chocolates, from truffles to cream- and caramel-filled assortments, are handmade and meltingly delicious. The shop's specialties are treats tied to the seasons, such as hand-painted, edible chocolate Easter eggs; Valentine hearts filled with truffles; and chocolate wine bottles packed with chocolate-covered almonds that are perfect for any celebration. Replace the Andre's label with your own and the glossy brown bottles make extraordinary wedding and anniversary gifts. Chocoholic Johnson Countians were thrilled when the Bollier family opened a second location, in Hawthorne Plaza.

The Better Cheddar
604 West 48th Street
(816) 561-8204

71st and Mission
Prairie Village, KS
(913) 362-7575
www.thebettercheddar.com
What sets a specialty gourmet shop apart from a grocery store are unique products and personal service. That's certainly the case at the Better Cheddar, where owner Ron Shalinsky and his gracious staff welcome you like family and encourage you to sample the wares. In fact there are so many chunks of cheeses, crackers with savory toppings, and decadent chocolate truffles to try, it's easy to have dinner while you shop.

Among the hundreds of gourmet selections are jars of the Better Cheddar's own proprietary brand; a dab of cranberry chutney on a gingersnap cracker is like getting a mouthful of Thanksgiving. There's food for thought as well: Hand-printed cards describe each cheese and offer suggestions for use. The Dutch aged cheddar with black pepper, you discover, is terrific with strawberries and makes a very grownup macaroni and cheese dish.

The Better Cheddar's Plaza store also sells a nice variety of wines (with a free tasting each Saturday from 2:00 to 4:00 p.m.), a perfect accompaniment to the gourmet picnic the staff can prepare with a little prior notice. And

their gift baskets are so legendary that regular customers order them delivered sight unseen.

Browne's Market
3300 Pennsylvania
(816) 561-0030
www.brownesmarket.com
When Ed and Mary Flavin opened this grocery store in 1887, it was to offer a taste of County Kerry to the thousands of Irish immigrants finding new homes here. The tradition continued when daughter Margaret married Jim Browne, and today the shelves are still stocked with treats from the homeland: sweets such as Hob Nobs and Cadbury Flakes, tweed caps, Aran knit sweaters, teas, and Claddagh windchimes. The deli case features bangers and mash, soda bread, and Irish stew. And everyone, no matter their heritage, enjoys the chocolate chip, chocolate oatmeal, and white chunk macadamia cookies. Show up on Cookie Tuesday and they're on sale. You might even see an impromptu Irish dance by the family's fifth generation. Browne's is the unofficial starting point for the city's huge St. Patrick's Day parade; the party starts as early as 7:00 a.m. with an authentic Irish breakfast.

Christopher Elbow Artisanal Chocolates
1819 McGee
(816) 842-1300
www.elbowchocolates.com
It's quickly become one of our favorite gifts for an open house or a birthday: a box of Christopher Elbow's chocolates. Each morsel is a work of art: glossy orbs that look like glass marbles, rainbow-colored pyramids, fat squares handpainted with swaths of color or dusted with cocoa. He infuses the truffles with unusual flavors such as Brazilian coffee, French lavender, Chinese five-spice, caramel banana, and delicate Earl Grey tea.

Christopher learned his trade as pastry chef for Shiraz and the American Restaurant before becoming a full-time chocolatier. His luscious creations are available in three sizes—two, four, or twenty-one melt-in-your-mouth wonders—each in an elegant, embossed white box tied with (what else?) a chocolate-brown bow. His gorgeous new digs in the Crossroads includes a "chocolate bar" where you can experience the world's most decadent hot chocolate.

Fervere Bread
1702 Summit
(816) 582-7323

Fred Spompinato makes breads with a tender texture and chewy crust that can be achieved only by hand kneading, lots of patience, and a special Old World oven. He named his tiny take-out bakery for the Latin word (pronounced *fur-VAIR-ay*) meaning passion. That may explain why Fred sold his first successful bread company years ago when it became more of a business and less of a craft.

Now he's up to his elbows in dough again and loving every sticky minute. Using organic flours and natural ingredients, he turns out dense, crusty loaves in six or so varieties, including an aromatic olive rosemary, a country French, and an oval wonder filled with walnuts, apples, and plump apricots. During winter his holiday gift to us is a cranberry pecan loaf enlivened with orange rind. No need to wrap it, Fred, we'll eat it here.

Fervere, which is in the bohemian neighborhood along with Blue Bird Bistro (see Restaurants) and a few artist studios, is open 11:00 a.m. to 7:00 p.m. Thursday through Saturday. There are always generous chunks of each bread, along with dishes of good olive oil for dunking, ready to sample before you buy.

Original Juan Specialty Foods Inc.
111 Southwest Boulevard
Kansas City, KS
(913) 432-5228, (800) 568-8468
www.originaljuan.com

Forget complaining about the heat and humidity of a summer day in Kansas—it's always hot at Original Juan's, where they cook up eighty-gallon vats of incendiary salsas and sauces, even fruit jellies, using chili peppers and little else. Even Wilber Scoville, the guy who devised the rating system for chilis, would whimper with one drop of Da' Bomb's The Final Answer. This deep-red sauce tops out at 1.5 million Sco-ville units and is available in a box that includes a lock and key. They're not kidding; you must be twenty-one or over to buy the stuff.

It's just one of about 150 products that are available through the company's Web site and catalog and at the retail counter on Southwest Boulevard. Not everything will cause your brow to sweat, though. They also carry Cheesecake in a Jar, a rich sauce to pour over ice cream or cake, and an award-winning artichoke and spinach cheese dip mix.

Planters Seed & Spice Company
513 Walnut
(816) 842-3651
www.plantersseed.com

At Planters the atmosphere is always festive, even without 35,000 people milling around the farmers' market down the street, as regulars show up for a monthly fix of coffee, bird seed, and half-ton bags of dog food. Not much has changed since it opened in 1924; the wooden floors may creak a little more now, but you can still get more than 200 varieties of herbs and spices in giant bins. The store also offers items such as chili seasoning and a wide variety of coffee beans. Along with a nice selection of loose teas in flavors such as mango, black currant, and vanilla, the store carries pretty teapots. The sales staff can help you create gifts using complementary items, such packets of chili seasoning and dried beans in a ceramic casserole dish or bags of flavored coffee beans and a grinder in a laminated box. A handy catalog provides additional inspiration.

A large portion of the store is devoted to gardening tools, flower bulbs, and decorative items, such as wind chimes.

The Roasterie
1204 West 27th Street
(816) 931-4000, (800) 376-0245
www.theroasterie.com

As a foreign exchange student in Costa Rica, Danny O'Neill fell in love with the rich, robust coffee served there. Fifteen years later his passion for the brew had him roasting beans in the basement of his Brookside home, and when he mastered the art of air roasting he knew he'd found his calling. He and buddy Norman Killman would roast in the basement, pack in the living room, and deliver the fragrant bags of beans to customers in Norm's '81 El Camino.

That was 1993. And although Norm swears he still has the car, he can certainly afford to drive something a little more exotic; the brand is sold in grocery stores and gourmet shops and served in Kansas City's top restaurants. In fact, several local chefs have commissioned their own special blends, so if you dig the java at the American Restaurant or the Classic Cup, you have Danny to thank. The company makes about forty blends and flavors in all, including a Kansas City Blend, a combination of Indonesian and Central and South American beans that's hearty yet smooth. But to be sleepless in Kansas City go for the Nitro Express, a darker roast with a pungent, smoky aroma and flavor. You can find the flavor-sealed bags at most area grocery stores. Tour the Roasterie's new facility Saturdays starting at 11:00 a.m. We bet there will be coffee.

Three Dog Bakery
612 West 48th Street
(816) 753-3647, (800) 4TREATS
www.threedog.com

Yes, we know the food here is for pooches, but it's so artfully done we couldn't resist. Besides, what better gift to take home to your best buddy than a Scotty Biscotti or Puppy Petit Four? Locals Dan Dye and Mark Beckloff started the company when they couldn't find healthy snacks for their three dogs, Dottie, Gracie, and Sarah Jean. Using dough made from whole wheat flour, unsweetened carob, and low-fat yogurt powder and a $2 bone-shaped cookie cutter, the duo concocted treats their girls loved.

Now Dan and Mark are rolling *in* dough.

Their products are available at Three Dog Bakery stores across the country (with one in Japan) and through selected Target stores. If you stop by the Plaza store you'll see several four-footed fans sampling the wares. You can also order through the dog-alog (a catalog simply wouldn't do) or the company's fun Web site.

HOME FURNISHINGS AND ACCESSORIES

Aesthetica
1801 Wyandotte
(816) 421-5455
www.aesthetica-kc.com

James Carver's creativity (he was a designer for Disney for years) is on parade in this shop filled with fascinating home decor, giftware, and gourmet food. The range of inventory may be wild—from precious gifts for baby to sophisticated martini glasses—but it's all so expertly selected and stylishly displayed, you'll want it all. Every purchase leaves the store with a gift bag and tissue, but pay a little extra and watch James do his magic. He'll create a gift package or clever container tied to a theme like a home spa or gourmet chocolates. In fact, James has an entire wall of his shop devoted to exquisite papers and ribbons, so the gift you take to a birthday bash might never get opened because it's just too pretty.

For personal gifts such as jewelry, handbags, and books, there's nothing like Aesthetica. And James even makes buying business gifts a breeze: Simply call him with a price range and he'll e-mail photos of options along with ideas for wrapping. Choose one and he'll do the rest, including shipping to the lucky recipient.

Black Bamboo
1815 Wyandotte
(816) 283-3000
www.black-bamboo.com

As an interior designer for an international architectural firm, Tim Butt envisioned beautiful and functional spaces for clients. Through his business travels, he was drawn to the simple, elegant lines of Asian and modern furnishings, so when he opened his new shop he filled it with a mix of each. He personally selected pieces from Burma, China, Thailand, Bali, Vietnam, and elsewhere.

In his handsome space, which formerly housed a vintage Corvette restoration shop, Tim gives each piece of furniture its due with room to breathe and great lighting. The inventory includes an ever-changing collection of antiques, such as a lovely blue-painted secretary from the mid-1800s, and sterling-and-jade jewelry and artwork.

The look of the place says expensive, but you might call it Asian minor: Prices range from $3.50 for a silk-screened greeting card that could easily be framed to a large cabinet handcrafted of Asian Yuma for around $3,000. In between is a wonderful array of sofas, chairs, side tables, and accessories—all reflecting Tim's keen sense of style. Lucky you; he also provides interior-design services.

Nell Hill's
501 Commercial
Atchison, KS
(913) 367-1086
www.nellhills.com

In the birthplace of Amelia Earhart, merchandise is flying out of the home furnishings store that's become one of the hottest retailers in the nation. Or perhaps the draft is *incoming* as vans and busloads of buyers from Omaha and Des Moines storm the place several times a year. During the holidays, when the store is aglitter with $300,000 worth of Christmas decorations, there's often a line snaking around the corner.

You might think, *What's the big deal?* at first sight of Mary Carol Garrity's modest two-story building on the corner, but, oh, what wonders await inside. Room after room is filled with European antiques next to all-American red-plaid sofas mingled with Indonesian tables topped with baskets, vases, and dishware. Everything is so artfully arranged you'll want to say, "I'll take the whole room, please."

No problem; delivery is free. But the affable Ms. G would rather help you develop your own look, a service she does every day for customers who bring in photos of rooms and a plaintive "Help me, please."

Personal service and inventory aside, some people come to Nell Hill's just for the price tags. The petite owner is a powerhouse when it comes to negotiating discounts, often importing tons of goods to get the best deals. She confides that she buys her wicker from the same village in the Philippines as Ralph Lauren but pays Pier 1 prices. Gifts such as silverplate bowls, sets of crisp white linen cocktail napkins, and wire baskets are so well priced it pays to just grab several and figure out who will get them later.

For more treasures, walk just a few paces to *the* G. Diebolt's (608 Commercial, 913-367-2395; www.gdiebolts.com), which features fanciful bedding, oodles of candles, mirrors, cashmere throws, and inspiration to create your own luxurious sanctuary, or her new antiques emporium, Garrity's, at 121 North Fifth Street (913-367-1523). Be sure to pick up a copy of Mary Carol Garrity's decorating books *Nell Hill's Style at Home* and *Nell Hill's Christmas at Home*. And watch for her new store to open in Briarcliff Village, closer to home.

Portfolio Kitchen & Home
8027 State Line Road
(816) 363-5300
www.portfolio-home.com

You won't leave this stunning showroom with a shopping bag, but you might come away with an entire new kitchen, bath, or dressing room worthy of any diva. Since opening a few years ago, owner Geri Higgins has become the go-to girl for Kansas City's most persnickety gourmets and style mavens. The showroom displays five complete kitchen environments, including a Zenlike haven, a loft-ready contemporary concept, and an Old World classic style. Though you might be tempted to simply point and say, "I'll take that one," you'll want to have the on-staff designers create your own dream kitchen. Geri takes full advantage

Here's one more reason to shop on the Country Club Plaza during your stay here: The parking is plentiful and free. Covered lots and on-street parking spaces are easy to find throughout the 4-block district.

of the showroom's refrigerators and multiple burners to turn Portfolio into party central several times a month when she hosts a fundraiser or other fabulous event. This is one A-list you'll want to join.

Pryde's Old Westport
115 Westport Road
(816) 531-5588
www.prydesoldwestport.com

It's a three-decade Kansas City tradition: When a young woman gets engaged, she heads to Pryde's to register *before* picking out her dress. Owner Louise Meyers has helped newlyweds, as well as college-bound seniors, singles, and empty nesters, outfit kitchens for more than twenty years. She's the pretty blonde in a dark green Pryde's apron greeting customers by name, making sure displays look inviting, and offering coffee to visitors. Say yes: Pryde's signature blend is so terrific you'll want to buy a pound or two to take home.

Or you might try using a trail of coffee beans to help you find your way back to the front door. The array of cutlery, cookware, dinnerware, linens, and serving pieces is so staggering you can get lost within the multi-floored, many-roomed space. Turn a corner and there's a wall of kitchen utensils you didn't know existed, barbecue tools of every design, candles, glassware, and more. Pryde's has a splendid collection of dinnerware to set an elegant or casual table, including England's finest stoneware, Portmeirion, and Emile Henry from France. But one of the store's best commodities is advice. Louise and her staff are more than happy to help you choose the proper tool for the task, demonstrate a pasta machine, or put together a gift basket for a bridal shower. Gift-wrapping is always free, and Pryde's can ship anywhere.

Retro Inferno
1500 Grand Boulevard
(816) 842-4004
www.retroinferno.com

Truth be told, collectors and interior designers on both coasts are more familiar with Rod Parks's collection of mid-twentieth-century furniture than many Kansas Citians are. With wall-to-wall primo modern designs in his groovy location, it's a sure thing you'll find the Herman Miller, Knoll, Dunbar, McCob, Russell Wright, or Heywood Wakefield piece you seek. Don't recognize the names? It doesn't matter; you'll identify the clean lines from any stylish Katharine Hepburn movie you've ever seen. These tables, credenzas, low-slung sofas, and stylish bars are shown next to white chairs sculpted like an open palm, boomerang-shaped cocktail tables, and Sputnik light fixtures from the fifties: just the stuff you could kick yourself for passing up at garage sales years ago. Or selling at your own!

Retro Inferno also sells accessories such as vintage cocktail shakers, Murano glassware, pink ice crushers, and even some vintage cocktail dresses that may have spent the evening at the Inferno Lounge, the disco that gave the shop its name. The nightclub is long gone, but the neon light lives on in Rod's front window. And you might even leave with a pocketful of cash; he buys quality vintage furniture and accessories, so that Electrolux gathering dust in the closet could pay for your trip. Here's an Insiders' tip: Park in back rather than the street; You may avoid a parking ticket. Hours are 11:00 a.m. to 6:00 p.m. Monday through Saturday.

JEWELRY

Helzberg Diamonds
Various locations at shopping malls and the Country Club Plaza
www.helzberg.com

From one tiny storefront in Kansas City, Kansas, this enterprise has become the personal jeweler to customers at more than seventy-five stores across the country. Morris Helzberg ℹ️ Some of the city's best gift shops are found in art museums. The Nelson-Atkins Museum of Art and the Kemper Museum of Contemporary Art both feature shops that offer books, posters, note cards, wearable art (such as jewelry and painted silk scarves), and handcrafted pieces such as vases and teapots.

began the dream in 1915, but it was his son, Barnett, then Barnett Jr., who grew it into one of the most successful retailers in the country. These marketing geniuses added an element of fun to the sometimes all-too-serious task of buying jewelry. In the 1930s the company offered free "aeroplane" rides with the purchase of a $49 Benrus Pilot watch, and to launch the new Country Club Plaza store Barnett Jr. brought in the Hope diamond, which the public could view for free if they made a contribution to the United Way.

This benevolent tradition continues today: Although retired from the gem business, Barnett Jr. and Shirley Helzberg are two of the most generous Kansas City citizens of all time. But it was their engagement in 1967 that sparked one of the store's most successful promotions, the "I Am Loved" pin. Barnett originally thought of the idea as a pre-engagement stall tactic. Since then the red-and-white pins have been used in schools to teach children self-esteem, sent to American troops in Vietnam, translated into eight languages, and featured in the "Charlie Brown" comic strip. To date the store has handed out more than thirty-five million of the red-and-white tokens of love.

Mazzarese Jewelry
4850 West 135th Street
Leawood, Kansas
(913) 491-4111
www.mazzarese.com

Like those of so many of Kansas City's finest jewelry stores, Mazzarese's traditions have been passed down through the generations. The youngest members are Tony and Tosca's son and daughter, Mark and Veronica, who have kept the family legacy of quality and brought in exciting new lines and ideas. With a gorgeous new store the company has even more room to show off its diamond creations from cherished lines as well as exclusive designs. Mazzarese is also known for its masterful array of timepieces, from diamond-encrusted look-at-me styles to classic tank watches. Along with stunning diamond and gemstone pieces, the store carries top-name sterling jewelry from John Hardy and a stellar collection of gifts for men.

Swirk Jewelry
310 West 47th Street
(816) 753-1949, (800) MR SWIRK
www.swirkjewelry.com

Seems like 1910 was a good year to open a jewelry store in the Midwest. Swirk's has built a loyal following buoyed by personal service, a small but lovely selection of diamond and gemstone jewelry, many estate pieces, and the fix-anything skill of its repair team. Here's where Kansas City brings its tired timepieces and broken bracelets. Visit the small shop above Buca di Beppo restaurant on the Country Club Plaza. You'll get a handshake whether you buy something or not, most likely from somebody named Swirk.

Tiffany & Co.
310 Nichols Road
(816) 531-7676
www.tiffanys.com

Our entire city opened a pale blue box tied with white ribbon when Tiffany came back to the Country Club Plaza a few glorious years ago. Since then we've been thrilled by the diamonds, been enchanted by the colored stones set in fantastical designs, and hoped our guests would bring us a hostess gift in that famous pastel package. And around here, anyone having a baby must get a sterling Tiffany rattle.

All the classics are to be found in this glittering store: engagement rings from demure to eye-popping, stunning pearl creations, and the finest tableware items and timepieces.

Heirlooms all. Manager Melinda Petet is famous for hosting the poshest parties here, usually for one of the many local charities. As guests of all ages sip champagne, they admire each other's bold Peretti cuff or Picasso drop— just two of the exclusive designer lines carried here—proving once again that although the Tiffany name has been around since 1837, the styles are endlessly fresh. And in case you're wondering, never fear; come in wearing jeans or furs. You'll always get friendly, courteous service.

Tivol
220 Nichols Road
(816) 531-5800

4721 West 119th Street
Overland Park, KS
(913) 345-0200

4131 North Mulberry Drive
(816) 891-2600
www.tivol.com

In 1910 when jeweler Charles Tivol opened a store in downtown Kansas City his ledger registered $105,000 the first year. Today the store often does that in one sale. It's come a long way from $95 diamond rings, but it's never wavered from a commitment to customer service. It doesn't hurt that Charles's son, Harold, has a knack for marketing; in fact the seventysomething still shows up in the company's clever ads.

The store moved to its current location on the Country Club Plaza in 1951, where it remains the area's crown jewel with breathtaking window displays and even more stunning creations inside. Top designer names are represented here, and in Kansas City the only proper engagement ring comes in a Tivol's black-and-gold box.

Harold swore he'd never move from the Plaza, and he hasn't, but when daughter Cathy accepted the reins she opened a second location in Hawthorne Plaza to cater to their customers out south. But don't let the luxurious surroundings keep you from entering. The friendly salespeople are happy to let

you try on a dozen diamond line bracelets, whether your wrist is clad in denim or mink. The latest in the Tivol string of pearls is the Briarcliff Village location, serving clients up north.

SHOPPING DISTRICTS

Brookside
Surrounding 63rd Street and Brookside Boulevard
(816) 523-5553
www.brooksidekc.com

This beloved Main Street-ish string of stores has retained its charm while continuing to grow thanks to the vibrant neighborhood surrounding it. More than seventy locally owned businesses are here, many for decades, from the ethnic treasures at World's Window to a fantasy world for little girls and their mommies at Lauren Alexandra (www.kcbebe.com), where a pink tutu has your name on it. Need clean undies? That's just one of the unique fragrances you'll find at 5B&Co. Candles.

Your little wizard will go ga-ga over Brookside Toy & Science, and Brookside Barkery & Bath will keep Fido in fine form. STUFF is a crazy quilt of marvelous gifts, decor, and art from over sixty local and national artists. Fine art is available at Leopold Gallery, and artful food can be had at Joe D's cafe, Avenues Bistro, or the wildly popular, quintessential sports bar called the Brooksider Bar & Grill. And the entire town cheered when our longtime treasure, the Dime Store, reopened, squeaky wooden floors and all. The new owners retained most of the favorite items, such as classic toys, art supplies, and household goods, but added such new goodies as an impressive display of paper goods.

Crestwood
55th Street between Brookside Boulevard and Oak Street
One of the city's first suburban shopping districts, Crestwood is in an area marked by its lovely homes and gardens. Naturally the block is filled with some of Kansas City's most

stylish shops, including MLB Designs (5504 Oak, 816-531-3133), a lavish collection of gifts, home decor and tabletop items, and jewelry; the Pear Tree, filled with must-have treasures for home and garden; and George Turbovich Designs (816-523-3974), an endlessly fascinating grouping of leather goods, accessories, and antiques hand-selected by its renowned interior-designer owner. Plan to spend a day as you peruse each antiques shop and boutique. To tide you over, there are cafes, including Aixois, where you can relax over lunch or dinner or take a cup of coffee to that comfy chair you spied at Bloomsday Books.

Crossroads Arts District
(1-mile-wide area between Downtown Kansas City and Crown Center)
www.kccrossroads.org
Every big city has one—a neighborhood where unique boutiques, antiques stores, showrooms, art galleries, and restaurants have popped up to become the trendiest place in town to shop. In Kansas City that destination is the Crossroads Arts District.

Part of its charm is that the studios and storefronts have emerged out of brick warehouses, abandoned office buildings, and lofts, many still sporting handsome concrete moldings and wooden beams. This is shopping the way it used to be, where the person behind the counter is the owner, friends gather over wine in the evening, and there's not a Starbucks in sight.

When a handful of the art gallery owners banded together to stay open late on Friday, First Friday was born. In past years it's become Kansas City's official street party, with crowds walking to the sixty or so galleries and artist studios, catching trolleys to visit ones that are a bit farther away, and shopping in stores that aren't in the typical shopping mall. Restaurants offer anything from a quick bowl of spicy noodles to a white-tablecloth, four-course meal.

And where art starts, lofts are sure to follow. The Crossroads and surrounding areas are the hottest addresses for loft-living, with new spaces being converted every month.

We've profiled several shops such as Aesthetica, Black Bamboo, Retro Inferno, and Webster House Antiques within this chapter; art venues such as Blue Gallery; and restaurants including Shiraz and Michael Smith.

Other must-see stops include High Cotton Home Furnishings (118 Southwest Boulevard, 816-471-3561) and Hudson Home, a showroom filled with fabulous modern furniture and lighting (1619 Walnut, 816-421-3649). You'll find information about and links to dozens more on the Web site, which includes a map. Or pick up a brochure when visiting any location within the neighborhood. The general boundaries are Truman Road to the north, Interstate 35 to the west, the KC Terminal railroad tracks to the south, and Troost Avenue to the east. Nearby hotels include the Westin and Hyatt at Crown Center and the Phillips House (see separate listings in Accommodations).

The Legends at Village West
1843 Village West Parkway
(At the intersection of Interstates 70 and 435)
(913) 788-3700
www.legendsshopping.com
Call it the shopping mecca a racetrack built. When the Kansas Speedway turned this vast acreage in Kansas City, Kansas, into the hottest thing going, shops soon followed. Cabela's appeals to every sports enthusiast, and you can decorate your entire home in the overwhelming inventory at Nebraska Furniture Mart. The Legends is the nifty open-air shopping and entertainment district to complete the mix with more than eighty tenants, including the city's first Adidas store and Cavender's western wear. The kid magnet, 20,000-square-foot T-Rex Cafe also has landed here first before it becomes a national phenom.

All in all, the Legends is a destination with 1.1 million square feet of retail space plus a luxury movie theater with a VIP section, Pin-Up Bowl (where you can pick up a spare along with a cocktail!). You'll find more than a hundred shops to keep you busy, including several exciting factory outlets from exciting fashion brands Ann Taylor, Banana Republic, Gap, and Brooks Brothers. Take a walking tour to learn more about famous Kansans who have been immortalized in bronze sculptures and medallions throughout the beautifully landscaped area. Makes you kind of proud to be from the Sunflower State. Fountains provide mesmerizing displays throughout the day (the same design team created the fountain at the Bellagio Hotel in Las Vegas).

Hungry for more? That's a good thing, because you have your choice of over thirty restaurants at the Legends, including Cheeseburger in Paradise, Yard House, where the burgers are hot and the beer is icy cold, Outback Steakhouse, and Kansas City's own Jazz—A Louisiana Kitchen. The Legends also hosts, well, legendary live music events including free summer concerts and family entertainment around the holidays. You can stay and play longer; simply book a room at the Great Wolf Lodge or, for a little romance, Chateau Avalon. Learn more about these in Accommodations.

Prairie Village Shops
71st and Mission Road
(913) 652-3306
www.prairievillageshops.com
Oh, to live in a cute ranch house in Prairie Village where you can walk to everything your heart desires. In this open air collection of shops, services, and boutiques you'll find one-of-a-kind treasures such as Curious Sofa, a gift and home decor emporium as clever as its name. Mady & Me is where the cutest kids in town shop, and Natural Wear appeals to women of style with classic to bohemian clothing. Stop by the Better Cheddar to taste your way through an incredible selection of imported and domestic gourmet goods and then choose a table at Cafe Provence, tout de suite.

Zona Rosa
Interstate 29 and Barry Road
(816) 587-8180
www.zonarosa.com

This exciting mixed-use district in the booming area north of the river hearkens back to the time of town squares where neighbors would gather to catch up with their weeks or listen to the local band. That's the theme behind this collection of more than eighty unique shops, including national chains and a few local boutiques, along with restaurants and services galore. It's all set in a pretty mix of architectural styles with plenty of green spaces, wide sidewalks, old-fashioned phone booths, and fountains (kids are welcome to splash around), encouraging you to park your car and actually stroll as you shop for the latest fashion at Ann Taylor or outfit your entire home at Ethan Allen.

Of course there's an ice cream parlor or two, and you can chill out with a martini at the Majestic Cafe, which is set between an upscale movie theater and a comedy club (see Nightlife for the laugh track). Enjoy a dinner and a movie there, or settle into a booth at any of the other restaurant choices including such local favorites as the Hereford House or Tomfooleries. Add in live music concerts in the summer, an Easter parade in spring, and enough holiday festivities to cheer up Scrooge and we know what you're thinking: Man, I could live here! Lucky you; you can. Zona truly is an urban center, complete with lofts above storefronts and restaurants. The open and bright floor plans appeal to young singles as well as empty nesters. Choose your new address on the Web site and we'll catch you at the Improv, right down in front.

SOUVENIRS AND GIFTS

The Best of Kansas City
314 Ward Parkway (Country Club Plaza)
Crown Center Shops
(816) 842-0200, (800) 366-8780
www.thebestofkc.com
One taste of our food and you'll want to take it all back with you. Now you can, with a gift basket from the Best of Kansas City. For years they've been putting together big, gorgeous gift baskets bursting with hometown products

like Laura Little's Fudge, Andre's Chocolates, Strawberry Hill nut loaves, Fritz's smoked meats, Hereford House Steak Sauce, and Wolferman's muffins. Nonfood items include CDs and books from local talent, coffee mugs, and caps. The two locations offer about twenty-five packages from sweet to savory.

Kansas Sampler
9548 Antioch Road
Overland Park, KS
(913) 383-2920

4849 West 117th Street
Town Center Plaza
(913) 491-3004

6858 Johnson Drive
(913) 432-3355
www.kansassampler.com
When you realize, Dorothy, that you're not in Kansas anymore, you'll wish you had some fun souvenir to remember your trip. Here's just the place to find it. Peg and Tim Liebert have put together a wonderful collection of Sunflower State–themed goodies such as T-shirts, sampler boxes filled with locally made gourmet food and goodies, books about the region, CDs from local artists, and Kansas magnets to add to your refrigerator collection. A favorite is the Pet Tornado and delicious sunflower-seed cookies.

ATTRACTIONS

Looking for a fabulous family vacation? Romantic weekend for two? A new place to call home? Congratulations! You've come to the right place. With so much to see and do, Kansas City is the perfect choice no matter how you define fun.

In fact, here's where our unique mix of citified culture (la-de-da) and Wild West rowdiness (yee-haw!) really pays off. You can spend your day contemplating a Rembrandt or attending a rodeo and then dine by candlelight or campfire . . . all within our city's boundaries.

History buffs will be taken aback; although another city is rightly called the gateway to the West, we were the *gate* that outfitted more than half a million travelers on the Oregon, California, and Santa Fe Trails during the mid-1800s. You can relive their stories at dozens of museums, historic sites, and restored antebellum homes. And if your taste runs to more modern architecture, things are looking up . . . way up. Our downtown skyline has nearly sixty art deco buildings from the 1920s and 1930s.

Naturally in this chapter you'll also see attractions that have wowed tourists for decades, such as our renowned Nelson-Atkins Museum of Art and the 14-block shopping mecca known as the Country Club Plaza. But for those frequent KC visitors who are thinking, *been there, done that,* get ready for a few surprises. A citywide cultural renaissance is taking place just in time for your visit. We're busy updating and renovating some of our most treasured landmarks and historical districts while adding new destinations on both sides of the state line. That means there's bound to be a snappy little bonus for the art lover, sporting nut, and shopaholic in your entourage. We're proud to show it all to you.

The attractions are grouped by category and listed alphabetically. Because hours frequently change, it's best to call for updated information. All attractions listed are in Kansas City, Missouri, unless otherwise noted.

You may wish to start at the Observation Points where you can see our city from on high.

ART MUSEUMS

Kemper Museum of Contemporary Art
4420 Warwick Boulevard
(816) 753-5784
www.kemperart.org

When locals describe Kansas City's *other* art museum, they simply say, "It's the one with the spider." This one could be the model for a sci-fi thriller. The sculpture by Louise Bourgeois weighs 1,600 pounds and is roughly the size of a New York apartment. A much smaller crawler can be seen on the building's exterior wall.

Opened in 1994, the museum is a gift from R. Crosby Kemper, recently retired as head of UMB Financial Corporation. At its core is the stunning collection of Kemper and his wife, Bebe, that includes works by Jasper Johns, David Hockney, Robert Motherwell, Georgia O'Keeffe, Willem de Kooning, and Frank Stella. A Dale Chihuly blown-glass chandelier is one of the most stunning displays.

If Wayne Thiebaud's *Cakes and Pies* painting makes you hungry, you'll find relief in Cafe Sebastienne. Consider this delightful restaurant part of the art tour because the walls are filled floor to ceiling with 110 canvases by Frederick James Brown. The works, commissioned by the Kempers, tell "The History of Art," and it's fun to pick out references to masters such as Picasso, Matisse, and Van Gogh. If you're stumped about a particular piece, the cafe has a printed guide.

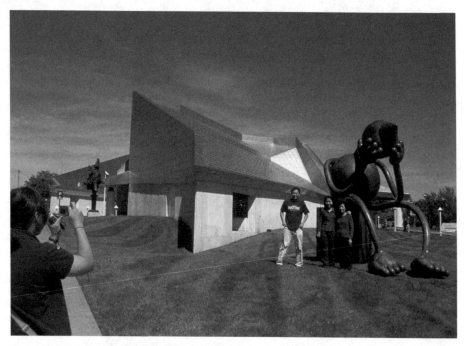

Crying Giant statue at the Kemper Museum. CVB OF GREATER KANSAS CITY

Along with permanent displays, the museum hosts exhibits throughout the year, usually by cutting-edge artists. Want one more reason to thank the Kempers? Admission is free. The museum is open every day except Monday, and the cafe serves lunch Tuesday through Saturday, Sunday brunch, and dinner Friday and Saturday. When you visit, take time to walk around the grounds of the Kansas City Art Institute next door; several of the students' sculptures are good enough to be in the museum.

Nelson-Atkins Museum of Art
See Close-up on page 154.

Nerman Museum of Contemporary Art
Johnson County Community College
12345 College Boulevard
Overland Park, KS
(913) 469-8500
http://gallery.jccc.net

Kansas City's stunning new contemporary art museum, designed by a world-class architect. We must be talking about the Bloch Building at the Nelson-Atkins Museum of Art, right? No, this praise is reserved for the new $15 million gallery at Johnson County Community College in Overland Park. Imagine the silence on the end of the line when museum director Bruce Hartman called big-time art dealers in New York to schedule a buying trip. Now imagine their surprise when they see the art displayed in this glorious new space designed by architect Kyu Sung Woo. It has placed Kansas firmly on the international art scene.

Named for local philanthropists (and revered collectors of postwar art) Jerry and Margaret Nerman and their son Lewis, the 38,000-square-foot space is the largest contemporary art museum in the four-state region and the only contemporary art museum in Kansas. Way to go, Nermans! You tell 'em, Kansas!

The Nelson-Atkins Museum of Art and Bloch Building Expansion

At the heart of Kansas City's vibrant art scene is the Nelson-Atkins Museum of Art, ranked among the top fifteen art museums in the United States. The city owes this Beaux Arts treasure to two primary people: the larger-than-life founder of the *Kansas City Star*, William Rockhill Nelson (see his profile on page 292–93), and a reclusive schoolteacher, Mary Atkins, who married late but well. Nelson bequeathed $11 million to the city for art acquisitions, and his daughter and son-in-law donated the family's twenty-acre estate, Oak Hall, for the site. At Mary's death, her late husband's estate was worth $1 million, enough to help fund the $3 million museum, completed in 1933. An imposing rectangle six stories high and larger than a city block, its classic design boasts thirty-two gigantic columns on both sides. Set far back on its sweeping, terraced lawn, it gives an air of a royal palace.

From literally nothing—not one single piece of art to its name—the Nelson has amassed nearly 35,000 pieces in its collection, from precious ceramic objects found in ancient Chinese tombs to an exceptionally beautiful Pawnee headdress dating to 1840. The Claude Monet *Boulevard des Capucines* is enchanting, while *Persephone* by local artist Thomas Hart Benton isn't nearly as shocking as when first, um, revealed.

But perhaps the most exciting acquisition isn't something that can hang on a wall—it literally *is* a wall, or actually several of them. The Bloch Building, which opened in June 2007, was deemed "the most anticipated building of 2007" by *Time Magazine*. This is, according to the *New Yorker*, not just architect Steven Holl's "finest building so far but also one of the best museums of the last generation."

Just don't be alarmed when you first spy this series of five irregularly shaped structures rising out from the east lawn. The size is deceiving; picture a sixty-seven-story skyscraper resting on its side partially submerged in the earth. The architect calls them lenses, and they are indeed constructed of milky glass. By day they look somehow unfinished, but at night they dazzle with a pale-blue glow. But it's what inside that counts: In contrast to the Nelson's ornate marble-lined vestibule (Holl himself calls the collaboration "the stone and the feather"), the three-story atrium is irregular in shape and crisscrossed with balconies and ramps. The interior walls beg to be touched—luminous polished white plaster and sections of the glass walls lead you through narrow corridors to the galleries belowground. The man *Time Magazine* named "America's best architect" has turned the space's ethereal light and shadow into its own art form.

The Bloch Building was made possible primarily by the co-founder of H&R Block, Henry Bloch, and his wife, Marion. The new building expanded the museum by 71 percent to some 400,000 square feet, providing space for the immense contemporary and African collections and the celebrated Hallmark Photographic Gallery. The latter is a gift from the Hall family—a truly remarkable collection of more than 6,500 works by 600 artists. One of its most haunting, and famous, photographs is Dorothea Lange's "Migrant

Mother, Nipomo, California." The galleries include canvases by Willem de Kooning, Jackson Pollock, and Franz Kline. And we've fooled plenty of new visitors by pointing them to Duane Hanson's lifelike *Museum Guard*, and saying, "Go ask that guard where the bathroom is." It will only work once.

With the expansion comes breathing room for the Nelson's massive collections of European, Asian, and American Indian art, much of which has never been seen for lack of space. In addition, there's a more thoughtful approach to the displays; decorative arts, paintings, and sculpture from similar periods are grouped together to provide a fascinating look at life during that time. Highlights include rooms decorated with European and American furniture and art from 1200 to 1960, including furniture by Frank Lloyd Wright, Gustav Stickley, and Ludwig Mies van der Rohe. Educational areas have also been expanded, including

The exquisite Temple Room within the Nelson-Atkins Museum of Art is part of a world-class collection. RICK McKIBBEN

the Ford Learning Center. The innovative programs available in this center are open to both children and adults. Classes are listed on the Web site, but please heed the fact that programs sell out quickly. Another tip is that members of the Nelson Friends of Art receive significant discounts for classes, along with other valuable privileges. Check membership levels, for as little as $50 a year, on the Web site.

Seven large sculptures by Isamu Noguchi sit in a contemplative space that serves as a visual bridge to the sculpture garden outside. Once again, the pieces are gifts from the Hall Family Foundation.

The Kansas City Sculpture Garden is delightful any time of day or night. This twenty-two-acre urban oasis is dotted with thirty stellar pieces of art by such masters as Renoir, Alexander Calder, and the Oldenburg–van Bruggen whimsical and often-photographed 18-foot-tall *Shuttlecocks*, from the Sosland family, which turn the green space into a giant's badminton court. And if you find your jaw dropping as you count the number of large Henry Moore pieces, yes, you're quite right: We have thirteen of these masterpieces. Once again, a tip of the hat to the generosity of the Hall family. Audio guides are available at the information desk. As you stroll the 0.7 miles, take care to notice that much of the time you're literally walking over the Bloch Building.

continued

Close-up

The acclaimed expansion has firmly put the Nelson-Atkins Museum of Art into the realm of art destinations. To fully appreciate the visit, you'll need at least two days, comfortable shoes, and help from the information desk. And if you're visiting with little art lovers, a "Discover" floor plan may be just as important as the "don't touch anything" talk you had in the car. Youngsters usually make a beeline for the *Armor for Man and Horse* from 1565, located in the original building's European gallery. Think you're carrying around a little extra weight? This poor chap's metal garb tops out at sixty pounds.

Never fear, a light meal is available at what *Travel Holiday* magazine called "the prettiest cafe in the Midwest," the open-air Rozzelle Court restaurant, with stone columns, massive trees, and a cascading fountain. The cafeteria-style line might pull you back from your mental vacation, but the menu of artistically arranged salads, delicious soups, and desserts won't disappoint. Rozzelle is open for lunch Tuesday through Sunday, 11:00 a.m. to 3:00 p.m. and dinner from 5:00 to 8:00 p.m. Thursday through Saturday. The new Museum Cafe in the Bloch Building tempts visitors with savory bites and wonderful desserts during the day on Tuesday, Wednesday, and Thursday and stays open until 9:30 p.m. Thursday through Saturday. Seasonal terrace seating looks onto the museum's spectacular new entry plaza with Walter De Maria's *One Sun / 34 Moons* as its centerpiece. This sculpture is situated over the parking garage—surely the most beautiful place for cars in the country—where it casts a heavenly glow. The watery view will cost you; parking is $5, but free for members.

Admission to the museum, however, is free. It's located at 4525 Oak Street, just a few blocks from the Country Club Plaza and within walking distance of several hotels, including the InterContinental, the Raphael, and the Southmoreland Inn (see the Web site for a handy list on the "Welcome" page). Hours are 10:00 a.m. to 5:00 p.m. Tuesday, Wednesday, and Sunday, and 10:00 a.m. to 9:00 p.m. Thursday through Saturday. The Bloch Building takes on its opalescent glow thirty minutes before dusk every night, then wink off at midnight Sunday through Thursday and at 2 a.m. Friday and Saturday. To plan your visit, check out www.nelson-atkins.org or call (816) 561-4000.

The spare, minimalist structure, composed of two glass and pale limestone boxes that jut out of the college's austere brick facade, is the architect's latest masterpiece. Kyu Sung Woo is also known for the Olympic Village in Seoul and the Arts of Korea Gallery at the Metropolitan Museum of Art. The cantilevered, 18,000-square-foot gallery block, set in a wedge-shaped lawn and sculpture court, is definitely a focal point of the busy intersection of College Boulevard and Quivira Road.

Bruce, known for his keen eye for art and his gregarious nature, asked for a signature building, but fundamentally a beautiful gallery space. It is that, indeed, with a 90-foot glass wall, skylights, and clerestory windows that fill the interior with light and connect with nature. Actually, JCCC has been famous for its outdoor Oppenheimer Sculpture Garden for years, gifts of Tony and Marti Oppenheimer that include the striking 6-foot *Walking Man (on the Edge)* by Jonathan Borofsky. The couple donated to the new museum's acquisitions as well.

The building's interior is a planned process of continual discoveries where elements are gradually revealed—giving visitors a sense of surprise at every turn. But it's the art that will have you swooning. Within the 4,000 square feet of permanent collection space you'll find the works of twenty-one big names, including Frank Stella, Leon Golub, Uta Barth, Brian Finke, Amy Sillman, and Aaron Young, as well as artists with Kansas City connections— James Brinsfield, Warren Rosser, and Eric Sall. Highlights are Kehinde Wiley's *Alexander the Great, Variation,* an immense painting of an African-American man, and Do-Ho Suh's *Some/One,* a shimmering, almost fluid suit of armor constructed of thousands of dog tags. Much of the work has been acquired in the past five years in anticipation of the new museum. There is also a changing art gallery, the Oppenheimer New Media Gallery, education and community spaces, and Cafe Tempo, which seats around one hundred.

The new museum joins the already remarkable collection of 400 sculptures and other artworks that have been displayed throughout the campus buildings and grounds for years. Where else but here can a student say, "I'll meet you in front of the Louise Bourgeois." It's art at its best— accessible to everyone.

CASINOS

In Kansas City you'll have a chance to go rollin' on the river. Sort of. Our riverboat casinos are, shall we say, permanently docked. But that doesn't mean you won't have a boatload of a good time as long as you're twenty-one or older. And here's an easy way to cruise over to the boats: Catch a ride on the Casino Cruiser, the No. 173 Metro Bus, which makes the loop from Crown Center and downtown hotels to the casinos. For information call the Metro at (816) 221-0660, jump on board www.kcata.org, or ask your hotel's front desk for more information.

Ameristar Casino Hotel
3200 Ameristar Drive
(816) 414-7000, (800) 499-4961
www.ameristarcasinos.com
You'll find two casinos for the price of one here, with more than 3,200 slot and video poker machines (the most in the city) plus more than 140 table games, including craps, roulette, and mini-baccarat. In fact, Ameristar boasts the largest poker room in the Midwest. Go fish.

This pleasure palace also holds the cards to lots of other entertainment. The Star Pavilion hosts top comedians, headline entertainers, and live professional boxing, and Depot #9 offers live music. You'll also find an eighteen-screen movie theater, an authentic Bavarian brewpub, an international buffet, a fine Italian restaurant, and nine cafes serving everything from Arthur Bryant's famous barbecue to fried rattlesnake to custom-made ice-cream cones. There's also an attached 184–guest room luxury hotel.

Argosy Casino
777 Argosy Drive
Riverside, MO
(816) 746-3100, (800) 900-3423
www.argosycasinos.com
Casino decor can range from over-the-top to elegant, and Argosy is definitely the latter. A

gorgeous new hotel pampers guests in 250 rooms, 8 exquisite suites, and a full-service day spa. The public areas and restaurants follow a romantic theme with midnight-blue skies and twinkling stars. It's particularly appealing in Journey Wood Fired Steaks, where chefs grill steaks to perfection over mesquite—a nice dining choice even if you don't plan to play. At Crazy Olives, order your favorite martinis, appetizers, and sandwiches to go with a side: live entertainment. Terrace Buffet's cozy environment will tempt you with breakfast, lunch, and dinner selections seven days a week.

For real action go from the dining table to a gaming table. There are forty-two in all, plus what *Casino Player* magazine calls "Missouri's loosest slots." You can try your luck at 1,800 of them for a nickel to $10 a pull. The Casino Stage Bar is where to find live entertainment Thursday through Saturday.

Harrah's North Kansas City
Casino & Hotel
One Riverboat Drive, North Kansas City
(816) 472-7777, (800) HARRAHS
www.harrahs.com

Harrah's offers the whole package: an exciting casino, a luxury hotel, five restaurants, and exciting live music in the rockin' VooDoo Lounge. You may never want to leave, especially when you see the gorgeous two-story casino. Take your winnings, or at least your hunger, to a buffet bonanza, Italian restaurant, or sizzling filet at The Range Steakhouse. Or count your coins back in your suite and order room service, available twenty-four hours a day. More good news? Harrah's recently put its money where its guests are with a $100 million makeover. That's a lot of chips!

Isle of Capri Casino
1800 East Front Street
(816) 855-7777, (800) THE ISLE (843-4753)
www.isleofcapricasino.com

Welcome to the islands, mon, and have a nice day. The Isle of Capri is like visiting a tropical resort with bright colors, a two-story waterfall,

When planning a day at an area attraction, don't forget that Kansas City's weather can change at the drop of a rain hat. Check the weather to see if you need to bring a warm wrap, umbrella, or sunscreen—or all three. Updated weather can be found online at www.kansascity.com.

lush landscaping, and the sound of island drums. If your button-down shirt gets in the way, simply replace it with a festive print at the Banana Cabana kiosk. The casino floor offers more than 1,000 slots and 30 table games and a chance to win big at Missouri's only Free Pull Machine. If you've worked up an appetite, Farradday's is ready to comply with New Orleans crawfish bisque or a steak. There's also Calypso's all-you-can-eat buffet, quick bites at Tradewinds Marketplace, or homemade chili and ice cream at Island O'Aces.

The Woodlands
99th Street and Leavenworth Road
Kansas City, KS
(913) 299-9797
www.woodlandskc.com

Until the Kansas Speedway showed up, this was the biggest thing to hit Wyandotte County in years. It's still an impressive racetrack, sitting off to the east of northbound I-435 with an electronic sign announcing race days. Greyhound races are held Thursday through Monday year-round. Horse racing season is October and November. If you miss the ponies in the off-season, don't despair; the Woodlands offers simulcast betting on out-of-state horse races. All race schedules are subject to change, and bettors must be eighteen or over.

Soon you can race to the nearest slot machine at the Woodlands. Wyandotte County voters recently approved a casino at the location. A temporary casino with as many as 800 slot machines will be replaced by a $40 million permanent casino and restaurant in the future.

The Woodlands also offers a fabulous Sunday brunch and other daily specials. And here's a real Insiders' tip: It's an ideal spot to park your RV when visiting the Kansas Speedway 2 miles away.

ENTERTAINMENT DISTRICTS

Oh sure, you'll want to spend at least one day on our famous Country Club Plaza. But don't miss our other areas that offer festivals and fairs along with enough nightclubs, unique shops, and restaurants to keep you entertained for an afternoon or a weekend.

The Country Club Plaza
Plaza Customer Service, 4745 Central
(816) 753-0100
www.countryclubplaza.com

No matter what you've read or heard about the Plaza, you're bound to be amazed by its beauty. Picture 15 blocks of Spanish-style buildings filled with retailers and restaurants, nightclubs and coffeehouses, antiques shops, and tiny boutiques. And in every corner and alleyway, courtyard, and median you'll discover a sculpture in bronze or marble, a lacy wrought-iron gate, a painted tile mural, a fountain, or flower bed. Entire books have been devoted to the Plaza, and you'll need three brochures just to try to see it all: a walking tour of artwork and fountains, a dining and entertaining guide, and a retail map. You'll find all of these and more at the customer service office at 4745 Central and reproduced on the Web site above.

Better yet, tuck the map in your pocket and simply walk around. Show up in spring and you'll share sidewalks with the 6-foot-tall Easter bunnies that have delighted generations of children and adults; this is also the season when flowering bulbs fill the gardens and people fill the sidewalk cafes. During summer you'll enjoy the free weekend music series, as well as the ice cream, iced cappuccinos, and icy martinis waiting at dozens of cafes and shops. In September the Plaza Art Fair turns the place into a giant neighborhood

i You can take home a piece of our famous Country Club Plaza—and more than just those few extra pounds you acquired from all the dining spots. The colorful banners you see lining the streets are available for purchase for around $40 (some are marked down) at the Plaza Customer Service office at 4745 Central. Call (816) 753-0100.

block party with 250 artists, live music, and food vendors. And starting on Thanksgiving night, miles of colored lights outline every spire and arch and swag—the Plaza's holiday gift to the world.

Plan to leave plenty of room in your suitcase; the Plaza puts Rodeo Drive to shame with more than 180 stores and boutiques. You'll find fashion's aristocracy, such as Armani, Brooks Brothers, BCBG, Ann Taylor, Betsey Johnson, St. John, and Burberry and three glittering floors of fashion, housewares, and giftwares at our hometown department store, Halls. Make yourself over at MAC Cosmetics or Aveda, or make over your home with something from Pottery Barn, Restoration Hardware, or Scandia Down. Younger kids will go for places like Discovery Channel; bigger kids will like the toys at Sharper Image.

Whew! Ready for a break? Then you'll love the fact that the Plaza is home to forty restaurants, bistros, and pubs, from one-of-a-kind eateries like re:Verse, Starker's Reserve, and Bo Lings Chinese Restaurant, to national favorites like McCormick & Schmick's, The Capital Grille, and Cheesecake Factory.

If you're ready to have someone else do the walking for a change, take a carriage ride with Pride of Kansas City Carriage (816-531-1999) or Surrey's Carriage (816-531-2673). These tours-on-the-hoof are fun during the day but really turn on the romance at night with white lights and glowing lanterns. There's even a pumpkin-shaped Cinderella's carriage! Or take a gondola ride on the landscaped ribbon of water known as Brush Creek. For around $45, Ambiance on the Water can provide a relaxing tour; draw the curtains and it's the ideal place to pop the question. The gondoliers are at your service from 6:00 to 10:00 p.m. Wednesday through Saturday, April to November, or by appointment at (816) 365-7101. And there's still time left to drop into Tommy Bahama's for that tropical print shirt you saw in the window. Parking is plentiful and free.

Crown Center
2450 Grand Boulevard
(816) 274-8444
www.crowncenter.com

In 1968 Joyce C. Hall, founder of Hallmark Cards, and his son, Don J. Hall, turned an eyesore called "Signboard Hill" into one of the city's most vibrant entertainment centers. Crown Center became one of the nation's earliest mixed-use developments and a model for how to do urban redevelopment right. You'll need a guidebook just to see it all, and thank goodness Crown Center offers a terrific one at the information booth on the lower level just past the main entrance. A separate map takes you past marvelous outdoor sculptures, including an Alexander Calder, plus fountains and landmarks throughout the eighty-five-acre complex and surrounding neighborhood.

You can get to nearly everything via a glass-enclosed elevated walkway called The Link that connects Crown Center with Union Station and the Hyatt Regency. But what makes this complex the "Rockefeller Plaza" of the Midwest is Crown Center Square, with fountains and terraced lawns where events take place all year. The Entertainment Pavilion with its free-form tent is home to free family activities, including concerts and outdoor movies, throughout summer, and from November to March it's transformed into the city's only outdoor ice-skating rink. Each winter the 100-foot mayor's Christmas tree becomes the square's glowing focal point.

Within Crown Center are more than fifty unique shops and restaurants, a movie complex, and two live stage venues: the American Heartland Theatre and the Coterie Family Theatre. The Hallmark Visitor Center provides a look at the greeting card company's history (you'll learn why the wackiest line is called Shoebox), and at Kaleidoscope kids can exercise their creative muscles. Parking is free for the first three hours; just remember to get your ticket validated at any retail shop or restaurant. Van-accessible handicapped parking is available on Grand Boulevard near the main entrance, and the parking garage includes handicapped parking with ramps to allow easy access. You can also rent strollers or check out wheelchairs at Customer Service.

Power & Light District
Downtown
www.powerandlightdistrict.com

This $850 million retail, entertainment, and housing district has brought Kansas City's long-slumbering downtown back among the living. And how! The 9-block center's first phase is complete, with more to come over the next few years, including plans for more than 1,000 condos and lofts. But for now, let's party like it's 1969, the last time anyone can remember the city's streets filled with so many shoppers and diners after offices close at 5.

The district connects the areas between Bartle Hall Convention Center, the new Sprint Center, and downtown's hotels. At its heart is the seventeen-story H&R Block world headquarters, that glowing green oval that also includes an art gallery and theater. And proving that they don't build 'em like they used to, two magnificent theaters were renovated as part of the mix—the Midland and the long-vacant Empire Theatre, which was renamed as AMC's flagship Main Street Theatre. AMC's world headquarters reside in the Power & Light Building that gives the district its name. Dining options are plentiful as well, with Kansas City favorites the Bristol Seafood Grill joining popular national names such as Gordon Biersch Brewery, Lucky Strike Lanes, and Famous Dave's Barbecue. Howl at the Moon offers a sing-along venue, while Mosaic Lounge's DJs spins your favorites all night long. Boutiques and art galleries make up the rest of the exciting list of tenants.

One entire block is reserved for Kansas City Live! a multilevel design with tented space for live music performances. Visitors and residents alike will be encouraged to stay and play with sidewalk bistros, pretty landscaping, and green spaces.

River Market
North of 5th Street from Broadway Bridge to Heart of America Bridge
(816) 842-1271
www.kc-citymarket.com

When it comes to attractions, this one really produces, literally. Since 1857 it's been home to the biggest farmers' market in the Midwest. But there's plenty happening here besides ripe tomatoes. The River Market is a laid-back neighborhood that's fun to explore on foot. You might even find a treasure to ship back home at the Kansas City Artists Coalition (816-421- 5222) at 201 Wyandotte, where a variety of artists show work from cutting-edge to classic.

Then follow your nose to Planters Seed and Spice Company at 513 Walnut, where you'll find bins overflowing with every fragrant herb, seed, and coffee bean imaginable. Antiques hunters will go nuts in the 30,000-square-foot Cheep Antiques (816-471-0092) at 500 West 5th Street. Other antiques are on view—this time reclaimed treasures from a boat that sank in 1856—at *Arabia* Steamboat Museum, 400 Grand Street (see listing in Museums).

When you need a break, head for River Market Brewery (500 Walnut), the first place to open (officially, anyway) when Prohibition ended. River Market also hosts wild and wonderful street parties with music and dancing nearly every weekend from spring through fall. Check the Web site or call for dates.

Village West
Intersection of I-70 and I-435
Kansas City, KS
(913) 788-3700
www.legendsshopping.com

This shopping, dining, and entertainment district surrounding the Kansas Speedway quickly became the state's biggest draw. Sports enthusiasts can find all camo, all the time at Cabela's (where little ones can stare for hours at the big fish in the huge aquarium), moms can outfit an entire home at Nebraska Furniture Mart, and we can all get a little retail therapy at dozens of specialty and fashion stores, many of which are the first ones to open in the Midwest.

Find a hot bargain at the Gap or Banana Republic outlet stores, then chill out over a cool drink at one of the many restaurants and bars. Stick around for the salsa lessons at Caliente Cuban restaurant or sing along with the bartenders at Cheeseburger in Paradise (believe us, these cheeseburgers *are* paradise, as are the mango mojitos). The mechanical bull is waiting for you at Saddle Ranch Chop House, where you may prefer to rope a steak and homemade cobbler instead. We guarantee kids will think the country's first T-Rex Cafe is dino-mite. Just save room for Sheridan's frozen custard after dinner.

If all that's not enough, Village West tempts you to stay longer with live entertainment, a 60-foot fountain display, and a walking tour that celebrates eighty famous Kansans (we're waiting for our plaque to go up any day now).

Westport
Westport Road between Main Street and Southwest Trafficway
www.westportkcmo.com

Westport got its start in 1833 when John Calvin McCoy built a trading post on the northeast corner of Westport Road and Pennsylvania. By 1836 the area's colorful population of fifty or so included scouts Kit Carson and Jim Bridger as well as John Sutter, a guy who skipped town to escape creditors and look for gold. The area also played a bloody role in the Civil War when the Battle of Westport became known as the Gettysburg of the West. Learn more at www.westporthistorical.org.

Today Westport is still a stopping point for thirsty and hungry travelers. Lucky for you, prairie dog is no longer on the menu; instead you'll find dining choices including award-winning Bluestem, chic (and gay-friendly) Bistro 303, and Westport Flea Market, home of the town's best burger—make that the *world's* best burger—plus bars and live music venues. And instead of spurs and cattle prods, shops offer candles, handcrafted jewelry, and garden art.

Most of us agree that a trip to Kansas City isn't complete without visiting Kelly's Westport Inn (500 Westport Road, 816-561-5800, www.kellyswestportinn.com), the city's oldest standing building. Built in 1837, it was once a grocery store operated by Albert Boone, grandson of Daniel. It was designated a national historic landmark in 1959, which means hands off on changing the creaky-floored structure. Frankly, current owners Pat and Kyle Kelly and their legions of loyal customers wouldn't have it any other way. This is the place to be on St. Pat's Day when the streets outside become a sea of green and a river of spilled beer.

Pick up a walking map of historic buildings and sites at Westport Merchants Association (816-756-2789) at 4123 Mill Street.

HISTORICAL CHURCHES

Cathedral of the Immaculate Conception
416 West 12th Street
(816) 842-0416
www.kcgolddome.org
In 1882 the dome of this neoclassic-style church was the highest point in the city. Today it's dwarfed by its steel-and-glass neighbors, but the gleam from the twenty-three-karat gold leaf outshines everything in sight. The dome was gilded in 1960, and the church was recently renovated. Masses are held at 12:15 p.m. Monday through Friday; at 2:30 and 4:30 p.m. on Saturday; and at 9:00 and 11:00 a.m., and 6:00 and 8:00 p.m. Sunday.

Community Christian Church
47th and Main
(816) 561-6531
www.community-christian. org

When Frank Lloyd Wright designed this church in the 1930s, technology couldn't produce the shaft of light he envisioned coming from the top of the dome. The beam would have to wait another sixty years for artist Dale Eldred to make it work, but even he wouldn't be around to see it. A year after his death, in December 1994, the Steeple of Light, which includes four xenon lights at 300 million candlepower each, was switched on. The lights shine heavenward every weekend and nightly through the holiday season.

The church itself is pretty amazing as well. Curved walls are covered with a textured white surface and, typical of Wright's style, the overall design is stark. But the brilliant architect knew what he was doing. Because he created a sanctuary without needless adornment, we can focus our attention on the things that matter most.

Community of Christ Temple and Auditorium
1001 West Walnut
Independence, MO
(816) 521-3045
www.cofchrist.org
With its silver spiral reaching skyward, the Community of Christ Temple is one of the country's most visually stunning structures. From the inside, looking up toward the ceiling as it rises 195 feet, the design becomes organic—a giant seashell glowing bright white.

In 1831 Joseph Smith designated Independence as the new site for the city of Zion, and today this international Mormon headquarters serves a denomination of 250,000 members. Visitors are welcome to experience the Worshiper's Path, a reflective walkway filled with symbolic artwork leading to the 1,600-seat sanctuary. The room is large, but when the 102-rank pipe organ is played, the very walls seem to vibrate with the powerful sound. Time your visit for one of the free recitals, which are held daily from 3:00 to 3:30 p.m. June to August and every Sunday from 3:00 to 3:30 p.m. September to May. Tours of the Temple are Monday through Sunday, but not from noon to 1:00 p.m., when the Daily Prayer for Peace is taking place. You are invited to take part; the service begins at 12:30 p.m.

The auditorium was designed in the 1920s and features a 5,800-seat chamber with seating in the round beneath a domed ceiling. President Truman made history here when he signed an executive order to desegregate the armed forces in 1948. Within the auditorium is the Children's Peace Pavilion, an interactive museum dedicated to promoting peace through example. The Pavilion is open Tuesday through Saturday 9:30 a.m. to 4:00 p.m. free of charge.

The Church of Jesus Christ of Latter-Day Saints
937 West Walnut
Independence, MO
(816) 836-3466
http://lda.org/placestovisit
Learn about the key role the Church of Jesus Christ of Latter-Day Saints (the Mormons) played in the early and often tempestuous history of Independence. The visitor center houses rare artifacts and artwork documenting the history and beliefs of the Mormons. Exhibits include a re-creation of a log cabin; the two-story mural titled *The Second Coming of Jesus Christ* is splendid. The center is 1 mile south of the Truman Library on the corner of River Road and West Walnut and is open from 9:00 a.m. to 9:00 p.m. daily for free guided tours.

Unity World Headquarters
1901 Northwest Blue Parkway
(816) 524-3550
www.unityworldhq.org
Unity Village's beautiful, 165-foot-tall bell tower can be seen for miles throughout the southwest part of the city; its teachings touch lives around the world. Unity has been offering nondenominational ministry, prayer, and education since 1889, and its monthly spiritual publication, *Daily Word* (www.dailyword .com), is translated into nine languages with an annual circulation of 1.3 million. Its Silent Prayer ministry receives more than two million requests for prayer assistance annually.

Unity Village's Mediterranean-style buildings, two of which are on the National Register of Historic Places, are situated among 1,400 acres of beautifully landscaped grounds, with meditation chapels, fountains, and reflecting pools. The showplace rose garden, with more than 800 rose bushes and fifty varieties, is at its prettiest June through October.

Free tours start at the visitor center and are available 9:00 a.m. to 4:00 p.m. Monday through Thursday, 10:00 a.m. to 1:00 p.m. Friday through Sunday. The guided walking tour, which includes a twelve-minute video presentation about Unity's history, takes about an hour and is equal to 2 city blocks; there are two flights of stairs. The tour can be modified to be wheelchair-accessible with advance notice. Guided tours must be booked in advance; call (816) 251-3578.

HISTORICAL HOMES

If you like looking at homes—really old homes—we've got 'em. Several of these mid-1800s era houses are on the National Register of Historic Places. Although you'll see a wide variety of styles, from simple cabin to opulent Victorian, there is a recurring theme. Most of these homes were directly on or near the famous trails heading west; in one case the backyard was turned into corduroy by thousands of wagon wheels. The homes are open for individual tours, or let Ann Malita-Smith of Kansas City Adventures (816-920-5513, www .kansascityadventures.com) plan a terrific itinerary of historic homes, churches, or other sites to match your interests. Ann lives in a 1909 shirtwaist in a lovely northeast neighborhood, so she respects old bricks, wood floors, and cranky furnaces.

Alexander Majors Historic House and Museum
8201 State Line Road
(816) 333-5556
www.heritageleaguekc.org

Today this nine-room house is surrounded by office buildings and banks, but in 1856 it served as an outfitting base for the growing Santa Fe Trail trade. Its owner, Alexander Majors, cofounded the Pony Express, which quickly became the largest overland freighting operation in the country, at one time employing 4,000 men and 3,500 wagons. But within eighteen months the telegraph displaced the need for wagons and riders and Majors lost his fortune. He would eventually get a job touring with a former employee, Buffalo Bill Cody, and his Wild West show. The house is filled with period furnishings, and the adjacent barn houses a working blacksmith shop and restored wagons. The site is open on weekends; closed during winter. Admission is $3.00 for adults, $1.50 for children.

Although the actual home is on the Missouri side of the state line divide, the front yard is in Kansas.

Bingham-Waggoner Estate
313 West Pacific
Independence, MO
(816) 461-3491
www.bwestate.org

If there ever was a superhighway in the mid-1800s, it was the Santa Fe Trail, and this estate had a front row seat. In fact, in 1999 wagon "swales" were discovered on the southern nineteen acres, which suggests this was a shortcut to the trail. You can see these paths by going behind the house, crossing the footbridge, and looking along a line of trees.

History was made inside the 1827 house as well. Of its many colorful residents, the most famous was George Caleb Bingham, an artist and early-day political activist who used brushstrokes to demonstrate his feelings about the Civil War. When a Union general issued the infamous command that left countless residents of Jackson County homeless, Bingham painted *Order No. 11* here. Other works are in the American Paintings section of the Nelson-Atkins Museum of Art. In 1870 he sold the home and moved to Kansas City.

The Waggoner family purchased the house in 1879 and produced its Queen of the Pantry Flour in the mill across the street. Three generations of this family occupied the home over the next hundred years. Today the house and its acreage are recognized as one of the more significant historical sites in western Missouri. Inside are many furnishings of the time, including a massive dining room table and a walk-in icebox. The home is open for tours from April to October and during the Christmas season. Admission is $4.00 for adults, $2.50 for seniors, and $1.00 for ages six to sixteen.

1859 Jail, Marshal's Home, and Museum
217 Main
(816) 252-1892
www.jchs.org

Just think: In the mid-1800s prisoners didn't have TVs or phones. Okay, no one did. But you'll still be amazed at these dungeon-like cells that held Frank James, William Clark Quantrill of Quantrill's Raiders, and others crossways with the law. Actually, the cell that held Frank James was opulently outfitted by his many adoring fans, and he took his meals with the jailer's family. But in other "guest" quarters, barred windows, double iron doors, and leg chains provide a chilling look at frontier justice. The jail and the marshal's home have been restored to period and contain an outstanding historical collection. Tours are given seven days a week March through December. Closed Thanksgiving, Christmas, January, and February. Admission is $4.00 for adults, $3.50 for seniors, $1.00 for ages six to sixteen, and free for under six.

Harry S. Truman Home
219 North Delaware Street
Independence, MO
(816) 254-9929

The simple charm of the Summer White House speaks volumes about the man who chose to be buried in his hometown rather than beside a towering monument in Washington, D.C.

Bess Truman's grandparents built the Victorian home in 1885; she grew up here, and she and Harry lived here when they weren't in Washington, D.C. The furnishings are just as they were when she died in 1982, right down to the dishcloth by the sink and Harry's hat by the door. The house is open year-round and tours are conducted every fifteen minutes. We suggest you arrive early because tickets are issued starting at 8:30 a.m. on a first-come, first-served basis. Tickets are available at the Truman Home Ticket and Information Center at Truman Road and Main Street, where you can watch a short slide show about the Trumans. Admission is $4.00, free for those under seventeen. Guided walking tours of the neighborhood leave from the center daily from 9:00 a.m. to 4:45 p.m. Memorial Day through Labor Day.

Harry S. Truman Office and Courtroom
112 West Lexington
(816) 795-8200

The office where the thirty-third U.S. president began his political career as a county judge is chiefly unchanged since the day he left for a higher calling. An audiovisual show traces Truman's life before his presidency. Tours are available Tuesday through Thursday and Saturday; the courthouse is closed on federal holidays.

Independence Square
(816) 252-0608
www.jchs.org

Independence has it all: infamous outlaws and a hometown hero, bloody border battles of the Civil War, and opulent homes. At its heart is Independence Square, which marked the beginnings of Harry S. Truman's political career and the journey for thousands heading west. Within the old-fashioned town square you'll find the 1859 Jail and Truman Office and Courtroom (described below) as well as antiques shops, unique stores, and restaurants. And

there's a phosphate or banana split waiting for you at Clinton's Soda Fountain (100 West Maple), where a young Harry once scooped ice cream and mopped the floor. He'd later say his weekly salary of three silver dollars looked like three million.

Jesse James Bank Museum
Court House Square
Liberty, MO
(816) 781-4458
www.stjomo.com

Did the James Gang really steal $60,000 from this bank in February 1866? We'll never know for sure, but it makes a great story. Regardless of who done it, this is the site of the first daylight peacetime bank robbery in the United States. You can tour the bank with its stone vault, iron safe, and Civil War–era teller's window. The bank museum is open year-round. Admission is $4.00 for adults, $3.50 for seniors, $1.50 for ages eight to fifteen, and free for those under eight.

Jesse James Farm and Museum
21216 Jesse James Farm Road
Kearney, MO
(816) 628-6065, (800) FUN-CLAY
www.jessejames.org

Where else but in the Wild West would people idolize a man who robbed trains and banks? But Jesse James wasn't just a typical hoodlum. His boldness and flamboyance—helped along by sensationalized newspaper articles and dime novels—turned him into a modern-day Robin Hood. There's more interest than ever in this local legend thanks to the new Warner Bros. release *The Assassination of Jesse James by the Coward Robert Ford*. Whew! That's a long title. All we need are two words: Brad Pitt. The actor, who was raised not far from here in Springfield, Missouri, plays the charismatic gunfighter. Jesse was born in this house in 1847, the son of a Baptist minister. The young man's religious upbringing apparently didn't take; after a stint in the Civil War he joined with other former Confederate guerrillas to lead the James Gang.

A tour of the home begins with a short film recapping the exploits of James and his older brother, Frank. Artifacts include Jesse's boots and spurs and Frank's letter of surrender. You can also stroll along the stream where the boys played as youngsters and pass Jesse's original burial site, where his mother once sold souvenir stones from his grave. The woman figured since visitors were taking them anyway, she might as well make a profit. Although there are no stones left unturned, the on-site gift shop offers books and souvenirs.

The famous bandit was shot in the back in 1882 and is now buried in Mount Olivet Cemetery in Kearney, about 20 miles northeast of downtown Kansas City. But there's always been talk that the bandit faked his death and lived out the rest of his life in the East. When his heirs agreed to have the body exhumed in 1995, the rumors were laid to rest (so to speak) when DNA and forensic evidence determined that the man in the grave really was Jesse. The home is open year-round and often hosts dramatic reenactments. Admission is $5.50 for adults, $4.25 for seniors, $2.50 for children eight to fifteen, and free for those under eight.

John Wornall House Museum
146 West 61st Terrace
(816) 444-1858
www.wornallhouse.org

Today this stately 1858 Greek Revival structure sits peacefully amid other lovely homes near Loose Park. But during three days in October 1864, the antebellum home's wide front porch was stained with blood when it served as an army hospital. The home's 500-acre farm was at the vortex of the Civil War's largest battle west of the Mississippi.

As a museum, the Wornall House provides an intriguing look at the lives of early settlers. Well-informed docents and staff take visitors through rooms filled with period furnishings, including a foursquare grand piano in the parlor and Lincoln rocker in the master bedroom. From October through May actors re-create a typical day in the mid-1800s. Several programs are mounted throughout the year, such as holiday candlelight tours and Civil War reenactments on the grounds. The museum is part of a twenty-five-stop driving tour of the Battle of Westport; other sites include Loose Park and a rise near the Big Blue River that was known as "Bloody Hill." Brochures are available from the Parks and Recreation Department (816-513-7500, 4600 East 63rd Street). The museum is open Tuesday through Sunday; closed in January. Admission is $6 for adults, $5 for seniors and students, and free for ages four and under. Call for hours, which change with the seasons.

Rice-Tremonti Home
66th and Blue Ridge Boulevard
(816) 358-7423

In 1844, Archibald Rice's 160 acres was a popular place to camp while waiting for spring before heading west on the trails. The homestead wasn't as fancy as some others still with us today, but that's the key to its fascination; its furnishings provide a glimpse into the way families lived in what was once wilderness. The home is now on the National Register of Historic Places.

One of the most interesting attractions is a replica of Aunt Sophia's cabin, where the family's slave lived. Sophia would cook the meals here and then carry them to the main house. Tours are available Saturday and Sunday from May through September.

Thomas Hart Benton Home and Studio
3616 Belleview
(816) 931-5722
www.mostateparks.com/benton

If you're a fan of this famous Kansas City artist, this tour is a must. If you're not familiar with his work, there's ample opportunity to discover it in the Benton section of the Nelson-Atkins Museum of Art and from a mural that fills a wall at the Truman Library.

His painting style was bigger than life, a colorful montage of voluptuous women, powerful men, and landscapes that seemed to rise and swirl as if in a tornado. The Benton home remains exactly as it was when the artist went outside to sign a painting and dropped dead in 1975. His brushes and paints, pipe, and harmonica are casually placed as if waiting for his big rough hands to take them up. His wife, Rita, died a few months later, but her famous spaghetti sauce lives on. Make sure to pick up a copy of her recipe in the kitchen. The tour is open seven days a week; admission is $2.50 for adults, $1.50 ages six to twelve. If you have time, stroll around the lovely Belleview homes district; minimansions line the streets, and the landscaping is exquisite, particularly in spring when the pink and white azaleas are in bloom.

Union Station
30 West Pershing Road
(816) 460-2222
www.sciencecity.com
After a second flood devastated the Union Depot in the West Bottoms, the city knew it needed to build a rail station on higher ground. Several years and $5.8 million later, the result was the City Beautiful movement's most spectacular testament to date. When Union Station opened on October 30, 1914, it was the third largest train facility in the world after New York's Grand Central and Pennsylvania Stations. More than 100,000 people jammed the 400- by 800-foot Grand Hall for the grand opening ceremony, with thousands more pushing into the football field–size North Waiting Room.

This magnificent Beaux Art structure was more than a train terminal; it was the city's town hall, where people came to dine at Fred Harvey's restaurant and dance on New Year's

i When you go to Union Station, remember that there really was a Union Station Massacre. It happened on June 17, 1933, when four people were killed during an attempt to free a notorious federal prisoner. You can still see the stray machine-gun bullet lodged in a wall near Union Station's east entrance.

i One of the most freewheeling ways to see our sites is on a Segway. Zip by Union Station, get a taste of the Crossroads Arts District, tour the Country Club Plaza, or take a Segway Safari at the Kansas City Zoo. Tours last from forty-five minutes to just over two hours (about the time it would take us to learn to operate the motorized wheels) and cost $40 to $80. Contact Segway Experience at (816) 531-0600 or www.segway experience.com.

Eve. "Meet me under the clock" was a common phrase as friends looked for familiar faces under the 6½-foot-wide dial. Army boots echoed through the marble halls as more than half of all World War II soldiers boarded trains here.

But by 1950s travel by rail was a thing of the past, and the station's depot was relegated to a walk-up window on one side. The last Amtrak train pulled out in 1985. The once-beloved station was forgotten, its now-empty halls echoing only with breaking glass, falling plaster, or the steady drip, drip of water leaking through a stained roof. Over the following decades several groups promised to rebuild it, but the projects failed one by one. Finally, city leaders had two choices: Restore it or tear it down.

They decided to bring it back to life, financed with a bistate cultural tax in 1996, the first such two-state, five-county program in the country. After more than $250 million and years of work, Union Station and its new Science City museum opened in November 1999. As you walk through the Grand Hall and North Waiting Room, be sure to look at the ornate ceilings 95 feet above you. These plaster swirls and ribbons, oak leaves, and rosette medallions—sky-blue, gold, and terra-cotta—were meticulously restored by artisans, including a team from Liverpool, England, that helped restore the fire-ravaged Windsor Castle. Crystal chandeliers, all 3,000 pounds of them, sparkle like new.

Union Station/Skyline. CVB OF GREATER KANSAS CITY

Union Station is once again a place to celebrate and meet friends under the clock before enjoying an elegant meal at Pierpont's, where the gorgeous bar alone is enough to make a conductor whistle. Within the massive station is Science City, an interactive museum for children with activities that prove science is everywhere in our lives. Adults and kids alike will enjoy the live theater and giant-screen Extreme Screen within the complex. For details, including ticket prices and times, see the Kidstuff chapter.

Vaile Victorian Mansion
1500 North Liberty
Independence, MO
(816) 325-7430
www.vailemansion.org
As pretty as a wedding cake, this thirty-one-room mansion features gables and towers,

lacy trim, and Gothic windows. Its highest peak is adorned with grillwork that looks like a crown, a fitting reference for a town called "Queen City of the Trails."

The house was built in 1881 for Harvey Merrick Vaile, a prosperous lawyer, rancher, and, as you'll see, rather wicked fellow. At one time the estate included a lake, boathouse, and lushly landscaped gardens. The home was just as elaborate within, filled with unheard-of conveniences like flushing toilets and a 48,000-bottle wine cellar. In the master bedroom a reclining woman (minus more than just her high-button shoes) was painted on the ceiling. Other interesting but less scandalous artwork appears elsewhere: As was the norm, the builder used inexpensive pine in the upper floors and then had it painted to look like more costly mahogany or cherry wood. If you look closely at the faux graining in the second-floor smoking room, you'll notice faces and animals incorporated into the swirls and dips.

After the owner's death in 1894, the home became a sanatorium and then a nursing home. It was nearly demolished before the DeWitt family bought it in the 1960s. The family, along with members of the Vaile Victorian Society, restored this home to a fare-thee-well and are pleased to invite you in. The group hosts a Mad Hatter's Tea Party in March, a strawberry festival in June, and holiday tours in December, when the home is beautifully decorated. The home is open seven days a week from April through October and certain days in December; please call for a current schedule. Admission is $4.00 for adults, $3.50 for seniors, and $1.00 for ages six through sixteen.

HISTORICAL MUSEUMS AND SITES

American Jazz Museum
18th and Vine
(816) 474-8463
www.americanjazzmuseum.com
Jazz. It was America's music, and in the 1920s and 1930s no place played it with more passion than Kansas City. Some of the greats, like Count Basie, Bennie Moten, and Charlie "Yardbird" Parker, got their start, made their name, or honed their craft here. Many stayed; some headed to the even brighter lights of New York. The American Jazz Museum is the first in the country devoted exclusively to this art form.

Dozens of interactive displays provide a glimpse of this historical, hysterical time when music poured out of dozens of nightclubs twenty-four hours a day. You can become part of it, if only for an hour or so, by listening to hundreds of the greatest jazz recordings ever made, including Ella Fitzgerald scatting through "A Tisket, A Tasket" and Big Joe Turner singing—what else?—"Goin' to Kansas City." Catch more than two dozen jazz performances on a video jukebox, and watch *Jazz*, an original film starring Jay McShann,

Max Roach, and Shirley Horn. Special displays, including the world's most expensive saxophone, honor talents like Charlie Parker, Louis Armstrong, and Duke Ellington.

Little hipsters aren't left out. In the Wee-Bop Room, children can play audio engineer at the mixing station; experiment with harmony, melody, and rhythm; and learn the range and sounds of different instruments. The museum is open Tuesday through Saturday 9:00 a.m. to 6:00 p.m., Sunday noon to 6:00 p.m. Admission is $6.00 for adults, $2.50 for children. A combination ticket to the American Jazz Museum and the Negro Leagues Baseball Museum costs $8.00 and $4.00, respectively.

Arabia Steamboat Museum
400 Grand Avenue
(816) 471-4030 (information),
(816) 471-1856 (group reservations)
www.1856.com
Who hasn't dreamed of finding buried treasure? Bob Hawley and sons David and Greg, along with Jerry Mackey and their families, put their dreams to work by uncovering the steamboat *Arabia* 132 years after it sank on its way from Westport to Parkville, Missouri. When the 171-foot boat went down, a quick-thinking crew got all 130 passengers off safely, with the exception of one lone mule. But 222 tons of goods drifted to a watery grave, including frontier-bound tools and dishware, shoes, and buttons . . . and 400 barrels of Kentucky bourbon. A few ladies were devastated to learn they wouldn't get the perfume they'd ordered from France.

Using an old river map, the Hawley and Mackey team located the boat in a cornfield one-half mile from the river's edge and began excavation in 1988. It would be three torturous weeks before they uncovered the splintered remains of the left paddle wheel. Soon the men were bringing up box after box of treasure. The museum is a fascinating look at these remarkably preserved supplies, which National Geographic *Traveler* calls "A King Tut's tomb . . . a time capsule of another age!"

Steamboat Museum at City Market. CVB OF GREATER KANSAS CITY

It's believed to be the largest single collection of pre–Civil War frontier artifacts in the country. Once inside, visitors will see a replica of the *Arabia*'s side-wheel paddle slicing through the water; there's even part of the walnut tree that was its downfall. After a short movie about the steamboat's history and its excavation you can ask questions, and often the person with the colorful answers is named Hawley.

You can then walk through the display areas by yourself or attend one of the tours—worth waiting for—that begin every half hour. Children eight years old and up will enjoy the museum, and it is wheelchair-accessible. A gift shop sells books about the *Arabia* written by Greg and David Hawley, including a cute children's book, and an 1856 perfume based on bottles found within the dig. Allow at least ninety minutes to see it all. Admission is $12.50 for adults, $11.50 for seniors, and $4.75 for ages four to twelve.

The museum is open seven days a week, closed on major holidays. The first tour begins at 10:00 a.m.; the last starts at 4:00 p.m. Food is not allowed in the museum, but an ice-cream parlor is just outside the entrance, and several casual-style restaurants are within walking distance. And here in Kansas City, we're eagerly waiting the excavation of a steamboat the Hawley family says was even grander than the *Arabia*. Stay tuned!

18th and Vine Historic District
1616 East 18th Street
(816) 474-VINE (8463)
www.americanjazzmuseum.org

From the 1920s through the early 1940s, the 18th and Vine neighborhood was the center of Kansas City's African-American culture, commerce, and entertainment. It's where jazz musicians like Charlie Parker, Count Basie, and hundreds of others played, and it's home base for the Negro Baseball Leagues. We pay tribute to their heart and soul in this $24 million, 50,000-square-foot complex that opened in 1997. Within its

Call ahead to find out if attractions offer tours, as these can greatly enhance your visit. One example is the *Arabia* Steamboat Museum in the River Market area, where the tour guide is occasionally one of the people who discovered the buried treasure. Often you can reserve space in the tour to guarantee your seat—not a bad idea during the busy summer or on weekends.

walls are separate museums devoted to jazz and the Negro Leagues (both described later in this chapter) as well as the Horace M. Peterson III Visitor Center, which tells of the contributions black citizens made to the city's social and economic development. The center also contains the Blue Room, a nightclub that re-creates the music's heyday. During the day this club is a minimuseum filled with artifacts; four nights a week it becomes a stage for some of KC's best jazz musicians. The Blue Room has its own entrance at 1600 East 18th Street. Call (816) 474-2929 for event schedules.

Two other attractions are close by. The Gem Theater Cultural and Performing Arts Center, a 500-seat facility that hosts dance and musical events, is across the street at 1615 East 18th Street, and the Charlie Parker Memorial is 1 block north between Vine Street and The Paseo. (You can read more about this tribute in Landmarks above.) The 18th and Vine District is five minutes from downtown and Crown Center, 2 blocks south of I-70 at the Paseo exit. Free on-street parking is available; the area is also served by Kansas City's Metro No. 108 Indiana bus and the trolley. For more details about the two main museums within the complex, see the American Jazz Museum and the Negro Leagues Baseball Museum listings.

Elmwood Cemetery
4900 Truman Road
(816) 231-0373, (877) 231-0373
www.historickcelmwood.org

Many of Kansas City's most important civic leaders were laid to rest in this European-style cemetery, their wealth and social status evident in enormous monuments and mausoleums. Even the grounds are historic, created by the city's most respected landscape architect, George Kessler. The forty-three acres served as an early drawing board for the parks and green spaces he would design during his career. Stop by the cemetery's office or go online for biographies of famous people buried here; guided tours are available for groups of ten or more with advance reservation. There may be a fee; certainly donations are always welcome at this not-for-profit historic treasure.

In a sea of massive monuments, the most impressive by far is the Armour Chapel, a stone Gothic sanctuary dedicated to the memory of meatpacking magnate Kirkland Armour (1854–1901). Other elaborate resting places belong to Jacob Loose, founder of Sunshine Biscuits, whose estate donated the land for Loose Park, and Kersey Coates, an influential leader who helped develop downtown's Quality Hill. His Coates House Hotel was one of the finest in the Midwest.

A much smaller tombstone was laid for a very large woman, 6' 10" Leannah Loveall Kearnes, also known as Annie Chambers. Kansas City's most notorious madam, Annie changed her ways late in life and left her City Market property to the City Union Mission. Along with famous people, more than 700 Civil War veterans are buried here, as well as many who died in border wars. There are also a large number of Jewish burials from Congregation B'nai Jehudah Temple in two southwest acres, all facing east.

Detailed biographies of several of these famous citizens can be found in Wilda Sandy's fascinating book, *Here Lies Kansas City*. Self-guided tours of Elmwood are welcome until dusk Monday through Friday. Please check with the office before attempting to take any monument rubbings. At this time there is no fee.

Truman Library. CVB OF GREATER KANSAS CITY

Harry S. Truman Library and Museum
500 West U.S. Highway 24
Independence, MO
(816) 833-1400
www.trumanlibrary.org

Independence is still wild about its native son, the thirty-third president, who grew up in this town. When the library opened in 1957 it became only the second such archive in the country.

Fresh from a $22.5 million renovation completed in 2001, the museum and library does more than just tell Truman's story. As he wished, it challenges visitors to explore the decision-making process of that era and how it affects our lives today. Two new permanent exhibits include "The White House Decision Center," a behind-the-scenes look that lets visitors take on the roles of the president and his aides in a re-creation of the West Wing. A

multimedia exhibit contains dozens of original artifacts and documents from before, during, and after Truman's presidency. Other features include the gravesites of Harry and his wife, Bess, the documentary film *Harry S. Truman: 1884–1972*, and a replica of Truman's Oval Office where you can listen to a tape of his voice and see the original THE BUCK STOPS HERE desk plaque.

This is a fascinating look at a leader who may be better regarded today than when he was in office, as we find a new appreciation for his honesty and frank-talking ways. And visitors are often surprised to discover the many ways Truman changed history: He proposed the first national health care plan, announced the end of the war in Europe, and signed peace treaties with other countries. He was also the president who dropped the first atomic bomb. The gift shop

Looking for a gift for your boss back home? Pick up a replica of Harry S. Truman's famous THE BUCK STOPS HERE desk signs, available in the gift shop of his museum. Just present it after you get that raise.

offers such keepsakes as replicas of Truman's famous THE BUCK STOPS HERE desk sign (for just 55 bucks) and pieces of the original red tape, which was strips of scarlet-colored twill used to bind U.S. documents during the Civil War. Now you know!

Museum admission is $7 for adults, $5 for over sixty-one, and $3 for ages six to eighteen. It's open seven days a week. Plan on spending at least one hour viewing the permanent displays and any special touring exhibit. Or consider making a day of it touring the other "Man from Missouri" attractions in Independence, including Independence Square and the Truman Home, both detailed in this chapter.

Johnson County Museum of History
6305 Lackman Road
Shawnee, KS
(913) 631-6709
www.jocomuseum.org
Although baby boomers might take issue with things from their childhoods ending up in a museum, the truth is that everyone will enjoy the 1950s All-Electric House. The ranch-style house, built in 1954 to showcase all the modern electric conveniences, was actually a model home in Prairie Village, a tidy Johnson County suburb. Now *this* was the life: a painting that slides back to reveal a black-and-white television, a remote control near Dad's recliner that closes the drapes and turns on the stereo, and a bedside dial that controls the lights throughout the house. Guess they hadn't discovered "clap on, clap off" technology yet. Other displays include actual home movies, toys from the '50s, and a snazzy 1955 two-tone Chevy Bel Air.

The main museum chronicles the county's growth from its beginnings as Indian Territory

in 1820, its change to farmland, then suburbs, and now its role as edge city and one of the fastest-growing areas in the two-state region. Exhibits show—through more than 500 artifacts, documents, photos, and maps—various and often competing versions of "the good life." The first inhabitants, the Shawnee, are represented by items such as ceremonial clothing and an 1859 edition of *Hymns in the Shawnee Language*. There are also interactive displays and profiles of thirty-three individuals who helped shape the area over the past 175 years. The museum is open from 10:00 a.m. to 4:30 p.m. Tuesday through Saturday and 1:00 to 4:00 p.m. Sunday. The All-Electric House is open Tuesday through Saturday from 1:00 to 4:00 p.m. Admittance to the museum is free; the house tour costs $2 for adults and $1.00 for children twelve and under. Poodle skirts not required.

Kansas City Museum of History and Science
3218 Gladstone Boulevard
(816) 483-8300
www.kcmuseum.com
Believe it or not, at one time this majestic building was a private residence. Well, they certainly don't make 'em like they used to. When lumber baron Robert A. Long built his villa called Corinthian Hall in 1911, it cost a whopping $750,000, unheard of in those days. He was content with everything except the view. To improve it he moved three 4,000-square-foot mansions down the street. Perhaps that's where the phrase "not in my backyard" originated. The palatial space is now the Kansas City Museum, which houses interactive displays about the pioneering spirit of our early settlers.

Kids in particular will enjoy exploring the culture of the Osage Indians, visiting Chouteau's trading post, and climbing aboard a covered wagon heading west. Everybody will go for the 1910 soda fountain, where they still scoop a pretty good ice-cream cone. A tour of the mansion gives you a taste of how fortune's favored lived . . . but who needs a bowling alley anyway? The planetarium hosts seasonal star shows and educational programs throughout the year.

Take a self-directed tour Tuesday through Sunday; student and group tours are also available with reservations. Call Union Station (816-460-2020). Admission is free, but suggested donation is $2.50 for adults and $2.00 for seniors and those seventeen and under.

Liberty Memorial and World War I Museum
100 West 26th Street
(816) 221-1918
www.libertymemorialmuseum.org

At this monument's groundbreaking ceremony in 1921, the crowd watched as General John J. Pershing and the four other principal Allied commanders took the stage. It was the first and only time these men appeared in one place. Five years later, before a crowd of 100,000, President Calvin Coolidge dedicated the country's only memorial honoring the men and women who died during World War I. The city had a reason to be proud; it had taken only ten days to raise the $2.5 million needed to build the monument. In today's dollars the contributions would be more than $20 million.

New York architect H. Van Buren Magonigle envisioned his 217-foot column as "an altar high raised in the sky with its flame of inspiration ever burning." That flame went out when the monument, crumbling and deemed unsafe, was closed in 1994. After a $30 million restoration project, the Liberty Memorial reopened with great fanfare on Memorial Day weekend 2002.

The project was financed by benefactors, private citizens, and the sale of granite bricks inscribed with names of brave loved ones long gone, including this author's father, John H. Van Luchene.

In 2007 extensive work was completed on the National World War I Museum, and it's as moving as the sight of the monument above. To enter the underground museum you'll cross a glass bridge and have one last view of the tower through the skylights before passing over a field of 9,000 red poppies, each one representing a man or woman who died fighting in the Great War. With over 50,000 artifacts, many never seen before, and interactive displays, it's a fascinating look at the physical, emotional, cultural, and political experiences during this time in history. Immersion galleries bring the combat to life through the eyes and ears of those who served. The museum store offers books, movies, music, and other materials related to WWI.

The museum is open Tuesday through Sunday, 10:00 a.m. to 5:00 p.m., with the last ticket sold to tour the tower at 4:15 p.m. Ticket prices range from $4 for children to $8 for adults, with an additional $3 to $4 to ride the elevator to the apex of the tower. Our advice is to do both; you'll save two dollars with a dual ticket, and the breathtaking 360-degree view of the skyline is priceless.

You can also experience that view at night at Tower after Hours the first Friday of each month from April to September, from 7:00 to 10:00 p.m. Tickets, available at the museum store, are $5 each.

Negro Leagues Baseball Museum
1616 East 18th Street
(816) 221-1920, (888) 221-6526
www.nlbm.com

Before the multimillion-dollar contracts, before the megabuck endorsement deals, there were men who played baseball just because they loved the game. And they continued to suit up and take the field even when major league teams shut them out because of their color. This museum, the only one of its kind in the country, follows the history of the Negro National League, beginning with its formation at the nearby Paseo YMCA in 1920. Out of that came the Monarchs, one of the league's most exciting teams thanks to players like Satchel Paige, Cool Papa Bell, Connie Johnson, and John Jordan "Buck" O'Neil. Oh, man, could these guys play ball.

Two short videos tell the stories of games played here and on the road, and an impressive display of memorabilia brings them to life. You'll see documents and photos that demonstrate the highs from wins and fans' adulation as well as the lows caused by segregation and racism. In this regard the exhibits transcend sports and hit at the very heart of our country at the time. Eventually the Negro Leagues ended for the same reason they started: sheer talent. The Brooklyn Dodgers recruited Monarchs player Jackie Robinson in 1945, and others soon followed. The leagues played their last game in 1960.

One of the museum's most striking displays is the Field of Legends, where life-size bronze players are positioned on a ball diamond. The ten statues represent the first Negro League players inducted into the Hall of Fame in Cooperstown, New York. Trivia games test your knowledge about these heroes.

The museum is open Tuesday through Sunday; admission is $6.00 for adults, $2.50 for twelve and under. Combination tickets to the Negro Leagues Baseball Museum and the American Jazz Museum are $8.00 and $4.00, respectively.

Union Cemetery Walking Tour
28th and Walnut
(816) 472-4990
www.kcmo.org/parks

When forty-nine-acre Union Cemetery was deeded in 1857, its planners thought it would provide enough burial space for the towns of Kansas and Westport for all time. Shortsighted? Not for two communities (we didn't become Kansas City until 1889) that had only 3,000 residents between them. It's estimated that 55,000 are buried here, including veterans from every American war and cholera victims by the score. Some of our city's most famous citizens lie here as well, individuals whose granite-etched names are repeated on city street signs, schools, and historic home sites. Alexander Majors, whose company founded the Pony Express, is here, as is artist George Caleb Bingham. Lesser known (except to those he assisted) is Tillman Crabtree, Kansas City's first policeman. One of his duties was to carry women across the city's muddy streets.

The cemetery is open for self-guided tours seven days a week from 8:30 a.m. to 3:30 p.m. Maps with biographies of the most famous are available in a small box near the entrance gate or at the sexton's cottage. Or contact the Union Cemetery Historical Society (816-472-4990), 227 East 28th Street Terrace, Kansas City, MO 64108. Be sure to bring large sheets of paper and charcoal pencils to create rubbings of interesting stones.

LANDMARKS

The Kansas City Power & Light Building
14th and Baltimore
www.skyscrapers.com
(click on "Kansas City")

The same year that New Yorkers were admiring their tallest skyscraper so far, the Empire State Building, we were agog at ours. In 1931 the Power & Light Building became the tallest building in Missouri. Architectural team Hoit, Price & Barnes knew this thirty-one-story art deco beauty would eventually lose its tallest-structure status, so they added a bonus: a 97-foot pillar of lights at top that cycle among white, amber, red, and green. The building's setbacks, which give it a telescoping look, are also dramatized at night with hidden floodlights. The art deco theme is repeated inside with a sunburst motif in the brass elevator doors, radiator grills, and even the water fountain.

Charlie Parker Memorial

The name of sculptor Robert Graham's 17-foot bronze head of Charlie "Bird" Parker is *Bird Lives*. He certainly does, through his music. The Kansas City, Kansas, native, who changed the sound of jazz, is memorialized on a plaza behind the American Jazz Museum in the 18th and Vine District.

Pioneer Mother

The inscription on this large bronze tells the story of thousands of women who gave up homes and families back east to start new lives. The passage from the Book of Ruth reads, "Whither thou goest, I will go and wither thou lodgest, I will lodge. Thy people will be my people, and thy God, my God." The sculpture is in Penn Valley Park, south of the entrance to the Liberty Memorial.

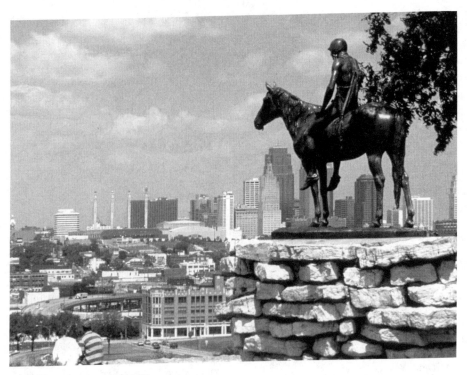

The Scout. CVB OF GREATER KANSAS CITY

Rosedale Memorial Arch
35th Street and Booth
Kansas City, KS

Based on the Arc de Triomphe in Paris, this monument pays tribute to soldiers who fought in World War I. It was designed by Rosedale resident John LeRoy Marshall and dedicated in 1923. The "War to End All Wars" wasn't, and seventy years later a monument was added to honor the soldiers of World War II, Korea, and the Vietnam conflict. High on a hill, the arch can be seen from miles away.

The Scout

This impressive statue of an Indian on horseback wasn't even meant to be ours; it rested here temporarily en route to its intended home at San Francisco's 1915 Panama-Pacific Expo. But Kansas Citians loved the sculpture so much they raised $15,000 to buy it. Now *The Scout* forever watches over our skyline from a hill in Penn Valley Park between Southwest Trafficway and Broadway, just off 31st Street.

Sky Stations/Pylon Caps
atop H. Roe Bartle Hall
13th and Central

When these metal sculptures were mounted on tall, slender pylons 200 feet above Bartle Hall in 1994, they became one of our most dramatic landmarks—and one of the most hotly debated. Some pundits refer to them as "three whirligigs and a curling iron." George Jetson may disagree, but R. M. Fisher's designs were influenced not by the space age but by the art deco designs found throughout our downtown skyline.

NEIGHBORHOOD DRIVES

Take a rubbernecking drive through some of our most beloved neighborhoods filled with charming Tudors or jaw-dropping mansions. Most of the stunners were built between 1900 and 1940, but there are some up-and-comers, particularly on the Kansas side. And take note of the number of trikes and basketballs in the driveways of homes costing $1 million or more. Where do these whippersnappers get all that cash? We know for sure it's not from writing travel guides. Following are some of our favorite drives.

Hallbrook
West of State Line, north of College Boulevard in Leawood, KS

What Hallbrook lacks in maturity—the area was developed just two decades or so ago—it more than makes up for in sheer glamour. Its villas and minimansions lean toward Spanish and country French in design. Look for one jaw-dropper that's based on Tara from Gone with the Wind.

Mission Hills
Southwest of State Line Road and 53rd Street, west of the Carriage Club

This lovely drive is another blessing from landscape architects and builders who let the lay of the land determine where streets and houses should be placed. Roads dip here and there, jogging gracefully around streams and skirting ancient trees. And the homes caught up in all this natural glory are simply magnificent. As you drive southwest you'll pass Mission Hills Country Club and Kansas City Country Club golf courses on the west.

Rich & Famous Tour
(913) 338-0129, (816) 763-9401
www.singlesmall.com/richtour

It's common knowledge that Jean Harlow, Walt Disney, and Ernest Hemingway lived in Kansas City at one time, but did you know Mickey Rooney, Red Skelton, Burt Bacharach, and stripper Sally Rand hung their hats—or fans, as the case may be—here as well? Local writer Don Davidson offers a fascinating drive-by tour of these homes as well as other celebrity's former abodes, including those of

Casey Stengel, actor Craig Stevens, Walter Cronkite, Ginger Rogers, and sports greats Marcus Allen and Joe Montana.

Former and current politicians, business owners, and media personalities are included, and you'll learn how Daniel Boone, Harriet Nelson, and other famous folks are connected to our town. There are more than one hundred homes in all, and Don describes them all in detail. A fun twenty-minute trivia quiz will see who's been paying attention. This is an ideal tour for groups from twenty to forty and lasts from 9:00 a.m. to 4:00 p.m. with a stop for lunch, is on your own. Coaches are equipped with restrooms, and there is an afternoon break. The fee depends on the total number in the group but is typically around $25 per person. Tours are by appointment only.

Ward Parkway
Beginning at West 53rd Street, southwest of the Country Club Plaza

No one will ask for your ticket to this attraction: It's a 4-mile drive on one of the country's most beautiful boulevards. We adore it, HGTV devoted an entire hour to it, and if you're visiting friends in Kansas City you're bound to get the grand tour at least once.

Ward Parkway has some of the priciest real estate in town. But even some locals don't know that it didn't cost a dime when J. C. Nichols began developing homes on these 500 acres near the turn of the twentieth century. Businessman Hugh Ward donated the land to the city but died before the papers were signed. His wife, Vassie James Ward, followed through on the plan and requested that it be named for her late husband.

The new boulevard became a magnet for money, and during the early 1900s some of the most prominent families chose to build their homes, villas, and mansions here. The Tom Pendergast house at 5650 Ward Parkway is one of the most famous, while certainly the most striking is the Corrigan-Sutherland House on the corner of 55th and Ward Parkway. In 1912 Barney Corrigan commissioned flamboyant Kansas City architect Louis Curtiss to design the splendid twenty-five-room home (a room for each of his eighteen children, with space for more, it would seem). The modern Art Nouveau style was constructed of concrete with a Carthage cut-stone facing and magnificent tree-motif stained glass. The estate cost around $200,000, but, alas, the sixty-six-year-old Corrigan didn't live to see it finished. He died on January 6, 1914, on his way to inspect the home's progress. The property was then purchased by the Sutherland lumber family, who remained here for several decades.

Though the homes' opulence turned this into a street of dreams, the green spaces made it a paradise. Today people jog, walk dogs, and bike along its tree-shaded sidewalks, and kids play tag football on wide medians that form miniparks. The boulevard was designed by renowned landscape architect George Kessler along with father-and-son team Hare & Hare. As for the remarkable fountains, sculptures, and urns that grace Ward Parkway, those were gifts from J. C. Nichols.

Westwood Hills
West of State Line Road on 50th Street
Although this is one of the smaller cities in both size (less than 1 square mile) and number of residents (around 390), it's earned the right to its nickname, "the Prettiest Little City in Kansas." Darling cottages and elegant estates are sprinkled along roads that dip and twist, and massive trees cross the streets to create overhead umbrellas. Be sure to stop in for a mango-flavored Jet Tea at the Hi Hat Coffee Shop (5012 State Line, 913-831-0341); there's enough ginseng in this golden-yellow smoothie to power your trip back home.

OBSERVATION POINTS

City Hall Observation Deck
414 East 12th Street
(816) 274-1444
www.kcmo.org
The only place to get a better look at the city is

from an airplane. Our stunning art deco–style City Hall provides a breathtaking view from its thirtieth floor open-air deck 425 feet above downtown. And while you're waiting for the elevator, check out the friezes and celestial-themed lighting fixtures in the lobby. The art continues outside with sixteen panels just above the sixth floor that depict major events in our city's history. This steel and limestone stunner, designed by architect firm Wight & Wight, was completed in 1937 at a cost of $5 million. The deck is open Monday through Friday from 8:00 a.m. to 4:15 p.m. To reach it take the lobby elevator to the twenty-eighth floor, and then take the stairs. There's no charge.

Cliff Drive
Gladstone Boulevard and Elmwood
www.cliffdrive.org
You're just in time to enjoy this 6-mile roadway that was recently restored to its turn-of-the-twentieth-century splendor. Although today the view from Cliff Drive isn't so hot—a jumble of train tracks and industrial buildings—it's a pleasant diversion with places to pull over and consider what it must have been like to negotiate the curves in a horse and carriage.

You can thank landscape architect George Kessler for retaining its natural beauty back in 1893 along with the surrounding 282-acre North Terrace Park. In fact you might see rappellers risking knees and elbows on the rugged limestone cliff that gives the road its name. For a more civilized look, stay in the car; that way you can also tool around the historic Northeast area, including the Scarritt Renaissance neighborhood bound by Independence Boulevard and the park. More than 120 homes and churches are listed as local historic landmarks. A good place to start is the Kansas City Museum on Gladstone Boulevard (see details in Museums), a mansion-turned-museum that hints at the area's opulence at one time.

Lewis and Clark Point
Eighth Street and Jefferson
www.lewisandclarktrail.com

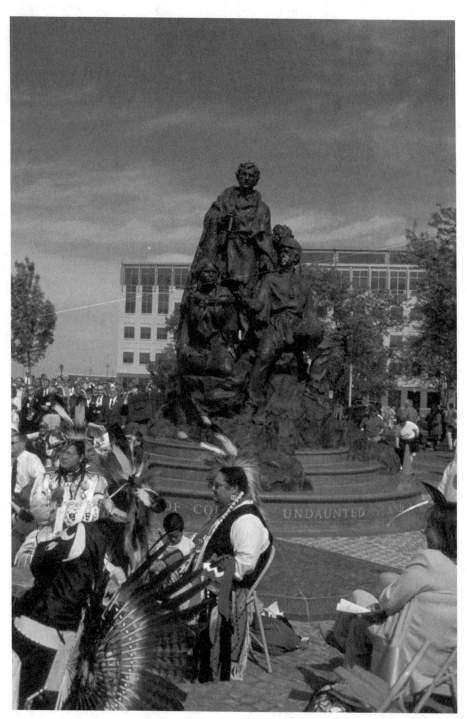

Lewis and Clark statue. CVB OF GREATER KANSAS CITY

i Looking for a bird's-eye view of our beautiful city? Take the elevator to the top of the Liberty Memorial's 217-foot column in the sky. You'll overlook our skyline and, just below the monument, our grand Union Station.

Stand at the bluffs overlooking where the Kansas and Missouri Rivers meet and try to imagine what Meriwether Lewis and William Clark were thinking on September 15, 1806. The expedition team was returning from an arduous trip to Oregon. They were exhausted and no doubt thirsty, but they wouldn't find refreshment here. Clark had deemed the Kaw "disagreeably tasted" on their first stopover two years earlier. No doubt.

The three-day encampment is now memorialized by Eugene Daub's sculpture *Corps of Discovery* at Jefferson and Eighth Streets on the bluffs of what is now Quality Hill. Dedicated in 2001, the 18-foot-high bronze depicts Lewis, Clark, their Shoshone Indian interpreter, Sacagawea, Clark's black slave, York, and Lewis's dog, Seaman. It's the nation's largest monument to honor the expedition. Check the back of Seaman's tail for a surprise: the artist's face!

OUT AND ABOUT

Deanna Rose Children's Farmstead
138th Street and Switzer Road
Overland Park, KS
(913) 897-2360
www.opkansas.org
Let's see: Old McDonald had a pig, and a cow, and a goat . . . and a *bison*? You'll find them all, along with chickens, sheep, and owls, at this fun-for-all twelve-acre farm in south Johnson County. It opened in 1976 and in 1985 was named to honor Deanna Rose, an Overland Park police officer killed in the line of duty.

It's always a fun excursion but especially so in spring, when newborn animals are popping up like daffodils. Although it's fun to watch them be bottle-fed, it's a positive giggle fest to feed the goats from your hands.

New to the area are a dairy barn, log fort, a country schoolhouse circa 1900, and a Kanza Indian encampment, complete with earthern lodge and tepees. For details skip over to Kidstuff.

The Kansas City Zoo
6800 Zoo Drive
(816) 513-5800
www.kansascityzoo.org
Take a wild animal safari without leaving the country at this natural-habitat zoo set in 200 rolling acres. The areas are divided into different "countries," which you can visit by walking, riding the train, or taking a safari boat ride. In Africa you'll see elephants giving each other mud baths to cool off on a summer afternoon, herds of sable antelope and impala running free, and giraffes necking. The Australian exhibit includes an aviary with twenty species of birds and mammals, and acres where kangaroo, emus, and dingoes roam. Here's where you can catch a ride on a camel or pony. Some of the older exhibits remain favorites, especially with kids who love to watch the sea lions splash in the pool.

Nocturnal Safaris give children a chance to play zookeeper for one night at a campout under the stars. This exciting, educational program is ideal for families, Scouts, and church groups for ages six and up. Reservations are on a first-come, first-served basis starting March 1.

You can also catch a flick (a really big one) at the Sprint IMAX Theatre, which boasts a 6½-story-tall screen and 12,000 watts of digital sound. Call (816) 871-IMAX for day and evening show times and ticket

i If you plan to visit such attractions as the Kansas City Zoo or the Nelson-Atkins Museum of Art more than once, you might save money by purchasing a membership card. Benefits often include free or discounted admittance, discounts on food or gifts, and invitations to special events. And a season pass at Worlds of Fun can quickly pay for itself.

Kansas Speedway. CVB OF GREATER KANSAS CITY

information. You can attend IMAX without visiting the zoo (tickets range from $4 to $10), but the best value is a combination ticket. Read more in Kidstuff.

Kansas Speedway
1333 Meadowlark Lane
Kansas City, KS
(913) 328-RACE (7223)
www.kansasspeedway.com
"It's purrrty," drawled NASCAR legend Richard Petty when he first saw this $260 million ICS-owned facility that opened in June 2001. It's also biiiig. In fact you could fit both Kauffman and Arrowhead Stadiums and their parking lots in the racetrack's infield. And while size does matter, this 1½-mile tri-oval track was designed for the comfort and convenience of the fans and racing. One example is the infield Fan Walk that gives racing

fans an up-close look at the garages, inspection stations, and Victory Lane. You can lap up more information in the Sports chapter.

Powell Gardens
1609 Northwest U.S. Highway 50
Kingville, MO
(816) 697-2600
www.powellgardens.org
This road trip for the soul begins with a 30-mile drive out of town, just enough time to listen to Vivaldi's Four Seasons while you anticipate what's coming up . . . literally. With 915 acres of perennial gardens, a shady rock and waterfall trail, wildflower meadow, and a lovely island garden set in the twelve-acre lake, the garden seems to offer some new display or event to treasure every spring. One of our favorites is the "Social Irrigation" cocktail party during every full moon in the

summer. Daiquiris and daylilies—we'll drink to that. Tickets are $15 for nonmembers, $10 for members, and reservations are required. And a 3.25-mile nature trail, a haven for butterfly- and birdwatchers, winds through lush forests and past orchids with perhaps a deer or two to spy. You can read more about this magical place in Parks, Lakes, and Recreation.

TOURS

Boulevard Brewing
2501 Southwest Boulevard
(816) 474-7095
www.blvdbeer.com

Since 1989 John McDonald has been single-handedly (well, actually he has 74 helpers now) resurrecting Kansas City's 150-year-old tradition as a brewery town. That's when he rolled out his first barrel of Pale Ale, and he has since added brews like Unfiltered Wheat, Dry Stout, and Bully! Port, which won a gold medal at Chicago's Real Ale Festival.

The quality remains the same, but John's upping the quantity, thanks to a $25 million, 70,000-square-foot expansion that opened in September 2006. So that's what selling 1.4 million kegs will buy you! The new facility will help quench a lot more thirsts; the goal is to release 700,00 barrels per year. Alas, it's available only in eleven states, but that's how John keeps on top of the quality.

You can get a minilesson on brewing on the Web site. Better yet, hop to it and attend a tour, Wednesday through Saturday by reservation only. You can also purchase some great merchandise with the company's cool logo at the brewery, online, and by phone.

Federal Reserve Bank of Kansas City
925 Grand Boulevard
(816) 881-2000, (800) 333-1010
www.kc.frb.org

If you promise not to walk in and chirp, "Show me the money," we'll let you in on this interesting tour. The guided walk-through includes an overview of the Fed's responsibilities in mone-

tary policy and regulation and a look at the bank's operating areas. The real fun comes, though, when you see the high-speed sorter that can count, sort, and destroy cash faster than a sixteen-year-old daughter: up to 100,000 bills an hour. The Money Museum tells the story of U.S. currency from its start during George Washington's administration to the current electronic processes. Coin collectors in particular will find the museum interesting. Tours, which last about ninety minutes, are given at 9:30 a.m. and 1:30 p.m. Monday through Friday. Call for groups of six or larger. And leave your money at home; the tour is free. Please note that the bank is moving to new headquarters near Crown Center. Call before planning your trip.

Harley-Davidson Final Assembly Plant
11401 North Congress
(816) 270-8488, (877) 883-1450
www.harley-davidson.com

Get your motor running at this facility, where you can watch the assembly-line action and drool over some shiny new rides. Tours are free, but there are a few rules. Children must be at least twelve years old and accompanied by an adult. No open-toed shoes are allowed. Anyone over eighteen will need a photo ID. Cameras are prohibited in the factory area, and all visitors will pass through a metal detector. But don't worry. Lockers are available to store your camera and the four pounds of keys that held up the security line.

Tours last approximately one hour. We suggest you call ahead, because tours are not available on holidays, during summer and Christmas shutdown, and when the plant is off-limits during special production work. The museum and tour center are open from 8:00 a.m. to 3:00 p.m., and logo merchandise is available in the gift shop. Some enthusiasts barely make it past the parking lot, which looks like one gigantic Harley dealership.

Historic Kansas City Foundation
201 Westport Road
(816) 931-8448

Some of us consider this passionate group our city's best friend. The foundation began in 1974 when concerned citizens, led by the irrepressible Jane Fifield Flynn, began trying to save historic structures from demolition. Since then they've rescued beauties like the Coates House, the President Hotel, and a group of apartment buildings on the Plaza known as Poets' Row. The group gives several public walking tours a year to showcase a different neighborhood or area such as Hyde Park, Union Station, and the Garment District. During these time-machine travels, volunteers describe architecture and tell interesting tidbits about famous residents. Most tours simply require showing up at an appointed time and paying $3 or so; others require preregistration and $10 to $15 each.

The foundation also hosts private walking tours for groups of ten or more with a two- to three-week advance notice. The donation is $5 per person. Tours last from one to two hours and some are adaptable for vans or buses. Potential areas include downtown's art deco buildings, River Market, 18th and Vine, and Northeast neighborhoods. Volunteers are also available for speaking engagements.

Kansas City Star Press Pavilion Tour
www.kcstartours.com

You read it here first, folks. The *Star* boasts one of the most modern newspaper plants in the world—certainly the prettiest one. That's it, the glowing green-glass rectangle just south of downtown. Two city blocks long with more than 420,000 square feet within four levels houses four 68-foot-tall Commander presses. These highly automated presses are fun to watch. For safety reasons, tourgoers must be at least eight years of age. There are other restrictions posted on the registration form available on the Web site. Note that there is considerable walking on the tour, but hey! To see how they print enough papers for one million readers a week, it's worth it. The *Star* also has an impressive number of items available for sale, including books.

The Roasterie
1204 West 27th Street
(816) 931-4000
www.theroasterie.com

Coffee is routine to most people; hit the button, wait for the hot brown liquid to appear. Slurp. Repeat. Well, we're not most people and we appreciate the talent in buying the best beans, lovingly roasting them, and giving them fun names like Full Vengeance and Nitro. The Roasterie produces award-winning coffee that is available at most local supermarkets, many of our fine restaurants, and online. And now you can learn how to savor the aromas and nuances that put coffee in the same category as wine and chocolate during an interesting, educational tour. Tours are offered every Saturday at 11:00 a.m. and reservations are a must. We're betting they have coffee waiting.

THE ARTS

Kansas City: the art capital of the world. Well, darn close anyway. When you factor in our museums, art spaces and galleries, orchestras, musical groups and soloists, and millions of dollars of public artwork like fountains, sculptures, and murals—well, it's enough to make any city seem downright highbrow. And the phrase "All the world's a stage" may well have been coined for Kansas City; we have more professional theaters than any other city our size in the United States. With more than 300 cultural organizations, our town is an exciting destination and, more important, a great place to live, work, and raise a family.

You can attribute our amazing cache of culture to early philanthropists like William Rockhill Nelson, who decided his adopted hometown deserved boulevards and a world-class art museum; J. C. Nichols, who gave us enough fountains to make even Rome seem second-rate. That city may boast more fountains, but we have more that actually work.

Current-day angels with names like Hall, Helzberg, Bloch, Kemper, and Kauffman keep the "home is where the art is" tradition going. And now they, along with thousands of musicians and singers, artists, writers, poets, and dancers who call Kansas City home, would like to share the wealth with you.

The listings in this chapter are presented in alphabetical order by category. All organizations are located in Kansas City, Missouri, unless otherwise noted.

ART MUSEUMS

The Kemper Museum of
Contemporary Art
4420 Warwick Boulevard
(816) 561-3737
www.kemperart.org

This dynamic art space features a dazzling core collection that includes work by Georgia O'Keeffe, Jasper Johns, Robert Motherwell, and Frank Stella. The museum also presents exhibits taken from its permanent collection as well as several shows a year starring internationally known artists such as Dale Chihuly and Herb Ritts. It's easy to find the place; just look for a gigantic spider sculpture on the front lawn. Yikes! The museum is open Tuesday through Sunday. Call for the times. Admission is free. The Kemper is described in detail in Attractions.

The Nelson-Atkins Museum of Art
4525 Oak Street
(816) 561-4000
www.nelson-atkins.org
This magnificent neoclassic building put Kansas City on the art map, not just in the country but also in the world. Along with pieces by Rembrandt, Renoir, and Caravaggio, the Nelson boasts one of the world's finest Oriental collections and more Henry Moore sculptures than anywhere outside the artist's hometown. Thanks to the extraordinary Bloch Building expansion, there's 70 percent more to love. We've included a close-up on the Nelson in the Attractions chapter. The museum is open Tuesday through Sunday.

i Find out about 150 other arts organizations, from individual graphic artists to puppeteers to orchestras, at the Arts Council of Metropolitan Kansas City Web site, www.artslinks.org. You'll also see a listing of events happening in and around Kansas City.

Nelson-Atkins Museum of Art. CVB OF GREATER KANSAS CITY

Nerman Museum of Contemporary Art
Johnson County Community College
12345 College Boulevard
Overland Park, KS
(913) 469-8500
http://gallery.jccc.net

How did we get so lucky? Two fabulous new art galleries opening in one year? We'd just put away our tuxes and gowns from celebrating the fabulous Bloch Building expansion at the Nelson-Atkins Museum when the invitation to the Nerman Museum's gala arrived.

Designed by esteemed architect Kyu Sung Woo, this $15 million museum—the largest contemporary art museum in the four-state region—has placed firmly Kansas on the international art scene.

The stunning minimalist gallery makes art the star with lots of white, light, and open spaces. And if you're wondering what a world-class museum is doing on the campus of a community college, you do not go to the head of the class. The new space is simply a way to display more of the already stellar collection that has been inside and out of the school for years. Central to this has been the Oppenheimer Sculpture Garden, gifts of Tony and Marti Oppenheimer. The couple donated to the new museum's acquisitions as well; the museum takes its name from major donors Jerry and Margaret Nerman and their son Lewis.

Read more about this glorious new space in Attractions. And during your tour, if you see a guy with a permanent grin on his face, that's Bruce Hartman, the museum's director. He's asking himself the same question: "How did I get so lucky?"

Welcome to the 'artland

You won't need a ticket to see some of Kansas City's most exciting odes to culture. Art is all around us, gracing parks and shopping areas, defining neighborhoods, fronting office buildings and libraries, providing beauty on brick walls. It's our public art, and many newcomers to our town are simply blown away at the amazing array.

In Attractions we listed two areas, Crown Center and the Country Club Plaza, that are really outdoor art galleries filled with sculpture, mosaics, and fountains. Tim Janicke, esteemed photo editor of the *Kansas City Star* Sunday magazine, collected a stunning array of our public art in a book, *City of Art*. It's available in local bookstores or through the *Star* (816-234-4436). While you're waiting for your copy, we'll take you on a brief tour of some of our favorite outdoor art, our fountains.

Our city's most beautiful landmarks were originally established to fill the needs of people and provide water for horses. There were plenty of takers; in 1910 the equestrian population of Kansas City was 70,000. Later fountains fed our desire for beauty and celebration. The City of Fountains Foundation (816-842-2299, www.kcfountains.com), established in 1973, partners with the Parks and Recreation Department of Kansas City to maintain existing fountains and help establish new ones. The foundation has a beautifully illustrated brochure to help you locate our liquid art around town.

The InterContinental Hotel
Corner of Wornall Road and Ward
Parkway
The hotel's front is defined by one of the tallest man-made fountains, a concave curtain of water 56 feet wide and 17 feet high. The waterfall provides a backdrop for a sculpture of the goddess of the hunt and her entourage of cherubs. Diana has an arm raised as if taking in the magnificent scene before her. But we think she's actually saying, "Hand me one of those fluffy robes, will ya?"

J. C. Nichols Memorial Fountain
47th Street and Nichols Parkway
Kansas City's signature fountain was dedicated in 1960 to the memory of J. C. Nichols, the developer of the Country Club Plaza, and Mr. Fountain as far as we're concerned. He was instrumental in turning our town into a water wonderland by acquiring fantastic fountains from Europe and shipping them home. This particular beauty depicts four equestrian figures that each represent a famous river of the world. The multiple water jets spray 30 feet from the center. Even in winter, when part of the fountain has become a blue ice sculpture, it is magnificent.

Fountain Displays
Forget statues on horseback; these three newer fountains offer gushing geysers. The Henry Wollman Bloch Fountain, in front of Union Station, sends dancing water 120 feet high, then lingers in mid-air before crashing to the

J. C. Nichols Fountain. CVB OF GREATER KANSAS CITY

ground. It propels two tons of water in a single gush—the equivalent of lifting a baby elephant—from 232 nozzles. The Crown Center Fountain offers a dancing water show every hour on the hour from noon until 10:00 p.m., synchronized to music recorded by the Kansas City Symphony. Kids of all ages chase the forty-nine water jets and forty-eight water shooters that spout up to 60 feet in the air. And at the Legends in Village West, wet is the word at the Civic Courtyard Fountain, which offers a two-tiered display that's mesmerizing to watch.

Boy and Frog Fountain
Nichols Road and Central
One of the Plaza's most endearing and amusing fountains, this charmer was purchased in 1929 in Florence, Italy. It shows a toddler who's surprised by a shower from a friendly bronze frog.

The Children's Fountain
North Oak Trafficway and Missouri Highway 9
Local sculptor Tom Corbin truly has captured the fountain of youth in this delightful display of six children frolicking in jets of water. The entire fountain itself is massive; the basin measures 60 feet by 100 feet.

Heritage Fountain
23rd and Topping
This spectacular tower of water in Blue Valley Park can be seen for miles around. Dedicated in 1977, this fountain stands on a site some 400 feet

continued

Local artist Tom Corbin sculpted these frolicking children at this sparkling fountain in North Kansas City. CVB OF GREATER KANSAS CITY

above the base of the park and consists of an 85-foot steel pylon with six-teen water jets at its summit.

The Town of Kansas 1850 Mural
204 West 3rd Street
Although this isn't a fountain, it does have a watery theme. Close to where our city began is a wonderful monument to the thousands of people who came here by way of the Missouri River. A mural on the side of a brick River Market building depicts a steamboat chugging along next to a raft in the muddy Missouri. Cows and a settlement are seen on the bluffs above, all under a cloudy Midwestern sky. The artwork, based on a well-known 1853 lithograph, was painted by Jesus Ortiz, Alisha Gambino, and Joseph Faus. River Market loft developer Mel Mallin came up with the idea, raised the money, got the building owner's blessing, and hired the artists. A few years later, this spunky octogenarian commissioned the same team to paint a mural depicting the Lewis and Clark Expedition's stop at our river area. It's located in the River Market area. Bravo, Mel!

DANCE

Kansas City Ballet
1601 Broadway Boulevard
(816) 931-2232
www.kcballet.org

This 50-year-old company of two dozen dancers is thriving under artistic director William Whitener, who has also contributed some of the troupe's newest ballets. Classical, modern, dramatic, and even comedic work makes up the rich and varied dance tapestry, and each year Whitener expands the repertoire. He enjoys shaking up the audience, and challenging the dancers, by bringing in new choreography and giving vibrant new life to pieces that haven't been performed in decades. One look at *Deuce Coupe,* set to Beach Boys tunes, and you'll realize this ain't your grandmother's ballet.

The tutus come back on, however, for other productions. Four are presented each season, including an annual *Nutcracker,* which is performed at the Midland Theatre during the holidays. Until the company makes its permanent home in the Kauffman Performing Arts Center, the other programs are at the Lyric Theatre. In addition, the dancers take their toe shoes on the road to grace stages at other venues. Ballet in the Park is a delightful series of free outdoor performances held each fall at green spaces throughout Kansas City, including Powell Gardens, the Loose Park Rose Garden, and the Crown Center Pavilion.

The Kansas City Ballet also offers dance classes for adults and children (in fact, only students enrolled in class can audition for parts in the *Nutcracker*). Along with ballet, programs in jazz, tap, yoga, and even tai chi are available. And you might want to keep those dancing shoes handy: Join the Ballet Barre, and you can party with other young professionals ages twenty-one to forty during happy hours before performances, salsa lessons, and other events. Membership dues are just $65; check the Web site.

Kansas City Friends of Alvin Ailey
218 Delaware, Suite 101
(816) 471-6003
www.kcfaa.org

We defy you to keep your feet from tapping along when the dancers match their steps to syncopated rhythms, bending bodies into human pretzels, leotards flying across the stage.

As the only official second home of Alvin Ailey American Dance Theatre, this organization not only hosts performances during the year, but it also instills a love of dance to youngsters through its innovative and powerful AileyCamp program. Designed to reach "at-risk" middle-school students in the Kansas City, Missouri, school district, this six-week summer camp uses dance to develop self-esteem and self-discipline and to foster creativity. It's heartwarming and inspirational to sit in the audience on the night the entire class performs in front of parents and siblings. You'll find yourself calling out right along with the proud parents sitting around you. In addition, KCFAA reaches over 35,000 young people each year through year-round programs that shatter racial, ethnic, and social barriers to promote awareness and respect.

FINE ART SPACES

Pick up a copy of *Review* (816-471-2343), a free publication devoted to visual arts in Kansas City, at midtown galleries and coffee shops and you'll see a list of at least 150 places where artwork is shown and sold on any given day. Although the majority is in galleries and studios, you can also find paintings just hanging around coffee shops, libraries, restaurants, and bank lobbies. Next stop: car washes. Before making your art discovery trek, call for information about hours and days open; a few are by appointment only, and many are closed one or two days a week.

Belger Arts Center
2100 Walnut Street
(816) 474-3250
www.belgerartscenter.org

One of the world's most impressive collections of works by Jasper Johns . . . in a warehouse? That's Kansas City, where art enthusiasts are everywhere. You can make special arrangements to view the John and Maxine Belger Family Foundation's collection of some of America's finest contemporary artists by calling the number above. Better yet, attend any of the regular art showings in the center's immense spaces in the Belger Cartage Services century-year-old building in the Crossroads Arts District. Since the first exhibition in 2000, the Belger has staged more than twenty major art shows, including an exciting variety of 2-D, 3-D, and 4-D artworks.

The galleries are free and open to the public Wednesday through Friday from 10:00 a.m. to 4:00 p.m., Saturday from noon to 4:00 p.m., and open until 9:00 p.m. on the first Friday of each month.

H&R Block Artspace
16 East 43rd Street
(816) 561-5563
www.kcai.edu/campus/artspace

When the Kansas City Art Institute got a grant from a Missouri cultural trust program, it was able to renovate a small warehouse near its campus into a gallery and arts education space. That cash infusion begot more, this time from benefactor Henry Bloch, and voilà: a home-away-from-school for art students. Open since 1999, the gallery hosts several exhibits a year that bring this concrete shell to life with ideas and vitality. Granted, a few exhibits have guests whispering, "Am I missing something, Edna?" but most are insightful works by very talented and as yet undiscovered artists.

Kansas City Artists Coalition
201 Wyandotte
(816) 421-5222
www.kansascityartistscoalition.org

Since 1975 the Kansas City Artists Coalition has provided support, exhibition space, and a voice for established and emerging artists both local and regional. More than 400 artists use its white walls as an ever-changing art gallery, and dozens of artists have nervously watched the public pick apart or praise their first exhibition here. Art lovers show up in droves (and SUVs) every February for the KCAC Benefit Art Auction, when some of the region's best artists donate work to be auctioned to the highest bidder. This is a chance for the artists to give back to an organization that played an important part in their early careers.

The coalition also produces the wildly popular Open Studios Tour every other year, with plans to make it an annual event. The first tour, which took place on two weekends in October 2000, exceeded all expectations. More than 213 artists in fourteen counties participated, gaining a new audience for their work and giving art lovers a chance to meet the artists and their environment. More than 19,000 art pieces were purchased, with total sales of almost $100,000. Not bad for four days!

LITERARY ARTS

Prospero's Books
1717 West 39th Street
(816) 960-7202
www.prosperosbookstore.com

Described as an artistic community masquerading as a used book store, this is the home of The Pit, Kansas City's largest open-mic poetry reading. And if you're picturing a handful of hopefuls waiting their turn, you'll be surprised to see the crowd. Each month between forty and one hundred writers show up to read original works to a sensitive and encouraging audience; after all, most of them have faced that microphone.

Readings begin at 5:30 p.m. on the fourth Sunday of each month. The bookshop also publishes some of the best work in *Prospero's Pocket Poets*. And if music is more to your liking, Prospero's turns into an intimate space for original music by some of the area's best songwriters on most Fridays and Saturdays. You'll hear a broad range of folk, Celtic, punk, jazz, and country.

The Writer's Place
3607 Pennsylvania
(816) 753-1090
www.writersplace.org

Entire books could be written *about,* not just in, this literary community center. The large stone structure with a turret was built as a private residence in 1909, then spent time as an apartment house, brothel, and church until becoming a homey place for writers to take classes, get advice, and share their work in 1992. You might call it a ghostwriter's place, because several workers and guests have seen, felt, or heard a presence they call Clara. Apparitions aside, the center houses a gracious lounge on the first floor, which is used for public events or smaller meetings, plus a gallery displaying art and texts. Classrooms, an extensive library, and offices take up the second and third floors.

The Writer's Place is a wonderful resource for local authors to share ideas, get tips from published writers, or commiserate over rejection letters. Several programs are held throughout the year, including book and poetry readings, a monthly book club, student writing competitions, and art exhibits. The public is invited to attend or participate for a small fee, and membership to the organization costs around $45 a year. And you may get to meet Clara.

MUSIC

Ah, the city where the blues and jazz officially met. Naturally we offer plenty of opportunity to explore the music scene of harmonicas, electric guitars, and drums. If you need a nudge, check out the dozens of nightclubs and restaurants offering live music seven days a week in the Nightlife chapter. But you'll also find classical music throughout our fair city. Hear that? Someone is tuning up right now. Please take your seat.

The Friends of Chamber Music
4635 Wyandotte, Suite 201
(816) 561-9999
www.chambermusic.org

In the late 1970s, Cynthia Siebert took a chance that Kansas Citians would sit through an evening of chamber music, let alone pay for the privilege. She was delighted by the enthusiastic response, and today as executive director she continues to bring in the world's finest chamber music, pianists, and early-music ensembles. To her credit, and to the audience's delight, she seeks out performers who bring passion and a freshness to their craft, not just a famous name. The fourteen-concert series takes place at four remarkable venues: the Folly Theatre, Grace and Holy Trinity Cathedral, Carlsen Center, and Redemptorist Church in midtown. Single tickets are not available but may be purchased in a minimum of three concerts. After that, they figure they have you hooked and you'll gladly pony up for an entire season subscription.

But here's a don't-miss free series for the entire family, Rob Kapilow's "What Makes It Great?" that introduces you and yours to famous musical selections (including Mussorgksy's lush "Pictures at an Exhibition"). Rob deconstructs the piece, asking talented chamber musicians to play bits and parts, asking questions, and generally delighting the audience. Check the Web site for times and dates of these three often sold-out performances, held at the Folly Theatre.

Kansas City Symphony
1020 Central, Suite 300
(816) 471-1100 (office),
(816) 471-0400 (tickets)
www.kcsymphony.org

With the hiring of Michael Stern as musical director in 2005, the symphony got the likable rock star it needed to bring the crowds back. He's handsome, charming, funny, and has a full head of beautiful hair—in short, everything you want in a conductor. A night at the symphony is whatever you make it: black tie or jeans, romance or revelry. Fond memories of the last time you heard "Symphonie Fantastique" or an exciting new venture into the music of Phillip Glass. You'll hear it here first, thanks to a full season that includes a dozen or so classical concerts at the Lyric Theatre, the Music Hall, and other venues such as Yardley Hall at Johnson County Community College.

The symphony also presents a Pops series of crowd pleasers like the Count Basie Orchestra or Neil Sedaka. Its Family Series introduces youngsters to the joy of classical music, pain free. Just try to keep a four-year-old from dancing in the aisle to "Snoopy Does the Samba." The symphony's musicians also take it on the road often for wonderful (and often free) concerts, like Celebration at the Station on Memorial Day, when cannons punctuate "1812 Overture" and fireworks dazzle thousands of patrons sitting in the green space between the Liberty Memorial and Union Station. Tickets vary by performance, with prices ranging from $15 to $40. Check online; the symphony sometimes has nonadvertised deals such as $13 tickets that are upgraded to the best available seats in the house—free. Now that's what we call a musical score!

Lyric Opera of Kansas City
712 East 18th Street
(816) 471-7344
ww.kcopera.org
Not crazy about opera? The Lyric may change your mind. Since 1958 it has been presenting glowing productions that have turned blasé audiences into opera lovers. What's the secret? For one thing, although the performances are in the original languages, supertitles shown above the stage let you know what that large man is bellowing about. Four productions are offered each season, including a blockbuster like *Aida* or *Madame Butterfly* and an American opera (for which supertitles may still be necessary). Long-term subscribers may have noticed an upgrade in singers and production values since 1998, when artistic director Ward Holmquist took the helm.

While the opera company awaits its new space in the Kauffman Center for the Perform-

ing Arts, it will continue to take the Lyric Opera stage. Its new office and set design center, in the Crossroads Arts District, is close by.

Quality Hill Playhouse
303 West 10th Street
(816) 421-1700
www.qualityhillplayhouse.com
When you're hungry for a sophisticated evening filled with the singable tunes of Cole Porter, George Gershwin, and Henry Mancini, this intimate theater has your seat ready. J. Kent Barnhart serves as emcee and musical director—and brilliant pianist—for cabaret reviews that have covered themes such as great duets, musical divas, and Sinatra songs. Kent's other talent (along with a quick wit and perfect timing) is choosing the right singers for the selections. In Kansas City he's blessed with some standout performers who can give us goosebumps with showstoppers like "My Man" from *Funny Girl* and "Try to Remember" from *The Fantasticks*.

The two-hour shows are slick and professional, and the small, seven-row arrangement ensures a great seat. The audience laps it up seven nights a week. To be sure, more than a few get in with a senior discount, but you'll also see plenty of young music lovers in the audience, especially those who appreciate haunting lyrics and music to hum all the way home. Quality Hill Playhouse produces four shows a year, with performances every night and matinees on Sunday and some weekdays. Single tickets are $23, with discounts for groups and seniors. Covered parking is adjacent to the playhouse, and Sienna Bistro (816-527-0220), serving lovely pastas, fish, and steaks, is right next door.

THEATER COMPANIES

Actors Theatre of Kansas City
30 West Pershing Road, Suite 850
(913) 677-5374
www.kcactors.com
This is a relatively new troupe of some of the city's most talented thespians who banded

together to present plays that don't get as much, well, play as they should. *Who's Afraid of Virginia Woolf?* made audience members appreciate their own spouses during a recent series, for instance. The productions aren't elaborate, but we'd put the quality of the acting against any in the country. ATKC schedules three plays each season during the summer, all performed at the H&R Block City Stage Theatre, relocated in Union Station. Tickets are available through the Central Ticket Office, 4949 Cherry Street in the University of Missouri–Kansas City Performing Arts Center, (816) 235-6222, or on the company's Web site.

American Heartland Theatre
Crown Center, Third Level Shops
(816) 842-9999
www.ahtkc.com

The actors must have been chanting "Break a leg!" nonstop when this theater opened on April 1 more than twenty years ago. Luck was obviously on its side, however, because the American Heartland continues to thrive. What keeps it so fresh is the variety of productions that include musical comedies, mysteries, and drama. Past seasons have offered *You're a Good Man, Charlie Brown, Rainmaker,* and its signature holiday presentation, *Nunsense.* If you don't laugh at the antics of this order of nuns (which includes the hapless Sister Amnesia), you may get your knuckles rapped with a wooden ruler.

The 420 seats rise sharply from the stage, ensuring that everyone has an unobstructed view. Unique features include a full-service

i Not sure what to wear to the ballet, symphony, or opera? Although opening night is usually business dress or evening wear, other performances are typically "anything goes." To learn more, including program guides, terms, and even when to applaud (when everyone else does!), check out the major performing arts' groups' Web sites. They'll also give you age restrictions for children.

bar (patrons can take beverages to their seats), a private suite for thirty-six guests, and free covered parking. Single ticket prices range from $19.00 to $27.50, with the holiday shows costing a few dollars more.

Barn Players
Little Theatre at Shawnee Mission Northwest High School
12701 West 67th Street
Shawnee, KS
(913) 381-4004

"Hey kids! I've got a barn, and my sister can sing and dance. Let's do a musical!" That's probably close to what happened in 1955 when this group held its first production, making it the longest continuously operating community theater in Kansas City. The group presents three productions a year, ranging from *California Suite* to *Little Shop of Horrors.* The group also has a scholarship fund for college-bound high school students interested in the performing arts.

The Coterie Theatre
Crown Center
(816) 474-6552
www.thecoterie.com

This professional theater for young adults has been a Kansas City favorite for more than twenty years, thanks to artistic director Jeff Church's mission to create an experience that all age groups can enjoy—with or without the kids in tow. The Coterie focuses on imaginative adaptations of beloved stories and fairy tales but isn't afraid to tackle deep subjects, like the Holocaust. The artistic integrity is so high that *Travel and Leisure* rated it one of the country's top-ten children's theaters. A new grant is allowing the Coterie to expand its classroom space and construct a lobby. See Kidstuff for information about auditions and tickets.

Heart of America Shakespeare Festival
Southmoreland Park
47th Street and Oak
(816) 531-7728
www.kcshakes.org

One of our most beloved summertime traditions started when a feisty redhead, Marilyn Strauss, brought her Tony award home and decided what this town needed was more Shakespeare. That was more than fifteen years ago, and since then, for four glorious weeks starting in late June we watch sword fights and ladies swooning from balconies as some of the city's finest actors bring the Bard's words to life. It all takes place under the stars in the tiny, urban Southmoreland Park near the Nelson-Atkins Museum of Art. Come early for the pre-show and either bring a picnic basket or purchase anything from hot dogs to salads, kettle corn to snow cones, and even wine and beer at the concession stand. You can rent lawn chairs for $5 rather than lug yours around, or better yet, get a reserved seat up front for $15. Call the office number listed above at least forty-eight hours before the performance date. There's no admission fee, but of course you'll want to donate to keep this wonderful theater experience alive.

Kansas City Repertory Theatre
UMKC Campus, 50th and Oak
(816) 235-2700
www.kcrep.org

From its humble beginnings in a wooden playhouse on the University of Missouri–Kansas City campus in 1964, this company has grown into a nationally respected theater that attracts actors and directors of national and international acclaim. For our money, though, it's the local actors we come to see. Before the curtain rises patrons are usually busy checking the program to see if favorites like Gary Neal Johnson, Merle Moores, and Mark Robbins will be appearing that night.

The Kansas City Rep produces six main productions during its September through June season, each running a minimum of twenty-four times. The repertoire includes classical and contemporary dramas and comedies, each beautifully staged, with costumes and lighting that are always top-notch. The Rep also gives the city a wonderful holiday gift, A Christmas Carol, when artisans and stylists create sets that are more fantastic every year. The not-for-profit organization's success is due in great part to a sense of continuity; in more than forty years it has had only three artistic directors, beginning with Dr. Patricia McIlrath, then George Keathley, who retired after fifteen years. Peter Altman assumed leadership in 2001.

The New Theatre Restaurant
9229 Foster
Overland Park, KS
(913) 649-7469
www.newtheatre.com

This dinner theater puts the emphasis on dinner, with a tempting buffet of entrees and side dishes that might have you wondering why they bother with a show. But you'll be glad you waited for the production; chances are the person on stage is a beloved TV star like Jamie Farr, Marion Ross, or Loretta Swit. With all that, plus nearly 700 seats in a beautiful stepped arrangement that gives everyone a great view, it's no wonder the Wall Street Journal calls this "the best dinner theater in the country."

Founders and co–artistic directors Dennis Hennessey and Richard Carrothers put on five shows per season, four of which star characters like Ritchie's Mom or Hot Lips. But audiences also enjoy seeing local actors on stage, like Lori Blalock, Jim Korinke, and Debra Bluford. Apparently it's a recipe that works. The New Theatre enjoys an average 94 percent attendance fifty-two weeks a year. And 40,000 to 50,000 of those people are out-of-towners, including several hundred who fly in from California and catch a show before heading to Branson or back home. Yes, indeed, it does cater to the mature audience. But you'll also see plenty of young adults laughing at the jokes. Ticket prices start at just $33 including the buffet, but better hurry. The majority of seats belong to season ticket holders.

Starlight Theatre
4600 Starlight Road in Swope Park
(816) 363-7827
www.kcstarlight.com

Starlight Theatre. CVB OF GREATER KANSAS CITY

Starlight opened its theater under the stars on June 25, 1951, with *Desert Song.* At the time about forty professional, self-produced outdoor theaters existed in the country; today only two remain, both in Missouri. During its early days, seasons consisted of ten shows that included operettas and new Broadway musical comedies. One of its unique features came from a disgruntled star. In 1958 Jerry Lewis was unhappy with the distance between the stage and the audience. An extension, paid for by the comedian, was built to cover the orchestra pit and remained in place until a new stage was built in 2000.

One "star" was a hard act to follow. Former President Harry Truman was happy to appear as himself in a play, until an appendicitis attack forced an early curtain call—into a waiting ambulance. By the 1970s, facing the exorbitant costs of mounting lavish Broadway musicals, Starlight turned to variety shows, and attendance dropped every year. Now the big shows are back, with five Broadway-style shows each May through September, including classics like *Sweet Charity* and *Hairspray.*

A $10 million, 12,000-square-foot, fully enclosed stage allows for huge, complex sets, such as a helicopter landing in *Miss Saigon.* The design incorporates two new towers to complement the existing ones that are the theater's trademark.

Tickets cost from $9 to $70—quite a range, but with 8,000 seats the cheap ones seem an acre away from the stage. You can tell the season ticket holders; they come armed with a chair cushion, binoculars, and an umbrella. You should, too. Starlight is also host to several top-name entertainers every year, from James Taylor to the Four Tops.

The audience has ample opportunity to dine under the stars, too. The Applause Club is a catered dining area open to season ticket holders only. The rest of us are happy to make do with the salads and sandwiches in the Encore! Deck. The concession stands sell hot dogs and other treats.

Theater League
Music Hall 301 West 13th Street
(800) 776-SHOW (7469)
www.theaterleague.org

Here's where Kansas City gets to see those thrilling Broadway productions like *Monty Python's Spamalot* and *The Lion King*, not long after they win Tony statuettes in New York. Sets are breathtaking displays, such as a miniature lake lit with thousands of candles for *Phantom of the Opera*.

The venue is pretty spectacular, too: the gorgeous 1930s art deco music hall at 13th and Wyandotte, with romantic private balconies overlooking the stage and sumptuous decor. Theater League mounts four major shows a year as well as special engagements such as concerts. And although individual tickets are available, it's the season ticket holders who get the best deals. With prices ranging from $140 to $200 per season, the package includes first dibs on special engagements and everything from free desserts to 50 percent discounts at several restaurants on the night of the performance.

Theatre in the Park
Shawnee Mission Park
79th and Renner Road
Shawnee, KS
(816) 464-9420 (info line),
(913) 631-7050
www.theatreinthepark.org

A summer night, a star-filled sky, and Curly singing something about a beautiful morning. There are few better ways to spend an evening than watching talented local actors and singers bring new life to classic Broadway shows, especially if you've packed a wedge of cold watermelon in your picnic basket.

The season consists of four musicals, and more than 3,000 people show up each night, far more than just parents of lead actors. The crowd attests to the fact that the talent is top-notch. Ticket windows open at 7:00 p.m., and our advice is to get there early because the line can get long. The programs begin at 8:30 p.m. A concession stand and public restrooms are available. Admission is $5 for adults, $3 for children ages four to twelve, and free for those under four.

Unicorn Theatre
3828 Main Street
(816) 531-PLAY (7529)
www.unicorntheatre.org

"Edgy," even "risky," are words often used to describe the topics portrayed on Unicorn's stage. In fact artistic director Cynthia Levin likes to describe it as contemporary, controversial, and consistent. Naturally it appeals to a dedicated audience of free thinkers who want something more to discuss post-performance than what the protagonist was wearing . . . or not.

The professional theater has produced more than 200 plays, with more than 45 world premieres, since it began in 1974 as an acting workshop in what is now the River Market area. In the late 1990s Unicorn moved to its current location in the midtown business district, transforming an old garage into a modern, intimate arrangement utilizing a thrust stage and a seating capacity of 150. Regular performances are shown Tuesday through Sunday, with ticket prices ranging from $12.50 to $25.00.

THEATER VENUES

The play's the thing—and so is the musical, comedy act, and concert. Kansas City is home to some stellar theaters, including three historic buildings that are nearly as interesting as what's on stage. And you can share in the buzz about our new Kauffman Performing Arts Center, due in 2009.

Carlsen Center and Yardley Hall
Johnson County Community College
12345 College Boulevard
Overland Park, KS
(913) 469-4445
www.jccc.net

Part of the behemoth community college campus on a windswept hill, the Carlsen Center is a 165,000-square-foot complex that houses four theaters, an art gallery, and an espresso bar along with classrooms and offices. Its size allows for a sweeping lobby with an 85-foot glass ceiling above a granite entry floor.

The exterior is brick, with a graceful arched doorway providing the only adornment, but it's the interior bricks that will catch your eye. Kansas artist Donna Dobberfuhl has created a series of figures that portray the history of theater, dance, and music. The carved-brick sculptures appear on the walls facing the entrance to Yardley Hall, an auditorium known for its superb acoustics and comfortable seating. Since its opening in 1991, the space has hosted such productions as Broadway plays and the Moscow State Symphony Orchestra, as well as current popular singers. More than 200 performances are held here every year, making the extensive free parking a real perk.

Folly Theatre
12th and Central
(816) 474-4444
www.follytheatre.com

Our only surviving theater palace from the nineteenth century, the Folly has gone through many names, including the Standard, the Century, Schubert's Missouri, and (unofficially) the Grand Old Lady of 12th Street. Despite a few face-lifts on the inside, the south facade given her by local architect Louis Curtiss is still intact. It's a stately face with simple lines embellished only with an elegant three-story Palladian window.

The theater originally cost $250,000 to build and opened September 23, 1900, with a series of touring vaudeville and burlesque comedies. It continued serving rather blue and rowdy fare until the Schubert family made the twenty-two-year-old legit at last. The Marx Brothers, Shirley Booth, and Humphrey Bogart performed here until once again the feathers were flying. In 1929 an unknown sixteen-year-old named Rose Louise Havoc made her debut here before she adopted her stage name, Gypsy Rose Lee.

The hall limped through the Depression and finally closed in 1974. Two local philanthropists, Joan Kent Dillon and William Deramus III, saved her from the wrecking ball and mounted a community effort to restore her beauty. The Folly reopened in November 1981 and has remained a vital part of our entertainment scene. She hosts the Friends of Chamber Music, the Harriman Arts Program of William Jewell College, and the Civic Opera Theater of Kansas City, as well as an international jazz series. When you visit the Folly, take a moment to realize that her bricks were laid by Civil War veterans.

Kauffman Center for the Performing Arts
16th and Baltimore
(816) 994-7200
www.kcperformingartscenter.org

A new crown jewel for the city is on the horizon—literally—on a hillside setting overlooking downtown to the north and Crown Center and our visual arts districts to the south. The Kauffman Center will be a world-class attraction consisting of 400,000 square feet of space. More than just audiences and civic leaders are thrilled about the news; the $326 million center will be home to the Kansas City Ballet, the Kansas City Symphony, and the Lyric Opera, companies in desperate need of growing room. In addition, the 1,600-seat concert hall and 1,800-seat proscenium theater will attract Broadway shows and other large productions.

The new addition to our cultural landscape comes by way of Julia Irene Kauffman, who heads up the Muriel McBrien Kauffman Foundation, named for her colorful mom. It was her late mother's dream to leave something so vital and lasting that this city would never forget her. Ms. Kauffman has committed $105 million to make that dream come true, one of the largest single gifts to a cultural project in the country. Another $200 million will come from private donors, foundations, and taxpayers.

The architect, Moshe Safdie, who has transformed urban areas from Canada to Jerusalem, is known for dramatic curves, intriguing textures, and a generous use of windows and open space. You can expect to see as many gardens as buildings in the 6-block setting that is scheduled to open in 2009.

The Midland Theatre
1228 Main Street
(816) 471-8600 (event line),
(816) 471-9703 (administrative offices)

Listed on the National Registry of Historic Places, the Midland is the grandest historic theater within a 250-mile radius of Kansas City. It was built by Marcus Loew in 1927 for an extravagant cost of $4 million.

One of only 300 theaters designed by celebrated architect Thomas Lamb, it's often been called Lamb's "favorite theater" and was certainly the most elegant of its day with over 6 million inches of gold leaf. Its five massive Czechoslovakian hand-cut crystal chandeliers, precious antique furniture, and spectacular wood and plasterwork are irreplaceable in today's market. The enormous auditorium seats 2,800 and is five stories high, with balconies and stylish opera boxes. It was the first theater in the country to have air-conditioning and is now among only twenty-five of its kind still standing.

The Midland presented silent pictures and stage shows during its early years. It was purchased by Kansas City's American Multi-Cinema (AMC Theatres) in 1966. The theater showed motion pictures until 1981, when once again it became the venue for Broadway plays, concerts, ballets, and special events. Stars such as Tony Bennett, Dolly Parton, and Harry Connick Jr. have performed on this stage during the past several years.

The Municipal Auditorium,
Music Hall, and the Little Theater
301 West 13th Street
(816) 513-5000
www.kcconvention.com

The Municipal Auditorium, an art deco wonder that was built in 1935 for $6.5 million ($2 million over budget), fills a city block with its hulking mass of limestone. Linear geometric designs and bas-relief medallions are its only external adornments, a severity that makes entering the grand foyer even more of a thrill.

The auditorium houses three large spaces—a multipurpose arena, the Music Hall, and an elegant little ballroom known as the Little Theatre—each with its own lobby, to accommodate any size or type of event including conventions, sporting events, exhibitions, concerts, plays, and lectures. It has been the scene of everything from political conventions to philharmonic performances to circuses.

The arena has seating for 10,500 people, and its unique roof-support system, which eliminated the need for pillars or posts, provides an unobstructed view from every seat. The 92-foot ceiling is high enough for a trapeze, and its 24,000-square-foot floor, built of oak two-by-fours, is strong enough to support an elephant—which it has. More college basketball Final Four games have been played here than in any other building in the nation. Now that's good hang time.

The Music Hall, built in 1936 as a home for the Philharmonic Orchestra, is entered through a splendid art deco lobby on 14th Street. It features pale gray Italian marble floors and walls, which create a nice echo until the room fills with theatergoers; chandeliers; and beautiful floor-to-ceiling murals. It seats 2,500 patrons in elegant splendor amid tones of burgundy, deep green, and gold and has an antique pipe organ that once accompanied silent movies. The Little Theatre is accessed through a door on 13th Street and boasts a sweeping doublewide stairway. The space seats 3,000.

KIDSTUFF

As you'll see, Kansas City is a great place to be a kid, raise a kid, or act like a kid again yourself. You can even pet a kid at a children's farmstead in southern Johnson County. From hands-on creative workshops to captivating historic sites, there's something for every tot and teen in your entourage. In fact, we're so kid happy here we don't have just one action-packed theme park, we have two.

And just to prove you can bring a kid to culture and still make him think, Kansas City offers lots of fascinating museums, including the interactive Science City at Union Station. There are plenty of indoor and outdoor activities so that youngsters can burn off all that energy, as well as kid-approved restaurants where they can gain it back.

Although we adore children, we're also partial to parents. That's why we tell you about several attractions that are cheap or absolutely free. You'll find other family activities and events to help fill the photo album in the Festivals and Annual Events chapter and the Attractions chapter. But the following ideas should keep the youngest members of your party busy for days. Soon you'll be hearing, "Mom? Dad? Can we move to Kansas City?"

The attractions in this chapter are listed alphabetically by kid-friendly category. All are located in Kansas City, Missouri, unless otherwise noted.

CREATIVE KIDS

Build-A-Bear Workshop
95th Street and Quivira
Overland Park, KS
(913) 307-0328
www.buildabear.com
Now here's a souvenir from Kansas City that won't land in the closet the moment you get home. At this colorful workshop in Oak Park Mall, your child gets to help construct his or her very own best buddy from twenty-five animal styles. The fun comes when they make it their exclusive toy by selecting a sound to place inside or even recording their own voiced message to replay any time they want. "You're the coolest!" comes to mind.

Your child can help create a birth certificate with name and "date of birth" or choose from seven storybooks starring the new pet. After a quick stuff and fluff, it's time to choose an outfit and accessories from a wardrobe of over 200 items. And to take the new furry friend home in style, there's even a Cub Condo carrying case. The basic plush animals are priced from $10 to $30; outfits are an additional charge.

Kaleidoscope
25th Street and Grand Boulevard
(816) 274-8301
www.hallmarkkaleidoscope.com
Every child is an artist at this workshop run by Hallmark Cards. In fact, the entire place looks like a giant greeting card, with themed areas where children ages five through twelve can spend an hour creating masks and other crafts with leftover materials from the card maker. Rather than being given a set project, children are encouraged to explore their own sense of color and design. Your child can come away from this visit with a new sense of expression and self-confidence.

Admission is free, limited to one fifty-five-minute session per child, and open to walk-in visitors on Saturday throughout the year and Monday through Saturday in summer. Reservations are required on weekdays during the school year and for groups of six or more at any time. Tickets are available starting at 10:00 a.m.

for walk-in sessions. Children must be accompanied by an adult. Call to check on what hours it's open.

Kaleidoscope also offers wonderful workshops taught by staff and volunteers where children can build or decorate a take-home project like a birdhouse or tie. There's a small fee for these programs, and reservations are required. And don't miss the free worksheets that detail additional activities families can do together at home; they're available at the receptionist's desk on the way out and can be downloaded from the Web site; get your five-year-old to show you how!

And here's another bonus: The Hallmark Visitor Center, also in the Crown Center complex, gives children in third grade and above a chance to learn how the Hallmark artists make their magic. Adults will adore the displays as well.

The center includes an interesting film on the creative process as well and an exhibit about Hallmark's history. Did you know it started right here in Kansas City? Kids get to make a bow to take home, and artists are around to demonstrate their skills and answer questions. This is free as well, but reservations are required for groups of ten or more or if you would like a guided tour. The visitor center is open Monday through Saturday. For more information call (816) 274-5672 or point your paintbrush to www.hallmark.com.

The center is wheelchair accessible and can accommodate children with special needs. Call the main number to determine which sessions are best for your child.

Though times and options change during the year, for the most part Kaleidoscope offers independent art sessions (when kids can create separately from the parent or caretaker) for ages five to twelve from 10:00 until 11:00 a.m. Monday through Friday; reservations are required. Walk-in independent art sessions are open beginning at 11:15, with another session starting at 12:30 p.m.

Adults get to play, too, at Family Art Sessions, which take place in the afternoon and on Saturdays. There must be one adult for every four children. Reservations are required for groups of twenty or more. Tickets are available starting at 9:30 a.m. at the entrance.

HAVE A BALL

Cool Crest Family Fun Center
10735 East Missouri Highway 40
Independence, MO
(816) 358-0088
www.coolcrest.com

The Patterson family has been entertaining everyone from tiny tots to tottering grandparents since 1950 at this 4½-acre playground. There's something to keep everyone happy, including four eighteen-hole miniature golf courses (watch the Green Dragon hazard; it's a doozie), go-karts, batting cages, and a 7,000-square-foot game room with video and pinball machines galore. The nifty fifties-style pizzeria serves up cheesy pies plus hot dogs, ice cream, and slushees. Cool Crest is lovingly maintained and seems to have another new attraction every year. Event planners can help make sure your birthday party or group outing is a success. Cool Crest is open year-round, and golf is available when weather permits. Prices vary based on activities. Because the hours vary depending on the day, call ahead for details.

Family Golf Park
1501 Northeast MO 40
Blue Springs, MO
(816) 228-1550
www.familygolfpark.com

If your kids can't find something exciting to do at this huge play area, it's time to ship them home. This beautifully landscaped park features thirty-six holes of miniature golf that wind through a lake setting, a par-3 golf course, putting green, game arcade, and bumper boats. Ker-splash! The golf practice facility is open year-round, and golf lessons are available for ages eight through twelve and thirteen through sixteen. Hours are 8:30 a.m. until 10:30 p.m. weekdays and until

11:30 p.m. on Friday and Saturday. Rates vary depending on the activities. Group packages make this an ideal place for kids' birthday parties. The staff can even arrange for pizza delivery and ice cream. And big people, listen up: You can reserve the golf park for corporate outings. Activities may include miniature golf, water balloon toss, bumper boat relay, and even a hula-hoop contest (sorry, sir—you'll have to ditch that tie). Check online for options and prices, or give them a call.

Incred-A-Bowl
8500 West 151st Street
Overland Park, KS
(913) 851-1700
www.incredabowl.com
When former Royals pitcher Danny Jackson and his wife, Jody, couldn't find an entertainment center the entire family could enjoy, they built one themselves, and it's a beauty. This 65,000-square-foot, state-of-the-art center includes a forty-lane computerized bowling alley, an arcade filled with more than a hundred of the latest interactive and virtual reality games, a three-story set of play tubes for the tikes, a new laser tag center, and a miniature golf course. Whew!

The complex's claim to fame, however, is Cosmic Bowling every Friday and Saturday night until 1:30 a.m., with groovy black lights, fog, glow-in-the-dark balls and pins, and upbeat music. Incred-A-Bowl also has a pro shop, gift store, and snack bar. Now if only those shoes weren't so dorky.

Call Incred-A-Bowl for opening and closing hours.

Jaegers Subsurface Paintball
9300 Northeast Underground Drive
(816) 452-6600
www.jaegers.com
What a brilliant use of our subterranean limestone caves! With 180,000 square feet in this paintball arcade, there are plenty of places to hide and go . . . splat! Players can choose from six to ten different games for any number of participants. The center is open daily

at various hours. Call for details. A three-hour session, including gun and paintballs, costs around $25 per player. Jaegers is located east of Interstate 435 and just north of the Missouri River.

HOT DOG! TIME TO EAT!

The Crayola Cafe $
2450 Grand Avenue
(816) 398-4820
www.hyattkc.com/crayola
This colorful restaurant in the Crown Center Shops caters to kids with a tin of crayons and ready-to-color placemats at each seat. And you'd swear a five-year-old—and a picky eater at that—dreamed up the menu. It features grilled-cheese sandwiches (crustless, of course), a double-decker peanut butter club, chicken drumsticks, and mac and cheese. Over twenty specialty fountain drinks and fruit smoothies keep the blenders buzzing. Parents can order theirs with alcohol (the piña coladas are great) along with grown-up menu items including sandwiches, salads, and pastas.

After lunch or dinner you can extend the color-me-happy experience at the adjacent Crayola Store. Along with oodles of crayons and logo-emblazoned clothes and accessories, you'll find interactive computerized displays and games.

Fritz's Railroad Cafe $
2450 Grand Avenue
(816) 474-4004
www.crowncenter.com
Get your vacation on track at this train-inspired restaurant in the Crown Center Shops. It's quite a trip to call in your order on the telephone at your booth and then watch it chuga-chug-chug to your table on an overhead electric train. The outrageous fun will delight your kids, and so will the menu of made-to-order burgers, hot dogs, sandwiches, and shakes. Parents will get on board as well, with tasty items like bowls of Fritz's famous chili.

Rainforest Cafe $–$$
11327 West 95th Street
Overland Park, KS
(913) 438-7676
www.rainforestcafe.com

Your kids will be wide-eyed and wonderstruck even before they sit down at this restaurant in Oak Park Mall. In this lushly vegetated place, thunder cracks, animals seem to come to life, and tropical fish mesmerize onlookers. It's almost too stimulating to eat, but when kids are handed their very own menu they usually change their minds. While they're having a blast, your children will be learning about ecology from talking trees and jabbering birds.

Birthday packages include invitations, treasure maps with crayons, and safari pith helmets (say that fast three times!). As for the food, prices are a bit high but portions are huge—and for a trip to the Amazon without boarding a plane, it might be worth it. There's even a full bar. Reservations are a must, particularly on weekends; walk-ins can expect at least an hour's wait.

T-Rex Cafe
1847 Village West Parkway
(The Legends of Village West) $–$$
Kansas City, KS
(913) 334-8888
www.trexcafe.com

Turn a corner at the shops in the Legends and—eeek! You've just come face-to-ugly-face with a life-size dinosaur! The first T-Rex in the country serves up fun, food, and even a little education for kids of all ages. From the moment you enter the doors, you're transported to a fascinating world filled with enormous animatronic dinosaurs. Even the kitchen gets in the act with a wood-burning oven, serving up prehistoric pizzas and rotisserie chicken. Little ones can tear into mac 'n' cheese or Dexter's Dino Dogs (three mini hot dogs), while carnivorous adults will be sated by a rib-eye steak or barbecue ribs.

Before or after the meal, eager tykes can unearth the past in the interactive Paleo Zone. Excavate fossils in the Discovery Dig, explore the mine to find hidden treasures, or pan for precious stones in the Discovery Creek. So that's where I dropped my wedding ring!

To remember the visit, T-Rex offers a wide variety of souvenirs including T-shirts and caps. Kids can even make their own new best friend in the first-ever Build-A-Dino Workshop. But for us, our memories of the Chocolate Extinction will do nicely; this brownie cake topped with ice cream, drizzled with fudge and caramel sauces, and topped with Butterfinger crumbs brings new meaning to the phrase "to die for."

ICE IS NICE

Crown Center Ice Terrace
2450 Grand Boulevard
(816) 274-8411
www.crowncenter.com

Kansas City's only outdoor ice rink is a scene worthy of Currier and Ives: couples, arm-in-arm, gliding across the ice to music, children in snowsuits making frantic arm circles to keep from falling . . . oops, too late. The setting for this living Christmas card is Crown Center, which appropriately enough is the Hallmark Cards headquarters. A free-form tent provides shelter so even during inclement weather the ice is perfect.

The terrace is open seven days a week, 10:00 a.m. to 9:00 p.m. from November through March. Fees are $6 per person and free for adults over sixty and children five and under; skate rental is $2. Groups of twenty or more save the rental fee, and the rink is available for private parties before or after regular hours; reservations are necessary for these activities. Bring plenty of quarters for the vending machines that dispense hot cocoa and cappuccino.

Pepsi Ice Midwest Skating Rink and Fitness Center
12140 West 135th Street
Overland Park, KS
(913) 851-1600
www.pepsiicemidwest.com

This sparkling, sprawling center features three ice rinks used for hockey and ice-skating competitions and practice. In fact this facility is home to one of the country's oldest ice-skating groups, the Silver Blades, and the only place in Kansas City to play adult hockey.

The ice is available for free skating at various times during the week, usually from 10:00 a.m. to early afternoon on weekdays, and two sessions on Saturday. Check the Web site or call for specific hours. Fees are $6.50 for adults, $5.00 for children under seven years of age, and $2.00 for skate rental. Lessons are also available, and the rink can be rented for birthday parties. The center also has a fitness center, game room, and deli.

Snow Creek Ski Lodge
MO 45,
5 miles north of Weston
(816) 640-2200
www.skisnowcreek.com

We'll admit Missouri is a few peaks short of Colorado, but that doesn't mean kids can't have fun on skis here. This ski lodge is on a natural hill with a 300-foot vertical drop and enough varied terrain to give beginners and experts a (ski) run for their money. Trails are accessed via two triple chairlifts, one double chairlift, and three rope tows. Thanks to fifty snow-making positions, the snow base ranges from 24 to 60 inches, enough to provide powdery fun for the crowds that pack this place on evenings and weekends. There are plenty of gentle slopes and flat areas for beginners to practice their wedges without getting blasted by the big kids.

A 10,000-square-foot lodge features a cafeteria, bar, and lounge and also houses the ski school and gift shop. The rental shop offers shaped skis with plenty of junior sizes, plus snowboards and ski boards—just the ticket for Jason's Run, an area with enough jumps, bumps, mounds, pipes, and tabletops to keep expert boarders counting the days until Snow Creek opens in mid-December. Weather permitting, the lodge stays open seven days a week through mid-March.

The park is always popular, but never more so than during the midnight sessions when lights turn the ice a pale gold and music adds to the party atmosphere. Midnight sessions start the last weekend in December, and on special nights the lodge is open until 3:00 a.m. Check the Web site or call for specific hours.

Prices range from $19 to $36 for a one-day pass, equipment rental another $16 to $20. Group rates and season passes are available. Lessons cost around $12 an hour for beginner or refresher; private lessons are also available. The Web site shows plenty of photos, including some pretty cool boarding competition. See you on the slopes, you snow bunny, you.

LIONS AND TIGERS AND GOATS, OH MY!

Deanna Rose Children's Farmstead
138th Street and Switzer Road
Overland Park, KS
(913) 897-2360
www.opkansas.org

If your children have never been up close and personal with a cow—or even if they have—they'll love this miniature twelve-acre farm. The farmstead opened in 1976 and in 1985 was dedicated in memory of Deanna Rose, an Overland Park police officer killed in the line of duty. This attraction is so wonderful it was the "extra credit" that earned Overland Park its rating as "most kid-friendly suburb in the U.S." by Zero Population Growth.

Within the barnyard are Bluefeather the bison, plus rabbits, pigs, chickens, sheep, and goats that like to play king of the mountain in their rocky playing field. In spring the place is filled with fuzzy little newborns; it's quite a treat to feed the babies from a bottle. Older animals, particularly the goats, are tame enough to eat from the palm of a two-year-old. Make sure you have enough film for your camera. You'll also want to bring plenty of quarters to buy feed from the vending machines.

The Kansas City Zoo

6800 Zoo Drive
(816) 513-5700
www.kansascityzoo.org

The Kansas City Zoo had humble but heartwarming beginnings when it opened in December 1909 as a shelter for abandoned circus animals. Since then it's gone through as many skins as a python. Two decades ago, as at many other zoos around the country, visitors could only stare at bored animals held behind cages. Today it's entirely different, with 200 acres of natural habitats that let the animals roam freely. And while there's no guarantee you'll see a lion—he may be snoozing in the brush out back—you'll appreciate the realistic environment almost as much as these beautiful beasts.

The zoo is continuing to grow and improve, and its endangered-species breeding programs are getting positive results and accolades from across the country. It's already the tenth largest zoo in the United States and, with 200 more acres available, could become one of the top zoological parks anywhere.

To really experience the new zoo, pick up a map at the entrance or, better yet, download a copy from the Web site to study before you arrive. You may want to alter your choice of footwear! Or take the train, which circles the central portion of the zoo with stops at Australia ($2.50 per person round trip); a tram, which runs to the African Market and back (75 cents each way); or a cruise on Lake Nakuru from the African Boathouse. Combo passes provide unlimited rides for $5 per person. Rides are seasonal; tickets can be purchased at admissions and at stations throughout the zoo. Golf cart tours are now available, or you can rent a stroller or a wheelchair, or even take a Segway Safari (sixty- to ninety-minute tours cost $50 to $70 and are available April through October).

There's plenty to see on foot, and the fun starts right in the front area called the KidZone. That's where you can ride on a cheetah or a rhino. Not real animals, of course; they are part of thirty-six hand-carved wooden animals that grace the new Endangered Species Carousel. Rides are $2 per person. Nearby is the new Discovery Barn, an enclosed, air-conditioned environment that lets you lock eyes with a lemur, squirrel monkey, or fascinating meerkat. Special exhibits take place here as well. Nearby is one of the most popular sights—the sea lion pool, where several times a day the sleek entertainers dive, splash, and bark in unison for their pay—fish tossed by their trainer. Get too close and you could get wet!

The Tiger Trail is a new area of the zoo, celebrating the return of the beautiful big cats. It's mesmerizing to watch the Sumatran tigers, Langka and Manis. Fewer than 250 are thought to exist in the wild. Then say "awww" over the baby red panda and laugh at the antics of the orangutans.

The Australian tour begins at an aviary with over twenty species of birds and mammals from the world's smallest continent. Then watch an entire community of kangaroos—we counted at least thirty—living in a natural habitat. Emus, dingo, wallaby, cassowary, and tree kangaroos can also be spied. If you want a bird's-eye view, take a camel ride; kids can also saddle up for pony rides.

One of the newest additions is the African exhibit, ninety-five acres of land that's home to more than 400 animals. Take a tour through Botswana, where the elephants roam, keeping cool by taking mud baths during summer's heat. Sometimes these pachyderms become Picassos as they paint on canvas, holding brushes in their flexible trunks. You can even purchase one of the masterpieces in the gift shop. Crossing into Kenya, animal lovers can gaze over seventeen acres of plains filled with sable antelope, beisa oryx, impala, and greater kudu . . . as in "kudu hand me the camera, please? I think I just saw a cheetah!"

Hop on a safari boat ride to tour Lake Nakuru, where you might see a baby hippo, or Kifaru Malika, the East African rhino, one of only 660 black rhinos in existence today. Want to see eye-to-eye with a giraffe? Then perhaps you'd like to picnic in the treetops while they forage for food nearby. Our zoo has been blessed with two giraffe births in recent years, and it's always a delight to watch these graceful animals grow up. And up.

In the Congolese Forest you'll see leopard, bongo, and lowland gorillas, and in Tanzania the chimpanzees will keep you entertained. In the final stop, Uganda, you'll view baboons, lemurs, jackals, and an enormous Aldabra tortoise.

The zoo hosts several events throughout the year, including a Halloween party called Boo at the Zoo, and Party for the Planet, which celebrates Earth Day.

Parents will also be glad to know there are several snack bars throughout the zoo as well as two sit-down restaurants. But, especially during the hot days of summer, it's a good idea to bring plenty of water along with sunscreen and hats.

The zoo also features the Sprint IMAX Theatre, which puts you right in the center of the action with a 6½-story-tall screen and 12,000 watts of digital sound. Recent shows included cave explorations and journeys into outer space. Call (816) 871-IMAX for day and evening show times and ticket information. You can attend IMAX without visiting the zoo (tickets range from $4 to $6), but the best value is a combination ticket.

But for our money, the biggest thrill for kids is a Nocturnal Safari, where they spend the night at a campsite after a day of playing junior zookeeper. Next morning, is that a tummy growling or a big cat waking up nearby? Never fear, the campers are safe and breakfast is waiting. This exciting, educational program is ideal for families, Scouts, and church groups for ages six and up. Reservations, which go as fast as a cheetah, start March 1, and the safaris run Friday and Saturday from late May through September. It's one more reason to become a member of Friends of the Zoo; FOTZ members pay only $30, nonmembers pay $35, and nonmembers who live out of town pay $40. Call (816) 513-5700, ext. 24673, for membership information.

The zoo is open daily year-round from 9:30 a.m. to 5:00 p.m. April 1 through October 14 and 9:00 a.m. to 4:00 p.m. the rest of the season, except for Sunset Safaris described above. It's closed Christmas Day and January 1. Admission is $9.50 for adults, $8.50 for seniors, $6.50 for ages three to eleven, and free for two and under. On Tuesday everyone gets in for $6. Parking is free and right outside the entrance.

There are other activities to keep your child, and you, entertained for hours. At the Fishing Pond, you can rent a pole for $3 on a strictly catch-and-release system. Pony rides and hayrides are available for $3 per person from 10:00 a.m. to 2:00 p.m. Monday through Saturday and noon to 4:00 p.m. on Sunday. Brick pathways wind through the park past flowers, vegetables, and shrubbery maintained by the Johnson County Extension Master Gardeners, and there's usually an expert or two on hand to tell you exactly how they get those begonias so perky. New attractions include an Indian encampment, a prairie playground, including a log fort, and a country schoolhouse.

Some of the recent additions are real gems: For around $4 kids can pan for gemstones in the new mine, and a play barn features an open-air bridge leading to two tube slides. The Tiny Tot play area is reserved for children six and under.

When those tuckered-out tykes are ready for lunch, the concession stand is ready with hot dogs and PB&Js, snacks, and juice. Though admission is free, donations are always welcome. The park is open 9:00 a.m. to 5:00 p.m., seven days a week, from early April through the end of October. Summer hours, 9:00 a.m. to 8:00 p.m., are in force Tuesday and Thursday from Memorial Day to Labor Day. Admission is free, but you'll gladly give a generous donation at the door: This kind of good old-fashioned fun is priceless.

LOOP-THE-LOOPS AND LOTS OF WATER

Worlds of Fun and Oceans of Fun
4545 Worlds of Fun Avenue
(816) 454-4545
www.worldsoffun.com
Kansas City sent the fun-o-meter off the charts when Worlds of Fun opened in 1973 with 175 acres of roller coasters, rides, and musical shows. The park continues to add new attractions and thrills every year. The need for speed was answered in 2006 with the Patriot, the longest and tallest inverted roller coaster in the region. Hold onto your hats (and stomachs) through more than two gravity-defying minutes that start by climbing a 149-foot lift hill before plunging you down a curved drop at nearly 60 mph. The 3,000 feet of track include an 89-foot vertical loop, inclined bank curve, and zero-gravity roll. No wonder flip-flops are not allowed! Daredevils must be at least 54 inches tall to ride. The Patriot joins the park's other whiz bang rides for kids of all ages.

The Mamba, ranked as one of the world's top-ten roller coasters, blasts riders 205 feet up, then drops 'em 184 feet at 75 mph. Your kids aren't making faces, Mom, they're just getting 3.5 Gs of fun. The Detonator lifts riders 200 feet in the sky, pausing just long enough to catch a breath before plummeting back to Earth. And the Boomerang is a twelve-story-tall scream machine that rockets forward and backward through corkscrew turns, upside-down loops, and 125-foot lifts at up to 50 mph. You might want to rethink those breakfast plans. Another popular ride is the Timber Wolf, a 4,320-foot roller coaster with hairpin turns and a unique 560-degree helix. A more sedate choice might be the Skyliner Ferris wheel, which provides a panoramic view from 60 feet up.

Worlds of Fun also keeps the smaller kids in mind with their very own Camp Snoopy. In this one-acre playland, the beloved Charles Schultz characters come to life and a small-scale tower ride can make your children feel like the big kids without getting scared. The Peanuts Playhouse is a new addition for the tykes. This three-story interactive funhouse lets kids slide and jump into 5,000 foam balls. A kiddy train and Red Baron airplane ride round out the activities.

To make your stay more enjoyable there are food concessions and stroller rentals available. Worlds of Fun is generally open daily from late May to early September at 10:00 a.m.; closing times are as late as 10:00 p.m. Get out the ruler, folks; here are the pricing policies: A single-day pass for adults and children 48 inches or taller is $37.95 plus tax. For children four years old and shorter than

48 inches, it's $11.95 plus tax. Same price for sixty-two years and up, and apparently they don't care how tall you are, Gramps. Kids age two and under get in free. Parking is $10 a day. Here's a hint: Before coming check the Web site for discounts. For instance, you can save up to $5 by purchasing tickets online, and a Ride & Slide pass gets you into both Worlds of Fun and Oceans of Fun for $49.95; a gate connects the two. And a recent promotion included a meal at Joe Cool's Backyard BBQ and admission for less than the regular admission price alone. Now *that's* pretty cool.

Next door is Oceans of Fun, a sixty-acre wet and wild adventure that includes a million-gallon pool with 4-foot-high waves, sandy beach, children's "sprayground," 43-foot water slides, and Castaway Cove, an adults-only pool with swim-up refreshments. Oceans of Fun is generally open daily from late May to early September at 10:00 a.m.; closing time varies. A single day pass for adults and children over 48 inches tall is $26.95; for children four years old and under 48 inches tall it's $12.95. Prices may change; call for specifics.

Now you can stay where the fun is. The Worlds of Fun Village resort features twenty cottages and twenty-two log cabins (which sleep up to six guests) and eighty-two deluxe RV sites so close to the thrills you can practically feel the whoosh of the Patriot roller coaster. A swimming pool, Jacuzzi, video arcade, laundry room, and shower facilities are available in the clubhouse, and there's twenty-four-hour security. Staying here gets you discounted tickets to the parks. RV sites are open early March through mid-November; cabins and cottages are available early April through the end of October. Check online for rates.

Zonkers!
The Great Mall of the Great Plains
Olathe, KS
(913) 393-3535
www.zonkers.com
Although Zonkers! is located in a huge discount shopping mall, you'll have no trouble finding

the entrance: Just look for the 15-foot-tall grinning ape. Inside is a day's worth of giggles, with bumper cars, laser tag, rides, and sports challenges that pay off in super prizes for ages two to twelve. Toddlers will find tubes, chutes, slides, and soft games that encourage hand-eye coordination. You can test yours by getting a buffalo chicken wing in your mouth without hitting your chin. In fact the Rhino Diner offers something for everyone in your group, including pizza, hot dogs, chicken fingers, milk, and soft drinks. Snacks like popcorn and cotton candy are also available.

Adults are encouraged to enjoy games and rides right along with the youngsters. If you're planning a birthday party for your little one, however, you can leave the entertainment to the friendly staff while you sneak out to shop at a few of the mall's stores. Zonkers! is all indoors, which makes it ideal during rainy or cold weather. It's open seven days a week as late as 10:00 p.m. Call ahead to check on opening and closing times for the day of your visit.

Admission is free, but rides require tokens. An all-day pass is $11.99, $5.99 for kids under 36 inches. Single ride tickets are available for $1.25. The Web site often has discount coupons ready to print.

MUSEUMS FOR YOUNG MINDS

Mention a museum to kids and watch how fast they run from the room. We understand. But if you can get them in the door of one of these exhibitions, you may have a hard time getting them to leave. Pick something your child is passionate about, like dinosaurs, or give him or her something new to learn about, such as astronomy. Suddenly that next science project is in the can.

When available we've listed the museum's Web site so you can preplan your visit to get the most out of your valuable time. Here's another plus: The wide variety of choices means there's something to interest every age group from toddlers to 'tweens and above. And don't miss our premier children's interactive museum, Science City.

Children's Museum of Kansas City
4601 State Avenue
Kansas City, KS
(913) 287-8888
www.kidmuzm.org

Imagine a museum where instead of warning your children to keep their hands to themselves, you get to say, "Go ahead and touch everything." At this wildly popular museum in the Indian Springs Marketplace, hands-on activities are designed to stimulate creativity, jump-start imagination, and teach motor skills and problem solving. There are role-playing sections where kids shop for groceries and ring them up using scanners. Backstage at the theater participants learn about lighting and sound effects and get to try on costumes and face paints. If they have a short poem, song, or speech, they can test it out on stage. And like they say, if you can make it in Kansas City, Kansas, you can make it anywhere. The wellness center has actual medical equipment including a stretcher, hospital bed, and crutches, a good way to help ease a child's fears before a scheduled hospital stay or doctor's visit.

The recycle center gives children, parents, and teachers an opportunity to pick up arts and crafts supplies on the cheap. And usually a new exhibit is making the rounds, such as a giant toothbrush that turns dental health into playtime or a puppet show.

The birthday parties are at the top of our list, however. You can choose a theme such as space travel or go all out with a Victorian Tea Party, where eight to ten little girls dress in fancy hats and clothes, dine on dainty food, and even get a Victorian etiquette lesson from the party hostess. At the Monster Morph, partygoers are transformed into monsters with costumes and face paint. Gruesome cupcakes and mysterious potions are served, a party we guarantee they'll remember for years.

The museum is open year-round, Monday through Saturday, from 9:30 a.m. to 5:00 p.m.,

Sunday 1:00 to 5:00 p.m. During the school year (September through May) it is closed on Monday. Admission is $3.50, free for under age two. Please be aware that the Children's Museum may be moving within the next few years, so please call or check the Web site before making your plans.

Science City at Union Station
30 West Pershing Road
(816) 460-2000
www.sciencecity.com

For children (or adults, for that matter) who consider science their least-liked subject, the Science City interactive museum will change their minds. Here, visitors learn that science is all around us in our everyday lives. And rather than viewing artifacts displayed behind glass, children are encouraged to play, interact, and learn with over fifty hands-on science activities. Land a space shuttle in a NASA-style simulator. Ride a bicycle over a high-wire 30 feet in the air. Explore new and exciting traveling exhibits each year inside the exhibit gallery.

Science City also showcases Dino Lab, the result of a partnership between Union Station and the University of Kansas. You can watch a scientist prepping real dinosaurs for display in this unique laboratory, the largest of its kind in the United States.

And here, they have camping down to a science with overnight camp-ins for children grades three to seven and their parents or group leaders. One adult is required for every five kids. Camp-ins run from 7:30 p.m. until 8:00 a.m. and cost around $35 per child, $25 for adults.

Science City offers plenty of places for pooped-out scientists and their parents to refuel without leaving Union Station. Get a quick bite at Union Cafe in the heart of the station. Or head across The Link, the enclosed elevated walkway kids consider a fun event all by itself, to Crown Center's food court and restaurants. Be sure to get your ticket or hand stamped at Science City if you plan to return.

Science City is open 9:30 a.m. to 5:30 p.m. Monday through Saturday and noon to

Toy and Miniature Museum. CVB OF GREATER KANSAS CITY

5:30 p.m. Sunday. General admission is $9 for adults, $8 for seniors, $7 for children four through twelve, and free for under three years of age. Parking is free for up to three hours; if you're staying longer, get your parking ticket validated at the event you're attending.

The Theater District, which is separate from Union Station, comes alive in the evening with four exciting stages. The City Extreme Screen's five-story-tall screen and two- and three-dimensional projection brings films to life. City Dome combines video, lasers, special effects, and multichannel sound to create a planetarium show that's out of this world. City Stage is a 200-seat live theater venue offering a variety of shows from musical revues to hilarious science demonstrations. Single theater admissions start at $6 for children and $8 for adults or can be purchased in combination with Science City. The Theatre District is open until 10:00 p.m.

and is located in the lower level on the west side of Union Station.

**The Toy and Miniature Museum
of Kansas City
5235 Oak Street
(816) 333-9328
www.umkc.edu/tmm**

Tell your children to "think small," and then take them to this fascinating museum filled with one of the world's most extensive collections of miniatures, antique toys, and folk art. Although girls of all ages are drawn to the exquisitely furnished dollhouses, boys will find plenty of interesting exhibits as well. They seem to love the transportation room with trains chugging overhead, and cast-iron scooters, stagecoaches, and cars are featured below. In the 15 Decades of Toys display, children see simple tin toys from the 1850s, cast-iron banks, an early teddy bear, Barbie and GI

Joe, Cabbage Patch dolls, and toys named for TV celebrities. Kids may get the biggest kick from parents pointing and saying, "I had one just like that!" And nearly everybody giggles at the sight of a naked doll, "Frozen Charlotte," named for a girl so vain she refused to wear her frock and froze to death. Kids, don't try this at home.

One of the museum's most enduring exhibits is the display of miniatures such as an American Indian bowl with 1/8-inch-long frog handles and an 8-inch-high English Georgian secretary desk with working locks and nineteen secret compartments. Wow! These objects are built to scale and often crafted from precious materials such as bone and sterling silver. Others were made of everyday items like wishbones, feathers, and pine cones. And don't miss the maze, a zigzag hallway lined with tiny room settings ranging from a turn-of-the-twentieth-century classroom to a study in the Palace of Versailles. Along with the regular exhibits there is often a special event scheduled, so plan on spending hours here.

Because there's so much to see within the twenty-four rooms on two floors, it's best to request a treasure hunt guide at the welcome center. Along with overviews of the rooms, the guide suggests questions to ask children, providing thought-provoking history lessons along the way. The museum, located on the beautiful tree-lined campus of the University of Missouri–Kansas City, is open 10:00 a.m. to 4:00 p.m. Wednesday through Saturday, and 1:00 to 4:00 p.m Sunday. It is closed Monday and Tuesday, on major holidays, and during the two weeks following Labor Day. Admission is $6 for adults and $4 for children ages three through twelve.

Wonderscope Children's Museum
5705 Flint Street
Shawnee, KS
(913) 268-4176, (913) 268-8130 (recorded message)
www.wonderscope.org
Although it's true that some other museums are fancier than Wonderscope, parents tell us that children beg to return here again and again. Located in the Flint Elementary building, Wonderscope is specifically set up for children from six months to ten years, one of the few places where toddlers will find plenty to do. A favorite section is the grocery store, where children get to shop for pretend groceries and scan the purchases. In the TV area your little Katie Couric or Matt Lauer can direct, film, and read the evening news. In the Raceways room, children can learn about gravity, speed, and acceleration using golf balls . . . are you sure Galileo started this way? And in the Hands of Mercy area, stories of current and former patients at Children's Mercy Hospital help teach children about medical care while they get a gentle lesson about compassion.

Special programs and events range from storytelling to the Gee Whiz science demonstrations. Budding preschool artists will enjoy the art workshops, while some kids head right for the indoor sandbox. Although food isn't allowed in the exhibit areas, you can enjoy lunch and snacks from home in the indoor picnic area; a soft drink machine is available. Wonderscope is also a favorite place for birthday parties; call for information about cost and availability.

The museum is open 10:00 a.m. to 5:00 p.m. Monday through Saturday and noon to 5:00 p.m. Sunday. Admission is $6 for ages three and up, $3 for ages one and two, and free for under one year.

RIDE 'EM COWBOY (AND COWGIRL)

American Royal Museum
and Visitor Center
1701 American Royal Court
(816) 221-9800
www.americanroyal.com
Okay, so your young 'uns don't get to ride a horse or rope a steer at this museum. But they can pretend they're riding Blaze as they try out a variety of saddle styles in the Tradi-

i When visiting Union Station's Science City, don't miss the Henry W. Bloch Fountain out front. This ever-changing liquid ballet pumps 9,225 gallons of water per minute through 232 computer-controlled jets shooting as high as 120 feet.

tions area. Lots of activities and displays keep little cowpokes entertained, and for students and 4-H members interested in agribusiness, this place is a must. The center opened in 1992 as a tribute to the hundred-year-old American Royal, Kansas City's annual horse and livestock shows, rodeo, and parade.

Kids get a kick out of stepping on a live-stock scale to compare their weight to that of pigs, chickens, and feeder steer. They can try their hand at an interactive livestock judging game and check out memorabilia from past rodeos and horse shows. And little girls can dream while gazing at a dazzling crown from the American Royal Queen contest.

The museum is open year-round, and trained docents are available for tours. Activities are scheduled throughout the year, including spring field trips when kids can take pony rides, make butter, grind wheat, plant a soybean, and learn how to line dance. Call extension 125 for specific dates and costs and to make reservations for specific events.

SEE WHAT'S IN STORE

Following are shops where your kids can spend their allowances, or the entire family can play, poke, and peruse without spending a dime.

Brookside Toy & Science
330 West 63rd Street
(816) 523-4501
www.brooksidetoyandscience.com
You don't need a child to enjoy this store; in fact there are plenty of solo adults walking around with big silly grins in place, reliving a childhood for an hour or so. Every conceiv-

able toy, game, and model car kit is here, along with a very nice display of telescopes and microscopes. As the name implies, this is science project headquarters, with science kits and educational toys to pique the imagination. Jim and Mary Jo Ward, who have owned this wooden-floored wonderland since 1964, take pride in the fact that they don't sell toy weapons of any kind.

Even for an independent store (rare these days) prices are competitive with the big chains. And here's another reason to shop here first: Kids are encouraged to bring in old toys in good condition to donate to less fortunate children.

For even more nostalgia, stroll down to the Dime Store, where you'll think you've stumbled into a time warp. This old-fashioned emporium is chockablock with sundries, toys, household goods, art supplies, and plenty of what used to be called penny candy.

Both stores are open daily and are within the delightful Brookside shopping district, an old-fashioned main street filled with unique shops, restaurants, and an ice-cream parlor. See the Shopping chapter for more.

Crayola Store
2450 Grand Boulevard
(816) 274-7500
www.crowncenter.com
Color this store fun! This visual and sensory experience captures the universal appeal of Crayola products in 60,000 square feet of color and creativity. Naturally you'll find all sorts of art supplies, backpacks, and toys starring the crayon colors, but there are also interactive games and a crayon-making demonstration to delight most ages.

Moon Marble Company
600 East Front Street
Bonner Springs, KS
(913) 441-1432
www.moonmarble.com
The owner of this store is a big kid himself, so children always have a blast here. Along with

keeping aisles filled with yo-yos, magic tricks, game boards, and old-fashioned tin toys, Bruce Breslow makes marvelous marbles while you watch. And of course there are plenty of the round wonders to buy—whole buckets of them—as well as collectible marbles from all over. Call or check the Web site for details about when Bruce will be demonstrating his skills.

Reading Reptile
328 West 63rd Street
(816) 753-0441
www.readingreptile.com

Walk into this cheery store once and you'll feel like one of the family. Since 1988 owners Pete and Debbie have been encouraging little readers with story hours, book clubs, and an annual two-day literary love-in when they bring together little readers, parents, and authors. Even when nothing special is happening, the Reptile is a cool place for kids. The Web site is good reading all by itself!

Zoom
Second level, Crown Center Shops
(816) 842-8697

We happen to love locally owned toy stores with cool stuff you won't find in big, national chains. That's the beauty of Zoom; every item is personally chosen because it's fun, educational, or a gift a child will treasure forever. Madame Alexander dolls fit into this last category, and Zoom offers an entire chorus line of the beautifully dressed little ladies. Science kits will fascinate both boys and girls, as will arts and craft packages and other activities for kids from infants to early teens.

Zoom's storefront is pretty spectacular all by itself with giant toys, along with windows and jigsaw tile out front. Inside, most kids beat a fast retreat to the Teddy Bear Express, where they can create their own stuffed buddy, even "custom-eyes" the blinkers. Record a favorite phrase or snippet of a song on the tiny chip to tuck inside. And of course the store carries those wildly desired Webkinz (if you have to ask, you don't have rug rats).

Kites, mobiles, books and more are all delightfully displayed, and what's more, there are people eager to help you choose just the right gift for any age.

If you can manage to drag your child away from the teddy bear outfits, you might notice Zoom's sister store a few doors down, called Bloom! It's a little girl's dream: every conceivable item in the Hello Kitty collection including home decor, hair accessories, fashion, makeup, and jewelry. Other famous and not-so-famous lines are represented here as well. And though the store appeals mostly to girls ages eight through 'tweens, plenty of moms have walked out sporting a pink Hello Kitty headband. Honest, honey, you can wear it, too.

TAKE IT OUTSIDE, KIDS

Kansas City is dotted with dozens of parks and lakes where kids can find enough beaches, nature trails, and campsites to fill a summer or a lifetime. You'll find descriptions of some of our favorite parklands in the Parks, Lakes, and Recreation chapter. In the meantime we'll introduce you to the following places created with kids in mind, including a park that's friendly to wheelchairs. Most parks are open from daylight to dusk daily. Call ahead for opening and closing times.

Ernie Miller Park and Nature Center
909 North Kansas
Olathe, KS
(913) 764-7759
www.erniemiller.com

Introduce your nature boy or girl to this 113-acre park that's been preserved in all its glorious natural state. Three trails wind through ecological habitats such as grassland, meadow, and forest. It's a terrific place for birding—look for woodpeckers, sparrows, owls, and woodland songbirds—as well as sighting other wildlife, like white-tailed deer. Pick up a pocket-sized guide at the Nature Center, where you can spend time with a terrific wildlife diorama and interpretive displays. General hours are 9:00 a.m. to 4:30 p.m. Monday through Saturday and 1:00 to 5:00 p.m. Sunday.

Penn Valley Skate Park
31st and Penn Lane
816-513-7500
www.kcmo.org/parks
Not to be outdone by Overland Park (see listing below), Kansas City Parks and Recreation opened a skate park on the west side of a beautiful urban park. It features a square shallow end with metal coping, clamshell-shaped midsection, and 10-foot-deep huge bowl. The park, open from 7:00 a.m. to 10:00 p.m. (unless wet or rainy) is for skateboarding and in-line skating only, and protective equipment must be used at all times. Competitive or demonstration events require special approval; call the number listed above. One blogger writes that "the trans throws you awesome." We're guessing that's a good thing. For links to other facilities in Kansas City (including Blue Springs and Independence), visit www.skateboard park.com.

Roller Hockey Rink
116th and Knox
Overland Park, KS
www.opkansas.org
This 120-foot by 65-foot rink at Indian Valley Park features a playing surface of color-coated asphalt with regulation height and width goal areas. A 5-foot-tall sideboard surrounds the playing area, and there are player benches located on both sides. Rules and safety suggestions are posted, but there are no supervisors on site. The rink, which is maintained by the top-notch Johnson County Parks and Recreation Department, is on a first-come, first-served basis. There are no fees for use.

Sheila Kemper Dietrich Park
27th Street and Gillham Road
The first things you'll notice about this midtown park are the vivid colors and high contrasts that are especially appealing to visually impaired children. This delightful play area, a concept that has become a national model, is designed to delight children of different ages with a variety of physical and development abilities.

Another thoughtful feature is the bright animal figures signing letters, a thrill for a hearing-impaired child who can read WELCOME. The park's surface is padded Astroturf instead of sand, so it's suitable for wheelchairs and safer for little ones just beginning to walk. Children will also enjoy playing on the giant pirate ship and bouncing on springy chairs.

Skateboard Park
138th and Switzer
Overland Park, KS
(913) 893-6354
www.opkansas.org
You've gotta love a community that spends $240,000 to build a facility devoted entirely to skateboarding. An Overland Park resource officer got the ball rolling in November 1997, organized students and parents at a local school to help, and convinced the city it was a keen idea. A committee member coordinated the landscaping as one of his Eagle Scout projects.

The area, complete with ramps, jumps, and rails for all skill levels, is popular with skateboarders and in-line skaters. On nice summer days there's usually a small crowd of people amazed at what these kids can do with a few inches of wood on wheels.

THEATERS FOR YOUNG THESPIANS

How many movie stars can pinpoint the moment they decided to become an actor? Plenty, and often that moment came while watching a play or musical as a child. Perhaps your youngster will catch the acting bug as well, or at least be entertained for an hour or so at one of these made-for-kids theaters. Some of them even offer acting classes (read more in the Education and Child Care section of the Relocation chapter), and one provides a forum for young playwrights.

The Coterie
2450 Grand Boulevard
(816) 474-6552
www.thecoterie.com

Since 1987 this professional acting company has been introducing young people to the joys of live performances. The subject matter is often thought-provoking, with such titles as *Free to Be . . . You and Me* and a look at the horrors of the Holocaust. But there's light-hearted fare as well, including a musical starring that silly Pooh Bear. The schedule, available on the Web site, lists the appropriate ages for each performance and often includes ideas for additional study on the subject, a useful feature for parents and teachers.

Regular performances are ongoing throughout the year but vary as to dates and times, so please call. You'll want to pick up the phone anyway; these productions are often sold out weeks in advance. Admission is $14 for adults; $8 for students, youths eighteen and under, and seniors. It's easy to add to the experience by attending after-performance workshops or by taking acting classes that are available for preschool through twelfth grade.

Each May the Coterie mounts a Young Playwright's Festival to showcase local talent. It also holds auditions for children and adults every spring; details can be found on the Web site or by calling. The Coterie is located within the Crown Center Shops.

Paul Mesner Puppets
707 West 47th Street
(816) 756-3500
www.paulmesnerpuppets.org

For more than two decades this talented puppeteer has been bringing children's books and classic fables to life using rod puppets (think Kermit and Miss Piggy) and beautifully crafted marionettes. Although the stories often have important messages, it's Paul's wisecracking humor that steals the show. Give him three minutes and you'll forget the variety of silly voices is coming from just one person behind the stage.

Programs, which are held at Unity Temple on the Plaza, usually run four times a year, typically in October, January, March, and July. Call or check the Web site for specific times and dates. Tickets are $6. During the rest of the season Paul and his troupe are touring the United States or giving shows at local festivals, events, and children's museums like Wonderscope. Some performances are available on videotape through Paul's company, Reading Reptile (816-753-0441), a children's bookstore, and Rainy Day Books (913-384-3126).

Theatre for Young America
(816) 460-2083
www.tya.org

For more than twenty-five years this company's mission has been to foster educational and emotional growth of children through drama. The good news is that children don't even realize they're learning; they're too busy laughing or getting immersed in the actions on stage. TYA, as it's called, mounts eight or nine shows a year in a range of subject matters from ancient to contemporary. The plays are appropriate for preschool ages and up. The staff and volunteers offer classes in voice, body movement, and conflict management. Individual classes as well as four-day and one-week residencies are available. A work-study program is also available, which allows teens (ages twelve to eighteen) to work on behind-the-scenes tasks such as lighting and assisting the director.

Classes take place at the award-winning Wonderscope Children's Museum, 5705 Flint Street in Shawnee, KS (see separate listing in this chapter), and performances are held at the H&R Block City Stage at Union Station, a wonderful facility with comfortable seats and excellent lighting and sound.

Performances last around an hour and are generally held Tuesday through Sunday throughout the year. Single admission prices are $6 per person, and group rates and season tickets are available. Call for times and dates of performances.

TWINKLE, TWINKLE, LITTLE STAR

You promised your child the moon and the stars; well, here's your chance to deliver. Kansas City is blessed with a number of observatories in both urban and suburban settings. Pick a cloudless night to introduce your little star to the wonders of the universe. And for the biggest Big Bang for your buck, head out to the giant telescope at Powell Observatory just north of Louisburg, Kansas.

Gottlieb Planetarium Shows
Union Station, 30 West Pershing Road
(816) 460-2020
www.unionstation.org
One of Kansas City's hidden gems, this planetarium hosts several fascinating kid-friendly programs, including an animated laser light show that includes favorite tunes from classic rock and retro hits. The 360-degree domed screen takes you on an incredible tour of the stars as they appear over Kansas City.

Tickets are $5.95 or free with the purchase of either a round-trip or express ticket from Union Station (details on Web site). The planetarium is open Tuesday through Sunday. Check the Web site for specific hours and programs, or see Union Station's details in the Attractions chapter.

Kansas City Museum
3218 Gladstone Boulevard
(816) 483-8300
www.kcmuseum.com
This museum, housed in a fabulous mansion, includes a planetarium with cool programs for school groups as well as seasonal shows just right for families. Winter Skies, for instance, is held December 11 through March 5. The program lets kids ages eight and up explore some of the most widely recognized constellations, including Orion the Hunter, Taurus the Bull, and Gemini the Twins. Showtimes are 1:30 p.m. on Friday and 1:00, 1:45, 2:30, and 3:15 p.m. on Saturday and Sunday. The cost is $3.50 per person. Call or check the Web site for other event information.

Powell Observatory
Lewis-Young Park
Louisburg, KS
(913) 438-3825
www.askconline.org
This, to use a purely scientific term, is the big Kahuna. Located far from the lights of the city, Powell Observatory has a reflecting telescope with a 30-inch mirror. It's the largest telescope in a five-state area and among the largest in the country that is available for public viewing.

Members of the Astronomical Society of Kansas City built and maintain the facility and host programs here such as "Starbright Saturday Night." Held every Saturday night from May through October beginning at dusk, the program includes a discussion about a current astronomical event and a short video. A tour of the observatory concludes with taking turns viewing the stars, galaxies, nebulae, moon, and planets through the 30-inch and 16-inch telescopes. The suggested donation is $3 per person. Bring lawn chairs or blankets, and don't forget the bug spray!

In addition to the huge display, society members are usually outside with their own telescopes and are happy to let visitors take a peek. The observatory is also open during major astronomical events; upcoming ones are detailed on the Web site. A map to the site, which is 20 miles south of Kansas City in Lewis-Young Park, is also included. You can also book the observatory for special groups such as Scout troops and birthday parties; reservations are required.

Warkoczewski Observatory
800 East 52nd Street
(816) 235-1606
Locate Orion faster than you can say . . . "Warkoczewski," through this 16-inch telescope mounted on the roof of Royall Hall on the University of Missouri–Kansas City campus. The observatory is named for the late Stanley Warkoczewski, a retired sound engineer who, along with his wife, Helen, spent ten years constructing the telescope in his basement before

donating it to the school. A member of the university's physics department, he often gave lectures on astronomy and taught many students how to build their own telescopes. Stan died in 1997 at the age of ninety-one, but we think he's up there, just to the east of Pegasus.

The observatory is open one hour after sunset on clear Fridays from April through November. It's best to call the number above to confirm that it will be available.

ANNUAL EVENTS AND FESTIVALS

Awhile back a gentleman wrote to the editor of the *Kansas City Star* complaining about what he considered a tragic lack of things to do in our town. Where, he implored, could he take his family when they came to visit in early July? For the next week or so, letters to the newspaper answered him with long lists of fascinating attractions . . . and more than a few offers to help him move out of town.

Perhaps he had missed the previous week's edition listing (for one Saturday alone) festivals celebrating Slavic, Greek, Scottish, African-American, and Hispanic cultures; three garden tours; a rock fest; a folk dance; three free jazz concerts; a fishing derby; the Monkees at the Midland; real monkeys at the zoo; a sailboat regatta; and Elvis Presley's cousin singing "Blue Suede Shoes." And that doesn't even include standbys such as Worlds of Fun, Oceans of Fun, the Truman Library, theaters, art exhibits, or lazy afternoons at a park or lake. Mister, if you can't find something to do in that group, you're not trying hard enough.

So here's our calendar for the rest of you. As you'll see, around here we'll throw a party or start a parade based on little more than that it's Tuesday. Perhaps our love of celebrating comes from our days as a pioneer town; make it through the winter with a few pigs left and one of those porkers will be the guest of honor at a community pig roast. Our Wild West roots also show up in rodeos and barbecues, including the granddaddy of 'em all, the American Royal, but those of you with more refined tastes won't be disappointed. Cultural activities are plentiful whether you're into dance, music, or fine arts. Flamenco guitar in a rose garden, check. *Nutcracker Suite* from a balcony, check. A 10-city-block outdoor art show, double check.

One of our finest treasures, our diversity, is evident in the number of ethnic festivals held throughout the year. You'll have a chance to taste spanikopita, kimchee, bangers and mash, or alligator on a stick (tastes just like chicken) while listening to a bagpipe, electric guitar, bouzouki, fiddle, steel drum . . . or accordion if you must.

Take a holiday—take two!—and few cities celebrate it better than KC. Dust off your best bonnet to join in an Easter parade. Fourth of July takes off with a bang and a boom with no fewer than twenty-four separate fireworks displays. Even our Halloween is spook-tacular, with a dozen haunted houses and pumpkin patches. Winter brings holiday tours of historic homes and the world's most thrilling display of Christmas lights. So come soon, and come often. No matter when you arrive we'll have something wonderful waiting for you.

The events are in Kansas City, Missouri, unless otherwise noted.

JANUARY

Country Club Plaza Holiday Lights
Just in case you haven't seen the Plaza illuminated with 75 miles of jewel-colored lights, you still have until mid-January before they're put away for another year. Then it becomes just your run-of-the-mill, 14-block Spanish-style outdoor shopping center with big-name shops, forty or so restaurants, and about a million dollars of artwork and fountains. Our favorite view can be seen coming down from the hill on Wornall that runs between the InterContinental and Raphael Hotels. It's a breathtaking moment as the entire postcard picture opens up.

Crown Center Ice Terrace
2450 Grand
(816) 274-8411
www.crowncenter.com

Put on your woolies and catch some frozen action at the city's only outdoor skating rink. You'll be warmed by the hot cocoa and the entire storybook scene. The hours are 10:00 a.m. to 9:00 p.m. daily, and skating lessons are available for little Winter Olympic wannabes. Admission is $6 and skate rental is $2. And when you're ready to duck inside, the entire Crown Center Complex is at your frozen feet.

Martin Luther King Jr. Celebration
William Jewell College
Liberty, MO
(816) 781-7700

Several communities and churches throughout the Kansas City area honor Dr. King's memory with music, dance, and educational programs so that children and teens can learn about his teachings. The City of Liberty has hosted one of the largest, "Building a Community: Shaping a New Generation," since 1985. Past years have showcased local groups including the Wylliams/Henry Danse Theatre and the William Jewell Concert Choir. The event is free to the public.

Snow Creek Ski Lodge
Weston, MO
(816) 640-2200
www.skisnowcreek.com

You can hit the ski slopes and still be home in time for dinner at Weston, Missouri, just forty minutes away. The mini-ski resort offers enough variety to give beginners and expert skiers an afternoon or evening of fun. The 24- to 60-inch base is courtesy of Mother Nature, helped along by fifty snowmaking machines, and trails are accessed via two triple chair lifts, one double chair lift, and rope tows. Après-ski activities take place in the lodge that sports a cafeteria, bar, and lounge, along with a rental shop where the hottest things going—literally—are the snowboards, thanks to the 2002 Winter Olympics. There's plenty

of time to practice your loops and jumps; weather permitting, the lodge stays open seven days a week through mid-March. Check out more of the cool news in Kidstuff.

FEBRUARY

Art Auction
Kansas City Artists Coalition,
210 Wyandotte
(816) 421-5222
www.kansascityartistscoalition.org

Hope you have some dough left after the holidays, because you'll want to buy something here. The Artists Coalition was formed in the early 1970s as a place where emerging artists could exhibit their work and learn a bit about the other side of creating: publicity and marketing. In 1984 they started this annual event to showcase about 200 artists in categories from ceramics and glass to pastels, found-art sculpture, and oils. For two weeks the work is displayed in the gallery, leading up to the night of the event, which includes a silent auction and live bidding. It's definitely an eclectic crowd, with art patrons in suits and cocktail dresses mingling with artists in blue jeans; sometimes it's the other way around. Actually, no one cares what you're wearing; it's just a wonderful opportunity to see a wide variety of artwork and meet the creators in one place. Appetizers and refreshments are included in the ticket price.

Groundhog Run
Hunt Midwest Underground Facility
Subtropolis
(816) 746-1414
http://mo-kan.easterseals.com

There may be 4 inches of snow on the ground, but it's a relatively toasty fifty-eight degrees in this underground cave. Nearly 3,000 runners vie for prizes in this 5K and 10K race. More than the balmy temperatures, the participants love the flat running surface. Entrants pay around $15, which gets them a T-shirt and the knowledge that they helped raise funds for a local charity.

Metropolitan Lawn & Garden Show
Bartle Hall, 13th and Central
(816) 931-4686, (816) 513-5000
www.kcconvention.com

What perfect timing! Just when Midwestern-ers can't take another day of gray skies and brown lawns, it's time for the Midwest's pre-mier lawn and garden show. Landscape designers try to outdo one another with fabu-lous displays of flowering bulbs, trees, and the latest in water gardens. One year's display included 6,000 square feet of waterfalls, foun-tains, ponds, and even a jumping water demonstration. Garden ornaments, outdoor furniture, and fountains are well represented, and garden experts present programs on lawn care; planting flowers, herbs, and veg-etables; and tree maintenance. And if you're still on the fence about fencing, patio materi-als, and decking, this is the place to ask ques-tions of the dozens of vendors on hand. The three-day event typically takes place in early February. Admission is $7 for adults; children under twelve get in free. See the description below for a two-for-one show price.

Remodeling & Decorating Show
Bartle Hall, 13th and Central
(816) 931-4686, (816) 513-5000

This may be the best deal of the year; you can attend this show and the Metropolitan Lawn and Garden Show for the same admission fee. Just wear comfortable shoes, because you'll be pounding the concrete for hours. Home-owners who are tackling a major remodeling job will find great products and ideas here, or at least someone to commiserate with. Even folks living in sparkling new houses will want to watch demonstrations on faux painting, wallpapering, and turning bedsheets into fancy curtain swags. More than 250 compa-nies, covering almost 200,000 square feet of exhibit space, show the latest home decorat-ing trends as well as products and services for roofing, skylights, kitchens and baths, spas, pools, and windows and doors. Demonstra-tions continue throughout the weekend. One year the Duct Tape Guys stuck around to

When attending an event at Bartle Hall, allow an extra twenty minutes for parking. The adjacent garage and lots charge $5 and fill up fast. It's often quicker to park a few blocks away (bring change for street meters) and walk back. With 40,000 spaces you're sure to find some-thing. Sometimes a shuttle service is available.

show audience members the many uses of the do-it-yourselfer's best friend. See the lawn and garden show for ticket information.

Harlem Globetrotters
Kemper Arena, 1800 Gennessee
(602) 258-0000
www.harlemglobetrotters.com

These court jesters have been entertaining Kansas City for decades, but their antics—and shooting arms—never seem to get tired. Audi-ence participation is a big part of the fun, and there's always a lucky little kid or pretty teen called out on the court. The history is as remarkable as that one-finger basketball trick; since 1927 the team has performed before over 120 million people in 115 countries. That's a lot of dribbling. Logo merchandise including balls, caps, and jerseys is available. Tickets start at $12.

Annual Kansas City Boat Show
Bartle Hall, 13th and Central
(816) 513-5000, (816) 931-4686
www.kcconvention.com

We may be landlocked, but Kansas City has more than its share of recreational lakes dot-ting the landscape, and the fabulous Lake of the Ozarks is just a few hours away. For more than twenty-five years this show, the Mid-west's biggest, has put thousands of boating and fishing enthusiasts, as well as party-cove sun worshippers, in the mood. It's a pretty awesome sight as Bartle Hall is transformed into a water wonderland complete with an indoor lake just to tempt you to finally buy that first boat, upgrade an existing one, or at least check out the latest fishing gear. All manner of luxury cruisers, fishing boats, ski boats, personal watercraft, and apparel are see-worthy. And if that's not enough, there's usually a celebrity guest appearance. (One year it happened to be a live alligator show.) You'll have plenty of opportunity to see more than a hundred boats on view; the show typically lasts Wednesday through Sunday. Adult tickets are $7; tadpoles under twelve get in free.

World of Wheels at Bartle Hall
13th and Central
(248) 650-5560
www.worldofwheels.com

You'll see plenty of flash, add-ons, and paint here . . . and that's just the bikini contest participants. Every year about this time, Bartle Hall practically vibrates with testosterone as they roll in every kind of hot rod, rebuilt classic cars, and fancy-detailed motorcycle imaginable. Some of the most popular displays are customized vehicles and bikes that feature incredible paint jobs and pounds of extra chrome. Proud owners vie for top prizes, others just show up to drool. The ticket price of $12.50 will also let you stand in line to ogle celebrities, women wrestlers, and scantily clad beauties . . . just don't ask to look under the hood. The show usually runs Friday through Sunday.

The RV Show
Bartle Hall, 13th and Central
(816) 513-5000
www.kcconvention.com

Once a year Bartle Hall becomes a superhighway with hundreds of motor homes, trailers, fifth-wheels, custom vans, campers, and minihomes that prove you actually *can* take it with you. And of course dozens of recreational vehicles are on display, ranging from a few thousand dollars to palaces-on-wheels that top out at more than $1 million. Vendors are also on hand with the latest in camping gear and every type of accessory, appliance, and aftermarket product available to make your home-away-from-home more comfortable.

Admission to this three-day show is $7; children under twelve get in free.

Mardi Gras Blues Pub Crawl
Various locations
(816) 531-7557, (913) 649-0383

Count 'em: twenty-one clubs, twenty-one bands, and several hundred of your best friends. It all adds up to the Kansas City Blues Society's annual portable party, when vans take you from club to club all over town. It's a great way to discover a new little joint in Westport or a happening place at 18th and Vine while you leave the driving to someone else. Tickets for the gig—always on Fat Tuesday—cost $10 in advance or $12 at the door of any participating club. The roster includes popular places like Grand Emporium, Blayney's, the Phoenix, and Winslow's City Market BBQ. The highest concentration is midtown, but you can start anywhere and hit as many clubs as you'd like. Just remember that eventually you'll have to navigate your own vehicle safely, so pick a designated driver.

Annual "Little House" Birthday Celebration
Cave Spring, 8701 East Gregory Boulevard
(816) 358-2283
www.cavespring.org

For anyone who loves Laura Ingalls Wilder's books, or the television show they spawned, this charming afternoon party is a must. Activities for young and old include storytelling and a chance for youngsters to experience the daily burdens of pioneer life by grinding wheat and churning butter. Old-fashioned games like sack races and egg tosses keep everyone entertained, plus there are arts and crafts and birthday treats. And here's an interesting twist: Adults get in free while children pay $5 in advance or $8 at the door. You can learn more about Cave Spring, a marvelous thirty-six-acre nature park and historic site, in the Parks, Lakes, and Recreation chapter.

Polar Bear Plunge
Shawnee Mission Park, 7900 Renner Road
Overland Park, KS
(913) 236-9290
www.kansastorchrun.org
Brrrrr! Since 1998 hundreds of folks have braved icy waters and potential head colds to jump into Shawnee Mission Park Lake. There'd better be a good reason, you say? There is: Money raised goes to benefit Special Olympics Kansas. Once participants stop shivering (tents are provided for changing into dry clothes), it's time to head to the post-plunge party at Barley's Brewhaus, 16649 Midland. Say, barkeep, can you warm that beer for me, please? Prizes are awarded for wimpiest plunge and most outrageous plunge wear, among others. Same-day registration is available for a $50 fee, and participants are encouraged to obtain sponsors to bring in more cold cash. The annual event is hosted by Kansas police officers. Special Olympics is an international program of sports training, education, and athletic competition for individuals with intellectual disabilities. In Kansas, more than 6,000 Special Olympians participate in twenty-one official sports.

MARCH

First Fridays in the Crossroads
Arts District
(816) 472-4546
www.kccrossroads.org
Although this street party–cum–gallery opening happens the first Friday of every month, the crowds really start showing up around March when the weather's better. This near-mile-wide downtown neighborhood, bounded by 15th Street and Interstate 35, is chock-full of artist studios, galleries, unique shops, and trendy restaurants. In most months a colorful trolley will take you around the area for free. Most galleries are open until 9:00 p.m.

Annual Easter Egg Hunt
Lake Jacomo
Blue Springs, MO
(816) 795-8200
www.jacksongov.org

A tisket, a tasket, grab your Easter basket and join this fun-filled morning when children from three years to third grade scamper for candy-filled eggs. Special guests, like Lulu Bell the Clown and the Easter Bunny, are usually on hand to cheer the little hunters on. A few "magic" eggs with special prizes are hidden among the others. Registration costs $5 and is limited to the first 600 participants, so early reservations are recommended. Make a day of it and enjoy the rest of Fleming Park, which includes the 970-acre Lake Jacomo.

Breakfast with the Easter Bunny
Powell Gardens
Kingsville, MO
(816) 697-2600
www.powellgardens.org
Could anything be sweeter than a three-year-old girl in an Easter bonnet or a toddler in his first tie? You'll see hundreds of them in all their pastel and plaid glory as they anxiously await the arrival of the Easter Bunny. While they're waiting they can dig into pancakes in flavors like blueberry, banana, and chocolate chip. Eggs, however, are not on the menu; they're saved for the Easter Egg hunt when kids up to age ten scatter throughout the gardens looking for plastic eggs filled with toys and candy. Seeing Powell Garden's display of thousands of spring bulbs is reward enough for most adults. Breakfast with the big guy is typically held the two Saturdays before Easter; the hunt follows the second date only. Breakfast is $6 for adults and children over three, $4 for under three, and it costs $5 to participate in the egg hunt, which includes garden admission. Reservations are required for both events.

Annual Home Show
Bartle Hall, 13th and Central
(816) 513-5000
www.kchba.org
Keeping up with the Joneses is a national obsession, and for over fifty years this show has been showing area residents how to do it right. At more than 600 displays in space equivalent to eight football fields you'll see the latest techniques, products, and services

available to remodel, decorate, secure, or beautify your home. There must be a dozen bubbling hot tubs alone. If you're in the market for a new home, you'll have a chance to meet with area builders and look through sample house plans.

And because this event is combined with the Kansas City Flower, Lawn, and Garden Show, you'll get expert advice on landscaping, or simply a chance to tiptoe through the tulips in the waterways and floral displays. Demonstrations showing everything from tree pruning to floral arranging are staged throughout the weekend; past shows have brought in nationally known experts like Mr. Fix-It. Concession stands offer hot dogs, snacks, and beverages. You can even take home more than just a bag full of product brochures; Wayside Waifs will be on-site with adorable, adoptable cats and dogs. In past years more than one hundred pets have found new homes at the show. The Home Builders Association of Greater Kansas City sponsors the four-day showcase. Admission is $7 for adults, $6 for seniors and students. Children twelve and under are admitted free.

Snake Saturday Parade and Festival
Downtown North Kansas City, MO
(816) 274-6000
www.nkc.org

Yes, Bridget, there is a St. Patty's Day parade north of the river, and it's a doozy. This pretty little community practically doubles in size—or at least in shades of green—as 100,000 people show up the Saturday before St. Patrick's Day for an all-day party. A parade winds its way downtown with more than 150 cars, bands, and floats, and the post-parade activities offer something for the entire family. Enjoy carnival rides, arts and crafts booths, and enough green beer to forever change the course of the Missouri River. Irish dance troupes and musical groups perform as well. The fun starts at 9:00 a.m. and is free.

Brookside St. Pat's Warm-Up Parade
Meyer Boulevard and Wornall
(816) 523-5553
www.brooksidekc.org

It's an impressive sight as floats, bands, clowns, community groups, antique cars, and dogs dressed in green wind their way through this pretty neighborhood. Come to think of it, with thousands of spectators, this parade is bigger than most cities put on all weekend, and we're just getting started. The parade starts around 2:00, but get here earlier because there are always fun goings-on like musical entertainment, dancing, food, and ale. But pace yourself: The big parade is less than twenty-four hours away.

St. Patrick's Day Parade
Downtown
(816) 931-7373
www.kcirish.org

Although our official St. Patrick's Day parade got a late start compared with some other cities, we soon showed them how to transform green crepe paper into a world-class float. Outrageous radio host Mike Murphy got the ball rolling on March 17, 1972, while having lunch (and perhaps a beer or two) with three friends at a downtown restaurant. They decided what Kansas City needed was a St. Pat's parade, by golly, so they whipped up a sign, put a green bow on somebody's dog, and began a tradition that's become the third largest parade in the country. These days about 350,000 people crowd the streets to cheer on more than 200 colorful floats, politicians in convertibles, high school marching bands, pretty girls dancing jigs, pipe and drum corps, an Elvis look-alike or two, and a contingency of kazoo players. It hasn't been without its problems; one year we watched in horror as a radio station mascot, a 40-foot inflatable fox with sunglasses and a guitar, got caught in overhead wires. They had to shoot him.

For those really in the spirit, the day starts at Browne's Market (3300 Pennsylvania Avenue), where an authentic Irish breakfast is served along with music and dancing as early as 6:00 a.m. After the parade it's traditional to join the masses on the streets of Westport. Once the crowds were so large they actually had to close the doors to Kelly's Westport Inn.

APRIL

Art at the Center
(formerly Art in the Woods)
Overland Park Convention Center
6000 College Boulevard
Overland Park, KS
(913) 895-6357
www.artkc.com
The Overland Park Arts Commission has been setting up this temporary art gallery since 1982. In 2003 it moved to a new home in the lower level of the new convention center. More than 120 artists are represented each year in the juried show, with work that includes photography, oils, watercolors, and abstracts. The art is for sale; prices range from $200 to more than $9,000. The free show is usually open for two or three weeks beginning in late April.

Civil War on the Border
Mahaffie Stagecoach Stop,
1100 Kansas City Road
Olathe, KS
(913) 782-6972
www.olatheks.org
As the first overnight stagecoach stop on the Santa Fe Trail outside Westport Landing, this place saw its share of wranglers, riders, and families heading west. It also got caught in the border skirmishes between Missouri and the Free State. In fact, these battles pre-dated the Civil War by four years. Reenactors dressed as infantry, cavalry, and artillery soldiers will relive Civil War days, as Yanks and Rebs mix it up during this two-day event. The cannon booms will be enough to knock you out of your seat! More cordial activities are on tap as well: an 1860 fashion show, a wedding, and a Missouri Town Dance. Demonstrations throughout the weekend will shed light on the frontier-town lifestyle, and the vittles and sarsaparilla will tide you over until the next stagecoach pulls up bound for Dodge.

Festival of Wines
American Heart Association Benefit
(913) 648-6727
www.kcwinefest.com
This is one party your cardiologist might actually prescribe. You'll get to consume some heart-healthy wine and raise money for the American Heart Association at the same time. Each year more than 1,500 big-hearted guests show up to sample 300 or so wines from some of the world's top vineyards. In just eight years it has become, according to USA Today, one of "the most popular wine festivals in the USA." The gala kicks off Friday night with a five-course wine dinner (at $200 a pop) starring a celebrity vintner such as Bob Mondavi. On Sunday the main event includes a grand wine and food tasting, live jazz music and dancing, and a live auction. Festivalgoers get a chance to schmooze with the winemakers while chefs from local restaurants demonstrate tips for cooking with wine. A live auction caps the evening as bidders vie for rare and fine wine lots, a trip to the California wine country, giftware, and restaurant certificates. Tickets to Sunday's event are $50 per person in advance and $60 at the door and include a commemorative wineglass and corkscrew. So far, thirsty donors have helped raise nearly $1 million for the cause. The gala is held at a different location each year. Call for current information.

Pembroke Hill School Clothesline Sale
State Line Road & Ward Parkway
(816) 936-1200
www.pembrokehill.org
This is without a doubt the most incredible garage sale in the Midwest. It takes volunteers weeks just to sort, tag, and display the wares, including everything from baby clothes to furniture, shoes to golf clubs, and antiques to jars of marbles. For those who don't know, Pembroke is a school for mostly privileged students, so their families' cast-offs often

sport designer labels. Oh, you'll still find the occasional lamp you wouldn't wish on your brother-in-law, but for the most part it's all primo stuff. Call the school for dates, or watch for the big banners displayed on the school grounds a week or two in advance. It costs $2 to shop from 9:00 to 11:00 a.m. on opening day (worth it!); otherwise it's free.

Kansas City Royals Opening Day
Kauffman Stadium
(800) 6ROYALS
www.kcroyals.com

The boys are back, the wait is over, and baseball season is officially open at "The K." Opening weekend usually falls within the first week in April, and people dress in blue and challenge their vocal cords. Sunday's game includes a special Kids Opening Day celebration including a postgame fun run and gifts. Learn more about this beautiful ballpark and the Royals in Sports.

Spring Homes Tour
(816) 942-8800
www.kchba.org

Find your new home or just see how the other half lives at the second largest scattered home show in the country. For more than forty years members of the Kansas City Home Builders Association have been giving us their best and most beautiful every spring with abodes ranging from $120,000 to over $4 million. Yowza! The last group usually boasts closets big enough to have their own zip codes. Many are fully furnished, giving lookers a chance to check out the latest in decorating trends. The tour spans eight counties and includes close to 500 homes. Free admission, but there is a price: You may not want to go home again.

Symphony Designer's Showhouse
Different location each year
(816) 968-9711
www.showhouse.org

Some of the area's most beautiful homes and talented interior designers come together once a year to create this benefit for the Kansas City Symphony. Each year a different home is selected, but it's always a magnificent specimen, often a minimansion along Ward Parkway. The empty house is open for a week or so in February for public previews before a single can of paint is opened and then closed while more than forty interior designers, landscape professionals, builders, architects, and artists work their magic. The finished showhouse is dressed to the nines, and it's interesting to see how each team of designers or individual interprets the room he or she has chosen to decorate. An on-site boutique sells a variety of goods such as jewelry, herb topiaries, and garden art. Preview tickets cost $5, and admission for the completed showhouse, which is usually open for three weeks, costs $15 at the door or $13 when purchased in advance at various outlets. No infants or children under eight years of age are admitted.

MAY

Abdallah Shrine Rodeo
Leavenworth County Fairgrounds
(913) 362-5300
www.shrinerodeo.com

Yippee ti yi yo! It's the biggest Shrine rodeo in North America, and we've got it. It's quite a thrill to watch 150 professional cowboys and cowgirls compete for big prizes in Brahma bull riding, steer wrestling, and calf roping. The one-handed bronc bucking event is done with and without a saddle (ouch), and cowboy wannabes get to catch and saddle a wild horse (double ouch). The clowns jumping in and out of barrels keep the competition light, and kids can get involved in a shoe race where they have to sprint across the arena, try on shoes from a barrel, and flip-flop back. The preshow is always a kick, with Shriners dressed in costume riding outrageously decked-out go-karts. Tickets are $8 to $12 for the two-day event.

Art in Columbus Park
9 blocks east of the River Market
www.urbanarts.info

This casual gallery walk is a bit like what the wildly popular First Fridays in the Crossroads felt like a decade ago; a handful of galleries and studios opening their doors, serving wine, and introducing artists to art lovers. The longest line isn't to get into an emerging artist's quarters, it's waiting for a table at Garrozzo's Italian restaurant, where the aroma of garlic overpowers any hint of oil paint. If standing in line isn't for you, there are several eateries with an open table in nearby City Market for before or after your crawl. The event is held every third Friday of the month, April through December, 6:00 to 10:00 p.m. It's free, but a small donation to keep the doors open and cheese and crackers on the table would be much appreciated.

Annual Bachathon
Grace and Holy Trinity Cathedral, 13th and Broadway
(816) 474-8260
www.ghtc-kc.org

All Bach, all the time. Some twenty-two years ago someone at this downtown cathedral got the bright idea that folks might like to hear six nonstop hours of the master's most famous concerti and cantatas. They were right, and today standing-room-only crowds fill the chapel to hear a twenty-eight-voice choral ensemble and masters playing the 33,000-pipe house organ. In years past selections have included the *Brandenburg Concerto V* and *Goldberg Variations*. Although most guests choose to listen to a few selections and quietly leave (wait here, I'll be bach), it's not unusual for true music lovers to stay put for the entire program. If that's you, bring a cushion for the pew. Cookies and beverages are available, and the surroundings are divine. Mostly Norman French in architecture, the

For up-to-the-minute listings of events, check the *Star* Friday Preview (www.kansascity.com), *The Pitch* (www.pitch.com), www.gointokansas city.com, and the current issue of *KC Magazine* (www.kcmag.com).

cathedral has a classic Gothic arch and two magnificent Tiffany stained-glass windows. The event is typically held the first Sunday in May and begins at 2:00 p.m., but you'll want to be there long before then to get a seat.

Antiques on the Common
Greenwood, MO (approximately 25 miles southeast of Kansas City)
(816) 537-7822

If only magazines like *Country Living* would stop showing up, we could keep this one-day antiques extravaganza our little secret. But nooooo, they have to tell the world about the goods brought in from dealers in fifteen states, the jaw-dropping prices—and the blueberry cream pie. It takes Claire Fellows about two months to set up all the tents and picnic areas, one day to sell out, and about two weeks to recuperate before she starts it all again for the September sale. Expect to find an enormous variety in every price range. If the $5,000 cabinet is too rich for your blood, check down the way; there's a less-rare version for $180. Other goodies include highly collectible tramp art, baskets, penny rugs, and tons of folk art. Ask Claire, who also owns Country Heritage and Friends antiques shop, for a flyer with directions and a list of places to stay while you're in town. And plan to get there early; about 1,500 or so shoppers with fire in their eyes and "I saw it first!" on their lips show up for this one.

Brookside Art Annual
63rd Street between Wornall and Main
(816) 523-5553
www.brooksidekc.org

The art fair season officially opens at this outdoor exhibit held in the charming village known as Brookside. It seems more tents are added each year, but still the sidewalks and streets overflow as 70,000 people wiggle their way in for a better look at silver earrings, a photo of the Plaza lights, an azure glass vase, or a pastel landscape.

About 195 artists are represented, grateful for a chance to talk to art lovers and sell work without paying commission. And because it is the first major show of the season, most of the artists do quite well, averaging $6,700 for the weekend. Children get a chance to create, too; at the Baptist Hospital tent they can create cards for patients. The art of eating well is also on display in food booths operated by local restaurants. A terrific addition for the past ten years or so has been the Share-a-Chair Silent Auction, where area artists decorate chairs, frames, and birdhouses that are then auctioned off. Proceeds benefit two local chapters of Habitat for Humanity. The fair, usually held the first weekend in May, also corresponds nicely with the opening of Joe D's wine bar patio, a terrific place to sit and admire your new prize.

Celebration at the Station
Union Station
www.celebrationatthestation.com

What could be more thrilling than our beloved Kansas City Symphony playing the "1812 Overture," punctuated by the sound of live firing cannons? It's a fitting finale to an evening of music set against the beautiful Union Station before turning around to see another majestic sight—fireworks against the Liberty Memorial. Grounds open at 3:00 p.m. with food, drink, and family entertainment before it's time to stake out the prime location for a picnic blanket. Some people simply plop down on the stone walls surrounding the area behind the Henry W. Bloch Fountain, temporarily quiet for the event. The rousing celebration is free.

Fiesta Hispanic
Bartle Hall
13th and Central
(816) 765-1992, (913) 706-7881
www.fiestakc.org

There's more entertainment than toys in a piñata at this festival honoring our city's vibrant Latino community. For two days puppeteers, Tejano singers, music and dance troupes, and exhibits keep the crowds entertained while an exhibit hall showcases the culture's proud heritage. It's a fitting tribute to national Hispanic Heritage Month. Admission is free.

Fiesta in the Heartland
Crown Center
(816) 472-6767
www.hccgkc.com

Just as not everyone wearing a "Kiss me, I'm Irish" button on St. Pat's Day has ties to Ireland, not everyone dancing salsa at this celebration is Latino. About 10,000 festivalgoers crowd City Market each May 1 to hear nationally known Tejano singers and Latino bands, practice salsa and cha-cha slide dances, and sweat off about three pounds in the jalapeño-eating contest. Olé! Less incendiary foods are available as well, including grilled tenderloin, tamales, and ice cream. Children will be treated to face painting, piñatas, and visits with sports teams' mascots.

Great American Barbecue Festival
Woodlands Race Track
Kansas City, KS
(913) 422-9599
www.thinkbbq.com

Gee, that's all we need, another barbecue festival. Kidding. Of course we love any weekend that includes 'cue, blues, and hot air balloons. Toss in a kiddie carnival and about the best darn fireworks display around and this newcomer to the barbecue contest game, held over Memorial Day weekend, is a winner. There are open and invitational contests; check the Web site for official rules and an application. In its first two years, the event raised more than $80,000 for local charities. That's nice, but can you point me to the rib-eating contest?

Kids Fishing Derby
Old Lake Jacomo on Beach Road
Blue Springs, MO
(816) 229-8980, ext. 16

Hey, kids, grab your fishing poles and head out to this fishing contest made just for little tadpoles. Since 1988 this one-day event, open to kids ages two through fifteen, reels 'em in with fun-filled activities and a casting contest. The first hundred kids to show up get a free cane pole; registration begins at 8:00 a.m. Children should bring an adult (aw, shucks), fishing pole, bait, and bucket to hold all that catch. Even if the line is a loser, every kid will take home a prize like fishing tackle and sporting goods.

Heritage Hikes
Various locations
(816) 235-1448 (Communiversity),
(816) 931-8448
(Historic Kansas City Foundation)
www.historickansascity.org
Each spring the Historic Kansas City Foundation and Communiversity join up for educational and entertaining strolls through the city's varied and vibrant neighborhoods and historic sites. Past hikes, which usually lasted three hours or so, have included the Northeast, downtown, and Hyde Park districts, giving walkers an up-close look at everything from Victorian homes to turn-of-the-twentieth-century warehouses-turned-condos. Reservations are necessary, and fees range from $10 for one hike to $25 for three. Other walking tours are hosted throughout the year for around $3 each; contact the foundation for dates and details.

Plaza Live! Courtyard Concerts
Locations around the Country Club Plaza
(816) 753-0100
www.countryclubplaza.com
You may not hear the tune "The Best Things in Life Are Free," but you'll experience it first-hand during this free music concert series that lasts from May through the fall. Some of the area's top musicians plug it in and lay it down at courtyards throughout the Plaza, including the Penguin located by Scandia Down, Mermaid near Eddie Bauer, and Neptune outside Houston's. The music ranges from jazz and pop to blues and Dixieland, with performers like Skip Hawkins Trio, Boulevard Band, Krazy Kats, Max Groove, Ida McBeth,

and Angela Hagenbach. Listen up from 5:00 to 8:00 p.m. Thursday and Friday and 2:00 to 5:00 p.m. Saturday and Sunday.

Truman Days
Independence Square
Independence, MO
(816) 325-7111
www.visitindependence.com
We prove we're still wild about Harry every year as we celebrate his birthday. It's a fine excuse to visit the museum, home, and courthouse that bear the name of the beloved thirty-third American president.

JUNE

18th and Vine Rhythm & Ribs Jazz Festival
Historic 18th & Vine District
(816) 474-8463
www.kcrhythmandribs.com
The jazz and blues aren't the only things smokin' at this jam-packed party; along with top-notch music, there's a barbecue contest going on, filling the air with the savory aroma of ribs and chicken. Think you've got what it takes? Enter to win and you could walk off with the "grand" prize. That's grand as in $1,000. But our money's on the talent on the number of stages situated around the grounds. You'll hear favorite local performers as well as national hit-makers such as Al Jarreau and George Benson. Now that was a sweet duet!

Kiddies have two full days of fun as well, with stilt walkers, face painting, and puppet shows. If you don't like barbecue (say what??), you can sink your teeth into other festival food like Cajun dogs and fajitas. Of course, beer, wine, and lemonade are available to quench your thirst. Bring blankets and chairs, and you might consider a beach umbrella to shield the sun, depending on the weather. Other activities include tours of the nearby Negro Leagues Baseball Museum. Tickets range from $20 to $30 with the lower price going for early online orders.

Corporate Woods Jazz Festival
Antioch and College Boulevard
Overland Park, KS
(913) 661-5459
www.jazzinthewoods.com

An opportunity to hear three days of nonstop music from Kansas City headliners—free? Count us in, along with about 40,000 other jazz lovers who've been showing up for the fresh air, great music, and Cajun sausages for more than fourteen years now. Lineups have included artists like Ken Navarro, the Greg Meise Quartet, Ida McBeth, Angela Hagenbach, and the New Red Onion Jazz Babies.

The venue couldn't be better. The rolling hills of Corporate Woods, a 294-acre office park blessed with thirty varieties of trees, picnic tables, jogging trails, and a winding woodland stream, provide opportunities to get some private time with your own Sophisticated Lady. As for the Cajun 'dogs, they're just one of dozens of festival foods to tempt you, including barbecue, onion blossoms, frozen margaritas, beer, and sweet treats. Several of the artists will have CDs for sale. Festival T-shirts and raffle tickets raise money for local charities. Bring lawn chairs, picnic baskets, kids, and dogs. Parking is plentiful around the corporate park.

Croatian Day Picnic
Fourth and Barnett
Kansas City, KS
(913) 788-9758

You'll find your thrill on Strawberry Hill at this annual celebration that's more than seventy-five years old. It's a chance to discover the all-too-often overlooked *other* Kansas City, a town with a rich heritage and vibrant neighborhoods of Slavic families. Lively polkas will get you dancing, but it's the food that will make you swoon: tender cabbage leaves stuffed with meat, onions, and rice; grilled sausages; and a flavorful sweet bread with layer after layer of ground walnuts and spices called povatica. Plus you'll have a chance to tour the Strawberry Hill Museum with parishioners of St. John's Catholic Church.

Dog-N-Jog Run-Fur-Fun
Mill Creek Park
(913) 596-1000
www.hsgkc.org

For over twenty years, 800 to 1,000 dogs and their owners have come out to enjoy this pretty park on the Country Club Plaza while they help contribute to the Humane Society of Greater Kansas City. Amazingly, the fur rarely flies, as most doggies enjoy the company. Plus they get massages and treats for rewards. Vendors are also on hand with pet-related products, and purebred rescue groups have terrific dogs available for adoption; in fact purebreds account for 25 percent of shelter animals. Participation in the fun run costs $15.

Downtown Overland Park Days
Metcalf Avenue between
78th and 83rd Streets
Overland Park, KS
(913) 642-2222
www.downtownop.org

This ain't your daddy's Old Overland Park; during this two-day event, the quiet downtown district rocks with R&B music, roving entertainers, a beer garden, and an old-fashioned street dance. An Avenue of the Arts features more than seventy local and regional artists and crafters, and the kids' carnival keeps little ones entertained with a petting zoo, clowns, and games. The farmers' market will stay open until all the luscious fresh produce has sold out, and even then you won't go hungry; more than fifty food vendors will tempt you with grilled chicken, barbecue, snacks, and frozen treats. Downtown's unique shops and restaurants will also be open to serve you. Donation is $2 at the gate.

Great Lenexa Barbecue Battle
Sar-Ko-Par Trails Park
Lenexa, KS
(913) 541-8592
www.lenexa-kansas.com

Mmmm, smell that hickory smoke? Just follow it to find one of the country's biggest barbecue battles. The word "battle" is right: Each year about 180 teams compete for the chance to take home the coveted trophy. A panel of 250 judges rates seven categories of meat, including brisket, pork, chicken, ribs, and sausage, and although that might sound like a cushy job, it's actually hard work. The fun begins on Friday evening as the smoke masters prepare giant cookers and closely guarded sauce recipes and then stay close through the night to regulate the heat. On Saturday morning while they're sweating out the judging, the rest of us can enjoy live music and kiddie games. The best part comes after the grand champion is crowned and the crowd is invited to taste the best barbecue in the state of Kansas.

Heart of America Shakespeare Festival
Southmoreland Park,
47th Street and Oak
(816) 531-7728
www.kcshakes.org
The play's the thing, and since 1992 this lively event has been our opportunity to brush up on the Bard. For four weeks from late June through July, professional actors, many of whom also appear at Kansas City Repertory Theatre, perform one or two of Shakespeare's plays on a rotating basis each Tuesday through Sunday. There is no performance on July 4. The plays are different each season, but you can expect a sword fight or two, love lost then found, and at least one episode of mistaken identity. And the setting is straight out of Romeo and Juliet: a lovely little park near the Nelson-Atkins Museum of Art.

Don't miss the preshow at 6:00 p.m., when actors do hilarious send-ups of the Bard's plays. Audience participation is heartily encouraged; nay, it's often mandatory as "volunteers" are plucked from the crowd of onlookers. The play begins at 8:00 p.m. Admission is free, but donations are welcome. A limited number of reserved seats are available for $15 and may be purchased through the Central Ticket Office (888-286-4849) at least twenty-four hours in advance.

Most folks simply bring a lawn chair, a blanket, and a picnic basket. Concession stands offer hot dogs, kettle corn, snow cones, and wine or beer.

Parkville Days Riverfest
English Landing Park
Parkville, MO
(816) 880-9026
www.parkvillemo.com
What an enchanting evening this makes, sitting under the stars listening to jazz with the fairy-tale spire of Park University glowing in the distance. Parkville has always had a getaway kind of feel to it thanks to an old-fashioned Main Street filled with antiques shops and galleries. The annual jazz fest turns the attention from shopping to its lovely park along the banks of the Missouri River.

There's always an impressive lineup of local musicians. And although it's highly unlikely you'll get bored with the music or tents of arts and crafts, you can always stroll along the groomed trails or visit the nearby nature sanctuary. See the Parks, Lakes, and Recreation chapter for more information about this 115-acre reserve. There's no charge for the jazz fest, and you may bring a cooler for snacks but no alcohol. Food, beer, wine, and other beverages are available at the festival.

Jazzoo
Kansas City Zoo
(816) 513-5800
www.jazzookc.org
Things can get pretty wild at this black-tie gala, and we're not just talking about exotic animals pacing a few hundred feet away. Jazzoo has Kansas City's social elite doing the jungle-boogie all night long, spurred on by music, dancing, and fine wines. And with the aroma of gourmet food prepared by eighty top chefs, it's amazing there aren't a few uninvited guests, like a hungry lion or two. At least the penguins know to dress appropriately. Tickets (at $150 a pop) usually sell out within days. Profits benefit the Zoo Learning Fund.

Juneteenth Celebration
Various locations
(816) 483-1300
www.juneteenth.com
With something for everyone—young and old, all races and backgrounds—this event has grown into a celebration of life. Black Archives of Mid-America Inc. has played host for more than twenty-five years, and each year the group outdoes itself with activities like a golf tournament at Swope Park, crowning of Mr. and Mrs. Juneteenth, a block party at the historic 18th and Vine District, and a motorcycle and car show. Kids have their own activities area with games, a chance to climb on a fire engine, and a share in the African-American culture. Local musicians keep the crowds entertained, while food vendors keep everyone happy with barbecue, grilled corn on the cob, and refreshments. The grand finale always showcases a top national musical group. The public is invited to attend the main celebration for free; other events, such as the golf tourney, include a registration fee.

Lake Fest
Missouri Town 1855
Fleming Park, Blue Springs, MO
(816) 795-8200
www.jacksongov.org
This is an incredible evening for the entire family, with boat and personal watercraft rides, water games, arts and crafts, and foods of the summer. Live entertainment and a fireworks display continue the fun into the night. The fun begins at 5:00 p.m. Admission is $7 per vehicle, $3 per walk-in.

Lee's Summit Festival of the Arts
Downtown Lee's Summit, MO
(816) 246-6598
www.downtownls.org
Invite some folks over to your block party and watch your population double overnight. That's what happens as soon as music—including rock, country, acoustic, bluegrass, and jazz—starts playing in every corner, alley, and parking lot within the 6-block downtown

area. Add more than 400 crafts, food, and commercial booths and, buddy, you've got yourself a festival. Plenty of people agree; the three-day fair, usually held the first week in June, can bring in as many as 80,000 guests. And just to prove they're good neighbors, admission is free.

Old Shawnee Days
57th and Cody
Shawnee, KS
(913) 248-2360
www.oldshawneedays.org
On any given day, Old Shawnee Town offers an interesting look at frontier living in the late 1800s. Its seventeen original and replicated structures include the 1843 territorial jail, a general store, a bank, and a funeral parlor. But during the annual Old Shawnee Days festival, the place really comes alive (even the funeral parlor) with a parade, carnival, battle of the bands, and big musical guests. Headliners have been '70s bands like Ozark Mountain Daredevils, Starship, Firefall, and Liverpool, a Beatles' cover band. Other activities have included historical reenactors, a live alligator wrestling show, and a cutest baby contest. No doubt these last two events were held on opposite sides of the fairground. All the usual festival food is available, and admission is free.

Riverfest
Berkley Riverfront Park
(816) 550-4722
www.kcriverfest.com
We take it back to where it all began for our town, the Missouri River, to celebrate Independence Day just a little early. Held in Berkley Riverfront Park just east of the City Market, what this annual event lacks in years (it started in 2004), it more than makes up in spirit. The weekend offers plenty of entertainment for all ages and interests including free-wheeling motocross, kids' carnival complete with face painting and magic shows, nonstop musical acts, and a spectacular fireworks display that can be seen all over the city. Things

can get toasty here around July, but we have a solution: a brewfest with tastes from local breweries. Just the thing to go with grilled hot dogs and other goodies.

Rose Day in the Park
Loose Park
(816) 784-5300
www.kcmo.org

We can't think of a more lovely way to spend the first Saturday in June than surrounded by thousands of rose bushes in Kansas City's prettiest urban park. This event is hosted by the Rose Society of Greater Kansas City, a club founded in 1931 to prove that roses could indeed grow here despite our Zone 5 rating and rather stubborn clay. And grow they do. The Laura Conyers Smith Municipal Rose Garden started with 120 bushes, and now the 2½-acre park has more than 4,000 plants in 125 varieties. This fragrant sea of pink and salmon, red and flame, lavender and deepest lipstick also includes a fountain and reflecting pool, benches, and pretty limestone and timber pergolas. The organization hosts other events throughout the year, including classes on caring for roses.

Scottish Highlands Games
Riverfront Park
Riverside, MO
www.kcscottishgames.org,
www.kcscot.com

It's amazing, Grace, what fun you can have at this annual festival filled with Celtic music and mirth. The traditional jigs, ballads, and reels go back to the sixteenth century, and favorites like "Scotland the Brave," "Caledonia," and of course "Amazing Grace" are easily recognized. You'll hear them all performed by bagpipes, drums, fiddles, bouzoukis, and voice. The Celtic harp, in fact, provides one of the most popular hands-on events, "Cuddle a Clarsach." Traditional costumes and dancing are also on tap, including the thrilling Scottish National style made popular by River Dance. Children will enjoy storytelling, face painting, and a chance to pose with Nessie, the Loch Ness Monster. And of course you'll have a chance to cheer on fifty or so big, burly men in kilts as they hurl sixteen-pound stones and Scottish war hammers for prizes (hopefully not at the audience). Tickets to the two-day event are $8, $3 for ages seven to twelve, and free for six and under. Bring two cans to donate to Harvesters Food Pantry to save $1 on each ticket.

St. Dionysios Greek Orthodox Church Festival
8100 West 95th Street
Overland Park, KS
(913) 341-7373

Why anyone would miss this festival is Greek to us. Every year for forty-six years, the church grounds have been transformed into an *agora* (marketplace) with a boutique filled with embroidered blouses, "worry beads," and sailor hats and a taverna set with succulent food. Fill your plate with leg of lamb, chicken baked in lemon sauce, a gyro sandwich, and traditional side dishes and pastries. While dining you'll be entertained by dancers clapping and twirling to the distinctive sounds of bouzouki. Eat fast—they need your table for dancing!

Parish members are proud of their heritage and their church, and tours are given throughout the two-day festival. The icons, bishop's throne, and the Pantokrator painted on the ceiling are beautiful . . . but isn't the music starting up again? Opa! Admission and parking are free, and proceeds from sales of food and goods go to benefit church community services.

Sugar Creek Slavic Festival
11520 East Putnam
Sugar Creek, MO
(816) 833-0192
www.slavicfest.com

Here's your chance to overcome your polka-phobia with a healthy dose of Slavic food, dance, and the happy sounds of accordion music. The festival started in 1986 to celebrate customs brought over from Slovenia,

Croatia, Hungary, Romania, and Poland in the mid-1800s. The savory food alone will make you want to add a few consonants to your surname, including sarma (stuffed cabbage rolls), kielbasa (Polish sausage), and povitica (rolled walnut bread). Traditional Slavic music and dancing are the mainstays of the two-day event, and guests have a chance to join in the kolo circle dances. This phrase may come in handy as you're finishing that second sausage: "Zedan sam," which means "I am thirsty." No problem; cold beer and beverages are just a dance step away. It's all happening at the Mike Onka Memorial Building, with proceeds benefiting North American Croatian Relief and local civic improvement projects.

Sunset Safaris
Kansas City Zoo
(816) 513-5800
www.kansascityzoo.org
During the dog days of summer, the zoo stays open every Thursday until 8:30 p.m. to take advantage of cooler evening temperatures. You'll be welcomed by train rides, music and games, and animals that are usually more active in the evening. Sunset Safaris run from early June through mid-August. Check the Web site or see Kidstuff for more information about the zoo.

JULY

Missouri River Miles 340 Canoe and Kayak Race
(913) 244-4666
www.rivermiles.com
"This ain't no mamma boy's float trip," the Web site warns, and it's true: just you, your canoe or kayak, and 340 miles of wind, heat, bugs, and rain. And leave it to Scott Mansker, the guy who founded this little cruise in 2006, to put it smack in the hottest time of the year, late July. This race will test your mettle from the first time your paddle hits the water in Kansas City to the last gasp in St. Charles. Did we mention you have just one hundred hours to finish? Your reward, other than a trophy, is

the chance to witness incredibly beautiful bluffs and forests, hear townspeople cheer you on along the route, and get your mug on the Web site for next year.

The inaugural year saw only fifteen competitors step up (ten finished); the second year brought out seventy-five canoes and kayaks with racers ranging in age from twenty-two to eighty-two. Go, Gramps! Though the competition promises to be a lot of hard work and some fun, it's also extremely well planned by experienced river rats. There are nine checkpoints along the route—which the Coast Guard has marked with mileage and channel markers—and racers are required to sign in and sign out.

Overland Park Civic Band Concerts
Santa Fe Commons Park,
81st and Santa Fe
Overland Park, KS
(913) 642-2222
Who says we've lost that small-town flavor? It's right here at this old-fashioned town-square park in sweet little old Overland Park. They strike up the band—usually ragtime, blues, or country—each Sunday evening beginning the first week in July and continuing through August. For more old-time fun, stroll the downtown area, window-shop, or stop in for a huge chocolate chip cookie at Mildred's Coffee Shop. The concerts are free; bring lawn chairs.

Summerfest
St. Mary's Episcopal Church,
13th and Holmes
(913) 645-7965
www.summerfestconcertsinkc.com
This four-program series is incredibly popular thanks to the talents of its ten-member chamber ensemble and a repertoire that appeals to a wide audience. Each program also includes a guest artist, such as a soprano soloist, who adds depth to the selections. After you've fed your soul, take care of the rest of you with a postconcert artist schmooze that includes a lavish spread of minisandwiches, hors d'oeuvres, sweets, and beverages. And as if all that

weren't enough, the concerts are presented in a stunning Gothic church that was built in 1888. Be sure to notice the high altar with deeply carved wood and the stained-glass windows. Summerfest has become quite the seasonal ticket, so early reservations are recommended. A subscription to all four concerts costs $50 until May 25, then it's $60. The programs are offered at 7:00 p.m. each Saturday and 5:00 p.m. each Sunday in July.

Theatre in the Park
Shawnee Mission Park,
79th and Renner Road
Shawnee, KS
(913) 312-8841 (info line),
(913) 631-7050
www.theatreinthepark.org

Thirty years ago this organization opened with a few boards laid on bricks and dressing rooms in nearby bushes. Today it's one of the hottest tickets in town as 3,000 patrons show up to watch Broadway productions like *Annie*, *Evita*, and *The Music Man* performed by non-professional actors, many of whom could one day be holding a Tony of their owny. The summertime experience gives hundreds of actors, dancers, and singers of every age group a chance to perform. Four different musicals are presented each season, and each runs for two weeks on weekends. The ticket gates open at 6:30 p.m., and because there are no prior sales, the line often starts an hour earlier; the programs begin at 8:30 p.m. A concession stand is on-site, as are public restrooms. Admission is $6 for adults, $4 for children ages four to twelve, and under four free. Bring a picnic basket and lawn chairs and be ready to cheer for somebody's kid.

Water Garden Tour
(816) 525-7664
kcwatergardens.com

Just when a cool splash of water would feel really good, the Water Garden Society of Greater Kansas City complies with an invitation to tour more than sixty area gardens. The offerings range from tiny koi ponds created by the homeowners to monstrous minilakes with waterfalls installed by professional landscape companies. Several have appeared in local and national garden magazines. Tickets, at $10 each, include a map and descriptive brochure and are available at several garden centers throughout the metro area. Check online for more information.

Wyandotte County Fair
The Woodlands
9700 Leavenworth Road
Kansas City, KS
(913) 788-7898
www.wycofair.com

This is the real deal, where 4–H kids show off their best calves (as in little cows, not leg muscles), pies, and dresses to win blue ribbons. For everyone else, just showing up is reward enough. A demolition derby, a youth rodeo, and a messy attraction called Mud Madness will keep you entertained until the fireworks display starts. The free stage offers country bands, gospel music, and folk dancing. The fairgrounds are wall to wall with tents filled with arts and crafts, carnival rides and games of chance, exhibits like chainsaw artists, clowns, a petting zoo, and a live shark show. In Kansas? Yep, plus enough cotton candy and funnel cakes to make the Whirly Bird off-limits.

You don't have to be in the 4–H club or even a Dot (our affectionate term for a Wyandotte County resident) to enter the competitions; anyone can bring a biggest tomato, best scrapbook, prettiest wreath, most impressive Lego construction, or chocolate chip cookies to vie for cash prizes. This author still treasures a State Blue Ribbon for banana nut bread won eons ago. But that's recent history; the fair has been around since 1863 and is now the largest county fair in Kansas and Missouri.

Entrance is free; wristbands for carnival rides are $16. Parking is $3. Check online for details and a coupon for additional savings.

Fourth of July Fireworks Displays and Festivals

Ever since private fireworks became verboten in KC, we've had to get our thrills at giant community displays. Let's see: a few Black Cats and sparklers or twenty minutes of dazzling jewels and diamonds exploding in the night sky overhead. We'll take the public fireworks, thank you very much. And you won't have to go far to see some spectacular shows; in fact, in some parts of the city you can watch several going off at once. Following are some of our favorites; a two-page spread of more listings can be found in the *Kansas City Star*. We've also included other family-friendly choices around the holiday.

Booms and Blooms
Powell Gardens
Kingsville, MO
(816) 697-2600
www.powellgardens.org

The sounds of the Missouri Symphony Pops will thrill you as fireworks light up the sky like giant multicolored chrysanthemums. Light jazz starts at 3:00 p.m., the conductor takes up the baton at 7:00, and the pyrotechnics start as soon as it's dark. Besides the booms, there are blooms like the eye-popping display of daylilies and other lush floral gardens. You can even stay cool with a stroll in a shady glen along a waterfall stream. Cafe Thyme offers a selection of crisp salads, tasty sandwiches, and desserts. Admission to the park is $8 for adults, $6 for seniors, and $3 for children.

Independence Day at
Missouri Town 1855
Lake Jacomo in Fleming Park
Blue Springs, MO
(816) 795-8200, ext. 1-260

You say you want an old-fashioned Fourth of July? How about the way they did it back in 1855? This re-created village from our city's early days really lives it up with patriotic speeches, a town parade, period costumes and music, and children's games that don't require batteries. And it all takes place at one of the prettiest parks in the city. Admission for the 9:00 a.m. to 4:30 p.m. event goes for $3 for adults, $2 for youth ages five to thirteen, and free for under five. Now you'll have just enough time to catch a nap before heading out to watch fireworks.

Lenexa Community Days
Old Town Lenexa, Santa Fe Trail Drive and Pflumm
(913) 541-0209
www.ci.lenexa.ks.us

Rise and shine early so that you can participate in the annual Freedom Run beginning at 7:00 a.m., and then catch your breath while enjoying a good old-fashioned community parade at 10:00 a.m. The rest of the day belongs to family games and activities, food vendors, and live music. For those of you still awake, the cities of Shawnee and Lenexa put on an awesome fireworks display at Shawnee Mission Park (5900 Renner Road) in the Theatre in the Park area. Bring lawn chairs and blankets. Admission is free to all events.

Star-Spangled Banner Spectacular
Corporate Woods Office Park
Overland Park, KS
(913) 829-8483
www.starspangledspectacular.org

You'll be watching the skies throughout this Fourth of July celebration, first when the Kansas National Guard flies overhead and then during a fireworks display that seems to go on forever. Musical entertainment, food and drinks galore, and an activity area for kids complete the deal. Even better, it's free.

Parkville July 4th Celebration
Historic downtown Parkville
www.parkvillemo.com

It's a full day of festivities starting with an old-fashioned parade plus a carnival, the American Legion's famous hamburgers, strawberry-topped funnel cakes, and sweet, sweet music. And there's nothing prettier than fireworks reflected in the Missouri River, so pick out the ideal spot for your picnic blanket early at lovely English Landing Park; this event usually pulls in 20,000 folks.

KC Fringe Festival
Various locations around Crossroads Arts District
www.kcfringe.org

Just a few years old, this robust collection of visual and performance art, fashion shows, music, dance, poetry and more takes place the last week in July at dozens of venues located within midtown. It's rather like a few days on a cruise ship; there are too many events on the agenda. You'll hear everything from rock bands to Celtic singers, find art to buy or watch local actors show off their knickers in a burlesque show. Other fashion shows display outfits created by local designers. A popular element of the festival is the Filmmakers Jubilee with indy film screenings in the Central Library film vault; yes, the theater is in an old bank vault. That's reason enough to attend. A small fee will get you a wristband and more fun than you can imagine. This is where to find emerging artists and wacky performers along with more mainstream talent.

AUGUST

Aviation Expo
Downtown Airport
(816) 471-4946
www.kcairshow.org

If things are looking up, it must be because the Blue Angels are in town. The U.S. Navy precision flight team is just one exciting element of the Aviation Expo. Other high-flying action includes the midair acrobatics of the U.S. Army Golden Knights Parachute Team, a demonstration team from Air Force A–10s, F–117s breaking the speed limit, and stunt pilots and wing walkers. Live music throughout the two-day show, a hot air balloon show at night, and free airplane rides for kids add to the list of activities, and forty food vendors serve up nachos, smoked brats, and snow cones.

Staged by the Mid-America Youth Aviation Association, the two-day expo helps educate young people about careers in aviation and related fields. Crowds have grown to more than 150,000 at the downtown airport, so parking elsewhere (such as the Crown Center) and catching a shuttle is a must. You'll find shuttle information on the Web site along with important safety tips like wearing ear protection and plenty of sunscreen. It gets mighty hot on that tarp, but that doesn't keep runners from participating in an early-morning race. Admission is $12; round-trip shuttle fare is $2.

Ballet in the Park
Various locations
(816) 931-2232, ext. 375
www.kcballet.org

With leafy trees serving as stage curtains, this series of free outdoor shows lets you get a bit of culture while wearing flip-flops and sipping lemonade. Since its start in the early 1980s, this has been one of the ballet troupe's favorite programs, both for the dancers and the audience. The diverse program ranges from ballroom dancing to neoclassic ballet, from dramatic work to modern pieces where bodies are twisted into "sculpture." The entire twenty-five-member company is featured in some capacity, giving some of the lesser known dancers a chance to star. Venues have included the Loose Park rose garden, Crown Center Pavilion, and Powell Gardens, so the surroundings are as lyrical as the artists. Performances are free and open to the public; bring lawn chairs or blankets. Dates change from year to year. Call for current information.

Blues and Bar-Be-Q Benefit
BB's Lawnside Bar-B-Q
1205 East 85th Street
(816) 822-7427
www.bbslawnsidebbq.com

How tough is this decision? Show up to hear thirteen bands, get some great barbecue, and drink cold beer while you contribute to a good cause. Past performers have included crowd-pleasers Four Fried Chickens and a Coke and Kelley Hunt. All proceeds go to the Sherwood Center, a United Way Agency that provides services for people with autism and related disabilities. Admission is $4 for adults; kids eleven and younger get in free. The event doesn't have a standard date; call for details.

Ethnic Enrichment Festival
Swope Park, Swope Parkway and
Meyer Boulevard
(816) 333-1124
www.eeckc.org
Twirling costumes, lively music, and an array of international cuisine; here's a chance to celebrate more than forty cultures that make our city so vibrant and appealing. For two days, usually the third weekend in August, you can enjoy a different performance on stage every half hour, including steel bands from Jamaica, Samoan dance groups, Scottish pipe bands, Mexican folkloric ballet, Japanese martial arts, and a parade of flags. Craft booths, food vendors, and educational activities are also on tap. Admission is $3 for adults; twelve and under are free.

Elvis Parade
20th & Central
(913) 744-3774
www.kyys.com
Put on your blue suede shoes, grab your teddy bear, and practice crooning, 'cause it's "now or never" to see more than a hundred parade entries, Elvis impersonators, and so much more. This hilarious, often embarrassingly bad festival has been sponsored by radio station KYYS (99.7 FM) for more than sixteen years. Thankyou, thankyouverymuch.

Festival of Butterflies
Powell Gardens
Kingsville, MO
(816) 697-2600
www.powellgardens.org
While 150,000 people watch for Blue Angels at the Air Expo, several hundred will be enchanted by other winged creatures closer to earth. More than 6,000 guests take turns watching the multicolored miracles in the garden's conservatory during the country's

largest butterfly exhibit. As cameras click, an orange-and-black Viceroy sips nectar from a purple ironweed flower, a blue Atala becomes a temporary hair bow on a three-year-old, and a rare orange-barred Sulphur flits by in iridescent splendor. More than twenty-three varieties emerge during this event, plus there are outdoor butterfly and hummingbird gardens, face painting for the children, and a catch-and-release party. It's a magical weekend that adds to the everyday wonder of Powell Gardens; you can read more about it in the Parks, Lakes, and Recreation chapter. General admission prices are in effect for the festival.

Kansas City Irish Festival
Crown Center
(816) 997-0837
www.kcirishfest.org
This annual festival should tide you over during those lean months between March 17 and the Labor Day Irish fest in Brookside. It's also simply a fine way to enjoy the warm weather and celebrate the area's Celtic origins.

A highlight of the two-day event is always the traditional and contemporary Irish music. In the past, local beauty and internationally acclaimed singer Connie Dover has thrilled the crowds along with favorites the Elders, Shenanigans, and Eddie Delahunt. The children's area offers games and arts and crafts like Celtic rubbings, along with Irish dancing, pipers, and exhibits for the whole family. Stout and ale flow, and authentic cuisine from across the pond is available. Tickets are $5 for adults; there is no charge for children under twelve.

Race for the Cure
Union Station
(816) 842-4444
www.komenkansascity.org
In August the streets around Union Station become a moving sea of pink as 20,000 T-shirted runners and walkers move toward the finish line and a cure. The Kansas City affiliate of the Susan G. Komen Breast Cancer Foundation has been going strong since 1993, moving

its course several times to accommodate the larger crowds. The 5K run/walk and 1-mile fun run appeal to a wide array of athletes, including those who wear photos of loved ones who have died from breast cancer or have survived it and those who are themselves fighting the disease. Water stations and cheering crowds keep the runners motivated, and music, festivities, and lots of food wait at the finish line. Registration fees range from $25 to $35. Call for this year's date.

Summer Skies
Kansas City Museum
3218 Gladstone Boulevard
(816) 483-8300

Learn to locate the constellations and stars just in time for that camping trip. You'll be able to find Scorpio, Sagittarius, Orion the Hunter, and the Summer Triangle from the museum's planetarium. Make a day of it and tour other exhibits, including photos and memorabilia from the Long family, who owned the original Corinthian Hall. Museum entry is $3.50 per person, and the star-filled event continues through early September.

SEPTEMBER

Antiques on the Common
Greenwood, MO
(816) 537-7822

Although antiques buffs try to keep this one-day sale a secret, word has gotten out and the crowds grow bigger every year. By now 1,500 or so fevered shoppers show up to dig through tent after tent of primo antiques and collectibles. Dealers from fifteen states bring in the goods, including early Americana, folk art, hooked rugs, redware (highly prized in New England), baskets, quilts, and country furniture with just the right amount of peeling paint. No matter what your budget ($5,000 or $10) you'll walk away with some treasure. And a full tummy: The blueberry cream pie, bratwurst, and chicken salad in a pita are all delicious. The brain behind it all is Claire Fellows of Country Heritage and Friends, a terrific

antiques store in Greenwood. Give her a call for directions and a list of motels and RV campsites; she might even send her recipe for Pig Pickin' Cake.

Art Westport
Westport Square
(816) 756-2789
www.artwestport.net

Westport's motto is if you can't beat the Plaza Art Fair in size, at least have yours a few weeks earlier. And it works. But this weekend-long street party succeeds for another reason: All the work is created by local artists, so there's a sense of community and continuity that gives shoppers a chance to buy from favorites year after year. Expect to see a great variety of styles and genres, including ceramics, oils, pastels, watercolors, metal sculpture, garden art, carved wooden boxes, and handcrafted jewelry. Food vendors line the streets, live music adds to the festival atmosphere, and the people-watching (as always) is as good as it gets. Admission is free, so you'll have extra cash for a new treasure.

Belton, Grandview & Kansas City
Railroad Company Train Rides
502 Walnut
Belton, MO
(816) 331-0630
www.beltonrailroad.org

It's all aboard for fun as this community relives its past as a railroad town in the 1920s. An authentically re-created open window train takes passengers on a forty-five-minute round-trip on Saturday, Sunday, and holidays from Labor Day through the end of October. Tickets cost $7.50 for ages three and older, $20 to ride with the engineer (no extra charge for blowing the whistle), and $10 to see the world in reverse from the caboose. Special seating is limited and on a first-come, first-served basis. Other activities are planned throughout the season, including ice-cream socials and educational field trips, and photos and documents from the railway's heyday are displayed in the gift shop.

Brookside Irish Festival
63rd and Wornall Road
(913) 338-1962
www.brooksideirishfest.com

'Tis a long way from St. Patty's Day, but apparently the 15,000 folks who crowd the streets of Brookside don't mind—or don't notice after downing a few Irish stouts. They show up in a sea of green to hear traditional music from local talent like the Elders, Eddie Delahunt, and Bob Reeder and to watch the flashing feet of O'Riada Academy of Irish Dance. Past years have also brought in national acts like Black 47, a group that mixes hip-hop and hard rock with traditional Irish music. Kids will keep busy with games and face painting, and parents may head right for the corned beef, scones, meat pies, and Irish whiskey. You might walk away with more than a hangover; raffle tickets are sold for trips to Ireland and big-screen TVs. Admission is $5; children twelve and under get in free. Money raised goes to a local Irish culture center.

Greek Festival
Greek Orthodox Church of the
Annunciation, 120th and Wornall Road
(816) 942-9100, (816) 491-1990

It's hard to imagine what our lives would be like without the influence of ancient Greece. Logic, geometry, medicine, and architecture (even words like *sophistication* and *philanthropy*) come from their world. Then there's the food. Here's a chance to experience it all (well, maybe just the food) at a celebration this parish has been hosting for more than forty-six years. You'll find enough gyros to feed an army, enough paper-thin phyllo dough to cover the world, and enough dancing to make Zorba proud. The crowds are so huge they need three food lines to serve hungry festivalgoers. But don't worry. We've saved some baklava for you. Admission and parking are free. The souvlaki plate will set you back $12.

Hidden Glen Arts Festival
Kansas Highway 10 and
Cedar Creek Parkway
Olathe, KS
(913) 961-ARTS (2787)
www.hiddenglen.org

You might say this art fair has a much larger canvas, the gorgeous, upscale homes and emerald-green golf course of Cedar Creek. But it's the hundred or so booths filled with fine art that will attract your immediate attention. Past favorites have included garden art crafted of recycled metal, delicate ceramic teapots, and gem-studded silver jewelry. Artists from ten states are available to discuss inspirations and techniques. Little squirts have storytellers, puppets, and a color wheel game to keep them busy while you shop. Admission and parking are free.

Lenexa Spinach Festival
Sar-Ko-Par Trails Park,
87th Street and Lackman Road
Lenexa, KS
(913) 541-0209
www.ci.lenexa.ks.us

Kids may shudder at the thought of a day devoted to spinach, but there's more to this festival than simply greens. It starts with a Kiwanis pancake breakfast and includes a polka dance, Popeye and Olive Oyl characters, and a tossing of the world's largest spinach salad, which is sold by the plateful to those who enjoy the leafy vegetable. The two-day event costs $1 for ages thirteen and older.

March of Dimes Annual Bikers for Babies
The Kansas Speedway
(816) 561-0175
www.marchofdimeskc.org/biker

This annual charity event brings a new meaning to the phrase "biker babe," as hundreds of motorcycle riders raise money to help save infants at risk. Participants are well rewarded with a free lunch, music and entertainment, great prizes, and a chance to ride through some of the Midwest's prettiest countryside. Past years have brought together 4,500 or so riders with total contributions of more than $430,000, and the crowd gets bigger every year. The fee is $35 per ride, but most participants spend months raising money for the cause. It's hard to say no to a guy in leather chaps.

Old Settlers Celebration
Downtown Olathe, KS
(913) 764-1050
www.olathe.org

No wonder this annual event is a blast; Olathe's had more than one hundred years to get it right. They certainly pack enough excitement into three days, including free concerts on Friday and Saturday nights starring big-time names of the '60s and '70s like Mitch Ryder, Gary Lewis and the Playboys, and Mark Lindsay from the Raiders. But the fun starts much earlier with carnival rides on Thursday and the state's biggest parade Saturday morning. More than 150 arts and crafts booths show off local talent, and ice cream keeps everybody cool.

One of the liveliest attractions is the gabfest that allows older residents to tell young whippersnappers about the good old days, like walking to school through 3 feet of snow. Barefoot. This celebration is a chance to discover a vibrant city with an interesting history, famous sons (including several governors, actor Buddy Rodgers, and J. C. Nichols, who developed the Country Club Plaza), and a name that means "beautiful" in the Shawnee Indian language.

Overland Park Fall Festival
Santa Fe Commons Park
Overland Park, KS
(913) 895-6357
www.opkansas.org

Get your Christmas shopping out of the way early at this outdoor arts and crafts show that's been steadily growing in size since 1980. Pace yourself; there are nearly 180 artists and crafters displaying hand-made treasures like jewelry, candles, ceramic dolls, stained glass, pottery, dried-floral wreaths, oil paintings, and personalized children's puzzles. Or save your money for the food booths with the usual summertime treats like Cajun sausages, kettle corn, snow cones, and beer. The farmers' market is also open, offering the freshest produce from nearby farms and orchards. Tables are set under big white tents, so even if it rains you can sit a spell while listening to local bands play crowd-pleasing blue grass, blues, jazz, and classic rock 'n' roll. Speaking of crowds, this event pulls 'em in, with attendance of about 18,000 over three days.

Pig-Pickin' Chicken-Lickin' Feast
Bingham-Waggoner Estate,
313 West Pacific
Independence, MO
(816) 461-3491

At the very least this annual festival wins the prize for the best hunger-inducing name. And you can bet you'll be licking your fingers after a dinner of roasted pig, Stroud's famous fried chicken, and lots of savory side dishes. Other down-home fun includes a quilt show, silent auction, banjo music, and clogging (that's folk dancing, folks). You can also tour the home that was a popular stop along the westward trails (read more about this site under Historic Homes in the History chapter). Advance reservations are required; tickets cost $10.

Plaza Art Fair
Country Club Plaza
(816) 753-0100
www.countryclubplaza.com

Some people save up all year to buy a fabulous treasure or two at this three-day event. They'll have plenty to choose from; more than 230 of the nation's top artists turn nine Plaza streets into one big outdoor art gallery. The quality of work is incredible. In a highly competitive jury process, more than 1,200 artists from some thirty-five states vie for the right to have their work seen by more than 275,000 art enthusiasts. Expect to see ceramics, fiber, glass, graphics and printmaking, metal, painting, pastels, photography, wood, and some of the most exquisite jewelry around.

While browsing you'll be treated to the aroma of Thai chicken pizza, Italian sausages, and black bean chili from more than two dozen Plaza restaurants. Desserts, icy margaritas, beer, and other beverages are also on the menu. Music fills the air as well, thanks to three stages offering everything from R&B to classical. Children can create their own masterpiece to take home in the Kid's Art Workshop or view other students' work at the Young Artist Exhibition tent. And of course it all takes place at the Country Club Plaza, which is a work of art all by itself. The Plaza Art Fair is a tradition that began in 1932 and just gets better with time.

Plaza Pzazz
Country Club Plaza
(816) 421-1753
www.rmhckc.org

As if the Plaza didn't have enough pizzazz, they throw a block party with music, dancing, and delectable food from the trendiest restaurants in town. The location couldn't be more chichi, either; the streets nestled along lovely Brush Creek on the Plaza are lined with booths and tents that are lit up with tiny white lights as the sun sets. The $75 ticket price goes to a very good cause: three local Ronald McDonald Houses that give shelter and support to families with seriously ill children. The charity serves more than 3,000 families a year. Tickets go as fast as an order of McDonald's fries.

The Kansas City Renaissance Festival
Bonner Springs, KS
(816) 561-8005, (800) 373-0357
www.kcrenfest.com

Buxomy wenches and men in tights? These fetching fantasies have been drawing crowds to this sixteenth-century shire every fall for more than twenty-seven years. Well, that and continuous entertainment, mouthwatering foods, and a wide array of handcrafted wares. Where else can you witness a sword fight, cheer a jouster on horseback, and flirt with a king, all in one afternoon? With sixteen acres and thirteen stages of music, plays, and zany comedies, there's almost too much to see in one day, so you'll be thankful the festival runs for seven weekends beginning Labor Day.

Each week sports a special theme; Lovers and Fooles, for instance, hosts the wedding of the century, and Pipes and Plaids brings out the bagpipes and kilt competition. Gypsies, bandits, beggars, the royal entourage, and dozens of other costumed characters stroll the sixteen-acre village, engaging visitors in skits and revelry. Music is around every bend: Celtic harmonies, bawdy pub songs and sea shanties, lilting tunes on harps and hammered dulcimers. The village's shaded lanes are lined with shops showcasing goods from more than 160 artisans, including puppets, beribboned hair wreaths, tooled-leather purses, and toy swords.

Kids are in their own little realm with elephant and camel rides, a petting zoo, and dozens of games such as Slay the Dragon and Drench a Wench. Some people show up just for the food, particularly roasted turkey legs big enough for two, pork chops on a stick, root beer floats, and eighty other delights including a rather modern invention, barbecue ribs. Cider Jack, wine, and ales are also available. The festival is open rain or shine and parking is free. Before you go, practice saying the standard greeting around Canterbury: "Huzzah!" Tickets are $15.95 for adults, $14.50 for students and seniors, $7.95 for children ages five to twelve and free for children under five. Check the Web site or call for discounted advance tickets.

Riverside Riverfest
Riverfront Park
Riverside, MO
(816) 741-3993
www.riversidemo.com

What this city lacks in history (it's only fifty years old) it more than makes up for in fun. Witness the number of activities it packs into one September weekend alone: a pancake breakfast, a vintage car show, a grand parade featuring the world-famous Anheuser Busch Budweiser Clydesdales, a carnival, a blues and jazz jam, a battle of the bands, a beauty contest, and two fireworks displays. Whew! There's plenty of entertainment for the kid-dies, too, including a petting zoo. The older crowd can sit it out at the bingo tents. The central event is free, and the fireworks display is priceless.

Santa-Cali-Gon Days
Independence Square
Independence, MO
(816) 252-4745
www.santacaligon.com

In the mid-1800s three routes—the Santa Fe, California, and Oregon Trails—led pioneers to new adventures out West, and they all began in or near Independence. This festival has grown in popularity in its thirty-plus years, topping out at some 250,000 visitors over the four-day span.

There's certainly enough to keep every one of them entertained. The Main Stage is always a big draw, with past performers like the Dixie Chicks, Clint Black, Eddie Rabbitt, and Asleep at the Wheel. The Community Stage hosts local talent, including Native American dancing, square dancing, and must-see events like watermelon seed–spitting contests. No con-test about who's got the best food roundup for the weekend; here you can choose from barbe-cue, jambalaya, hamburgers, corn dogs, ice cream, lemonade, and dozens more. In fact, more than 300 commercial food and game booths are here, along with a large carnival midway. And the juried craft show has been ranked among the top in the nation by the crafters themselves.

For those interested in the historical sig-nificance of the trails, the Missouri Free Trap-pers exhibit portrays the life of the pioneers. Four days of fun, free admittance and parking . . . what more could you want? How about discount tickets for the carnival rides on the Web site? You'll also find information about free shuttles—a must, especially on Saturday afternoon.

Strut with Your Mutt
Brookside
(816) 761-8151
www.waysidewaifs.org

Put on the dog while you help raise funds for the Wayside Waifs animal shelter. This walkathon is held every fall, and part of the fun is entering different contests like cutest pooch, best costume, or the owner and pet who most resemble each other (scary judging when the entrant is a wrinkled sharpei). Plus there are vendor booths and doggie treats galore. $30 gets you a T-shirt and possibly a slobbery thank-you from a schnauzer.

Kansas City Symphony
Labor Day Concert
Shawnee Mission Park
(816) 471-0400
www.kcsymphony.org

You haven't lived until you've heard the Kansas City Symphony begin the first notes of the "William Tell Overture" just as the sun is set-ting behind a canopy of trees. This popular Labor Day tradition always includes selections the audience instantly recognizes, even if they can't recall the name, such as Copland's "Rodeo" or "The 1812 Overture." It's a fine way to introduce youngsters to classical music. The program begins at 7:00 p.m., which gives you plenty of time to enjoy the park's lake, rolling hills, and leash-free dog area. Read more about this popular green space in Parks, Lakes, and Recreation.

OCTOBER

CANstruction
Various locations
(816) 329-5000
www.canstruction.org

This annual event builds its own excitement as eleven teams of architects, engineers, and contractors compete to design and build giant structures made entirely out of canned goods. Has anyone entered the leaning tower of pizza sauce yet? At the close of the month-long exhibition, the canned goods are donated to the Harvesters Food Pantry. Admission is free, but you're encouraged to bring at least one can of food or a nonperishable item to view the display.

Christmas in October
(816) 531-5259
www.christmasinoctober.org

You've gotta love a community that comes together for two weekends each October to clean up, fix up, and rehabilitate homes belonging to low-income homeowners who often are elderly or disabled. This nonprofit group was started in 1984 by Richard W. Miller and John P. McMeel (of Andrews McMeel Publishing) with a couple of hammers and a few willing friends. These days about 7,000 skilled laborers and hardworking volunteers tackle the jobs.

Over the years this group has improved more than 8,000 homes in neighborhoods throughout the metro area, often enabling residents to remain in their homes with dignity and pride. Union craftspeople like electricians, plumbers, carpenters, and roofers handle the major repairs during the first weekend. A week later a horde of energetic workers with paintbrushes, rakes, and wheelbarrows show up to finish the job. There's a mighty big payoff for a few days of sore muscles and Eggshell Gloss in your hair: joyful tears from an eighty-five-year-old lady who will have a warmer house this winter.

Fall Parade of Homes
(816) 942-8800
www.kcparadesofhomes.com

At this annual show you'll find about 500 reasons to buy a new home as more than 200 builders from eight counties tempt you with their finest houses. You can tour as many as you'd like in every lifestyle and price range, from less than $95,000 to more than $1.6 million. Just why does any one family need seven bathrooms, anyway? Many of the most exclusive homes are dressed to the nines by area interior designers, so you'll come away

with lots of decorating ideas. To add to your choices, downtown lofts and condos have been added to the tour. Books with floor plans are available at most of the homes, and a tour map is available online.

FilmFest Kansas City
Various locations
(816) 421-2900
www.filmkc.org

What's the difference between FilmFest Kansas City and those big-deal festivals like Cannes or Sundance? Well, although we can't offer you a glimpse of Robert Redford, at least in Kansas City you'll see films. That's right, even if you're not an industry mover and shaker or member of the media, you can buy a ticket and see fifty or so movies from around the world. Aspiring filmmakers will also be interested in workshops and a chance to schmooze with producers, screenwriters, and directors. The movie lineup offers something for every taste, including sci-fi thrillers, musicals, foreign films, shorts, cinematic masterpieces, and potential blockbusters from established names. The weeklong event includes the KAN-ED filmmaking program, the precursor to the KAN Film Festival, a competitive event held every June in Lawrence, Kansas.

Historic Kansas City Homes Tour
(816) 931-8448

Ever drive by a beautiful home and wish you could peek inside? Now you can, with the owner's blessings. Each fall the Historic Kansas City Foundation chooses one neighborhood to feature, always an area filled with turn-of-the-twentieth-century jewels that have been carefully preserved or lovingly restored. Past tours have included the fabulous Scarritt-Renaissance and Hyde Park neighborhoods. Tickets are $10 and can be purchased at the site. Proceeds help continue the foundation's mission of restoring, renewing, and rediscovering historic buildings, homes, and areas of our city.

**Hyde Park Historic Homes
Tour and Festival
Hyde Park Neighborhood
(816) 561-HPNA (4762)
www.hydeparkkc.com**

Get close and personal with some of the loveliest homes in Kansas City at this annual tour. You'll see everything from charming shirtwaist bungalows to stately stone mansions, brought back to glorious turn-of-the-twentieth-century grandeur by hardworking homeowners. Tour guides (often the residents themselves) discuss the home's history, interesting details about the restoration, and sometimes-spooky tales about ghostly visits. Typically five homes are on the list, all within a pleasant stroll.

**Junior League of Kansas City
Holiday Mart
Overland Park International Trade
Center, 115th and Metcalf
Overland Park, KS
(816) 444-2112
www.jlkc.org**

Get on your mark, get set, shop! Lots of ladies finish their entire holiday shopping list in one fast-paced afternoon at this annual buyer's paradise. More than one hundred gift boutiques are side by side, offering jewelry (silver, gemstone, and estate pieces), home decor, gourmet foods, apparel, pewterware, and collectibles. Many of the area's most popular shops are represented as well, including Nell Hill's from Atchison, Kansas, and Locust Grove of Weston, Missouri. Clothing booths tend to carry unique fashions like fringed leather jackets, elaborately decorated vests and hats, and fun accessories not available anywhere else in town. And of course you'll find Christmas decorations galore, including tree-trimmers, ornaments, dried floral wreaths, and exquisite Santas with price tags of $300 or more. For the most part, though, prices are so reasonable you'll be glad you grabbed a shopping basket at the door. Single-day tickets are $10 in advance and $8 at the door; multiday tickets, good for all four days, are $18. Call the number above for ticket outlet information.

**Lee National Denim Day
(800) 944-5633
www.denimday.com**

How cool is this? Wear jeans to work and instead of getting reprimanded you're considered a good citizen. Local business Lee Jeans sponsors this now-national event, with money going to the Susan G. Komen Breast Cancer Foundation. So take that $5 bill out of your jeans pocket and send it in.

**Weston Irish Festival
O'Malley's Pub, Short and Welt Streets
Weston, MO
(816) 640-5235
www.westonirish.com**

In Weston they turn Octoberfest into O'Toberfest with three days of fun. What else can you do when your name is Sean O'Malley and you own an Irish pub? How nice that he invites all his friends and guests to join in as dozens of top-notch Celtic singers, dancers, and musicians entertain. Headliners have included internationally known Connie Dover, who happens to be a Weston resident when not touring, the Elders, and the Shenanigans. Of course there's also plenty of Irish food and drink, authentic jewelry and clothing to buy, and CDs to have the artists autograph. Gate passes range from $8 to $10 a day. Children under twelve are free, but you may want to plug the little ones' ears when Bob Reeder starts in with his naughty limericks.

Halloween Events

We turn into the City Boo-tiful near the end of October, when you can find about forty Halloween activities all over town (look for current lists in the *Star*), including haunted houses, acres of pumpkins, and nonscary festivals for little trick-or-treaters. As they say at the pumpkin patch, you can take your pick.

**Blue Valley Recreation Pumpkin Patch
Blue Valley Recreation Complex
Overland Park, KS
(913) 685-6000
www.bluevalleyrec.org**

For children seven and under, this is better than a bag full of Snickers bars. They'll be having so much fun, and get so tuckered out, they may not miss the door-to-door candy collecting. Activities include hayrides, clowns, face painting, and a moonwalk, and everybody gets a pumpkin to take home. A small fee and preregistration are required.

Boo at the Zoo
Kansas City Zoo
(816) 513-5800
www.kansascityzoo.org

Looking for a ghoulishly good time for your young trick-or-treaters? This is a not-so-scary place where they can trick-or-treat from twenty candy stops, watch puppet and sea lion shows, and participate in zookeeper chats and animal feedings. And of course they'll get to see the real live versions of their little kitty-cat costumes. This all-day party is usually held the weekend before Halloween, and usual admission prices ($6.50 to $9.50) are in effect.

Halloween Family Concert Fest
Johnson County Community College
Overland Park, KS
(913) 895-6357
www.opkansas.org

How about a safe alternative to trick-or-treating that's certainly easier on the dental bills? And instead of getting a bag of sugar your kids get a dose of classical music. Don't worry about their getting bored; they may not recognize "Peter and the Wolf," but "Star Wars" will definitely ring a bell. Other activities include costume contests and prizes. There's no charge.

Powell Pumpkin Patch
25695 Spring Valley Road
Louisburg, KS
(913) 837-2212

Drive thirty minutes just to get lost? That's part of the fun at this pumpkin patch with a twenty-acre maze, the largest in the Midwest. Walking through the mile of trails will take at least

thirty minutes, and your reward is a chance to pick out the prettiest or at least most carve-worthy pumpkin from thirty acres of the orange globes. Admission is free; pumpkin prices vary by size.

Spooktacular at Powell Gardens
Powell Gardens
Kingsville, MO
(816) 697-2600
www.powellgardens.org

This two-day fall festival includes storybook characters, games, costume contests, and lots of treats in a friendly setting. And— mum's the word—the gardens are simply beautiful this time of year. Bring your own trick-or-treat bag. Prepaid registration of $5 to $7 is required.

The Beast
1401 West 13th Street
(816) 842-4280
www.kcbeast.com

Can you tell we've gotten to the haunted house section of our list? This one is billed as "America's largest haunted house," and though we can't vouch for that, it is guaranteed to scare your socks off. Instead of having visitors walk in a line, the Beast has an open design so that guests can wander at will through several themed areas. This may not be appropriate for young children or even older kids who are easily traumatized.

It's open weekends in September and October and then nightly from mid-October until early November. The haunting starts at 7:00 p.m. and lasts until the fog lifts. Yikes! Admission is $20. Combo tickets to The Beast and the Edge of Hell are the best deal, at $33; check online for coupons.

The Edge of Hell
1300 West 12th Street
(816) 842-4279
www.edgeofhell.com

They call this theater the granddaddy of all haunted houses, and you'll wish Gramps were here to hold your hand. It's Kansas City's biggest and oldest fright fest, with a huge advantage over the others: a five-story slide. See The Beast for ticket information.

NOVEMBER

American Royal Livestock
Horse Show & Rodeo

See the Close-up in this chapter and get ready to rodeo, pardner.

A Christmas Carol
Kansas City Repertory Theatre
4949 Cherry Street
(816) 235-2700, (888) 502-2700
www.missourirepertorytheatre.org

Even after more than twenty-five years, we never grow tired of seeing this Christmastime treat featuring outstanding costumes, staging, and acting. The chain-rattling ghosts floating in air are hair-raisingly believable, the ending is always happy, and by the time Tiny Tim makes his final memorable statement, you truly will feel blessed. Tickets for thirty-nine performances (late November through the end of December) go on sale as early as October, and early reservations are a must for the best seats. It's the perfect way to wrap the entire family in the holiday spirit. Parking is free and plentiful around the UMKC campus. Adult tickets range from $27 to $33 depending on seats; youth tickets (eighteen and under) are $18. The Rep always offers three or four signed performances per season.

Crown Center Ice Terrace
2450 Grand
(816) 274-8411
www.crowncenter.com

Something to look forward to all year long: outdoor ice-skating in Crown Center Square. Opening day for the season is usually the first week in November, with a free early-morning skate from 6:00 to 9:00 a.m. including complimentary hot chocolate and doughnuts. Free morning skates continue while the terrace stays open, through late March. Regular admis-

sion is $6 per person plus $2 skate rental. The hours are 10:00 a.m. to 9:00 p.m. Sunday through Thursday and 10:00 a.m. to 11:00 p.m. Friday and Saturday. It's lovely to skate when you can see stars, as long as that doesn't mean you've just taken a fall. How many cups of cocoa am I holding up?

The Fairy Princess
Union Station
(816) 483-8300
www.unionstation.org

Create a delightful memory as children whisper their wishes to the Fairy Princess, and with a wave of her wand, a gift magically appears! Her highness is always a vision in layers of netting and a glittering crown, and children of all ages are instantly enchanted. Wishes come true every Saturday from late November until just before Christmas. Visits are free with Union Station admission. Photos are $5. It's an experience they'll never forget; this author certainly never has.

Handel's Messiah
Community of Christ Auditorium
Walnut and River
Independence, MO
(816) 235-6222
www.cofcrist.org

When King George II heard George Friederic Handel's Messiah for the first time, he gave it a standing ovation. You'll do the same after hearing the 350-voice Independence Messiah Choir and the Kansas City Symphony perform the stirring oratorio. The two groups practice for months for this one performance, a nine-decade gift to the community. The staging adds to the evening: a beautiful church, a monstrous 113-rank organ, and a chorus dressed in tuxedoes and evening gowns rising before you on stepped platforms. By the time the "Hallelujah Chorus" begins, you can't help but join in. The perfor-mance is held every year on the Saturday before Thanksgiving. Tickets range from $12 to $28 and are available starting in early September. Don't miss it.

Home for the Holidays Tour
Various locations
(913) 685-2802
www.jcym.com
We'll bet your home would look spectacular if you had a professional interior designer and dozens of elves decorating it for the holidays. That's what happens during this popular tour when the Johnson County Young Matrons choose five gorgeous homes in an upscale area, lavish them with about a ton of ornaments and fresh greenery, and then invite the rest of us in to drool. The tour is typically held on a weekday, so hundreds of workers call in sick and hope their bosses don't show up until after dinner. Advance tickets cost $12 and are available at area grocery stores. The price increases to $15 at the door—worth every penny for the decorating ideas you'll take back to your own home.

Holiday Lighting Ceremonies and Displays

Santa doesn't need Rudolph to locate Kansas City. By the first of December we're lit up like a . . . well, like a Christmas tree, as every community adds its own special holiday display. Following are some of the best and brightest.

Christmas in the Park
Longview Lake Campground
Lee's Summit, MO
(816) 795-8200
www.lees-summit.mo.us
Children will have their little faces plastered to the car window when you drive slowly through this display of 175 animated figures illuminated by nearly 300,000 lights. To join them, take Interstate 470 to View High Drive, south to Third Street, and follow the signs, or just listen for the oohs and ahhs coming from vans full of kids. Free, but donations of $1 per vehicle or $1 per person for buses go to help nearly forty local charities. The lights turn on in late November and continue through December 31.

Mayor's Christmas Tree Lighting Ceremony
Crown Center Square
(816) 274-8444
www.crowncenter.com
The holiday season is officially here when this 100-foot tree arrives in Crown Center Square the first week in November. Then it's dressed in thousands of lights and ornaments in time for the lighting ceremony the evening after Thanksgiving. The mayor of Kansas City and a celebrity guest flip the switch for more than 7,000 white lights on the tree and an additional 50,000 illuminating Crown Center Square. This glowing tree stands as a symbol of the Mayor's Christmas Tree Fund, which has helped more than 40,000 less fortunate families over the past nine decades. Even after the holidays the tree has a special purpose: Its wood is used to make commemorative ornaments sold the following year to benefit the charity.

The tree lighting is a magical finale to a day that begins when Santa appears in his horse-drawn carriage before settling into his temporary home in Crayola Christmas Land. He'll be available for photos and to listen to secret wishes.

Overland Park Mayor's
Lighting Ceremony
Between 78th and 83rd Streets
west of Metcalf
Overland Park, KS
(913) 642-2222
Santa arrives a little early at downtown Overland Park, but that's just fine with the kids waiting to take a picture with the jolly old elf. Parents will get in the spirit too, with carolers, holiday crafts for sale, gay music, free cider and cookies, and an electric light parade. The mayor lights the Christmas tree at dusk, and the party continues with free carriage rides for those who bring two canned goods to donate to Harvesters.

Christmas Card Lane
Mission Ridge III
Olathe, KS
(913) 764-2913

This neighborhood of more than 200 homes all join together to create giant holiday card displays, lines of luminaries, and twinkling front-yard trees. The display usually runs from Thanksgiving until December 31 and is located north of 151st and west of Ridgeview at Ridgeview and Frontier. No charge, but we'd gladly pay.

Country Club Plaza

This legendary scene is perhaps our city's most treasured tradition when, starting each Thanksgiving night, more than 75 miles of jewel-toned lights illuminate every spire and swag of the Spanish-style architecture. Even when the temperature is ten degrees below zero, a crowd shows up to help with the countdown as a celebrity guest pulls the switch. For the past few years the drama has escalated, with a spectacular fireworks display at the InterContinental Hotel.

Mission Hills, KS

63rd and Ensley and Eisenhower Lake

We're not sure how this started—as a lark or a mistake—but a few years ago a homeowner tossed a string of white lights into a tree and let it fall naturally. The result was an illuminated modern art sculpture. The look caught on and now dozens of neighbors join in to create a sea of sailboat shapes along the streets of this pretty neighborhood.

Ward Parkway and Romany Road between 69th and 71st Streets

Make this your second stop after viewing the Plaza lights. It's a fantastic sight, with hundreds of tree trunks wrapped in tiny white lights. The glowing circles are amazing when viewed in perspective from Ward Parkway.

DECEMBER

Christmas in Weston
Downtown Weston, MO
(816) 640-2909
www.westonmo.com

For more than twenty years this charming town has been getting all dolled up for the holidays and inviting us to visit. There's plenty to make the forty-minute drive worth your time: a walking tour of five historic homes, wandering street carolers, carriage rides through town, and visits with Father Christmas. Many of the antiques shops, stores, and boutiques offer hot cider and cookies, too. Tickets are $25. And if you're so enchanted you want to visit Weston again, you'll find information in Day Trips and Weekend Getaways.

Drive-Through Living Nativity
Rockwood Baptist Church
10035 Westport
Independence, MO
(816) 252-6155

More than fifty characters and live animals depict thirteen scenes in the life of Jesus, creating a moving experience that reminds us of the true meaning of the holiday. Although there is no charge, donations are accepted. The drive is usually open for a week beginning the first of December.

Jazz Community Carol Fest
Community Christian Church,
4601 Main Street
(816) 561-6531
www.webjazz.net

Ever hear "Silent Night" performed with a syncopated beat? You will at this happening, happy event that pairs classic holiday tunes with two dozen of Kansas City's finest musicians. Enough gospel and classic renditions are tossed in to keep everyone in the mood; it's simply not Christmas until you've heard Ida McBeth sing "O Holy Night." The $20 tickets go fast for this joyful treat that always falls on the first Sunday afternoon in December.

The Gardener's Railway
Powell Gardens
Kingsville, MO
(816) 697-2600
www.powellgardens.org

Model train enthusiasts will love watching G-gauge trains wind their way through a dwarf forest and lush greenery. Everyone else will

Ropin', Ridin', and Ribs

In Kansas City, when you mention the *party*, chances are you're talking about the American Royal. We've been celebrating this combination grand parade, rodeo, and livestock competition since 1899, so it's definitely here to stay. But for most of us, the American Royal doesn't mean ropin' and ridin', it means ribs. As in barbecue.

Carolyn Wells, the smoky-voiced executive director of the Kansas City Barbeque Society (the group that sanctions nearly one hundred competitions across the country), calls it the Super Bowl of barbecue. Local cartoonist Charlie Podrebarac refers to it as the Woodstock of barbecue. Even the *New York Times Magazine* has gotten in the act, dubbing it the Academy Awards of barbecue.

All we know is that if you're new in town and looking for the competition, you won't need a map. Just look for the blue smoke rising from hundreds of cookers taking their own sweet time transforming briskets, ribs, pork butts, and sausages into tender morsels to be offered up to about 600 judges the next day. Have mercy, it smells divine as forests of hickory, oak, apple wood, and cherry give off a sweet and pungent perfume. Adding to the aromatherapy are whiffs of onion, peppers, and molasses as teams mix up carefully guarded sauce recipes or stir big pots of barbecue beans to make the most of meat drippings and chunks of brisket.

Each year teams from around the country show up at the West Bottoms, smokers in tow, to vie for more than $60,000 in prizes and trophies as big as a side of beef. About sixty-five elite teams, champions all, compete in the International Invitational contest, with about 350 or so more entering the open cook-off.

The annual bash provides plenty of entertainment even for noncookers. It seems more than barbecue is being judged as teams try to outdo one another by personalizing their roped-off areas with outlandish decorations, inflatable palm trees, and live bands. Even the teams' names are a hoot, like Bite My Butt, Pig Newton, Drinkers with a Bar-B-Que Problem, and Any Pork in a Storm. The winners get more than bragging rights and some cash; a title from the American Royal can mean a real boost to business if you own a barbecue restaurant, sell your own sauce brand, or market a smoker.

There is, of course, another side to the American Royal, and without it we probably wouldn't be as well known for our barbecue. The livestock show speaks to Kansas City's century-old importance in the food chain. Here, too, some of the country's best ranchers and 4-H members come to compete for big prizes in categories like Angus bulls, heifers, lamb, and swine.

The American Royal Rodeo is one of the top ten in the country sanctioned by the Professional Rodeo Cowboys Association and offers such

Ropin' and ridin' at the American Royal Rodeo, an annual event that showcases our Wild West heritage. RICK McKIBBEN

events as barrel racing, saddle bronco riding, calf roping, and the ever-popular mutton bustin'. A Mexican Rodeo Extravaganza salutes the Mexican cowboy heritage with folkloric dancing, mariachi bands, and charro bronco riders. Even folks who don't care about the fine art of lassos show up for the big-name entertainment after the events. Country crooners like Willie Nelson, Faith Hill, Clint Black, and others have appeared. A huge parade down Main Street begins the whole shebang with more than 7,000 participants, including sixteen saddle clubs, twenty-five floats, and twenty-three bands. A children's rodeo, a horse show, and agricultural exhibitions round out the weeklong extravaganza. So now you know the answer to "Where's the beef?" It's right here in Kansas City, especially in October. A new addition is a barbecue competition just for youngsters.

All the staged events take place at the American Royal Complex, west of downtown in the West Bottoms. For more information, mosey on down to the Web site at www.americanroyal.com or call (816) 221-9800. And if you plan to come, remember: Cowboy boots are more than just a fashion statement.

be thrilled just to shrug off jackets in the toasty confines of a glass-encased conservatory. And there's still plenty to see throughout the rest of the gardens even in the sepia tones of winter. Regular admittance fees apply: $5.50 for adults, $2.50 for children ages five to twelve.

The Nutcracker
Midland Theatre
(816) 931-3330
www.kcballet.com

This holiday classic continues to astound audiences, both young and old, with its magnificent sets, costumes, and special effects. (The Mouse King is truly sinister!) The performance features the beloved music of Peter I. Tchaikovsky, choreography by Todd Bolender, three casts of professional artists from Kansas City Ballet, and more than one hundred youngsters ages seven to seventeen selected from Kansas City Ballet School. Children love the fantastical characters and perk up when they hear music they recognize. And the setting, the historic Midland Theatre with its gilt trimming and rich velvets, adds to the magic. Tickets range from $15 to $60.

Winter Skies
Kansas City Museum
3218 Gladstone Boulevard
(816) 483-8300

Here's a wonderful way to introduce children to the heavenly world of astronomy or reacquaint yourself with favorite stars and constellations like Orion, Gemini, Taurus, and Sirius, the brightest star in our winter sky. The museum's planetarium presents two or three programs each Friday and Saturday through mid-March. Tickets cost $3.50 per person.

New Year's Eve Celebrations

Prove you can par-*tay* with the best of them with bubbles, balloons, and boogalooing at your choice of big galas or more intimate affairs. In addition to those listed below, dozens of hotels, nightclubs, casinos, and restaurants offer packages from $40 per person to more than $1,000. In one recent year, the *Kansas City Star* listed more than fifty party events. Pop!

Hyatt Regency Crown Center
2345 McGee Street
(816) 421-1234, (816) 435-4152
www.hyattnye.com

Just you, your sweetheart, and 4,000 of your closest friends. Sound romantic? It certainly is *exciting,* especially at the stroke of midnight when they release 20,000 balloons. The evening also includes spacious entertainment areas, an indoor laser light show, and a pyrotechnic display. Packages include champagne, buffets, and open bars starting at $180 for singles hoping for a last-minute match and $275 for couples.

Union Station's New Year's Celebration
(816) 460-2020
www.unionstation.org

It's been a tradition since 1933 to ring in the New Year at Union Station. At this grand palace there's plenty of room to find a cozy spot for a midnight kiss (dibs on under the clock) or link up with friends to toast the New Year. The evening includes more than just champagne; you can also visit Science City and see live stage shows in the Theater District. Prices start at $60.

Velvet Dog
400 East 31st Street
(816) 753-9990
www.martinicorner.com

This disco explosion has been the grooviest New Year's bash around since 1996. The crowd becomes one big groove-machine while dancing to a jukebox full of funky '70s disco hits, and next door the Empire Room's DJ takes requests for Bee Gees favorites. Better practice spelling out "YMCA" before you call for reservations. A $30 advance ticket ($40 at the door) will get you into both clubs and includes a limited open bar. This is a definite twenties crowd.

PARKS, LAKES, AND RECREATION

Kansas City and Mother Nature? We're like *that*. She blessed us with a landscape of shimmering lakes, lush green spaces, golden prairie grass, and acres of woodlands. Everywhere you look we're surrounded by the great outdoors, which might account for the dozens of sports activities and organizations you'll read about in the Sports chapter.

But for now let's see just how easy being green can be. Kansas City, Missouri, alone has 188 parks, including the third largest metropolitan park in the country, and more than 130 miles of boulevards and parkways covering some 10,000 acres. Downtown parks, sometimes shaded more by skyscrapers than sycamores, give city workers a respite from phones, faxes, and meetings long enough to enjoy lunch alfresco, listen to a jazz concert, or ogle the annual Elvis Parade. More about that later.

In addition, the city is ringed by hundreds of lakes, woods, and parks, places where you can commune with nature, possibly feed apples to bison, and most definitely feed your soul. With an abundance of rolling acres, fragrant floral displays, lakes overflowing with sporting amenities, and cool, sandy beaches, it's easy to say, "You bet!" when someone tells you to take it outside.

And how we do love our gardens. Kansas City gardeners have fought clay, rocks, and a pernicious Zone 5 to create some of the country's most stunning groupings of flowers and plantings. Drive down any street and you'll notice the fruits of their labor as front doors are defined by masses of flowers. Each season brings another reason to celebrate. Spring's irises, tulips, and daffodils give way to mounds of impatiens, splashy azaleas, and daylilies, and then mum's the word each fall. Where the sun won't reach, we plant hundreds of hostas. Backyards are filled with koi ponds, Japanese gardens, shady decks, and New Orleans–style courtyards. And while you may not want to stop the car to peer over a stranger's gate, you can get inspiration and fresh air at one of our public gardens described here. We highly recommend our 915-acre Powell Gardens for starters.

There's far more to describe than one chapter will allow, so in the Close-up we've listed area parks and recreation departments and garden clubs where you can learn about other green spaces, special events, and classes. You may also want to peruse the Annual Events and Festivals chapter for special events regarding flora and fauna throughout the year. Perhaps there's a water garden tour or butterfly festival near you.

Chances are by the time you have that picnic basket ready, you'll have discovered a pastoral spot on which to spread a blanket. To help you find it, we've divided this chapter by activity type. Listings are in Kansas City, Missouri, unless otherwise noted.

LAKES

Fleming Park
Missouri Highway 40 on
Woods Chapel Road
Blue Springs, MO
(816) 795-8200
www.jacksongov.org
You bet they're happy campers in Jackson County; they're also happy boaters, fishing enthusiasts, swimmers, and hikers. Fleming Park, a 7,800-acre paradise just fifteen minutes east of Kansas City, offers all these activities and more with two lakes, a swimming beach, picnic shelters, archery range, hiking, and camping facilities. We provide

No man is an island . . . but we have one in the area. Twelve-acre Nelson Island is the only publicly accessible island in the Kansas River. It's located at the northern terminus of Mill Creek Streamway Park.

camping information in the Accommodations chapter, or call (816) 229-8980 for a free campground guide.

Winding through the grounds are six trails that offer blufftop and lakefront vistas, as well as your choice of a quiet stroll or a challenging hike. The park is also where you'll find Missouri Town 1855, an antebellum farming community of more than twenty-five buildings dating from 1820 to 1860. This living-history museum uses original furnishings and equipment, interpreters in period attire, and rare livestock breeds to depict the lifestyles of the mid-nineteenth century. Take a self-guided tour or watch for annual events like Children's Day in June, when kids can take out the ear-buds and participate in a gunnysack race or pie-eating contest.

Take a safari ride through the one hundred–acre Animal Enclosure and you can stare a bison in the eyes and watch a family of elk play in a pasture. And, yes, please do feed the animals; be sure to bring apples and pears. Tours are given Saturdays throughout the summer, and tickets ($5 for adults, $3 for seniors and kids from two to thirteen) are available the day of the tour at Missouri Town; preregistration is not available. Call (816) 229-8980 for more information about this wild ride.

The Kemper Outdoor Education Center is a haven for nature lovers, nestled on the east side of Lake Jacomo in the Fleming Park Nature Preserve. The center features aquariums, live displays of reptiles (go ahead, *you* touch it), a bird viewing area, and a display of rocks and minerals. The forty-acre site boasts butterfly gardens, ponds, beehives, wildlife-feeding stations, and a 1-mile nature trail through wetlands, tallgrass prairie, and wood-lands. Kemper Gardens is a popular spot for summer weddings where the bridge over the garden pool waterfall makes a lovely altar. Okay, we've fed the bison, said "I do," and filled up on blueberry pie. Now, get set to get wet at one of Fleming's two lakes.

Blue Springs Lake

Powerboats, water skis, tubes, and personal watercraft are all familiar sights on this 720-acre lake. Anglers try their hands at striped bass, bluegill, largemouth bass, and catfish. Bring your own boat or rent one at the marina (816-795-1112), where you'll also find lakeside gasoline pumps, concession stands, and (let's think positive here) a fish-cleaning station. You can also pick up your state fishing license at the marina.

Or you can beach it at Blue Springs' sandy shoreline. Get energetic with a swim, volleyball game (balls are available for rent), paddleboat, kayak, or canoe, or simply work on that tan. Certified lifeguards are on duty, and showers, restrooms, and full concessions are available, so you can simply show up with your bathing suit and a towel. Oh, and you'll need $3.00 for adults or $2.25 for kids fifteen and younger. The fun starts Memorial Day.

Lake Jacomo

Set sail on this breathtaking 970-acre lake located in the heart of Fleming Park. Enjoy colorful sailboat regattas, or jump aboard a pontoon boat where the livin' is easy. The marina (816-795-8888) provides everything you'll need for a day at the lake: boat rental, concession stands, state fishing license, and tackle shop. And get that frying pan ready for some crappie, bluegill, largemouth bass, and walleye: Jacomo is an angler's dream come true.

Lake Jacomo is the place to be on any balmy day, but it's particularly appealing during special events like July's Lake Fest, when thousands of folks line the shores and take lake cruises, watch a regatta, and enjoy a spectacular fireworks display. The annual Easter Egg Hunt brings out hundreds of kids to look for goodies.

Wyandotte County Lake Park
91st Street and Leavenworth Road
Kansas City, KS
(913) 596-7077
www.kckpl.lib.ks.us/wyco/parks
You could easily imagine you're in the Lake of the Ozarks while driving through this 1,500-acre parkland with bluffs, heavily timbered woods, and gently rolling hills. Its 400-acre lake is where about half of Wyandotte County first placed a worm on a hook, and many of them return every spring to continue the drill. Some get an earlier start; boating and fishing are allowed from the last Saturday in February through November 30. Call about hours and permits. A horse trail and children's playground are other possibilities, and be sure to show up for free model railroad rides each second Saturday of the month from April through November.

WyCo Lake, as we call it, has sixteen shelter houses, each with water, electricity, restrooms, and playground equipment; there's a reservation fee for each. Other picnic areas are free to the first group there with the potato salad. The handsome James P. Davis Hall provides air-conditioned comfort for up to 150 guests. The lake is also home to the Korea-Vietnam Memorial, the only monument in the United States to honor soldiers from both wars. Dedicated in 1988, the structure includes a wall of marble fronted by two life-size bronze statues representing 111 who died from Wyandotte County. Kansas City sculptor Tom Corbin donated his time to create the bronzes, and a dozen labor unions donated thousands of hours to the project.

PARKS AND GARDENS

Antioch Park
6501 Antioch Road
Merriam, KS
(913) 831-3355
www.jcprd.com/parks
The Johnson County parks district purchased this park in 1956 (its first acquisition) and has turned it into one of the most popular community parks in the metropolitan area. Although at forty-four acres it's not the largest, they've packed it with lots of activities like tennis and basketball courts, two small catch-and-release fishing lakes, and an accessible playground called Dodge Town where kids can climb in and out of the hotel and general store. Four picnic shelters offer tables, grills, drinking fountains, and restrooms and can be rented for around $30 for a half day from the parks department.

The park is also home to the Helen Cuddy Rose Garden and Memorial Arboretum, a picturesque wedding site found on the northwest corner of the park. More than 650 rose bushes grace the grounds, reflecting late centenarian Helen Cuddy's favorite flower. The peaceful garden, which has held many weddings over the years, also encloses a cascading fountain, a sundial, and a perennial bed containing iris, lamb's ear, hibiscus, crocus, and other old-fashioned favorites. A walkway will take you through the small arboretum, and picnic tables, a small lake with stepping-stones, and a children's play area will beckon you to stop for a while. You can remember loved ones by contributing a planting; for more information call (913) 831-3355. The metro's first exclusively Vietnam memorial was recently constructed here to honor those who served.

Barney Allis Plaza
12th Street and Wyandotte
(816) 513-5000
Tucked between the Bartle Hall Convention Center and downtown hotels sits a city park that serves as an unofficial town square. It's a popular place to get a quick bite from a street vendor, link up with friends after work, and attend Party at the Barney block parties. Trees provide shade, and a large sloping fountain sits on the north end. To the east is the Kansas City Sports Walk of Stars, a monument to local greats that hasn't yet, if you'll forgive the pun, quite gotten off the ground. During summer months, the lunchtime crowd is

i Although there's no charge to enjoy most of the green spaces we've described, you will need a little green to rent a shelter or a boat or spend the day at a beach. Call the numbers shown for fee information or to reserve your space. And call early; many of the most popular shelters are reserved far in advance.

treated to free noon concerts that could be jazz, blues, ragtime, or classical guitar, or silence of a dozen laptops; free wireless Internet access is available here. And every August, Barney meets the King as a dozen or so Elvis impersonators don outlandish white jumpsuits, oversize sunglasses with attached sideburns, and sparkly belt buckles to hold a parade. Hundreds turn out to watch the quirky tribute and vote for the best outfit. Thankyou, thankyouverymuch.

Bonner Springs Park
Interstate 70 North
Bonner Springs, KS
(913) 596-7077
www.bonnersprings.org

This 540-acre park is kept busy year-round with more than just picnics and volleyball. Located adjacent to the Agricultural Hall of Fame, the park houses the Verizon Amphitheatre, where top-selling musical groups perform outdoor concerts. Each fall the area becomes an Old English village during the Renaissance Festival (read about this in Annual Events and Festivals). When the electric guitars and jousting stop, the park offers space for outdoor activities like tennis courts, ball fields, and shady picnic areas.

Deanna Rose Children's Farmstead
13800 Switzer Road
Overland Park, KS
(913) 897-2360
www.opkansas.org

A favorite destination for families thanks to its petting zoo, wagon train rides, and other activities, the farmstead also contains a delightful garden maintained by the Johnson County Extension Master Gardeners. Surrounded by a white picket fence, the old-fashioned garden contains a butterfly garden; herbs; shade garden planted with hostas, lilies, and columbine; and a vegetable garden, all along a winding brick walkway. Usually a garden expert is there, measuring the marigolds or tending to tulips, so you might get some advice during your visit.

English Landing Park
Parkville, MO
(816) 505-2227
www.parkvillemo.com

This long and narrow sixty-four-acre greenway stretches along the natural bends and limestone bluffs of the Missouri River, providing wonderful views from its hiking trails, picnic shelters, and playgrounds. Most of the amenities are just across a turn-of-the-twentieth-century truss bridge. You'll find lots of folks enjoying ripe peaches and other fresh produce from the farmers' market alongside the trail. The park hosts several festivals throughout the year, including the Parkville Jazzfest and Christmas on the River.

For even more adventure, head to the Parkville Nature Sanctuary, which offers 115 acres of woods and wetlands, a waterfall, a beaver colony, and a glimpse of the area's storied past as a river town. You'll find a trailhead just north of the soccer field parking lot. And if you've had enough of the great outdoors, head back to Parkville's Main Street, where shops, galleries, and a wide array of restaurants await.

Heritage Park
159th Street and Pflumm Road
Olathe, KS
(913) 831-3355
www.jcprd.com/parks

This 1,160-acre park was dedicated on Independence Day 1981 and includes enough amenities to warrant a parade. Facilities include ten picnic shelters; a forty-five-acre lake; a marina with pedal boat and sailboard rentals; concession stands; play areas; fields for softball, soccer, and football; and an

The Men Who Turned Kansas City Green

When people visit Kansas City and swoon over our vast parks and boulevards, they're paying tribute to landscape architects George Kessler and the father-and-son team of Sid and Herbert Hare.

When a twenty-one-year-old George Kessler came to town in 1890, he saw little more than scattered homes on little hills, occasionally separated by junglelike foliage. He soon partnered with William Rockhill Nelson, who owned and edited the *Star* and who was desperate to turn the little town into a picturesque and pleasant city. Together they, along with other concerned citizens like August Meyer, created the City Beautiful project. By 1895 Kessler was replacing shacks, dumps, and rickety signboards with verdant hillsides, tree-shaded lakes and walks, and smooth, spacious boulevards.

For thirty years he worked with the Kansas City Park Board to create Gladstone Boulevard and Cliff Drive, the Paseo, and Liberty Memorial and to turn a depressing Vinegar Hill into the majestic Penn Valley Park. Kessler did more than just green-up Kansas City. During his forty-year career he designed twenty-six communities, twenty-six park and boulevard systems, nearly fifty parks, and forty-six estates and residences in twenty-three states, Mexico, and China. You can learn more about his work through the George Kessler Society (P.O. Box 6685, Kansas City, MO 64123–0658; www.georgekessler.org).

Sid Hare started his career as superintendent at Forest Hill Cemetery, where he became a national authority on expanding the roles of cemeteries as botanical gardens, bird sanctuaries, and arboretums. In 1910 he started a landscaping consulting firm with his son, Herbert, who had studied with the famous Frederick Law Olmsted. During their twenty-eight-year partnership, father and son continued Kessler's tradition of wide, beautiful boulevards and parks throughout Kansas City's landscape.

Their trademark was winding roads contoured to natural topography, preserving trees and valleys, and retaining (or creating) scenic vistas. In 1913 J. C. Nichols hired the Hares to work on the Country Club District area. In addition to laying out approximately 2,500 acres, the firm designed the grounds for many homes, including some of the fifty-acre estates that made up the original Mission Hills. Herbert was responsible for designing settings for many of the imported sculptures and fountains that Nichols placed throughout his developments.

Hare & Hare also collaborated with architect Edward Buehler Delk in planning Nichols's Country Club Plaza. Other memorable works include the Rose Garden in Loose Park, which Sid completed in 1937, a year before his death, and the setting for the Nelson-Atkins Museum of Art. Herbert went on to contribute projects throughout the country, including Kansas City's masterful Linda Hall Library arboretum. He passed away in 1960, soon after completing plans for Lake Jacomo.

The legacy of Kessler and Hare & Hare continues today through programs like MetroGreen, a large-scale system of interconnected corridors that will span more than 1,000 miles to link city to countryside, suburb to urban area. More than a system of trails and bike paths, MetroGreen will conserve the unique native landscape—bluffs and woodlands and prairies, parks and boulevards—to ensure that future generations will enjoy them as well.

i   Although perhaps you'll never have a park named for you like Mr. Swope, Powell, or Loose, you could leave a legacy with a park bench, tree planting, or rose bush. Several of our public parks and gardens can arrange for a lasting memorial in your honor.

eighteen-hole championship golf course and driving range. We're tuckered out just thinking about it.

One of its most unique features is the Black Bob Shelter House, which is on an island and also accessible by foot from the marina area. It can handle up to 300 and is available by reservation only. The shelter includes thirty tables, a large barbecue grill, electricity, and restrooms—a good thing, because it's the only district shelter that allows 3.2 beer. Extremely popular, it is often rented months (even years) in advance.

Kauffman Legacy Park
4800 Rockhill Road
(816) 932-1200
www.kauffman.org

This exquisite walled sanctuary is one more lasting legacy from Ewing and Muriel Kauffman. And although it's not large, there is much to see as you walk through each display. Brick pathways lead you past elegant ironwork, sculptures, and stained-glass windows providing a delightful mix of vistas and textures. A teak bench provides a place to pause and murmur a quiet thank-you to the Kauffmans, whose gifts are ever blooming. Garden pavilions provide shade, and pergolas brace bright blossoms nodding on vines. A lush mix of flowers and plants is changed three times each year, so the garden looks completely different from month to month.

A reflecting pool runs the length of the Parterre Garden, where slender female sculptures by local artist Tom Corbin are captured in midpirouette. The octagonal pool in the Green Garden offers an ever-moving water display, and shhh . . . there's one more area to be discovered. The secluded Secret Garden

really does have a secret: three hidden fountains that shoot arcs of water above your head at random moments. At least once a day someone feels a drop from above and asks, "Is it raining?" The garden is open every day except some holidays, and there is no admission fee. No pets are allowed except assistance dogs.

Linda Hall Library
5109 Cherry Street
(816) 926-8747
www.lindahall.org

Most people come to the Linda Hall Library seeking knowledge and information. With more than one million volumes, it is the largest privately supported library of science, engineering, and technology in the United States. But those seeking tranquility will find it in the fourteen-acre urban arboretum with 450 or so trees representing 160 varieties. In late April the tree peonies, saucer-size beauties in vibrant colors, begin to bloom; they constitute one of the largest collections in the Midwest. By May the antique shrub roses scent the air as you stroll by. A butterfly garden is planted with happy marigolds, color-box zinnias, Mexican sunflowers, and nectar-rich fennel. A new area contains fifty species of indigenous perennials. Tours of the gardens can be arranged, or you may pick up a printed guide at the library's front desk for $5.

Loose Park
51st and Wornall Road
(816) 561-9710
www.kcmo.org/parks

Loose Park wasn't always so serene. At one time this was the site of the bloody Civil War Battle of Westport, but today the only reminders are historical markers placed throughout the seventy-four acres. An 8-foot-high bronze statue of Jacob Loose watches over the garden named in his honor. And early-morning joggers, Plaza workers breaking for lunch, late-afternoon lovers, and children tossing bread crusts to the ducks are all drawn to this space up the hill from the Plaza.

Welcome to Paradise

Set among gently rolling hills, Powell Gardens is one of the Midwest's most treasured places, offering 915 acres of vivid plants bursting with color, winding pathways along brooks and waterfalls, windswept meadows, and some of the region's most striking architecture. Luckily, this scene of serenity is a mere 40 miles away.

Your tour begins at the visitor center, a handsome stacked-limestone building that houses a conservatory, classrooms, a delightful gift shop, and Cafe Thyme, where upscale buffet food is served for lunch, Sunday brunch, and dinner during special events.

When you're ready to explore the grounds, you can take a free trolley ride to the different areas or cross the bridge on foot to the Island Garden set in a twelve-acre lake. This is a showplace for native and exotic water plants, rock gardens, and ornamental trees—nearly 800 varieties of plants in all. A three-pooled cascading water garden acts as the focal point. The island's north side allows for an uninterrupted view of the stunning Marjorie Powell Allen Chapel, a wood, glass, and stone triangle in the sky designed by famed Arkansas architect Fay Jones.

After leaving the water garden, head to your right past the Wildflower Meadow. There you'll enter the cool and serene Rock and Waterfall Garden, dressed in every shade of green imaginable in delicate ferns and nearly fifty varieties of hostas. Sweet pinks and white appear in flowering trees in spring, and in summer raspberry-colored azaleas provide a burst of color. Hidden among these enchanted woods are picturesque decks and secluded benches for cuddling or taking time to reflect.

Just over a bridge is the 3½-acre Perennial Garden, the largest in the Midwest, with more than 5,000 plantings, including many chosen specifically as come-hithers to butterflies. In summer the place nearly pops with orange, deep reds, and brilliant yellows as 250 varieties of daylilies lift their trumpets to the skies. The curving walkways take you through twists and turns to a peaceful pavilion overlooking the lake.

Back at the visitor center you can enjoy a crisp salad or tasty sandwich or buy a book or garden tool in the gift shop. Here's also where you may take part in a class on growing orchids, constructing a birdhouse, or making holiday wreaths from natural elements. Outdoor festivals and events include the popular Booms and Blooms over Fourth of July weekend, with live music and an impressive fireworks display, and Ballet in the Park with the Kansas City Ballet. Several times a year members of the Astronomical Society of Kansas City present stargazing demonstrations.

More than 100,000 visitors enjoy the gardens (816-697-2600, www.powell gardens.org) each year. General admission April through October is $8 for adults, $7 for seniors, and $3 for children ages five to twelve. From November to March the price is $2 less. Just one hint before you head out: Bring plenty of film.

Close-up

Parks and Recreation Departments

Most cities within our metroplex have their own parks and recreation departments, staffed and managed by those wonderful men and women who plan outings; clean away debris; and keep our lakes, parks, trails, and public gardens so idyllic. Here's how to reach them. And when you do, you might say thanks!

Missouri
www.mopark.org

Kansas City
Kansas City Missouri Parks & Recreation, (816) 513-7500

Cass County
Belton Parks & Recreation, (816) 331-0336

Clay County
Clay-Platt Baseball League, (816) 734-3733

Clay County Parks & Recreation, (816) 532-0803

North Kansas City Parks & Recreation, (816) 274-6008

Liberty Parks & Recreation, (816) 792-6009

Grandview Parks & Recreation, (816) 763-3900

Jackson County
Jackson County Parks & Recreation, (816) 795-8200

Raytown Parks & Recreation, (816) 358-4100

Platte County
Platte County Parks & Recreation, (816) 858-3338

Kansas
www.jcprd.com

Johnson County
Blue Valley Parks & Recreation, (913) 685-6000

Johnson County Parks & Recreation, (913) 831-3355

Within Loose Park is the Laura Conyers Smith Municipal Rose Garden, with a reflecting pool, a fragrant display of hundreds of colorful blooms, and a small lake with a tranquil lily pond. Although Jacob Loose's widow, Ella, who commissioned the park in 1927, had requested athletic fields, we're secretly glad someone dropped the ball, so to speak. Without shouts of fouls and scores, Loose Park provides a restful, peaceful retreat.

Overland Park Arboretum &
Botanical Gardens
179th and Antioch
Overland Park, KS
(913) 685-3604
www.opkansas.org
This hidden, 300-acre gem in south Overland Park is most definitely growing, with new ecosystems, thirteen gardens, four conservatories, and a handsome learning center. Five

Lenexa Parks & Recreation,
(913) 541-8592

Wyandotte County
www.kckpl.lib.ks.us/wyco

Mission Community Center,
(913) 722-8200

Kansas City, Kansas, Parks &
Recreation, (913) 596-7077

Olathe Parks & Recreation,
(913) 764-6163

Bonner Springs Parks & Recreation,
(913) 422-7010

Overland Park Parks & Recreation,
(913) 895-6350

Gardening Organizations and Resources

The Loose Park Garden Center
5200 Pennsylvania Avenue
(816) 784-5399

This is the headquarters for several garden clubs, where meetings, shows, and workshops take place. The horticultural reference library has about 1,500 books on every bloomin' thing. It's open 8:00 a.m. to 4:00 p.m. weekdays. The Garden Center Association of Greater Kansas City, an umbrella group with about 1,000 members, meets here. Its newsletter, *Garden Bulletin,* is published bimonthly and includes a calendar of events. Membership costs $15 a year. For information call the number above.

Master Gardeners' Hotlines

These are the experts to call when your dahlia's drooping or your tomatoes are toast. Armed with state horticultural training courses and scads of experience, the volunteers can answer your questions or direct you to other resources. The Johnson County Master Gardeners work at the Deanna Rose Farmstead, 137th and Switzer in Overland Park. The hotline (913-764-6306) is staffed 9:00 a.m. to 4:00 p.m. weekdays. The Missouri Extension hotline (816-833-8733) is open 9:00 a.m. to 3:00 p.m. weekdays. Or contact the Master Gardeners' automated Info-line, (913) 393-1913 or www.outreach.missouri.edu/extensioninfoline.

miles of wood chip–covered hiking trails meander through the area and across two 75-foot bridges spanning Wolf Creek. The trails become slightly more challenging along limestone bluffs rising above the southern banks of the creek. Views from here are marvelous, and if you linger long enough you might see a crane or other waterfowl silently land.

Eight natural ecosystems, from prairie grassland and dense woods to a wildflower meadow, provide a surprise at every turn. The highlight is the Erickson Water Garden, with four waterfalls and a bog with more than one hundred natural plantings that attract birds, butterflies (more than 500 varieties have been identified here!), and two-footed nature lovers. Benches scattered around the area invite you to rest and listen to the restful sounds of cascading water and laughing children.

The Marder Woodland Garden is a relatively new addition with massive stone pillars supporting wooden arbors at its entrance and overlook. It's a romantic spot with the sound of falling water resonating through towering trees. And your little nature boy or girl will have fun following a spiraling walkway or watching frogs frolic in a pond in the Children's Discovery Garden. Plants and trees are identified here, as they are throughout the garden. An easy, half-mile asphalt trail provides a nice stroll.

The visitor center hosts programs and social events and contains a small gift shop and concession stand. Enjoy your refreshment on the sunny patio. When visiting, please note that you cannot reach the arboretum by going south on Antioch. Take U.S. Highway 69 south to 179th Street, turn right, and go west about 0.5 mile. Large signs will indicate the entrance on your left. Admission is free, but donations are accepted.

Shawnee Mission Park
7900 Renner Road
Shawnee, KS
www.jcpard.com/parks

More than three million visitors enjoy this 1,250-acre park every year, more than any other park in the state of Kansas, making the district wonder why it doesn't open a tollbooth. Lucky for us, it's a public park and anyone can enjoy its many natural wonders along with a few treasures where Mother Nature got some human help.

Facilities include a 150-acre lake for boating, fishing, and sailboarding, twelve shelters and numerous picnic areas, horseback and nature trails, an archery range, and a marina. A sandy beach with a concession and bathhouse appeals to sun-lovers. There's a $3.00 fee for Johnson County residents, while others pay $3.50. Shelters range in size from Shelter No. 3 with a lake view and seating for thirty-two to No. 10 in the Walnut Grove area with three grills, twenty tables, and seating for 160. Please invite us to *that* party. In fall this park has a splashy show of colorful foliage that rivals New England. Colorful trees line the main road that circles the park; take one and head to the south side of the park where a 5-story observation tower provides a breathtaking view of the jewel-tone leaves.

Shawnee Mission Park is also home to Theatre in the Park, a popular summer theater venue (see The Arts for more information), and the John Barkley Visitor Center, which has an exhibit on the history of parks in Johnson County. Pet owners, however, make a mad dash to the dog park, a seventy-acre fenced area that is leash-free. With access to the lake, it's a favorite with labs, who gleefully swim out to retrieve sticks. Leashes are required everywhere else.

Swope Park
Swope Parkway and Meyer Boulevard
(816) 513-7500
www.kcmo.org/parks

Topping out at 1,769 acres, Swope Park is the largest city park in Kansas City and one of the most expansive in the country. The land was donated by millionaire Thomas H. Swope and dedicated on June 25, 1898. It contains two golf courses; areas for softball, soccer, rugby, and Frisbee; horseback trails; and a day camp for kids. And, yes, you can rough it in the middle of a city: Hiking enthusiasts can take a guided scenic tour along the hill south of the Lake of the Woods.

The Lakeside Nature Center (4701 East Gregory Boulevard, 816-513-8960) within Swope Park is Missouri's largest wildlife rehabilitation center, caring for more than 3,300 native animals and birds. The center also has a 1,000-gallon aquarium and offers educational programs for all ages, including birdwatching, animal tracking, streamside hikes, and nature photography. The nature center is open 9:00 a.m. to 5:00 p.m. Tuesday through Saturday and noon to 4:00 p.m. Sunday. Admission is free, and the center is open year-round, closed Monday. Swope Park is also home to the 8,000-seat Starlight Theatre as well as the Kansas City Zoo and Sprint IMAX Theatre.

TRAILS

Drive around this suburban area and you might dismiss it as row after row of housing developments, shopping centers, and office buildings. But thanks to city fathers with vision, Johnson County, Kansas, is a place of green spaces, meandering streams, and pocket parks, with about 140 miles of trails for walking, hiking, and biking. You just need to know where to look. The following will give you a good head start, but to really get a lay of the land, the Johnson County Park and Recreation District (913-438-7275, www.jcprd.com) offers maps and descriptions. And if you plan to take a phone, park rangers are available through the dispatcher by calling (913) 782-0720.

The Indian Creek Trail and Tomahawk Creek Trail system in Overland Park provides more than 30 miles of hiking and biking leisure. The Indian Creek portion joins Quivira Park at 119th and Quivira and extends to Leawood City Park, where it dips under Interstate 435 and through commercial, residential, and office areas. The areas are shaded, a few park benches are scattered around, and you'll see a charming little waterfall along the way. You can also access the trail at several points, including Corporate Woods office park, where a drinking fountain and picnic shelter mark the entrance to a partially hidden bridge.

i When exploring our many walking and biking trails, remember it's "Yield to the right and pass on the left." When approaching walkers from behind on a bike or in-line skates, it's courteous, not to mention safer, to announce "To your left" to allow them time to move over.

Tomahawk Creek Trail runs behind Blue Valley Recreation Fields near 138th Street and Antioch Road, and from Nieman Road and 135th Street around St. Andrew's Golf Course to the Deanna Rose Children's Farmstead, which makes a great stop along the way (see Kidstuff for information about this delightful place). The trail connects with a trail at Miller's Woods.

Mill Creek Streamway Park crosses four counties as it travels along Mill Creek from Woodland Road north to Kansas Highway 10 in Olathe and then continues north through Lenexa, Shawnee (where it dips into Shawnee Mission Park), and Merriam to the Kansas River. If you made it all the way, celebrate with a little dance on twelve-acre Nelson Island, the only public-accessible island in the Kansas River, where the trail ends. Mill Creek includes wheelchair-accessible parking, drinking fountains, and shaded picnic areas.

SPORTS

Ballgames! Getcher red-hot ballgames here! In Kansas City we love our sports. Always have, always will, whether our teams are winning or not. And our sports town status began long before the Royals and Chiefs suited up. It started in 1884 when the Kansas City Unions baseball team first took the field.

But it was the Kansas City Monarchs, those champs of the Negro Leagues, that really put us on the map. Satchel Paige, Jackie Robinson, and Buck O'Neil were so important to the sport and this city that we built the country's only Negro Leagues Baseball Museum (www.nlbm.com). You can read more about this terrific memorial in the Attractions chapter.

And no other city in America can rival our history of college tournament basketball. A tournament—Big Six, Big Seven, Big Eight, Big Twelve—has been played in Kansas City every year, sometimes twice a year, since 1946. But it started long before that. In 1937 what is now known as the NAIA tournament, the nation's oldest, began at downtown Municipal Auditorium. By the time the NCAA Tournament final came here in 1940, 10,000 fans packed the stands and March Madness became an official affliction. The NCAA returned in 2005 after a short stint in Texas. And after an eight-year absence, the NAIA returned to Kansas City in 2002. We remain the undisputed Tournament Town.

We're not always watching sports . . . sometimes we're participating in them. You'll find plenty of athletic activities to keep you in liniment, including golf, cycling, hiking, and running. We're also big on joining clubs so that we can talk about our sports when we're not watching or playing; for instance, for a city without a single snowcapped mountain, we have one of the country's largest ski clubs.

You'll get contact information in this chapter. But first, let's hit one out of the ballpark.

The listings in this chapter are grouped by spectator, participation, family, and kids' sports. The facilities are located in Kansas City, Missouri, unless otherwise noted.

SPECTATOR SPORTS

Kansas City Brigade
(913) 383-8020
www.kcbrigade.com
2006 was the inaugural year for the team, part of the Arena Football League. Local ticket holders no doubt will recognize the burly guy with the sweet grin; that's co-owner Neil Smith, who earned two Super Bowl rings during thirteen years with the Kansas City Chiefs and the Denver Broncos. So the guy knows sports. And the Brigade Girls know how to get a crowd enthused. These five beauties in blue will be moving with the team to the exciting new Sprint Center downtown. Season tickets for the 2008 season go for $68 to well over $1,000. Premium single-day tickets start at just $9, even for those games that are broadcast nationally on ABC.

Kansas City Explorers
(816) 513-5630
www.kcexplorers.com
With fifteen years as members of World Team Tennis under their white belts, the Explorers pack 'em in at what must be the prettiest venue in the league. Their court is

i By the time you read this, Kansas City will be welcoming you to the Sprint Center for additional sports franchises and big-name concerts in our revitalized downtown area.

Kauffman Stadium. CVB OF GREATER KANSAS CITY

at Barney Allis Plaza, in the heart of our downtown. Evening games when the lights come on in the art deco skyscrapers, the famous Bartle Hall Pylons stand tall against the night sky—well, it's breathtaking. Add the *ka-pop, ka-pop* of that tennis ball and it's all the night music you need. Season grandstand seats go for $140, but the best deal is a four-pack of box seats for just $200. You can imagine that with only 2,600 seats total, they tend to go fast.

Kansas City Royals
Kauffman Stadium,
Truman Sports Complex
(816) 921-8000, (800) 676-9257
www.kcroyals.com
Here's a trivia question for you, sports buffs: What local team name in the late 1880s sounded a lot like the Red Sox? Give up? It

was the Kansas City Blue Stockings. Honest. More than a century later we're still on that side of the color wheel, but you can bet there are more people cheering at the Kauffman than at the old Muehlebach or Municipal Stadiums. For one thing, The K, as we affectionately call it, seats 40,625 fans.

The stadium was named for Ewing Kauffman, who purchased the Kansas City Royals in 1968 and turned the team into one of the most successful franchises in baseball. They won six division championships and two American League pennants. We showed our appreciation by building a fancy new Royals Stadium in 1973, and they proceeded to fill it with two million fans a year more than eleven times. Now *that's* a lot of beer and peanuts. The stadium is one of the fan-friendliest arenas in pro sports. Behind the fence in right field is a 322-foot-wide fountain, the largest privately owned water display in the world, that puts on a dazzling show between innings and when one of our boys hits a home run. In left field is a 30-by-40-foot Sony JumboTron video display board that was the largest in the country when installed in 1990. Water jets and fireworks filled the sky on October 27, 1985, when Kansas City won the World Series title with an 11–0 victory over the St. Louis Cardinals.

We said thanks to Mr. K on July 2, 1993, when the twenty-one-year-old Royals Stadium was renamed in his honor, and there wasn't a dry eye in the dugout or stands. A month later tears came again as the only owner the team had ever had died at the age of seventy-six. But George Brett gave us something to cheer about in 1999 when he became the first member of the Royals to be inducted into the Major League Baseball Hall of Fame.

Kansas City ushered in a new era when David Glass took over ownership in 2000. And although we haven't returned to the glory days of 1985—yet—there's always this season. Tickets range from $8 to $30. Soon the winning team (a girl can dream, can't she?) will have a stadium that's slicker than ever, thanks to the $250 million renovation package voters approved in 2006. Just don't expect the bases to be loaded all at once; this phase-in plan will be completed by Opening Day 2010. What can you expect? Well, an additional 39,000 seats, an exciting Walk of Fame area, an eye-popping high-def scoreboard, and a wide concourse that spans the stadium. A new restaurant in right field will feature fare from local eateries, although we've always thought the ballpark franks and Frosty Malts ("Git yer Frosssty Malllllts!") hit a home run. And that 6-inch-high pile of peanut shells under this seat? Not mine. Fans with money to burn can show off in fancy new home-plate suites.

Kansas City Chiefs
Arrowhead Stadium
(816) 920-9300
www.kcchiefs.com

Other teams hate to play at Arrowhead Stadium, and it has less to do with the opposition than the fans. Kansas City boosters are known as the loudest and most enthusiastic in the National Football League. Crowd noises have been known to challenge even the most seasoned veteran's concentration; even squinting up at that sea of blood-red jackets, hats, and sweatshirts can be intimidating.

Fans have had plenty of practice chanting in unison; of the nearly 80,000 seats, most are occupied by season ticket holders. The rest are usually snapped up when single-game tickets, ranging from $54 to $103 a pop, go on sale in late July. Purchase these through Ticketmaster, (800) 676-5488 or www.ticketmaster.com. Whatever your ticket stub says, you'll pay dearly for parking; right now it's $22. The gates open 3½ hours before kickoff to allow for the second sport at Arrowhead: tailgating. And nobody does it better than the KC fans.

Around here, pro football isn't a game, it's a lifestyle. Entire sections of department stores are devoted to Chiefs apparel. Every fall Chiefs flags fly from cars and front porches. Then there are the tailgate parties, when the parking lot takes on a blue haze from row after row of grills sizzling up hot dogs and burgers. The competition is nearly as fierce as what's to come, with groups trying to outdo one another and TV cameras recording the action. You'll see everything from barbecue ribs, baked beans, and cold beer to chilled baby lobster with fine wine. We'll stick with brats, please, with plenty of mustard and kraut.

Kansas City football, too, has had a long history. It started in 1924 with the Blues (that color again!), an NFL team that changed its name to the Cowboys a year later. In 1963 Lamar Hunt moved his Dallas Texans to Kansas City and named them for the city's mayor, H. Roe Bartle, whose nickname was "Chief." The team won the American Football League championship in 1967 and 1970. On January 11, 1970, the Chiefs won the Super Bowl, and in 1972 they moved into their new stadium in the Harry S. Truman Sports Complex.

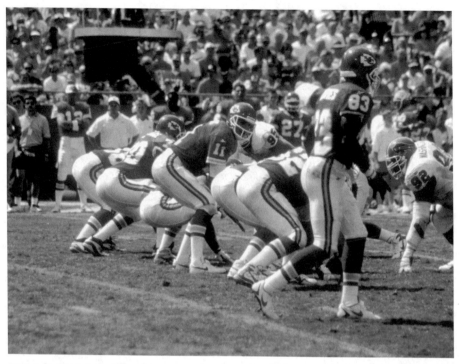

Kansas City Chiefs football team. CVB OF GREATER KANSAS CITY

Kansas City Roller Warriors
Hale Arena at Kemper and other venues
(913) 636-7894
www.kcrollerwarriors.com

Like watching fast women? Wearing knee pads and game faces? Then the KC Roller Warriors—our local dames on roller skates—can offer just your kind of evening. Considering the team names, such as the Knockouts and Victory Vixens, you can expect some outrageous bouts. The grunts and yelps are enhanced with the sounds of local bands that rock out during the games.

The Warriors team, the story goes, is "the angry mutant love child" of skaters Dirty Britches and Princess Anna Conda (Brooke Leavitt and Mandy Durham), who founded the league in 2004. The Web site itself is hilarious, with bios and photos of each player, complete with a cigarette hanging from red lips, a baby on a hip, or a hapless opponent being shoved headfirst into a locker. Though the teams promise to "capture your heart and skate all over it, until it bleeds," don't be afraid. These fast-paced spectacles are actually great fun for kids as well as adults. The brawling broads (and they love it when you call 'em that) play six at-home games; tickets are $13 in advance and $18 at the door. Kids get in for half-price. Games are usually sold out and, frankly, so is the beer.

Kansas City T-Bones
CommunityAmerica Ballpark
1800 Village West Parkway
Kansas City, KS
(913) 328-5618
www.tbonesbaseball.com

What do you call a baseball team from the land of sizzling steaks? The T-Bones, of course, and the action can be as hot as a platter of beef. Members of the Northern

Close-up

Sprint Center

13th Street and Grand Boulevard
(816) 283-7300
www.yourkcarena.com

Is it a spaceship? A giant, glowing pillbox hat? No, it's the Sprint Center, the 18,500-seat arena that helped launch the revitalization of Kansas City's downtown. Open in fall 2007, the $276 million project will host sports and concert events. Beyond that, the arena is home to the College Basketball Experience and the National Collegiate Basketball Hall of Fame, sponsored by the Kansas City–based National Association of Basketball Coaches. It will house memorabilia and exhibits and provide a wonderful venue for events and induction ceremonies. This shrine to hoops alone is expected to bring over 150,000 visitors to the center its first year.

And speaking of hang time, the arena's construction involved some pretty precarious moments as 12-foot-by-5-foot glass panels—2,204 in all if you're counting—were carefully installed into the exterior of the 130,000-square-foot structure. The result is a stunning sight that changes with the light of the day, from golden to pink, then glows green at night as a beacon to fans of sports and music.

As a long-needed downtown arena, the Sprint Center anchors the exciting Power & Light District, a twenty-four-hour-a-day entertainment and retail neighborhood.

League, which was founded in 1993 as a way for talented players to continue careers after leaving Major League life, these guys really put on a show. Part of the fun is the stadium itself, the CommunityAmerica Ballpark, built in 2003 with a retro feel that includes plenty of attention to fan comfort and fun. For instance, although there are only 4,365 seats, not a one has a bad view. The farthest from the field is a mere 50 feet, so everyone can hear the crack of the bat and the hum of a fastball. A wide concourse allows you to watch the game even while catching a snack at the concession stand. Parents love the children's play area, where they can keep an eye on the kiddies and the on-field action. Little fans will want to spend time with Sizzle the Bull, the entertaining mascot (his sign is Taurus, if you must know).

Tickets are retro as well, starting at just $6 for general admission up to $18. Check out season-ticket plans that get you into all twenty-four home games. Or bring nineteen of your buddies and score the Home Run Party Deck, including Arthur Bryant's barbecue for $500. Did we mention parking is free?

Kansas City Wizards
(816) 920-9300
www.kcwizards.com

When it was announced that the new major league soccer team in Kansas City would be known as The Whiz, the management got what they wanted: plenty of attention. When the jokes threatened to overcome the players' potential, the name was changed to the Wizards in 1996. Ahhhh, that's better. The new name and jerseys must have worked; the team won the MLS Cup in 2000. If that's like winning the Super Bowl of soccer, it's appropriate because the Wizards' owner is Lamar Hunt, who also bankrolls the Chiefs.

The Wizards play their home games at Arrowhead Stadium; the season runs from April through September. Tickets cost $12 to $19 for adults and $8 to $13 for youths.

PARTICIPATION SPORTS

Bike or run along our many trails, swing a golf club, bowl a few strings, or take to the ice. We figure you've got to stay active just to burn off all that barbecue. No matter what your pleasure or passion, you'll have an opportunity to play it here. And if you're into fishing or sailing, check out our extraordinary array of lakes in the Parks, Lakes, and Recreation chapter.

Biking

Kansas City has its share of biking enthusiasts, who enjoy our wide streets and miles of trails. The only thing missing is designated bicycle lanes throughout the metro. This may change in the next few years; the MetroGreen plan aims to encourage more two-wheeled transportation with hundreds of miles of trails linking urban to suburban areas. Until that happens, if you do venture out on your Schwinn, do so with caution. Wearing a helmet goes without saying, but also follow all motor traffic rules, be alert, and, above all, make yourself known to drivers. For companionship on the open road, plus information about scenic bike rides and annual charity rides, contact one of the clubs below.

Favored paved trails include the Blue River Parkway, which starts in Minor Park at Red Bridge Road in Kansas City; the Mill Creek Streamway Park, which extends more than 17 miles from the Kansas River to downtown Olathe; and the Indian Creek and Tomahawk Biking and Hiking Trails in Overland Park, which run about 10 miles along the northern edge of I-435. Access points include Corporate Woods and Leawood Park.

i Of the nearly two million people living in the KC metro area, an estimated 270,000 are golfers. No wonder, then, that we've raised some winners. Pros from our town include Tom Watson, Matt Gogel, Bruce Lietzke, and Tom Pernice Jr. (PGA Tour) and Amy Alcott (LPGA Tour).

Johnson County Bicycle Club
www.jcbikeclub.org

This group started in the late 1960s as part of the local parks and rec department and went solo in 1973 with about thirty members. Today nearly 300 riders are involved, which means you can find a buddy or group strapping on a helmet to hit the road nearly every day. It sponsors three annual rides of up to 100 miles and holds monthly meetings to demonstrate new equipment and discuss how gel-padded bike shorts are the best garments ever invented. Throughout the year, volunteers host free rides that vary in speed, distance, and starting location but frequently begin or end at a restaurant to further the club's unofficial motto, "Ride to eat, eat to ride!" Membership dues are $20 a year, and many of the events are open to nonmembers for a fee. Find more information on the Web site, or write to P.O. Box 2203, Shawnee Mission, KS 66201-2203.

The Kansas City Bicycle Club
(816) 436-5641
www.toto.net/kcbc

This club, established in 1963, sponsors everything from beginner rides to all-day marathons for those who have to see what's over the next hill. The KCBC also has a United States Cycling Federation–sanctioned racing team and hosts the Tour of Kansas City race every fall. Quarterly meetings are held at a different location each time and always include an interesting ride and a picnic. A monthly newsletter keeps members current on upcoming events, newly discovered tours, and training techniques. Annual dues are $20 ℹ️ Shave some dollars off your golf game by opting for early-bird savings or twilight hours.

for individuals, $25 for families, and $35 for sustaining members.

Fencing

Kansas City Fencing Center
9900 Antioch
Overland Park, KS
(913) 579-9535
www.kcfencing.org
Fencing helps develop agility, strength, speed, and discipline. If not, what's the point? This program is taught by some of the country's finest, including head coach Kelly Williams, the top-ranked female saber fencer in the United States. Now she's training others to succeed: Her students have placed in the top eight in United States Fencing Association competition in every age group. Classes are available for beginning, intermediate, advanced, and expert level fencers in three categories: saber, foil, and épée. Intro classes, which include two one-hour classes per week, range from $65 to $85 per month and provide equipment. Open sessions using your own equipment are also available.

Golf

Kansas City has been in love with golf since 1894, when two Scottish duffers created the town's first course in what is now the Hyde Park neighborhood. Did we say "course"? It was actually nothing more than a deserted cow pasture near 36th and Gillham Road. Two years later a group of the original players started Kansas City Country Club, an elite organization that celebrated its golden anniversary in 1996.

By the early 1900s courses began to dot the landscape, and the increased interest attracted some of the finest golf course designers of the day, including A. W. Tilling-

hast and James Dalgleish. Kansas City was becoming known as a golfing town. More courses, both private and public, sprang up, and the city played host to a PGA event for more than a decade. All that practicing paid off. Kansas City native Tom Watson has won the PGA Tour Player of the Year six times and eight Majors and has been considered one of the top all-time players since turning pro in 1971. Another native, Matt Gogel, is also making a name for himself.

As interest in golf grew, spurred by Tom Watson's success, Kansas City began to see a need for more public courses, and dozens of city and county greens were developed during the 1980s and 1990s. Today more than one million rounds of golf are played annually on seventy-two courses (forty-six public and twenty-six private) in the Greater Kansas City area. And new courses are added every year to keep up with the demand. You can bet that prime home lots next to new golf courses go fast. Our private courses are superb, and we hope you'll have a chance to play on at least one during your visit; many of them have reciprocal privileges for members of other clubs. In this chapter we'll concentrate on our beautiful public courses.

Please note that this list is not inclusive. Get an overview and list of events at www.kansascitygolfer.org, www.kcgolfer magazine.com, and www.kcmetrogolf.com, where you can even book tee times. We've listed courses with a wide range of fees.

Deer Creek Golf Club
7000 West 133rd Street
Overland Park, KS
(913) 681-3100
www.deercreekgc.com
With its 162 acres of rolling terrain and plenty of mature trees, sand, and water, well-traveled golfers may immediately identify this as a Robert Trent Jones Jr. course. It's certainly one of his most beautiful. Jones has crafted not one but two signature holes into this masterpiece. The No. 3 hole is a 422-yard hole that plays between a creek on

the left and a bunker on the right. To make it you'll have to drive it dead-on. And if you didn't care for that water hazard the first time around, you won't care for the second signature shot. It comes at No. 15, a 22-yard par 3. Monday through Friday fees are $70, $10 more on weekends.

Heritage Park Golf Course
16455 Lackman Road
Olathe, KS
(813) 829-GOLF (4653)
www.jcprd.com

This popular course isn't a walk in the park, although it is in one. The course has proven its level of difficulty by being used for U.S. Open qualifying rounds. The 16th hole is the one that can trip you up on this Don Sechrest–designed course. The 215-yard, par-3 hole requires 190 yards of carry over a body of water. We'd like to have a take in that used golf-ball concession. Fees range from $14 to $20 weekdays and $16 to $26 Friday through Sunday and holidays.

Ironhorse Golf Club
15400 Mission Road
Leawood, KS
(913) 685-GOLF
www.ironhorsegolf.com

This 189-acre course has quickly become an area favorite, winning top honors from readers of *Ingram's* magazine and accolades from *Golf Digest*. It was designed by Dr. Michael Hurdzan, and every effort was made to maintain the natural landscape, which gives the course a mature look that will only improve with time. The par-72 championship eighteen-hole layout offers a distinct challenge on every hole, and the creek that meanders through the course affects play on no fewer than fifteen holes. Ironhorse features bent grass greens, zoysia fairways, and bluegrass and fescue roughs. Golfers can choose from five tee complexes per hole. Total yardage varies from 6,900 yards from the back tees to 4,783 from the forward tees.

The upscale homes that surround the course are as magnificent as the grounds. Fees are $45 to $70, with discounts for Leawood residents. Cart fees are $16.

Longview Lake Golf Course
11100 View High Drive
(816) 761-9445

Near one of the area's most picturesque lakes, this course features varying elevations, elevated tee boxes, and a little longer play. The Scottish-style links offer something for every skill level. Signature holes both include water. No. 8 is particularly challenging because of the pond running along the left side. And one of the prettiest views on the course provides its biggest trouble spot on No. 12, which is played next to Longview Lake. Weekday greens fees are $37, $41 Friday through Sunday. A cart will cost you $6. And consider showing up four hours before twilight, when the all-you-can-play buffet is open and costs just $24 including the cart.

Overland Park Golf Club
125th and Quivira
Overland Park, KS
(913) 897-3809
www.opkansas.org

The biggest hazard here is finding a place to park at 5:00 p.m. Keep driving, though, because playing here is a pleasure. Around 125,000 rounds of golf are played at OPGC per year, a tribute to its beauty, location, and value. On weekdays you'll pay $20 to walk and $34 to ride; $23 to walk and $34 to ride on weekends.

With forty-two sand bunkers on thirteen holes and two lakes affecting five holes, you might as well say each hole is a challenge. The course is sited high on a hill in Overland Park with extraordinary views. As you can imagine, tee times go fast, so it's best to call several days in advance. This course also offers a popular par-3, nine-hole ladies' league, and for a community course has a decent pro shop, instructors, and snack bar.

Close-up

Kansas City, Start Your Engines

To visualize just how big the Kansas Speedway is, consider that both Kauff-man and Arrowhead Stadiums, plus their humongous parking lots, would fit into its infield, with room left over for one particular race driver's ego.

The $260 million International Speedway Corporation–owned facility opened in June 2001 and gave Wyandotte County a sound that drowns out even the rumble of racing motors: *ka-ching!* Season tickets went flying out the door, with 40 percent of total ticket sales going to Kansas residents. Fans from forty-six states and four Canadian provinces grabbed up the rest. Individual seat prices range from $225 to $330.

Those lucky enough to get seats are not disappointed. The 82,000-seat, 1.5-mile tri-oval NASCAR track was designed for the comfort and conven-ience of the racing teams and the fans. The final phase will expand seating to 150,000. Thanks to a beautifully planned low infield and elevated back-stretch, every seat from rows 1 to 65 has an unimpeded view of all four turns and the backstretch. And although the seats are great (especially those per-sonalized with the owners' names), the Fan Walk is even better. Guests access the infield via a tunnel located south of the grandstand. Within the infield fans get an intimate look at the garages, inspection stations, and Vic-tory Lane. An opening in the fence provides a chance to obtain autographs.

Fans might have to wait to get a driver's scribbled name, but they won't have to wait for much else. ISC and its designers did their homework and found out that racing fans hate to stand in line, so the Kansas Speedway has sixteen ticket windows, eighteen concession stands (including those selling barbecue), fifty portable food kiosks, and twelve restrooms. That last statistic is very good news for fans who consume 26,203 gallons of beer dur-ing a NASCAR Nextel cup series. Put another way, it's enough liquid refresh-ment (including beer from our city's own Boulevard Brewery) to fill a stock car's gas tank 1,191 times.

A new way to enjoy the experience is the Pit Stop Pub, a hospitality area open during September's NASCAR races. For $300, you'll enjoy breakfast, lunch, and a snack, guided pit tours, and live entertainment during the two-day event. Make reservations through the main ticket office.

Or to really get in the driver's seat, attend one of the five driving schools that take place at the speedway, including the Richard Petty Driving Experi-

Swope Park Memorial Golf Course
Interstate 435 and Gregory
in Swope Park
(816) 513-8910
www.swopememorialgolfcourse.com
This course is carved out of Swope Park, at 1,769 acres one of the country's largest met-ropolitan parks. The area is also home to Starlight Theatre, the Kansas City Zoo, a hik-ing trail, and a nature conservatory. But with land this vast you'll feel completely insulated from the world in this natural beauty.

A. W. Tillinghast built the course in 1913, and although it's a shorter course than many

Vrroom! Treat yourself to one of the country's most fan-friendly NASCAR racetracks, the new Kansas Speedway in Wyandotte County. CVB OF GREATER KANSAS CITY

ence and the Mario Andretti and Jeff Gordon racing schools. Toll-free numbers for these companies are found on the Kansas Speedway Web site's FAQ page.

An even better view, along with a wet bar and private bathrooms, is available in one of sixty-eight luxury suites. The privilege costs plenty; after a one-time administrative fee of $7,000, the rooms go from $29,000 to $70,000 a year with a four-year minimum commitment. *Ka-ching* indeed. Each one sold out immediately; now there are plans to build one hundred more.

Drivers appreciate the design as well. Veteran driver Bill Elliott said it may be the best ever built. Creature comforts include garages that measure 5 to 10 feet larger than those at most tracks, increased amperage for trailer hookups, and a terrific family center and playground for their children.

Sound good? That's what everyone else thought, too. Tickets to the 2001 inaugural season were sold out, and every season has followed suit. Most of the season ticket holders renewed, which they can do for thirty years, and those on the waiting list snagged any that were left. But it's not too late to get on the next list. Or simply wait until ISC decides to add a few thousand more seats. And you can still see this gorgeous new track; several nonracing events are held here each year, including a barbecue cookout and races to raise money for charities. To find out more about tickets and events, contact Kansas Speedway (913-328-RACE, www.kansasspeedway.com), 1333 Meadowlark Lane, Kansas City, KS.

more contemporary ones in Kansas City, it has many excellent features. That is, if you're ready for a challenging game. Two of Kansas City's toughest holes are here. No. 17 is slightly uphill, and adding to the tension is a bunker in the middle of the fairway. And on the 14th hole, bunkers to the left of a right turn 250 yards out can make you wonder why you ever took up the sport. Perhaps the reasonable fees will cool you off: Nine holes will cost you $12, with a $6 cart fee; eighteen holes cost $23.

Tennis

Head out with your tennis racket to any park in the city and you're bound to find a net with your name on it. Many are free or available for a dollar or two; a few have lights that are often coin operated. During nice weather we recommend calling ahead to reserve court time.

Happy Rock Park
7600 Northeast Antioch Road
Gladstone, MO
(816) 436-2200
Four lighted courses are located in this Clay County park that gets its name from a twist on the city's name. There's no charge for court time, which can mean some wait time, but you'll have other activities to keep you entertained. The eighty-acre park offers playgrounds, fitness trails, soccer fields, and beautiful open land that's just right for sailing Frisbees or flying kites.

Indian Creek Recreation Center
7401 West 103rd Street
Overland Park, KS
(913) 895-6385
www.opkansas.org
Although these eight courts have no lighting, they're popular until dusk when players seem to be enjoying the great outdoors as much as a good backhand. A tennis pro is on hand during summer, and a playground, picnic shelter, and paved fitness trail are nearby. Overland Park offers thirty tennis courts in all within its park system; this one is the largest.

Plaza Tennis Center
4747 J. C. Nichols Parkway
(816) 784-5100
www.kcmo.org/parks
These are quite possibly the most glamorous tennis courts in the country, with architecture that echoes the Country Club Plaza, and the landscaped Brush Creek walkway within view. Recently expanded to add lockers, showers, and a pro shop, these fourteen lighted courts include a stadium with seating.

The gorgeous new digs have attracted professional, college, and regional champi-onships. Lessons and racquet stringing are available. Court fees range from $4 to $8 per hour with an additional $1 for lights, and reservations are taken up to twenty-four hours in advance. Annual cards are available from $50 for juniors to $225 for families; benefits include three-day prior reservations, waived court fees, and other discounts.

Running and Walking

By the time spring shows her pretty head, plenty of us are hitting the streets to gear up for road races. You'll have lots of chances to get your race-day T-shirts here; there seems to be a fund-raising run or walk every weekend. Following are three of the largest. If you'd like a few pointers before you sign up, we've included information about a local running club.

AIDS Walk
(816) 931-0959
www.aidswalkkansascity.org
The region's largest AIDS fund-raising event brings together around 3,500 people to raise money and awareness for the men, women, and children living with HIV/AIDS in the Kansas City area. The 2007 event alone raised $430,000 for research and programs. The run is usually in April, and past sites have included Mill Creek Park on the Country Club Plaza.

Groundhog Run
(816) 746-1414
This race takes place in the Hunt Midwest Underground Facility Subtropolis, a huge, underground labyrinth big enough to handle an eighteen-wheeler. The runners aren't too hep on the course's twists and turns, but they dig the fifty-eight degrees in the middle of winter. The race is held every February. Get there early; this one attracts 3,000 or so runners, and the space, naturally, is limited.

Kansas City Track Club
(816) 333-RACE (7223)
www.kctrack.org

Run a few miles, get a free beer. Sounds like a plan. This track club devotes its time to teaching people how to run, keeping them motivated and safe and then rewarding them with some of the best parties around. A long-standing tradition is the 4- to 12-mile Wednesday night fun run that ends at some member's house for potluck dinner. It usually draws forty to seventy members, and visiting runners are always welcome. Other outings include Sunday-morning long runs and Thursday-night speed sessions.

The club also puts on seventeen or so races a year, including the St. Pat's Run; the Dog-N-Jog Run-Fur-Fun, featuring 980 dogs and their masters; and the Brew to Brew, a 42-mile killer that starts at the Boulevard Brewery in Kansas City and ends at the Free State Brewing Company in Lawrence. Certainly the most scenic course is the annual Cliffhanger 5K walk/run held at the historic Cliff Drive in the Gladstone Boulevard area. Although the limestone cliffs provide some challenge, seeing the waterfall fountain is worth it. A $15 membership gets you discounts and newsletter updates.

Trolley Run
(888) 543-7223, ext. 4
www.trolleyrun.org
Following along Kansas City's long-gone urban trolley track, this is Kansas City's largest run and the fourth largest 4-mile run in the United States. It's actually just a festive street party, because the course is so flat and scenic you won't feel like you've worked at all. Starting in the Waldo area at 75th and Wornall, the run takes you through some of our loveliest old neighborhoods, where dogs and kids line the streets to cheer you on. Keep going: The final reward is a view of the lushly landscaped Brush Creek, a below–street level, 0.75-mile concrete ribbon that has a tiered waterfall at the west end.

The race ends on the Country Club Plaza with music, lots of food, and high-fives all around. On top of that the race, now sponsored by Sabates Eye Center, is held in April, one of our best months weatherwise. If all

that doesn't convince you, perhaps this will: Money raised goes to help the Children's Center for the Visually Impaired, an organization that provides training and help to blind and visually impaired infants and children.

Sailboat Racing
Jacomo Sailing Club
Lake Jacomo
Blue Springs, MO
(913) 707-8818
www.jacomosailingclub.org
This club has been promoting the sport of sailboat racing since 1958, before the lake was even completed. And you've got to love any organization that calls a meeting in the middle of a crystal-blue lake on a Sunday afternoon. Although the majority of its members like nothing better than a good competitive regatta, some members just come out to watch, cheer, and enjoy the day on the club's nicely equipped pontoon boat. The club offers training sessions for new members, and each June they hold an Open Sail, sort of like an open house but with boats. It's a great opportunity to learn more about the sport, see the different types of fleet boats, and get wet. If you decide to join, an associate membership costs $40 a year and includes all privileges except competing for trophies. A $95 per year membership entitles sailors to skipper their own boat and compete for trophies.

FAMILY SPORTS
Bowling

Interest in this sport seems to ebb and flow depending on how people feel about the shoes. It's popular once again, not only with long-term leagues and little kids but also with teens seeking a fun Friday out with friends. Several bowling alleys in Kansas City cater to the young crowd with laser light shows and booming music.

AMF College Lanes
10201 College Boulevard
Overland Park, KS

(913) 451-6400
www.amf.com

A real plus for people staying at the Doubletree Hotel across the street, this center offers thirty-two lanes, seven billiards tables, and a lounge along with a small arcade. They crank up the music for X-treme Bowling, when black lights make the pins and balls glow, dude. And for groups of four, a Fun Pack is the way to go: $10 each will get you shoe rentals, two hours of bowling, a pitcher of soda, popcorn, and a one-topping pizza.

Incred-A-Bowl
8500 West 151st Street
Overland Park, KS
(913) 851-1700
www.incredabowl.com

This 65,000-square-foot, state-of-the-art center includes a forty-lane computerized bowling alley, an arcade filled with a hundred of the latest interactive and virtual reality games, and a three-story set of play tubes for the tykes. Teens in particular really go for the Cosmic Bowling every Friday and Saturday night, when black lights, fog, glow-in-the-dark balls and pins, and upbeat music take the pain out of a gutter ball. The fun continues until long past midnight. Incred-A-Bowl also has a pro shop, gift store, and snack bar.

Camping

Basswood Country Inn and RV Resort
15880 Interurban Road
Platte City, MO
(816) 858-5556, (800) 242-2775
(reservations only)
www.basswoodresort.com

At this resort, which *Peak Magazine* calls "perhaps the most beautiful wooded lakefront setting in the Kansas City area," you can stay at a cabin or set up camp overlooking the lake. Stay where Bing Crosby and Harry Truman did, at one of this resort's cabins, or camp out at a spot overlooking the lake. Actor Matthew McConaughey stayed here in his custom Airstream trailer to promote *Sahara*. We're feeling hot already. There are 119 full-hookup RV sites (30 and 50 amp) plus twenty water/electric-only sites for tents and pop-ups, including fourteen deluxe sites with patios. Guests can use the two picnic shelters, play-ground, spacious laundry facilities, and super-clean bathhouses with shower stalls and vanities. A meeting hall is available for parties and family reunions.

You'll have plenty to do with four freshwater lakes stocked with catfish, bass, crappie, and carp, plus a swimming pool, volleyball court, and walking trails through the wooded acreage. A convenience store offers videos (perhaps *White Christmas?*) and basic groceries. Basswood Resort, open year-round, is just 5 miles from the Kansas City International Airport. Sorry, ladies; Matthew is long gone.

Jackson County Parks and Recreation Campgrounds
(816) 229-8980
www.co.jackson.mo.us

The county offers three public campgrounds with a total of 236 camping sites, all about fifteen minutes from Kansas City proper. They are available by reservation for stays up to fourteen days, and at least one camper must be twenty-one or over. The camping facilities include showers, restrooms, attendants, picnic tables, and ice. Check out the handy new online reservation service.

Longview Lake Campground is part of a 5,000-acre park that includes a 4-mile nature trail, horse park, swimming beach, and twenty-seven-hole public golf course. The 930-acre lake has a full marina with wheelchair-accessible fishing docks. The campground is open April 27 through September 30. Its 119 sites include 59 with electricity at $14 to $17 per day and 60 tent-ready at $10 to $13 per day.

Lake Jacomo Campground is within beautiful Fleming Park, at 7,800 acres, the largest parkland in Jackson County. At its heart is 970-acre Lake Jacomo, and there's the smaller Blue Springs Lake as well. Attractions include a nature preserve, Audubon center, marina, swimming beach, hiking trails, and more. The campground has sixty large, tree-lined sites, ten full hookups, thirty-eight electric, and twelve tent, which cost from $10 to $23 per day. The site is open year-round; call for specific availabilities.

Blue Springs Lake Campground, also within Fleming Park, is open April 13 to October 31 with fifty-seven sites (twenty full hookup, seventeen electric and water, twenty electric) that range from $14 to $23 per day.

Fishing

With all our lakes and parks, you're sure to reel in the largest walleye, crappie, channel catfish, or largemouth bass you've ever seen. Since the region covers two states and nearly a dozen counties, fishing permits vary. But for the most part, Missouri requires a $3.00 per day nonresident permit, and Kansas charges $3.50 per day. You'll find information about our major lakes, including Jacomo, Blue Springs, and Wyandotte County, in the Lakes, Parks, and Recreation chapter. Following are some additional fishing spots.

Lake Olathe
625 Lakeshore Drive
Olathe, KS
(913) 971-8521
www.kdwp.state.ks.us
You're sure to find a place to capture a competition-size catfish, bass, or even trout somewhere in these 170 acres. There's even an assist from Old Saint Nick; each year the parks and recreation division tosses retired Christmas trees into the area around the fishing piers to create nesting places for fish.

Shawnee Mission Park
7900 Renner Road
Shawnee Mission, KS
(913) 831-3355
www.jcprd.com
Anglers seeking bluegill, carp, and bass show up at this 150-acre lake, one of the most popular in the region. Boat rentals are available, but you'd better reserve yours early; each spring and fall the lake is stocked with rainbow trout. Now that's good eating.

Smithville Lake
DD Highway
Smithville , MO
(816) 532-4217
www.nwk.usace.army.mil/smithville
When people around here say they're "gone fishin'," chances are this is their destination. Just 20 miles north of downtown Kansas City, Smithville's 7,200 acres provide plenty of reeling action. The lake is stocked with tiger musky, walleye, bass, crappie, and several species of catfish for an afternoon of fishing and a fine fillet that night. Boats are available for rent at the two full-service marinas, and five multilane boat launch ramps ensure easy accessibility to the water. And you're in luck: Smithville has 777 campsites, one-third with electrical hookups. Call (816) 532-0803 for reservations.

Ice Skating

Crown Center Ice Terrace
2450 Grand Boulevard
(816) 274-8411
www.crowncenter.com
Kansas City's only outdoor ice rink opens to great fanfare each November and continues until March—and by that time skaters are often dressed in T-shirts and shorts! The terrace is open seven days a week, 10:00 a.m. to 9:00 p.m. Fees are $6 per person, and skate rental is $2. Groups of twenty or more save the rental fee; and the rink is available for private parties before or after regular hours. A vending machine dispenses hot cocoa and cappuccino, and soft drinks for those balmy early spring days.

Pepsi Ice Midwest Skating Rink and Fitness Center
12140 West 135th Street
Overland Park, KS
(913) 851-1600
www.pepsiicemidwest.com
You're apt to see Olympic-quality skaters practicing spins and jumps at the home of the

Silver Blades, one of the country's oldest ice-skating groups. Competitions and practice take up quite a bit of ice time, but free skating is available during the week from 10:00 a.m. to early afternoon on weekdays and two sessions on Saturday. With three ice rinks, this center also hosts hockey practices and games. Fees are $6.50 for adults, $5.00 for children under seven years of age, and $2.00 for skate rental. Lessons are also available, and the rink can be rented for birthday parties. This giant new center also has a fitness center, game room, and deli.

Miniature Golf

Cool Crest Family Fun Center
10735 East Missouri Highway 40
Independence, MO
(816) 358-0088
www.coolcrest.com
This 4½-acre playground has been getting families together for fun since 1950. You'll have plenty of opportunity to practice your short game (and patience) because Cool Crest offers a total of four eighteen-hole miniature golf courses. Other activities include go-karts, batting cages, and a 7,000-square-foot game room with video and pinball machines galore. And to continue with the blast-from-the-past theme, a '50s-style pizzeria serves up pies with all the toppings. After an afternoon here you'll find yourself singing along to their decades-old jingle, "It's a fun, family kind of place!"

Family Golf Park
1501 Northeast MO Highway 40
Blue Springs, MO
(816) 228-1550
www.familypark.com
So you're not ready to spend thousands of dollars on golf lessons, clubs, and shoes? You can still have fun knocking a ball around at this course. This beautifully landscaped park features thirty-six holes of miniature golf winding through a lake setting. The center also includes a par-3 golf course, putting green, game arcade, and bumper boats. Ker-

splash! The golf practice facility is open year-round; golf lessons are available. Hours are from 8:30 a.m. until 10:30 p.m. weekdays and until 11:30 p.m. on Friday and Saturday. Rates vary depending on the activities. It's great fun for the entire family.

Snow Skiing

Kansas City Ski Club
(913) 383-9006
www.kcskiclub.org
Go figure. Here we are, miles away from a mountain, and we have one of the largest ski clubs in the country. And it's active without a flake in sight. With 3,000 members, there's always a group getting together to play volleyball or golf, socialize at an area bar, or take canoe trips in the summer. Oh, yes, and ski. The fifty-year-old club sponsors about thirty-one ski trips each year with destinations as diverse as Colorado, New Mexico, Canada, and Spain. The membership more than pays for itself in what you'll save on each trip. Besides that, it's one of the best ways to meet singles in the area.

Snow Creek Ski Lodge
Missouri Highway 45,
5 miles north of Weston
(816) 640-2200
www.skisnowcreek.com
When ski buffs aren't in a car or van heading to Breckinridge or Vail, you might find them at this ski lodge that opened in 1985. People who expect the Midwest to be flat as a flapjack will be surprised to see a 300-foot vertical drop and enough varied terrain to give beginners and experts plenty of action. Nine intermediate trails are served by two triple chairlifts and one double chairlift, and rope tows get you to the beginner area. The snow base usually ranges from 24 to 60 inches, thanks to fifty snowmaking machines.

A lodge features a cafeteria, bar, and lounge and also houses the ski school and gift shop. The rental shop offers shaped skis with plenty of junior sizes, plus snowboards and ski boards. Jason's Run has enough jumps, bumps, mounds, pipes, and tabletops to keep expert boarders happy. The park opens in mid-December and stays open through mid-March if the weather cooperates. It's open seven days a week, offers night skiing beginning in late December, and stays open until 3:00 a.m. for special events.

KIDS' SPORTS

Baseball

Mac-N-Seitz Training Academy
13705 Holmes
(816) 942-9992
www.mac-n-seitz.com

When two former Major Leaguers, Mike Macfarlane and Kevin Seitzer, became dissatisfied with the baseball training their sons were receiving, they started this top-rated academy in Martin City. Housed in a new facility complete with indoor and outdoor practice fields, batting cages, bullpens, and a fitness center that rivals any in the metropolitan area, here youngsters can get the training they need to succeed in the sport while having fun. Along with coaches' clinics, the center offers membership programs that include group and private lessons, filming and video analysis, and training camps. A baseball membership is $65 a month; softball, $55.

Skateboarding and Roller Hockey

Roller Hockey Rink
116th and Knox
Overland Park, KS
www.opkansas.org

Kids love this regulation, 120-by-65-foot rink at Indian Valley Park. The surface is coated for safety (well, at least it's safer), and a 5-foot-tall sideboard surrounds the playing area. Player benches are on each side. Rules and safety suggestions are posted, but there are no supervisors on-site. The rink is maintained by the Johnson County Parks and Recreation Division, and there are no fees for use.

Skateboard Park
138th and Switzer

Overland Park, KS
(913) 893-6354
www.opkansas.org

After the popularity of iceboarding competitions in the 2002 Winter Olympics, this sport is sure to skyrocket. This small park was created thanks to a grassroots effort that began with an Overland Park resource officer. $240,000 later, the community got its center in 1997, complete with ramps, jumps, and rails for all skill levels. It's popular with skateboarders and in-line skaters.

FITNESS CENTERS/ HEALTH CLUBS

With three pages of health clubs listed in the Yellow Pages, it's a wonder we're still ranked as one of the country's fattest cities. Here's where those who are fit stay that way, or at least check out the cutie on the next treadmill.

24 Hour Fitness
www.24hourfitness.com
Metcalf Super Sport
12075 Metcalf Avenue
(913) 338-2442

Metcalf Active
7420 Metcalf Avenue
(913) 362-2404

Olathe Active
13511 Mur-Len Road
(913) 829-4503

Ward Parkway Center Sport
8600 Ward Parkway
(816) 276-2466

The Athletic Club of Overland Park
10440 Marty
Overland Park, KS
(913) 383-9060
www.athleticclubop.com

You'll have no excuse not to get in shape at this premium fitness center. Its cardio theater includes banks of treadmills, elliptical machines, and rowing machines, and a cycle studio puts you through the paces during a spinning class. A full-size basketball gym, nine racquetball and handball courts, and even a sand volleyball court are here. The complex also includes an indoor pool; separate area for free weights; and studios for yoga, Pilates, and aerobics. You'll also find locker rooms and lounges that are downright plush, plus a cafe that serves a variety of healthy meals, snacks, and fruit smoothies. Or you can blow that workout on a beer. Massage and spa therapies, nutrition services, a pro shop, and a day care center round out the mix.

Shawnee Sport
11311 West Shawnee Mission Parkway
(913) 248-0724
The world's largest privately owned fitness center chain made a big splash in Kansas City by opening first two, then five workout centers. Clubs are categorized by the number of amenities; although they're all pretty beefy, the Super Sport facility in south Johnson County really rocks with a bank of treadmill and elliptical training machines that almost guarantees a no-wait workout; a basketball court and large group cycling area for spin

time; executive locker room; saunas; juice bar; and a wide variety of group classes that include Pilates, weight-and-cardio combos, and even a few that incorporate belly dancing. The personal trainers at this location are also top rate, including Tom, who will personally kick your butt if you miss an appointment. Check online for membership discounts; during the summer months, for example, rates are as low as Tom's body fat.

YMCA
Various locations
(816) 561-9622
The YMCA of Greater Kansas City includes twelve branches throughout the metropolitan area. Although the equipment and services vary, most have weight rooms, indoor and/or outdoor tracks, locker room facilities, and cardio equipment. Some have pools, and several offer child care. The YMCA also holds true to the "Christian" part of its name by catering to families and children. Kids are encouraged to cultivate healthy bodies and minds through sports activities, craft classes, and other programs. The YMCA of Kansas City, Kansas (913-371-4400), has two locations.

DAY TRIPS AND WEEKEND GETAWAYS

Why anyone would want to leave the pleasant confines of Kansas City is beyond us. But the three small towns in this chapter have enough appeal to pull anyone away from a plate of our famous ribs. Each one has a unique personality and enough attractions to make it well worth the short drive.

But instead of jumping on the highway after dinner, why not slide under a down-filled duvet at a bed-and-breakfast? Each town offers irresistible options, from an antiques-filled estate to a rustic but romantic working ranch. Besides a sumptuous breakfast the next morning, staying overnight gives you one more day to explore a museum, scout out another art gallery, or stop by that pretty park you passed on the way.

There you have it: three destinations that feel like a century away. Best of all, you'll hardly need to top off your gas tank. You can be checking out that cute little antiques shop or sinking your teeth into a square of home-made fudge in less than an hour.

And now, let's get started by doing what so many travelers did in the late 1800s: heading west.

LAWRENCE, KANSAS

Lawrence is a marvelous mix of quirkiness and cosmopolitan flair that can be found only in a college town. Toss in a couple of four-star restaurants, great music venues, and . . . well, we won't expect you back tonight. In fact, for some tourists a weekend became a week that turned into forever. The town is booming thanks to graduates who stay on and visitors who fall in love with the laid-back pace, vibrant arts scene, and parks and lakes just a short walk or bike ride away. Its historical buildings also rate points: In 2000 the National Trust for Historic Preservation named Lawrence one of the dozen most distinctive and unique destinations in the country.

The varied collection of downtown shops is also a draw. At the heart of the 5-block district is Massachusetts Street, which you'll soon call "Mass" like everyone else. The tree-lined avenue is an outdoor art gallery thanks to a successive series of one-year exhibitions of sculptures by national artists. Thirty more outdoor artworks and murals serve as a nice introduction to the galleries and museums around town. On select Fridays throughout the year, most galleries join in the Gallery Walk, where artists mingle with guests. Check the Web site (www.visitlawrence.com) for dates. A sampling of art showrooms includes Phoenix Gallery, specializing in custom stained glass, ceramics, textiles, and prints; Borderline Gallery (6 blocks east of Mass on 9th), with unique artwork like copper clocks and raku ceramics; and Silver Works, a gallery of exquisite handcrafted jewelry and crafts. Most shops are located between 6th and 11th Streets on Mass, but don't overlook some gems on adjacent side streets. Parking lots on Vermont Street and parts of a garage on New Hampshire Street (see the Web site for a handy map) provide two hours of free parking—a good solution to the hassle of parking meters.

The apex of arts activities is the Lawrence Arts Center (785-843-ARTS [2787]), in the 900 block of New Hampshire. The center features exhibitions by area and nationally known artists and is home to the professional Prairie Wind Dancers and Seem-to-Be Players Children's Theatre Company.

You'll also find enough home furnishing stores to turn every University of Kansas dorm room into a palace. Many of these rival

Kansas City shops for style and variety. Popular ones include the Bay Leaf (725 Mass) for gourmet cookware (just follow your nose to the coffee-of-the-day that's brewing; they also carry exotic loose teas). Antiques abound as well: you'll hit the jackpot at the Lawrence Antique Mall (830 Mass), where more than seventy dealers are ready to help you fill that empty car trunk or suitcase for the trip home. With so many choices (and the Midwest's well-known antiques bargains), you might want to keep the number for a rental van handy.

Plan to spend at least an hour at the Blue Heron (921 Mass), where they take an artful approach to life with contemporary and traditional furnishings and accessories from quirky to refined. If your footgear isn't made for walking, head into Footprints, where they stock 10,000 Birkenstock sandals. While you're slipping on a pair, take time to admire the mural of agricultural landscapes created by local artist Missy McCoy. Stop in au Marché, a European-style grocer that stocks a nice selection of gourmet cheeses, pâtés, and sausages. They can create a picnic lunch to go, perhaps to serve on a dish from Hobbs, a fun shop that specializes in reproduction dinnerware from famous restaurants around the world.

Spending the day surrounded by college students might make you yearn for a makeover. Rejuvene Day Spa (785-865- 4372) can comply with a facial, massage, and body wrap. Images Salon (9th and Louisiana, 785-843-2138) puts the "ahhhh" in "spa" with detoxing body wraps, stone massages, and head-to-toe luxuries. Retail shops offer everything from lingerie to vintage resale clothes.

Hungry yet? No doubt you've been tempted by the sight of a dozen or more sidewalk cafes all along Mass. If you prefer a more upscale choice—although still friendly—save your appetite for one of Larry Town's superb restaurants. We give ten points out of ten for Ten, the restaurant in the Eldridge Hotel (see details later in this section). Start the evening with the locals at the Jayhawker bar right next door, where the martini list is as lively as the conversation. Or have your vodka in the spicy red sauce over pasta at Ten while your date digs into the New Zealand lamb chops. The desserts are big enough to share. Ten is open for breakfast (with buffets on both Saturday and Sunday), lunch, and dinner. Teller's was one of the first restaurants to make Lawrence a dining destination and is still one of the best; here's where to order salads, pasta specials, and more—and then check out the restrooms, just past the converted bank's safe.

Pachamama's (785-841-0990, 800 New Hampshire, www.pachamamas.com) has a new location closer to the action. Chef Ken Baker turns fresh, local ingredients into memorable meals. Witness his peppered smoked pork tenderloin with soufflé'd garlic-cheese grits, or wood-fired breast of duckling on smoky greens. And his vanilla bean crème brûlée? Oh, mama. The restaurant serves dinner seven nights a week and hosts Patio Grills on Tuesday, as well as Friday wine tastings. Reservations are a must.

More casual fare, like soups and sandwiches, is found at the Free State Brewing Company (636 Mass, 785-843-4555, www.freestatebrewing.com), the first legal brewery in Kansas since pioneer days.

Before or after dinner, consider catching a performance at the Lied Center of Kansas (15th and Iowa, 785-864-ARTS [2787]), a dazzling $14.3 million multipurpose facility that's home to KU's concert series, Swarthout Chamber Music, and Broadway and Beyond performances. Past seasons have included *Chicago*, the Girls Choir of Harlem, and the Baryshnikov Dance Project. The University Theatre (15th and Naismith Drive on the KU campus, 785-864-3982, www.kutheatre.com) presents a wide array of plays and musical performances, including the popular Kansas Summer Theatre.

Perhaps other nightlife is calling you. Lawrence offers some of the Midwest's most exciting live music venues, like the Bottleneck at 737 New Hampshire and the Granada on Mass, offering heart-thumpingly loud music from rock to alternative. Liberty Hall on Mass is a restored opera house that provides a beautiful setting for live entertainment as well as cinematic releases.

When you're ready to turn in, Lawrence has several dreamy options. The Eldridge Hotel (7th and Mass, 785-749-5011, 800-527-0909, www.eldridgehotel.com) is the only Lawrence business in the same spot it occupied during Kansas Territorial Days and throughout the Civil War. A new hotel was built on the site in 1924, and it has been recently renovated into an all-suite hotel with 48 luxury suites. A honeymoon suite has a shower built for two. Rates range from $135 to $285; check www.visitlawrence.com for special deals like the Bed-and-Breakfast Package for $89.

The Halcyon House Bed and Breakfast (1000 Ohio Street, 888-441-0314, www.the halcyonhouse.com) is a charming European-style inn whose structure was built in 1885. Nine rooms are filled with antiques and flourishes and range from the Nooks and Crannies with a shared bath for $55 to the private Carriage House with its own luxurious bath and fireplace for $149. Awaken to the smell of coffee brewing and fresh baked breads. Breakfasts might include scrambled eggs, buttery waffles, fresh fruit, and homemade muffins.

About 15 miles from Lawrence is the Circle S Ranch (3325 Circle S Lane, 785-843-4124, www.circlesranch.com), a country inn that offers plush quarters within a 12,200-acre working ranch. Although the architecture is stylishly rustic (you'll love the hammered copper front door and wraparound porch), the twelve guest rooms with private baths feature antiques and luxurious bed linens. You won't want to miss the hot tub in a silo! The best amenity, however, might be the view of cornflower-blue skies, rolling hills, and meadow flowers. The land has been in the owner's family since the mid-1880s. Room rates (from $155 to $175 for rooms, $190 to $215 for third-floor suites) include a ranch hand breakfast with all the fixins. Read more about this relaxing destination in the Accommodations chapter. Your

hammock is waiting under the giant oak tree.

After breakfast at your hotel or bed-and-breakfast, you can return to downtown to catch all the shops and galleries you missed, or head to one of the area lakes and parks. Anyone who thinks the Kansas prairie is a dull patch of green is in for a pleasant surprise. The Prairie Park Nature Center is a seventy-one-acre park adjacent to seven acres of virgin prairie with 180 species of wildflowers and native grasses that flow like shimmering satin with the wind. You can explore more than a mile of trails that pass through prairie and wetlands and end at a seven-acre urban lake. Interpretive signs along the path point out habitat elements and identify wildlife.

Located just 3 miles southwest of Lawrence is Clinton Lake, with 7,000 acres for boating, swimming, and fishing. Five developed areas offer bridle, hiking, and mountain biking trails; camper hookups; primitive camping sites; and a complete marina along with a restaurant and convenience store. For more information call (785) 843-7665.

To experience Lawrence, travel west on Interstate 70 from Kansas City, exit at the first Lawrence exit (204), and turn left (south) onto 2nd Street. A visitor center is located in a historic train depot at North 2nd and Locust Streets. For more information call (785) 865-4499 or (888) LAWKANS (529-5267), or visit the Web site, www.visitlawrence.com.

WESTON, MISSOURI

Blink twice when you reach Weston and you'll wonder where you left the time machine. Antiques shops, a clothing store like none other, more than its share of historic homes, and two fine-dining restaurants should keep you busy for a day or a weekend. Lucky for you Weston has some appealing bed-and-breakfast options and one historic downtown hotel. The hamlet's official tagline might be "the town that time forgot," but you never will.

If it hadn't been for a Missouri River flood in 1881 that shifted the river 2 miles away into

i Most small towns tend to "roll up the sidewalk" early. That's certainly true in Atchison, Kansas, and Weston, Missouri, where restaurants tend to close at 9:00 p.m. and there are few nightspots. If you're after relaxation and romance, these towns are fine choices. But if you like variety, from art to music to theater, Lawrence is your kind of getaway.

Kansas, Weston could have been a major metropolis instead of a side trip. Most of us send a silent thank-you to that watery presence every time we visit this town that's magically stuck in the mid-1880s.

Weston was the first city founded in the six-county Platte Purchase of 1837, and today it remains a hamlet of 1,700 residents—all, it would seem, living or working in a pre–Civil War building or antebellum home. In all, 22 blocks of buildings are listed on the National Register of Historic Places, including the Price-Loyles Home (718 Spring Street, 816-640-2383), an 1857 three-story Federal-style home that was occupied by four generations of Daniel Boone's descendants. The home, filled with original family furnishings and toys, is open for tours. See more of the town's past at the Weston Historical Museum, which features artifacts depicting life here from prehistoric times to World War II.

Main Street has antiques as well, but these are the kind you can buy. In fact, Weston is a magnet for antiques shoppers from surrounding states. With fourteen or so Old World emporiums lined up side by side, shoppers look like human rickrack as they go from door to door seeking peeling-paint cabinets and sponged bowls.

Several stores mix old with new, such as the Acorn, where you'll find vintage furniture and linens along with new garden art. If you're a fiend for rare Depression glass, make a beeline to db's Antiques, home to one of the largest collections of this highly collectible glassware in the Midwest. And not only will you find that perfect silk pillow at Nelson and Taylor Interiors, but the in-store decorating team will help you coordinate an entire room to go around it. Next door is anything but vintage! At nti2 you'll find an eye-popping display of contemporary furnishings and gifts, including a 'tween section that will keep that younger shopper racing for your charge card. Renditions offers an extensive array of handcrafted Arts & Crafts furniture and accessories with such well-known names as Hile Furniture, Porteous tiles, and gorgeous mica lamps. If you need a pine table to display that new lamp, Youngblood Gallery most likely has it, along with other antiques and giftware. After all, they've been a Main Street beacon for more than twenty-two years.

One of the most remarkable shops in the region is a few miles out of town. Locust Grove Antiques (25180 Highway JJ, 816-640-3203) carries a collection of antique and new furniture and accessories arranged in small habitats that make it easy to say, "I'll take the whole room!".

When you're finished sprucing up your home, consider a new outfit at Missouri Bluffs Boutique and Gallery. This is truly the Bermuda Triangle of the Midwest; it's a fact that women who walk in here are never seen again. The store is wall-to-wall with clothing that marries rustic with romance: embroidered and bejeweled vests, sweeping velvet skirts, suede jackets with 6-inch fringe, and hats festooned with fabric roses and netting. You'll also find case after case of jewelry, including artist Kelly Johnson's beaded pins and masks. Red-and-black cowgirl boots to go with your new getup? Size 7, coming up.

By now you're starving, and Weston can oblige. The Vineyards (505 Spring Street, 816-640-5588, www.thevineyards restaurant.com) serves lunch and dinner in an 1845 antebellum home that is delightful during the day and turns intimate with candleglow at night. Cheryl Hartell is a spirited young chef with quite a talent with fresh ingredients and sauces. Start your meal with her baked Brie or house salad with blue cheese crumbles and delightful vinaigrette that fans have been begging her to bottle.

Dinner recommendations include a daily risotto, filet of beef with Merlot sauce and grilled portobello mushrooms, or French-cut pork chops with a caramelized apple, fennel, and red onion sauce. The extensive wine list includes selections from Weston's own award-winning Pirtle Winery. Cheryl hosts wonderful wine-tasting dinners, including one she calls Pinot Envy. Clever girl. The Vineyards is open for lunch Wednesday through Saturday and dinner Wednesday through Sunday. A Sunday brunch menu includes items like a beef tenderloin, mushroom, and smoked Gouda omelet. Reservations are recommended.

Save enough time to visit the winery (502 Spring, 816-640-5728, www.pirtlewinery.com) across the street. Housed in a historic church with a wine garden and tasting room, Pirtle's is known for its honey mead, a slightly sweet wine that gives honeymoon its name. The shop is open daily from 10:00 a.m. (it's cocktail hour somewhere in the world!) to 6:00 p.m.

Another favorite dining choice is Avalon Cafe (608 Main Street, 816-640-2835, www.avaloncafeweston.com). This 150-year-old home makes an appealing backdrop for chef David Scott's masterpieces, especially wild game such as elk and duck. The Weston Trio takes the guesswork out of ordering; it usually features a wild-game dish plus a fish and steak with a selection of marvelous sauces. For lunch the baked Brie is a gimme. Depending on the season, the melting-cheese dish will include fresh strawberries or grilled eggplant and zucchini, along with buttery baked garlic to slather on French bread. Add a salad and it's plenty to share with a friend for lunch. Avalon is open for lunch and dinner Tuesday through Saturday. Reservations are a must.

If you'd prefer frivolity to fine dining, take a trip to Ireland at O'Malley's 1842 Pub (Short and Welt Streets, 816-640-5325, www.westonirish.com), carved out of three limestone brewery cellars built 55 feet below-ground. You'll definitely want to tipple an O'Malley's Irish Cream Ale (or two). This popular beverage is produced in the same location first established in 1842. After a number of setbacks (including a fire and a little thing called Prohibition) that were enough to drive anyone to drink, the operation is back making original nineteenth century–style beers. Sean O'Malleys's pub hosts several big events a year, including a St. Patty's Day celebration. If you're lucky, local Celtic singer Connie Dover will be home from touring and grace the room with her enchanting voice. If not, balladeer Bob Reeder might turn the same room blue with his repertoire of naughty limericks.

Blues and greens are the colors at Weston Bend State Park, where a scenic overlook offers a view of the Missouri River, Fort Leavenworth in Kansas, and beyond until the line of trees turns into a mist. A hiking trail that meanders through the woods and along the edge of the bluff also has great views of water, prairie, and rugged cliffs. Hikers and bicyclists have the 3-mile paved loop trail all to themselves. Secluded picnic sites, a playground, and open shelter are awaiting your afternoon getaway. For longer park visits, a campground with basic and electric campsites, modern restrooms, hot showers, and laundry facilities is available. For information, or to reserve a campsite, call (816) 640-5443 or go to www.mostateparks.com.

For most of us, however, a getaway means just that: leaving the laundry, cooking, and cleaning to someone else. If that's you, Weston has places for pampering. The Inn at Weston Landing (500 Welt Street, 816-640-5788, 877-249-5788, www.innatwestonlanding.com), is a Celtic-style hideaway that is part of the original Weston Brewing Company built in 1842. The inn's four spacious rooms (all with private baths) have distinct personalities. The Andrew O'Malley room reconstructs a delightful cottage on the southern tip of Ireland's Clew Bay with a fireplace, hand-blown windowpanes, and spinning wheel. You might imagine the scent of heather on the highlands in the Rosine Fleming room. New owners Mike and Cyndee Bohaty have added such amenities as queen beds and a hot tub in the garden while keeping the authenticity. One of Cyndee's

most requested breakfasts is strawberry parfaits, asparagus and mushroom quiche,
bacon, and homemade scones.

The Benner House Bed and Breakfast (645
Main Street, 816-640-2616, www.benner
house.com) is a fine example of steamboat
gothic architecture. It was built in 1898 for
George Shawhan, who owned what is now
known as the McCormick Distillery. Strolling
from the shops and restaurants, you'll notice
the house right away with its wraparound
porch, quaint gingerbread details, and large
windows overlooking the veranda. Inside,
hosts John and Julie Pasley have filled the
home with antiques, including a pump organ
that dates back to 1911.

Breakfast will be waiting after a night's
rest in one of the four upstairs guest rooms,
each with private bath. The front bedroom
offers a view of downtown and features a yo-
yo quilt and oak bedroom set. Across the hall,
a brass bed and Main Street view make the
room a favorite with guests. Other amenities
include a hot tub set in the backyard garden,
a parlor for socializing, and a sitting room
where you can curl up in a rocking chair with
a book. Rates start at $110. The Benner
House is an ideal place for a wedding for up
to fifty guests.

The Hatchery House Bed and Breakfast
(618 Short Street, 816-640-5700, www
.hatcherybb.com) is a handsome Federal-
style home built in 1845 that got its name for
the number of children "hatched" here
throughout the years. Present-day innkeepers
Bill and Anne Lane have hatched some pretty
swell ideas themselves, such as filling the four
guest rooms with lovely antiques and keeping
the original wood-burning fireplaces intact.
We feel a winter trip coming on. Shop for your
own antiques downtown but be back in time
for wine and cheese in the parlor before
heading back out for dinner. A nightcap will
be waiting before you take the stairs to your
upstairs room, each named for a historic figure. Payne's Pineapple Room is an oversize
beauty with treetop views. Each room has a
private bath. Say good morning to early-bird

coffee and rolls, or wait for the sumptuous
farmhouse breakfast.

If you prefer a "downtown" stay, then the
Saint George Hotel (500 Main Street, 816-640-
9902, www.thesaintgeorge.com) has a suite
waiting for you. Built in 1845 and recently renovated, the twenty-six–guest room hotel has
amenities the steamboat captains it once
served could never fathom. High-speed Internet access, massage showerheads, and a
continental breakfast are some of the perks.
Rates range from $99 to $279. Other unique
in-house treats include the Wine Bank Bar and
the River Bend Bakery, where the cinnamon
rolls will be calling your name.

Weston tempts you with festivals and
special events throughout the year, including antiques shows in March and April, one
of the reasons *Midwest Living* ranked it one
of the top-ten antiques destinations in the
Midwest. In June a citywide garage sale
brings in the bargain hunters, and four summer weekends are devoted to free music in
the park featuring regional talent. A July 4
festival includes a parade, street fair, and
fireworks, and two ice-cream socials keep
you cool in August.

In October the town celebrates the German and Irish families that made Weston
home in the 1800s with an Octoberfest and a
three-day Irish Festival. The annual Applefest,
held in October as well, brings together more
than forty folk artists; a garden market; food
vendors selling everything from turkey legs to
homemade root beer; live music; a parade;
and everything you could possibly make
apples into, including apple butter, fritters,
cider, and dumplings. You can also celebrate
the harvest at the source; two nearby
orchards offer such fall treats as pumpkin
patches, hayrides, caramel apples, and free
cider. Call Vaughn Orchard and Country Store
(816-386-2900) and Weston Red Barn Farm
(816-386-5437) for details.

Before the first frost, townspeople begin
planning the annual Candlelight Homes Tour in
December, when five historic homes are
dressed for the season. Street activities feature

carolers, carriage rides, and a chance to whisper wishes to Father Christmas.

Weston is 30 miles northwest of Kansas City; take exit 20 off Interstate 29 and follow the signs. For information visit www.weston mo.com. A visitor center at 502 Main Street has brochures on shops, lodging, and restaurants. Please be aware that many of the shops and restaurants are closed on Monday.

ATCHISON, KANSAS

A trolley ride past grand Victorian mansions on brick-paved streets, sweeping views of the Missouri River valley from a tree-shaded park bench, and a hot fudge sundae at an old-fashioned soda fountain downtown: If this sounds like an idyllic afternoon, then this lovely riverfront town is for you.

When you come to Atchison you'll be following in the footsteps of the Kansa Indians, who gave the state its name, and Lewis and Clark, who passed through on July 4, 1804. Fifty years later Atchison became one of the first settlements in the Kansas Territory. The town was named for David R. Atchison, then president of the Missouri Senate, who became president for a day when Zachary Taylor refused to take office on a Sunday.

Its location at the westernmost bend of the Missouri River turned the town into a leading commercial center, a role that was expanded when the Atchison, Topeka & Santa Fe Railroad was founded in 1860. Soon bankers and railroad magnates were building impressive mansions and minicastles, many of which still line 3rd, 4th, and 5th Streets.

Other settlers were building grand stone structures as well; the Benedictine monks established St. Benedict's Abbey (1020 North 2nd Street, 913-367-7853, www .kansasmonks.org) in 1858. It's easy to tell the church didn't come until a century later. A student of Frank Lloyd Wright, Barry Byrne, designed this handsome limestone structure with a 44-foot-high nave ceiling. His wife created many of the interior frescoes. Self-guided tours are available, and if you

Sometimes tiny shops and 10-table restaurants keep strange hours, so to keep from driving 40 minutes only to see a display of CLOSED signs on doors, call to check on open days. In Weston, for instance, it seems the whole place shuts down on Monday.

wish to spend more time in this spiritual setting, weekend retreats can be arranged. Contact Father Matthew Habiger (913-367-5340) for details.

In 1863 the Benedictine Sisters established Mount St. Scholastica College for women, and in 1938 their beautiful chapel (801 South 8th Street) was dedicated. The interior is rich with beautiful marble, including pillars that contain many fossils. A large rose window, stained-glass windows, and a magnificent Romanesque vaulted ceiling make this worth a look. Tours can be arranged by calling (913) 367-6110. The chapel overlooks the river, and a park bench under an ancient tree provides a pleasant stop.

Enough reflection—now it's time to shop! Atchison's claim to fame, of course, is as the birthplace of Amelia Earhart. But these days another woman is putting the town on the map. Mary Carol Garrity's famous home interiors store, Nell Hill's (501 Commercial, 913-367-1086, www.nellhills.com), is a phenomenon that's been covered in *Victoria* magazine, *Kansas City Home Design,* and even the *Wall Street Journal.* Customers from Topeka, Omaha, and of course Kansas City make regular road trips to stock up on European antiques, home furnishings, accessories, and gifts at jaw-dropping prices. Don't worry about getting it all home; Mary Carol ships. And be sure to ask about her interior design book while you're there.

Other antiques shops on Commercial Street are worth checking out as well. This outdoor pedestrian plaza is landscaped with brick walls, seasonal plantings, and fountains. Hungry? Pop into Marigold Bakery and Cafe (913-367-3858), a cozy place for crisp salads, sandwiches on focaccia, and homemade pies. Take an extra cookie to go. Or belly up to the lunch counter at one of two vintage soda fountains. Most downtown locations are open every day except Sunday.

Garrity's Encore, 121 North 5th Street (913-367-1523), is Mary Carol's "new" place for "old" items—as in antiques—as well as her exciting new furniture line. Does this woman *never* sleep?

Now that you've experienced the town's sanctuaries (both religious and 400-count Egyptian cotton) it's time to discover its history. The visitor center (913-367-2427, 800-234-1854, www.atchisonkansas.net) is historical itself, housed in the restored Santa Fe Depot at 200 South 10th Street. Open every day except major holidays, the center provides maps, a brochure, and a gift shop for souvenirs of your visit. The same address is home to the County Historical Society Museum, which has artifacts from steamboats and wagon trains, and the Atchison Rail Museum, owned by a voluntary group of railroad enthusiasts who operate a miniature railroad during the summer.

The depot is also where you can catch the Atchison Trolley for a forty-five-minute narrated tour past eighteen sites on the National Register of Historic Places. The ride departs each hour on the hour on different days and times from May through October and during special events. Fares are $4 for adults, $2 for children four to twelve. As you *clack, clack, clack* over brick streets you'll see some of the most impressive Victorian homes in the Midwest as well as the Romanesque-style post office that was completed in 1894. You may want to hop off at one of the following stops to explore.

The Evah C. Cray Historical Home Museum (815 North 5th Street, 913-367-3046) is a twenty-five-room mansion that offers a look at the opulence of the Victorian era. Built in 1882, it is distinguished by a three-story fairy-tale tower, ornate fireplaces, and original chandeliers. The carriage house has a video viewing room, country store, and exhibits. A minimal fee is charged. The museum is open daily May through August, closed November through February, and open Friday through Monday all other months. Got that?

The Muchnic Art Gallery (704 North 4th Street, 913-367-4278) is in a spectacular Queen Anne mansion that was built in 1885 for lumber merchant George W. Howell. His profession dictated the home's lavish use of carved woods, such as the intricate parquet floors of walnut, mahogany, and oak and faces carved on the ornate newel posts in the lower hall; the eight faces are said to represent the Howell family. Cast-bronze hardware and stained glass in the conservatory are other masterful touches. H. E. Muchnic, founder of LFM (now Atchison Casting), purchased the home in 1922 for $9,000. The furnishings and paintings on the main floor are just as when the Muchnic family lived here. Since 1970 the second floor has been dedicated as exhibition space for the Atchison Art Association. The home is open on weekends and Wednesday afternoons from March through December; there is a small fee.

The Amelia Earhart Birthplace Museum (223 North Terrace Street, 913-367-4217, www.ameliaearhartmuseum.org), also on the trolley route, is a pretty Gothic Revival cottage built in 1861 by the famous flyer's grandfather, Judge Alfred G. Otis. The Ninety-Nines, a women's pilot organization Earhart helped found in 1929, now operates the museum, which features period furnishings. Open daily, but hours vary throughout the year. Donations are appreciated.

You'll find more memorials to the aviatrix at the International Forest of Friendship at Warnock Lake. A life-size bronze gazes over the grounds and a forest that was established during the town's bicentennial. Each June,

i If you're planning to stay at a bed-and-breakfast, the host can become your new best friend even before you sign the register. Call before your visit, if possible, to request information about upcoming events, what not to miss, and restaurant recommendations. That way you can get the most from your visit.

Close-up

Downtown Parkville, MO

(816) 505-2227
www.parkvillemo.com
This riverfront village is a charming little getaway for a day of shopping, yet is close enough to drop in for lunch. The real pull is its mix of two dozen one-of-a-kind shops and galleries filled with gifts, decor, and fine art. Home Embellishments (816-505-1022) is like an always-open art fair representing work from more than sixty artists. Look for wacky metal masks, steel garden sculptures of frogs and flowers, folk art frames, funky jewelry, and a collection of knobs and pulls. Across the street, at 201 Main Street, is River's Bend Gallery (816-587-8070), with gorgeous etched-glass vases, whimsical ceramic and glass martini glasses, wearable art including painted vests and flowing tunics, vivid pastel landscapes you'll want to get lost in, and silver and pewter jewelry at terrific prices.

A short walk up Main Street, Dixie Dunnaway turned a charming home into an even more charming shop called Rivendell (816-746-9506). It's the place to find gorgeous lamps, picture frames, and throw pillows. You'll wish your home could smell as good as La-De-Da, and it can (816-741-6711). This delightful shop sells pretty sachets, glycerin soaps in flower designs, unusual candles, and potpourri, all wonderfully displayed among stylish upholstered chairs, rattan and metal tables, and lamps. One brick wall is filled with room-making clocks inspired by antiques from Paris, London, and Portobello.

Ready to drop? You'll have your choice of restaurants ready to recharge your energy level. Cafe des Amis (816-587-6767) serves country French fare on a lovely treetop deck. The pizzas at Stone Canyon (816-746-8686), especially the roasted potato and chicken version, are legendary. Or work off your meal with a stroll along the groomed trails that meander through 115 acres of river valley woods and wetlands, complete with a romantic waterfall. Read more about this nature sanctuary in the Parks, Lakes, and Recreation chapter.

new plaques are set into a walkway to honor people involved in aviation and space exploration. Trees representing all fifty states and more than thirty-five countries are planted here, including the "Moon Tree," which was grown from a seed taken to the moon aboard Apollo 14. It is encircled by a memorial to the ten astronauts who have lost their lives.

A deck on a hill within the lake provides a spectacular view of the Amelia Earhart Earth-

work. Kansas artist Stan Herd created this one-acre portrait of permanent plantings and stones in 1997. Now it's time to plant yourself in a booth at the River House Restaurant (913-367-1010) at 101 Commercial. Here you'll find elegant dining in a century-old building that has been a railroad hotel, peanut butter factory, and bordello. There's a pun in there somewhere, folks; we'll let you work on it. Lovely views of the river are part of the restaurant's many charms, but the big draw is the menu, which includes grilled steaks, seafood, and salads. Lunch and dinner are available Monday through Saturday.

If you prefer something more casual, Jerry's Again (121 North 5th, 913-367-0577) tempts you with salads, soups, and sandwiches. In fact, a shopping trip to Garrity's Encore upstairs usually ends right here with a slice of one of Virginia's legendary pies. Paolucci's (113 South 3rd, 913-367-6105) is a family establishment that provides a taste of Italy in this small town. A vast take-out menu includes meatball sandwiches, but we'd prefer dining in to dig into a platter of shrimp scampi or pasta with sausage. The lounge next door is a lively spot for a before- or after-dinner drink.

Ready for bed? Part of the allure of tiny towns is that lodging choices always seem to include a bed-and-breakfast. Atchison has two delightful options. St. Martin's Bed and Breakfast is perched on a stone wall and provides a glorious view of the river from the back patio. You may never want to leave the luxury of the spacious Gold Suite, with its grand king-size bed, claw-footed bathtub, and shower for two. Four other rooms are available, including the ultraromantic Anna's Room in shades of taupe and mauve with a dreamy view.

All rooms have a private, adjoining bath and are $95 per night. Owners John and Janet Settich are well known for their continental breakfasts, which include made-from-scratch baked goods like pumpkin bread, cheddar cheese biscuits, and cinnamon rolls and a delightful platter of fresh fruit and gourmet cheeses. Cereals and yogurt are also available. John is an amateur historian of the town and can tell you fascinating stories and suggest must-see attractions. St. Martin's is at 324 Santa Fe Street. Call (913) 367-4964 or (877) 367-4924. You may view the rooms online at www.stmartinsbandb.com.

But you'll find reasons to visit Atchison other than cinnamon rolls and biscuits; there seems to be a special event nearly every weekend, especially in summer. Things really start jumping in March for the St. Patrick's Day parade, with floats downtown and

corned beef and cabbage at the Elks. Later in the month, get on track for the annual Artrain, when five railcars serve as art galleries and studios for local and regional artists. In May 3 downtown blocks are transformed into the Kiwanis Spring Flea Market, and the following week the Antique Airport Fly-in displays vintage aircraft at the airport named for the town's famous daughter. That same month, the Riverbend Art Fair features artists from a six-state area with live music, children's activities, and food vendors.

In July a celebration on the 4th serves up food, music, and fireworks at the Amelia Earhart Stadium, and two weeks later the Annual Amelia Earhart Festival treats residents and guests to outdoor concerts, arts and crafts, food, a carnival and street dance, and a spectacular fireworks display on the Missouri River. In October the Atchison Homes Tour lets us peek into some of the fabulous old homes. Tickets are $15, and money raised goes to the Mount St. Scholastica Academy. The Oktoberfest Arts and Crafts Festival is a downtown event with more than one hundred arts and crafts vendors plus German food and music. And count us in for the Haunted Homes Tour, which extends through Halloween. This narrated trolley tour takes you around "the most haunted town in Kansas." Perhaps Sallie will make an appearance; you can read about the famed "Heartland Ghost" at www.prairieghosts.com. The tour costs $5, and children from four to twelve get a goodie bag. The rest of us just get goosebumps.

The trolleys are rolled out again for the annual Tour of Lights each December, an hour's round-trip of festive holiday lights and decorations all around Atchison. Fares are $4 for adults and $2 for children. For more information on all these events, call the Atchison Area Chamber of Commerce at (913) 367-2427 or (800) 234-1854. Details are also available on the Web site, www.atchisonkansas.net. To reach Atchison, head north on I-29, take exit 20, and follow Missouri Highway 273 to Missouri Highway 45. Go north on MO 45 to U.S. Highway 59, and then go west 4 miles to the town.

MEDIA

Perhaps Kansas Citians have so many media choices because more than half of us live in the Show-Me State. Our need-to-know mentality can be appeased through a breathtaking variety of ways, including five daily newspapers, a handful of weeklies, ten television stations, twenty FM and twenty-three AM radio stations, and a growing list of public interest Web sites. And whatever your livelihood or hobby, from golf to computers, fine dining to fitness, chances are there's a special-interest publication to help you do it better, find out where to enjoy it, or at least commune with others who share your passion.

Following are some of our more interesting means of communicating, listed by category. Companies are located in Kansas City, Missouri, unless otherwise noted.

DAILIES

The *Examiner*
410 South Liberty
Independence, MO
(816) 254-8600

500 West R. D. Mize Road
Blue Springs, MO
(816) 229-9161
www.examiner.net
The *Examiner* is owned by Morris Communications Corporation, which serves the towns of Independence, Sibley, Buckner, Blue Springs, Grain Valley, and Oak Grove under its two mastheads: the *Independence Examiner* and the *Blue Springs Examiner*. This century-old newspaper is published afternoons Monday through Friday and Saturday morning. Local home delivery costs $100 per year.

The *Kansas City Kansan*
8200 State Avenue
Kansas City, KS
(913) 371-4300
www.kansascitykansan.com
Strong political leadership (finally!) and exciting new tourism destinations west of the state line have given this daily more to cheer about in the past few years. The paper has covered Wyandotte and northern Johnson Counties since 1921, so the fourteen-year-old 4–H'er who once had his prize-winning pig pictured in the paper might now be turning his bifocals to the monthly senior section. In fact community news is the strong suit of the *Kansan* for folks who feel slighted by the big paper across the river. Published Tuesday through Saturday with a circulation of 10,000. Subscriptions cost $85 per year.

The *Kansas City Star*
1729 Grand
(816) 234-7827
www.kansascity.com and www.kcstar.com
Although the *Star* is the only daily newspaper that serves the entire metroplex, it has never used its "only game in town" status to deliver less-than-stellar reporting. It mirrors our town's tragedies and triumphs with insight and depth. And despite the nationwide trend of decreasing newspaper readership, the *Star* remains a vibrant and growing communicator. Indeed, a preholiday edition can weigh as much as your Thanksgiving turkey!

The paper's five metropolitan bureaus contribute a neighborhood feel to each zoned issue. Its editorial coverage has evolved with the lifestyle interests of its readers, adding a daily FYI/Living section that deals with fitness, family, pets, home fashion, and just enough celebrity gossip to keep us from turning to supermarket tabloids. The Thursday Preview provides a week's worth of entertainment and arts coverage throughout the region. The *Sunday Star Magazine* brings us profiles of people, places, and events in our area worth a closer look.

On-staff photographers provide sometimes humorous and often poignant glimpses of the city's inhabitants. When journalists like Eric Adler share stories about hometown heroes, we cheer; when his four-part series features a teenager fighting drugs and a tough home life, hundreds of us mail checks to pay for her college tuition. Sportswriter Mike Polanski's prose is so remarkable that even nonsports buffs often turn to his section first. Kevin Collison is our eyes and ears for downtown development.

The paper's online version displays news, story archives, and extensive links to other area sites. A classified section lets viewers search for a house, car, or job from their computer screens. Daily delivery costs $198 a year; Saturday and Sunday–only delivery is $144. Newsstand cost is 50 cents. See the Close-up in this chapter for a look at the history of the *Star*.

The *Olathe Daily News*
514 South Kansas
Olathe, KS
(913) 764-2211
www.olathedailynews.com
This community paper is the place to find news about local schools, business, and social events in the booming southwest

Along with the *Kansas City Star*, the Nelson-Atkins Museum of Art, and our city's many boulevards, parks, and gardens, William Rockhill Nelson left another, more furry legacy. He imported squirrels from neighboring states and let them loose in Kansas City's new green spaces. So some fall, as you're watching the long-tailed creatures leap around in search of acorns, you can say, "Nuts to you, Mr. Nelson."

region of the metroplex. Daily circulation on Tuesday through Saturday is around 8,000 except on Wednesday, when it jumps to 42,000 and includes a Home Living section with new home community profiles, real estate listings, and gardening and home decorating tips. Yearly subscriptions are $111.

WEEKLIES

The *Business Journal*
1100 Main Street, Suite 210
(816) 421-5900
www.bizjournals.com/kansascity
Kansas City's edition of American City Business Journals Inc. is delivered to nearly 11,000 offices each Friday. Its editorial focus—banking, sales and marketing, business owner profiles, growth strategies—is geared to decision makers in companies with fewer than one hundred employees. Each issue takes an in-depth look at a business category such as family businesses, health care, or banking. The annual *Book of Lists* is an excellent tool for area salespeople and job seekers; it names top managers and lists revenue for segments such as manufacturing, minority businesses, advertising agencies, property managers, lenders, architects, and travel industries. The print version has added lifestyle coverage. The online version is easy to navigate and provides links to the publisher's forty-one other city journals. An annual subscription gets you fifty-three issues plus the *Book of Lists* for $94; the newsstand price is $1.75 per copy.

The *Call*
1715 East 18th Street
(816) 842-3804
www.kccall.com
"We call it like it is" was the motto of Chester A. Franklin, an ambitious businessman and community activist who founded one of the nation's most respected African-American papers in 1919. The paper quickly developed a reputation as an advocate for social justice, with articles about lynchings, police

brutality, segregation, and discrimination in housing and employment. In 1955 Lucille Bluford took the helm after writing for the paper for more than two decades. Known for her thoughtful and thought-provoking columns, Bluford has been called "the conscience of Kansas City." Her own conscience guided her when she sued the University of Missouri for not allowing her to attend its school of journalism in the late 1930s. She lost the case, but in 1984 she received the school's Honor Medal, and five years later MU presented her with an honorary doctorate of humanities. But this petite lady's highest honor came not in bronze but in bricks: The Kansas City, Missouri, Public Library system named a new branch library at 3050 Prospect for her in 1988. Bluford died on June 13, 2003, two weeks shy of her ninety-second birthday. The *Call* has a paid circulation of 20,000 and costs $26 a year. Single issues cost 50 cents.

The *Independent*
4233 Roanoke Road
(816) 471-2800
www.kcindependent.com

If you're *anyone* in Kansas City society, your engagement, wedding, and birth announcements will have been covered by the city's oldest magazine; if your last name appears on a street sign, building, or museum anywhere in town, chances are your photo accompanied the write-up. Since 1899 the city's crème de la crème have turned these oversized black-and-white pages to see who wore what designer's gown to the latest ball or to muse about gentle gossip in "Over My Shoulder." The readership represents Kansas City's most influential, active, and civic-minded citizens . . . and certainly some of its most affluent. The average household income is $335,000, with an average net worth of $3.1 million. The *Independent* arrives in polished brass mailboxes on Saturday morning forty-five times a year and is available at a select number of newsstands. The annual subscription price is $45.

The *Leaven*
12615 Parallel Parkway
Kansas City, KS
(913) 721-1570
www.theleaven.com

The weekly newspaper of the Archdiocese of Kansas City in Kansas is distributed free to families who belong to Catholic parishes throughout Wyandotte, Johnson, and Leavenworth Counties. Each issue covers national and local news, book reviews, and a calendar that lists upcoming social and educational events, retreats, and meetings. The commentary pages answer questions regarding religion and provide a deeper look into the current Sunday's scripture.

The *Pitch*
1701 Main Street
(816) 561-6061
www.pitch.com

This free weekly with an 80,000 circulation is the city's most recognized alternative tabloid. The editor boasts that the paper is dedicated to "hard-hitting journalism, smart criticism, lively features, and good old-fashioned muckraking," but the real reason folks pick it up is to see what band is playing at the Hurricane or what food critic Charles Ferruzza thinks of the new restaurant in town. In fact, anyone who whines "There's nothing to do in Kansas City" has somehow missed tripping over stacks of the *Pitch* in doorways of bookstores, coffeehouses, and bistros and in red kiosks all over town. Its calendar offers the area's most complete coverage of live music, dance, and theater (including some in Lawrence, Kansas, a college town about half an hour away). And for a paper with such a Gen-X base, it provides a respectable listing of events for kids. Even the ads are pretty entertaining; here's where to find outlets for any vice from martinis to water pipes, sexy lingerie to sex partners (you might need to read the abbreviation code for any designation beyond SWM in the personal ads titled "Romance" and "Wildside").

The annual Best of Kansas City issue—usually in mid-October—has the typical "best

William Rockhill Nelson

Many of us read all about it in the *Kansas City Star*, the venerable newspaper founded by William Rockhill Nelson on September 18, 1880. In Kansas City this newspaperman from Indiana saw a town where he could make both money and a difference—and he eventually did both. His other legacies include our park and boulevard systems and the art gallery that bears his name.

Nelson quickly showed his business acumen by charging 2 cents for his paper instead of the nickel that the other three dailies already in print did. The last of his competitors, the *Kansas City Journal*, held on until 1942. As Nelson's fame and legend grew—thanks in great part to his unconventional tastes and famed battles with the establishment—he was often interviewed by national magazines like the *Saturday Evening Post*. Theodore Roosevelt became a personal friend who often came to Kansas City to seek his advice.

Nelson's paper's reach expanded along with his waistline when in 1891 he delivered the *Weekly Kansas City Star* to country towns throughout Kansas, Missouri, Nebraska, Colorado, and Oklahoma. For 25 cents a year subscribers were treated to reprints from the daily *Star* and the editor's political views.

By 1901 he had purchased the *Kansas City Times*, a morning daily, and began calling his empire "the twenty-four-hour *Star*." The *Star*'s afternoon edition ceased in 1990. In 1911 the paper moved to its current location, a redbrick Italian Renaissance–style building at 18th and Grand where there were no private offices. Nelson said the layout was designed so that everyone could feel equal; employees knew it was so the boss could keep his eyes on them.

By the time he died on April 13, 1915, Nelson's fortune was estimated at between $5 million and $10 million and the *Star*'s circulation was more than 200,000. His will stipulated that after the death of his heirs the entire fortune would be converted to cash and given to the arts. His majestic home, Oak Hall, is now the site of the Nelson-Atkins Gallery of Art. He had already made our city a work of art; he used his paper to campaign for paved roads and streets, sidewalks and streetlights. And he was instrumental in creating the city's parks system in 1881 when he hired landscaper George E. Kessler to design a boulevard and park system that is still considered one of the finest in the world.

As for the *Star*, Nelson thought it couldn't continue without him. But survive it has, and has thrived under the helm of talented and forward-thinking managers and through pens of award-winning journalists. Its reporters and editors have won eight Pulitzer Prizes and four Polk Awards. Yet its most famous reporter wasn't around long enough to earn more than a paycheck: Ernest Hemingway joined the staff in October 1917 but left the

A big man with big dreams for Kansas City, William Rockhill Nelson pushed forward the city's beautiful park and boulevard systems, among other accomplishments. SPECIAL COLLECTIONS DEPARTMENT, KANSAS CITY PUBLIC LIBRARY, KANSAS CITY, MISSOURI

next April to drive ambulances in the war. Hemingway credited a *Star* editor, C. G. "Pete" Wellington, with teaching him to write clearly and provocatively. The paper's style sheet at the time admonished, "Use short sentences. Use short first paragraphs. Use vigorous English." Okay.

When Nelson's daughter, Laura Nelson Kirkwood, died in 1926, the paper was sold in accordance with his will. With financial help from her husband, Irwin, thirty *Star* employees purchased the paper for $11 million. In 1977 it was sold to Capital Cities Communications Inc. for $125 million; it later became part of the Knight-Ridder chain, and today it is part of the McClatchy family.

During the 1980s, under editor James H. Hale, the *Star* greatly expanded its zoned suburban operations and extended its coverage of business and sports, just in time to herald the city's first baseball championship in 1985. Hale's fifteen-year tenure also saw a continuation of Nelson's philanthropic legacy by establishing Project Warmth, which has raised millions of dollars and tons of clothes and blankets for the city's poor.

The *Star* has explored innovative methods of delivering news and information through technology. StarTouch, an interactive telephone news and information service, was launched in 1991; within four years the system was logging six million calls a year. And in 1996 the paper decided to embrace the emerging news source that threatened its readership: It introduced a multimedia site in cyberspace just two years after the phrase "World Wide Web" first appeared within its newsprint pages.

And the *Star* continues to find ways to assist the community through programs like Stars in Education, which provides newspapers and training materials to schools; Hooked on Books, a citywide program that delivers books to school libraries; a recycling program; and sponsorship of ongoing health and business seminars.

brunch" categories along with a few fresh options such as best guilty pleasure. Just thinking about those answers gives us goose-bumps. The paper's online incarnation provides a repeat of the printed page with added links to other sites, Web-exclusive features, essays, and blogs that will make you blush. The writing style is not for the timid.

MAGAZINES

Ingram's
2049 Wyandotte Street
(816) 842-9994
www.ingramsonline.com

For more than a century this monthly, and its predecessor, *Corporate Report,* has been a staple among area business leaders. The average reader's annual income is close to $229,000, and nearly half are millionaires. Each issue contains editorials about law, sales and marketing, technology and e-commerce, profiles of the city's movers and shakers, coverage of area philanthropic activities, and a short calendar of upcoming events. The magazine does a fine job at promoting Kansas City's strengths by profiling a geographical portion of the city including schools, economic growth, and real estate options. There's stiff competition to make the magazine's annual Corporate Report 100, a list of Kansas City's fastest-growing companies, and perhaps even tougher competition for the annual best-of survey published each August. Within days plaques declaring "Best Barbecue" or "Best Golf Course" start going up all over town. *Ingram's* is delivered free of charge to qualified readers; subscriptions are available for $45 per year.

KC Magazine
7101 College Boulevard
Overland Park, KS
(913) 894-6923
www.kcmag.com

Every city has one: a glossy magazine that celebrates the region's most interesting people and places. Lucky for us, *KC* is a beaut with

great writing and photography. Published monthly, each issue offers late-breaking takes on around-town happenings, profiles of hometown celebrities, tips on making your space more livable, and handy guides to restaurants and events. Once a year the magazine publishes the Best of Kansas City survey in which community readers provide their own favorites along with readers' top picks. *KC* is $4.95 per issue. An annual subscription is $18.00.

Kansas City Home Design
7101 College Boulevard
Overland Park, KS
(913) 894-6923
www.kansascityhomedesign.com

Although *Home Design* shares its editorial staff, office space, and a handful of writers with *KC Magazine,* it is by far the more elegant, better-dressed sister. In each issue, two or three homes, often belonging to our town's toniest couples, are profiled along with stunning photography to show us how the other half lives and entertains. And after drooling over a four-page photo essay of a dinner party, complete with recipes, you'll feel as if you'd been a guest. Other topics include gardening, home renovations, coverage of high-profile society events, and the art scene. The title also appears on an annual coffee table book repeating ten of the most spectacular homes of the past issues. The magazine is published bi-monthly; subscriptions are $18.

Kansas City Homes and Gardens
4121 West 83rd Street
Prairie Village, KS
(913) 648-5757
www.kchomesandgardens.com

The fact that Kansas City can support two home and garden magazines is testament to our appreciation for graceful living, lovely gardens, and gracious entertaining. This magazine also has a lake living section to appease the hundreds of residents who spend summer weekends at the Lake of the Ozarks, four hours south of Kansas City. Published monthly, the magazine costs $26 for an annual subscription, $4.95 for an individual copy.

SPECIAL INTEREST PERIODICALS

Camp
1600 Genessee, Suite 525
www.campkc.com

A print and online resource for the local (and growing) lesbian, gay, bisexual, and transgender community, *Camp* covers arts and entertainment previews upcoming events such as the Gay Pride Parade, and touches on health and social issues. The publication also offers a roster of businesses that cater to and support this thriving group. Reporters also sign in on travel destinations that are gay friendly. One of *Camp*'s most celebrated covers featured a photo of then-mayor Kay Barnes, a politician who was a strong LGBT advocate. Dressed in an attractive purple running suit, she led the 2006 AIDS Walk. The tabloid is available at bookstands and musical venues throughout the city.

Dos Mundos
902-A Southwest Boulevard
(816) 221-4747
www.dosmundos.com

Dos Mundos, or *Two Worlds*, has provided a bilingual forum for Kansas City's vibrant and growing Hispanic population since 1981; 80 percent to 90 percent of the information is translated. The readership is diverse: Of the more than 110,000 Hispanics living in the Kansas City metropolitan area, only about 60 percent are of Mexican origin. The remainder are mostly Puerto Ricans and Cubans. Along with national news, *Dos Mundos* covers local news, sports, and entertainment and provides a much-needed focus on Hispanic heritage. The 70,000 circulation covers the greater Kansas City area with nationwide distribution accounting for 5 percent. Published biweekly, an annual subscription costs $35.

JAM (Jazz Ambassadors Magazine)
P.O. Box 36181
Kansas City, MO 64171
(913) 967-6767
www.kcjam.org

One of the finest regional jazz magazines in the country, *JAM* has covered the Kansas City jazz scene since 1986. It is distributed free to 500-plus Kansas City Jazz Ambassador members (one more great reason to join this organization), and available free at local jazz venues, record stores, bookstores, and libraries. Whether your musical taste runs to jazz, Dixieland, or bebop, *JAM* is the place to find where musicians are jamming at nightclubs and festivals, learn more about our town's musical heritage, and read where to board the bus for the next pub crawl. *JAM* is produced in even-numbered months.

Kansas City Small Business Monthly
P.O. Box 754
Shawnee Mission, KS 66201
(913) 432-6690
www.kcsmallbiz.com

Small and emerging businesses in the area have a friend in publisher/editor Kelly Scanlon. Her monthly tabloid covers need-to-know topics such as how to keep employees happy, watch out for the latest computer virus, cope with rising health care costs, decide whether to incorporate, measure trade show results, market globally, and write a sales script. And that was just October. Each issue also profiles a successful business, provides strategies for home offices, and includes a comprehensive calendar of seminars and events. There's even a handy guide for the biggest problem facing entrepreneurs today: where to get a decent lunch in fifteen minutes. The online version is extremely well designed and offers additional articles about marketing, sales, and cash flow. The annual "Entrepreneur's Guide" is a keeper, covering legal, marketing, e-commerce, taxes, real estate, education, and training subjects. *Small Business Monthly* is distributed free to qualified readers and is available by subscription for $8 a year.

Review
1708 Campbell
(816) 471-2343
www.ereview.org

This monthly glossy magazine covers Kansas City's impressive art scene through previews of upcoming exhibitions and art events, gallery and studio listings, reviews of current works, and artist-on-artist interviews. Here's where to locate art in places outside the galleries: coffeehouses, flower shops, restaurants, and libraries. If you're not familiar with the talent and variety of work to be found within our town, this publication may surprise you. Available free at many bookstores and galleries around town.

Verge
P.O. Box 3040
Kansas City, KS 66103
(816) 531-8500
www.vergekc.com

An upscale magazine that celebrates Kansas City's vibrant gay and lesbian community, *Verge* also appeals to straights who want to keep up with the latest fashion trends and nightspots. *Verge* covers the entire lifestyle options for this demographic that represents a high disposable income along with a passion for arts and culture. Social issues are also included, such as gay adoption and testing your "gaydar."

The magazine is issued at will, at least for now, but has plans to become a bi-monthly publication. It's available by subscription or in kiosks and newsstands around town.

TELEVISION

Hundreds of dinners got cold as an estimated 100,000 people crowded around 7,500 television sets throughout the city when our first station, WDAF–TV, went on the air at 6:00 p.m. October 16, 1949. To beam those signals the station built a 724-foot antenna, which was the highest man-made structure in Missouri at that time. It became the seventy-ninth TV station in the country. Viewers were treated to three hours of programming every day, starting with a locally produced children's show sponsored by Frito-Lay; during the rest of the day many people tuned in just to watch the test pattern.

The *Kansas City Star* owned WDAF–TV from sign-on until it was indicted by a federal grand jury for monopolistic advertising practices and forced to sell the station in 1958. A year after its first airing, WDAF became an NBC affiliate, a designation it continued until 1994, when it switched to the Fox Network.

Kansas City's pioneer station holds bragging rights to a number of firsts in the market, including the first to offer color, stereo, Doppler radar, twenty-four-hour programming, and a helicopter for traffic and news reporting.

Today the helicopter from WDAF–TV vies for air space with KMBC–TV's eyes-in-the-sky. But when it comes to on-air time, Kansas City has its favorite personalities. The patriarch is Larry Moore at KMBC–TV, who started as a reporter with the station in 1968 and became primary news hawker in 1972. His warmth has earned him a wall full of awards, such as News Anchor of the Year and one of Kansas City's Ten Top Celebrities. But it's his community involvement that has earned him such accolades as Man of the Year. Moore helped organize the Dream Factory in 1984, a nonprofit that has helped grant the wishes of nearly 2,500 seriously ill youngsters; the anchor has helped raise $400,000 annually to send kids to Disneyland, get them computers, and travel around the country to meet favorite celebrities. Moore, a cancer survivor, was also lauded by the American Cancer Society for his educational series urging early detection. The entire community watched and sent prayers as he lost his dark, wavy hair to chemotherapy before he bounced back to the robust health he enjoys today.

At KSHB–TV one of the personalities is also known for a luxurious head of hair—or fur, in this case. It's Stormy the weather dog, who accompanies meteorologist Gary Lezak on his speaking engagements at retirement communities and schools and often appears on the air.

You might be interested to know that the KCTV tower at 125 East 31st Street is taller than the Eiffel Tower in Paris. The KC tower stands at 1,067 feet; the Parisian structure—although admittedly more beautiful—is 1,024 feet tall.

Along with cable programming, Kansas City supports nine local stations, including network affiliates and one independent station. The stations are listed along with their non-cable channels. Kansas City also has two cable companies, Time Warner and Comcast. For these channel settings, check the last page in Star TV found in the *Kansas City Star* Sunday paper.

WDAF Channel 4 (Fox)
KCTV Channel 5 (CBS)
KMBC Channel 9 (ABC)
KCPT Channel 19 (PBS)
KCWE Channel 29 (CW)
KSHB Channel 41 (NBC)
KPXE Channel 50 (ION)
KSMO Channel 62 (MyNetworkTV)

RADIO

Kansas City joined the country's love affair with radio in the spring of 1922 when a furniture dealer and a radio supplier joined forces to put the city's first commercial station, WOQ, on the air. A few weeks later religious programming and poetry readings were being broadcast from the RLDS Church (now Church of Christ) on WPE. WDAF, whose call letters live today, used the airwaves for a more lively purpose as it broadcast the Coon Sanders Nighthawks Orchestra live from the Muehlebach Hotel starting that June. Kansas City radio played an even bigger part in the history of jazz when, in 1935, a record producer heard Count Basie's Barons of Rhythm carried live from the Reno Club at 12th and Cherry Streets on his car radio hundreds of miles away.

Sadly, it's harder to dial in a jazz tune on a local station today as contemporary hits and album rock have taken over the airwaves. A few stations offer jazz programming at various times throughout the week, and KCIY–FM 106.5 provides what it calls "smooth jazz" from a variety of contemporary artists like Diana Krall and David Sanborn. Classical music lovers also go wanting in Kansas City, since its only all-classical station, KXTR, left its FM status in 2000. It now has far less reach on its new home at KXTR, 1660 AM.

Drive-time listeners hoping to get away from the in-your-face ramblings of radio personalities can tune to KCUR–FM 89.3, a non-commercial station that broadcasts National Public Radio and Public Radio International programming. Popular locally produced programs make up the rest of the broadcasting day; at 10:00 a.m. every other Friday foodies listen to restaurant reviews on Walt Bodine's program, while Chuck Haddix (aka Chuck Haddock) shares his passion for blues, soul, and jazz—along with 250,000 recordings housed in the Miller Nichols Library—every Friday and Saturday from 8:00 p.m. to midnight on "Fish Fry." Another music lover got his start on KCUR: Bill Shapiro's "Cyprus Avenue" debuted on the station in 1978 and today his "intelligent rock and roll" can be heard on fifty radio stations across the nation. It's aired from noon to 2:00 p.m on Saturday in Kansas City.

Other stations are listed below.

News/Talk

WIBW 580 AM, www.am580wibw.com
KFEQ 680 AM, www.680kfeq.com
KCMO 710 AM, www.710kcmo.com
KMBZ 980 AM, (popular call-in forum for sports fanatics) www.kmbz.com
KCXL 1140 AM, www.kcxl.com
KCTE 1510 AM, www.1510.com

Christian/Gospel/Family Value

KCCV 760 AM, www.bottraradionetwork.com
KGGN 890 AM (Urban gospel), www.kggnam.com
KCWJ 1030 AM, www.kcwj.org
KEXS 1090 AM, www.kexs.com
KGNM 1270 AM, www.kgnmradio.com

KCNW 1380 AM (Catholic programming),
www.wilkinsradio.com
KPRT 1590 AM, www.kprt.com
KCCV 92.3 FM,
www.bottraradionetwork.com

National Public Radio/Cultural/ Classical/Jazz

KUPN 1480 AM
KXTR 1660 AM, www.kxtr.com
KCUR 89.3 FM, www.kcur.org
KKFI 90.1 FM, www.kkfi.org
KCMW 90.9 FM
KANU 91.5 FM

Country

KFKF 90.1 FM, www.kfkf.com
KBEQ 104 FM, www.q104kc.com
WDAF 106.5 FM, www.wdaf.com

Adult Contemporary

KOKO 1450 AM
KMXV 93.3 FM, www.mix93.com
KRBZ 96.5 FM

KUDL 98.1 FM, www.kudl.com
KSRC 102.1 FM, www.star102.com
KKJO 105.5 FM

Rock/Rhythm/Soul (including Oldies)

KCMO 94.9 FM, www.oldies95.com
KZPL 97.3 FM, www.973theplanet.com
KQRC 98.9 FM, www.989therock.com
KYYS 99.7 FM, www.kyys.com
KCFX 101.1 FM, www.kcfx.com
KLZR 105.9 FM, www.lazer.com
KCJK 105.1 FM, www.1051jackfm.com

Others

WHB-810 AM (Sports), www.810whb.com
KPHN 1190 AM (Business), www.radio
disney.com
KMEX 1250 AM (Spanish)
WDAF 610 AM (Sports), www.61sports.com

Urban/Hip Hop

KPRS 103.3 FM, www.kprs.com
KMJK 107.3 FM, www.magic1073.com

WORSHIP

We have, as theologian Martin Marty said when he saw a 1998 *Kansas City Star* poll on religion, "a real believing town here." Indeed. Ninety-six percent of those surveyed said they believed in God or a higher power, 95 percent believed in miracles, 85 percent believed in life after death. And we put our faith to work. Fifty-two percent of Kansas Citians attend worship services weekly, 68 percent pray daily, 23 percent read scripture daily, 16 percent read it several times a week, and 40 percent volunteer for charity.

Through the years, even during our rough-and-tumble early days, we have built monuments to faith in buildings that reach toward the heavens: the dizzying spiral of the Community of Christ Temple, the majestic Unity Tower, the shining golden dome of the Cathedral of the Immaculate Conception, the Steeple of Light piercing the night sky from the Community Christian Church near the Plaza. And a new heaven-sent symbol is being planned for the United Methodist Church of the Resurrection in Leawood, Kansas, home to the fastest-growing Methodist congregation in the country.

There are slightly more than 2,000 congregations here, representing more than a dozen faiths. In addition to the more familiar Protestant, Roman Catholic, Jewish, Eastern Orthodox, and Islamic groups, there are Hindu, Buddhist, Sufi, Baha'i, Native American, Sikh, Jain, pagan, Unitarian Universalist, and New Age groups.

And to keep pace with the faithful in the suburbs, new houses of worship—huge structures, even some megachurches, defined as those with over 2,000 in attendance—are being built at an amazing pace. Yet even some of these supersize structures are outgrown before the last pew is in place. Our frantic expansion is getting noticed. John Vaughan, director of Church Growth Today, a research center in Bolivar, Missouri, says "to have this kind of growth and this kind of construction is phenomenal. For the size of the city, it makes it even more impressive."

And the fervor of the heartland is evident in the fact that two of the churches mentioned, Community of Christ and Unity School of Christianity, are world headquarters. The third is the Church of the Nazarene.

It certainly was for Joseph Smith III, who in 1852 took the helm of the largest Mormon splinter group to found the Reorganized Church of Jesus Christ of Latter-Day Saints in Independence, Missouri. Why this place? Because the Midwest town is where his father, Joseph Smith, had determined Jesus Christ would return to Earth. When the elder Smith was killed in 1844, the son continued his teachings here in the city of Zion. The growing congregation built their massive auditorium in 1920 and later the temple with its splendid 300-foot spiral roof that resembles a seashell.

The campus, 1001 West Walnut, Independence, serves as the spiritual center for 250,000 members in more than fifty states. Along with a museum, the campus contains the Children's Peace Pavilion, an interactive museum dedicated to promoting peace through example. The Worshiper's Path, a reflective walkway filled with symbolic artwork, leads to the 1,600-seat sanctuary. Guests are welcome to visit, and organ

i A list of churches, synagogues, and other houses of worship in the area, including links to those with Web sites, can be found at www.kansascity guide.com/church/index.htm.

recitals are held at various times of the year. You are also invited to take part in a Daily Prayer for Peace beginning at 12:30 p.m. You may contact them at (816) 521-3045 or www.cofchrist.org.

Unity World Headquarters, with its beautiful 165-foot-tall bell tower, is situated among 1,400 acres of beautifully landscaped grounds with meditation chapels, fountains, and reflecting pools. It is home to a magnificent rose garden with more than 800 rose bushes and fifty varieties. Founded in 1889 by American clergyman and educator Charles Fillmore and his wife, Myrtle, the nondenominational religion combines teachings from Christian Science, Hinduism, Theosophy, New Thought, and others.

Unity has been offering ministry, prayer, and education since 1889. Its monthly spiritual publication, *Daily Word*, is translated into nine languages with an annual circulation of 1.3 million, and its Silent Prayer ministry received two million requests for prayer assistance in 1999. Free tours start at the visitor center (1901 Northwest Blue Parkway, 816-524-3550, www.unityworldhq.org) Monday through Friday year-round; weekend tours are also available May through October.

The Church of the Nazarene is the third religious organization to be headquartered in Kansas City. The church moved to its present home at 6401 The Paseo shortly after it was organized October 8, 1908, in Pilot Point, Texas.

The International Center provides support services to more than 1.4 million members worshiping in more than 12,600 churches in the United States, Canada, and 143 other world areas. Its publishing house is 5 miles north of the center at 2931 Troost Avenue and is the largest publisher of Holiness (Wesleyan) literature in the world. It prints more than 500,000 books annually.

Although today religious headquarters and even community churches can take over entire blocks or acres of land, Kansas City's first house of worship was a log cabin built in 1834 at what is now 11th and Pennsylvania. It was called

i Roman Catholics wishing to attend Mass in Latin may do so at a beautiful Gothic church built in 1924 at 2203 Parallel Avenue in Kansas City, Kansas. Blessed Sacrament Church holds daily Latin Mass Monday, Tuesday, Wednesday, and Friday at noon, low Mass on Sunday at 7:30 a.m., and high Mass at 10:45 a.m. Call (913) 321-1958 for more information.

"Chouteau's church" because it was funded by the extended family of Francois and Berenice, who came here in 1820 as the first white settlers. It is the oldest worshipping congregation in Kansas City. Various missionaries built the log cabin and two brick structures, none of which are standing today.

In 1845 Father Bernard Donnelly, a pioneer priest, came to the area. Thanks to his Irish charm as much as his pastoral leadership, he soon became a legend among the settlers and native tribes. In 1880 the area was officially designated a diocese, and Bishop Hogan was named the first bishop.

When the Immaculate Conception Church was relocated to its present site at 416 West 12th Street in 1882, it was the tallest building in Kansas City, Missouri. People bought tickets just to ascend the staircase to see the view. The church became the Cathedral, or the Mother Church, for the newly formed Diocese of Kansas City in 1884. In 1895 one of the most unusual carillons in the city was installed in the tower; the ten bells are named after saints. The largest of these, St. Thomas, is most often rung.

The church was renamed the Cathedral of the Immaculate Conception in 1893. It is always a lovely site, its graceful lines and stained-glass windows giving visual and spiritual respite among its taller neighbors. But when the sun turns the twenty-three-karat gold dome into a shimmering glow, it's simply beautiful. Call (816) 842-0416.

In 1974 the Cathedral of the Immaculate Conception entered into a covenant with the neighboring Episcopal cathedral, Grace and

Holy Trinity. This stone structure is quite impressive as well and contains two Tiffany stained-glass windows.

One religious landmark, the striking B'nai Jehudah synagogue at 69th and Holmes, has been torn down. Yet even its destruction follows the Jewish values and congregational concepts of shalom—the promotion of harmony in all things. Taking its place will be the University Academy, a charter school that will serve more than 1,000 students in grades six through ten. The congregation's new home, at 123rd and Nall in Overland Park, Kansas, (913-663-4050, www.bnaijehuda.org), serves a growing faith community that spans more than 130 years.

In 1870, twenty-five Jewish families gathered, pledged $800, and rented a hall at 6th and 8th and Main Streets to form the first Jewish congregation in Kansas City, Missouri. Founders included Civil War veterans who had fought on both sides of the conflict, a saloon-keeper, store owners, clerks, and at least one gold prospector.

They called themselves B'nai Jehudah, "children of Judah." It became one of the pioneer congregations of Reform Judaism in America, and its rabbis and hundreds of its people have played prominent roles in the economic, social, and political life of Greater Kansas City from an early day to the present. Today membership numbers about 1,700 families.

The congregation's modest first temple, built in 1875 at 6th and Wyandotte, was replaced ten years later by a more substantial structure at the southeast corner of 11th and Oak, opposite the present City Hall. By 1908 the growing congregation needed more space and so built an imposing new structure at Linwood Boulevard and Flora Avenue. Temple membership more than doubled soon after World War II, with the majority of members moving farther south. This led to relocating the facilities to 69th and Holmes in 1957 with a new religious school, social hall, and chapel. Ten years later the sanctuary was added. Designed by Kansas City architect

Clarence Kivett, the broadly spiraling temple rising nearly 90 feet high was meant to evoke one of the oldest structural forms, the Bedouin tent.

One more area church is of note, both for its architect and for its tower made of light instead of steel. But the heavenly beam almost didn't happen. When Frank Lloyd Wright designed the Community Christian Church (816-561-6531) in the 1930s, technology couldn't produce the shaft of light he envisioned coming from the top of the dome. Sixty years later artist Dale Eldred, who was teaching at the Kansas City Art Institute, created a system to send four xenon lights toward the skies. But not even he lived to see the display. The artist died before the Steeple of Light was finally switched on in December 1994. The lights are on every weekend and nightly during the holiday season. You may visit the church at 47th and Main.

A modern-day church is making history as well. The United Methodist Church of the Resurrection (913-897-0120, www.cor.org) at 137th Street and Roe Avenue in Leawood, Kansas, is the fastest growing United Methodist church in the country. With its expansion plans it is poised to become the largest as well. Led by the charismatic Reverend Adam Hamilton, the congregation has grown from a handful of families meeting in a funeral home chapel in 1990 to more than 13,000 today.

When the church's 10-year expansion plan is complete, the structure will encompass almost one million square feet of worship,

The *Kansas City Star* publishes a section each Saturday called "Faith" profiling congregations and individuals, listing upcoming faith events, and providing advertising for area churches, synagogues, and other places of worship. Each week two members of the newspaper's panel of religious leaders answer a reader's question. Once the reincarnation was covered by a Buddhist lama and a Baptist minister.

educational, fitness, and multipurpose space and a 7,000-seat sancutuary. That's larger than Kemper Arena and Bartle Hall combined.

With its amazing growth, some question the church's ability to serve its congregation's spiritual needs. But those who attend are impressed. The key to the Church of the Res-urrection's (or COR, as it's often called) suc-cess is its mission to build a faith community for those who don't go to church and have lit-tle or no religious background.

There is no doubt that when this many people come together with one goal, things get done. The COR was recently the Commu-nity Blood Center's third largest donor, behind Sprint and Hallmark. Its congregation pro-vided 5,000 sack lunches to children in West-port, helped build sixteen homes for Habitat for Humanity, sponsored 300 children through Compassion International, and donated liter-ally tons of clothing and food to area shelters and food pantries.

We've talked about cathedrals and churches created so that people of one faith can come together to pray, do good work, seek solace, and rejoice in the glory of their God. Kansas City is also home to a church that has no central denomination, the Pil-grim Chapel (816-753-6719, www.pilgrim chapel.org).

This tiny English Gothic church at 3801 Gillham Road was built in 1941 as a congrega-tion for the deaf and hard of hearing—a rare example of a religious building constructed by and for a special-needs membership. The Pil-grim Lutheran Church for the Deaf closed in 1987, and today under the leadership of ordained ministers Roger and Elizabeth Cole-man, the facility is open to people of all faiths. All religions are welcomed: Christian, Jewish, Buddhist, Hindu, Muslim, or New Age.

Behind these massive stone walls and heavy oak doors, people come to worship and meditate, hold wedding or funeral cere-monies, or simply pause in the middle of a

i The increasing number of faithful can make it tough to find a seat in church as well as at breakfast. By 11:00 a.m. restaurants serving brunch are packed with churchgoers. Be prepared to wait at First Watch, a breakfast-and-lunch-only restaurant with locations around the city, as well as eateries like the Bristol in Overland Park. Some places take reservations.

hectic day. And what they find is something extraordinary, both spiritually and struc-turally. Architects incorporated special accommodations for lip-reading and hand signing. For instance, sightlines were impor-tant, so the pulpit was built high enough that everyone could see clearly from every posi-tion. The rows of windows were positioned to eliminate glare. And its miniature Gothic dimensions created an unplanned benefit for the hearing: perfect acoustics with no echoes and no dead spots.

The church is beautiful in both its simplic-ity and its special touches. The stained-glass windows of rose and amber provide a pinkish-golden hue, and the oak parquet flooring is laid in lively geometric squares. Even the 24-inch-thick stone walls are special. Instead of the ghostly white of native Missouri lime-stone, Pilgrim Chapel was built of Wisconsin limestone, a putty-gray color that weathers well. The sacred space has no ornamentation; the lines are clean and pure. And in keeping with the intradenominational theme, there are crosses, a menorah, and portraits of yogis, symbols that can be brought out for a service, then put away.

In 1999 Pilgrim Chapel was placed on the National Register of Historic Places. And across the country there are only a few cities that have anything remotely similar to this tiny space where everyone is welcome. It is a fitting tribute to the City of Faith.

RELOCATION

All right already, we've convinced you to move here. Congratulations, neighbor. You're going to love living in the heartland. We've helped you pick your neighborhood, line up some festivals, locate parks and lakes, and find where to get a great meal. Now let's move you in.

To smooth your move we've divided this chapter into topics of major interest to those planning—or just contemplating—a move to Kansas City: Neighborhoods and Real Estate will help you decide where you want to live. Once you've settled on a location, Getting Started will help you get hooked up to utilities. Getting Legal provides basic information about licenses you'll need, and Getting to Know You introduces those little nice-to-know services in town. In Kansas City we take our children's education and well-being seriously. Education and Child Care highlights that commitment, and Higher Education takes the search for knowledge to the next level—for you as well as your kids. As you'll see in Health Care and Wellness, the city's health care infrastructure is second to none, and although we might not be the first place to pop into your mind when you think *retirement*, perhaps we should be. Check out the Retirement section of this chapter and decide for yourself.

Whatever your reasons for making the move, welcome to Kansas City!

The listings are in Kansas City, Missouri, unless otherwise noted.

NEIGHBORHOODS AND REAL ESTATE

Kansas City real estate agents fight over who gets to take the couple from California on a tour of available homes. Once the visitors get a gander at the five-bedroom beauty on two acres for the same price as a two-bedroom bungalow in San Jose, they'll practically wrench the contract out of the agent's hand.

A recent survey conducted by the National Association of Homebuilders ranked Kansas City No. 1 in housing affordability among metropolitan areas with populations over one million. Let's compare apples to apples, or in this case a four-bedroom, two-and-a-half-bath home in a neighborhood that would appeal to a middle-manager transferee. According to Coldwell Banker's 2006 Home Price Comparison Index, that exec would pay just shy of $192,000 to live in Kansas City versus $551,000 in Deerfield, Illinois. A similar home in Spokane, Washington, will run nearly double ours, and trust us: You'll love our coffee just as much. Moving from La Jolla, California? See how far your $1.87 million will go in the heartland, as in a mansion in Mission Hills, an equestrian estate, or a three-story chateau on one of our pristine lakes. No wonder one California transplant thought an ad for a $130,000 home here was for the down payment alone.

Is it any wonder *Money* magazine named Overland Park, Kansas, No. 6 in its Top 100 Places to Live in 2006? This pretty suburb excelled in such categories as low crime rate, short commute distance, job growth, green spaces (there are seven public golf courses here), and median home prices around $20,000 less than the Best Places average. Tiny Parkville, Missouri, got a pat on the back from *Men's Journal* in 2007; it was the only Midwest community to be named one of the 50 Best Places to Live.

Families will be happy to know they're welcome here; we rank No. 3 among large metropolitan areas for relocating, according to Worldwide ERC. But singles—bring it on! We moved up eight spots to No. 30 in *Forbes* magazine's Best Cities for Singles in 2006, based on our nightlife, culture, job growth, and "coolness" factor. Dig it. Both of those rankings were helped by what *AmericanStyle* magazine found when it named us one of its annual Top 25 Arts Destinations in 2006.

Factor in our low tax burden and the picture gets even better. According to the Tax Foundation, homeowners in Missouri pay 10.49 percent of their income in local and state taxes, and Kansas homeowners pay 10.88 percent. Both numbers are well below the national average of 11.33 percent.

In fact Kansas City ranks well below the national average in cost of living and costs for housing, utilities, and grocery items. According to the American Chamber of Commerce Researchers, we are one of the nation's best bargains. Our residents average about 28 percent above the national median in real income, which combines "affordable" with "cost-effective." That means we have more disposable money for shopping, dining out, and recreation. No wonder big retailers like Nordstrom can't get here fast enough. Let me at those Johnson County shoppers!

Kansas City also offers solid business opportunities for both corporations and employees. *Expansion* magazine rated Kansas City No. 3 on its 50 Hottest Cities in the U.S. for 2006, based on our central location and low cost of living. *Fortune* has referred to our town as one of the best places for doing business. Perhaps more important in terms of lifestyle, the same magazine listed Kansas City as most beloved by its own resident executives.

Perhaps one reason the execs are so happy is that they're not behind the wheel. Kansas City is second only to San Antonio for freeway miles per capita, which means our workforce has a faster and easier commute than other cities our size. On average, most commuters get to the office before the cup of coffee gets cold, in about twenty minutes. One executive who left behind a ninety-minute commute each way in Chicago said living ten minutes from his office has meant a true lifestyle change. He has more time to spend with his family, can easily make a 5:00 tee time, and has far less stress.

Giant corporations are proud to call Kansas City home. Sprint Nextel's 3.9 million–square-foot world headquarters houses 10,000 employees. Hallmark Cards, one of the world's best-known brands, with sales of $4.2 billion, is based here.

H&R Block, the nation's largest tax preparation firm, was founded in Kansas City in 1955 and employs 86,500 worldwide. Its move to downtown Kansas City helped revitalize that area. American Century Investment Inc., the mutual fund giant, with $50 billion in assets, was begun in Kansas City, and here it stays. And other large corporations are locating here to reap the rewards of our central location and wealth of educated, friendly workers. *Management* magazine rates us among the top twenty-five "Hottest Real Estate Markets." Once transferred employees get a chance to experience the Midwest lifestyle and buying power, they're thrilled to call Kansas City home.

Although these corporate giants have helped grow our economy and attract a top-notch work force, Kansas City remains a hotbed of entrepreneurial and small business activities. In fact, 99 percent of local companies employ 250 or fewer workers, accounting for 64 percent of total employment. They find plenty of support through training and specialized programs. *Entrepreneur* magazine rates Kansas City as one of the best three cities for supporting small business, and *Inc.* magazine has called us "an entrepreneur's dream." Our diversity—a healthy mix of big corporations and small companies—is one reason we tend to weather a recession better than most other cities do.

Our job force is consistently ranked among the most educated and productive in the United States, but we realize there's more to life than just work. We are, above all, a city of balance.

We tend to take our city's riches for granted, but newcomers are often surprised at our varied and vibrant arts culture. The Nelson-Atkins Museum of Art features one of the world's finest collections of Asian art and has more Henry Moore sculptures than any place this side of the Atlantic. The museum has completed its dramatic expansion—the Bloch Building—which elevated its standing even more. Down the street, the Kemper Museum of Contemporary Art showcases works by Dale Chihuly and Louise Bourgeois.

Music lovers have the Kansas City Symphony, Lyric Opera, Chamber Music series, and jazz concerts at the Folly Theatre. Art galleries abound here, especially in our revitalized inner-city Crossroads Arts District that's home to dozens of small showrooms and artist studios. And just on the horizon is the $340 million Kauffman Center for the Performing Arts, which will make a monumental addition to our city's skyline and way of life. Yet with all our highbrow offerings, one of our most appealing aspects is our mix of cultures. You can enjoy an evening of Beethoven on Saturday night and spend Sunday afternoon at a blues jam.

And we like to exercise our bodies as well as our minds. Long known as a major league sports town, we offer more recreational amenities than most cities our size. With hundreds of parks, lakes, golf courses, recreation centers, and public pools in every community, we offer ample opportunities for family entertainment and a healthy lifestyle. In fact, *Men's Health* magazine ranks Kansas City second in cardiovascular fitness and fourth for running and jogging.

Head out to Lake Jacomo on any given Sunday and it looks like a movie set for Happy Town USA as people fish for bluegill and glide through a sailboat regatta, little kids play soccer, teens take up volleyball, couples bike along trails, dogs catch Frisbees, and Dad catches a snooze under an oak tree. Look up and you'll see kites doing a graceful figure eight in our clean, fresh prairie wind, and hot air balloons dotting the sky with a rainbow of color.

You'll find all four seasons beautifully represented here. Outdoors, in fact, is where Kansas City really shines. Real estate agents tell stories of newcomers who expect to find dusty streets with tumbleweeds scuffing the car door and instead are enchanted by our lush green spaces and acres of forests.

People who have never seen the marvelous seasonal transitions are delighted in spring when our Bradford pear trees turn pink and white and daffodils line every sidewalk. Summers in Kansas City become a paintbox of greens with luxurious lawns and trees in full force, and gardens and flower boxes are ripe with colorful blooms. In autumn we open our jewelry box to decorate trees with purple, deep red, brilliant orange, and gold. And perhaps there's not a more precious sight than a four-year-old at the window with the news that "It's snowing!"

The City of Fountains is also a wellspring of education. We boast a network of highly rated public schools, private and parochial schools, top-notch technical and vocational programs, and private and state-affiliated colleges and universities. Parents are involved in their students' school programs through parent-student-teacher programs and are quick to vote "yes" when it comes to updating existing schools, building new ones, and improving services.

Many of our public schools and their educators have received state and even national recognition, including Teacher of the Year honorees, Triple A–rated schools, and Blue Ribbon awards from the U.S. Department of Education. Graduating students find a wide variety of choices, whether they seek the small student-teacher ratio of a private college like William Jewell or the excitement of the University of Missouri–Kansas City, with 13,000 students. Graduate degree programs abound, offering working adults a chance to take classes part time while maintaining their careers.

With our great schools, friendly neighborhoods, and abundance of recreational opportunities, Kansas City is a great place to raise a family. In fact, Overland Park, Kansas, is the "kid-friendliest" suburban area in the country (among those with populations over 100,000) according to the Washington-based group Zero Population Growth. The group looked at factors like education, environment, health, public safety, and community life.

On the other side of town, Lee's Summit, Missouri, is one of only seventeen cities nationwide, according to Homeadvisor.com, that meet the highest criteria in terms of school ratings, sunny days, and cost of living index below the national average. And Kansas city earned a spot on *Expansion Management* magazine's list of the Top 20 Best Cities for Business Attraction in 2007.

Wellness is also an element that puts Kansas City ahead. It's significant that people come here from all over the country to obtain premium health care. More than sixty hospitals and specialized clinics stand ready to meet any medical need, from the birth of a baby to the rarest forms of cancer. Greater Kansas City is also home to award-winning medical research based at the University of Missouri School of Medicine, the University of Health Sciences, and the University of Kansas Hospital, which was recently ranked thirtieth in the nation for its heart program by *U.S. News & World Report*, and that was before the judging panel witnessed the new state-of-the-art Center for Advanced Heart Care, which opened in October 2006.

In 2000 they were joined by the Stowers Institute for Medical Research, a $195 million, 600,000-square-foot facility funded by James Stowers Jr., founder of American Century Investments. With its current endowment of $1 billion, the center is devoted to studying gene-based afflictions such as cancer, Alzheimer's disease, and rheumatoid arthritis. Largely due to the Stowers project, eight primary research institutions are collaborating through the Kansas City Area Life Sciences Institute, with a goal of making our city one of the nation's top-ten centers for life sciences and biotechnology research in the years ahead.

Add to the mix our Midwestern friendliness and small-town values, and it's easy to see why people who have grown up here wouldn't want to live anywhere else. And people who move here realize they've stumbled upon the nation's best-kept secret.

What newcomers find is more than just a vibrant city. We're an exciting mix of neighborhoods as varied as can be. And naturally, for a metropolis that encompasses more than 9,100 square miles and nineteen counties in two states, housing options are diverse. Urban offerings include River Market warehouses converted to sleek lofts, upscale apartments that overlook the Country Club Plaza and Crown Center, and downtown condos not far from where our city began. In fact, urban-minded singles and urbane empty-nesters have around 4,000 lofts, condos, and apartments waiting for them ranging in price from just over $100,000 to more than $2 million for a view that will have you singing, "Kansas City, here I come."

If you're willing to put in some sweat equity, you can find century-old homes in historic districts that need your tender loving or expertise with a sledgehammer. For considerably more you can own a restored 1909 colonial Revival minimansion complete with original stained-glass windows and a fireplace in every room.

Looking for land, lots of land, under starry skies above? We can set you up with a suburban lifestyle next to a lush golf course or a country estate with room for horses or overlooking a shimmering lake. More modest means will still land you in a desirable neighborhood of trim ranch houses where strollers and yellow Labs are part of the landscape.

You'll have your pick of neighborhoods and homes here, and chances are for far less money than you'd ever imagine possible. And you'll be amazed at how quickly you'll be welcomed into the neighborhood. No matter what your interests, you'll soon find a garden club or singles' group to join, an invitation to a Chiefs' tailgating party, or another soccer mom who's happy to let you take Tuesday.

Let's take a drive around the neighborhoods. Notice all the people waving? Yes, we really are that friendly in Kansas City.

Ready for the grand tour? We divide this section into counties, then by city. Each community, whether it's populated by 334 or 134,000, is governed by a mayor and city council. Granted, this gets a little confusing when a dividing street has a different speed limit depending on whether you're heading north or south. But on the plus side, having so many communities with their own histories and sense of pride means more festivals and Fourth of July fireworks displays for the rest of us.

Missouri

Cass County

www.casscounty.com

If you prefer the quiet, scenic countryside to a metropolitan environment, you may want to explore some of the many advantages Cass County's cities provide. From its rural beginnings, Cass is becoming a hot ticket in terms of new business and residential development thanks to a low cost of living, efficient transportation, and room for expansion. Its diverse economic base includes biotech firms and manufacturers, and new, attractive industrial parks are popping up throughout the region.

Cass County students receive a superb education in ten school districts that do an excellent job balancing studies with healthy recreational programs. Parents will also like the fact that their dollars go far here in terms of quality housing. Well-kept older homes, bright new subdivisions, or a custom-built estate: You'll find it all in Cass.

And where new homes are built, retail and services are sure to follow. The county has exciting new shopping districts to take care of its residents. Families can also "take it outside" at any number of nearby parks, lakes, and golf courses. Some of the most popular fishing and boating lakes are nearby, including Lake Winnebago, RainTree Lake, and the natural paradise known as Lake Jacomo. Take your pick from the following Cass County cities.

BELTON

www.belton.org

A sleepy little town that has seen remarkable growth lately as families move south to get nice homes for far less than in town, Belton has its own school district and a population of around 24,000. It's a bit of a drive to the airport (about forty-five minutes), but you can be on the Plaza in about twenty minutes. Homes tend to be traditional and cost from $60,000 to more than $1 million for mansions sitting on enormous estates.

LAKE WINNEBAGO

Ah, this is the life! Although some people simply maintain a vacation home here, most choose the resort-type amenities every day. Yet even with its Lake of the Ozarks feel, it's just thirty minutes from downtown.

Housing options are attractive, diverse, and amazingly affordable when compared with resort-caliber cities across the nation. Students attend the highly rated Lee's Summit school district, and health care and shopping options are all within easy reach. About 900 lucky folks live here, and there's always room on the lake for one more boat. Homes range from $90,000 to more than $250,000.

RAYMORE

www.raymore.com

Known as a small rural farm community years ago, recently Raymore has had the greatest percentage of population increase of any Kansas City suburb. The population numbers around 8,000 right now, but the growth will continue. Close to Belton, you can expect the same twenty-minute drive to the Plaza. Or you can stay home and have a cookout with your neighbors; this is a friendly place. Home prices range from $60,000 to $500,000.

Clay County

www.claycogov.com

Surrounded by the natural beauty of rural landscapes, yet with the convenience of urban living, Clay County offers the best of both worlds. In fact, 20 percent of Kansas City, Missouri, extends into Clay. Its residents are proud of the eclectic mix of neighborhoods, its colorful history, and exciting growth.

Clay County is the fourth largest county in the metroplex, ranking third in both total retail sales and total effective buying income. Just fifteen minutes from downtown Kansas City, it has attracted giant companies like Citicorp and Union Pacific to its 400-square-mile confines. In fact, the small community of North Kansas City is home to more than thirty of the Fortune 500. Liberty boasts such highly visible names as Ferrellgas and the Hallmark Cards Distribution Center.

Education is a priority as well. Students are served by the respected North Kansas City and Liberty school districts. Also found in Liberty is William Jewell College, a four-year private resident college that is highly regarded nationwide. Newcomers to Clay County enjoy the balance of small-town living and metropolitan attractions. Lakes and parks await, and there's excitement to be had as well at two riverboat casinos. And you can bet little ones will love living near Oceans of Fun and Worlds of Fun.

Sound good? When you're ready to move here, you'll have a variety of housing choices, from Tara-like estates on acreage to historic older homes. And if a friendly neighborhood is your style, Clay also offers lots of new subdivisions.

GLADSTONE

www.gladstone.mo.us

Sometimes referred to as Happy Rock, this community of some 27,200 is about 10 square miles in area and is completely surrounded by Kansas City North. It's a great place for families, thanks to its proximity to Smithville Lake, Worlds of Fun, and Oceans of Fun. The airport is just twenty minutes away. Homes tend to be ranch or traditional and cost $60,000 to $400,000.

LIBERTY

www.ci.liberty.mo.us

Historic charm, small-town spirit, and recreational amenities galore appeal to families living in this 27-square-mile city. Its population is on a steady incline (an 18 percent increase each decade since 1940), yet Liberty has a friendly, country town appeal.

As one of Missouri's oldest settlements, Liberty is home to a number of well-preserved original structures like the Jesse James Bank. But families won't need to rob a bank to live here; home prices are favorable. You can choose anything from renovated older homes in quiet neighborhoods for $100,000 to country estates on sprawling acreage for $1 million or more.

NORTH KANSAS CITY

www.nkc.org

Boasting a large and diverse economic base, North Kansas City is home to more than a thousand businesses that include some of the world's leading corporations. Yet neighborhoods offer the peace and relaxation of well-kept homes set on tree-lined streets.

A highly developed park system offers ball fields, playgrounds, swimming, tennis, and walking trails. And its 5,000 residents can find a full calendar of professional sports events, plus entertainment and shopping at the nearby River Market and Country Club Plaza.

Housing options run the gamut from small starter homes to nice-size family homes ranging from $75,000 to well over $1 million.

Jackson County

www.cojackson.mo.us

Named for General Andrew Jackson at the height of his popularity, this county is blessed with beautiful rolling hills, wooded sites, and mature greenery. It's the population center of the metroplex, so within its nearly 605-square-mile area are densely populated urban centers as well as growing cities like Lee's Summit and a variety of small towns.

It offers the region's most diversified and exciting cultural avenues, yet affordable and attractive housing options still abound. You'll have your choice of lovingly restored historic homes, sleek renovated lofts, cottages in tree-lined neighborhoods, lakeside estates, and affordable reverse ranch-style homes in new subdivisions.

An excellent network of educational opportunities are here, including two highly rated two-year community colleges, plus the University of Missouri at Kansas City, Kansas City Art Institute, Avila College, Rockhurst College, and DeVry Institute. When it's time to put down the books, Jackson County provides the area's most vibrant entertainment districts. The River Market, Country Club Plaza, and Westport are all here, providing four-star restaurants, charming bistros, and world-class shopping.

Jackson County is also at the heart of our cultural center with its showpiece, the Nelson-Atkins Museum of Art, as well as the stellar collections of the Kemper Museum of Contemporary Art. Art galleries and studios are here as well, too many to count, because a new one seems to pop up every week.

For more recreational activities (although a day shopping on the Plaza can get your heart racing), the county has the 1,800-acre Swope Park, home to the Kansas City Zoo, a wonderful nature center with educational facilities and hiking trails, and a golf course. Swope Park also has the exciting Starlight Theatre, one of the most successful professional outdoor theaters in the country.

Yet with all its many delights, Jackson County real estate is surprisingly affordable. Homeowners have a wide array of choices in charming older neighborhoods, downtown high-rises, new subdivisions, and luxurious lakeside locations. Here, too, is where many young professionals and empty nesters find the city's most exciting apartments and condominiums, including those on the Plaza or Crown Center that provide "city" living at its best.

BLUE SPRINGS
www.bluespringsgov.com
The original pioneers found this area to be the ideal stopover due to the abundance of clear, clean water from a nearby spring at the mouth of the Little Blue River. Water is still quite a draw for this community. Lake Jacomo and Longview Lake are nearby, and you'll have your choice of fourteen city parks. Three golf courses mean there's no waiting for tee times. About 50,000 lucky people make their homes here and send their children to AAA-rated Blue Springs schools.

Home prices can still be a bargain, beginning at $80,000, but can easily escalate to $1 million for estates on spectacular lands.

GRANDVIEW
www.grandview.org
Situated on the southern edge of Jackson County, Grandview's residents value a stable neighborhood environment yet enjoy the convenience of major interstates a few miles north. A major intersection, the Grandview Triangle, has been redesigned to make commuting a piece of cake. About 25,000 people live in Grandview, and houses range from $45,000 to around $200,000.

INDEPENDENCE
www.ci.independence.mo.us
One of our most vibrant historical areas, this is a great place to visit and an even better place to live. After all, it was good enough for Harry S. Truman. About 111,000 people can proudly say the buck stops here, and it can for you, too, for $50,000 to $300,000.

Besides offering a wealth of historical sites, Independence is close to downtown, the Plaza, and the airport. Travel to each is around fifteen to twenty minutes.

KANSAS CITY
www.kcmo.org
Over half a million people live in Kansas City, and who could blame them? You could write an entire book about its lifestyle, fountains, food, and friendliness . . . hey! We did!

The city is made up of three distinct major areas: midtown, where homes cost $20,000 to $400,000; Country Club Plaza, where you would pay between $50,000 and $2 million; and south Kansas City, where homes range from $80,000 to $750,000. Kansas City is also where to find exciting lofts and condominiums in the River Market, downtown, and the West Bottoms. Prices range from $100,000 to well over $1 million.

Although it takes a bit of a drive to get to

the airport (from thirty to sixty minutes), look what's nearby: the Plaza, the zoo, Crown Center, the River Market, Nelson-Atkins Museum of Art, and the stay-and-play Power & Light District downtown.

LAKE LOTAWANA

www.lake-lotawana.mo.us

Ideally situated just 20 miles from downtown Kansas City, this lake community offers both summer and year-round homes centered on a sparkling 600-acre lake. It's the perfect backdrop for magnificent waterfront estates. Its 2,200 residents enjoy a vacation-like lifestyle and needn't spend a million dollars to achieve it. Small bungalows and lake cabins are still available for less than $100,000, but there are also showplaces that cost $1 million or more.

LAKE TAPAWINGO

Just west of Blue Springs and close to the urban amenities of Lee's Summit and Kansas City, this small lake community provides a tranquil setting. The lake itself is small, which is how the 890 or so residents like it: no loud motorboats to break the peaceful sound of children playing Red Rover at dusk. Although you'll still see small cottages dotting the rolling wooded landscape, homeowners with real buying power have discovered this beauty and have built magnificent lakeside estates worth well over $1 million.

LEE'S SUMMIT

www.lees-summit.mo.us

Located in eastern Jackson County, Lee's Summit is the third largest city in Missouri based on geographic size. With more than ninety subdivisions, it's also the fastest growing community in the Kansas City area.

Families love it here thanks to an awardwinning school district and plenty of recreational opportunities at nearby Longview Lake and Lake Jacomo. Arrowhead Stadium is a fifteen-minute drive. You'll see a wide variety of architectural styles in the neighborhoods, from traditional to contemporary. Expect to pay from $80,000 to $1 million, which would get you a palatial home on a golf course.

RAYTOWN

www.raytown.mo.us

When Raytown was incorporated in the 1950s, it had a population of 850 in a 2-mile-square land area. Today it has grown to 12 square miles and a population of 31,850. It's close to some of the area's most beautiful lakes, including Blue Springs, Longview, and Lake Jacomo.

Home prices are very reasonable here. You'll see bungalows, ranches, Victorians, and traditionals ranging from $60,000 to more than $250,000.

Platte County

www.co.platte.mo.us

Overlooking the point where the Missouri and Kansas Rivers meet, Platte offers the rolling hills, dramatic limestone overlooks, and lush woods that appeal to so many homeowners. It's home to one of the country's most fetching river towns yet is just minutes away from the vibrancy of downtown Kansas City; in fact, Platte County offers some of the most stunning views of the city's skyline.

Executives who travel on business find this region ideal, with the airport just minutes away. Or you can work close to home at one of dozens of new office and industrial parks that have sprung up here.

The nearly 12,000 students enrolled in four public schools get a quality education thanks to excellent schools and a strong student-teacher-parent system. Undergraduate and graduate programs are also available from Park University and Webster University.

As for lifestyle, many Kansas Citians enjoy visiting towns in Platte for their "day trip" amenities, including antiques shops, galleries, and unique restaurant choices. Lucky for the county's population of nearly 69,000, all that fun is in their own backyards. So are beautiful riverfront parks, lakes, and acres of wetlands that make fishing a joy.

PARKVILLE

www.parkvillemo.com

Nestled in the natural beauty of wooded hills and the limestone bluffs of the Missouri River, ℹ️ Just moved into town and miss your old friends? You can make new ones through the New Neighbors League. Whether you're interested in gardening, travel, antiquing, wine tastings, golf, bowling, or canasta, you'll find a group to join. Check out www.kcnnl.com.

this is a highly desirable area. It's home to Park University, and its historic downtown area is filled with antiques shops, restaurants, and art galleries. A nature center and riverside park add to its charm.

Parkville affords an extraordinary view of the Kansas City, Missouri, skyline. To get there takes only fifteen minutes, and the airport is a pleasant fifteen-minute drive. About 5,500 people live here, and the architecture varies from traditional to historic, with some cozy cottages around $100,000, to fabulous homes costing more than $1 million.

RIVERSIDE

www.riversidemo.com

As a Northland suburb of Kansas City, Riverside is known for its pleasing small neighborhoods, large industrial parks, and extensive business district. With a population of fewer than 3,000, it offers a small-town spirit with easy access to the region's finest cultural, educational, and social amenities. Home styles and prices vary greatly, from $75,000 to $250,000.

WEATHERBY LAKE

Only fifty-seven years old, this delightful community is centered on a man-made lake set in panoramic rolling hills and lush woods. The community originally was developed as an enclave of summer homes, but people found it too hard to leave at the end of the season. Now Weatherby supports neighborhoods ranging from lake cabins to gorgeous estates. City leaders were smart enough to put strict zoning laws into place early to maintain the area's rural and rustic feeling, which its 1,700 residents find so appealing. Homes range from less than $80,000 to more than $500,000.

Kansas

Johnson County

www.jocoks.com

We've always known Johnson County was in a class all its own in terms of beautiful parks and lakes, lovely neighborhoods, and excellent schools. But the rest of the nation has caught on: *Fortune* magazine calls it one of the premier counties in the nation in terms of business climate and exceptional quality of life. Its many attributes have attracted such corporations as Sprint Nextel, Applebee's International, Black and Veatch, Yellow Corporation, Universal Underwriters, Farmers Insurance, and FedEx.

Nationally recognized for its superb public schools, Johnson County offers many choices for private education and parochial schools. The area is also home to excellent opportunities for higher education, including the award-winning Johnson County Community College, and satellite campuses of Baker University, St. Mary College, MidAmerica Nazarene University, Ottawa University, and the Edwards Campus of the University of Kansas. These programs allow working adults to obtain bachelor's or master's degrees while remaining close to home and work. Excellent health care choices are within the county's boundaries as well.

The living is easy in Johnson County, thanks to the first-rate recreational opportunities at its many lakes, parks, and recreational centers. Golfers can choose from some of the most challenging and luxurious public and private courses in the metro. And if shopping is your sport, look no further. Overland Park alone offers more than forty open-air plazas as well as enclosed modern complexes with hundreds of shops, department stores (can you say Nordstrom?), restaurants, and theaters. Historic sites and museums, even ones kids will love, are within JoCo's boundaries.

Its many attributes have made it one of the fastest growing counties in the Kansas City area and state. In fact, Johnson County accounts for 71 percent of the total population growth in Kansas, adding approximately 10,000 new residents each year. And yet with all its natural beauty, tremendous growth, and clean, attractive cities, Johnson County's home prices are among the lowest of any area. From a quaint historic home to a custom master-piece on a wooded lot, you can afford the lifestyle you deserve. Following are snapshots of Johnson County's various locations.

COUNTRYSIDE

How about holding a block party where the entire city shows up? That's a real possibility in this delightful little community of just 312 citizens and 133 homes. It's bound by Nall and Lamar Streets, 61st Street to the north and Shawnee Mission Parkway to the south, creating a square-mile garden. You just have to love a neighborhood whose city tree is the red cedar and city bird is the house wren.

Homes are so choice here that people stand in yards and ask residents, "Are you leaving soon?" as if you're in a prime parking space. The answer is no, usually. Who would want to leave paradise? Houses in Country-side, for the most part, are cute bungalows, some ranch style, and prices can go from $100,000 to $200,000 or so. Good luck. Coun-tryside recently became part of the City of Mission but retains its own homes association.

DESOTO

This has long been a sleepy little town of just over 3,200 residents, but that's all been changing in the past few years. DeSoto's loca-tion between Lenexa and Lawrence on Kansas Highway 10 makes it a prime place for resi-dential, retail, and commercial growth. And with ready access to the desirable lifestyles of both Lawrence and Kansas City, you might say DeSoto is the best of both worlds. Its progres-sive school system, which also serves resi-dents of western Shawnee, is another plus. The Plaza is still only twenty-five minutes away; the airport, forty.

Right now home prices are relatively low, considering that so many of the homes include acreage, but that will start to change. Prices range from $90,000 for a simple ranch

to $400,000 plus for an estate set way back on vast acreage. Got horses?

FAIRWAY

www.fairwaykansas.org

This is one of the most desirable addresses, thanks to a storybook setting of pretty ranch homes and stone cottages with small but beautifully landscaped yards. The landmass is only about 1 square mile, but it packs in around 3,900 people, and they love the small town in a big-city atmosphere. And the loca-tion? Let's just say it got its name from the three panoramic golf courses nearby.

Its proximity to the Plaza (just five to ten minutes away) plus parks and the excellent Shawnee Mission School District make this area ideal for singles and for couples with young children. Homes here are snatched up as soon as they hit the market; in fact in the crazy days of the mid-1990s, here's where you might have seen bidding wars on a perfectly manicured lawn. Look for prices from $100,000 to $900,000.

LAKE QUIVIRA

Located in both Johnson and Wyandotte Counties, Lake Quivira affords residents a lakeside lifestyle that is still conveniently located in town. Distinctive homes and tran-quil neighborhoods are found in this gated community of around 1,900. Swimming, boat-ing, and sailing are all part of the allure, plus a jogging track around the area's 1.3 square miles. Home styles vary greatly from small older bungalows to stunning contemporary showhomes. Prices range from $100,000 to well over $1 million.

LEAWOOD

www.leawood.org

Answer "Leawood" to a question of where you live and you instantly get more respect. Pure snobbism? Not really. Leawood just hap-pens to be one of the prettiest places around, with lovely homes with nice-size yards and a convenient location (ten minutes to the Plaza, twenty to downtown) that still feels like it's out in the country. Perhaps that's because it used to be. Leawood dates back to territorial days and was built on farmland acquired by early settlers. Over 29,000 live in this area that primarily sits between State Line and Mission Roads and extends from 83rd Street south to 202nd Street.

The city was named for the original landowner, Oscar G. Lee. The spelling was changed slightly by the developer. Leawood offers a pleasing mix of older, well-kept neighborhoods along tree-lined streets and vibrant new subdivisions. And with its "halfway mark" between the Country Club Plaza and Town Center Plaza, shopping doesn't get much better. Expect handsome traditional homes from $250,000 to upward of $5 million. You heard us.

LENEXA

www.ci.lenexa.ks.us

Ah, suburbia. Lenexa sits in west-central Johnson County, south of Shawnee, and is home to more than 40,000 people. You can see the city's roots as a town along the Santa Fe and Oregon Trails in late-nineteenth-century buildings that still stand in Old Town Lenexa.

Residents are family oriented; during summer there's a festival or celebration every week, including a barbecue contest in June, the Spinach Festival in September (perhaps you shouldn't mention that one to your kids), and the Chili Challenge in October. Maybe it's a good thing Lenexa offers so many recreational opportunities to work off all those calories. Shawnee Mission Park, Sar-Ko-Par Trails Park, Ernie Miller Nature Park, and the Johnson County Arboretum are close by.

The Plaza is about a twenty-minute drive, and it's forty minutes to the airport. Look for

i You can check out hundreds of homes during the Home Builders Association of Greater Kansas City's Parade of Homes. These tours are held for two weeks each spring and fall, and the homes are typically professionally decorated. Contact the association for dates at (816) 942-8800, or check www.kchba.org.

generally traditional architecture in the price range of $100,000 to more than $500,000.

MERRIAM

www.merriam.org

Welcome to Worlds of Fun . . . in Merriam? In 1880 famed architectural designer George Kessler turned forty acres of wooded hills into a lovely park area, complete with a lake, tennis courts, and boating. And at the turn of the twentieth century, Kansas Citians were coming to the Hocker Grove Amusement Park's dancing pavilion, skating rink, and rides. The amusement parks have closed, but Merriam still offers a wonderful lifestyle for its 12,000 residents. With the city's ready access to the highway system, the Plaza is just twelve minutes away, the airport about twenty-five.

Home prices in Merriam vary dramatically depending on whether the house is a two-bedroom bungalow or a five-bedroom reverse ranch on a landscaped lot. Expect to find homes between $80,000 and more than $300,000.

MISSION

www.mission-ks.org

A charming 'burb in the northern section of Johnson County, Mission offers neighborhood shopping centers, excellent schools, and tree-lined streets. And location? You can practically be on the Plaza before you find your charge card. The airport is thirty minutes away. Homes here are typically traditional or ranch style, with a few fairy-tale Tudors tossed in for looks.

The excellent Shawnee Mission School District is a draw for families, but first-time homebuyers often shop here first for homes in the $80,000 range. Larger homes can run higher than $300,000.

MISSION HILLS

www.missionhills-ks.gov

The Beverly Hills of Kansas City, Mission Hills is status plus. Exclusively fine homes—there are no shopping centers to ruin the line of expansive lawn after lawn. And it may be the most impressive art gallery in town: Sculptures and fountains are dotted within its 2.5-mile radius, gifts from developer J. C. Nichols.

The city also contains three of the area's finest golf clubs. This is the only city of its size in the country that can claim this distinction. There are 1,327 homes and villas here in a delightful range of styles that makes rubber-necking fun. You'll see colonial, Tudor, contemporary, Spanish, traditional, and a handful of contemporary homes. Prices range from around $300,000 (a bargain if you can find one) up to $6 million. Pull your Mercedes or Beemer out of the garage and you can be at the Plaza within five to ten minutes, to the airport in thirty.

MISSION WOODS

www.missionwoodskansas.com

Exclusive, exquisite, and in demand. Occupying twenty acres of land, yet with only 165 or so residents, Mission Woods has the distinction of having the lowest population of any of the incorporated cities of Johnson County. Homes here quietly go on the market (you'll never see a yard sign) and are quickly sold.

Amenities include a nearby golf country club, tennis club, several parks, and both private and parochial schools. Thanks to its location at the intersection of State Line Road and Shawnee Mission Parkway, the Plaza is at its doorstep.

This is truly one of the most beautiful little cities in the country, and the privilege of living here will cost between $500,000 and $2 million, but we know of a recent $4.5 million sale. All things considered, that may well be a bargain.

OLATHE

www.olatheks.org

From the Indian word for "beautiful" (pronounced Oh-LAY-thuh), this city covers 50 square miles. Its size holds many advantages, including two airports, Johnson County Executive and the Industrial Airport, and its own award-winning school district.

It's also home to Hillsdale Lake, a gigantic recreational area, and Olathe Medical Center. Homes here range from $75,000 for a modest

starter home (ideal for singles, young couples, and retirees) to more than $2 million for a gorgeous estate overlooking the lake at Cedar Creek. Its diversity means you'll see architecture in a variety of designs, from traditional to Spanish, California contemporary to prairie style.

OVERLAND PARK

www.opkansas.org

Overland Park has shaken off its roots as a bedroom community to become a vibrant city with its own personality. Today it's home to 170,318 (no, make that 170,319!) with a population growth that's one of the fastest in the metro. Families in particular love it here, and it's been rated among the best places in the country to rear children. Schools are excellent, and it's blessed with nearby parks, lakes, and mile after mile of hiking and biking trails. Other pluses are the Johnson County Arboretum and Deanna Rose Children's Farmstead.

And you'll have just the place to buy all those cute kids' clothes, as well as your own fashions. Overland Park is home to Oak Park Mall, one of the largest malls in the state and the only one with Nordstom as its anchor. The Plaza is just a twenty-minute drive, and the airport another ten minutes or so.

Overland Park is a great place to work as well as live; when we call Corporate Woods an office park, we mean just that. Architecturally stunning buildings are set in forty acres of wooded, rolling hills with walking paths, streams, and picnic areas that make lunch break a minivacation. And the multimillion-dollar Sprint Nextel complex is here as well. Look for two-story traditional homes for the most part, for mortgages from $100,000 to $1 million.

PRAIRIE VILLAGE

www.pvkansas.com

"Charming" is the word that most comes to mind to describe this hamlet of established neighborhoods with an abundance of trees and ten parks. Located just west of State Line and south of Mission Hills, this is a real draw for affluent singles and families who enjoy a i Make friends fast through New Friends of Kansas City, a social organization where women can meet other women who share the same interests, whether it's antiquing, playing cards, attending sports events, or trying new restaurants. Though the membership is limited to women only, there are plenty of activities that include spouses. Membership is $20 a year. Visit www.newfriendsofkc.com.

small-town atmosphere that's close to everything. Prairie Village is home to two delightful open-air shopping centers, Corinth Square and the Prairie Village Shops, which means a grocery store, a gift shop, and an ice-cream parlor are just a stroll or bike ride away. No wonder people who grew up here tend to stay in the neighborhood.

Big-time shopping and entertainment venues on the Plaza are a short ten minutes away; although the airport is a thirty- to forty-minute drive, you won't want to leave home very often. The typical Prairie Village home is traditional, Cape Cod, or ranch, costing from $120,000 to more than $500,000.

ROELAND PARK

www.roelandpark.net

This is a quaint, older neighborhood in the northeast corner of Johnson County with plenty of pluses. It's ten minutes away from the Plaza and ten to fifteen minutes from downtown and is within the desirable Shawnee Mission School District.

The population is around 7,000, and home styles tend toward traditional, ranch, and bungalow. Prices generally run from $100,000 to $250,000.

SHAWNEE

www.cityofshawnee.org

Shawnee Mission Park alone is enough reason to want to live in this Johnson County community. It offers the Theatre in the Park, a fabulous lake, and a 450-foot-tall observation tower. Hey! I can see my house from here!

There are twenty-one other parks to explore as well. Other recreational opportunities, at least for teenagers, can be found at the nearby malls, including Oak Park Mall and the Great Mall of the Great Plains. And the Plaza is a quick ten-minute drive away.

Shawnee has nearly 50,000 residents and is one of the fastest growing cities in the state. Look for traditional-style homes in the $80,000 to $600,000-plus range.

SPRING HILL

www.springhillks.org

Located in northeast Kansas, Spring Hill straddles the Johnson and Miami County lines, giving residents amenities of a big city in a rural setting. Incorporated in 1885, Spring Hill has recorded strong residential and commercial growth in the past few years and expects that to continue.

It has about 2,500 residents, and an additional 6,000 people live outside its boundaries but within the school district. And like the good neighbors they are, they work together to address community needs. This city is about twenty to thirty minutes from Interstate 435, the main artery. Houses tend to be on large-acreage lots, many with separate garages. The house prices are as varied as the style of homes available, from $50,000 to well over $500,000.

STANLEY

Early settlers in this area purchased their home lots for about $10 an acre, and although you can add some zeroes to that now, the lifestyle is worth every penny. Stanley was annexed by Overland Park in 1985 but feels like its own little world with rolling, wooded acres. Many of the homes take advantage of the landmass, with homes set half an acre away from the road down a curving path. Several estates have horse pastures.

Stanley is at the heart of the top-rated Blue Valley School District and is close to Town Center Plaza and fine restaurants. Architectural styles vary greatly, from Colorado lodge to traditional. Prices range from $140,000 to more than $500,000.

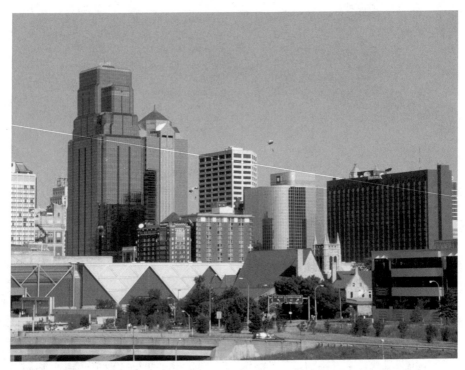

Downtown skyline. CVB OF GREATER KANSAS CITY

WESTWOOD

www.westwoodkansas.com

Looking like a picture postcard of everything you could want in a neighborhood, Westwood offers well-manicured lawns, beautiful older homes, and picturesque neighborhoods. Its tidy size, just 1 square mile, gives it a small-town feeling. Parks and walking trails make Westwood great for families, and a health club with tennis courts and swimming pool are pluses. Ideally situated close to the Plaza and Overland Park, Westwood provides its 1,800 residents with the best of the metroplex.

Home styles range from darling bungalows to handsome Spanish-style structures. Expect to pay from $150,000 to $1 million or more.

WESTWOOD HILLS

www.westwoodhills.org

Although at just three-quarters of a square mile, Westwood Hills is one of the smaller

cities, it is one of the loveliest residential choices. It is filled with charming neighborhoods, serene streets lined with mature shade trees, and a showcase of eclectic architectural styles. Many are storybook Tudor-style with stone or brick set amid lush landscaping.

The award-winning Shawnee Mission School District makes this an ideal community for families as well as young professionals. A very desirable address; expect home prices from $200,000 to $2 million.

Wyandotte County

www.wycokck.org

Named for the Wyandot Indians who once made this area their home, Wyandotte County, or WyCo, is steeped in the history of the Old West yet offers a progressive lifestyle. With its central location along river bluffs overlooking the confluence of the Missouri and Kansas Rivers, it offers easy access to the entire region. The airport is just ten to fifteen minutes away, and downtown Kansas City, Missouri, from five to ten minutes.

This county offers something even more appealing to homebuyers: Some of the lowest home prices in the Greater Kansas City area. Triple-A school districts also rank high on the plus side; the New Stanley School, for instance, was singled out for the state's "Next Century" program of excellence. Health care is also tops here thanks to the University of Kansas Hospital's well-respected programs.

Within the county are exceptional recreational opportunities, including the Agricultural Hall of Fame, an outdoor music theater, and the 1,500-acre natural wonder known as Wyandotte County Lake Park. Among its many amenities are playgrounds, tennis courts, horse paths, and a 400-acre lake for fishing and boating.

If sports are your game, you'll have the Woodlands Race Track for dog racing and simulcast horse racing, and the spectacular Kansas Speedway, a $250 million NASCAR facility with state-of-the-art features. Homebuyers, start your engines!

BONNER SPRINGS

www.bonnersprings.org

On the western edge of Wyandotte County, Bonner has easy access to many areas of interest, such as Verizon Amphitheater, where headline musical acts appear, and the Renaissance Festival takes place in the fall. The Kansas Speedway is nearby as well.

With a population of around 6,750, the city has its own school district. Homes generally go for $60,000 to more than $500,000.

KANSAS CITY

www.wycokck.org

The Wyandot Indians first settled here in 1840, and its oldest home is the Grinter House, whose owner operated a ferry across the Kansas River (which we call the Kaw) in 1857. Today KCK is home to several ethnic groups. Strawberry Hill has a strong Slavic community, and the Rosedale and Argentine

areas have Mexican American settlements. Both groups celebrate their heritage with several festivals during the year.

The city provides excellent access to the other Kansas City's downtown district. It's about five minutes across the Lewis and Clark Viaduct, the Plaza is a ten-minute drive, and it's just twenty minutes to the airport. With a strong government in place, KCK is coming into its own. Home prices cover quite a spread, from starter homes in the $40,000 range to grand new estates with large lots for $400,000. The city also has a hidden gem in its historic Westheights Manor neighborhood, where homes average $200,000.

Real Estate Companies

Kansas City is home to hundreds of real estate companies and thousands of agents, most of whom are licensed on both sides of the state line. Although some of these professionals specialize in certain areas of the region or in specific categories such as historic homes, sleek condos, or estates with surrounding acreage, most will be happy to locate whatever home you seek.

Some neighborhoods and subdivisions are so desirable they have their own real estate offices, such as Hallbrook in Leawood and Cedar Creek in Olathe. However, any Realtor can take you on a tour of the area.

It's often tricky to find a Realtor in a new city. We suggest you ask friends and family for references; if they've had a good experience with an agent, they'll be thrilled to tell you about it. And if you're being transferred for business, often your company's human resources department can make recommendations.

If in doubt, call the Kansas City Regional Association of Realtors (913-498-1100, www.kcrar.com). The Web site includes links to related organizations such as the National Association of Homebuilders and area home inspectors. You'll also find a link to a list of available homes in the area that are shown by Realtor members, or go to www.heartland mls.com. You can find homes by location,

To shop for a home in your pajamas, simply click on www.realtor.com/kansascity and you can scan about 4,000 homes. You can select your potential abode by region, zip code, price range, or other criteria, such as number of bedrooms and whether you want treed acreage or lakefront living.

price range, or categories such as maintenance provided or acreage. The Better Business Bureau of Greater Kansas City (816-421-7800) is another resource to make sure you're working with a professional firm you can trust.

The following real estate firms were selected based on experience, customer service, and sometimes their expertise for specific areas of homes. This is by no means a complete list; Kansas City has around 7,000 members of the real estate board, and the phone book alone shows ten pages of offices, individual brokers, and agents. The offices shown here are the top area producers, based on gross sales, according to a recent issue of the Kansas City edition of the *Business Journal*.

The real estate companies here are in Kansas City, Missouri, unless otherwise noted.

Prudential Kansas City Realty
8101 College Boulevard
Overland Park, KS
(913) 491-1550, (800) 444-7206
www.kansascityhomes.com
Although not the largest company in terms of agents, this company packs a punch in sales. According to statistics compiled by the *Kansas City Business Journal,* in one year alone this company sold over 4,000 properties with an average price of $254,000. No wonder this young-but-mighty company was honored with a Gibraltar Award for being one of the top fifty in the PREA network in 2005. One of the company stars is Nancy Ward (913-981-2840), who handles a variety of properties, from a $240,000 condo on the Plaza to a castle on a lake for nearly $8 million. Kathy Stone (816-410-5535), a member of the Multi-Million-Dollar Club, specializes in homes in

town, from a darling Prairie Village ranch to a stunning Georgian colonial for $1.7 million.

Reece & Nichols
11500 Granada
Leawood, KS
(913) 491-1001
www.reeceandnichols.com
Reece & Nichols has such a winning combination of marketing strength and hardworking agents that it's the second largest real estate company in the United States. Closer to home, it's involved in nearly half of all sales in the Kansas City area. Let's put a dollar figure on that, shall we? All told, the company's gross sales in 2005 were over $5.5 billion. We're sold. It now boasts more than 2,200 agents in just over sixty-two branch offices, reaching all areas of Kansas City and beyond in new homes, resales, and land.

Exclusive services include "My Home," a personal tracking system that lets you create custom home searches online. When a home matching your criteria comes on the market, you'll be contacted, often before it shows up in the listings. Reece & Nichols also takes the guesswork out of finding home services and products by listing agent–recommended vendors throughout the metropolitan area in categories such as appliance repair, brick and stone contractors, plumbing, and pest control.

The company has a full-time relocation department (913-469-8300, 800-821-6565), staffed by experts who can take you by the hand and lead you through all the details involved in moving.

And before you think Reece & Nichols is too big to care about someone looking for a bungalow for under 100 Gs, remember that the company is made up of lots of individual offices. You'll be a big deal when you call.

One example is the office at 9035 Metcalf in Overland Park, Kansas, where broker and manager Terri McGowen serves as mentor, motivator, and leader to ninety top-notch sales associates. Downturn in the market? Not for Terri's team. They had their best year yet when others were complaining about a lack of listings and sales. You can reach this upbeat professional or one of her associates at (913) 402-2500.

Although Gail Dicus (913-239-2002, gaildicus.com) can find or sell your home anywhere in Kansas City and beyond, she specializes in Leawood and the coveted estates in south suburban Johnson County. This effervescent pro and her team of seven sold over $24 million in 2006 alone. Kathy Koehler of the Koehler Bortnick Team (913-239-2067, koehlerbortnick.com) is so successful, she even publishes her own properties-for-sale magazine, which is available on her Web site and at many area grocery stores. Grant Lundberg (816-560-1273) can set you up—way up—in an upscale high-rise condo, either on the Plaza or in the heart of the Crossroads Arts District.

RE/MAX

That red-white-and-blue balloon stops you every time. There are thirty RE/MAX offices in Kansas City that share the attention-getting logo with more than 4,100 other independently owned RE/MAX offices around the world. Having a network with offices in thirty-eight countries and on six continents gives them marketing moxy and ongoing training opportunities—and gives you a leg up when you're ready to buy that second home in Mexico, where they have offices. Following are some of the top-performing RE/MAX offices in town; each is independently owned and operated.

RE/MAX Metropolitan
6321 Walnut
(816) 444-7900

From starter homes to lavish estates, Pam Turner's team can locate it for you. One agent, Drew Hertel (816-769-7708), must be doing something right; he's been named Best Realtor of the Year by readers of *KC Magazine* for three years running, and top Realtor by the *Independent* subscribers in 2006. Perhaps it's his well-deserved tagline: "KC's Luxury Living Expert."

RE/MAX First Realtors
11251 Nall Avenue
Leawood, KS
(913) 338-1880, (800) 394-1880
www.firstkc.com

RE/MAX First has been serving clients in both Kansas and Missouri since 1992, but the seventy-six sales associates were at work long before that. They each average more than fifteen years of experience, and along the way they have earned enough awards and plaques to nearly require a separate office and full-time duster.

RE/MAX State Line/Suburban Real Estate
10200 State Line Road
Leawood, KS
(913) 649-3100
www.realtykc.com

With a whopping 98 percent customer satisfaction rating, this is one successful office.

One experienced Realtor in this office is Scottie Broderick (913-312-3620), who practically invented the phrase "It's my pleasure." A full 95 percent of her listings come from repeat customers or referrals.

Realty Executives
www/realtyx.com

With more than 675 associates and thirty-five locations in the Kansas, Missouri, and Nebraska area, this company has connections. It's part of a worldwide network with locations in all fifty states, twenty-one countries, and five Canadian provinces. That kind of power provides clients with some super bonuses, like an international corporate relocation division and major savings in intrastate moving expenses. Following are some of the offices in Kansas City under the Realty Executives banner.

Realty Executives of Kansas City
11115 Ash Street
Leawood, KS
(913) 642-4888
www.realtyx.com

This hardworking team of more than 217

agents and brokers recently moved into the top spot in overall sales for Realty Executives offices.

Other winning Realty Executives offices are Metro One (816-525-7000) in Lee's Summit and Realty Executives Area Realtors (816-453-9100) in Gladstone.

Century 21 Heartland Realty
7709 West 151st Street
Overland Park, KS
(913) 681-8215, (800) 581-8215
www.century21heartland.com

If Century 21 is the world's largest residential real estate company, this office is one of the reasons. As the No. 1 Century 21 office in the metropolitan area for four years straight, as well as being rated top office in Kansas twice, this is one motivated team. The company has three locations in Johnson County.

The office makes it easy to buy or sell a home. Buyers can answer a few questions on the Web site and receive automatic updates when their dream home becomes available. Sellers can choose "Market Analysis" on the same site to learn the fair market value of their home. Heartland also has a full-time relocation agent on staff to help you transfer to your new home.

Coldwell Banker
www.coldwellbanker.com

Looking for a real estate company that's secure? Coldwell Banker fits the bill—it's been around since 1906. One of the reasons is the growth in the number of its independently owned and operated offices: 3,000 offices globally with more than 75,000 sales associates. The John Moffitt & Associates team (www.coldwellbankermoffitt.com) is the top dog here, with offices in Overland Park (913-491-6800) and Blue Springs (816-224-8000). John also opened the Urban Living Center (1705 Baltimore, 816-268-4555) in the heart of the Crossroads Arts District to appeal to modern-day pioneers rushing to buy or rent condos and lofts. John's nothing if not versatile; as a Realtor and developer, he's involved with spectacular homes and condos in Leawood, Kansas, as well, including the wooded enclave Hazelwood and the luxury Parkway 133 Villas at 133rd and Roe. This team taps into the special services available through a giant like Coldwell Banker, including the international Concierge program that provides deep discounts on everything from car rentals to custom closets. You can even print the coupons using your computer.

Crown Realty
2099 East 151st Street
Olathe, KS
(913) 782-1155
www.crownrealty.com

Since 1973 this family-owned agency has been getting buyers into the saddle, literally. As specialists in horse and rural properties, these seventy professionals in five offices can find you the right home whether your taste runs to Green Acres or Dallas. Dallas, indeed; their biggest transaction to date took place in late 2001 and included ninety-two farm properties running along two counties and reaching into both Kansas and Missouri. One buyer, one seller, $13.9 million. Must have been a lot of Christmas bonus checks at Crown.

If you're more the city type, a Crown agent can find you a sleek loft or in-town Tudor just as easily. But if you're coming to Kansas City with a horse trailer, this should be your first stop.

Keller Williams Realty
8005 West 110th Street, Suite 100
Overland Park, KS
(913) 906-5400
www.kw.com

Keller Williams is an innovative firm that has been in the forefront of using the Internet to make buying and selling a home faster, easier, and less stressful. The company has fifty agents in the Kansas City area who put technology to good use.

New Home Developments

These are new homes in resortlike areas that

are offered exclusively by on-site real estate offices. With one stop you'll be able to view several homes in the development, usually decorated to the nines, along with a look at available land. Expect to be overwhelmed; these areas usually are built around a luxurious golf course or lake (or both) and are affiliated with some of Kansas City's finest builders.

Cedar Creek Realty
KS Highway 10 at the
Cedar Creek Parkway exit
Olathe, KS
(913) 829-6500
www.cedarcreek-kc.com

Long, graceful vistas of deep forests, emerald-green freeways, and stone bluffs with waterfalls and stepping-stones: Could life get any more relaxing than this? Not for the 900 families that call this paradise home. Cedar Creek is made up of neighborhoods set among rolling hills in southwest Johnson County, centered on a 65-acre sailing and fishing lake, 1,500 acres of undisturbed natural green space, and the gorgeous Shadow Glen Golf Club. It's all part of a 4,500-acre master-planned community that will offer more neighborhoods to keep up with the demand. It will also expand on the adjacent retail shops and a 700-acre office park and eventually include a hotel.

It's already a city you may never want to leave; among the amenities are its own fire station, elementary school, indoor gymnasium, lighted tennis complex, miles of hiking and biking trails leading through some of the most stunning landscape in the region, and four private parks, including one of 600 acres. Ready to move in? We thought so. You'll find a wide variety of home styles here, from all-brick traditional to Colorado contemporary with prices ranging from the mid-$300,000s to well over $2 million. And folks who move to Cedar Creek find something else: friendly neighbors. The area has several informal special interest clubs to join, such as early-morning walkers, a Bible-study group, and a gourmet dinner club.

Find out why the Greater Kansas City Home Builders Association calls this "Kansas's Best Single Family Community." But hurry. Resales go fast. New lots go even faster.

The National
6701 Birkdale
Parkville, MO
(816) 587-HOME (4663)
www.thenationalgolfclub.com

Say, isn't that Tom Watson playing one hole ahead of you? It certainly could be at the National Golf Club. The hometown hero built this course and belongs to the club. You can join him by owning one of these breathtaking homes built amid massive oaks and sycamores, perched on limestone bluffs, or overlooking the lake and incredible course. Homes range in price from the upper $300,000s for villas in the Links to a French-style knockout with a tile roof and outdoor fireplace for $3 million. The lower-level golf cart storage will come in handy, because the lucky homeowner will have a private cart path to the club.

The National's clubhouse is pretty spectacular as well, with 40,000 square feet of amenities including a dining room that's actually one of the best restaurants in town. It has hosted wine tastings with another famous Watson, Tom's brother Ridge, who owns a vineyard in Carmel. Another impressive guest has been former University of Missouri basketball coach Norm Stewart, who showed up for a fireside chat. Check out the homes available online, and then call the office to arrange a private tour. You might just see Tom.

Other New-Home and Resale Resources

For Sale by Owner
10635 Roe
Overland Park, KS
(913) 498-FSBO (3726)
www.fsbo-kc.com

This service makes locating a commission-free "fizz-bow" a piece of cake. The Web site lists properties in Kansas and Missouri and provides a photo, description, and price along with the owner's phone number and e-mail address, if available. You'll see everything from houses in midtown for $45,000 to luxurious retreats in the upper ranges for sale by owners and builders.

The Pearson Company has been Kansas City's leader in private home sales since 1996 and provides excellent services for both buyers and sellers, including paperwork assistance and access to attorneys if necessary. Along with the Internet listing, the company distributes 30,000 copies of its free listing magazine every month to shopping centers, grocery stores, airports, and hotels.

Homefinder.com

A service of the *Kansas City Star,* this Internet site lets you search listings from the *Star* and real estate brokers from all over the Kansas City area. You can also locate an agent who meets your needs, get information such as an affordability calculator, and get tips on moving.

Homes for Sale
(913) 621-HOME (4663)
www.kchomes.com

Chuck Boyles Inc. publishes three big, fat magazines showing resale property, acreage, builders, new construction, and new-home communities in the Greater Kansas City area. Areas covered are Kansas, Suburban North, and Jackson/ Cass Counties. The free guides are distributed biweekly to grocery stores, bookstores, and some retailers across town, or you can request one sent free of charge by phone or online. The Web site also has links to Realtors and homes for sale.

Kansas City New Homes Guide
(913) 385-2772
www.kcnewhomes.com

This glossy magazine covers new-home subdivisions throughout the entire metro area in a well-organized format. Comprehensive maps are included for each area, along with a listing for each community by price range, home size, builder name, and contact information. This magazine is also a boon for new residents, as it lists helpful phone numbers for each area's chamber of commerce, utility contacts, and attractions. The magazine is distributed free each month to area grocery stores, libraries, and other outlets.

Condominiums, Lofts, and Apartments

Our affordable real estate costs make it possible for the vast majority of residents to buy homes (nearly 75 percent in Johnson County alone), but often an apartment is the way to go. We offer a dazzling variety of options, from sleek lofts overlooking downtown to minicities situated around a lake in the suburbs.

In fact, condo living is one of the fastest growing markets in the area. Since the early 1980s developers have been converting century-old warehouses into loft spaces at an amazing rate, yet they can't keep up with the demand. At this writing thousands of units are being offered throughout the River Market, downtown, and Quality Hill areas, with more on the way. The high-ceilinged, open spaces appeal to young professionals as well as empty nesters who are thrilled to give up yard maintenance in lieu of a balcony with a breathtaking view of downtown at night. Following are a few of the more notable selections in town.

Conover Place Lofts
5th and Wyandotte, River Market
(816) 421-0572
www.conoverplace.com

This premier loft development in the vibrant River Market district offers such amenities as inside garages, a workout room and pool, 13- to 20-foot ceilings, fabulous stainless-steel kitchens, polished concrete floors, and huge windows overlooking the downtown skyline. Toss in the exposed-brick walls and heavy-timbered ceilings and it's a glossy-magazine shot of upscale urban living. A two-bedroom complete with a 266-square-foot terrace goes for around $449,000—that is, if you move fast.

Mallin/Gibson Loft Properties
201 Wyandotte
(816) 471-6789
www.kclofts.com

Mel Mallin, a lovable and sharp-as-a-tack octogenarian, is considered the grandfather of loft living in Kansas City. He fell in love with the bohemian lifestyle while courting his wife in New York's SoHo neighborhood after World War II and decades later decided to try to sell the idea to his hometown. He nearly lost his shirt. Live downtown? In a big brick box without walls? But Mel persevered, kept to his "For God's sake, cheer up!" mantra, and today is one of our town's most successful and respected real estate developers.

His company, which includes his son-in-law, Dana Gibson, is beloved by tenants for its old-fashioned service.

Oh, and did we mention he has great lofts available? The locations are in the hot and happening River Market area, with the farmers' market, restaurants, and entertainment at your doorstep. These are true lofts, with all the romance of those days Mel remembers from New York: open floor plans, high ceilings, exposed-brick walls, majestic wood columns and beams, wood floors, and plenty of windows. Options include the Art Space at 201 Wyandotte, which was originally built in 1900 and renovated in 1985. Your neighbors include several artists and the Kansas City Artists Coalition, an organization so dear to Mel's heart that a gallery space has been named in his honor. Then there's Delaware Lofts at 219 Delaware, with forty apartments ranging from 625 to 3,000 square feet. Landmark Lofts, 425 Washington, are located in a handsome brick structure that was originally built in 1885; renovations were completed in 1998.

One Park Place
307 East 31st Street
(816) 756-2221
www.oneparkplacekc.com

Reece & Nichols is the exclusive agent for one of the Midwest's most exciting condo projects, one of two buildings honored by the American Institute of Architects. Homes here start at $400,000 and go up with the view, which is a jaw-dropping look at Union Station, the downtown skyline, and even a smidge of the river.

The twentieth floor penthouse is where we want to be on July 4th to see fireworks all over the city. Amenities here are unmatched as well and include a lavish lobby and entertainment area complete with catering kitchen, a wine room, complete fitness center, 24/7 staff and concierge service, and even a pet grooming area for when your pooch isn't outside enjoying the 176 acres of green space at your doorstep. An indoor saltwater lap pool, outdoor pool, and his-and-her saunas will keep you in shape for all the entertaining you'll want to do in your stunning condo with primo finishes and appliances. A ten-year tax abatement sweetens the deal.

Other Resources for Apartments

The *Kansas City Star* maintains an online listing of apartments (www.apartments.com), where you can search all developments throughout the Kansas City metro area. Options range from studios starting at $350 to major league palaces in the sky for $2,000 or more a month. The site also provides information about renter's insurance, moving, and more. And of course you can always find an apartment the old-fashioned way, through the newspaper. On Saturday the *Star* publishes a separate guide showing apartments available; in Sunday's real estate broadsheet, you'll find houses for rent.

The *Pitch* includes a few choice apartments around town, usually in the coolest inner-city areas near the Art Institute, the Plaza, and Westport. Here, too, is where you'll find listings for roommates wanted. You can pick up a copy free at hundreds of outlets throughout the city.

Apartments for Rent (913-888-1200) is a slick magazine that showcases more than 300 rental units throughout Kansas City, including lofts, apartments, corporate housing, and even senior communities. Many of the ads include special deals, such as first month's rent free or $100 savings with a year's lease. The publication is available free at grocery stores and convenience stores around town, or go online (www.forrent.com) to see the goods.

GETTING STARTED

Naturally you'll want to get the lights, water, and gas turned on and the telephone hooked up, so we'll start with the basics. Sounds easy, until you remember that the Kansas City metro area comprises more than 150 cities in a nineteen-county area (more or less, depending on who's counting). To make it more confusing, some counties use two or more utility companies. This creates a new version of the old joke: How many newcomers does it take to turn on the lights? Two: one to find out whom to call and the other to bang his head on the wall. If you can get through this maze of numbers, more power to you.

That task taken care of, we can move on to more interesting things like how to learn more about Kansas City and where to meet new friends. We'll also cover some essentials about living here and provide valuable resources. Most important, we'll clue you in to some of the top services that are often so hard to find when you're new to a city: hair stylists, dog trainers, florists, landscapers, and more. These are names we've culled over the years from hundreds of interviews, lots of referrals, "best of" surveys in local publications, and personal experience.

Utilities

If you have questions about what service provider serves your area, check with your Realtor, landlord, homeowners association, or city or county clerk. When you call the utility customer service representative, be prepared to make a security deposit to establish service. Requirements for service deposits vary and are usually based on an amount totaling two months' worth of bills.

Most deposits are refunded after one year or when service is terminated. Water deposits range from about $20 to $75 or more, but rural dwellings can have a much heftier fee—as much as $1,500—if a meter must be installed. Just one more thing to ask your Realtor before you sign on the dotted line. Following are the basics. And honestly, once you make it past the conundrum of our utility providers, you're home free. With the lights on.

Electricity

MISSOURI

Aquila
Platte, Clay, Ray, and western Jackson Counties
(816) 421-6600
(800) 303-0762
www.aquila.com

Independence
(816) 325-5000
www.ci.independence.mo.us/pl

Kansas City Power & Light
(Western Cass and Jackson, southern Clay and Platte, and most of Johnson Counties)
(816) 471-5275
www.kcpl.com

Platte-Clay Electric Cooperative
(Northern Platte, northern Clay, and Ray Counties)
(800) 431-2131

KANSAS

Board of Public Utilities
(Kansas City, KS)
(913) 573-9190
www.bpu.com

i To get underground utility lines marked before digging, call (800) 344-7483 in Missouri and (800) 344-7233 in Kansas.

Westar
(Olathe, Bonner Springs,
Leavenworth, Lawrence, DeSoto)
(800) 794-4780
www.westarenergy.com

Gas

MISSOURI

Aquila
(Platte, Clay, Ray, and western Jackson
Counties)
(816) 421-6600
www.aquila.com

Missouri Gas Energy
(Jackson, Platte, Clay, Ray,
and Cass Counties)
(816) 756-5252
www.missourigasenergy.com

KANSAS

Atmos Energy
(Portions of Johnson, Wyandotte,
Leavenworth, and Douglas Counties)
(800) 621-1867
www.atmosenergy.com

Kansas Gas Service
(Parts of Johnson, Wyandotte, Franklin,
Miami, Douglas, Anderson, Osage, and
Leavenworth Counties)
(800) 794-4780
www.oneokkansasgas.com

Water

MISSOURI

Missouri Water Department
(Kansas City)
(816) 221-6505
www.kcmo.org

KANSAS

Board of Public Utilities
(Kansas City, Kansas)
(913) 573-9000
www.bpu.com

Water One
(Johnson County)

(913) 895-1800
www.waterone.org

Telephone

AT&T
Residential customers
(800) 464-7928
www.att.com

Birch Telecom
(888) 772-4724
www.birch.com

Everest
(913) 825-3000
www.everestkc.com

Sprint Nextel
(800) SPRINT1
www.sprint.com

Time Warner Cable
(816) 222-5776
www.timewarnercable.com

Cellular Phone Service

Southwestern Bell Mobile
(800) 331-0500

Sprint Nextel
(800) SPRINT1
www.sprint.com

Verizon
(800) 922-0204
www.verizonwireless.com

Cable

Comcast
(888) 266-2278

DirecTV
(816) 421-4004
www.directv.com

Time Warner Cable
(816) 222-5776
www.timewarnercable.com

Trash

Many homeowners associations provide curbside trash pickup as part of their dues. And many cities in the metropolis offer a curbside recycling program or have developed convenient drop-off centers at churches and shopping areas. Check with your Realtor or your homeowners association contact. For more information on recycling, call the Mid-America Regional Council's recycling hotline at (816) 474-TEAM.

The following companies cover the greater Kansas City area; you may also contact them for information regarding items for recycling.

Deffenbaugh Disposal Service
(913) 631-3300

Hickman Disposal Service
(913) 831-2072

REB Trash Service
(913) 779-6592

Post Offices

To locate a post office near you, visit www.usps.gov. Get a handy online guide at http://moversguide.usps.com.

GETTING LEGAL

Motor Vehicle Registration

In Kansas City we rely on our vehicles to get us around, and we have the highway miles to prove it. With three interstates, four interstate linkages, and ten federal highways, you can get just about anywhere you want in twenty minutes or less.

Now let's get you legal and on the road. In both Kansas and Missouri, license plates are issued upon vehicle registration. Each state has different rules and procedures. Find out specifics on current requirements, and necessary inspections, fees, and locations at the following Web sites:

Missouri
http://dor.mo.gov

Kansas
www.ksrevenue.org/dmv

Voter Registration

Generally registration for voting must be completed at least twenty days prior to primary or general elections. However, in Jackson, Cass, Clay, and Platte Counties, residents must wait twenty-eight days after registration to be eligible to vote. In Johnson County it's fourteen days. You must reregister each time you change your residency or name.

Application information includes your name, birthplace, birth date, mailing address, telephone number, place of previous registration, and usually your Social Security number. An oath or signature is required to verify that all information is true.

To register in both Kansas and Missouri, you must submit information with a current address and meet the following requirements: You must be a U.S. citizen or have a naturalization number if you were born outside of the country, be at least eighteen years of age, and meet the residency requirements for your voting precinct.

Registration centers are located throughout the metroplex, and any of the centers below can direct you to the one most convenient to you. Kansas residents have the option of mail-in registration. In Missouri, that option is restricted to those who are unable to travel to a registration center in person.

Johnson County Board of Election:
(913) 782-3441
Kansas City, Missouri, Board of Election:
(816) 842-4820
Wyandotte County Board of Election: (913) 334-1414

Driver's License and Permit

To receive a driver's license with full privileges in either Kansas or Missouri, you must be at least sixteen years of age. New Kansas residents must pass only a vision test if your out-of-state license is current.

In Missouri, if your out-of-state license is valid, you are required to take a vision and road sign recognition test. If your current license has been expired for more than ninety days, you will be required to take the driving and written test as well.

Kansas offers a special restricted license for young adults at least fourteen years old for the purpose of going to or from school or work; this license requires the written permission of a parent or guardian.

Missouri

Licenses are issued on a six-year basis (every three years for those older than sixty-nine), and new residents are required to apply immediately. Bring a valid out-of-state license. You'll be required to pass a vision and road sign recognition test. If your license has expired you'll need to take a written test and will be sitting in a car with a Missouri State Highway Patrol officer. Contact the following office for examination and testing; there may also be an area office closer to you:

Kansas City
(816) 889-2461
http://dor.mo.gov

Kansas

Licenses are issued every four years, and new residents are required to apply immediately. Bring your valid out-of-state driver's license with you. New residents must pass only a vision test, unless your current license has been expired for more than ninety days. Then a driving and written test is required. (We were serious when we said to apply immediately.) For examination and testing, contact one of the following offices:

Johnson County
(913) 826-1800

Wyandotte County
(913) 573-2821

Hunting and Fishing Licenses

Licenses are required in both states for fishing as well as hunting small and large game. In Kansas the waiting time after registration is sixty days. In Missouri new residents are eligible for a license after thirty days. And just wait till you see the bass in Lake Jacomo!

The cost for licenses varies depending on your age (seniors and youth get reduced rates), residency status, and the duration of the license. Nonresident licenses carry significantly higher price tags. Fishing licenses can be purchased for as long as one year or a mere twenty-four hours. They're available for purchase at local sporting good stores and most public lake marinas. For current rates or questions on specific game stamps or licenses, contact the respective state offices:

Missouri Department of Conservation
(816) 356-2280
www.mdc.mo.gov

Kansas Department of Wildlife & Parks
(913) 894-9113
www.kdwp.state.ks.us

GETTING TO KNOW YOU

Area convention and visitor bureaus are great sources for newcomers to town as well. Keep in mind that nearly every city within the vast metropolis has its own center ready to welcome you with brochures, maps, and information. Check the telephone book for contact information. Following are the organizations that cover the entire metropolitan area.

Convention & Visitor's Bureau
of Greater Kansas City
(816) 221-5242
www.kansascity.com
This should be your first call, even before you move. These fine folks will set you up with information about Kansas City in general as well as contacts for your particular area of town. Plus they'll give you a dandy little coupon book with free or discounted admissions to several attractions around town.

Kansas City Area Chamber of Commerce
(816) 221-7440
www.kcchamber.com

Online Visitor's Guide
www.visitkc.com, www.experiencekc.com

Gifts, Grooming, and Various Good Things to Know

You're new in town. Where do you find your new best friend, your confidant, the most important person in your life . . . in other words, your hair stylist? Pick a name out of the phone book? We think not. There are other fine salons in town, but following are a few where you and your locks will be treated incredibly well. After you're coifed or trimmed, we'll introduce you to other services that are difficult to find.

Day Spas and Salons

Bijin Salon & Day Spa
6960 Mission Road
Prairie Village, KS
(913) 671-7777
ww.bijinsalon.com

Mario Tricoci Salon & Day Spa
111 Nichols Road
(816) 931-9922

Par Exsalonce
11849 College Boulevard
Overland Park, KS
(913) 469-9532
www.parexcalonce.com

Serenity the Rejuvenating Day Spa
7211 West 95th Street
Overland Park, KS
(913) 341-0025
www.serenitydayspa.net
When Judy Hohn's doctors couldn't diagnose her various aches and pains, she found relief through massage. That was decades ago, and now her spa is providing the same healthful benefits to clients. Along with a variety of massage options they offer mani-

i One of the best ways to get in tune with a new city is through its daily newspaper. In our case it's the Kansas City Star. You can find it at newsstands throughout town, or subscribe by calling (816) 234-STAR (7827). And the newspaper's Web site, www.kansascity.com, is a twenty-four-hour gateway to local news, weather, events, and more.

cures, pedicure, and facials. Make a day of it with a beauty package or invite your girl-friends for a spa party.

Florists

Most large grocery stores have floral departments these days, and the quality and variety are good enough for a gift on the way home or to cheer a sick friend. But when you need a floral design guaranteed to impress a boss or delight your sweetheart, the following florists can arrange it.

Beco Flowers
1922 Baltimore
(816) 472-4242
www.becoflowers.com
A serene collection of baby artichokes in a wooden bowl. A fat pineapple in a base of bright gerbera daisies. Collette Keenan and Rebecca Ederer like to play with their food. These talented florists also do amazing things with flowers, from show-off displays for an entryway to sweet floral bouquets. There is no minimum price for orders. The florist is also an art gallery, called the CUBE, which showcases a different artist's work every month.

Dan Meiners Studio
1700 Wyandotte
(816) 842-7244
www.danmeiners.com
If you want to get a "Wow!" from someone, send one of Dan's arrangements. His work can be contemporary or very traditional depending on your needs, and he's known for incorporating unusual vessels and groupings. Dan

Good Phone Numbers to Know

Fire, police, sheriff, and ambulance: 911
Child abuse: (800) 392-3738
Missouri Poison Control Center: (816) 234-3430
Kansas Poison Control Center: (913) 588-6633
Directory assistance (local): 1411
Local from pay phones: 411
Weather forecast: (913) 831-4141
Road condition information (Kansas Highway Patrol): (913) 782-8100
Legal Aid of Western Missouri: (816) 474-6750
Legal Aid for Wyandotte and Leavenworth Counties: (913) 621-0200

and his talented staff are also high society's first call for weddings and special events. At his new shop, the giftware and home decor are nearly as spectacular as the flowers.

Matney Floral Design
2708 West 53rd Street
Fairway, KS
(913) 362-5419
If the flowers at a black-tie gala get more attention than the ball gowns, Chuck Matney is probably to blame. From a single exquisite orchid to stunning arrangements that use Granny Smith apples in tall vases, his designs are fresh, inventive, and in perfect taste.

Making New Friends

Perhaps the toughest thing about moving to a new city is meeting people who share your interests. You should have no trouble in Kansas City; in fact newcomers are often surprised when strangers strike up a conversation at the bookstore, grocer's produce section, and in the elevator. We even have an entire club to welcome you with open arms. And if you're single, check out the many opportunities to meet someone new.

Matchmaking Services

If it's time to let a professional handle your love life, the following are a few companies that can take you in hand.

Heart to Heart Introductions Inc.
(913) 491-9110
www.hearttoheart.com
This company is the compatibility specialist and will screen and match potential clients with a low-key approach. Fees vary.

It's Just Lunch
(816) 421-5600
www.itsjustlunchkansascity.com

Supper Club
(913) 851-8400
www.kcsupperclub.com
Three women, three men, one table. What could be intimidating about that? This service provides a way to meet other singles during a casual dinner at one of Kansas City's best restaurants. The clientele tends to be successful, attractive professionals.

SINGLES GROUPS

Singles of the world—unite! Sometimes new cities can seem like couplesville, but Kansas City has some terrific organizations where like-minded singles can meet, whether they're looking for a date or a way to volunteer their time.

Colonial Presbyterian Church
9500 Wornall
(816) 942-3272
www.colonialkc.org

One of the city's most expansive organizations to meet others through activities, parties, and outings. Groups are generally divided by age from twenties to sixties and beyond. All denominations are welcome.

Friends of Art Solos
(816) 751-1246
www.nelson-atkins.org
This group, which is sponsored by the Nelson-Atkins Museum of Art, has so many varied and interesting activities that happily married couples are jealous. Actually, anyone can attend the events, but it's a boon for singles. You'll be invited to attend parties throughout the metro area, dinners in the glamorous Rozzelle Court, and visits to artists' studios.

Johnson County Unos
(913) 262-7658
This group, which meets at Pius X Church in Mission, Kansas, provides social and spiritual contact for widows and widowers throughout the metropolitan area.

Midwest Singles Dances
(816) 254-6493
www.midwestsinglesdances.com
Gotta dance? You'll find a willing partner at these weekly dances held at hotel ballrooms throughout the area. The age range is from mid-thirties through late sixties, and attendance can be high, as many as 160 to 250.

Singles Available for Community Service
St. Joseph Hospital,
Interstate 435 and State Line at
Community Service Building D
www.sacskc.com
Volunteer your time to a worthy cause and possibly make a love-match? Sounds like the perfect combination to us. This group gets involved with organizations like the Harvesters, Big Brothers and Big Sisters, and Special Olympics. Show up the first Thursday of every month at 7:00 p.m. and they'll put you to good work.

Village Singles
Village Presbyterian Church
6641 Mission Road
Prairie Village, KS
(913) 262-3195
www.members.aol.com/villagers
One of the best ways to meet singles in town through a variety of club activities, trips, classes, and parties.

SPECIALTY GROUPS
New Neighbors of Kansas City
www.newfriendsofkc.com
Clean your social calendar! Join this fun-loving group of women and you'll be kept busy with shopping trips, tours, gourmet dinners, and luncheons complete with speakers. This lively bunch also gives time and money to charities.

Pet Projects

Here's where to find a new pet in Kansas City, how to report a lost one, or where to have yours trained, groomed, and housed when you're out of town.

Keep in mind that in Kansas and Missouri, each community develops and maintains rules and regulations for pet registration, leash laws, and other pet-related policies. For details in your community, contact your local city courthouse; numbers are listed in the blue government section of the telephone directory.

If you find a lost dog or cat or lose your beloved family pet, call the numbers below. The Kansas City Star also provides a free listing in its daily "Lost or Found" section. Call (816) 234-4000 to place a notice. The shelters

i Meeting other singles can be easy in Kansas City, if you know where to look. Lots of available single parents meet while taking their children to parks or kid-friendly activities on weekends. The Deanna Rose Children's Farmstead is a popular place, and we know two great people who met at Kaleidoscope. See Kid-stuff for more ideas.

are also the best place to find a new buddy. Visit in person or check out the online adoptions and just try to keep from losing your heart to a new little Fido or Fluffy.

Animal Haven
9800 West 67th Street
Merriam, KS
(913) 432-7548
www.animalhavenkc.com

Humane Society of Greater Kansas City
(913) 596-1000
www.hhskc.org

Lakeside Nature Center
(To report an injured or abandoned wild animal in Missouri)
(816) 513-8960
Pet owners are lucky that one of the world's most respected pet behavior authorities lives and practices in Kansas City. Dr. Wayne Hunthausen has trained hundreds of other veterinarians as well as pet owners around the world on how to keep dogs from biting, barking, or ruining your carpet—and how to keep cats out of the houseplants.

Wayne has also provided expert advice on programs such as *20/20, PBS Health Week*, and *Today*. He's available for consultation and has produced a video for families called *Dogs, Cats and Kids* to teach children how to act around animals. His Westwood Animal Hospital also offers services in animal health and surgery, training, and has excellent boarding and grooming facilities.

Lost Dog Registry
(816) 333-0020

Operation Wildlife
(Helps with wild animals found injured in Kansas)
(913) 631-6566

Wayside Waifs
(816) 761-8151
www.waysidewaifs.org

Publications and Books

We cover local magazines and newspapers in Media, but here's a refresher course about Kansas City–based periodicals or books that belong in your mailbox or on your coffee table.

Kansas City: An American Story

This gem of a book by Rick Montgomery and Shirl Kasper, published by the *Kansas City Star*, is a comprehensive, richly illustrated account of a river town that made it big. The book came out in time for our 150th birthday, and we can't imagine a better gift. It's available for around $50 at area bookstores or through the *Star*. Call (816) 234-4636 and ask for "Star Books." Other titles have covered everything from barbecue to a major flood.

KC Magazine

Every great city deserves a great city magazine, and ours says it all: *KC*. In each monthly issue you'll meet the town's movers and shakers, find out where bartenders are shaking the best martinis, and see who wore what to last week's gala. Fabulous homes, restaurant reviews, and fashion features round out the must-read mix. Sign up for the magazine's A-List to get the scoop on exclusive parties and special discounts. *KC Magazine* is available by subscription and on newsstands all over the city. Visit www.kcmag.com or call (913) 894-5923.

Tours

When you go to Paris, you take a tour. Rome, same thing. In Kansas City you can simply drive around to acquaint yourself with our many charms, or you can hire a tour guide to take you to all the most interesting attractions. It's also a great way to learn about Kansas City's history and see our most impressive attractions while somebody else drives, and at least you'll have no problem with the language. Here are some ways to go sightseeing. We list other options in Getting Here, Getting Around and Attractions.

ℹ️ Here's a tour of Kansas City's past that doesn't even require a vehicle. On www.kcstories.com you'll read memoirs from older Kansas Citians who participated in writing teacher Michael Humphrey's Thousand Stories project. These are fascinating essays from people who lived through the Great Depression, went to work on Kansas City's streetcars, and watched stage acts at long-gone palace theaters.

ACCESS Kansas City
6400 West 110th Street
(816) 753-0200
www.accesskc.com
This company excels in providing successful events, including decor, entertainment, transportation, and accommodations.

Agenda: Kansas City
5290 Foxridge Drive
(916) 268-4466
(888) AGENDA KC
www.agenda-kansascity.com
This experienced team can create an entire itinerary for a group or individuals with a variety of transport options including limos, luxury buses or vans, or even our colorful trolleys.

Historic Kansas City Foundation
Three cheers for this organization for fighting to keep Kansas City's historical buildings and districts alive and well. Volunteers offer guided tours by advance appointment and can provide self-guided tour brochures on areas like the Historic Northeast District, Quality Hill, and the Plaza. They also host walking tours at various times of the year and an annual fund-raiser when they offer tours of homes in wonderful neighborhoods. Call (816) 931-8447.

Experience KC
415 Delaware Street
(816) 872-3299, (866) 533-0757
www.expkc.com

Specializing in developing creative, unique group tours, this company offers one-stop-shopping ease.

Passage Unlimited
This group offers customized tours from the African-American perspective. Choices include jazz, the Underground Railroad, historic sites, and more for groups of ten or more. For more information call (816) 483-4919.

Weddings Kansas City Style

Planning a wedding for yourself or someone else is stressful enough; we can't imagine handling all the details if you're new to the area. Your first stop should be to the newsstand to pick up the latest copy of *KC Weddings*, a wonderful magazine that covers every element of getting married in town, including catering, musicians, gowns, reception sites, and photographers. It's published by Grand Communications, a subsidiary of the *Kansas City Star*. Call (816) 234-4234 for back issues, or visit www.kansascity.com/kcweddings/.

Following are two tried-and-true professionals who can help make this important ceremony . . . well, a piece of cake. You'll find romantic honeymoon ideas in the Accommodations chapter.

Final Touch Studios
(wedding coordinator, florist)
(913) 492-5864
www.finaltouchstudios.net
Rosemary Dennis is a miracle worker. She can whip up the most incredible floral displays and bouquets, coordinate the reception hall, and hire the band, baker, and limousine so that you won't have to worry about a thing. She brings the most important element to the party: resourcefulness. We've seen her rip up a slip to create lovely pew bows when the bride's mom left them at home. Not really, but we know she could. Rosemary also creates incredible arrangements with silk and dried arrangements for clients and interior designers.

i Until a few years ago we had to dial only the seven-digit number to reach anyone in the metropolitan area. Today you'll need to dial the area code if it's different from the one you're dialing from. If you forget, you'll hear, "We're sorry. Your number cannot be completed as dialed. Please check the number and dial again."

Simple Elegance
(913) 397-9932

Kendra Brown is the wedding coordinator Rosemary Dennis recommends when the bride needs the whole works, from hiring the caterer to fluffing the train before the walk down the aisle. Her company's name says it all; her weddings tend to be elegant and very romantic.

EDUCATION AND CHILD CARE

Our city's commitment to education shows up in one of the first questions parents ask when shopping for a home: "How are the schools around here?" The answer, particularly in our suburban areas, is "excellent." Here in the heartland, Junior isn't the only one bringing home a bright-red A on his report card; many of the institutions in our thirty-six school districts have achieved the highest distinctions awarded by their states.

That's not to say they all make the grade. Our largest district, Kansas City, Missouri, with 32,000 students in seventy schools, is plagued by the same problems most other urban cities have: poor attendance, below-average test scores, and low graduation rates. And these troubles remain despite spending $2 billion to create impressive magnet schools with themes like science, foreign languages, performing arts, and college preparation.

Yet families with inner-city addresses still have excellent options such as Montessori, private schools (both religious and nonreligious), and twenty charter schools, which are independent public schools designed and operated by educators, parents, community leaders, and others.

These institutions, along with our top-notch suburban public schools, have elevated our overall educational rankings to some of the highest in the nation. Banners boasting A-plus rankings are posted next to glass cases crowded with 3-foot-tall basketball trophies. Elementary schools proudly show off Blue Ribbon certificates at parent-teacher meetings. And quality schools help produce students who are eager to continue their education: Greater Kansas City's 82 percent high school graduation rate beats the national average by at least seven points. In three Johnson County districts, more than 90 percent of the graduates are college bound.

We take a look at some of the elementary and secondary education choices available, both public and private, as well as list resources for day care programs within the metroplex. In the following section we graduate to our many fine colleges and universities as well as other learning options for adults and seniors.

Public Schools

Following is an overview of area public schools that have achieved impressive state and national honors. The accolades are shared by administrators, teachers, and students, as well as the parents who stay involved in school activities and tend to vote "yes" on school bonds. The schools are listed alphabetically by state.

Missouri

BLUE SPRINGS
www.bluespring-schools.net

Jackson County's second largest district has two high schools, four middle schools, and twelve elementary schools; yet despite this escalating enrollment, it has garnered state and national recognition. Thanks to a $30 million bond election, which received an 85 percent approval, a districtwide technology program will make computers accessible to each staff member and student. *Expansion*

Management magazine consistently bestows its highest Gold Medal award on the district, and the *Wall Street Journal* named it one of the top ten in the nation.

GRANDVIEW

Students who live in south Kansas City don't have a problem finding their lockers; they go to one school from kindergarten through eighth grade. And the kids aren't the only ones singing this one-school system's praises: The state named it one of the best small schools in language arts and science. The district's high schools also receive high marks from the state in journalism, art, music, and business, and 75 percent of its students participate in extracurricular activities.

INDEPENDENCE

www.indep.k12.mo.us

For a district that's more than 135 years old, Independence looks remarkably fit. It has been accredited with distinction by the Missouri Department of Education, making it the largest district in the state to be so honored. Two of its high schools have received A-plus ratings, and three elementary schools are national Blue Ribbon winners. Its twenty-first-century early childhood education program is a model for the nation.

NORTH KANSAS CITY

www.nkcsd.k12.mo.us

Parents, businesses, and community members work together in this district through projects such as YouthFriends, Partners in Education, the Community Committee, and educational foundations. The results are schools that consistently earn A-plus rankings and students who score above state and national averages. The district also features the GED Online series, a pilot program for the state, as well as all-day kindergarten, summer enrichment classes, and before- and after-school child care. High school graduates who meet academic requirements are eligible to receive free books, tuition, and fees for two years at a community college or vocational school in Missouri.

PARK HILL

www.parkhill.k12.mo.us

In southern Platte County parents, educators, and students work together through programs like Parents as Teachers and Community Education. This commitment has helped earn the district Accredited with Distinction status from Missouri as well as a Gold Medal from *Expansion Management* magazine. In 1999 Park Hill's superintendent was named the state's Superintendent of the Year. Students in the district have earned perfect SAT scores and the state Heisman trophy for athletics.

Kansas

BLUE VALLEY

www.bluevalleyk12.org

Serving more than 20,500 students in thirty schools, this southern Johnson County district has earned a reputation for high academic performance. Fourteen schools have received the prestigious Blue Ribbon Award. Graduating seniors were offered more than $30.2 million in college scholarships. The district has also implemented successful community outreach programs, including SHARE (Seniors Helping and Refining Education), which places senior citizens in the schools to share time and talents, and YouthFriends, which pairs adults with children who benefit from individualized attention.

DESOTO

www.usd232.org

Administrators in the fastest growing school district in Kansas planned for growth by building eleven new facilities in the late 1990s. And not just any square box will do: The elementary school design has won international acclaim as a "Kid Friendly School." Technology plays a big part in learning, with computers in each classroom and additional computer labs for students that include CAD (computer-aided drafting) units.

KANSAS CITY

www.kckps.org

With more than 20,000 students speaking sixteen languages, this district is making a concerted effort to expand special programs for students with limited English proficiency. Stanley Elementary is the district's only year-round elementary school. In 2001 voters approved a $120 million bond to upgrade technology, air-condition schools, and make other improvements. And thanks to a $10 million grant from the Ewing Marion Kauffman Foundation, the "First Things First" program will be expanded to the entire district. This program, which has been tested at a few schools since 1998, has achieved remarkable results. At Wyandotte High School suspensions dropped 57 percent, and at Washington High 289 students, one-quarter of the enrollment, increased their reading levels by three or more grades in just one year. The dropout rate has been cut in half.

OLATHE

www.olatheschools.com

An expanding student population makes this southwest Kansas district the fourth largest in Kansas, but it may be the teachers who put it on top. Among their honors are twelve Presidential Awards for Excellence in math and science teaching and fourteen National Blue Ribbon Awards from the Department of Education. Voters recently passed a $60 million bond to continue the district's good works.

SHAWNEE MISSION

www.smsd.org

This school district challenges students to do their best through such initiatives as the International Baccalaureate Program, an advanced system of studies that earns students college credit, and the Center for International Studies, which gives students in grades nine through twelve an opportunity to develop skills in Arabic, Chinese, Japanese, Russian, and geopolitics. National Merit Scholarships are well represented here; recently forty-four district students took home honors.

Private Schools

The Kansas City area offers a variety of choices for private education at the elementary and secondary levels. The Missouri Council for American Private Education publishes a directory of the state's private schools for around $10. For more information write to the organization at 334 Nantucket Drive, Ballwin, MO 63011 or call (314) 214-8255.

The Kansas State Board of Education publishes the annual Kansas Educational Directory listing private schools in the state. The directory is available at libraries, online at www.ksde.org, or by calling (785) 296-4961.

Nearly every Catholic Church in Kansas City has an affiliated school where children receive an outstanding education along with lessons in religion. For information about schools call the specific church directly or the area's diocese. In Missouri contact the Roman Catholic Diocese of Kansas City–St. Joseph at (816) 756-1850 or www.diocese-kcsj.org /schools. In Johnson and Wyandotte Counties in Kansas, contact the Archdiocese of Kansas City in Kansas at (913) 721-2082 or www.archkckcs.org.

For information on schools affiliated with the Lutheran Church in Kansas and Missouri, contact the Director of Lutheran Schools in Missouri (314-268-1508) or Kansas (785-357-4441).

Many of our prestigious private schools teach children from tots to teens, so students don school colors from the morning they arrive in a stroller until the afternoon they drive away in their SUV or Mom's BMW. Combining as many as five grade levels is a practice that instills a sense of family and school spirit that extends far beyond the campus gates. A diploma from one of these schools, coupled with a diploma from a top university, can almost guarantee an interview with Kansas City's best companies; alumni tend to look after their own.

The schools listed here are arranged alphabetically by state.

Missouri

Barstow
11511 State Line Road
(816) 942-3255
www.barstowschool.org

In 1884 two Wellesley College grads, Mary Barstow and Ada Brann, came to Kansas City to establish a local school comparable to the independent schools in the East. With the financial backing of several notable city leaders, including William Rockhill Nelson and August Meyer, their School for Girls was officially opened. Although lofty in goal—Brann's motto was "to educate a woman is to educate a nation"—the school had humble beginnings. The first class consisted of five girls sitting in a sparsely furnished parlor at 1204 Broadway. The school moved frequently, all within the posh Quality Hill area, and by 1897 began accepting a few boys in its college preparatory program. That same year Brann returned to her home in New England, which left the dynamic redhead, Barstow, to continue the school. It thrived after moving to a four-story schoolhouse in an apple orchard at 15 Westport Road—what is now an CVS drugstore parking lot at Westport and Main. Parents of ninety-three students paid $62.50 per term.

In 1909 boys were admitted to the lower school only, and by 1923 Barstow had a new home at 50th and Cherry in the flourishing Rockhill section of town. By 1954 the school's enrollment of 170 was expected to quickly double after the board voted to allow coeducation. This created a need to move to forty acres "in the country" at 115th and State Line Road. The new school was dedicated on May 5, 1962, where it stands today surrounded by lovely neighborhoods and massive estates. All 645 students, from preschool through twelfth grade, share the campus, providing a sense of family in the communal lunchroom and extra cheering power during varsity pep rallies.

Pembroke Hill School
5121 State Line
(816) 936-1200
www.pembrokehill.org
Alumni still call their alma mater Pem-Day from when this private school was known as Pembroke–Country Day, an all-boy school founded in 1910. Some of Kansas City's most prominent families sent their sons to Pem-Day

and their daughters to Sunset Hill, which opened in 1913. The two schools had many similarities: Both were highly regarded and independent; teachers often taught at both institutions; and several activities, especially theatrical programs, involved students from both campuses. When the two schools merged in July 1984, the newly named Pembroke Hill School adopted traditions from both facilities. For example, students voted to keep Pem-Day's colors of red and blue on the school's banner; the motto "Freedom with Responsibility" came from Sunset Hill. Another beloved tradition remains from the girls' school days: May Day, complete with music, poetry, and dancing around the Maypole, is observed each spring.

PHS is located on two campuses less than a mile apart near the Country Club Plaza; it's quite a stirring sight to see a football game in play while driving past the field on your way to dinner on fall evenings. Make sure to lower your car window to get the full effect. The school offers an extended day program until 6:00 p.m. for children through fifth grade, a service that continues during winter and spring breaks. And its students learn the importance of giving back to the town that has provided so much: All upper school students must complete sixty hours of community service before graduation; many easily surpass this requirement. Currently 1,200 students are enrolled from age two through twelfth grade.

St. Teresa's Academy
5600 Main Street
(816) 501-0011
www.stteresasacademy.com
The oldest school in Kansas City remains one of its best. This Catholic, independent college-preparatory school for young women was founded in 1866 and is sponsored by the Sisters of St. Joseph of Carondelet. Students are treated to a twenty-acre collegelike campus in one of the most elegant residential areas of Kansas City, Missouri, near Loose Park. A newly renovated quadrangle draws students

from more than seventy elementary schools and various ethnic, social, and economic backgrounds. In 2001, 100 percent of St. Teresa's graduates continued their education, with more than 60 percent receiving academic scholarships. Many of these had a head start on their secondary education by earning up to thirty hours of college credit. The school emphasizes a well-rounded experience by encouraging involvement in sports (it has one of the most respected athletic programs in the area) and community service. Volunteering a minimum of ninety hours is a prerequisite to graduation. The academy enrolls just over 500 students.

Kansas

Christots Country Day School
21403 Midland Drive, Shawnee
(913) 422-5684
www.christots.com
With activities that include gardening, music, and visiting the school's rabbit and baby goats, it's enough to make you want to revert to childhood. Students from eighteen months to third grade also learn phonics, geography, math, science, and computer skills through a Montessori-based teaching discipline. The school is set in wooded acreage, and the children spend plenty of time outdoors participating in games and watching for the deer that live just beyond the facility's fence. The school has been in operation since 1986; all classes are led by certified teachers.

Hyman Brand Hebrew Academy
5801 West 115th Street, Overland Park
(913) 327-8180
www.hbha.edu
In 1966 parents who wanted to provide a Jewish day school for their children rented space at Ohev Shalom Synagogue and began with thirty-three students. In 1973 a high school department was added. Over the years the academy has moved several times to adjust to its growing enrollment needs; in fall 1988 it found its permanent home when the architecturally stunning Jewish Commu-

nity Campus opened in south Overland Park. Since then space has been added to support a biology lab, fine arts center, Judaic studies rooms, two computer labs, and a foreign language classroom. Speaking of language skills, the admissions form states that new applicants entering grades four through twelve must be able to read and write Hebrew. The children come from a variety of racial, national, and economic backgrounds (over 50 percent receive financial assistance), yet all are being raised in the Jewish faith. Currently 270 students are enrolled from kindergarten to grade twelve.

Kansas City Christian School
4801 West 79th Street, Prairie Village
(913) 648-5227
www.kcchristianschool.org
The hallmarks of this fifty-year-old institution are its Biblical integration, character training, and parental involvement. In fact, parents don't just bake cookies for the booster club, they sign a form promising to be active in their child's academic and spiritual upbringing. Advanced placement classes in English and math provide college credit. The 14:1 student-to-teacher ratio helps turn out quality students, and the Discover Program caters to students with learning disabilities. The emphasis is on academic competence as well as compassion; for example, many teens in the class of 2000 spent their senior trip in the sunshine, but instead of frolicking in Ft. Lauderdale they were constructing classrooms in a tiny village in northern Belize. The school enrolls 575 students from preschool to twelfth grade, representing more than a hundred churches from across the area.

Child Care

Kansas City is a family-oriented community with hundreds of day care options for working parents. Churches offer programs ranging from daily child care to weekly "mom's day out" relief, and the phone book is filled with Montessori and other organizations that accept children from several weeks of age through kindergarten and beyond. National companies such as Kindercare and La Petite Academy are well represented.

Several agencies provide resources and referrals to help you find a competent center, including the Johnson County Child Care Association (913-341-6200), Heart of America Resource and Referral (800-753-9981), and Day Care Connection (913-962-2020).

The two state organizations that oversee day care licensing and registration are the Missouri Department of Health's Bureau of Child Care Safety and Licensure (816-325-5860) and the Kansas Department of Health's Johnson County Branch of Health and Human Services Child Care Programs (913-894-2525).

HIGHER EDUCATION

Kansas City, it should be noted, is a university town. Never mind that the homecoming parade is an hour or so away. In fact the traffic you hear on crisp fall evenings is alumni driving to the University of Kansas in Lawrence, the University of Missouri–Columbia, or Kansas State University in Manhattan to cheer at ballgames before heading to favorite beer joints from school days. But woe is the couple with mixed allegiances; the ride home from a game between dueling schools can be pretty chilly. After all, one team has to lose.

Yet despite the lure of these Big Twelve schools, degree seekers can choose in-town options without sacrificing prestige. Several of our colleges are nationally recognized for excellence yet offer students smaller class sizes for more personal attention. And don't worry that the little darlings will be denied interaction with other cultures by staying close to home; we draw students from around the world.

High school grads can select from an array of universities, community colleges, and trade schools. Several out-of-town entities maintain classrooms within our geographical area, an ideal way for working adults to obtain a four-year or advanced degree.

In addition, to help fuel our reputation as

the life sciences center of the country, we have a number of respected schools in the health care field training medical doctors and researchers. Other professional schools offer degrees in chiropractic, dentistry, and osteopathy. See the Health Care and Wellness chapter for these options.

We cover some of Kansas City's classiest institutions and then take a look at other learning choices for adults and seniors, including dance and cooking classes. There could be tap shoes or a sauté pan in your future.

The listings are arranged in alphabetical order by type of institution and are located in Kansas City, Missouri, unless otherwise noted.

Two-Year Institutions

Johnson County Community College
12345 College Boulevard
Overland Park, KS
(913) 469-8500
www.jccc.net
Hear the deep, grinding sound of a bulldozer? Must be another building going up at Johnson County Community College. In the sleepy suburb of Overland Park sits a community college with the sheer size and academic power to rival many four-year universities. JCCC's eighteen redbrick buildings are linked by walkways and gardens dotted with outdoor sculptures and rimmed by thirteen parking lots. The Regnier Center for Business Technology and the Nerman Museum of Contemporary Art have just opened. No wonder first-timers need a map to get around; each fall campus security staffers help a dozen or so dazed students find their cars.

The campus has to be immense to support its enrollment: With more than 34,000 students each semester, JCCC is the third largest institution of higher education in the state. It offers a full range of undergraduate credit courses that form the first two years of most college curricula as well as more than fifty one- and two-year career certificate programs that prepare students to enter the job market.

Its Center for Professional Education is the largest continuing education program in the region, enrolling more than 12,000 students in more than 600 certification workshops and seminars each year. More than 150 companies take advantage of training courses tailored for them and presented at the college or on-site at the workplace. And more than 11,000 people attend JCCC's public events, including a writers' conference, travelogue series, and youth programs.

But it's the three-year Chef Apprenticeship program that's brought the school national acclaim. Here's where some of the country's best chefs have trained; in fact the school has placed extremely well in international cooking exhibitions, usually bringing home gold and silver medals.

The 234-acre campus is also home to the Carlsen Center, one of the most sophisticated performing and visual arts complexes in the city. Within its space is the 1,250-seat Yardley Hall. (Read more about the Carlsen Center in The Arts chapter.)

Take a virtual tour of JCCC on its Web site or stop by in person. It's easy to find, particularly during warm weather when kite enthusiasts use its windswept hillside to maneuver huge, brightly colored flying contraptions.

Metropolitan Community Colleges
3200 Broadway (administrative center)
(816) 795-1000
www.mcckc.edu

Metropolitan Community Colleges is actually a system of five colleges—Blue River, Longview, Maple Woods, Penn Valley, and the Business & Technology Center—in nine locations throughout the Kansas City area. More than 40,000 students choose these schools every year for more than just economic reasons (although parents are thrilled with the $80 per credit hour cost). These modern facilities on beautiful campuses offer more than seventy career certificates or transfer degrees in technology, health care, and business, even auto mechanics and veterinary sciences.

Yet educational quality isn't short-changed. For instance, in 2000 Longview Community College was one of four institutions named "College of the Year" by *Time Magazine*/the *Princeton Review*, putting it right up there with Sarah Lawrence and Cornell University.

Four-Year Colleges and Universities

Avila College
11901 Wornall Road
(816) 501-2400
www.avila.edu

Avila's history started in the seventeenth century when the Sisters of St. Joseph of Carondelet in France crossed the Atlantic and half a continent to begin St. Teresa's Academy, a private school for girls. In 1916 the Sisters founded St. Teresa College on the same campus and in 1963 moved the college to fifty acres at the edge of Kansas City for a new location and a new name. In 1969 Avila opened its enrollment to men. Today more than 2,000 students from more than a dozen countries and all parts of the United States are drawn to Avila each year.

The Catholic college has continued the Sisters' pioneering ways. It was the first college in Kansas City to offer programs in nursing, gerontology, and social work. It is also the first (and currently only) four-year college in the city to offer a paralegal program approved by the American Bar Association and one of only twenty-three colleges in the country to offer a four-year degree in radiological technology.

Park University
8700 Northwest River Park Drive
Parkville, MO
(816) 741-2000
www.park.edu

It's hard enough to keep students focused on lessons, but when the classrooms are high on a limestone bluff with views of the Missouri River peeking through leaves that change colors with the seasons, it must be downright impossible. Yet the 1,000 or so students attending this four-year coeducational Christian institution continue to excel.

The campus is arguably the most beautiful in the Midwest, thanks to its picturesque site overlooking the bend of the river, the quaint town of Parkville, and the skyline of downtown Kansas City, Missouri. Opened in 1875, the buildings were constructed of native limestone; in fact the campus is a geologist's dream, with fossils from the Paleozoic period visible in building blocks and stone stairways. The boulder at the entrance of Copley Hall is a glacial deposit. Poets might find inspiration in walking the 800 acres of woodlands, waterfalls, and wildflowers.

The main campus is home to the School of Arts and Sciences, Nursing Bridge program, accelerated weekend and evening courses, and graduate programs in education and business administration. Its School for Extended Learning, which has served the non-traditional, working adult student since 1972, has forty-three campuses in twenty-one states across the United States. Of these sites, thirty-four are on military installations.

A diverse population is treated to Park's charms: The student body represents thirty states and more than fifty foreign countries. And more than 85 percent of undergraduate students receive some form of financial aid in the form of grants, loans, and work-study positions.

It was the students who built the school's most stunning building, Mackay Hall, to pay for tuition. Construction of the limestone building—topped with a 135-foot-tall clock tower—began in 1886 and took seven years to complete. Another impressive site is Herr House, an upper-class residence hall built in 1927 that sports a handsome lounge and large rooms with—get this—*walk-in closets*.

But perhaps the university's most inspiring site is the Black History Wall located near the 6th Street entrance. The landmark is inscribed with the names of four African-American employees who contributed to Park's rich history, including Spencer Cave, head groundskeeper from 1875 until his death in 1946 and who, one alumnus said, "taught us more than our professors."

Rockhurst University
1100 Rockhurst Road
(816) 501-4000
www.rockhurst.edu
The spirit behind Rockhurst University was born in 1521 when a Spanish soldier took a cannonball in the leg at Pamplona. That soldier, later to be known as St. Ignatius of Loyola, used his recovery time for spiritual growth, which led to the formation of the Society of Jesus. The Jesuit tradition of service to others through a liberal education came to Kansas City in 1910 with the founding of Rockhurst University.

Today the university serves approximately 3,000 students (about 72 percent Catholic) at the main campus in Kansas City's cultural district and the Ignatius Center of Rockhurst University/Saint Louis University, located in suburban Kansas City. Rockhurst alumni are achievers; one in ten is president, chief executive officer, or owner of his or her own company or organization. There's even a presidential appointee: Hector V. Barreto, class of '83, became head of the U.S. Small Business Administration in 2001.

Older students also choose Rockhurst for a superior education. Its Continuing Education Center, through subsidiary National Seminars, is the nation's largest provider of adult continuing education. And Rockhurst's Executive Fellows MBA program boasts an alumni list that includes more than 400 top leaders in major organizations throughout the Kansas City area and the nation.

"The Rock" has been ranked consistently as one of the top fifteen universities in the Midwest by *U.S. News and World Report*, listed in *Barron's* "Best Buys in College Education," and received accolades in *Money* magazine. And it hosts PeaceJam, an annual event where Nobel Peace Prize winners and students discuss global issues and perform community service projects together, making it perhaps the only forum where you could hear, "So what do you consider the biggest threat to peace in the Middle East . . . and could you hand me that hammer, please?"

In fact, 96 percent of students participate in community work. They're also active in internship and co-op work programs thanks to the university's ties with local companies and its nonprofit leadership program. Yet there's time for sports as well: The Hawks and Lady Hawks routinely participate in national play-offs in soccer, volleyball, and basketball.

University of Missouri–Kansas City
5100 Rockhill Road
(816) 235-1111
www.umkc.edu

In the heart of Kansas City's cultural and entertainment zone stand the red tile–roofed buildings of the University of Missouri–Kansas City. The campus was established in 1933 when local philanthropist William Volker, presented the school with a forty-acre parcel in the Rockhill district. The main campus is named in his honor.

Soon other colleges were merging with the school to form an arts and sciences focus. The Kansas City School of Law joined in 1938, followed by dental, pharmacy, medical, and nursing schools. Today thirteen schools and colleges offer more than 125 degree options to more than 14,000 students. In 1963 the University of Kansas City became part of the 160-year-old University of Missouri system, joining three other campuses located in Columbia, Rolla, and St. Louis.

UMKC is also home to the Henry W. Bloch School of Business and Public Administration; the Conservatory of Music; Kansas City Repertory Theatre, the premier resident theater company of the Midwest (read more about this in The Arts chapter); National Public Radio's local affiliate, KCUR–FM (see Media); and a Gallery of Art.

The campus also has the area's largest academic library system, with more than five million volumes, including the Linda Hall Library of Science and Technology, second only to Harvard University Library in scientific material. Miller Nichols Library houses several fascinating exhibits on Kansas City's history; for example, get a taste of our jazz heritage,

complete with recordings, at "Club Kaycee" at www.umkc.edu/orgs/kcjazz.

Although the school's facilities are state of the art, the seventy-year-old ivy-covered stone buildings and tree-lined walkways retain an aura of pre–World War II innocence and a slower pace.

William Jewell College
500 College Highway
Liberty, MO
(816) 781-7700
www.jewell.edu

Being named *Time* magazine's "Liberal Arts College of the Year, 2001–2002" is impressive, indeed, for a school that was derided for being on the edge of civili-zation when chartered in 1849. Named for Dr. William Jewell, a prominent physician from Columbia, Missouri, the college adheres to the principles of a century and a half ago: Provide a superior quality education while retaining its Missouri Baptist heritage. The college became coeducational in 1921.

Jewell pulls from some of the most academically talented students in the region; in a recent entering class of 300, nearly 10 percent had graduated as valedictorian or salutatorian. These top achievers can choose from several advanced programs including the Oxford Honors Program, which combines British tutorial methods of instruction with a year of study in Oxford or Cambridge.

One of the college's strengths is its incoming freshman program that links new students with five mentors, including two faculty members and three students. Newbies get acquainted fast thanks to team-building exercises held at the new Tucker Leadership Lab. This same facility, including rock climbing walls and towers, challenging rope and bridge courses, and the "Sweet Chariot" 250-foot swing ride, is also popular with corporate teams and not-for-profit groups.

A sense of camaraderie can also be found by joining a fraternity or sorority or a Bible-study group or by helping construct houses in the inner city through Habitat for Humanity.

i At Kansas City Art Institute's annual Student Ceramic Sale, held on campus a few weeks before Christmas, you can snag great artwork at remarkable prices. Call KCAI at (816) 474-5224, or visit www.kcai.edu for details.

And class sizes are kept small, averaging 15 students, so that the nearly 1,200 students enjoy one-on-one attention.

Graduate and Master's Programs

Adults who want to further their careers have plenty of options through universities that offer MBAs, including schools that have primary campuses in Kansas City and off-site universities that have developed a satellite presence in town.

Baker University School of Professional and Graduate Studies
6600 College Boulevard
Overland Park, KS
(913) 491-4432
www.bakerspgs.edu

Working adults can complete a degree almost as fast as they can say the name of this program. Well, almost. Students can obtain an undergraduate degree in just three years of intense work. Baker's SPGS also offers accelerated MBA and MSM degrees as well. It's quite a commitment; students typically attend one three-hour class a week with interim group study assignments. With a main campus in Baldwin City, Kansas, the university maintains satellite locations in Overland Park, Kansas, and Lee's Summit, Missouri.

Henry W. Bloch School of Business and Public Administration
5100 Rockhill Road
(816) 235-1111
www.umkc.edu

This school, located at the University of Missouri–Kansas City campus, offers both an MBA, which can be completed as a part-time student, and an Executive MBA, which is a twenty-one-month, intensive program with classes that meet every other Friday and Saturday. One of the school's strongest points is its connections with and support from area businesses that can lead to job placement.

MidAmerica Nazarene University
2030 East College Way
Olathe, KS
(913) 782-3750
www.mnu.edu

Busy professionals can complete an MBA degree within two years at MidAmerica with the help of other students, caring instructors, and a personal laptop computer that's part of tuition. Here, courses are laid out in a structured manner in which each class builds upon the last to provide a feeling of integrated knowledge. This system is one reason the university has such a successful completion rate for its program.

University of Kansas Edwards Campus
12600 Quivira Road
Overland Park, KS
(913) 897-8400
www.edwardscampus.ku.edu

Now adults in Kansas City can chant "rock chalk Jayhawk" while driving just a few miles to campus. The master's program is designed to meet the needs of a typical student, who is thirty-three years old, works full-time, and has a family; most classes meet one night a week, and computer labs are open days, evenings, and weekends.

Mini-Medical Schools

These sessions may be just what the doctor ordered if you've ever wondered what makes you tick or what progress is being made to diagnose and treat various diseases. Two Kansas City medical schools have opened their doors to the public through classes taught in lively, understandable formats by some of the schools' top physicians and researchers. Although "graduates" won't come away with a medical degree, it's a sure thing they'll be more proactive about their

Kansas City Art Institute

If you could point to one reason our town is so flush with art galleries and artist studios, it's the Kansas City Art Institute. Young creative minds come here from forty-five states and five foreign countries to study with some of the best instructors in the world. And if at first they grumble about being stuck in a cowtown, they soon fall in love with our exciting, urban city, and many of them stay after graduation.

Yet as a frontier town in the mid-1880s, Kansas City was an unlikely place for the founding of an art school. It began in 1885 when a small group of art enthusiasts organized a Sketch Club to "talk over art matters in general and to judge pictures." The club moved into quarters in the Deardorf Building at Eleventh and Main Streets and held its first public exhibition in the spring of 1887. The Kansas City Art Association and School of Design was incorporated in July of that year.

As the rowdy town's first cultural institution, KCAI has enjoyed support from prominent business and civic leaders, starting with Howard Vanderslice, who in the 1920s purchased a stone mansion and surrounding eight acres at 44th and Warwick for the school. Four years later the Art Institute renamed the residence "Vanderslice Hall." Today the school shares its neighborhood with the Nelson-Atkins Museum of Art and the Kemper Museum of Contemporary Art.

The college recently expanded its campus within the Southmoreland Neighborhood by purchasing two properties at 43rd and Walnut and opening the H&R Block Art Space, a gallery for contemporary work by students and other artists. The new Jannes Library, situated in a stately old mansion known as the Cunningham Estate, recently opened.

The private four-year college awards bachelor of fine arts degrees in ceramics, design/illustration, fiber, painting and printmaking, photo and new media, sculpture, and art history or creative writing with a studio art emphasis. The 600 students join an impressive roster that includes Walt Disney, painters Jackson Pollock and Keith Jacobshagen, ceramicists Richard Notkin and Akio Takamori, sculptor Robert Morris, and photographer Thomas Barrow.

For more than three decades KCAI has hosted a lecture series, open to students and the public, starring some of the world's most respected artists and scholars.

KCAI also offers many outreach programs, including evening and weekend continuing education courses for credit and noncredit, family studio workshops, and a high school summer residency program. Student exhibits are held twice a year on campus, providing an opportunity for the public to experience and buy the work on display.

For more information contact the Kansas City Art Institute at 4415 Warwick Boulevard, Kansas City, MO 64111; (816) 474-5224; www.kcai.edu.

own health care, and without living through a thirty-six-hour intern shift.

KU School of Medicine
3901 Rainbow Boulevard
Kansas City, KS
(913) 588-1227
www.kumc.edu/som/minimed

When KU School of Medicine decided to offer these sessions a few years ago they hoped for 50 students. They got 250, with 100 on the waiting list. The eight-week sessions cover the same medical and research topics medical students receive. The curriculum changes each year, but past programs have covered cancer research, pain management, trauma center techniques, and diabetes. The result is a public that's informed and more at ease about communicating with their own physicians. Tuition is $95 and includes a detailed notebook covering each topic, a reception with the instructors before each session, and a gift (one year it was scrubs!) presented during the graduation ceremony. Some scholarships are available.

UMKC School of Medicine
2411 Holmes Street
(816) 235-1801
www.med.umkc.edu

This fascinating seven-week fall session covers topics such as asthma, women's health, stroke, and complementary and alternative medicine. Each one-hour presentation is followed by a question-and-answer session, often the most popular part of the evening. All age groups have attended, from one very sharp teen to an incredibly feisty eighty-nine-year-old woman. On graduation night students receive a certificate, T-shirt, and tour of nearby Truman Medical Center. The tuition is $35, and registration is required, as this is always a sellout.

Other Learning Experiences

With so many credit and noncredit classes available around town, adults can expand their minds or their waistlines. You'll find classes for sports enthusiasts (think sailing and ice-skating) in the Parks, Lakes, and Recreation chapter.

Communiversity
5327 Holmes
(816) 235-1448
www.umkc.edu/commu

Called the university without walls, this is a mixed bag of adult education classes taught by volunteer instructors at various homes, gardens, and classrooms throughout the city. Want to learn how to buy a house, and then decorate it the feng shui way? Learn breathing techniques from a "recovering lawyer"? Here's where to find these and dozens of other classes in categories like Arts and Crafts, Inner and Outer Paths (yoga to reading auras), Food (tamales and paella to dim sum), and Business and Legal Issues that tackle reading an investment prospectus or writing a news story. This last one is taught by a Pulitzer Prize–winning news correspondent. Other teachers, called conveners, include professional chefs, financial planners, and artists.

Classes cost between $9 and $16 each; materials, if needed, are extra. Communiversity offers two semesters a year, starting in August and January. The free printed catalog is available at the office located on the UMKC campus or at bookstores, coffee shops, and other outlets around town a month or so before classes begin. The online version is up and running by then as well. Popular classes fill quickly.

The Culinary Center of Kansas City
7917 Foster
Overland Park, KS
(913) 341-4455
www.kcculinary.com

Follow your nose to Old Overland Park and join fellow culinarians, both skilled and novice, in hands-on cooking classes and demonstrations. The classes are fun and educational, and the best part is you get to taste the results afterward.

Instructors are chefs from some of Kansas City's top restaurants as well as other talented area cooks. CCKC has four to eight classes per week, and many of the favorites sell out as soon as the twenty-page newsletter hits the mailboxes. Popular offerings include a Wine Country Dinner, with comice pear and Stilton salad, crispy crusted salmon with thyme-infused zucchini broth, and black bottom coconut cream pie; and a Bistro Dinner Under the Tuscan Sun, with penne *puttanesca,* honey-glazed pork tenderloin with fennel, and winter pears in wine served with Gorgonzola and walnuts. Are you drooling on the page yet? Classes are matched to the season, so you'll learn barbecuing techniques in summer and holiday entertaining tips in winter. There are plenty of basic cooking classes as well, covering topics such as choosing a knife or stocking the pantry.

Classes are held in a lovely space, a cross between a Tuscan country house and villa in the south of France, that's also available for private parties, weddings, and corporate team-building events. Join the Frequent Fryers Club and get a discount on your fifth class.

New Writer's Workshop
6000 Lamar
Mission, KS
(816) 630-7063
www.kansascitywriters.com
If you long to unleash your writing potential or want to find out how to get your work published, this is the course for you. New writers will find a relaxed, supportive atmosphere and an instructor (always a published writer) who will help develop creativity, writing skills, and marketing techniques. Classes are held mornings for eight consecutive sessions each fall and cover fiction, nonfiction, and poetry. The fee is $50.

Theatre for Young America
Acting Classes
Mission, KS
(816) 460-2083
www.tya.org

Some students at this theater and education center are seeking acting careers; others simply want to improve their voices, body movements, creativity, and self-esteem. Classes for ages three through eighteen are taught by professional actors and experienced theater craftspeople. The center also provides work/study programs to give students a chance to learn scene crafts, lighting, directing, and other behind-the-scenes skills. The classes are affiliated with the not-for-profit Theatre for Young America; for more information on performances see the Kidstuff chapter.

The Writers Place
3607 Pennsylvania
(816) 753-1090
www.writersplace.org
Newcomers to the craft of writing as well as frequently published sages come together in this grand stone mansion in Kansas City's elegant Valentine Neighborhood. Before its rebirth as classroom, library, and literary community center for readers and writers, the handsome building—complete with turret—spent time as a private home, brothel, and church. It could even serve as inspiration for one genre of fiction: the ghost story: Some say it's haunted.

William Hickok and local writer Gloria Vando founded the Writers Place in 1992 with the goal of providing a venue where writers could come together and discuss their work. They can also improve it, through a series of courses and workshops on everything from fiction writing and poetry to dialogue, usually taught by regional published authors.

The Writers Place also hosts ongoing events, open to the public, that include book discussions, poetry readings, and dramatic presentations. Fund-raising events are always a lively soiree. The organization currently has 1,000 members; dues are $40 per year for individuals, $60 for families, and $20 for students.

HEALTH CARE AND WELLNESS

When moving to a new city, even more important than locating the nearest ice-cream parlor is finding the closest hospital. In Kansas City, chances are you'll have one practically in your backyard.

Even more good news is that many of our hospitals are nationally known for specialties like cardiac care, cancer diagnostics and treatment, and even kidney transplants. Chalk it up to the fact that Kansas City is home to three medical schools: the KU Medical Center, known for its outstanding research programs; the University of Missouri–Kansas City, offering a unique six-year program combining B.A. and M.D. degrees; and the University of Health Sciences, with a focus on osteopathy. Practitioners of chiropractic have the highly respected Cleveland Chiropractic College. While we're busy training the best physicians and health care workers in the world, they're busy falling in love with this town. After graduation they tend to plant their comfortable white shoes right here.

We're also making medical breakthroughs that can help eliminate disease, speed the recovery process, and improve the patient's quality of life. For instance, our neurosurgeons were the first in the region to operate on tumors and lesions near the brainstem that were once thought to be inoperable. Heart surgeons performed the first endoscopic vein removal from the leg in the Midwest; the resulting incision was less than 2 inches long instead of the previous method, which created a scar the length of the leg.

And our KU Hospital was one of the first hospitals to perform deep-brain stimulation surgery to help control tremors associated with Parkinson's disease. It has performed more of these surgeries than any other hospital in the world.

Kansas City is fast becoming a world leader in the exciting field of life sciences with the opening of the Stowers Institute for Medical Research. This $200 million facility is devoted to finding cures to gene-related diseases like cancer and Alzheimer's. Find out more about this biomedical research center in this chapter's Close-up.

As for immediate care, we'll start our rounds by covering the area's three largest health care organizations with multiple facilities and then follow up with individual medical centers and other health care providers. And we promise, no "cutting-edge" jokes.

All institutions are located in Kansas City, Missouri, unless otherwise noted.

Saint Luke's Health System

www.saintlukeshealthsystem.org

This organization consists of three hospitals, a home health and wellness agency, fifteen physician practices, and thousands of affiliated physicians in the Kansas City metropolitan and surrounding regions. Following is a look at each hospital in the immediate area.

Saint Luke's Hospital of Kansas City
4401 Wornall Road
(816) 932-2000

For more than a century, Saint Luke's has been serving the health care needs of a growing city. Founded in 1882 as a fifty-bed institution at 10th and Campbell Streets, the hospital moved to its present location near the Country Club Plaza in 1923, when a six-story, 150-bed facility was dedicated. Today the hospital campus covers more than 8 square blocks and includes more than a dozen major facilities. The 623-bed tertiary-care hospital offers more than fifty-six medical specialties through its network of 484 physicians.

One of its primary focuses is on cardiac health. The Mid America Heart Institute, located at the Wornall Road campus, is the No. 1 preferred heart care facility in the region. The institute performed the world's first coronary angioplasty for an acute heart attack in 1980, revolutionizing heart attack treatment worldwide. This 210-bed specialty heart center is complemented by six groups of doctors who specialize in cardiac and pulmonary research and care.

St. Luke's Hospital is also highly regarded

i Most of the larger hospitals and health care groups provide community outreach programs including nutritional counseling, fitness programs, CPR training, and even babysitting classes. Many of these programs are free or inexpensive. Call around; often the hospitals publish schedules in a newsletter or on their Web sites.

for its cancer prevention, diagnosis, and treatment centers. Its Centers for Breast Care of the Cancer Institute provides the latest in imaging and diagnostic techniques, including stereotactic core biopsy.

Saint Luke's Northland Hospital
5830 Northwest Barry Road
(816) 891-6000
Smithville Campus
601 South U.S. Highway 169
(816) 532-3700
www.saintlukeshealthsystem.org
One medical staff of more than 247 active physicians serves the two campuses. The Barry Road facility is an eighty-bed general acute-care hospital including a special-care nursery. The Smithville location opened in 1938 as the first Northland hospital. Today it encompasses ninety-two beds.

Saint Luke's South
12300 Metcalf Avenue
Overland Park, KS
(913) 317-7000
This seventy-five-bed facility offers a range of health care services including emergency, physical and occupational therapies, happy-mom-happy-baby birthing suites, prenatal services and a Level II nursery, cardiac diagnostic testing and rehabilitation, sleep disorder center, pain management clinic, and radiology services, along with surgery center.

Saint Luke's South was designed to be exceedingly patient friendly, with new technology such as wireless communication, electronic patient records, and bedside registration. Now that's a brilliant idea! It also

offers a 90,000-square-foot medical office building on its campus.

Additional Services

Shawnee Mission Medical Center
9100 West 74th Street
Overland Park, KS
(913) 676-2000
www.shawneemission.org
Back in the days of $4 house calls, residents of northeast Johnson County had few choices when it came to health care. Eight doctors practiced in the county, and the nearest hospital was a four-bed facility in Gardner, Kansas. Thanks to two doctors, Al Armbruster and Donald Smith, Shawnee Mission Hospital opened in 1962. Its fifteen-acre campus was donated by J. C. Nichols, a gift that was appraised at nearly $6.5 million at the time. Dr. Smith delivered the first two babies born at the 102-bed hospital.

Today the campus has expanded to fifty-four acres, which includes a 383-bed acute care hospital, a freestanding outpatient surgery facility, a community health education building, five medical office buildings, an employee child care center, and a community fitness course.

A member of the Adventist Health System, it has 640 physicians on staff and employs 2,500 associates. Its primary medical services are cardiovascular, women's care, surgery, and outpatient programs.

Other programs associated with Saint Luke's follow.

Ask-A-Nurse
(816) 932-6220, (800) 932-6220
www.saint-lukes.org
Stubbed toe? Chest pain? Is it a cold or the flu . . . or perhaps that potato salad that sat out all day? You can get immediate answers to your medical questions twenty-four hours a day, seven days a week through this free service. It's also a handy way to find out about upcoming community education classes and register at the same time. And if you're new in town, you can find a physician (within the Saint Luke's family, of course) who meets your specific needs.

The Stowers Institute—Hope for Life

In 1994 Jim and Virginia Stowers decided they wanted to give back some-thing "more valuable than money" to the millions of investors in American Century mutual funds who made their success possible. As cancer survivors, they decided to put their fortune to work to find the causes of cancer and other gene-based diseases.

Starting with an initial gift of $50 million, they created the Stowers Insti-tute as a nonprofit medical research organization. They purchased the ten-acre site formerly occupied by Menorah Hospital in the heart of the city and began construction of the 600,000-square-foot complex in 1998. Since then the Stowers have followed their initial gift with stock and cash that raised the institute's endowment above $2 billion.

The center is well on its way to turning Kansas City into "Biomed Valley," attracting top researchers and scientists from around the world. And although experts tried to convince the Stowers that the best-of-the-best would never transfer to Kansas City, they were soon proved wrong. Dr. Bill Neaves, the institute's president, and Dr. Robb Krumlauf, its scientific direc-tor, are beginning to staff the facility with the world's top minds. They tend to be impressed with the city, but they are overwhelmed by the institute. Its laboratory and research support space is unsurpassed. And the buildings and grounds at 1000 East 50th Street are simply magnificent. The general architect is the Kansas City firm of Peckham Guyton Alvers & Viets, but MBT Architecture of San Francisco, one of the few firms in the country specializ-ing in research facilities, designed the laboratory and research spaces.

The landscaped grounds include waterfalls and walking trails, and the building's entrance is defined by a 31-foot double helix sculpture. The sculp-ture and the glass panels in the library's fireplace contain the institute's slo-gan, "Hope for Life."

At its opening, the center was staffed with four laboratories headed by independent scientists. Since then it has recruited additional scientists and highly ranked experts in bioinformatics and transgenic technology. When fully operational, the institute will house at least fifty independent research programs focused on understanding the genes and proteins that control how cells in our bodies divide, differentiate, migrate, and die. By studying these fundamental processes in cells, scientists hope to discover how genes cause many diseases, particularly cancer. For more information about the Stowers Institute, log on to www.stowers-institute.org or call (816) 926-4000.

The Stowers center served as a catalyst for the Kansas City Area Life Sci-ences Initiative, a coalition of businesses, hospitals, and universities with a common goal: to improve the quality of life.

The Cancer Institute
(913) 676-8156

This oncology partnership, affiliated with Saint Luke's Health System, provides the community with a wide variety of services from a single source.

The institute collaborates with Kansas City's academic and research communities to provide research, therapies, and ongoing care. Specific services include inpatient oncology treatment, radiation therapy, breast centers at Menorah Medical Center and Saint Luke's Hospital, the Blood and Marrow Transplant program, a gynecologic oncology practice, and Gamma Knife services at Research Medical Center.

Crittenton Behavioral Health
10918 Elm Avenue
(816) 767-4101

Located on a picturesque 156-acre site near Longview Lake in southeast Kansas City, Crittenton is Kansas City's premier provider of psychiatric care for children and their families.

Founded in 1896, the center has evolved into a comprehensive system of care that includes acute inpatient hospitalization, partial hospitalization, community-based services, and prevention services. On any given day, more than one hundred children and young people receive treatment in one of the therapeutic programs. Additional behavioral health programs, for children and adults, are available at several locations through the system. These include addictions services and assessment centers.

Home Care and Hospice
(816) 756-1160

As the largest full-service home care organization in Kansas City, this organization provides home health services to help patients remain independent and decrease the time they need to spend in the hospital; hospice services, which provide caring medical and emotional support to patients and their families during the last days of life; plus home pharmacy infusion, medical equipment, and private-duty services.

Carondelet Health

This national network of hospitals is operated by the Sisters of St. Joseph Health System. In Kansas City they operate the two hospitals described below, as well as other facilities and services, including St. Mary's Manor, Carondelet Manor, and Villa Saint Joseph long-term care facilities; and home care services, a hospice, a pharmacy, and eight physician offices under the Carondelet name.

Saint Joseph Health Center
1000 Carondelet Drive
(816) 942-4400
www.carondelethealth.org

Established in 1874 as the first private hospital in Kansas City, today this facility has 300 beds and is served by more than 720 staff physicians. With its handsome central atrium and architecture, it looks more like a hotel than a hospital. Patients also like the smaller waiting rooms spread throughout the place rather than having one huge Grand Central Station with screaming kids and four television sets, all tuned to a different station. The attached Medical Mall has a nice food court that beats most cafeteria choices hands down.

Saint Joseph's specialized services include Level II trauma care, a chest pain center, cardiac and pulmonary rehabilitation center, Lifeflight Eagle air medical services, and family-centered maternity care including neonatal intensive care.

Also on-site are an asthma center; the pain management center; a sleep lab; and programs for wellness, sports medicine, and nutrition.

i The Web site of Leawood's American Academy of Family Physicians, www.familydoctor.org, has health information fact sheets in both Spanish and English, self-care flowcharts, drug data, and more. By the way, Kansas City is home to the international headquarters of the American Academy of Family Physicians.

St. Mary's Hospital of Blue Springs
201 West R. D. Mize Road
Blue Springs, MO
(816) 228-5900
www.carondelethealth.org

This 111-bed acute care hospital opened the first Birthing Center in Missouri, providing a homelike environment for families. The hospital also has a twenty-four-hour emergency room, Lifeline, hospice care, pain clinic, mobile CT scanner, and physical therapy unit.

Ongoing community wellness programs include coping with diabetes, prenatal and postnatal education, and CPR classes. St. Mary's Manor, a skilled nursing and residential care facility, is located adjacent to the hospital campus.

HCA Midwest
(816) 508-4000
www.hcamidwest.com

Through this network of twelve state-of-the-art hospitals and multiple treatment facilities, HCA offers superb care in the Greater Kansas City area. Whether you need a heart transplant, or just a doctor with a heart, HCA can handle it. In fact, HCA offers seven Chest Pain Centers, each accredited by the nationally recognized Society of Chest Pain Centers.

Thanks to a recent $450 million capital investment, this health care system can pull from some of the nation's leading medical and nursing schools. More than 3,000 physicians serve patients through primary care, inpatient and outpatient services, employer health programs, home health and hospice care, and wellness programs. Hospitals within the HCA umbrella include Baptist-Lutheran Medical Center, Overland Park Regional Medical Center, Independence Regional Health Center, Medical Center of Independence, Research Medical Center, and Menorah Medical Center (see separate listings for most of these).

Menorah Medical Center
5721 West 119th Street
Overland Park, KS
(913) 498-6000
www.menorahmedicalcenter.com

Menorah first opened its doors on Rockhill Road in Kansas City in 1931 and moved to its new location in 1996. The new campus includes a 158-bed acute care hospital, doctors building, and outpatient clinics. It may be the most beautiful facility in the city with its handsome architecture, fountains, and gardens that can be viewed from patient rooms and waiting areas. An appendectomy in fifteen minutes? Sure, doc, but did you see the daffodils in bloom?

Within the 110,000-square-foot center is a sophisticated cardiology center including open-heart surgery, angioplasty, pacemakers, diagnostics, and a full range of modern cardiac care. The Family Birthing Center has twelve luxurious birthing suites that cater to new parents by providing private baths and showers with a jetted tub, sleeping facilities for Dad or a support person, and in-room private dining. We'd like to make a reservation for Friday, please.

Other patient-care touches include a pre-op pediatric party where younger patients get a firsthand look at the operating room to help ease any fears. They can also try out the kid-size electronic jeep they'll be driving into surgery. A kosher kitchen takes care of the special needs of Jewish patients, and the arboretum is a tranquil garden with a walking trail that beckons caregivers and patients to relax.

Overland Park Regional Medical Center
10500 Quivira Road
Overland Park, KS
(913) 541-5000
www.oprmc.com

This center was among the first health care facilities to bring quality patient care to southern Johnson County. Opened in 1978, today it encompasses a 249-bed acute care hospital, three medical office buildings, three pharmacies, and offices for more than 385 physicians.

Overland Park Regional offers several services that set it apart from other centers in the area. For instance, it has the only nationally verified Level II Trauma Program in Johnson County, including twenty-four-hour emergency services. It also offers a Stroke Prevention and Recovery Program through its emergency department.

The hospital's Diabetes Wellness center is recognized for excellence by the American Diabetes Association. Its Burn and Wound Care Program is known as one of the region's most comprehensive. And the Geropsychiatry Program offers special care for the elderly, including crisis stabilization in the twenty-four-bed unit; comprehensive psychiatric, medical, and neurological evaluations; individualized, ongoing treatment programs; and free follow-up visits.

Overland Park Regional is also home to a Sleep Disorders Center that evaluates, diagnoses, and treats patients with sleep problems. There's no question that new parents have a hard time sleeping, but they'll have a nice time with delivery thanks to the center's Pre-Delivery Program that includes "Birth Day Beepers" for the dad or birthing coach and twenty luxurious suites that pamper the new family. You can even let friends and family across the world see the new little miracle through the "StorkBytes" program that allows you to put your baby's photo, first name, and vital statistics on a Web site. And if problems should arise, the center has Johnson County's only Level III Neonatal Intensive Care Unit, providing the highest level of care for premature or sick infants.

Research Psychiatric Center
2323 East 63rd Street
(816) 444-8161

This center offers a full continuum of behavioral health services, including inpatient and partial hospitalization programs, as well as a CareNet Clinic that provides crisis intervention, outpatient counseling, and community support groups. The forty-member medical staff and one hundred–member allied staff provide services available to the Greater Kansas City area.

The center's Senior Adult Inpatient Treatment is known regionally and nationally for its quality and longevity. Patients are treated based on their needs, either as high-functioning

seniors or those who suffer from organic or chronic mental illness. Separate treatment programs are available through the Child and Adolescent Program, which includes a tutorial system that helps patients from ages thirteen to eighteen keep up with schoolwork.

Baptist-Lutheran Medical Center
6601 Rockhill Road
(816) 276-7000
www.b-/mc.com

When Baptist Medical Center and Trinity Lutheran Hospital merged in 2000, they created a new entity to serve the south Kansas City community better. Licensed for 354 beds, the medical center is located on a thirty-seven-acre campus that includes outpatient facilities, medial office buildings, and a Pavilion Health Club that's dedicated to the rehabilitation and prevention of illness and disease. Baptist-Lutheran has approximately 1,000 employees and more than 700 physicians on its medical staff.

In addition to the traditional hospital services such as emergency, critical care, surgery, and other offerings, the center maintains the Center for Radiation Therapy; the Goppert Family Care Center, an extended-hour program that treats all aspects of the community's health needs; and the Center for Eye Surgery, which provides glaucoma and cataract surgery and features two suites specifically for laser procedures. The Pain Management department (816-276-7094) provides services relating to acute and chronic inpatient and outpatient situations. Patients can be referred by their physicians or self-admitted.

The medical center is involved with several community activities. It teams with the Yellow Cab Company to provide free rides home to people who can't (or shouldn't) drive from restaurants, parties, or bars during the holidays. Since its inception, Holiday Cab has provided more than 23,000 rides. Baptist-Lutheran is the exclusive local provider of the Lifeline twenty-four-hour emergency response system. Subscribers keep a small pager with them at all times, so help is just a push-button away.

Numbers for Health-Related Questions or Emergencies

Look to these organizations for help. Crisis lines are answered twenty-four hours a day.

Life-Threatening, Police, and Fire Emergencies: 911

AIDS Counseling & Information Hotline: (800) 590-2437

AIDS Testing Council of Greater Kansas City: (816) 751-5166

Al-Anon, Alateen: (816) 373-8566

Alcoholics Anonymous: (816) 471-7229

Alzheimer's Disease & Related Disorders Help Line: (913) 831-0003

American Cancer Society of Wyandotte & Johnson Counties: (913) 432-3277

American Diabetes Association: (816) 361-3361

American Heart Association: (913) 648-6727

American Lung Association: (816) 842-5242

American Red Cross: (816) 931-8400

ANSWER Network Teen Suicide Hotline: (800) 784-2433, www.teenanswer.org

Arthritis Foundation: (816) 753-2220

Battered Women's Hotline & Shelter: (816) 861-6100

Domestic Violence Network: (816) 995-1000

Kidney Foundation: (913) 262-1551

Mental Health Crisis Hotline: (888) 279-8188; TDD (800) 955-8339

Narcotics Anonymous: (816) 531-2250

Poison Control Center, Kansas: (913) 588-6633, (800) 332-6633

Poison Control Center, Missouri: (800) 366-8888

Rape Crisis Hotline: (816) 531-0223

Safehome Sexual Assault Hotline & Shelter: (913) 262-7273

Substance Abuse Center: (913) 362-0045

Sudden Infant Death Syndrome Resources: (913) 649-6996

Suicide Prevention Hotline: (913) 831-1773

Physician referrals

The following are referral centers that are not tied to any particular hospital or health care group.

Cass County Referral: (816) 884-3291

Jackson/Clay/Platte County Referrals: (816) 531-8432

Kansas Medical Society (serving Johnson and Wyandotte Counties): (913) 432-9444 www.msjwc.org

West Central Missouri Medical Society: (816) 679-4135

INDEPENDENTLY OPERATED HOSPITALS

Children's Mercy Hospital
2401 Gillham Road
(816) 234-3000
www.childrens-mercy.org

You and your child will immediately know this is a special place when you see the lobby filled with bright colors, children's artwork on the walls, and physicians who often wear Hawaiian shirts instead of white jackets.

The hospital's history can be traced to 1897 when two sisters, Dr. Alice Berry Graham, a dentist, and Dr. Katharine Berry Richardson, established the Free Bed Fund Association to treat "sick, crippled, deformed and ruptured" children from families that couldn't afford health care. Today the Children's Mercy health care system includes the state-of-the-art, 194-bed hospital in Kansas City, busy outpatient clinics in midtown, and a hospital in suburban Johnson County (described separately).

The hospital serves children from birth to age eighteen and provides outpatient care in thirty-five pediatric subspecialties. Children's Mercy has the region's only Level I pediatric trauma center and emergency department as well as a Level IV neonatal intensive care nursery.

Along with providing the very best care possible, the hospital caters to young patients' emotional needs. Little ones are encouraged to bring a favorite stuffed animal or doll along with them, which promptly receives a bracelet that matches the child's. Kids can get an online tour of the hospital with Mercy Bear, with helpful tips for parents along the way.

The hospital continues to expand its services, thanks to several generous gifts from Kansas City citizens and annual fund-raising efforts. It is involved in a ten-year, $129 million expansion that will increase services at the two locations and continue its ongoing research programs in genetics, cancer, neonatal, immunology, and nursing. The sisters who began this service with one child more than a century ago would be proud to see that their work continues: Children's Mercy provides more than $20 million in charity care per year.

Children's Mercy South
5808 West 110th Street
Overland Park, KS
(913) 696-8000

This facility brings the nationally recognized pediatric expertise closer to families in the south metropolitan area. It offers convenient access to outpatient pediatric surgery, sixteen pediatric specialty clinics, a short-term stay inpatient unit, after-hours clinic, and radiology services. More important, it continues the central hospital's renowned kid-glove treatment for little patients that takes much of the fear out of surgery and medical procedures.

University of Kansas Hospital
3901 Rainbow
Kansas City, KS
(913) 588-5000

KU Med West
7405 Renner Road
Shawnee, KS
(913) 588-1227
www.kumed.com

For nearly a century the hospital at the University of Kansas Hospital has been providing leading-edge medicine and care to the people of the region. The hospital was separated from the University of Kansas system and placed under its own authority in 1998.

As the region's only true academic medical center, the physicians at KU Hospital are dedicated researchers, scientists, and educators. Their achievements are many. Neurosurgeons were the first in the region to operate on tumors and lesions near the brain stem that were once thought inoperable. Heart surgeons performed the first endoscopic vein harvesting in the Midwest, creating an incision a mere inch and a half long rather than one the length of the leg.

KU Hospital was one of the first hospitals in the world to perform deep-brain stimulation surgery, which significantly controls tremors associated with Parkinson's disease and other brain disorders; it has performed more of these surgeries than any other hospital in the world. The hospital also performed the first kidney transplant in the state and has the first and only liver and pancreas transplant program in the area. A heart transplant program opened in 2002. Its Kidney Institute is one of the top programs in the world in fighting polycystic kidney disease. Its new 110-bed Center for Advanced Heart Care facility, across the street from the main hospital, opened in October 2006. Honestly, the architecture and art displayed throughout are so beautiful the staff is having a hard time getting patients to leave after they are healed. The amenities are pretty artful as well with private rooms, overnight accommodations for visitors, and a decentralized nursing setup that means a caring health care provider is just steps away.

The facility also has the region's only burn center certified by the American College of Surgeons and the American Burn Association. And its new heart-lung program features the most advanced diagnostic and treatment technology in the region. A $23 million investment added two state-of-the-art catheterization labs, operating suites, and therapeutic procedures. Its PET (positron emission tomography) scanner is the most accurate imaging technology available for tracking cancer and heart disease, allowing doctors to view a patient's internal organs at the cellular level.

Along with treating more than 200,000 inpatients and outpatients a year, KU Hospital provides health and wellness programs to another 10,000 people. For instance, about 3,700 people line up in their vehicles for a flu shot every fall. "I'd like fries with that" is not an option.

North Kansas City Hospital
2800 Clay Edwards Drive
North Kansas City, MO
(816) 691-2000
www.nkch.org
For more than forty years this hospital has

expanded to meet the growing needs of its community north of the river. Today it's a fully equipped 350-bed regional medical center with more than 550 physicians representing forty-five medical specialties.

It's perhaps known best for its superb maternity unit, which treats the birthing process as the magical time it is. For example, the private labor, delivery, recovery, and postpartum rooms are designed to pamper Mom and baby with all the comforts of home, including a specially designed birthing bed, private bath with jetted tub, television, and VCR. Dad can rest on a foldout sleeper chair and enjoy meals at the dining table. To celebrate the big moment, parents receive a decorative birth announcement and a diaper bag filled with gifts, including a logo T-shirt. No wonder more than 1,800 births take place here every year. Extraordinary medical care is close by if needed: The Level II neonatal intensive care nursery is on the same floor.

Cardiac care is also a specialty. North Kansas City Hospital was the first health care provider in Kansas City to use minimally invasive techniques for open-heart surgery. This advanced surgery offers less discomfort and a quicker return to home and everyday activities. To diagnose and treat heart problems before surgery is necessary, the hospital offers one of the area's most advanced cardiac catheterization labs.

North Kansas City Hospital has also made strides in its cancer treatment program. It was the area's first medical facility to eliminate the need to remove the prostate when cancer is confined to the area. And new gastrointestinal procedures take advantage of fiber-optic technology to allow the detection of polyps in the colon and remove them without major surgery. The center also offers the Northland's only hospital-based radiation therapy services.

Its new Health Services Pavilion is just what the patients ordered. This $94.8 million facility consists of six levels and offers expanded outpatient services in one easily accessible location. Along with plenty of covered parking, the center has large, visitor-friendly waiting areas;

Tiny Town, a section designed just for kids; and a health and wellness center for fitness and rehabilitation programs.

Olathe Medical Center
20333 West 151st Street
Olathe, KS
(913) 791-4200
www.ohsi.com

Founded in 1953 as the Olathe Health Foundation, the hospital established new facilities at its present location in 1987. When it built the expansive campus it was truly out in the boondocks. Today it's surrounded by homes, shopping centers, and office parks.

The 150-bed center's comprehensive patient services include anesthesiology, dermatology, diabetic, education, cardiac care and rehabilitation, community service, emergency medicine, general surgery, laser surgery, and MRI. Also on-site are facilities for pain management, oncology treatment, speech and audiology, support groups, and wellness programs. Many of Olathe Medical Center's more than 300 active staff physicians have offices located on the center's health campus and at health care facilities of Olathe Medical Services, Inc. The new Miami County Medical Center in Paola, Kansas, is a subsidiary.

Providence Medical Center
8929 Parallel Parkway
Kansas City, KS
(913) 596-4000
www.providence-health.org

The Sisters of Charity opened Providence Hospital in 1920, and in 1976 the center relocated to a new building on a spacious campus in western Kansas City, Kansas. In 1994, Saint John Hospital in Leavenworth, Kansas, became an affiliate of Providence to further expand regional health care delivery.

The mission continues to focus on Providence's special identity as a Catholic hospital while expanding its services. Some of these programs include a radiation oncology center, a cardiac center offering open-heart surgery and rehabilitation; geropsych services, and a broad range of general and specialized surgical services including neurosurgery and ophthalmology.

Along with the 400-bed hospital, the campus maintains Providence Place, a 90-bed nursing facility that provides diverse health education and screening programs.

Additional Services

Kansas City Hospice
Main Office: 9221 Ward Parkway,
Suite 100
(816) 363-2600
www.kansascityhospice.org

For more than twenty years, Kansas City Hospice has provided medical, emotional, and spiritual support to area residents approaching the last stage of life. More than 130 professional staff in three Kansas City Hospice offices serve more than 2,000 Kansas and Missouri families each year, regardless of their ability to pay.

These families receive individually tailored care from a team that can include nurses, medical social workers, home health aides, art and music therapists, bereavement counselors, chaplains, and specially trained volunteers. Together they manage pain and provide caring, gentle support.

The Carousel Program (913-894-8228), Kansas City's only pediatric hospice in the region, cares for newborns through teenagers.

The organization's new resale shop, Top Drawer, offers great bargains on gently used clothing and estate items. People who donate

> Finding the right doctor in the Yellow Pages is nearly impossible. To save time, and to make sure the doc matches your particular needs—including coverage by your insurance—call the referral centers shown in this chapter. Most hospitals and groups also provide referrals, but be aware that the list will come from their own rosters.

their goods have excellent taste: Offerings include designer duds, furs, and antiques. Located at 3826 West 95th Street, Leawood, Kansas, in the Ranch Mart Shopping Center. Call (913) 642-2292 for hours.

The Rehabilitation Institute of Kansas City
3011 Baltimore
(816) 751-7700
www.rehabkc.org

The Institute is a not-for-profit Heart of America United Way agency that helps children and adults with disabilities realize their highest physical, social, and vocational potential. Programs include community integration, day treatment, and outpatient medical services. It is also one of the largest vocational rehabilitation centers in the state of Missouri, with extensive work evaluation, counseling, and placement programs. The institute has a team of more than a hundred full-time staff who help those disabled by stroke and spinal cord injury along with those affected by birth, childhood, or adult-onset diseases.

More than 1,700 people come to the institute each year to increase their functional capacity through medical rehabilitation; another 1,800 patients receive vocational rehabilitation to enhance their employment opportunities. Programs are available at six locations throughout Kansas City and outlying areas.

Visiting Nurse Services of Health Midwest
(816) 531-1200
www.vnakc.com

Established in 1891, this not-for-profit home health care agency offers the area's most comprehensive range of in-home services. As a United Way agency, it cares for adults throughout metropolitan Kansas City and surrounding rural areas regardless of the patient's ability to pay.

Home care can be as simple as providing skilled services that allow an older adult to live independently, such as physical therapy and nutritional counseling, or as complex as administering chemotherapy. Nursing visits, personal care assistance, and antibiotic treatments can all be handled in the comfort of the patient's home.

Mental Health

Johnson County Mental Health Center
Northeast: 6000 Lamar, Suite 130
Mission, KS
(913) 831-2550

Southwest: 1125 West Spruce
Olathe, KS
(913) 782-2100
www.jocogov.org/mentalhealth

This community mental health center provides professional assistance to service the emotional and mental health needs of Johnson County residents. Programs include individual, family, and group counseling and treatment.

Fees are based on the client's ability to pay. A twenty-four-hour crisis service is available for situations requiring immediate attention; the after-hours emergency number is (913) 384-3535.

Mental Health Association of the Heartland
739 Minnesota Avenue
Kansas City, KS
(913) 281-2221
www.mhah.org

This center is dedicated to promoting the mental health of the community and improving the quality of life of persons with mental illness through advocacy, education, and support. A new service for people diagnosed with a mental disorder who just want to talk can be reached at (913) 281-2251. The Teen Help Line is (913) 281-2299.

Two Rivers Psychiatric Hospital
5121 Raytown Road
(816) 356-5688
www.tworivershospital.com

Set in a serene, parklike environment, this eighty-bed facility provides short-term treatments for adults, children, and adolescents suffering with mental illness or chemical dependency. Some of the services offered are a Masters and Johnson Trauma and Dissociative Disorders program, eating disorders treatment, on-site accredited school program, and free assessments.

Underlining its treatment is a commitment to safety and confidentiality. The center is CHAMPUS approved and has received accreditation with commendation from JCAHO.

Diagnosis and treatment are available twenty-four hours a day, seven days a week.

Western Missouri Mental Health Center
1000 East 24th Street
(816) 512-7000
www.med.umkc.edu
This academic training and research center provides acute care to the seriously mentally ill in its role as the regional inpatient and emergency psychiatric hospital for the state of Missouri and the University of Missouri–Kansas City School of Medicine. The center also operates supervised housing, prevocational services, and outpatient substance abuse treatment.

RETIREMENT

We'll be the first to admit that Kansas City hasn't made its reputation as the retirement center of the universe. Maybe we should. After all, the wonderful attributes that make this town great for families—low cost of living, a wealth of recreational choices, vibrant arts and culture environment, friendly people, and excellent health care options—make it a terrific place to retire. And if you're leaving one career and thinking about starting another, our network of college courses and entrepreneurial programs will help you get started, you young whippersnapper, you.

Best of all, we treat older Americans as the gems they are. Want proof? The Shepherds Centers of America started right here in Kansas City. This seniors-helping-seniors program helps participants maintain independent and productive lifestyles while they enjoy new-

One of the best ways to make friends in Kansas City is through volunteering, and perhaps there's no better place to lend a hand than at your friendly neighborhood hospital. You can serve as an escort for patients or even as a rocker in the nursery!

found creative outlets. Activities range from meal delivery, to legal counseling, to classes in art, to writing, to travel. Today the concept has been copied at more than a hundred centers nationwide, with new sites opening every year.

Kansas City is also home to one of the country's most respected retirement communities, John Knox Village, which has been instrumental in developing programs and excellent living options for seniors for more than thirty years. In fact, our senior communities are so stellar, Mom and Dad might have to fight off their kids wanting to move in with them. Again.

You'll find the right living arrangement to fit your lifestyle, including luxurious villas with a health club, salon, and garden outside your door; assisted care facilities; and even services that care for patients with Alzheimer's.

Let's take a look at all the services and programs available for our mature residents. You might find yourself fudging on your birth certificate just to be able to participate.

Opportunities are listed in alphabetical order by category, followed by a Retirement Communities section. Organizations are located in Kansas City, Missouri, unless otherwise noted.

Education

It's never too late to learn. Teachers and professors adore having mature students in the classroom to provide a unique view on a subject and serve as role models for the younger generation. Many of our universities and colleges offer discounts to seniors; check out "Colleges and Universities" in this chapter's Higher Education section. In addition, our parks and recreation departments offer educational programs in everything from art to tap dancing. You'll find individual listings in the Parks, Lakes, and Recreation chapter.

And if you live in Johnson County, you're really in luck; there's a club just for you at JCCC. Read on.

Brown & Gold Club
Johnson County Community College
12345 College Boulevard
Overland Park, KS
(913) 469-8500, ext. 4305
www.jccc.net/academic/brownandgold

If you're a Johnson County resident age fifty-five and older, this is your ticket to ride. For a mere $10 a year you can take credit classes free (some restrictions apply), get discounted fees for continuing education courses, and attend parties, special lectures, and events throughout the year. Since the club began in 1972, more than 5,000 members have joined. Programs include travel, from trips as close as Overland Park's New Theatre Restaurant to a ten-day Caribbean cruise; social events such as a dance for St. Valentine's Day; special lectures; and discounted or free tickets to entertainment at the college's Carlsen Center. It's enough to make you lie about your age.

SeniorNet
Johnson County Community College
(913) 469-2323
www.seniornet.org

Keep in touch with friends around the world, learn more about health issues, or sell your rocking chair on e-Bay. Older Americans are jumping onto the computer with help from programs like SeniorNet. This nonprofit organization provides computer instruction and access to an online network in an easy-to-learn and fun environment.

SeniorNet has more than 22,000 members in the Western Hemisphere and more than 125 sites across the country. In the Kansas City area, classes are taught at several locations, including KCPT, the public television station, and the Johnson County Community College

campus in Overland Park. Membership is $35 a year. For information or to join, contact the area coordinator, John Duff, at the number shown above.

Recreation

In Kansas City, seniors can keep active and healthy, thanks to a plentitude of programs through organizations like banks and savings and loans. Check with yours to see if they host travel groups and special events. Several area hospitals also offer programs specifically geared toward older citizens. These include free or reduced-cost health screenings and classes for CPR, fitness, and nutrition. For more information see the Health Care and Wellness chapter.

Our parks and recreation departments provide dozens of programs for seniors. Each county has its own parks and rec department; you'll find them listed in Parks, Lakes, and Recreation.

Classic Senior Games
Jackson County Parks and Recreation
(816) 795-8200, ext. 1278

Each September, this Olympic-style event brings out the competitive nature in men and women who don't feel fifty years old. But that's the *minimum* age for these games; you'll also see plenty of participants pushing eighty. Sports include swimming, tennis, track and field, and horseshoes. Medals are awarded for a variety of categories. This four-day event is recognized by the United States National Senior Sports Organization.

50 Plus Program
Johnson County Park and
Recreation District
(913) 831-3355
www.jcprd.com, www.50plusprogram.com

Arts and crafts classes, group travel, cards and games, gardening . . . do these folks ever slow down? Johnson County's 50 Plus Program offers so many classes and events there's no time to grow old and creaky. A recent list of springtime activities included West Coast

One of the best ways to stay active is to volunteer. Share your expertise as a SCORE volunteer, serve as an usher, serve at a soup kitchen, or pull weeds at a community garden. You'll find opportunities in this section, or contact the Heart of America United Way (816-235-6675), which can match your interests with an organization that needs you.

Swing, Latin Rhythm Workout, Working with Digital Photography, Hands-On Investing, Basic Spanish, and a rather curious class, New Spouse Checklist. Travel opportunities have included trips to China and the Yangtze River, Spain and Portugal, and Branson, Missouri.

Other programs include regular health screenings at reduced or no cost, CPR training, yoga, and joining friends for regular nature walks. What are you waiting for?

Senior Arts Council
(913) 897-4165
This group began in 1977 as a way for senior arts and crafters to showcase their talent and continue to learn new creative skills. Each meeting, held the last Monday of each month at 1:00 p.m., includes a guest artist or speaker. The fee is $10.

Senior Peers Actively Renewing Knowledge (SPARK)
4825 Troost
(816) 235-2870
www.umkc.edu/spark
You've got to love this acronym, eh, Sparky? This program, hosted by the University of Missouri–Kansas City and affiliated with Elderhostel Institute for Learning in Retirement, provides courses each summer at the school's campus. Noncredit courses touch on such topics as computers, the Internet, Spanish, music, and Kansas City history.

Most classes meet once a week for four, six, or eight periods. An annual SPARK membership costs $51 and includes three classes and admission to various social activities

throughout the year. There is a fee, usually around $10, for each additional class. Call the number above for more information. Persons with speech or hearing impairment may call Relay Missouri at (800) 735-2966 (TT), or (800) 735-2466 (voice).

Shepherd's Center of Kansas City Central
5200 Oak (and other locations)
(816) 444-1121
www.shepherdcenters.org
The Shepherd's Center movement was started in 1972 by twenty-five Catholic, Jewish, and Protestant congregations in one area of Kansas City. The goal was to create programs that would enrich the lives of seniors, help them to remain independent, and to celebrate life.

The first center was a smashing success from the start. Each Friday, 400 to 500 men and women took classes on everything from painting and journaling to learning to play bridge. Soon the center was helping 4,000 people stay active and engaged in life. The genius of the program is that it is an interfaith ministry by and with older adults rather than a ministry to them. Many of the programs are taught by senior volunteers.

Shepherd's Center soon became a model for other programs throughout the country, and an ad hoc committee was formed in 1973 to respond to requests from other communities. The Shepherd's Centers of America was incorporated a year later. Today this organization coordinates nearly one hundred independent Shepherd's Centers throughout the country. Centers in the Kansas City area provide classes in foreign language, computers, tai chi, and creative writing; there are dozens of classes and groups.

In addition, senior volunteers go into the community to help their neighbors. A few of the twenty-five services are Meals on Wheels to deliver a hot noontime meal to those who can't leave their home; Wheels That Care, providing free transportation to doctor's visits, pharmacies, and grocery stores; Respite Care to offer short-term relief for caregivers of homebound loved ones; and Care Home Contacts, to visit nursing home residents who don't have family or friends. There are other Shepherd's Centers throughout the city. Contact the number above or go online to learn more.

Services

American Association of Retired Persons
700 West 47th Street, Suite 110
(866) 389-5627
www.aarp.org
It's a rite of passage: Turn fifty and get a big packet of information from AARP. Frankly, we can't imagine anyone who would say no to this collection of benefits for $12.50 a year. A sampling includes discounts on everything from lodging and car rentals to cruises and information and resources on health, fitness, and insurance, as well as legal and consumer issues. And with more than thirty million members, AARP is the largest advocacy group for older adults in the United States.

Joining the local chapter will net you invitations to social events, provide opportunities to volunteer your time and expertise, and give you access to the organization's home-delivery prescription drug service and much more. Plus, your spouse gets in free whether he or she is fifty or not. Membership also includes subscriptions to the monthly AARP Bulletin and the bimonthly *Modern Maturity*.

AARP's 55 Alive/Mature Driving Program
700 West 47th Street, Suite 110
(866) 389-5627
www.aarp.org
This program is just what is says: teaching older Americans how to drive defensively. The comprehensive, eight-hour course covers topics such as age-related changes that can affect vision, hearing, and physical strength. Check with your auto insurance carrier; some agencies provide discounts to seniors who have completed the course.

Area Agency on Aging–Johnson County
11875 South Sunset, Suite 200
Olathe, KS
(913) 894-8811
(Press "1" for Aging Information)
www.jocoks.com/humanservices-aging
The goal of the AAA is to help older adults in Johnson County maintain independence and dignity in their own homes and in the community. A few of the programs include in-home services such as minor repairs and preparing for winter; noon meals and fellowship at senior centers and through home-delivered meals for homebound seniors; legal services and insurance counseling; and client assessment referral and evaluation (CARE), which provides preadmission assessments for persons considering nursing facilities or long-term care services.

In addition, the Catch-a-Ride program (913-477-8105) provides older adults and persons with disabilities with a free ride to grocery stores, senior centers, and health care appointments.

Area Agency on Aging–Kansas City
600 Broadway, 300 Rivergate Center
(816) 474-4240
www.marc.org
This initiative of the Mid-America Regional Council serves older residents in Cass, Clay, Jackson, Platte, and Ray Counties in Missouri. Some of the programs and services include providing hot meals and activities at senior centers; delivering meals to residents who are unable to leave their homes; offering adult day care services and homemaker and personal care services such as grocery shopping; providing transportation to medical appointments, and offering advocacy in legal and consumer situations.

Generally, the MARC adult programs are available to those age sixty and over, regardless of income. There are no predetermined fee scales, but participants are encouraged to make voluntary contributions to offset the cost of the services they receive. In addition, a limited number of programs are available to those between the ages of eighteen and fifty-nine with significant disabilities.

Volunteering

That friendly face who shows you to your seat at the ballet? That's a volunteer, and not only does she get to meet new people and contribute to the community, she gets a free seat for the *Nutcracker*. Pretty sweet, indeed. Kansas City provides thousands of opportunities for seniors to donate time, talent, and expertise. You've read about some of them here, such as the seniors-helping-seniors programs through the Shepherd's Centers. In addition mature adults can mentor at-risk youth, read to little kids, teach English to immigrants, and yes, serve as ushers or guides at one of our many cultural centers. Call your favorite venue found in The Arts chapter; chances are they're holding a nifty uniform in just your size.

Following are other worthwhile volunteer opportunities.

Catholic Charities
(913) 621-1504
2220 Central Avenue
Kansas City, KS
www.catholiccharitiesks.org
The volunteer opportunities at this organization are as big as your heart. This nondenominational group is always grateful for people who serve at community kitchens, read to small children, mentor youths in need, set up households for immigrants, and serve as hospice caregivers. Catholic Charities helps more than 75,000 people every year; you can make it 75,001.

Heart of America United Way
(816) 235-6675
www.hauw.org
The umbrella organization services hundreds of not-for-profit groups throughout the greater Kansas City area and serves as a resource center for volunteer opportunities. Give them a call to match your talents with a need, or show up at their annual Day of Caring, held every June. This communitywide service event mobilizes volunteers from over 126 companies, federal agencies, and labor unions.

Retired & Senior Volunteer Program (RSVP)
www.hauw.org/rsvp
This program gives seniors a chance to learn new skills and share their expertise with others while making new friends through volunteering. Opportunities include serving as ambassador at the airport, becoming a resource guide at Union Station, or mentoring students at area schools. Contact the United Way at Jackson, Clay, and Platt Counties at (816) 474-5111, ext. 245; in Wyandotte County it's (913) 371-3674. Or call the Johnson County Volunteer Center, (913) 341-1792.

The Service Corps of Retired Executives (SCORE)
4747 Troost
(816) 235-6675
www.scorekc.org
If you've ever run a company, managed a department, or written a brochure, someone in the business world needs your talents. This organization pairs retired executives with small business owners in need of advice. Sponsored by the Small Business Administration, the program has experts in virtually every area of free enterprise, including management, finance, marketing, and human resources.

The Kansas City chapter's volunteers join more than 11,500 nationwide who donate their time and talent to help nearly 300,000 entrepreneurs every year. The satisfaction that you helped should be enough, but sometimes there are more immediate bonuses, like the one a businessman in Johnson County who provided advice to a young woman starting a candy company got. He has enough chocolate to last another lifetime.

i One of the best things about turning sixty in Johnson County is getting a free subscription to *Best Times*. This monthly publication of Aging International Action of Johnson County provides information about services and events for seniors. Call (913) 477-8242 for subscriptions.

Retirement Communities

John Knox Village
400 Northwest Murray Road
Lee's Summit, MO
(816) 524-8400, (800) 892-5669
www.johnknoxvillage.org

This forty-acre retirement community is practically its own town. Residents find everything they could need or want for the best years of their lives, including a variety of housing options, a maintenance-free lifestyle, plenty of activities, and a full continuum of health care services.

There are nearly 15,000 homes at John Knox, providing more than seventy floor plans including apartments, cottages, duplexes, town houses, and single-family homes. All maintenance and utilities (except telephone) are included in a monthly fee. No shoveling snow or cutting the lawn, but many of the residents enjoy tending the garden. And with all those chores done for you, you'll have more time to enjoy the fitness center, two swimming pools, fishing lake, nine-hole golf course, bowling alley, and 2,000-seat pavilion for dances and shows.

The Village also offers plenty of choices when it comes to dining. The Villager Restaurant has sit-down table service and a Sunday Family Brunch once a month. A more casual choice is the cafeteria-style dining room with a spectacular view of the golf course and lake. And for date night, take your sweetie to the Fireside Dining Room, with dishes that range from soup and sandwiches to grilled tuna steak.

Part of the real joy of living here are the ongoing activities like craft lessons, musical groups, a variety of clubs to join, and trips to take as a group. Security is another benefit; the campus has its own security force with officers patrolling the area twenty-four hours a day, 365 days a year. Residents also have access to health and wellness programs and services, including nutritional and rehabilitation services. And because John Knox Village is a continuing care retirement community, it also offers access to twenty-four-hour nursing care, an assisted living facility, a fully accredited, 430-bed skilled nursing center complete with an Alzheimer's unit, a physician's clinic, and the adjacent 102-bed acute care Lee's Summit Hospital, all on the campus.

Residents may choose to pay an annual rental fee or enter into an entry fee agreement that's available in four different levels of care.

Town Village Leawood
4400 West 115th Street
Leawood, KS
(913) 491-3681
www.townvillage.com

You've got a lot of living to do, and Town Village is just the place to enjoy it. It's close to entertainment, outdoor activities like parks and golf courses, and some of the best shopping and restaurants in the region, so you'll have plenty to keep you busy. But you might find yourself spending most of your time at this campus, especially once you taste the four-star quality food served in the light-filled dining room. No mush here; how about Cornish game hens, trout amandine, chicken stir-fry, or another one of the delicious entrees that rotate on a four-week cycle, so diners are never bored.

Other amenities include arts and crafts, an indoor pool, resident gardening area, fitness center, and a Cultural Guild, which brings in artists, musicians, and actors to entertain the residents. Spacious apartments are available, from studios through two-bedroom, two-bath homes.

Village Shalom
5500 West 123rd Street
Overland Park, KS
(913) 317-2600
www.villageshalom.org

A retirement village with its own award-winning art gallery? This beautiful campus in south Johnson County was designed as a nurturing—even exciting—environment for seniors. Near the Jewish Community Campus, Menorah Medical Center, and a number of activities, it provides fellowship for those who value Jewish traditions. The villas, apartments, and suites are beautifully designed for comfort and luxury, and the grounds are landscaped with lovely gardens and walking paths.

Community-oriented services include Rachel's Cafe, a kosher dining room; a day spa; and the ElderSpa Wellness Center. The Epsten Gallery is a two-story, museum-quality art showroom that features exhibits from around the world. In addition, within the community are a full-service bank, children's outdoor playground for visiting family members, and a social hall and synagogue.

Village Shalom offers maintenance-free villas, apartments, and Shalom Suites, which provide assisted living or skilled nursing services. The Weinberg Health Center has additional facilities to meet the special needs of those residents with Alzheimer's and other diseases.

INDEX